Scott Foresman - Addison Wesley
MATH

AUTHORS

RANDALL I. CHARLES

Carne S. Barnett   Diane J. Briars   Warren D. Crown
Martin L. Johnson   Steven J. Leinwand   John Van de Walle

Charles R. Allan • Dwight A. Cooley • Portia C. Elliott
Pearl Ling • Alma B. Ramírez
Freddie Lee Renfro • Mary Thompson

Scott Foresman
Addison Wesley

Editorial Offices: Menlo Park, California • Glenview, Illinois
Sales Offices: Reading, Massachusetts • Atlanta, Georgia • Glenview, Illinois
Carrollton, Texas • Menlo Park, California

http://www.sf.aw.com

The friendly characters who help you in this book with math tips, remembering, and problem solving are Zoombinis™. They are used with the permission of Brøderbund Software and can be found in the interactive problem-solving software, *Logical Journey of the Zoombinis®*, © 1996 Brøderbund Software and TERC, available from Brøderbund Software, Novato, California. For more information, write Brøderbund at P.O. Box 6125, Novato, CA 94948-6125, or call (415) 382-4740.

Cover artist Robert Silvers was taking photographs and playing with computers by the time he was ten. Eventually he melded his interests in computer programming and photography to produce a program that divides images into a grid and matches them with images from a database. The results are mosaics such as the one on this cover.

CHAPTER 1

Data, Graphs, and Facts Review 6

Theme  WORLD WIDE FRIENDS

Data File  6

Team Project What's Different? What's the Same? 8

Technology Resources

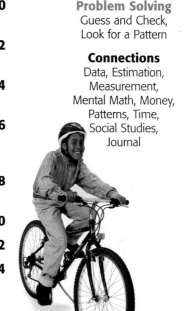

Review and Maintenance appears in green type; Problem Solving in red type

CHAPTER 2

Whole Numbers and Decimals: Place Value, Adding, and Subtracting 48

Theme FASCINATING FACTS

Data File 48
Team Project
  The Earliest Calculator 50
Technology Resources

Problem Solving
Draw a Picture, Guess and Check, Look for a Pattern, Make an Organized List

Connections
Algebra, Data, Estimation, Mental Math, Money, Patterns, Literature, Science, Social Studies, Journal

Problem Solving
Draw a Picture

Connections
Algebra, Data, Estimation, Measurement, Mental Math, Money, Patterns, Fine Arts, Health, Journal

Problem Solving
Use Objects/Act It Out

Connections
Algebra, Data, Logic, Money, Probability, Time, Geography, History, Literature, Science, Social Studies, Technology, Journal

Multiplying Whole Numbers and Decimals 108

Theme  ALL AMERICAN NUMBERS

Data File 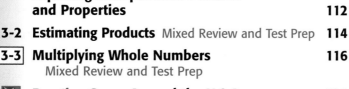 108
Team Project Road Trip! 110
Technology Resources

Geometry 266

Theme

Data File **266**
Team Project That's a Wrap **268**
Technology
Resources

Review and Maintenance appears in green type; **Problem Solving** in red type

CHAPTER 7

Fractions and Mixed Numbers 298

Theme

WATER, WATER, EVERYWHERE!

Data File 298
Team Project Raindrops Keep Fallin' 300
Technology Resources

CHAPTER 8
Fraction Operations and Customary Linear Measurement 344

Theme **Fraction Action with Hobbies**

Data File **344**
Team Project Critter Riddle **346**
Technology Resources

CHAPTER

9

Fractions and Multiplication 400

Theme *Food Around The* W🌍RLD

Data File **400**
Team Project Yummy, Yummy Recipes! **402**
Technology Resources 🖩 💿 🖥

Problem Solving
Look for a Pattern,
Use Objects/Act It Out

Connections
Algebra, Data, Measurement,
Patterns, Time, Fine Arts,
Geography, Journal

Problem Solving
Look for a Pattern

Connections
Data, Logic, Measurement, Time,
Fine Arts, Geography, Music, Journal

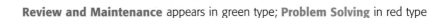

Review and Maintenance appears in green type; **Problem Solving** in red type

Length, Perimeter, and Area 436

Theme

Data File   436
Team Project Tangram Animals 438
Technology Resources 🖩 💿 🖥

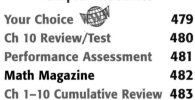

Measurement 484

Theme THINGS TO BUILD

Data File **484**
Team Project Turn Up the Volume **486**
Technology Resources

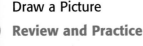

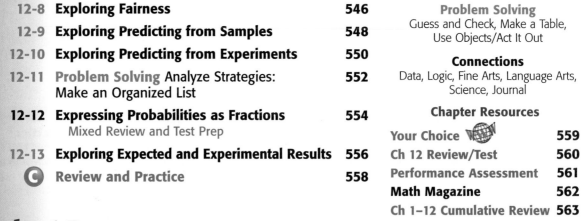

GET READY!

Welcome to Math Class

Do you recognize me? I'm the **Get Ready** Zoombini. My friends and I can't wait to help out this year in math class.

I'll help with **problem solving!**

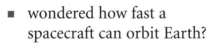
I'll help you **remember**. You won't forget with me around!

STAY SHARP!

I'm great at giving helpful **math tips!**

Did you know? I'll let you in on lots of fun facts.

SPACE SHUTTLE

Math is everywhere—not just in math books. We will introduce you to real students who use math every day to help understand the world around them. Have you ever:

- wondered how fast a spacecraft can orbit Earth?

- compared populations of endangered species?

- figured out how to build a ramp for inline skaters?

- discovered the patterns in a Filipino tinikling dance?

The math we learn together will help us do all that and more. So what are we waiting for? Let's launch into a new year!

Reviewing Skills

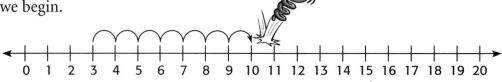

You Will Meet
real people who use math every day

You already know lots of math! Let's review basic facts before we begin.

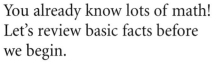

Review addition facts. Find each sum. You can use a number line to help.

1. $3 + 7$ **2.** $2 + 9$ **3.** $9 + 8$ **4.** $8 + 4$ **5.** $5 + 4$

6. $6 + 9$ **7.** $8 + 6$ **8.** $4 + 7$ **9.** $5 + 7$ **10.** $6 + 5$

Monica keeps track of weather data on page 348.

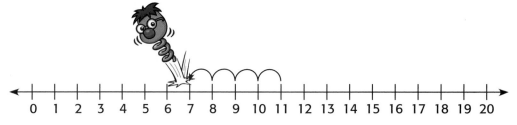

Review subtraction facts. Find each difference. You can use a number line to help.

11. $11 - 4$ **12.** $12 - 7$ **13.** $18 - 9$ **14.** $10 - 3$ **15.** $14 - 8$

16. $15 - 9$ **17.** $17 - 8$ **18.** $13 - 6$ **19.** $11 - 5$ **20.** $9 - 4$

21. Review multiplication facts. Copy and complete the multiplication table. Look for patterns.

Josh delivers recycling news on his school's TV station. See him on page 172.

x	3	4	5	6	7	8	9	10	11	12
3	9						27			
4		16				32		40		
5			25	30	35					
6			30	36					66	
7		28			49					
8	24					64				96
9							81			

Math Tip
Multiply the numbers across the top of the table by the numbers down the side of the table.

Review division facts.

22. $24 \div 6$ **23.** $72 \div 9$ **24.** $18 \div 3$ **25.** $60 \div 10$ **26.** $22 \div 11$

27. $25 \div 5$ **28.** $56 \div 8$ **29.** $64 \div 8$ **30.** $49 \div 7$ **31.** $28 \div 7$

Math Tip
Patterns and mental math can help you solve some math problems.

Patterns Complete each pattern.

32. 1, 2, 4, 7, ▪, ▪, ▪   **33.** 1, 2, 4, 8, ▪, ▪, ▪

34. 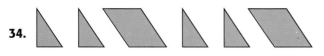 ___ ___ ___

Mental Math Use mental math to find each answer.

35. $36 + 12$ **36.** 32×3 **37.** $25 - 10$ **38.** $3 + 50$ **39.** $100 \div 4$

Add, subtract, multiply, or divide to solve the riddle. Match each letter to its answer in the blank below. Some letters are not used.

40. $7 + 8$ [K]   **41.** $36 \div 4$ [U]

42. $15 - 5$ [I]   **43.** 7×5 [D]

44. $6 + 7$ [A]   **45.** 6×6 [V]

46. $16 - 9$ [L]   **47.** $3 + 9$ [P]

48. $16 \div 4$ [F]   **49.** $10 - 6$ [G]

50. 10×3 [C]   **51.** 9×7 [O]

52. $5 + 6$ [H]   **53.** $35 \div 7$ [S]

54. $4 + 6$ [Y]   **55.** 5×4 [B]

56. $17 - 5$ [J]   **57.** $56 \div 7$ [N]

58. $14 - 9$ [B]   **59.** $48 \div 8$ [T]

▪   ▪   ▪   ▪   ▪
___   ___   ___   ___   ___
30   63   9   8   6

What must an astronaut do backward in order to lift-off?

Problem Solving

Introduction to Strategies

Problem Solving Strategies

- Use Objects/Act It Out
- Draw a Picture
- Look for a Pattern
- Guess and Check
- Use Logical Reasoning
- Make an Organized List
- Make a Table
- Solve a Simpler Problem
- Work Backward

Choose a Tool

How does a detective solve a case? Detectives, just like math students, depend on **strategies.** A detective might make a list of suspects or draw a map to organize the facts and solve a case. You can do that, too!

Here is a math mystery that an archaeologist needs help solving. Is there a pattern in the designs on this ancient wall? How many Xs would have been used in the sixth design? You can use strategies to solve the problem.

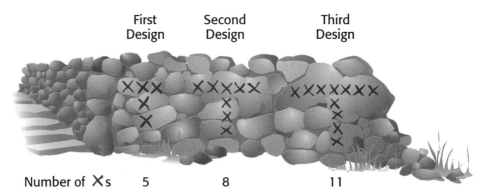

	First Design	Second Design	Third Design
Number of Xs	5	8	11

Nathan, Sue, and Joe each solve the problem a different way.

Draw a Picture and Look for a Pattern

I need to add 1 X to each end and the bottom of the T shape for each design. On the sixth design I can count how many Xs I have.

I need 3 new Xs for each example. There are 3 new designs to get to the sixth.

$3 \times 3 = 9$
$9 + 11 = 20$

Design	1	2	3	4	5	6
Xs	5	8	11	14		

+3   +3   +3   +3

Talk About It

1. How many Xs are needed for the sixth design?

2. Which strategy would you have chosen to solve this problem? Why?

3. Why do you think there are several ways to solve this problem?

Try These

Use any strategy to solve.

1. Does Bryan have enough shirts and pants to wear a different outfit each day of the week? Explain.

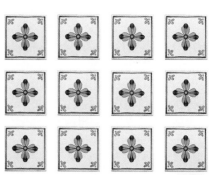

Bryan's Clothes			
Shirts	👕	👕	👕
Pants			

2. Ken, Tami, Bobbie, Desiree, and Alan want to play a video game. They have 40 minutes. Only 2 can play at a time. Is there enough time for each to have at least 10 minutes? Explain.

3. Tony has 12 tiles. How many different ways can he place them to make a rectangular design?

4. **Journal** Keeping a math journal is a great way to check your progress. Write a short entry describing what you'd like to learn this year, or describe a favorite problem you already know how to solve. Check your journal during the year. You may be surprised by how much you learn!

Chapter 1
Data, Graphs, and Facts Review

In Touch Online
Page 9

SECTION A

Reading Graphs, Describing Data, and Facts Review

9

These line plots show the measurement of arm spans for several girls and boys. How many girls have an arm span of 54 in.?

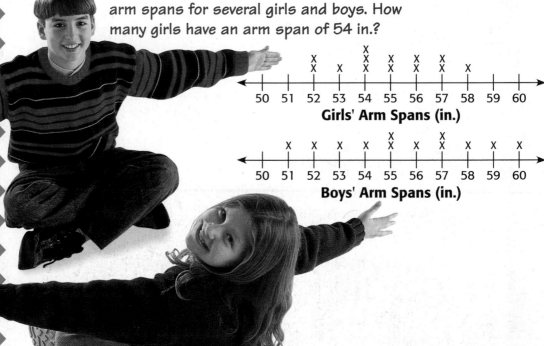

Girls' Arm Spans (in.)

Boys' Arm Spans (in.)

Making Graphs and Facts Review

**Plotting Time
Page 25**

Which country has the greatest number of students per 100 who read for fun every day?

Students Who Read for Fun Every Day	
Country	Number of Students per 100
Taiwan	17
Ireland	40
France	39
United States	29
Israel	43
Canada	36
Korea	11

Surfing the **W**orld **W**ide **W**eb!

How much time do you spend reading each week? What do you read? Skim over to **www.mathsurf.com/5/ch1** to find out more about other students' reading habits.

TEAM PROJECT

WHAT'S THE DIFFERENCE? WHAT'S THE SAME?

How are you and other students alike? How are you and they different? What are school days like for students around the world? Find information to answer these questions and then show your results.

Make a Plan

- What would you like to know about other students at your grade level in the United States or in the world?

- How much data will you need to give an accurate picture? Where can you find this information?

- How can you best present your findings?

Number of School Days in a Year	
Country	**School Days**
Germany	240
Haiti	175
Korea	251
Mexico	200
United States	180
Zimbabwe	225

Carry It Out

1. Decide on four topics to investigate.

2. Research your topics. Learn about students from around the world.

3. Make a table like the one shown or a graph to show your research results.

4. Paste your tables and graphs on posterboard for display.

Talk About It

- How are you different from other students? How are you alike?

Present the Project

- Present the results of your investigation.
- How are the different results presented?

Reading Graphs, Describing Data, and Facts Review

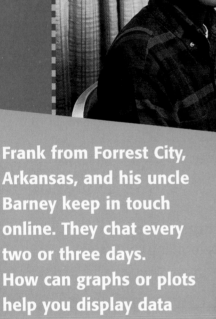

Frank from Forrest City, Arkansas, and his uncle Barney keep in touch online. They chat every two or three days. How can graphs or plots help you display data about chatting online?

Skills Checklist

In this section, you will:

☐ **Review Basic Facts**

☐ **Read Graphs**

☐ **Read Line Graphs**

☐ **Read Stem-and-Leaf Plots**

☐ **Find the Range, Mode, and Median**

☐ **Solve Problems by Using a Guide and by Choosing an Operation**

☐ **Explore Algebra by Finding the Rule**

GET READY!

Brushing Up On Basic Facts

Review facts. Find each answer.

1. $9 + 7$	**2.** 4×8	**3.** $49 \div 7$
4. $18 - 9$	**5.** $32 \div 8$	**6.** $8 + 3$
7. 9×3	**8.** $16 - 9$	**9.** 5×6

Reading Graphs

You Will Learn

how to use graphs to analyze data

Vocabulary

pictograph
uses pictures or symbols to show data

bar graph
uses vertical or horizontal bars to show data

line plot
uses symbols above a number line to show data

Learn • • • • • • • • • • •

A **pictograph** compares data and information. This pictograph gives information about class sizes in different countries. Each symbol stands for 4 students.

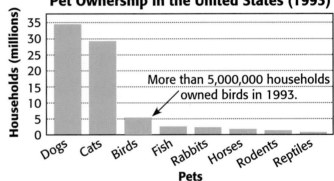

Class Size	
Spain	🏠🏠🏠🏠🏠🏠|
Japan	🏠🏠🏠🏠🏠🏠|
United Kingdom	🏠🏠🏠🏠🏠
United States	🏠🏠🏠🏠|
Germany	🏠🏠🏠🏠|
Canada	🏠🏠🏠🏠🏠

🏠 = 4 students
🏠 = 2 students
🏠 = 1 student

United Kingdom

$5 \times$ 🏠 $= 20$ students

United States

$$
\begin{array}{r}
4 \times \text{🏠} = \quad 16 \\
\text{🏠} = +\ 2 \\
\hline
18 \text{ students}
\end{array}
$$

A **bar graph** is also used to compare data.

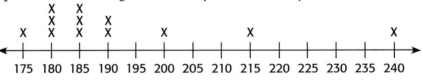

Pet Ownership in the United States (1993)

Households (millions): 0, 5, 10, 15, 20, 25, 30, 35

Pets: Dogs, Cats, Birds, Fish, Rabbits, Horses, Rodents, Reptiles

More than 5,000,000 households owned birds in 1993.

A **line plot** compares data by showing clusters of information. This line plot tells how long the school year is in many countries.

```
            X   X
            X   X   X
    X       X   X   X       X           X                       X
 ◄──┼───┼───┼───┼───┼───┼───┼───┼───┼───┼───┼───┼───┼───►
   175 180 185 190 195 200 205 210 215 220 225 230 235 240
```

Length of the School Year in Different Countries (days)

The three Xs above 180 mean that three countries have 180 school days.

Talk About It

In the pictograph, what does part of a school mean?

Check •

Using Data Use the graphs to answer **1** and **2**.

1. Did more households own cats or dogs in 1993? Explain.

2. **Reasoning** When would you use a pictograph, a bar graph, or a line plot?

Practice

Skills and Reasoning

Using Data Use the graph to answer **3–5.**

3. What kind of ball can travel about 145 mi/hr?

4. About how much faster does a served tennis ball travel than a hit table-tennis ball?

5. Why do you think the numbers across the bottom of the graph begin at 90?

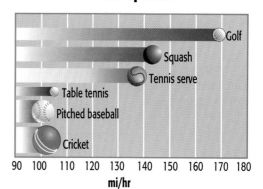

Ball Speeds

Using Data Use the Data File on page 6 to answer **6–8.**

6. Measurement What was the arm span for the most girls shown on the line plot?

7. How many boys' and girls' arm spans are represented on the two line plots?

8. How many boys and girls on the line plots have an arm span that is less than 55 in.?

9. Explain why a bar graph was used in **3–5** and a line plot in **6–8.**

Problem Solving and Applications

Using Data Use the graph to answer **10–13.**

10. At what age does the average person have 21 teeth?

11. About how many teeth does the average 28-year-old have?

12. How many more teeth does the average 38-year-old have than the average 58-year-old?

13. Estimation Does the average person have a greater or lesser number of teeth as he or she gets older?

14. Collecting Data Find examples of pictographs, line plots, and bar graphs in magazines and newspapers. Explain how they are used.

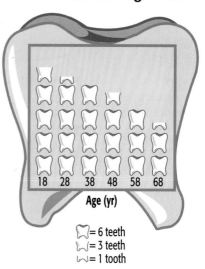

Teeth of the Average Person

Mixed Review: Basic Facts

Mental Math Find each sum or difference.

15. 6 + 5	**16.** 8 + 6	**17.** 15 − 9	**18.** 11 − 2	**19.** 12 − 7
20. 9 + 5	**21.** 4 + 8	**22.** 17 − 8	**23.** 13 − 5	**24.** 7 + 6
25. 11 − 3	**26.** 5 + 7	**27.** 9 + 2	**28.** 13 − 6	**29.** 6 + 6
30. 6 + 3	**31.** 5 + 8	**32.** 8 − 3	**33.** 14 − 6	**34.** 15 − 7

Reading Line Graphs

You Will Learn
how to use line graphs to analyze data

Vocabulary

line graph
shows increases or decreases over time

scale
the marked intervals on a graph

interval
the fixed distance between the numbers on the scale of a graph

vertical axis
up-and-down number line on a graph

horizontal axis
left-to-right number line on a graph

coordinates
ordered number pair used in graphing

Learn

Are you feeling a bit crowded wherever you go? Maybe you have good reason!

A **line graph** may be used to show trends and how data changes over a period of time. This line graph shows the change in the number of people per square mile in the United States between 1940 and 1990. The point with **coordinates** (1960, 51) is above 1960 and to the right of 51.

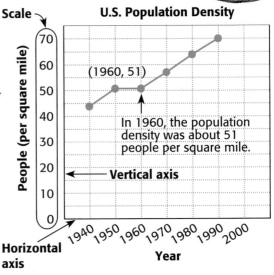

You can use the graph to see trends in the population density from 1940 to 1990. The population density has increased by 26 people per square mile over 50 years.

Talk About It

1. About what was the approximate population density in 1970? How do you know?

2. By 2004, about how many people per square mile do you think there will be?

Check

Math Tip

A broken scale uses this symbol (ξ) to show that some numbers are missing.

Use the line graph to answer **1–3**.

1. What do the numbers on the horizontal axis represent? What is the scale?

2. Give the coordinates that represent the average high temperature on September 21.

3. **Reasoning** What would you expect as the average high temperature in Chicago on September 17?

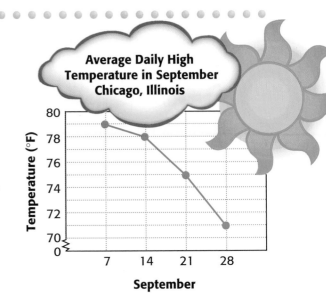

Practice •••••••••••••••••••••••••••••

Skills and Reasoning

Use the line graph to answer **4–9**.

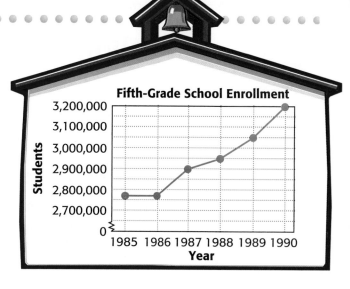

Fifth-Grade School Enrollment

4. About how many fifth-grade students were in school in 1986?

5. Write the coordinates that represent the number of fifth-grade students in school in 1987.

6. In which year was the enrollment the highest?

7. What is the scale on the vertical axis?

8. In which two years was the enrollment of fifth graders about the same?

9. Between which two years was there the least increase in enrollment: 1986–1987 or 1987–1988?

Problem Solving and Applications

Using Data Use the line graph to answer **10–13**.

The graph shows the change in the number of children between the ages of 5 and 13 in each group of 100 people in the United States.

10. Does this line graph show an upward trend, a downward trend, or neither? Explain.

11. **Collecting Data** The data for the line graph was collected before the year 2000. So, the population for 2000 was a projection. Find the most recent estimate or actual data for 2000.

12. **Critical Thinking** Make a projection for 2010.

13. **Social Studies** What if a line graph showed the number of people per 100 that are 65 years old or older. Do you think this graph would show an upward or a downward trend? Explain.

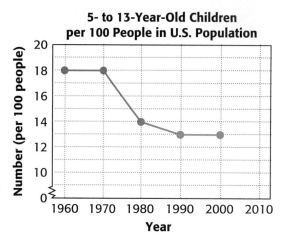

5- to 13-Year-Old Children per 100 People in U.S. Population

Mixed Review: Basic Facts

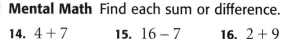

Mental Math Find each sum or difference.

14. $4 + 7$
15. $16 - 7$
16. $2 + 9$
17. $11 - 7$
18. $14 - 8$

19. $8 + 9$
20. $12 - 4$
21. $14 - 5$
22. $3 + 8$
23. $10 - 7$

24. $15 - 6$
25. $7 + 9$
26. $15 - 7$
27. $4 + 9$
28. $17 - 9$

Reading Stem-and-Leaf Plots

Frank from Forrest City, Arkansas and his uncle use their computers to keep in touch.

Learn

Although Frank and his uncle live in different cities, they don't let the distance come between them.

Frank jotted down the number of minutes each time they chatted online in August. Are most of their chats less than a half-hour?

Minutes per Chat
25 20 23 15 18 32 15 22 8 31
5 23 11 21 30 16 10 28 12 45

One way to organize Frank's list is in a **stem-and-leaf plot**. This kind of graph organizes data visually. It makes data easy to understand.

The tens digit of a number is the **stem**. The ones digit of a number is the **leaf**.

4	5 4 | 5 represents 45.
3	2 1 0
2	5 0 3 2 3 1 8
1	5 8 5 1 6 0 2
0	8 5

The shape of the leaves shows most chats are greater than 9 minutes and less than 30 minutes.

Frank and his uncle usually chat for less than a half-hour.

Math Tip
This row shows the data 15, 18, 15, 11, 16, 10, 12.

Talk About It

Why is zero used as a stem in the stem-and-leaf plot?

Check

Use the data to answer **1** and **2**.

Number of Calls to the Homework Line in 10 Days

25	26	9	24	18
6	12	7	18	20

Stem-and-Leaf Plot

2	5 6 4 0
1	8 2 8
0	9 6 7

1. Which numbers are stems? Leaves? What does each stand for?

2. **Reasoning** On how many days were more than 15 calls made?

Skills and Reasoning

Use the stem-and-leaf plot to answer **3–5.**

Annual Library Spending on Books ($ per person by state)

Stem	Leaf
0	6 8 9 7 8 7 9 8
1	9 1 2 3 0 8 6 2 0 9 3 7 6 0 4 6 5 3 6 2 4 3 2 0 9 2
2	4 1 2 8 4 5 2 1 3 2 0 4 4 2 1
3	6

3. What is the least amount spent by libraries? The greatest amount?

4. **Patterns** In what order are the stems arranged from top to bottom?

5. **Patterns** Make a statement about the amount spent per person on books by libraries in most states.

Problem Solving and Applications

Using Data Use the stem-and-leaf plot to answer **6–8.**

6. The exact figures for passengers using two different Paris, France, airports are 29,630,222 (Charles de Gaulle) and 26,617,556 (Orly). Where would you expect to find these figures located in the stem-and-leaf plot?

7. Do the two Paris airports combined have as many passengers as the airport with the greatest number of passengers? Explain.

8. O'Hare Airport in Chicago is the world's busiest airport. Where is its location on the plot? What does this data represent?

9. **Journal** Write about a situation in which you might use a stem-and-leaf plot.

World's 20 Busiest Airports in 1994 (millions of passengers)

6	6
5	2 3 1 4
4	2
3	5 0 3 0 5
2	5 6 6 7 7 7 7 8 9

Every year, over a quarter of a million commercial flights take off and land at O'Hare Airport.

Mixed Review: Basic Facts

Mental Math Find each product.

10. 3×5	**11.** 7×2	**12.** 4×0	**13.** 6×1	**14.** 4×9
15. 5×2	**16.** 8×1	**17.** 6×5	**18.** 9×0	**19.** 7×9

STAY SHARP!

PRACTICE AND APPLY

Range, Mode, and Median

You Will Learn
how to find the range, mode, and median for a set of data

Vocabulary

range
difference between greatest number and least number

mode
number that occurs most often

median
middle number when data are in order

Learn •

Suppose you wanted to buy a mountain bike. The line plot below shows the prices of different mountain bikes.

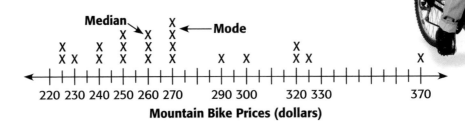

Mountain Bike Prices (dollars)

range   greatest number ($370) – least number ($225): $145

mode   number that occurs most often in a set of data: $270

median   middle number when data are ordered: $260

There can be more than one mode. If the number of data items is even, the median is halfway between the two middle numbers.

You can find the mode and median of the test scores in this line plot.

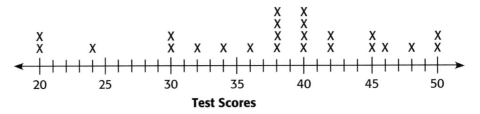

Test Scores

Problem Solving Hint
To find the median, put data items in order from least to greatest.

There are two modes: 38 and 40. There are 24 scores, so the median is halfway between the 12th and 13th scores. The median score is 39.

Talk About It

Will a set of data always have a range, a mode, and a median? Explain.

Check •

Using Data Use the Data File on page 6 to answer **1–4.**

1. Compare the ranges for girls' and boys' arm spans.

2. Which plot has only two modes?

3. Is the median of the girls' or boys' arm spans greater?

4. **Reasoning** Do boys or girls tend to have longer arm spans?

Skills and Reasoning

Use the line plot to answer **5** and **6**.

This line plot shows the number of books 25 students read during summer vacation.

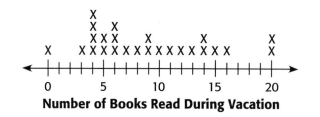

Number of Books Read During Vacation

5. Give the:

  a. range   **b.** mode   **c.** median

6. Aretha said, "About half the children read fewer than 8 books." Julio said, "About half the children read more than 8 books." Who is correct? Explain.

Use the stem-and-leaf plot to answer **7** and **8**.

This stem-and-leaf plot shows the number of regular season games won in the last 20 years by the National Basketball Association champions.

4	9 7 4
5	7 6 7 2 9 8
6	1 0 2 3 7 5 2 5 2 7
7	2

7. Give the: **a.** range   **b.** mode   **c.** median

8. Is the mode or the median a better number for describing the middle of a set of data? Explain.

Problem Solving and Applications

Using Data Use the pictures to answer **9–11**.

This picture shows the prices of 7 different youth helmets.

9. What is the median price for the helmets?

10. Money Only the $29, $30, and $33 helmets got better-than-average ratings by a consumer product rating organization. Which helmet would you buy? Explain.

11. What If A new helmet comes onto the market priced at $31. What would the new median price for a helmet be?

12. Critical Thinking One of the $250 mountain bikes in the line plot on page 16 got a very poor rating. What would be the effect of leaving this data item out of the line plot?

Mixed Review: Basic Facts

Mental Math Find each product.

13. 6×4 **14.** 2×8 **15.** 7×3 **16.** 5×6 **17.** 4×7

18. 8×6 **19.** 9×3 **20.** 5×8 **21.** 9×4 **22.** 7×7

Problem Solving

Analyze Word Problems:
Introduction to Problem Solving

You Will Learn
how to solve problems using a guide

Learn • • • • • • • • • • • • • • • • • •

The 4-step guide below can help you solve many kinds of problems. How many students did not choose movies or soccer?

Favorite Things to Do on Saturdays

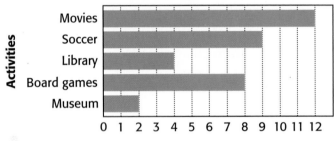

Activities: Movies, Soccer, Library, Board games, Museum

Number of Students

▶ **Understand**	Read the problem carefully. Find the information you need.	4 students chose the library, 8 chose board games, and 2 chose museums.
	Find the question.	How many did not choose movies or soccer?
▶ **Plan**	Think about what you need to do.	You need to combine the number who chose libraries, board games, and museums.
▶ **Solve**	Use the plan.	$4 + 8 + 2 = 14$
	Find the solution.	14 students did not choose movies or soccer.
▶ **Look Back**	Decide whether the answer makes sense.	35 students in all $- 21$ choosing movies or soccer 14 The answer makes sense.

What can you do to understand a problem?

Use the bar graph on page 18. How many more students like indoor activities than outdoor activities?

1. What information do you need to answer the question?

2. What operations would you use to solve this problem?

3. How many students like to spend time indoors?

4. How many like to spend time outdoors?

5. How many more like to spend time indoors than outdoors?

Problem Solving
Practice

Using Data Use the data in the bar graph on page 18 to answer 6—9. Choose the number sentence you would use to solve each problem.

6. In another survey of 35 students, 17 said they like to go to the movies. How many more is that than this survey?

   Ⓐ $17 + 12 = 29$ Ⓑ $17 - 12 = 5$

7. In a survey of 16-year-olds, three times as many students chose the library as in the survey on page 18. How many is that?

   Ⓐ $3 + 4 = 7$ Ⓑ $3 \times 4 = 12$

8. The students who chose movies were in 6 different classes. If the same number of students in each class chose movies, how many students in each class chose movies?

   Ⓐ $12 \div 6 = 2$ Ⓑ $12 \times 6 = 72$

Problem Solving
Strategies

- Use Objects/Act It Out
- Draw a Picture
- Look for a Pattern
- Guess and Check
- Use Logical Reasoning
- Make an Organized List
- Make a Table
- Solve a Simpler Problem
- Work Backward

Choose a Tool

9. **Money** The students who chose movies bought the tickets shown. How much did they pay in all?

   Ⓐ $12 + \$3.50 = \$15.50$ Ⓑ $12 \times \$3.50 = \$42$

Use any strategy to solve each problem.

10. **Money** Three soccer players said they rent equipment. They each pay $8.00. How much do they pay in all?

11. **Money** Robbie returned 3 books late to the library. He paid a total fine of $0.75. If the fine on each of the books was the same, how much did he pay for each book?

12. **Journal** How are the "Plan" and "Solve" steps different?

Problem Solving

Analyze Word Problems: **Choose an Operation**

You Will Learn
how to solve problems by choosing an operation

Learn •

Sally was paid $6 each week for 5 weeks to care for plants. How much did she earn?

Work Together

To choose an operation for a problem, think about the action taking place.

Add	Multiply
Combine groups.	Combine equal groups.
Subtract	**Divide**
Take away. Compare. Separate.	Share equally. Make equal groups.

▶ **Understand** What do you know?

What do you need to find out?

▶ **Plan** What will you do to find the answer? She was paid the same amount each week. Need to find the total amount.

What is the key action? Combine equal groups.

▶ **Solve** What operation will you use? Multiplication: $5 \times \$6 = \$30$

What is the answer? She was paid $30 for the 5 weeks.

▶ **Look Back** How can you check?

Talk About It

Suppose Sally was paid $5, $6, $6, $4, and $7 for 5 weeks' work. What operation could you use to find how much she was paid in all? Explain.

Choose the operation for each problem. Then solve each problem.

Brandon washed and waxed cars during the summer. He charged $3 to wash and $7 to wash and wax a car.

1. How much more did Brandon charge to wash and wax than just to wash a car?

2. He earned $18 on the cars he only washed.

   a. How many cars did he wash?

   b. How much did he earn by washing and waxing 6 cars?

   c. How much did he earn in all?

Problem Solving Practice

Write the operation needed for each problem.
Then solve each problem.

3. Marissa had 13 lawn-watering customers. That was more than she could handle, so she gave 5 of them to Beth. How many customers did Marissa keep for herself?

4. **Money** Luis collects the same amount from each customer on his paper route. He collected $28 one week from 4 customers. How much did they each pay?

5. Tina has finished all but 2 of her dog-walking jobs. She walks 11 dogs in all. How many dogs has she already walked?

6. **Time** John has been watching his little brother for 3 hours. His parents will not be home for another 4 hours. How long will John have watched his brother by the time his parents return?

7. In order to buy the new outfits she wants, Helen needs a total of 12 customers for her crafts business. She already has 5. How many more customers does she need?

8. **Using Data** The array shows how much Brian spent on supplies for each of his lawn-mowing customers. How much did he spend?

9. Janice increased her babysitting rate by $1 per hour. Now she will earn $12 for 4 hours of work. How much did she charge per hour before she raised her rate? What strategy did you use?

Problem Solving Strategies

- Use Objects/Act It Out
- Draw a Picture
- Look for a Pattern
- Guess and Check
- Use Logical Reasoning
- Make an Organized List
- Make a Table
- Solve a Simpler Problem
- Work Backward

Choose a Tool

PROBLEM SOLVING PRACTICE

Exploring Algebra: What's the Rule?

A	B
2	12
5	30
8	48
9	54
12	72

Problem Solving Connection

■ Look for a Pattern

■ Guess and Check

Vocabulary

variable
a letter that stands for a number or a range of numbers

Problem Solving Hint

Be sure to try a rule on several pairs of numbers.

Explore •

You can find a rule that relates numbers in a table.

Work Together

1. Find the rule for this table.

   a. Look at the first pair of numbers, 2 and 12.

   b. How do you think they are related?
      Try adding. 2 + 10 = 12

   c. Does adding 10 work for the second pair?
      5 + 10 = 15, not 30

   d. Go back and try again.
      Try multiplying.

   e. Does it work for the second pair?
      How about the third pair? The fourth?

   f. Write the rule.

2. Find the rule for each table. Then copy and complete it.

a.

A	B
24	3
32	
48	6
56	
64	8

b.

A	B
5	12
10	
15	22
20	
25	32
30	

c.

A	B
7	2
9	4
11	6
13	8
14	
17	
18	13

Talk About It

How many pairs should you test to see if your rule works?

Connect

When using a table, you can tell how the numbers in column B relate to those in column A in words or using a **variable** such as *n*.

A	B
0	0
1	5
3	15
6	30

Using Words: Multiply by 5.

Using a Variable: $n \times 5$

A	B
7	1
14	2
28	4
49	7

Using Words: Divide by 7.

Using a Variable: $n \div 7$

Practice

Find the rule for each table. Give the rule using words and a variable.

1.

A	B
9	3
15	5
24	8
30	10

2.

A	B
1	10
3	30
7	70
10	100

3.

A	B
0	0
8	1
24	3
56	7

4.

A	B
1	6
2	7
3	8
4	9
5	10

Copy and complete each table. Give its rule using words and a variable.

5.

A	B
4	20
5	
7	35
12	

6.

A	B
9	1
36	
72	8
90	

7. Geometry Readiness

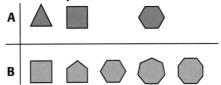

Write each rule using a variable.

8. 7 more than a number   **9.** Divide a number by 10   **10.** Multiply a number by 1

Write each rule using words.

11. $n \times 34$ **12.** $n \div 13$ **13.** $n \times 3$ **14.** $n - 4$ **15.** $n + 2$

 Copy and complete each table. Use your calculator if you wish.

16. rule: $n \times 7$

A	0	7	12	19
B				

17. rule: $n \div 6$

A	36	186	300	666
B				

 18. Journal Explain how you can find a rule for a table.

SECTION A
Review and Practice

Vocabulary Choose the best word to complete each sentence.

Word List	
pictograph	mode
variable	line plot
stem	range

1. The number that occurs most often in a set of data is called the ____.

2. A ____ uses pictures or symbols to show data.

3. A ____ is a letter that stands for a number or range of numbers.

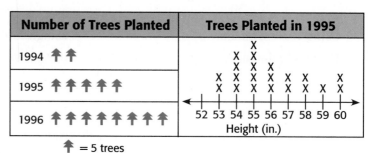

Number of Trees Planted	
1994	🌲 🌲
1995	🌲 🌲 🌲 🌲 🌲
1996	🌲 🌲 🌲 🌲 🌲 🌲 🌲

🌲 = 5 trees

Trees Planted in 1995 — Height (in.): 52 53 54 55 56 57 58 59 60

(Lesson 1) Use the pictograph or the line plot to answer **4** and **5**.

4. What pattern do you see in the number of trees planted?

5. How many trees are 55 in. or taller?

(Lesson 2) Use this line graph to answer **6** and **7**.

6. What is the weight of the baby at 3 months?

7. What can you predict about the baby's weight at 15 months?

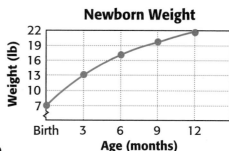

Newborn Weight

Weight (lb): 22, 19, 16, 13, 10, 7
Age (months): Birth, 3, 6, 9, 12

(Lessons 3 and 4) Use this stem-and-leaf plot to answer **8–10**.

8. What is the greatest amount spent by one person at the book fair?

9. List the stems and the leaves.

10. Give the range, median, and mode for the money spent at the book fair.

Dollars Spent at the Book Fair per Person

0	4 6 4 2 5 9
1	0 6 3 8 0
2	2 0 1

(Lessons 5 and 6) Solve.

11. Out of 12 students surveyed, 5 owned dogs and 3 owned cats. How many did not own a cat or a dog?

(Lesson 7) Copy and complete each table. Write its rule using a variable.

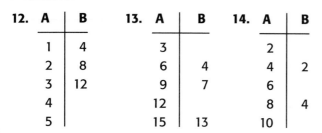

12. A	B		13. A	B		14. A	B
1	4		3			2	
2	8		6	4		4	2
3	12		9	7		6	
4			12			8	4
5			15	13		10	

15. **Journal** Explain how you can write a rule in two ways.

Skills Checklist

In this section, you have:

☑ Reviewed Basic Facts

☑ Read Graphs

☑ Read Line Graphs

☑ Read Stem-and-Leaf Plots

☑ Found Range, Mode, and Median

☑ Solved Problems by Using a Guide and by Choosing an Operation

☑ Explored Algebra by Finding the Rule

REVIEW AND PRACTICE

B Making Graphs and Facts Review

Elayna from New Jersey enjoys riding the New York City subways. She is recording data for a stem-and-leaf plot to show how long it takes in minutes to get from one station to another on the subway line. What will the stems show? What will the leaves show?

GET READY!

Brushing Up On Basic Facts

Review facts. Write each using numbers and symbols. Then find each answer.

1. the product of seven and five

2. the difference of eleven and three

3. the sum of eight and four

4. thirty-six divided by six

Skills Checklist

In this section, you will:

☐ Learn About Scales and Bar Graphs

☐ Explore Making Line Graphs

☐ Explore Making Stem-and-Leaf Plots

☐ Solve Problems by Using Logical Reasoning

☐ Review Basic Facts

Scales and Bar Graphs

You Will Learn

how to choose a scale when you make a bar graph

Remember

The scale tells you what units are used on the axes of a graph.

Learn	• •

I scream, you scream, we all scream for ice cream!

Adults and children in the United States eat more ice cream than anyone else in the world, but the Australians aren't far behind.

The two bar graphs show the same data, but they use different scales.

Which graph has a scale that makes it easier to give a closer estimate of the amounts produced?

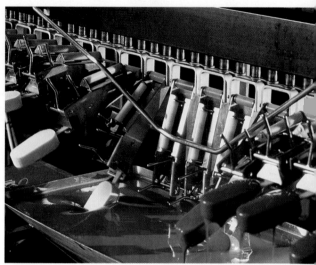

In 1992, U.S. companies used machines, like this dipping unit, to make over 3 billion liters of ice cream.

Example 1

The first graph makes it easier to give a closer estimate of the amounts produced.

This scale increases in 2-qt units.

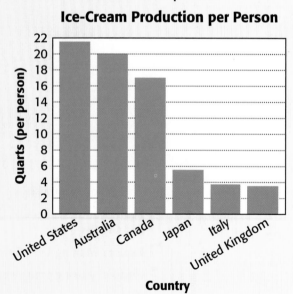

This scale increases in 5-qt units.

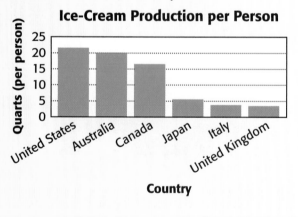

You can also use horizontal bars to show data in a bar graph.

Example 2

Make a horizontal bar graph for the data in this table.

Most Popular Ice Cream Flavors			
Flavor	**Number of People per 100**	**Flavor**	**Number of People per 100**
Butter pecan	|||||	Chocolate	||||| ||||
Vanilla	||||| ||||| ||||| ||||| ||||	Strawberry	|||||

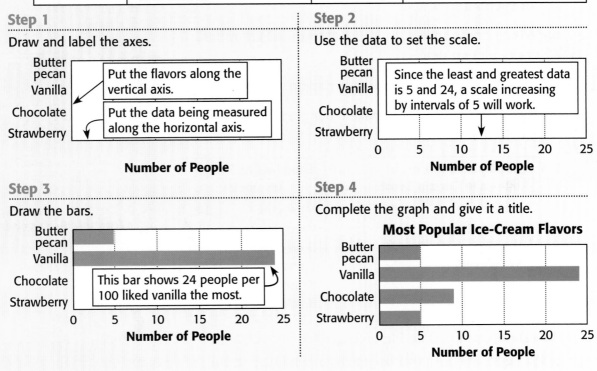

Step 1

Draw and label the axes.

Put the flavors along the vertical axis.

Put the data being measured along the horizontal axis.

Step 2

Use the data to set the scale.

Since the least and greatest data is 5 and 24, a scale increasing by intervals of 5 will work.

Step 3

Draw the bars.

This bar shows 24 people per 100 liked vanilla the most.

Step 4

Complete the graph and give it a title.

Most Popular Ice-Cream Flavors

Talk About It

Would a scale with intervals of 20 work for the graph in Example 2? Explain.

Check

Choose a scale and make a bar graph of the data in each table.

1.

Number of Years Between Invention and Use in $\frac{1}{2}$ of U.S. Homes	
Technology Invented	**Number of Years**
Cable Television	39
Telephone	74
VCR	30
Television	21

2.

Population of Native American Peoples, 1990 Census	
Native American Peoples	**Population (thousands)**
Cherokee	308
Navajo	219
Chippewa	104
Sioux	103
Choctaw	82

Skills and Reasoning

Using Data Use the bar graphs to answer **3–6**.

3. What is the scale on Graph A? Graph B?

4. Do both graphs record the same amount of vitamin C for each kind of juice?

5. Which graph implies that the amount of vitamin C varies a great deal?

6. Which graph is easier to read? Explain.

Science Choose a scale and make a bar graph of the data in each table.

7.
Top Speeds (mi/hr) of Athletes in Certain Sports	
Cycling	140
Rollerskating	26
Running	28
Skateboarding	53
Skiing	124
Speedskating	30

8.
Loudness of Sounds (decibels)	
Jet engine	140
Loud music	110
Heavy traffic	90
Conversation	60
Whispering	20
Rustling leaves	10

Using Data Use the Data File on page 7 to answer **9–12**.

9. What scale could you use to make a bar graph for the data table?

10. What labels would you use for your horizontal and vertical axes?

11. Make a bar graph to show the data.

12. Describe how a graph with intervals of 5 would look different from a graph with intervals of 10.

Problem Solving and Applications

Using Data Use the data to answer **13–16**.

13. Make a bar graph with the data in the table.

14. Does it make sense to say that all 6-to-11-year-olds watch exactly 21 hr of television every week? Explain.

15. What is the range of the data?

16. **What If** 18-to-24-year-olds watch television 2 hr less each week. Find the median of this new data.

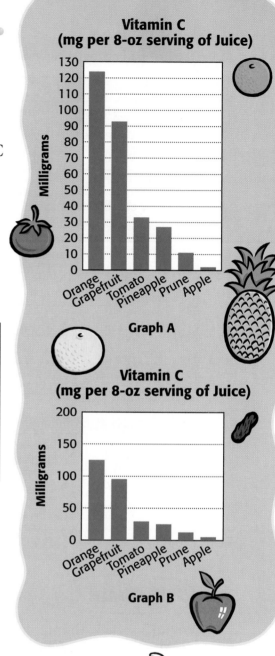

Graph A

Graph B

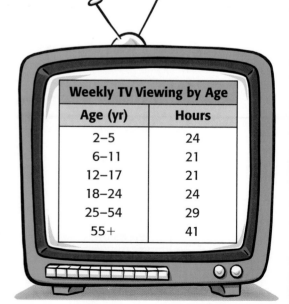

Weekly TV Viewing by Age	
Age (yr)	Hours
2–5	24
6–11	21
12–17	21
18–24	24
25–54	29
55+	41

Problem Solving and CAREERS

Software companies look for new ideas and for people to develop them. In 1995, consumer reporters rated the top computer games as follows.

Prices and Ratings of Top-Rated Computer Games (1995)		
Game	Average Price	Score (out of 100)
The Lost Mind of Dr. Brain	$41	82
Eagle-Eye Mysteries in London	$45	70
Where in the World is Carmen Sandiego?	$54	80
Nile: Passage to Egypt	$43	68
SimCity 2000	$55	68
Theme Park	$45	63
Gizmos & Gadgets	$45	69
Science Sleuths	$33	65

Computer programmers, like these, develop and design video games.

17. Make a horizontal bar graph of the price data.

18. Make a vertical bar graph of the scores.

19. Compare the graphs. What can you tell a friend about top-rated computer games and their prices?

20. What is the range of the prices?

21. What is the mode of the prices?

22. What is the range of the scores?

23. What is the mode of the scores?

24. Collecting Data Find out about how much the starting salary is for a person who works with computers.

25. Journal Describe the steps you take in making a bar graph from the data given in a table.

Mixed Review: Basic Facts

Mental Math Find each quotient.

26. $30 \div 5$ **27.** $16 \div 2$ **28.** $8 \div 1$ **29.** $20 \div 5$ **30.** $45 \div 9$

31. $14 \div 2$ **32.** $63 \div 9$ **33.** $35 \div 5$ **34.** $36 \div 9$ **35.** $15 \div 5$

36. $18 \div 2$ **37.** $72 \div 9$ **38.** $7 \div 1$ **39.** $40 \div 5$ **40.** $27 \div 9$

Exploring Making Line Graphs

Problem Solving Connection

- Draw a Picture
- Find a Pattern

Materials

- grid paper
- ruler

Explore

Elayna rides the New York City subway on school holidays. Can you tell from the data in the table about how many people will be riding the subway with Elayna at 2 P.M.?

New York City Subway Riders					
Hour	9 A.M.	11 A.M.	1 P.M.	3 P.M.	5 P.M.
Number of Riders (thousands)	203	114	118	207	300

You can make a line graph to estimate the number of riders.

Elayna, from Jersey City, New Jersey, goes to New York City to visit museums.

Remember

To find the ordered pair (2, 3), move 2 to the right on the horizontal axis, move up 3 on the vertical axis.

Work Together

1. Use grid paper.

   a. Title the graph and draw the axes.

   b. Put the times on the horizontal axis.

   c. Find the range and choose a scale for the vertical axis.

   d. Place a point on the graph for each ordered pair.

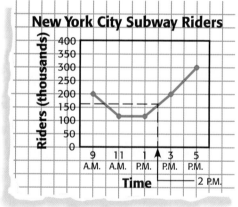

   e. Use line segments to connect the points.

   f. Find a point on the horizontal axis halfway between 1 P.M. and 3 P.M. Use a ruler to find the point on the graph directly above 2 P.M.

   g. Then use the ruler to find the number on the vertical axis directly left of this point. Record the coordinates.

2. About how many thousands of riders were on the subway at 2 P.M.?

Tell how your graph helped you find out about how many riders were on the New York City subway at 2 P.M.

Connect •

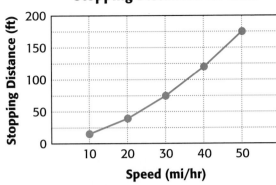

Stopping Distances for Cars

You can use line graphs to see trends, or changes over time, in data.

The graph shows that stopping distances increase greatly as speed increases. For example, the stopping distance at 60 mi/hr would be much greater than 175 ft.

Practice •

1. Use this table to make a line graph.

2. Use the graph to determine about how many riders there would be at 6 P.M.

3. Between which two times shown on the graph does the number of riders change the least?

New York City Subway Riders	
Hour	Number of Riders (thousands)
5 P.M.	350
7 P.M.	132
9 P.M.	60
11 P.M.	37
1 A.M.	9

4. **Science** Waves caused by the eruption of underwater volcanoes or earthquakes are called *tsunamis*. They can travel about 1,000 km/hr over the surface of the water. In open water, the waves might be 1 m tall, but they are often 50 m tall by the time they reach land. Use the data in the table to make a line graph that shows the height of the waves at different distances from land.

Katsuchika Hokusai's *In the Well of the Great Wave of Kanagawa.*

Distance from Land (km)	1	5	10	15	20	25	30
Height of Waves (m)	45	32	20	10	5	1	1

5. **Journal** Explain how a line graph can be used to help you make predictions.

Exploring Making Stem-and-Leaf Plots

Problem Solving Connection

- Draw a Picture
- Look for a Pattern

Explore •

The list shows the number of minutes it takes several students to get to their schools.

Minutes to School				
17	36	82	9	20
78	40	19	39	19
90	27	45	76	34
62	33	45	61	59
15	30	11	55	16

Work Together

Make a stem-and-leaf plot to show the minutes to school data.

1. List the stems you will need.

2. Record the numbers in your stem-and-leaf plot. Remember, each stem represents a tens digit and each leaf a ones digit.

Talk About It

3. Describe your stem-and-leaf plot. Do all the stems have leaves? Do all the stems have about the same number of leaves? Explain.

4. Which stem has the greatest number of leaves? Explain.

Connect

Stem-and-leaf plots help you see how the data is clustered, or grouped.

Test Scores in Mr. Hartke's Class
62 84 77 68 75 92 87 85 79 82
80 94 77 69 81 90 78 86 65 76
85 92 74 86

```
6 | 2 8 9 5
7 | 7 5 9 7 8 6 4
8 | 4 7 5 2 0 1 6 5 6
9 | 2 4 0 2
```

Most of the test scores are between 70 and 89.

Practice

Using Data Use the table to answer 1–10.

1. Make a stem-and-leaf plot for the American League data.

2. Make a stem-and-leaf plot for the National League data.

3. Which league had a champion with fewer than 30 home runs?

4. Which league had more champions who hit 30–39 home runs?

5. Which league had more champions who hit 40–49 home runs?

American League and National League Home Run Champions, 1976–1996					
Years	Home Runs		Year	Home Runs	
	AL	NL		AL	NL
1976	32	38	1987	49	49
1977	39	52	1988	42	39
1978	46	40	1989	36	47
1979	45	48	1990	51	40
1980	41	48	1991	44	38
1981	22	31	1992	43	35
1982	39	37	1993	46	46
1983	39	40	1994	40	43
1984	43	36	1995	50	40
1985	40	37	1996	52	47
1986	40	37			

6. Which league had more champions who hit more than 50 home runs?

7. What is the median number of home runs for the American League?

8. What is the median number of home runs for the National League?

9. **Patterns** Describe the shapes of the stem-and-leaf plots for the American and National Leagues.

10. **Journal** Explain how organizing data from a table in a stem-and-leaf plot helps you "see" the data better.

As of 1996, Eddie Murray was 11th on the all-time list of major league players with 3,218 hits.

STOP and Practice

Find each sum or difference.

1. $\begin{array}{r} 5 \\ +4 \\ \hline \end{array}$	2. $\begin{array}{r} 13 \\ -4 \\ \hline \end{array}$	3. $\begin{array}{r} 9 \\ +5 \\ \hline \end{array}$	4. $\begin{array}{r} 7 \\ +8 \\ \hline \end{array}$	5. $\begin{array}{r} 17 \\ -9 \\ \hline \end{array}$

6. $\begin{array}{r} 8 \\ -8 \\ \hline \end{array}$	7. $\begin{array}{r} 14 \\ -8 \\ \hline \end{array}$	8. $\begin{array}{r} 12 \\ -3 \\ \hline \end{array}$	9. $\begin{array}{r} 6 \\ +6 \\ \hline \end{array}$	10. $\begin{array}{r} 5 \\ -0 \\ \hline \end{array}$

11. $0+7$ 12. $6+7$ 13. $12-5$ 14. $15-5$ 15. $4+6$

16. $\begin{array}{r} 23 \\ +12 \\ \hline \end{array}$	17. $\begin{array}{r} 10 \\ +14 \\ \hline \end{array}$	18. $\begin{array}{r} 35 \\ -10 \\ \hline \end{array}$	19. $\begin{array}{r} 44 \\ -22 \\ \hline \end{array}$	20. $\begin{array}{r} 60 \\ -10 \\ \hline \end{array}$

Find each product or quotient.

21. $\begin{array}{r} 7 \\ \times 5 \\ \hline \end{array}$	22. $\begin{array}{r} 4 \\ \times 6 \\ \hline \end{array}$	23. $\begin{array}{r} 3 \\ \times 2 \\ \hline \end{array}$	24. $\begin{array}{r} 9 \\ \times 6 \\ \hline \end{array}$	25. $\begin{array}{r} 8 \\ \times 8 \\ \hline \end{array}$

26. $15 \div 3$ 27. $12 \div 6$ 28. $14 \div 2$ 29. $45 \div 5$ 30. $36 \div 9$

31. 4×0 32. $15 \div 3$ 33. $72 \div 9$ 34. 4×8 35. 0×7

36. $4\overline{)28}$ 37. $7\overline{)42}$ 38. $9\overline{)63}$ 39. $2\overline{)18}$ 40. $8\overline{)40}$

41. $36 \div 6$ 42. 6×8 43. $30 \div 5$ 44. 7×9 45. 3×9

Error Search

Find each answer that is not correct. Write it correctly and explain the error.

46. $7\overline{)35}$ with quotient 8 47. $\begin{array}{r} 7 \\ +8 \\ \hline 56 \end{array}$ 48. $\begin{array}{r} 8 \\ \times 4 \\ \hline 36 \end{array}$ 49. $\begin{array}{r} 9 \\ -2 \\ \hline 7 \end{array}$

50. $45 \div 9 = 6$ 51. $12-7=4$ 52. $1 \times 1 = 2$ 53. $2 \times 3 = 5$

54. $7 \times 4 = 24$ 55. $6+6=1$ 56. $12-9=3$ 57. $56 \div 8 = 48$

Helping Hands!

You can use your fingers to do multiplication by nines.

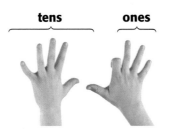

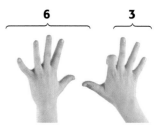

To multiply 7×9, count 7 fingers, starting with the pinky on your left hand. Bend down the seventh finger.

To get the answer, consider the fingers to the left of the bent finger as tens and the fingers to the right of the bent finger as ones.

For 7×9, 6 fingers to the left of the bent finger represent 6 tens, or 60. The 3 fingers to the right represent 3 ones. That's 63 in all!

On your paper, draw hands to represent each of these facts. Include the tens and ones above each finger. Find each product.

58. 2×9 **59.** 5×9 **60.** 8×9 **61.** 9×9 **62.** 3×9

Number Sense   Evens and Odds

Look at these diagrams.

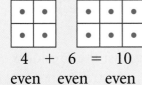

$$4 + 6 = 10$$
even even even

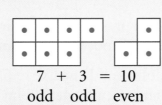

$$7 + 3 = 10$$
odd odd even

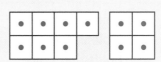

$$7 + 4 = 11$$
odd even odd

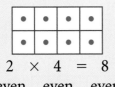

$$2 \times 4 = 8$$
even even even

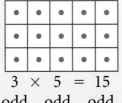

$$3 \times 5 = 15$$
odd odd odd

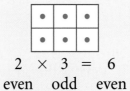

$$2 \times 3 = 6$$
even odd even

63. What is the result when you add
  a. two even numbers?
  b. two odd numbers?
  c. an even and an odd number?

64. What is the result when you multiply
  a. two even numbers?
  b. two odd numbers?
  c. an even and an odd number?

Write whether each sum or product is even or odd without doing the operation.

65. 3×3 **66.** $5 + 4$ **67.** $7 + 5$ **68.** 4×5 **69.** 3×8

Problem Solving

Analyze Strategies: Use Logical Reasoning

You Will Learn
how to solve problems by using logical reasoning

Learn •

Four friends are president, vice president, treasurer, and secretary of the Game Players Club. The president speaks first at meetings and Kim speaks next. John and Lana like to play against the president and vice president. Mario's brother is the secretary of the club. Which office does each friend hold?

Work Together

▶ **Understand**   What do you know?
What do you need to find out?

▶ **Plan**   How will you find out what you need to know?   Read the clues in order. Use logic to write what you know in the table.

▶ **Solve**   Write *yes* in the table if the player holds that office. Write *no* if the player does not.

Reading Tip
Look for the answer in the table.

- The president speaks first and Kim speaks next. Kim is not the president.

- John and Lana like to play against the president and vice president. John and Lana aren't president or vice president. Mario must be the president. Kim must be the vice president.

- Mario's brother is the secretary. John must be the secretary. Lana must be the treasurer.

What is the answer?

Player	John	Kim	Lana	Mario
President	no	no	no	yes
Vice President	no	yes	no	no
Secretary	yes	no	no	no
Treasurer	no	no	yes	no

▶ **Look Back**   How can you check the answer?

Another Example

Helen, Sam, Shannon, and Jack are the last ones left in a game of musical chairs. Use the clues and the picture to identify which student is wearing each color.

What You Read

a. Helen is across from the student wearing yellow.

b. Jack is just behind Shannon.

What You Know from the Picture

a. Helen is wearing red so Shannon must be wearing yellow.

b. Jack is wearing blue.

c. Sam must be wearing green.

 **Talk About It**

How does logic help you find the answer?

Check

Problem Solving
Understand
Plan
Solve
Look Back

1. Adam, Carol, Edwin, and Gail participate in swimming, tennis, baseball, and roller hockey. Carol plays tennis. Adam hates the water. If Edwin plays baseball, in what sport does each participate?

   a. What information is given directly?

   b. Which questions must be answered?

   c. Which clue helps you decide what sport Adam does **not** play?

   d. How can you find Gail's sport?

   e. Which sport does each play?

2. Four tournament players sat around a square table. The champion was on Mai's right. Jeffrey was across from Mai. Ann was on Jeffrey's right and across from Nicole. Who was the champion?

Apply the Strategy

Use logical reasoning to solve each problem.

3. The game room snack menu has pretzels, popcorn, chips, and trail mix. Joseph and John each choose two snacks, but neither chooses the same snack. Joseph never eats pretzels. John hates popcorn. Both boys agree that pretzels and chips do not go together. Which snacks did each choose?

4. Each year, club members rate new games. This year, *Minute by Minute* came in last. *Baloney* barely beat out *Guess What*, but was behind *My Hero*. *The Pits* came in just ahead of *Minute by Minute*. *You Need an Operation* was ahead of *Baloney* but just behind *My Hero*. In what order did the club members rate the games?

Problem Solving Strategies

- Use Objects/Act It Out
- Draw a Picture
- Look for a Pattern
- Guess and Check
- Use Logical Reasoning
- Make an Organized List
- Make a Table
- Solve a Simpler Problem
- Work Backward

Choose a Tool

Choose a Strategy

Use any strategy to solve each problem.

5. The board game that the club members chose for the tournament this year can be played by either 3 or 4 players. There are 12 players in the tournament. What is the least number of boards they will need?

7. **Money** The club members have $80.00 saved for buying games this year. They want to buy *Tantrum* for $20 and *Fooled Me* for $15. They want to spend all the money and buy at least 5 games. How many of each game should they buy?

9. The greatest score you can get when playing *Fooled Me* is 450 points. The greatest score for *Tantrum* is less than the greatest score for *My Hero* which is 225 points. Put the games in order from least to greatest score.

6. **Time** One game says that you have no more than 1 minute to take your turn. If you make your move in 45 seconds, how much less than 1 minute did you need?

8. *It's My Party* was rated by 20 club members. 8 more liked it than disliked it. How many club members liked the game?

10. One game has red, blue, and yellow counters. How many 2-color counter combinations can you make? List them.

Problem Solving and TECHNOLOGY

Most cars do not travel as fast as jet planes, but there are some that do. Two of them, the *Spirit of America* and the *Thrust SSC*, seek the world record.

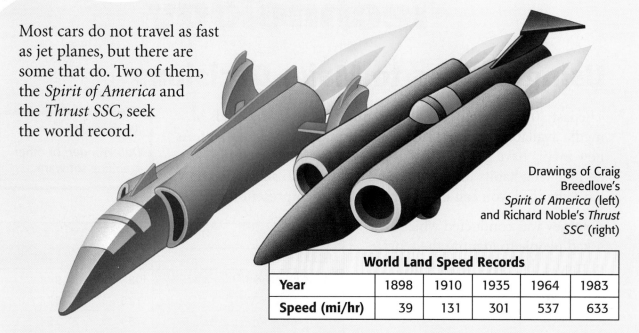

Drawings of Craig Breedlove's *Spirit of America* (left) and Richard Noble's *Thrust SSC* (right)

World Land Speed Records					
Year	1898	1910	1935	1964	1983
Speed (mi/hr)	39	131	301	537	633

Using Data Use the data to answer **11–14.**

11. What is the difference in speed between the first record shown and the 1983 record?

12. Between which two years shown was there the greatest increase in the speed record?

13. **Science** Sound travels at about 760 mi/hr. How many miles per hour faster than the 1983 record will either car have to travel to reach the speed of sound?

14. **Measurement** Together, the *Thrust SSC* and the *Spirit of America* weigh 23,000 lb. The *Thrust SSC* weighs 5,000 lb more than the *Spirit*. How much does each weigh? Give the strategy you used to solve the problem.

15. **Journal** Explain how using a table can help you solve a logic problem.

Mixed Review: Basic Facts

Mental Math Find each quotient.

16. $16 \div 4$	**17.** $27 \div 3$	**18.** $48 \div 8$	**19.** $24 \div 6$	**20.** $56 \div 7$
21. $24 \div 3$	**22.** $42 \div 6$	**23.** $63 \div 7$	**24.** $32 \div 4$	**25.** $72 \div 8$
26. $42 \div 7$	**27.** $36 \div 4$	**28.** $56 \div 8$	**29.** $18 \div 3$	**30.** $48 \div 6$
31. $12 \div 3$	**32.** $54 \div 6$	**33.** $49 \div 7$	**34.** $81 \div 9$	**35.** $21 \div 3$
36. $36 \div 9$	**37.** $64 \div 8$	**38.** $18 \div 2$	**39.** $20 \div 4$	**40.** $25 \div 5$

Technology

Using Graphs to Make Decisions

The last 30 years have seen an amazing growth in the kinds of media available for Americans' education and entertainment. As new media have gained popularity, other reading, listening, and viewing habits in America have changed. To show how they have changed, you can use a variety of ways to present the data.

Materials

DataWonder! or other graphing software

A survey was conducted which asked people to identify the types of media they used during the course of a year. Hourly totals were then calculated.

HOURS PER YEAR			
MEDIA		1986	1996
1	Network TV	985	948
2	Cable TV	126	377
3	Daily Newspapers	184	164
4	Books	88	101
5	Home Video	22	55
6	Recorded Music	173	287
7	Movies in Theaters	10	11

Work Together

Use graphing software to organize the data into a report so that it can be easily understood.

1 Open a **Full Data Table** in the software program.

- Enter this data table. Use the Helper option under the File menu if you need help creating the table.

2 Graph the data in your table.

- Choose **Show Graph** from the **Graphs** menu.

- Next, choose **Vertical Bar** from the Graphs menu, or click on the vertical-bar icon at the top of the graph window.

Math Tip
You can change the width of columns.

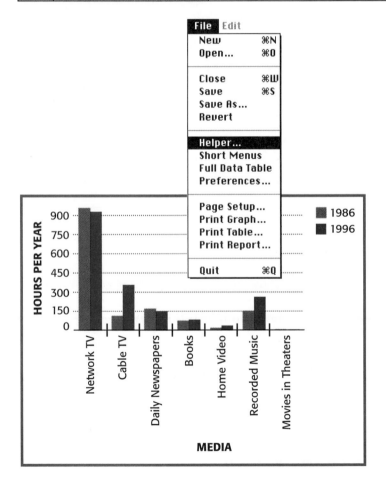

3 Put this graph into your **Report** window.

- Select **Show Report** from the **Report** menu.

- Select **Insert Graph** from the **Report** menu.

- Give your graph a title and **Print Report**. Close this **Report** window.

4 Now create a second data table.

- Pull down the **File** menu and select **New.**

- Create a table using this information.

- Choose **Line Graph** from the **Graphs** menu, or click on the line-graph icon at the top of the graph window.

5 Open a new **Report** window. Insert your new graph into it. Give the graph a title.

Exercises

Answer **1–4** in the Report window. **Print Report** when you finish.

1. Look at your double-bar graph. Which medium was used by the greatest number of people in 1986? In 1996?

2. Which two media showed the greatest increase in use over the 10-year period?

3. Look at your line graph. How does the number of people watching prime-time television change between Wednesday and Friday?

4. Which graph is better at demonstrating how data change as time passes?

Extensions

Answer **5** and **6** in the Report window. **Print Report** when you finish.

5. How would knowing which media had seen the greatest increase in number of hours used help you make advertising decisions? In which media would you choose to advertise? Explain.

6. **Reasoning** Why is the data for Movies in Theaters almost invisible on the bar graph? How could you use the Change Scale option to show this data? What changes can you see on the graph?

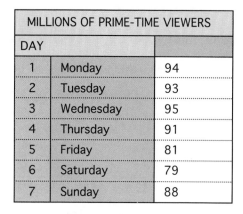

MILLIONS OF PRIME-TIME VIEWERS		
DAY		
1	Monday	94
2	Tuesday	93
3	Wednesday	95
4	Thursday	91
5	Friday	81
6	Saturday	79
7	Sunday	88

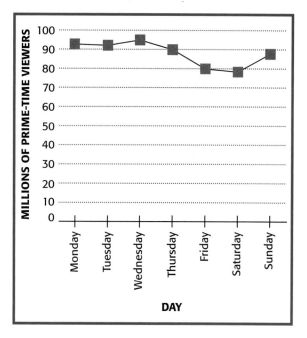

Review and Practice

(Lessons 8 and 9) Use these graphs to answer 1–6.

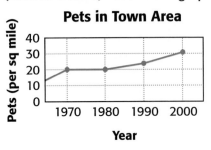

Pets in Town Area

Dog Hair Length

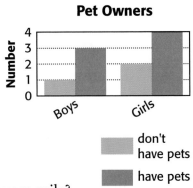

Pet Owners

1. In which year did the town first have at least 20 pets per square mile?

2. What can you predict about the number of pets per square mile in the town in the year 2010?

3. Which graph shows that beagles have the shortest hair?

4. About how many inches longer is a sheepdog's hair than a terrier's?

5. How many more boys have pets than don't have pets?

6. How many more girls than boys have pets?

(Lesson 10) Use the table to answer 7–10.

7. Make a stem-and-leaf plot for the OK Videos data.

8. What is the median number of videos rented?

9. What is the range of the number of videos rented?

10. What is the mode for the number of videos rented?

Video Rentals at OK Videos	
Date	Number of Videos Rented
October 1	20
October 2	15
October 3	22
October 4	18
October 5	26
October 6	30
October 7	26

(Lesson 11) Use logical reasoning to answer each.

11. Put these four students in order by age from least to greatest. Al is older than Cindy but younger than Beth. Either Dave or Beth is the youngest.

12. Ed, Fred, Gail, and Holly form a construction group. There is a painter, plumber, electrician, and carpenter. Ed and Fred will not paint. The carpenter's name begins with H. The electrician's name is shorter than the plumber's. Who does each job?

13. **Journal** Describe how you would graph the point (2, 3) on a coordinate grid.

Skills Checklist

In this section, you have:

☑ Learned About Scales and Bar Graphs

☑ Explored Making Line Graphs

☑ Explored Making Stem-and-Leaf Plots

☑ Solved Problems by Using Logical Reasoning

☑ Reviewed Basic Facts

YOUR CHOICE

Choose at least one of the following. Use what you have learned in this chapter.

① Personal Pulse

Count how many times your heart beats in one minute by placing two fingers firmly under your thumb where your wrist and hand meet. Record your pulse for 1 min, once every 5 min, over the span of 1 hr (you will have 12 entries). Then make a stem-and-leaf plot to find the rate at which your heart most commonly beats.

② Sports Logic

Solve this problem using logical reasoning. Inez, Jake, Kate, and Lou each like one of these sports: baseball, tennis, biking, and basketball. Jake, Kate, and Lou like sports that require the use of a ball. Jake's sport requires a court and a racquet but Kate's doesn't require either. Who likes each sport?

③ Age Action

At Home Find out the ages of ten friends, family members, or members of your community. What is the range, mode, and median age for your group? Use a calculator if you wish.

④ Over Time

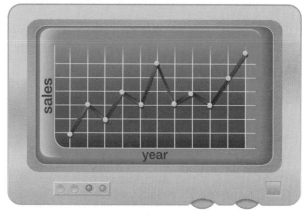

Pick a topic of your choice from **www.mathsurf.com/5/ch1**. Choose a topic that will give you data over a period of years. Then make a line graph for your data. Be sure to label the vertical and horizontal axes.

Review/Test

Vocabulary Match each word or words with its meaning.

1. For the set: 8, 2, 3, 4, 5, 9, 8; it is 8.
2. For the set: 8, 1, 7, 9, 6; it is 7.
3. For the set: 8, 2, 3, 9, 8; it is 7.
4. An ordered number pair used in graphing
5. Shows trends over a period of time
6. A scale across the bottom of a graph
7. The marked intervals on a graph
8. Can be used to organize data by their digits

a. stem-and-leaf plot
b. coordinates
c. line graph
d. mode
e. median
f. range
g. scale
h. horizontal axis

(Lessons 1–4 and 8–10) Use the table or the stem-and-leaf plot to answer **9** and **10** and **13–15**.

Soccer Ball Sales	
Number Sold	**Year**
50	1995
45	1996
30	1997

9. Choose a scale and make a bar graph to show the number of soccer balls sold.

10. How would you represent the number of soccer balls sold in 1995 in a pictograph? What scale would you use?

11. Choose a scale and make a line graph to show the sales of soccer equipment over these 6 months: January: $3,000; February: $3,500; March: $4,250; April: $4,000; May: $4,000; June: $3,500.

12. Do you predict that July's soccer equipment sales will be greater than or less than June's?

13. What are the leaves for the stem 8?

14. Find Janele's median spelling grade.

15. What is the range for Janele's spelling grades?

Janele's Spelling Grades

7	8 5
8	5 6
9	5 0 5

(Lessons 6 and 7) Copy and complete each table. Give its rule using words and a variable.

16.
A	2 3 5	10
B	5 6	11

17.
A	10 8	4 2
B	5 4 3	

18.
A	3 5	9 11
B	1	5 7

(Lessons 5 and 11) Use logical reasoning to solve the problem.

19. Mac, Ned, and Opal played a game in which the highest score wins. Opal beat Mac but lost to Ned. Who had each of these scores: 9, 8, 6?

CHAPTER 1
Performance Assessment

Which activities keep you and your friends busy in the afternoons and evenings during the school year? Survey 12 of your friends to answer that question. Ask each person what activities he or she does from the time school is out until he or she goes to bed.

1. **Decision Making** Decide which 12 friends you are going to survey and which activities you will include. You may not know exactly which activities you want to include until you start surveying.

2. **Recording Data** Copy and complete a table like the one shown. Use your data to make a bar graph.

3. **Explain Your Thinking** How did you choose the title of your graph? What helped you to decide on a scale?

4. **Analyze Your Data**
   Write a summary about the data on your graph. Include the following information:

   a. What was the most popular activity?

   b. Were there any activities in which everyone surveyed participated?

   c. What might you conclude about the results of your survey?

Activity	Number of People Who Do This Activity
Do homework	
Eat	
Watch TV	
Play soccer	
Play baseball	
Play football	
Read	
Baby-sit brothers and sisters	

5. **Critical Thinking** Would you expect to get the same results if you had surveyed 12 other friends? Compare your results with the graphs of two other surveys. What do you think would be the same or different about your graph if you had surveyed 12 teachers?

Math Magazine

Picture This! The artist Niki Glen helped over 120 students at Thew Elementary School in Tempe, Arizona, plan and paint a mural for their school. The mural is titled "Dwelling Diversity." It shows many aspects of historical Native American life in five regions of the country and how the customs differ in each region.

The mural is 6 ft tall and 16 ft wide. Students drew small sections of the mural on grids. They then transferred their pictures to the larger painting using coordinates from the small grids.

Niki Glen and the students have more murals planned for the future.

Try These!

1. Draw a picture. Use these coordinates in order.

   $(3, 2) \rightarrow (3, 11) \rightarrow (2, 11) \rightarrow (10, 15) \rightarrow (14, 13) \rightarrow (14, 16) \rightarrow$

   $(16, 16) \rightarrow (16, 12) \rightarrow (18, 11) \rightarrow (17, 11) \rightarrow (17, 2) \rightarrow (3,2)$

   Mark each coordinate on a grid, then connect them in order. What have you drawn? Use a larger grid and draw the picture again. Are the pictures identical? What is the same and what is different?

2. Draw a picture on grid paper that uses simple line segments. Record several coordinates for the picture on a separate sheet of paper. Trade coordinate sheets with a classmate and draw one another's pictures. How does your picture compare with the original picture?

Cumulative Review

Test Prep Strategy: Make Smart Choices

Look for patterns.

What are the next three numbers in this table?

L	1	2	3	4	5	6
M	1	4	9	▪	▪	▪

- Ⓐ 11, 13, 15
- Ⓑ 8, 10, 12
- Ⓒ 16, 25, 36
- Ⓓ 102, 103, 105

Begin with 1. You get 1 if you multiply 1×1. Multiply 2×2 to get 4, and 3×3 to get 9. The rule is: multiply the number in L by itself to get the number in M. The next three numbers would be Ⓒ 16, 25, and 36.

Write the letter of the correct answer. Choose any strategy.

1. Which figure is a triangle?

   Ⓐ   Ⓑ   Ⓒ   Ⓓ

2. Monday, Sam had 4 problems in math for homework. Tuesday, he had 8. Wednesday, he had 16. If his teacher follows the same pattern, how many problems should Sam have on Thursday?

   Ⓐ 20   Ⓑ 24   Ⓒ 32   Ⓓ not here

3. Which does **not** have the same product as 4×6?

   Ⓐ 2×12 Ⓑ 3×8 Ⓒ 7×3 Ⓓ 24×1

4. A square has how many equal sides?

   Ⓐ 1   Ⓑ 4   Ⓒ 2   Ⓓ 6

5. Complete this sentence: $3 \times n = 27$.

   Ⓐ 8   Ⓑ 9   Ⓒ 81   Ⓓ not here

6. Which operation would you use to determine how many pennies each of 18 children will get if there are 54 pennies to share equally?

   Ⓐ addition   Ⓑ subtraction   Ⓒ multiplication   Ⓓ division

7. Find the difference between 13 and 5.

   Ⓐ 7   Ⓑ 18   Ⓒ 2   Ⓓ 8

8. What type of graph uses symbols to represent data?

   Ⓐ pictograph   Ⓑ bar graph   Ⓒ line plot   Ⓓ stem-and-leaf plot

9. Which rule best describes the pattern in this table of data?

   Ⓐ $n \times 6$ Ⓑ $n + 5$ Ⓒ $n + 6$ Ⓓ $n \times 1$

A	1	2	3	4	5
B	6	7	8	9	10

10. Which of the following is equal to $81 \div 9$?

    Ⓐ $6 + 4$ Ⓑ $27 \div 9$ Ⓒ 3×5 Ⓓ not here

Test Prep Strategies

- Read Carefully
- Follow Directions
- Make Smart Choices
- Eliminate Choices
- Work Backward from an Answer

REVIEW AND PRACTICE

Chapter 2
Whole Numbers and Decimals: Place Value, Adding, and Subtracting

FASCINATING FACTS

SECTION

A

Understanding Whole Numbers 51

Where would you like to live? Lots of people have decided on California, Florida, Texas, and Georgia in the last 100 years! Which state's population was about equal to the sum of two other states' populations in 1990?

From Russia to
West Virginia
Page 51

**Population of Four States
1890, 1990**

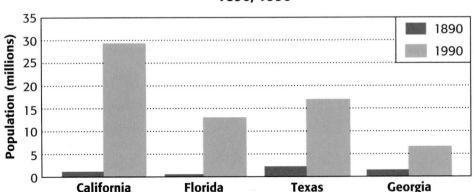

Understanding Decimals

This chart shows the highest mountain on each continent. Which continent boasts the highest mountain?

65

World Mountains

Continent	Mountain	Height (mi)
North America	Mount McKinley	3.848
South America	Cerro Aconcagua	4.324
Europe	Mont Blanc	2.987
Asia	Mount Everest	5.498
Africa	Mount Kilimanjaro	3.663
Australia	Mount Kosciusko	1.386
Antarctica	Vinson Massif	3.194

Get in the swim.
Page 65

Surfing the World Wide Web!

To learn more about mountains and mountain climbing, hike over to **www.mathsurf.com/5/ch2**. Use the data you find to make your own mountain table.

Adding and Subtracting Whole Numbers and Decimals

81

If you are mountain climbing, you'll need your strength. According to the bar graph below, what is the most common type of tissue in your body?

Body Tissue by Weight

Weight (lb)

0.50
0.40
0.30
0.20
0.10
0

Brain Muscle Blood Skin Liver Bone Other

Body Tissue

It's a maze!
Page 81

TEAM PROJECT
The *Earliest* *Calculator*

For centuries, the Chinese, Japanese, and Russians used the world's first calculator, the abacus, to add, subtract, multiply, and divide. You can make an abacus and count or compute on it.

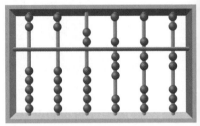

Chinese *abacus* showing 10,872

Make a Plan

- What do you need to make an abacus?
- Where can you find information on how to use it?
- Who will do the research, and who will do the construction?
- Who will demonstrate the use of the abacus for the class?

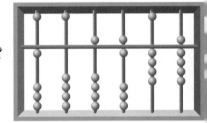

Japanese *soroban* showing 105,649

Carry It Out

Make your abacus and learn to use it.

a. Collect your materials and research.

b. Make the abacus and practice showing different numbers.

c. Demonstrate how to count to at least 25 for the class.

Talk About It

- How did your team build an abacus?
- Where did you find the details about the abacus? How did you find out how to count on it?
- Did anyone figure out how to add or subtract on the abacus?

Russian *scety* showing 427.5

Present the Project

Plan a class demonstration of all abacuses. Are there differences in teams' abacuses? Have the class suggest ways to add or subtract.

A Understanding Whole Numbers

Anna is a Russian immigrant who came to West Virginia in the early 1990s. In 1994 there were 1,822,021 people living in West Virginia. This was an increase of 99,171 people since 1990. How could you find out how many people lived in West Virginia in 1990?

GET READY!

Place Value with Greater Numbers

Review addition and multiplication. Find each sum or product.

1. $600 + 50$ **2.** $80 + 4$ **3.** $80 + 9$

4. $300 + 70 + 4$ **5.** $200 + 7$ **6.** $100 + 30$

7. 3×10 **8.** 6×100 **9.** 8×10 **10.** 4×100

Skills Checklist

In this section, you will:

☐ **Explore a Million**

☐ **Read and Write Numbers Through Millions and Billions**

☐ **Explore Place-Value Relationships**

☐ **Compare and Order Numbers**

☐ **Round Numbers**

Exploring a Million

Explore •

Suppose a bank exchanges ten worn-out dollar bills for ten new ones every day. It would take 100,000 days, or over 250 years, to exchange 1 million dollars.

Work Together

1. Use patterns to learn about 1 million. Continue the pattern. What would the shape of a 10,000 block be? Describe its measurements.

Number	10,000	1,000	100	10	1
Block	?	Cube	Flat	Long	Cube
Shape	?	Cube	Flat	Long	Cube

2. What would the measurements of a 100,000 block be? Draw its shape.

3. What would be the measurements of a million block? Draw its shape.

4. About how many million cubes do you think would fit in your classroom? How could you find out? Explain.

5. Describe any patterns you see in the shapes of the blocks.

6. Describe any patterns you see in the numbers.

Connect

Here are some other ways to think about 1 million.

1,000,000 pennies = 200,000 nickels = 100,000 dimes = 40,000 quarters = 10,000 dollars

1 day = 1,440 minutes   1 month = 43,200 minutes (30 days)

1 year = 525,600 minutes (365 days)   2 years = 1,051,200 minutes

In its lifetime, one ladybug can eat more than 50,000 aphids. Twenty ladybugs can eat more than 1,000,000 aphids.

Practice

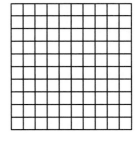

Patterns Use patterns to answer **1** and **2**.

1. How many small squares are there on
   a. 1 sheet?   **b.** 10 sheets?   **c.** 100 sheets?

2. **a.** Estimate how many sheets of this grid paper you would need to have a million small squares. Then multiply to find out. How close was your estimate?

   b. Suppose you had another type of grid paper that is 12 × 12. Would you need a greater or lesser number of sheets to show a million small squares? Explain.

3. **Write Your Own Problem** Write about how big a million is. Use patterns.

4. **a.** Use a calculator to reach 1,000,000 by adding 100,000s. Here's how: Enter: 0 ⊞ 100,000 ⊟. Keep pressing ⊟. Stop at 1,000,000. How many times did you press ⊟?

   b. How many times do you think you will have to press ⊟ in order to reach 1,000,000 by 10,000s? Use your calculator to check. How close was your estimate?

5. **Critical Thinking** If you saved $100 a month, how many months would it take until you could exchange your savings for 1,000,000 pennies? How many dollars would you have? Would you want to make the exchange?

6. **Using Data** Use the facts from *Did You Know?* on page 52 to answer each question.

   a. Does the average $100 bill "live" for over 1,000,000 minutes?

   b. Does a $1 bill "live" for over 1,000,000 minutes? Explain.

7. **Journal** Explain how you could figure out how old you are in minutes.

Place Value Through Millions

You Will Learn

how to understand, read, and write numbers through millions

Materials

calculator

Vocabulary

digit
symbol used to write numbers:

0, 1, 2, 3, 4, 5, 6, 7, 8, 9

period
a three-digit group of numbers, separated from other groups by a comma

ways to write numbers
standard form
expanded form
word form

Math Tip

The place-value chart helps you read greater numbers. You say: "230," then at the comma you name the period, "million."

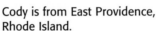

Learn •

Cody collects and recycles aluminum cans. He'll never run out of cans to recycle since about 230,136,986 cans are made daily!

Cody is from East Providence, Rhode Island.

A place-value chart shows the value of each **digit** in this number.

Millions Period			Thousands Period			Ones Period		
hundreds	tens	ones	hundreds	tens	ones	hundreds	tens	ones
2	3	0 ,	1	3	6 ,	9	8	6

This number can be written in several ways.

Standard form 230,136,986

Expanded form

200,000,000 + 30,000,000 + 100,000 + 30,000 + 6,000 + 900 + 80 + 6

Word form

two hundred thirty million, one hundred thirty-six thousand, nine hundred eighty-six

What pattern can you find in the place names in each **period**?

Check •

Write each number in standard form, expanded form, and words.

1. 3,406,237   2. 60,000,000 + 100,000 + 8,000 + 10 + 5

3. four hundred sixty million, two hundred six thousand, six hundred two

4. **Reasoning** Write the greatest 9-digit number possible with 1 in the hundred millions place. You can't repeat digits.

Skills and Reasoning

Write each number in word form.

5. 4,056,070 **6.** 314,805,771 **7.** 27,000,357 **8.** 39,040,002

Write each number in standard form.

9. forty-three million, five hundred nine thousand, four hundred fifty-eight

10. nine hundred twelve million, thirty-one thousand, three hundred one

11. 500,000,000 + 4,000,000 + 300,000 + 10,000 + 9,000 + 100 + 8

12. 70,000,000 + 800,000 + 90,000 + 4,000 + 200 + 10 + 6

13. Look at these numbers. | 4,000 400,000 4,000,000 |

    a. Write each number in word form.

    b. How are the three numbers alike?

    c. How are the three numbers different?

Problem Solving and Applications

14. Money How long would it take you to spend a million dollars if you spent

    a. $1,000 each day? **b.** $100 each day? **c.** $10 each day?

15. Literature In *The Little Prince* by Antoine de Saint-Exupéry, the businessman of the fourth planet says he owns "five hundred and one million, six hundred twenty-two thousand, seven hundred thirty-one" stars. Write this in standard form.

 16. Science Recycling 1 can saves enough energy to run a TV for 3 hr. If 170 million cans are recycled daily, how many hours of TV could you watch from this recycling?

Mixed Review and Test Prep

Find each sum or difference.

17. 7 + 8 **18.** 18 − 9 **19.** 728 − 9 **20.** 17 + 18

 Algebra Readiness Copy and complete.

21. $5 + n = 15$ **22.** $n - 20 = 32$ **23.** $n \times 7 = 0$ **24.** $239 - n = 239$

25. $n \times 1 = 8$ **26.** $2 + n = 12$ **27.** $n - 10 = 15$ **28.** $15 + n = 15$

29. Find the correct answer. 70 − 52 = ▮

    Ⓐ 28 Ⓑ 22 Ⓒ 45 Ⓓ 18

Exploring Place-Value Relationships

Problem Solving Connection

- Make an Organized List
- Guess and Check

Materials

- place-value chart
- calculator

Vocabulary

exponent
a number that tells how many times another number is used as a factor

$$2 \times 2 \times 2 = 2^3$$

base   exponent

Explore • • • • • • • • •

Suppose you've just invented a great computer game and you have $1 million to place ads in newspapers, magazines, and on TV. It's up to you to decide the best way to spend the money.

Work Together

Type	Network TV	Local TV	Magazine ad	Newspaper ad
Cost per Ad	$100,000	$10,000	$1,000	$100

1. How many newspaper ads could you buy for the price of one magazine ad? For the price of ten magazine ads?

2. A network TV ad is how many times as expensive as a newspaper ad?

3. Suppose you have only $10,000 to spend on ads. Which types of ads can you afford to buy? Which types of ads are too expensive?

Did You Know?

In the 1997 Super Bowl, a 30-second commercial cost $1.3 million.

4. How many ads of each kind could you buy for $10,000?

5. Decide how you would spend a $1-million ad budget. How many of each type of ad would you buy?

Talk About It

6. Share your plan to spend $1 million. How does your plan differ from those of your classmates?

7. Discuss how you kept track of how much you were spending.

8. How did the place-value chart help you figure out how much you could spend on each kind of ad?

Connect

Our place-value system is based on groups of ten.

Powers of Ten		Factors	Exponent Form
10 ones	= 10	10	10^1 ←exponent
10 tens	= 100	10×10	10^2 base
10 hundreds	= 1,000	$10 \times 10 \times 10$	10^3
10 thousands	= 10,000	$10 \times 10 \times 10 \times 10$	10^4
10 ten thousands	= 100,000	$10 \times 10 \times 10 \times 10 \times 10$	10^5
10 hundred thousands	= 1,000,000	$10 \times 10 \times 10 \times 10 \times 10 \times 10$	10^6

You read "10^6" as 10 to the 6th power.

Practice

1. How many 10,000s make 100,000?

2. How many 100,000s make 1 million?

3. How many 1,000s make 100,000?

4. How many 1,000s make 1 million?

Write each number using exponents.

5. 1,000   6. 100,000   7. 100   8. 1,000,000   9. 10,000

10. **Patterns** What relationships between the exponent and the number of zeros do you notice in **5–9**?

 Algebra Readiness Copy and complete.

11. $10^n = 10,000$ 12. $10^n = 1,000,000$ 13. $n^2 = 100$ 14. $n^5 = 100,000$

15. A number has a 3 in the ten thousands place. You multiply it by 10. Where will the 3 be in the product? Explain.

16. **Using Data** Use the fact from *Did You Know?* on page 56 to find how many $10,000 local TV ads you could buy for the price of one 30-second commercial during the Super Bowl.

17. **Science** Scientific notation is based on powers of ten. A number greater than or equal to 1, but less than 10, is multiplied by a power of 10. You write 1,000 as 1×10^3 in scientific notation. Write in scientific notation:

a. 10,000   b. 100,000

c. 1,000,000

 18. **Journal** Explain how our place-value system is based on the powers of ten. Give an example.

Place Value Through Billions

India 919,903,000

China 1,190,431,000

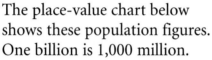 **Learn**

Did you know the world's population in 1994 was over five billion? The two countries with the largest populations in 1994 were China and India.

The place-value chart below shows these population figures. One billion is 1,000 million.

	Billions			Millions			Thousands			Ones		
	hundreds	tens	ones	hundreds	tens	ones	hundreds	tens	ones	hundreds	tens	ones
World			5 ,	6	4	2 ,	1	5	1 ,	0	0	0
China		1 ,	1	9	0 ,	4	3	1 ,	0	0	0
India			9	1	9 ,	9	0	3 ,	0	0	0

In words, China's population was one billion, one hundred ninety million, four hundred thirty-one thousand.

Talk About It

How is 5,600,000,000 like 5,600? How is it different?

Did You Know?

Together India and China make up about 2 billion of the world's population.

Check

Write each number in standard form.

1. one billion, five hundred million
2. fifteen billion
3. four hundred billion, nine hundred
4. **Reasoning** Compare the populations of China and India. Is the value of the 3 greater in China's or India's population figure? Explain.

Skills and Reasoning

Write each number in standard form.

5. two billion, five hundred million

6. twenty-five billion

7. nine hundred billion seventy

8. thirty-six billion, four hundred

Copy and complete.

9. 702,411,000,800 = _____ billion, four hundred eleven _____, eight hundred

10. 14,000,920,000 = fourteen billion, nine hundred twenty _____

11. How many 100,000,000s are in three billion? In thirty billion?

12. The world's population is 5,642,151,000. Give the value of each five.

Problem Solving and Applications

13. Collecting Data Find examples of millions and billions in newspapers or magazines. How are greater numbers used?

Social Studies Use the table to answer **14–17.**

14. Which continent or region has a population of over one billion?

15. Which continent or region has the least population?

16. Which continents or regions have populations over 500 million?

17. Write the value of both 3s in Asia's population.

Population by Continent or Region (1994)	
North America	289,000,000
Latin America; Caribbean	474,000,000
Europe	509,000,000
Asia	3,344,000,000
Africa	701,000,000
Former USSR	296,000,000
Oceania; including Australia	28,000,000

Mixed Review and Test Prep

Find each sum or difference.

18. $9 + 9 + 9$ **19.** $13 - 4$ **20.** $3 + 7 + 8$ **21.** $25 - 6$ **22.** $42 - 3$

Patterns Copy and complete.

23. $10 \times \blacksquare = 1,000,000$ **24.** $100 \times 1,000 = \blacksquare$ **25.** $\blacksquare \times 10,000 = 1,000,000$

26. Mental Math Find the sum. $200 + 30 + 7 = \blacksquare$

    Ⓐ 300   Ⓑ 507   Ⓒ 210   Ⓓ 237

Comparing and Ordering

CALIFORNIA
29,760,021

ILLINOIS
11,430,602

NEW YORK
17,990,455

TEXAS
16,986,510

Florida
12,937,926

You Will Learn

how to compare and order whole numbers

Remember

< means "is less than"

> means "is greater than"

= means "is equal to"

Learn

This map shows the 1990 census counts for the five most populated states.

You can compare and order populations using place value.

Example 1

Compare the populations of New York and Texas.

Begin at the left. Find the first place where the digits are different.

17,990,455   16,986,510

Both numbers have 1 ten million.

17,990,455   16,986,510

7 millions > 6 millions

So, 17,990,455 > 16,986,510.

New York's 1990 population was greater.

Example 2

List the states in order of population from least to greatest. Compare the numbers two at a time.

11,430,602 < 12,937,926

12,937,926 < 16,986,510

16,986,510 < 17,990,455

17,990,455 < 29,760,021

The order from least to greatest is: Illinois, Florida, Texas, New York, California.

Talk About It

How can you use place value to compare 153,452 and 154,102?

Check

Copy and complete. Write >, <, or =.

1. 647 ● 691   **2.** 101,719 ● 101,790   **3.** 98,767 ● 89,767

Order these numbers from greatest to least.

4. 1,555,400   1,555,387   2,000,800   1,439,999

5. Reasoning If a number is greater than 110,000,000 and less than 111,000,000, what digit will be in the one millions place? Explain.

Practice

Skills and Reasoning

Copy and complete. Write >, <, or =.

6. 111,500 ⬤ 97,578

7. twenty-one hundred ⬤ 2,077

8. 100,000,040 ⬤ one hundred million, forty

9. 954,933 ⬤ 945,888

10. 540 thousand ⬤ 55,039

11. 619,466,312 ⬤ one billion, five hundred million

12. 254,362,130,465 ⬤ 254,384,721,031

Order these numbers from least to greatest.

13. 464,351 989,942 981,999 744,345

14. 11,058,754 12,875,000 20,000,000 12,446,000

15. 12,422,323,112 16,487,706,541 12,580,944,016 14,991,328,692

16. What digit could be in the ten millions place of a number that is greater than 50,000,000 and less than 100,000,000? Explain.

Problem Solving and Applications

Using Data Use the Data File on page 48 to answer **17–20**.

17. Which of the four states had populations less than 15 million in 1990?

18. Which of the four states shown had the greatest population in 1890? About what was that population?

19. Does the state that had the least population in 1890 have the greatest population in 1990? Explain.

20. **Critical Thinking** Which state in 1990 had about 8 times its 1890 population? Explain.

Mixed Review and Test Prep

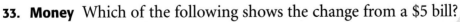

Find each answer.

21. 7×8

22. 9×9

23. 8×9

24. 0×17

25. $18 - 7$

26. $3 + 7 + 8$

27. $137 - 0$

28. $10 + 21$

29. $\begin{array}{r} 9 \\ \times 7 \\ \hline \end{array}$

30. $\begin{array}{r} 8 \\ + 3 \\ \hline \end{array}$

31. $\begin{array}{r} 29 \\ - 0 \\ \hline \end{array}$

32. $\begin{array}{r} 36 \\ + 0 \\ \hline \end{array}$

33. **Money** Which of the following shows the change from a $5 bill?

Ⓐ $1.98   Ⓑ $0.98   Ⓒ $1.02   Ⓓ $9.02

JOE'S MARKET
SHOP
&
SAVE
bread...... $2.59
apple 0.38
eggs 1.05
Total $4.02
THANK YOU

Rounding Numbers

Learn • • • • • • • • • • • • •

Anna came to the United States from Russia in 1991. She, like tens of millions of Americans, began her life in a different country. From 1820 to 1990, about 56,994,000 people immigrated to the United States.

You can use **number lines** and place value to round numbers.

Anna (center) and her friends live in Charleston, West Virginia.

Example 1

Round 56,994,000 to the nearest ten million.

56,994,000 is closer to 60,000,000 than to 50,000,000. To the nearest ten million, 56,994,000 rounds to 60,000,000.

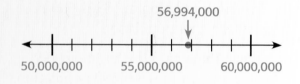

Example 2

Round 8,430,000 to the nearest hundred thousand.

Underline the digit in the place to which you want to round: 8,4̲30,000

Look at the digit one place to its right. If it is 5 or greater, round the underlined digit to the next greater number. If it is less than 5, round to the underlined digit.

8,4̲30,000   3 < 5

8,430,000 rounds to 8,400,000.

Talk About It

How do you know that 55,000,000 is halfway between 50 and 60 million?

Check •

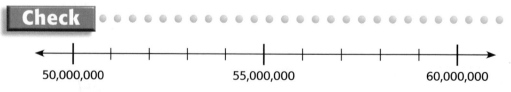

1. Use the number line to help you round 56,890,000 to the nearest 10,000,000.

Round to the nearest hundred thousand and to the nearest million.

2. 18,736,544   3. 5,399,485   4. 8,039,245   5. 3,754,666

6. **Reasoning** If 453,000,000 rounds to 450,000,000, to which place did you round?

Practice

Skills and Reasoning

7. Use the number line to help you round 11,436,890 to the nearest million.

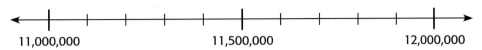

11,000,000   11,500,000   12,000,000

Round to the nearest hundred thousand.

8. 527,900   **9.** 1,094,650   **10.** 12,873,422   **11.** 4,333,500

Round to the nearest million.

12. 5,430,982   **13.** 103,827,361   **14.** 27,099,323   **15.** 36,499,999

Round to the nearest ten million.

16. 94,270,009   **17.** two hundred fifty-three million

18. 2,583,000,000   **19.** 675,000,000

20. If 336,785,398 rounds to 300,000,000, to which place did you round?

Problem Solving and Applications

21. **Critical Thinking** What is the greatest number that rounds to 1,200,000 when rounded to the hundred thousands place?

Using Data Use the table to answer **22** and **23**.

22. **Estimation** An announcer said, "The game was played in front of a sell-out crowd of more than 90 thousand people." At which stadium did the game probably take place?

23. **Estimation** If the announcer said, "A sell-out crowd of a little more than 100 thousand people," which stadium did she probably mean?

Stadium	Capacity
Rose Bowl	106,721
Michigan Stadium	101,701
Los Angeles Coliseum	93,761
Sugar Bowl	80,982

Mixed Review and Test Prep

Algebra Readiness Copy and complete.

24. $17 + n = 22$ **25.** $n - 9 = 18$ **26.** $n \times 3 = 12$ **27.** $n - 0 = 17$

28. $n + 6 = 14$ **29.** $6 \times n = 12$ **30.** $20 + n = 33$ **31.** $n - 4 = 29$

32. In which number does the 3 have a value of thirty thousand?

    Ⓐ 3,645,007   Ⓑ 35,442,618   Ⓒ 5,103,482   Ⓓ 16,435,798

SECTION A
Review and Practice

Vocabulary Match each with its meaning.

1. number line
2. digit
3. period

a. a three-digit group of numbers
b. a line that shows numbers in order
c. symbols: 0, 1, 2, 3, 4, 5, 6, 7, 8, 9

(Lesson 1) Write the value in dollars for each.

4. ten $10 bills   5. one hundred $1,000 bills   6. ten thousand $100 bills

(Lesson 3) Copy and complete.

7. $10 \times \blacksquare = 3,000$ 8. $\blacksquare \times 80,000 = 800,000$ 9. $10^{\blacksquare} = 1,000,000$

(Lessons 2 and 4) In the number 86,320,051,700, write the value of:

10. 5   11. 2   12. 3   13. 8   14. 1   15. 6

16. Write sixteen billion, thirty-one million, one hundred sixty in standard form.

(Lesson 5) Copy and complete. Write >, <, or =.

17. 43,862 ● 43,826   18. 368 thousand ● 36,800   19. 4,312,829,999 ● 4,312,830,000

(Lesson 6) **Using Data** Use the table to answer **20** and **21**.

State	Native American Population, 1990
Oklahoma	252,420
California	242,164
Alaska	85,698
Texas	65,877
Oregon	38,496
Florida	36,335

20. Which state has a population of about:
   a. 66,000 Native Americans?
   b. 35,000 Native Americans?

21. How would you estimate the Native American population of Oregon to the nearest thousand?

22. **Journal** Explain how you would order 54,893, 54,695, 53,999, 58,735, 54,889 from least to greatest.

Skills Checklist

In this section, you have:

☑ Explored a Million

☑ Read and Written Numbers Through Millions and Billions

☑ Explored Place-Value Relationships

☑ Compared and Ordered Numbers

☑ Rounded Numbers

B Understanding Decimals

The swimmers are neck-and-neck. It's down to the wire. One swimmer touches the wall just fractions of a second before her competitors.

How can you use decimals and place value to describe and compare winning times?

GET READY!

Rounding Decimals

Review whole numbers. Round to the nearest thousand.

1. 34,801   **2.** 10,399   **3.** 98,700   **4.** 19,382

Write the number in standard form.

5. two million, one hundred seventy-three thousand, eight hundred fifty-four

Tenths and Hundredths

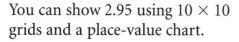

Learn

Olympic records are made in decimal fractions of a second.

Gold medal winner Brooke Bennett beat the bronze medalist by 2.95 seconds in the 1996 Olympics.

You can show 2.95 using 10 × 10 grids and a place-value chart.

You write this decimal as 2.95. You read it as "two and ninety-five hundredths."

For decimals less than one, write a 0 in the ones place. Read 0.36 as "thirty-six hundredths." Read 0.8 as "eight tenths."

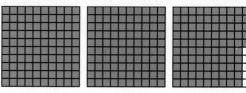

hundreds	tens	ones		tenths	hundredths
		2	.	9	5
		0	.	3	6
		0	.	8	

Talk About It

Describe any patterns you see in the place-value chart. How could you extend these patterns?

Check

Write each decimal shown.

1.

2.

Use grids to show each decimal.

3. 3.19   **4.** 2.07   **5.** 1.15

6. Reasoning The 1996 Olympic Women's 200 Meter Freestyle was won by a margin of 0.41 seconds. How can you describe this time in tenths and hundredths?

Skills and Reasoning

Write each decimal shown.

7. 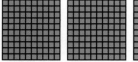   **8.**

Use grids to show each decimal.

9. 1.47   **10.** 2.07   **11.** 1.36   **12.** 3.85   **13.** 1.60

Write each number in decimal form.

14. 80 hundredths   **15.** 8 hundredths   **16.** 8 tenths   **17.** 8

18. one and fifty-six hundredths   **19.** three and seven hundredths

20. Is it possible to show 0.73 by shading only entire columns on the grid? Explain.

21. Which is greater, 2.36 or 2.57? Do you have to look at the hundredths place to decide? Explain.

Problem Solving and Applications

Using Data Use the data in the table to answer **22–24.**

22. Write the number of seconds that has a 3 in the ones place. Explain your choice.

23. Which numbers have a 3 in the tens place? How can you tell?

Times for Women's 800 Meter Freestyle Heat, 1996			
Swimmer	**Country**	**Minutes**	**Seconds**
Brooke Bennett	United States	8	32.38
Dagmar Hase	Germany	8	33.55
Kerstin Keilgass	Germany	8	36.33
Kirsten Vlieghuis	Netherlands	8	39.73

24. Which number or numbers has a 3 in the hundredths place? How can you tell?

25. **Patterns** Using the numbers 2, 3, and 8 in the ones, tenths, or hundredths places, how many decimals can you make? List them. Explain how you would make the greatest decimal.

Mixed Review and Test Prep

Copy and write >, <, or = to complete.

26. 3 + 5 + 1 ● 9   **27.** 18 − 11 ● 9   **28.** 3 × 6 ● 6 × 3   **29.** 81 ÷ 9 ● 10

30. Which of the following is equal to one million?

Ⓐ 10^3 Ⓑ 10^4 Ⓒ 10^5 Ⓓ 10^6

Exploring Equivalent Decimals

Problem Solving Connection
Draw a Picture

Materials
10 × 10 grids

Vocabulary
equivalent decimals
decimals that name the same amount

0.7 = 0.70

Remember
If there is zero in the hundredths place of a 2-digit decimal, you can change to tenths easily.

0.40 = 0.4

Explore •

Equivalent decimals are decimals that name the same amount.

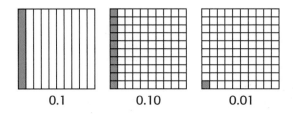

0.1   0.10   0.01

0.1 and 0.10 are equivalent. 0.01 is not equivalent to either.

Work Together

Use 10 × 10 grids to help you.

1. Show each decimal using grids. Then tell which two numbers in each group are equivalent.

   a. 0.2   0.20   0.02

   b. 3.0   0.30   0.3

2. Shade a grid for each of the following numbers. Name the equivalent decimal.

   a. 0.8   **b.** 0.60

3. Name two other equivalent decimals. Shade grids to show they are equivalent.

Talk About It

4. How can you tell if two decimals are equivalent?

5. Give an example of how zeros make a difference when writing equivalent decimals. Explain.

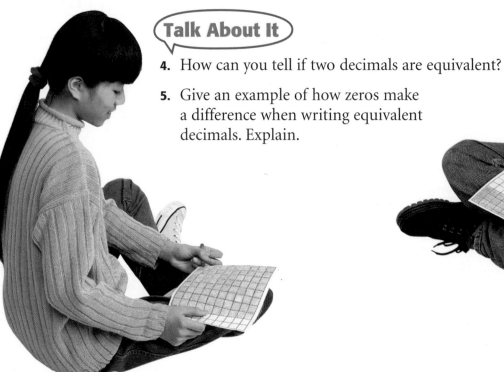

Connect

Zeros are important when writing equivalent decimals.

3 tenths   30 hundredths

          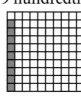

0.3   =   0.30

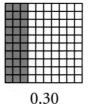

Math Tip
Writing a zero in the wrong place can change the value of a decimal.

You can see that 0.9 and 0.09 are not equivalent.

90 hundredths   9 hundredths

0.90   is greater than   0.09

Practice

Write two decimals that name each shaded part.

1.   **2.**   **3.**   **4.**

Write each as an equivalent decimal using tenths.

5. 0.90   **6.** 0.10   **7.** 0.70   **8.** 0.30   **9.** 0.50

Write each as an equivalent decimal using hundredths.

10. 0.5   **11.** 0.8   **12.** 0.2   **13.** 0.4   **14.** 0.9

In each group, write which decimals are equivalent.

15. 0.6   0.60   0.06   **16.** 0.07   0.7   0.70   **17.** 0.90   0.09   0.9

18. 0.1   0.01   0.10   **19.** 0.08   0.8   0.80   **20.** 0.30   0.3   0.03

21. Money At the grocery store, you see these two packages of cheese. Which is the better buy? Explain.

22. Critical Thinking Michael says he will plant 0.6 of his garden with corn and 0.6 of his garden with tomatoes. Will his plan work? Why or why not?

23. Journal Explain why you can write an equivalent decimal in the hundredths for any decimal in tenths.

CHEDDAR CHEESE
0.7 lb
for $2.49

CHEDDAR CHEESE
0.70 lb
for $2.31

Thousandths

You Will Learn
how to show, read, and write decimals to thousandths

Learn

A person who is 5 feet 3 inches tall is almost one thousandth of a mile tall! A thousand people of that height stretched out head-to-foot would cover a mile. You can use grids and place-value charts to show decimals in thousandths.

Example 1

Show, read, and write the decimal for $\frac{1}{1000}$.

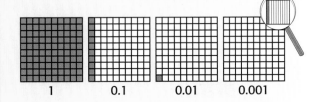

| 1 | 0.1 | 0.01 | 0.001 |

You write: 0.001   You read: one thousandth

Example 2

Mt. Rainier in Washington state rises about 2.729 miles above sea level.

Show its height with the place-value chart.

ones	tenths	hundredths	thousandths
2 .	7	2	9

You read 2.729 as "two and seven hundred twenty-nine thousandths."

Talk About It

How are thousandths related to hundredths? To tenths?

Did You Know?
The Pacific Ocean is deeper than Mt. Everest is high. The Mariana Trench in the Pacific is 6.782 miles deep!

Check

Write each number in decimal form or in word form.

1. one and three hundred sixty-seven thousandths

2. two and fifty-two thousandths

3. 0.408   **4.** 1.503   **5.** 0.619   **6.** 3.007

7. **Reasoning** Between what two numbers does 0.001 fall on this number line? Explain how you know.

0	0.01	0.02	0.03	0.04	0.05

Skills and Reasoning

Write each number in decimal form.

8. 6 thousandths

9 600 thousandths

10. 6 hundredths

11. 6 tenths

12. 6

13. three and three thousandths

14. five hundred six thousandths

15. two and forty-four thousandths

16. Which is greatest and which is least: 1.7, 1.07, 1.007? Explain.

17. Critical Thinking Write the greatest possible decimal in thousandths.

Problem Solving and Applications

Using Data Use the Data File on page 49 to answer **18–20.**

18. Which mountain is the highest? Explain how you found your answer.

19. Look at the height of Cerro Aconcagua. Which number is in the thousandths place? What part of a mile is this?

20. How many thousandths of a mile higher is Mount McKinley than Mount Kilimanjaro?

21. Write Your Own Problem Use the data in *Did You Know?* on page 70 to write your own problem about the Mariana Trench.

Cerro Aconcagua (*SAYroh* AH *kawng KAH gwah*), the highest mountain in the western hemisphere, is located in Argentina.

Mixed Review and Test Prep

Find each sum or difference.

22. 22
  + 38

23. 90
  − 78

24. 103
  − 10

25. 13
  27
  + 9

26. 88
  + 22

 Mental Math Find each product.

27. 10
  × 3

28. 100
  × 3

29. 200
  × 3

30. 500
  × 3

31. 50
  × 30

32. Which of the following is the sum of 499 and 201?

Ⓐ 600   Ⓑ 601   Ⓒ 700   Ⓓ 710

Decimals on the Number Line

Learn • • • • • • •

Everyone loves a parade! On Thanksgiving, Crystal joins the two million people at the Macy's Thanksgiving Day Parade.

Crystal stands at 77th Street and Central Park West, where the parade begins. Her friend, Erica stands at 59th Street, where the parade turns.

Crystal and Erica watch the Thanksgiving Day Parade in New York.

Example 1

Find the distance between Crystal (C) and Erica (E) in miles.

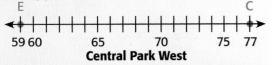

E C
59 60   65   70   75 77
Central Park West

Each block is 0.05 mile. The friends stand 18 blocks apart, so count by 0.05s: 0.05, 0.10, 0.15, ... 0.90. They are 0.90 mi apart.

Example 2

Suppose Crystal and Erica agree to meet at 64th St. and Central Park West. What part of a mile will Erica walk? Use a number line to show the distance.

miles
0   0.05   0.10   0.15   0.20   0.25

59   64

Erica walks 0.25 mi.

(**Talk About It**)

How can you show tenths on a number line?

Check •

1. Copy and complete.

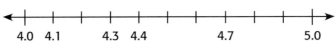

4.0 4.1   4.3 4.4   4.7   5.0

2. Name the number shown by each letter.

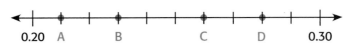

0.20 A   B   C   D   0.30

3. **Reasoning** Is 2.2 or 2.24 closer to 2? Explain.

Practice

Skills and Reasoning

4. Copy and complete.

7.0 7.1 7.2   7.4   8.0

5. Name the number shown by each letter.

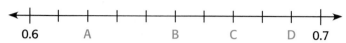

0.6   A   B   C   D   0.7

Use the number line shown to answer 6 and 7.

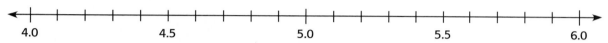

4.0   4.5   5.0   5.5   6.0

6. Name two numbers between 4.5 and 5.0.

7. Name two numbers between 5.5 and 5.6.

Use the number line shown to answer 8–10.

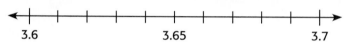

3.6   3.65   3.7

8. Name three numbers between 3.6 and 3.7.

9. Is 3.07 between 3.6 and 3.7? Tell how you know.

10. Is 3.65 the half-way point between 3.6 and 3.7? Explain your thinking.

Problem Solving and Applications

11. Measurement A marching band in a parade carries a flag that measures 2.28 m in length. Is it closer to 2.2 m or 2.3 m?

12. Estimation How far is each distance? Estimate the distances to the nearest tenth of a mile.

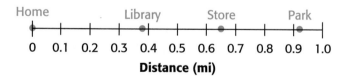

Home   Library   Store   Park

0   0.1 0.2 0.3 0.4 0.5 0.6 0.7 0.8 0.9 1.0

Distance (mi)

a. Home to library

b. Home to store

c. Home to park

d. Store to park

Mixed Review and Test Prep

Algebra Readiness Copy and complete.

13. $16 \times n = 160$ **14.** $2 + 30 = n$ **15.** $n + 479 = 479$ **16.** $37 \times n = 37$

17. Which of the following is greater than 7×8?

Ⓐ 15   Ⓑ 9   Ⓒ 56   Ⓓ 58

Exploring Comparing and Ordering Decimals

Problem Solving Connection
Draw a Picture

Materials
10 × 10 grids

Remember

3 < 5 means
3 is less than 5.

5 > 3 means
5 is greater than 3.

Explore •

To compare and order decimals you can use 10 × 10 grids or a number line.

Work Together

Compare 0.54 and 0.59.

0.54   <   0.59 (or 0.59 > 0.54)

1. Color 10 × 10 grids to compare each pair of decimals.
   Write >, <, or =. Check your answer on the number line above.

   a. 0.58 ● 0.63   **b.** 0.65 ● 0.56   **c.** 0.61 ● 0.58

2. Compare these decimals two at a time. 0.53, 0.6, 0.5, 0.55, and 0.58.
   Then order them from greatest to least.

How can number lines help you order numbers from least to greatest?

Connect

You can use place value to compare and order decimals.

Compare 2.364 and 2.368.

Start at the left, look for the first place where the digits are different. Compare the digits.

8 thousandths > 4 thousandths   2.368 > 2.364

Order 2.364, 2.368, and 2.36 from greatest to least.

Compare numbers two at a time.

2.368 > 2.364   2.364 > 2.36

So the order from greatest to least is 2.368, 2.364, 2.36.

Math Tip

In 2.364 and 2.368 the numbers in the thousandths place are different.

Practice

Copy and write >, <, or = to complete.

1. 0.2 ⬤ 0.06   **2.** 0.5 ⬤ 0.45   **3.** 0.99 ⬤ 1.0   **4.** 0.6 ⬤ 0.59

5. 0.3 ⬤ 0.33   **6.** 0.3 ⬤ 0.30   **7.** 1.5 ⬤ 1.32   **8.** 2.8 ⬤ 2.09

Using Data This table shows batting averages midway through a season for six major league baseball players. Use the table to answer 9–12.

9. Which player has the highest batting average?

10. Which player has the lowest batting average?

11. Order the batting averages from highest to lowest.

12. **What If** Another player, with a batting average of .358, was added to the chart. Where would his average be in the order?

13. **Health** In the United States, the average amount of cheese eaten per person is 26 lb a year, or 0.5 lb a week. Which people on the list eat more than the weekly average? Which people eat less?

14. **Journal** Explain how placing decimals on a number line helps you order them.

Batting Averages		
Player	**Team**	**Average**
Burks	Colorado Rockies	.339
Alomar	Baltimore Orioles	.353
Piazza	Los Angeles Dodgers	.341
Grace	Chicago Cubs	.337
Rodriguez	Seattle Mariners	.362
Knoblauch	Minnesota Twins	.352

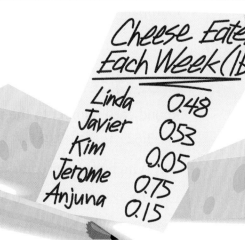

Cheese Eaten Each Week (lb)

Linda   0.48
Javier   0.53
Kim   0.05
Jerome   0.75
Anjuna   0.15

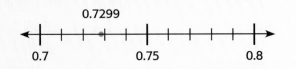

Rounding Decimals

You Will Learn

how to round decimals to the nearest tenth or hundredth

Learn

When is a dollar not worth a dollar? When it comes from another country! On August 23, 1996, the Canadian dollar was worth only 0.7299 that of the U.S. dollar.

You can round this value to the nearest hundredth or tenth.

Example 1

You can show dollar values on a number line and round to the nearest hundredth.

0.7299 rounds to 0.73.

0.7299

0.7   0.75   0.8

You can also look at the digits to round.

Example 2

Round to the nearest hundredth.

0.7299	Underline the place to round to.
0.7299	Look at the digit to its right.
9 > 5	If 5 or more, increase the digit to the left by 1. If less than 5, just use the digit to the left.

0.73

The hundredths digit increases by 1.

The Canadian dollar is worth about $0.73.

Round to the nearest tenth.

0.7299

0.7299

2 < 5

0.7

The tenths digit remains the same.

The Canadian dollar is worth about 0.7 of the U.S. dollar.

Did You Know?

Other places, like New Zealand, Hong Kong, and Australia, use "dollars" of different values.

Talk About It

Compare rounding to the nearest hundredth to rounding to the nearest tenth.

Check

Round each number to the place of the underlined digit.

1. 3.<u>6</u>2   2. 0.<u>0</u>81   3. <u>1</u>.98   4. 2.3<u>6</u>7   5. 0.<u>3</u>45

6. Which number could be rounded to 0.58?

Ⓐ 0.589   Ⓑ 0.57   Ⓒ 0.59   Ⓓ 0.577

7. **Reasoning** Name two different decimals that could be rounded to the hundredths place as 0.38.

Practice

Skills and Reasoning

Round each number to the place of the underlined digit.

8. 6<u>2</u>.79   **9.** 1.0<u>8</u>8   **10.** 0.<u>9</u>3   **11.** 45.5<u>1</u>5   **12.** <u>3</u>.607

13. 0.9<u>9</u>8   **14.** <u>9</u>.86   **15.** 1.<u>1</u>05   **16.** 5.5<u>5</u>5   **17.** 36.<u>9</u>81

18. <u>3</u>.54   **19.** 18.<u>0</u>9   **20.** 0.0<u>7</u>6   **21.** 3.0<u>1</u>0   **22.** <u>1</u>.09

23. <u>0</u>.7   **24.** 0.<u>7</u>45   **25.** <u>4</u>.499   **26.** 5.<u>0</u>76   **27.** 0.5<u>4</u>9

28. Name two decimals with digits in the thousandths place that could be rounded to the tenths place as 0.3.

Problem Solving and Applications

Using Data Use the table to answer **29–31**.

29. About how many cents is a Hong Kong dollar worth?

30. Which of the three dollars is worth the most? Do you need to round to find the answer?

Country	Value of "Dollar" in U.S. Dollars August 29, 1996
New Zealand	$0.6921
Hong Kong	$0.1293
Australia	$0.7905

31. If you had a New Zealand dollar and a Hong Kong dollar, about how much would you have in U.S. dollars?

32. **Collecting Data** Look up the value of the Canadian, Australian, Hong Kong, and Singapore dollars in a newspaper, magazine or an on-line service. Answer **29–31** again using today's data.

33. **Mental Math** Sharad owes Jessica 68¢, but he only has dimes. What's the nearest amount he could give her?

34. **Money** Look at the circle graph of how Tamika spent her allowance this week. Round each item to the nearest dollar.

    a. On what item did she spend the least amount?

    b. About how many dollars did she spend?

Tamika's Weekly Spending

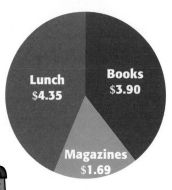

Lunch $4.35   Books $3.90   Magazines $1.69

Mixed Review and Test Prep

 Algebra Readiness Copy and write >, <, or = to complete.

35. 3 + 5 + 8 ● 3 + 5 + 7   **36.** 17 − 0 ● 17   **37.** 18 × 1 ● 18   **38.** 7 + 0 + 4 ● 7 + 4

39. **Patterns** Which of the following continues the pattern?

    10, 100, 11, 110, 12, 120, ■, ■, ■

    A 13, 130, 14   **B** 130, 140, 150   **C** 13, 130, 140   **D** not here

Problem Solving

Analyze Strategies: Draw a Picture

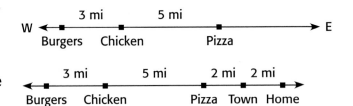

You Will Learn

how drawing a picture can help you solve problems

Problem Solving Hint

When the information is confusing, drawing a picture may help.

Learn • • • • • • • •

Suppose the road leading to your home from the west has 3 restaurants. One serves chicken, one burgers, and one pizza. The chicken place is 3 mi east of the burgers, 5 mi west of the pizza, and 7 mi west of town. Your home is 2 mi east of town. How close is the nearest restaurant to home?

Work Together

▶ **Understand**

What do you know?

What do you need to know?

▶ **Plan**

How will you solve the problem?

Draw a picture.

▶ **Solve**

Draw a picture to show the restaurants.

Complete the drawing.

Use the picture to solve the problem.

```
        3 mi        5 mi
W ←———■————————■——————————————■——→ E
    Burgers  Chicken        Pizza

        3 mi        5 mi        2 mi  2 mi
   ←——■—————————■———————————■——————■————■——→
    Burgers  Chicken     Pizza  Town  Home
```

What is the answer?

The pizza restaurant is nearest, 4 mi from home.

▶ **Look Back**

How can you check your answer?

Talk About It

Why is Draw a Picture a good strategy to use here?

Draw a picture to solve.

1. Suppose you are going out one evening to the movies with Jo and Mo. Your parents will pick them up. Jo lives 6 mi north of your house and Mo lives 3 miles east of Jo. The movie theater is 7 mi east of Jo's house. You stop for a snack at a diner that is 2 mi south and 4 mi west of the theater.

   a. How far have you traveled by the time you get to the diner?

   b. How far are you from home and in what direction?

   c. Does Jo or Mo live closer to the diner?

Problem Solving
Practice •

Problem Solving
Strategies

- Use Objects/Act It Out
- Draw a Picture
- Look for a Pattern
- Guess and Check
- Use Logical Reasoning
- Make an Organized List
- Make a Table
- Solve a Simpler Problem
- Work Backward

Choose a Tool

Draw a picture or use any strategy to solve each problem.

2. Four girls are waiting in line for movie tickets. Beth is ahead of Kelly. Lisa is behind Kelly. Beth is behind Erika. What is the order of the girls in line?

3. On Sam's street there are some traffic lights and stop signs. After 3 stop signs, he comes to the first traffic light. The number of stop signs decreases by 1 between traffic lights after that. The last signal is a stop sign. How many traffic lights are there? How many stop signs?

4. Bob is older than Jeff. Amir is younger than Jeff. Glenn's age is between Amir's and Jeff's. What is the order of the boys by age from youngest to oldest?

5. A pizza restaurant is planning to set aside four rooms for parties. Copy the picture at the right. Show how the four tables can be separated from each other by building only three walls.

6. A chicken dinner for four costs $7 more than spaghetti. If spaghetti costs $17, how much does chicken cost?

7. **Fine Arts** Four famous artists were born in the 17th, 18th, 19th, and 20th centuries. Their names are Van Gogh, Rembrandt, Goya, and Kahlo. Kahlo was not born in the 18th or 19th century. Rembrandt was born before the others. Van Gogh was born in the 19th century. Draw a number line to show in which century each was born.

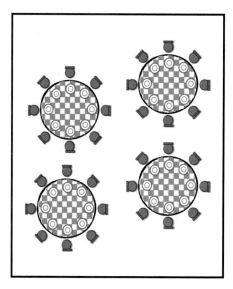

PROBLEM SOLVING PRACTICE

SECTION B
Review and Practice

(Lesson 7) Write each number in decimal form.

1. 63 hundredths   **2.** five and 30 hundredths   **3.** 6 tenths   **4.** 8 hundredths

5. 2 and 9 tenths   **6.** 4 hundredths   **7.** 12 hundredths   **8.** 3 tenths

(Lesson 8) For each group, write the equivalent decimals.

9. 0.3   0.30   0.03   **10.** 0.08   0.80   0.8   **11.** 0.05   0.5   0.50   **12.** 0.2   0.20   0.02

(Lesson 9) Write each number in decimal form.

13. 4 tenths   **14.** 40 hundredths   **15.** 4 thousandths   **16.** 40 tenths

(Lesson 10) Name the number shown by each letter.

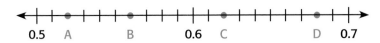

0.5   A   B   0.6   C   D   0.7

17. A   **18.** B   **19.** C   **20.** D

21. **Measurement** Little League bats can have a maximum diameter of 2.25 in. Is this diameter closer to 2 or 3 in.?

(Lesson 11) Copy and complete. Write >, <, or =.

22. 0.3 ⬤ 0.08   **23.** 0.45 ⬤ 0.3   **24.** 0.89 ⬤ 0.9   **25.** 0.05 ⬤ 0.15

26. 2.61 ⬤ 2.2   **27.** 1.264 ⬤ 1.268   **28.** 28.03 ⬤ 28.030   **29.** 2.93 ⬤ 2.9

(Lesson 12) Round each to the place of the underlined digit.

30. 4.7̲1   **31.** 0.09̲5   **32.** 1.2̲5   **33.** 0̲.583

34. 5.69̲8   **35.** 3.8̲64   **36.** 0.5̲79   **37.** 1.02̲2

(Lesson 13) Draw a picture or use any strategy to solve the problem.

38. Four students were waiting to play a computer game. Their names and ages were: Al, 10; Bea, 11; Chet, 12 and Di, 11. Neither the oldest nor Al was first in line. Di was between Bea and Chet. What was the order of the students in line?

39. **Journal** Explain how rounding 364 to the nearest ten is like rounding 3.64 to the nearest tenth.

Skills Checklist

In this section, you have:

☑ Learned About Decimals Using Tenths, Hundredths, and Thousandths

☑ Explored Equivalent Decimals

☑ Written Decimals to Hundredths on the Number Line

☑ Explored Comparing and Ordering Decimals

☑ Rounded Decimals

☑ Solved Problems by Drawing a Picture

REVIEW AND PRACTICE

Adding and Subtracting Whole Numbers and Decimals

Thousandths, Ones, Hundredths . . . Sorting through decimals and whole numbers can be like trying to get through a complex maze like this maze in New Jersey. The maze is called the Unami maze in honor of the Lenni-Lenape who planted corn there years ago. But knowing the rules gives you the direction you need to succeed!

What do you need to know to add and subtract whole numbers and decimals?

Place Value with Whole Numbers and Decimals

Review place value. Copy and complete.

1. 23 = ■ tens ■ ones
2. 0.23 = ■ tenths ■ hundredths
3. 5.81 = ■ ones ■ tenths ■ hundredths
4. 6.07 = ■ ones ■ tenths ■ hundredths
5. 0.514 = ■ tenths ■ hundredths ■ thousandths

Skills Checklist

In this section, you will:

☐ Estimate Sums and Differences

☐ Add and Subtract Whole Numbers

☐ Explore Adding and Subtracting Decimals

☐ Add and Subtract Decimals

☐ Solve Problems by Choosing an Operation

Estimating Sums and Differences

Vocabulary
front-end estimation
a way to estimate a sum by adding the first digit of each addend and adjusting the result based on the remaining digits

Learn

John collected 1,004,024 pennies. They were worth $10,040.24 and weighed almost 7,000 lb.

This table shows the weights and values of some pennies.

Weights and Values of Pennies		
Number	(lb)	($)
144	1	$1.44
288	2	$2.88
576	4	$5.76
1,152	8	$11.52

John Tregembo, from Plymouth, Michigan, collected his pennies from 1982 to 1995.

If you have 6 lb of pennies, about how many pennies do you have? You can find 6 pounds of pennies by subtracting 2 from 8 or by adding 4 and 2. You can estimate by rounding or **front-end estimation**.

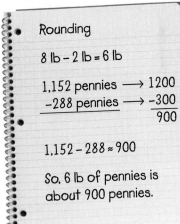

Rounding

8 lb – 2 lb = 6 lb

1,152 pennies ⟶ 1200
–288 pennies ⟶ –300
                         900

1,152 – 288 ≈ 900

So, 6 lb of pennies is about 900 pennies.

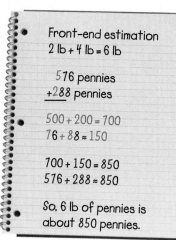

Front-end estimation
2 lb + 4 lb = 6 lb

576 pennies
+288 pennies

500 + 200 = 700
76 + 88 ≈ 150

700 + 150 = 850
576 + 288 ≈ 850

So, 6 lb of pennies is about 850 pennies.

Math Tip
You can use ≈ to show about or "approximately equal."

Talk About It
Why was one estimate higher than the other?

Check

Estimate each sum or difference.

1. 520
  + 375

2. 884
  − 406

3. $7.07
  − 3.59

4. 621
  432
  + 561

5. $9.82
  + 3.12

6. **Reasoning** If you round $9.75 and $25.82 to the nearest dollar, will your estimated sum be more or less than the actual sum?

Practice

Skills and Reasoning

Estimation Estimate each sum or difference.

7. $\begin{array}{r} 123 \\ -\ 67 \end{array}$	8. $\begin{array}{r} \$8.56 \\ +\ 4.65 \end{array}$	9. $\begin{array}{r} 627 \\ +\ 346 \end{array}$	10. $\begin{array}{r} \$5.89 \\ -\ 3.94 \end{array}$	11. $\begin{array}{r} 807 \\ -\ 289 \end{array}$
12. $\begin{array}{r} 637 \\ 87 \\ +\ 182 \end{array}$	13. $\begin{array}{r} 294 \\ 348 \\ +\ 666 \end{array}$	14. $\begin{array}{r} \$10.89 \\ -\ 3.55 \end{array}$	15. $\begin{array}{r} 499 \\ +\ 503 \end{array}$	16. $\begin{array}{r} \$5.58 \\ -\ 1.90 \end{array}$

Estimate. Copy and write >, <, or = to complete.

17. $47 + 59$ ● 100

18. $\$15.99 - \$6.00$ ● $\$10.00$

19. $23 + 87$ ● 120

20. $37 + 43 + 59$ ● 140

21. $333 + 777$ ● $1,000$

22. $\$99 - \$12$ ● $\$80$

23. If you increase both addends when rounding two numbers to add, what can you say about your estimated sum? Explain.

Problem Solving and Applications

Using Data Use the table on page 82 to answer **24–26.**

24. About how many pennies are in 5 lb?

25. About how much more is 8 lb of pennies worth than 2 lb of pennies?

26. **Critical Thinking** Explain how you could find the number and value of any number of pounds of pennies from 1 to 15.

27. **History** Abraham Lincoln became President in 1861. The Lincoln penny was coined in 1909. About how many years later was that?

28. **Logic** A nickel weighs more than a penny so there are fewer nickels than pennies in a pound. Would you rather have a pound of nickels or a pound of pennies?

Mixed Review and Test Prep

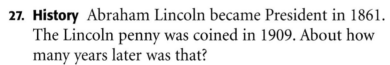

Find each product.

29. 8×3

30. 9×8

31. 7×6

32. 3×9

33. 7×8

Using Data Use the circle graph to answer **34.**

34. Which two categories made up about a third of the Antico's expenses?

Ⓐ other, housing

Ⓑ food, housing

Ⓒ other, food

Ⓓ other, transportation

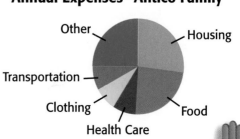

Annual Expenses—Antico Family

Other, Housing, Transportation, Clothing, Health Care, Food

Adding and Subtracting Whole Numbers

You Will Learn

how to add and subtract 3-digit to 5-digit whole numbers

Learn • • • • • • • • • • • • • • • •

The longest scheduled nonstop airline flight covers 7,969 miles between New York and Johannesburg, South Africa.

The table below shows some shorter airline distances in miles between some cities in the United States.

	Chicago	D/FW	LA	Miami	NY
Chicago	—	798	1,745	1,197	740
Dallas/Ft. Worth	798	—	1,246	1,110	1,383
Los Angeles	1,745	1,246	—	2,342	2,475
Miami	1,197	1,110	2,342	—	1,090
New York	740	1,383	2,475	1,090	—

Find the distance for a trip from Los Angeles to Chicago to New York to Miami. You can add to find the total distance.

Example 1

Step 1

Add ones.

Los Angeles to Chicago: 1,74**5**
Chicago to New York: 74**0**
New York to Miami: + 1,09**0**
                                            5

Step 2

Add tens.
Regroup as needed.

  1
1,7**4**5
   7**4**0
+ 1,0**9**0
      75

Step 3

Add hundreds.
Regroup as needed.

 1 1
1,**7**45
   740
+ 1,**0**90
   575

Step 4

Add thousands.

 1 **1**
1,745
   740
+ **1**,090
 3,575

Remember

You sometimes need to regroup in more than one place.

The distance for the trip was 3,575 miles.

Estimate to check the reasonableness of your answer.
1,700 + 700 + 1,100 = 3,500. 3,575 is close to 3,500, so the answer is reasonable.

Example 2

You can subtract to compare distances.
How much farther is it from New York to Miami than from Chicago to Dallas?

Step 1	Step 2
Subtract ones. Regroup as needed.	Subtract tens. Regroup as needed.

Step 1:
$$\begin{array}{r} 1,0 \overset{8}{\cancel{9}} \overset{10}{\cancel{0}} \\ -798 \\ \hline 2 \end{array}$$

Step 2:
$$\begin{array}{r} \overset{9\ \ 18}{\cancel{10}} \overset{8}{\cancel{9}} \overset{10}{\cancel{0}} \\ 1,0\cancel{9}\cancel{0} \\ -798 \\ \hline 9\,2 \end{array}$$

Step 3	
Subtract hundreds.	Estimate to check.

Step 3:
$$\begin{array}{r} \overset{9\ \ 18}{\cancel{10}\ \overset{8}{\cancel{9}}\ \overset{10}{\cancel{0}}} \\ 1,\cancel{0}\cancel{9}\cancel{0} \\ -798 \\ \hline 2\,9\,2 \end{array}$$

Estimate to check.

$$\begin{array}{r} 1,090 \rightarrow 1,100 \\ -798 \rightarrow -800 \\ \hline 300 \end{array}$$

292 is close to 300, so the answer is reasonable.

It is 292 miles farther from New York to Miami than from Chicago to Dallas.

You can use regrouping to subtract with zeros.

Example 3

Step 1	Step 2	Step 3
Subtract ones. Regroup as needed.	Subtract tens.	Subtract hundreds.

Step 1:
$$\begin{array}{r} \overset{9\ \ 9}{\cancel{10}\ \overset{9}{\cancel{10}}\ \overset{10}{\cancel{10}}} \\ 1,\cancel{0}\cancel{0}\cancel{0} \\ -93 \\ \hline 7 \end{array}$$

Step 2:
$$\begin{array}{r} \overset{9\ \ 9}{\cancel{10}\ \overset{9}{\cancel{10}}\ \overset{10}{\cancel{10}}} \\ 1,\cancel{0}\cancel{0}\cancel{0} \\ -93 \\ \hline 0\,7 \end{array}$$

Step 3:
$$\begin{array}{r} \overset{9\ \ 9}{\cancel{10}\ \overset{9}{\cancel{10}}\ \overset{10}{\cancel{10}}} \\ 1,\cancel{0}\cancel{0}\cancel{0} \\ -93 \\ \hline 9\,0\,7 \end{array}$$

Chicago 798 mi
Los Angeles 1,246 mi
Dallas

Talk About It

1. How does place value help you to add and subtract?

2. How did you first regroup 1,000 in Example 3? What did you do next?

Check

Find each sum or difference. Then estimate to check your answer.

1. $\begin{array}{r} 14,536 \\ +8,192 \\ \hline \end{array}$

2. $\begin{array}{r} 45,329 \\ -6,847 \\ \hline \end{array}$

3. $2,003 - 684$

4. $387 + 492 + 49$

5. **Reasoning** Find $9,000 - 7,999$ mentally. Explain why it is easier to do mentally than by writing it out.

Skills and Reasoning

Find each sum or difference. Then estimate to check your answer.

6. 787
    + 309

7. 403
    − 221

8. 647
    + 983

9.   353
    + 4,777

10. 487
    + 39

11. 4,103
    − 685

12. 17,842
    − 6,397

13. 12,345
    + 67,890

14. 10,000
    − 3,842

15. 4,759
    + 98

16. 849
    − 783

17. 500
    − 377

18. 409
    − 97

19.   37
    498
    27
    + 35

20. 483
    55
    142
    + 344

21. $3,000 − 188$ **22.** $4,892 + 373 + 5,688$ **23.** $13,021 − 7,896$ **24.** $39 + 387$

25. $11,110 − 379$ **26.** $876 + 549$ **27.** $2,788 + 349$ **28.** $6,007 − 4,982$

29. $345 + 8,745 + 10,007 + 428 + 31$ **30.** Subtract 7,367 from 8,023.

31. Find the difference of 3,426 and 5,210.   **32.** Find the sum of 1,403, 298, 5,017, and 912.

33. Find the sum of 3,892, 11,569, 3,382, and 347.

34. Find $8,998 + 6,999$ mentally. Explain why it is easier to do this sum mentally than by writing it out.

35. Find $8,000 − 6,001$ mentally. Explain your reasoning.

Problem Solving and Applications

 Algebra Readiness Copy and complete.

36. $1,317 + n = 2,428$ **37.** $30,000 − n = 29,996$ **38.** $4,300 + 817 = n$

Using Data Use the data on page 84 to answer **39** and **40**.

39. Find the longest possible round trip. What is the distance? If you include three different cities, what is the longest trip and its distance?

40. **Geography** Plan the shortest possible New York to Los Angeles trip with one stop in between. Explain your reasoning.

41. **History** A 1963 stamp commemorating the Emancipation Proclamation was designed by the African American artist Georg Olden. How many years ago was this stamp issued?

Problem Solving and SOCIAL STUDIES

Mary Bethune, an African American educator, had a dream and $1.50.

She was the founder of a school for African American girls that became Bethune-Cookman College in Daytona Beach, Florida. She carefully recorded every contribution she received. Here is a list of some contributions, large and small.

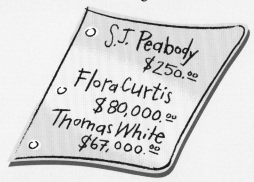

S.J. Peabody $250.⁰⁰
Flora Curtis $80,000.⁰⁰
Thomas White $67,000.⁰⁰

42. Money If a donor said he would double Peabody's donation, how much would he give?

43. Money What was the total of the donations from Curtis and White?

44. Time Mary Bethune started her school in 1904 and was involved with it until her death in 1955. How many years did she work with the school?

45. Journal Explain how regrouping in addition problems differs from regrouping in subtraction problems. Give examples.

Mixed Review and Test Prep

Find each product.

46. 3×9 **47.** 8×8 **48.** 9×4 **49.** 7×8 **50.** 2×6

Find each quotient.

51. $81 \div 9$ **52.** $56 \div 7$ **53.** $48 \div 6$ **54.** $21 \div 7$ **55.** $63 \div 7$

56. Algebra Readiness Copy and complete. Write the rule.

A	2	5	8	12
B	5		11	

57. Which of the following shows the other facts in the fact family for $9 \times 7 = 63$?

Ⓐ $9 + 7 = 16$
$9 - 7 = 2$
$63 \div 7 = 9$

Ⓑ $7 \times 9 = 63$
$63 \div 7 = 9$
$63 \div 9 = 7$

Ⓒ $7 \times 9 = 63$
$7 + 9 = 16$
$9 + 7 = 16$

Ⓓ $7 \times 9 = 63$
$63 \div 7 = 9$
$7 + 9 = 16$

THE COVER-UP GAME

Players
2–4 players

Materials
4 number cubes, each numbered as follows

1: 0, 1, 2, 3, 4, 5

2: 6, 7, 8, 9, 0, 1

3: 2, 3, 4, 5, 6, 7

4: 8, 9, 0, 1, 2, 3

game board

2–4 sets of different-colored markers

scratch paper

pencils

Object
The object of the game is to place a marker on each digit on the game board in the fewest number of turns.

How to Play

1. Each player selects a set of colored markers, then tosses a number cube to decide who starts.

2. The first player tosses all 4 number cubes, then makes and solves an addition exercise using the digits shown on the cubes.

3. The player places a marker on the game board for the ones and tenths digits that correspond to the sum.

    Example

$$\boxed{3} . \boxed{4}$$
$$+ \boxed{9} . \boxed{4}$$
$$1 \boxed{2} . \boxed{8}$$

Only one marker of each color is allowed on any space.

4. Play continues in counter-clockwise fashion around the board.

5. The first player to place his or her marker on every digit on the board is the Grand Winner.

Talk About It

1. How did play change during the game?

2. What strategy did you use to get a specific answer?

More Ways to Play

- Play the game using subtraction instead of addition.

- Use two extra number cubes. Extend the game board by adding a "tens" or "hundredths" section.

Reasoning

1. Suppose you needed an answer with a 6 in the tenths place. What two numbers would you hope to toss?

2. Suppose you needed an answer with a zero in the ones place. What two numbers would you hope to toss?

3. If you tossed a 6, 4, 2, and 7, could you place a marker on the 9 tenths square? How? Could you place a marker on the 9 ones square? How?

Exploring Adding and Subtracting Decimals

Problem Solving Connection

- Use Objects/ Act It Out
- Draw a Picture

Materials

- 10 × 10 grids
- 2 colors of crayons or colored pencils

 **Explore** • • • • • • • • • • • • •

You can use 10 × 10 grids to help you understand how to add and subtract decimals.

Work Together

Use 10 × 10 grids to find the sum and difference of 0.53 and 0.28.

1. 0.53 + 0.28

   a. Shade 5 columns and 3 more squares to show 53 hundredths.

   b. Using a different color, shade 28 more squares.

   c. Count the shaded squares to find how many hundredths there are in all.

   d. Write the sum.

2. 0.53 − 0.28

   a. Shade 5 columns and 3 more squares to show 53 hundredths.

   b. Cross out 2 columns and 8 more shaded squares to show subtraction of 28 hundredths.

   c. Count the shaded squares that were not crossed out.

   d. Write the difference.

Use 10 × 10 grids to find each sum or difference.

3. 0.54 + 0.32   **4.** 0.13 + 0.79   **5.** 0.38 + 0.46

6. 0.64 − 0.18   **7.** 0.83 − 0.17   **8.** 0.42 − 0.09

 **Talk About It**

How is adding or subtracting decimals like adding and subtracting whole numbers?

Connect

· ·

You can use what you know about addition and subtraction of whole numbers to add or subtract decimals. Find the sum and difference of 0.25 and 0.19.

What You See

Find 0.25 + 0.19.

What You Write

$$\begin{array}{r} 1 \\ 0.25 \\ + 0.19 \\ \hline 0.44 \end{array}$$

Add as you would with whole numbers.
Regroup as needed.

Math Tip

Remember the decimal point.

Find 0.25 − 0.19.

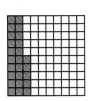

$$\begin{array}{r} 1\ 15 \\ 0.2\cancel{5} \\ - 0.19 \\ \hline 0.06 \end{array}$$

Subtract as you would with whole numbers.
Regroup as needed.

Practice

· ·

Use grids or drawings to find each sum or difference.

1. 0.42
    + 0.78

2. 4.32
    − 1.83

3. 3.28
    + 1.37

4. 1.12
    + 3.09

5. 0.90
    + 0.11

6. 2.7
    − 1.6

7. 3.42
    − 2.79

8. 4.7
    + 0.5

9. 0.72
    − 0.58

10. 6.1
    − 0.9

11. 3.21 + 4.37 + 2.7

12. 3.9 − 2.8

13. 0.98 − 0.69

14. 4.47 − 3.28

Algebra Readiness Copy and complete. Use grids or drawings to help you.

15. $1.40 - 1.4 = n$

16. $3.44 + 3.03 = n$

17. $3.20 - n = 2.10$

18. $1.11 + n = 6.10$

19. **Money** Explain how you could show 2.83 using dollars, dimes, and pennies.

20. **Critical Thinking** Would quarters and nickels be good models for adding or subtracting decimals? Explain.

21. **Journal** Explain how grids help you when you subtract. Draw pictures.

Adding Decimals

You Will Learn

how to add decimals to hundredths

Learn

The Unami Farm cornfield maze in Somerset, New Jersey covers 6 acres. The maze was named in honor of the Lenni-Lenape Indians who planted corn there long ago.

This diagram shows part of a maze. The lengths of parts of Path A, a path that does not lead to the exit, are labeled.

2.0 m
1.45 m
3.6 m
PATH A

Example

What is the total length of Path A? Add. 3.6 + 1.45 + 2.0

Step 1	Step 2	
Write the numbers. Line up the decimal points. Write zeros to help show place value.	Add as you would with whole numbers. Place the decimal point.	Estimate to check that your answer is reasonable.
3.6**0** 1.45 2.0**0**	3.60 1.45 + 2.00 ‾‾‾‾‾ 7.05	Round each addend to the nearest whole number. 4 + 1 + 2 = 7 7.05 is close to 7, so the answer is reasonable.

Path A is 7.05 meters long.

Talk About It

Why do you line up decimal points when you add decimals?

Did You Know?

The world's largest hedge maze is in Great Britain. It has 2,700 m of paths!

Check

Find each sum.

1. $5.52 + $3.47

2. 5.07 + 3.7

3.   4.19
    0.07
 + 6.2

4. $6.98
    3.24
 + 7.49

5. **Reasoning** In the example above, 3.6 was written as 3.60. Would it be correct to write it as 3.06? Explain.

Skills and Reasoning

Find each sum.

6. 5.31
    + 7.49

7. 3.02
    + 4.57

8. 3.02
    + 0.95

9. 6.30
    + 0.46

10. 5.29
    + 4.16

11. 3.42
    0.58
    + 2.65

12. $3.59
    0.87
    + 1.25

13. 0.73
    1.73
    + 0.17

14. 4.8
    3.6
    + 5

15. 1.01
    2.12
    + 3.23

16. $10.98
    +   3.25

17. 4.5
    + 0.54

18. 2.5
    + 5.25

19. 9.99
    + 3.28

20. 16.0
    + 1.60

21. $2.1 + 5.4 + 4$

22. $1.07 + 3.01 + 0.22$

23. $0.74 + 0.43$

24. $5.7 + 5.07$

25. $2.6 + 0.72$

26. $1.8 + 0.12 + 5.6$

27. $0.24 + 1.08$

28. $6.02 + 4.18$

29. Find the sum of $3.89 + 2.54$.

30. Add 1.04 and 3.99

31. Explain why you can not write 7.1 as 7.01

Problem Solving and Applications

32. Path B in the maze is made up of paths of lengths: 2.1 m, 4.07 m, 3.11 m, and 0.98 m. How long is Path B?

33. Probability If you have $0.50, name all the possible combinations of coins you could have if you do not include pennies.

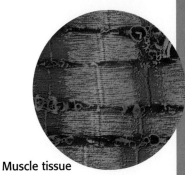

Blood tissue

Using Data Use the Data File on page 49 to answer **34–36**.

34. Science Which combinations of two tissue types make up half (0.50) or more of the human body?

35. Science What is the total for the body tissue parts by weight?

36. Write Your Own Problem Look at the bar graph. Write a question that can be answered using the data from the graph.

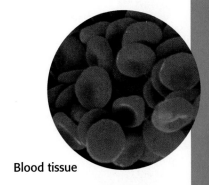

Muscle tissue

Mixed Review and Test Prep

Find each difference.

37. $309 - 89$

38. $147 - 38$

39. $333 - 134$

40. $111 - 21$

41. Money Which combination of coins is **not** worth $0.75?

Ⓐ 5 dimes, 5 nickels

Ⓑ 6 dimes, 3 nickels

Ⓒ 6 dimes, 15 nickels

Ⓓ 2 quarters, 2 dimes, 1 nickel

Subtracting Decimals

You Will Learn

how to subtract decimals to hundredths

Learn • • • • • • • • • • • • • •

Mawsynram, India, gets the most rain in the world. Its average rainfall is 466.80 inches. Some average annual rainfalls for cities in the United States are shown in this bar graph. You can see that "matching" cities do not get "matching" rainfalls.

Did You Know?

In the United States, Alabama gets the most rain with an average annual rainfall of 64.64 inches.

Average Annual Rainfall (in.)

City	Rainfall
Portland, ME	43.84
Portland, OR	30.36
Albany, NY	41.25
Albany, GA	45.63
Springfield, MO	55.78
Springfield, IL	31.45

Scale: 25 30 35 40 45 50 55 60

Inches of Rainfall

Example 1

How much more rain does Portland, Maine, get than Portland, Oregon?
To find the difference, subtract as you would with whole numbers.

Step 1	Step 2	
Line up the decimal points. 43.84 30.36	Subtract. Place the decimal point. $\overset{7\ 14}{4\ 3.\cancel{8}\cancel{4}}$ $-3\ 0.3\ 6$ $\overline{1\ 3.4\ 8}$	Estimate to check 43.84 → 44 30.36 → −30 $\overline{\qquad 14}$ 13.48 is close to 14, so the answer is reasonable.

Portland, Maine, gets 13.48 more inches of average rainfall than Portland, Oregon.

Example 2

8.2 − 3.75

Step 1	Step 2	
Line up the decimal points. 8.20 $-$3.75	Subtract. $\overset{\overset{11}{}}{\underset{}{8}}\overset{7\overset{\cancel{1}\;10}{}}{\cancel{8}\,.\,\cancel{2}\,\cancel{0}}$ $-\;3\,.\,7\,5$ $\overline{4\,.\,4\,5}$	Estimate to check. 8.20 $\rightarrow$ 8 $-$3.75 $\rightarrow$ $-$4 $\overline{4}$ 4.45 is close to 4. The answer is reasonable.

You can use what you know about subtracting decimals to subtract money.

Example 3

$18.00 − $3.52

Step 1	Step 2	
$$$18.00 $-$3.52	$\overset{7\;\overset{9}{\cancel{10}}\;10}{\$1\,\cancel{8}\,.\,\cancel{0}\,\cancel{0}}$ $-3\,.\,5\,2$ $\overline{\$1\,4\,.\,4\,8}$	Estimate to check. $$$18.00 $\rightarrow$ $$$18 $-$3.52 $\rightarrow$ $-$4 $\overline{\$14}$ $14.48 is close to $14. The answer is reasonable.

Talk About It

When you subtract $3.52 from $18, as in Example 3, why do you need to write $18 as $18.00?

Check

Copy and complete.

1.
```
    12
  8 ■■
  9.3 7
- 6.4 8
  ■.8 ■
```

2.
```
    6 ■
  5.7 ■
- 0.57
  5.■ 3
```

3.
```
    ■
  ■■ ■
$ 8.0 0
- 5.7 9
  2.■ 1
```

4.
```
     ■
   ■■ ■
 $9.0 3
- 7.2 9
 $1.7 ■
```

5.
```
      ■
  ■ ■ 13
  2.■ 3
- 0.9 7
  ■.9 ■
```

Find each difference.

6.
```
  0.56
- 0.3
```

7.
```
$18.99
-  9.99
```

8.
```
  0.9
- 0.38
```

9.
```
  0.57
- 0.29
```

10.
```
$1.29
- 0.40
```

11.
```
$13.07
-  8.88
```

12.
```
  4.33
- 0.43
```

13.
```
$11.11
-  9.87
```

14.
```
 13.03
- 9.29
```

15.
```
 15.06
-11.99
```

16. **Reasoning** What do you do when the number in the hundredths place in the top number is less than the number in the hundredths place in the bottom number? Use 0.73 − 0.58 as an example.

Skills and Reasoning

Find each difference.

17. $6.99
    − 3.99

18. 14.0
    − 3.71

19. 25.50
    − 0.78

20. 7.9
    − 0.63

21. 4.22
    − 3.66

22. 13.92
    − 4.55

23. $5.00
    − 2.59

24. 7.9
    − 6

25. 3.0
    − 0.5

26. 1.07
    − 0.89

27. $2.22
    − 1.99

28. 7
    − 0.37

29. 7.45
    − 3.96

30. 1.98
    − .59

31. 13.2
    − 11.37

32. 4.5
    − 0.56

33. 3.70
    − 3.07

34. $12.99
    − 8.68

35. 7.09
    − 6.99

36. $10.00
    − 0.99

37. 7 − 3.56   38. 0.99 − 0.06   39. 13.8 − 3.75   40. 0.9 − 0.03

41. Find the difference between 8 and 4.53.   42. Subtract 6.8 from 23.6.

43. If you have a 0 in the hundredths place in the top number and a 9 in the hundredths place in the bottom number, how do you subtract?

 Algebra Readiness Copy and complete.

44. $1.9 − n = 0.9$ 45. $n − 0.99 = 2.19$ 46. $7.45 − n = 6.17$

Problem Solving and Applications

Using Data Use the bar graph on page 94 to answer **47–49**.

47. Which of the two "matching" cities has the greatest difference in rainfalls? What is the difference?

48. Find the cities with the least and greatest rainfalls. What is the difference between the rainfalls?

49. Find the difference between the average annual rainfall in Mawsynram, India, and the city in the bar graph with the highest annual rainfall.

Using Data The smallest camera that is for sale is a circular Japanese petal camera. It has a diameter of 1.14 inches and a thickness of 0.65 in. Its focal length is 0.47 in. In contrast, the world's largest camera is 8.83 ft high, 8.25 ft wide, and 46.0 ft long.

50. How much greater is the small camera's diameter than its thickness?

51. Is the small camera's focal length more or less than 0.5 in.? How much more or less?

52. If you had a box that was 1 in. by 1 in. by 1 in., would the small camera fit in it?

53. **Write Your Own Problem** Design your own camera. Describe it using decimals. Then price it (under $100). If you sold it to someone with a $100 bill, how much change would you get?

54. **Journal** Explain how to subtract decimals, using an example. In your example, use at least one zero in the top number.

Mixed Review and Test Prep

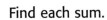

Find each sum.

55. 70 + 36   **56.** 12 + 317   **57.** 999 + 7   **58.** 836 + 745

59. 71 + 3,629   **60.** $209 + $348   **61.** 8 + 80 + 800   **62.** 39 + 93 + 309

Find each quotient.

63. 81 ÷ 9   **64.** 48 ÷ 6   **65.** 56 ÷ 7   **66.** 49 ÷ 7   **67.** 42 ÷ 6

68. 36 ÷ 4   **69.** 30 ÷ 6   **70.** 27 ÷ 9   **71.** 18 ÷ 3   **72.** 45 ÷ 5

73. **Money** A roll of film and its processing cost $5.59 and $12.50. About how much change would you get from a $20 bill?

Ⓐ about $2.00   Ⓑ about $18.00   Ⓒ about $7.00   Ⓓ about $19.00

STOP and Practice

Find each sum or difference.

1.	657 + 643	**2.**	846 − 189	**3.**	$521 + 605	**4.**	382 − 78	**5.**	4,006 − 387

6.	25,590 − 1,691	**7.**	15,465 + 53,809	**8.**	25,486 − 648	**9.**	$11.59 + 11.49	**10.**	$26.00 − 22.34

11.	8.90 3.57 + 5.03	**12.**	3.67 6.84 + 14.00	**13.**	7.8 3.09 + 4	**14.**	6.08 7.09 + 8.91	**15.**	3.1 2.01 + 5.06

16. 15.8 − 4.61   **17.** 237.05 − 25.671   **18.** 5.3 + 6.12 + 11.094

19.	1.72 + 0.67	**20.**	4 − 0.5	**21.**	3.23 + 2.85	**22.**	15.5 − 5.05	**23.**	$12.92 − 6.76

24.	351 468 + 629	**25.**	54,700 23,405 + 43,617	**26.**	1,219 2,400 + 3,042	**27.**	7.2 1.8 + 9.6	**28.**	17.17 5.82 + 6.54

29. 19.5 − 9.5   **30.** 17.13 − 5.03   **31.** 9.08 − 2.5   **32.** 8.3 + 2.1 + 3.6

33. 28.32 + 106.5 + 67.44   **34.** 4.7 + 4.07   **35.** $22.50 − $8.75   **36.** $390 + $77.99 + $32.01

37. $30.00 − $6.45   **38.** 2.2 + 9.5 + 20.7   **39.** $17.98 + $15.50   **40.** 12.92 − 6.83

Error Search

Find each sum or difference that is not correct. Write it correctly
and explain the error.

41.	$6.09 + 3.41 $9.40	**42.**	15,983 − 9,044 6,949	**43.**	5,000 − 3,008 2,998	**44.**	4.07 + 0.16 4.23	**45.**	$8.36 − 8.29 $0.17

Cover Up!

Add or subtract. Match each letter to its answer in the blank below. Some letters are not used. Answer the riddle.

What goes up a chimney down, but can't go down a chimney up?

8.03	9.18	330	$42.81	339.97	$5.48	2,562	10.02	10.02	8.03

46. $18.79 + $24.02 (M)   **47.** $3.05 + $2.43 (R)   **48.** $57.65 − $11.34 (I)

49. 3.8 + 1.52 + 4.7 (L)   **50.** 11.78 − 2.60 (N)   **51.** $16.62 − $8.71 (Y)

52. 3,008 − 456 (D)   **53.** 1,368 + 1,194 (E)   **54.** 1.5 + 6.08 + 0.45 (A)

55. 365.09 − 24.11 (O)   **56.** 240.35 + 99.62 (B)   **57.** 273.48 + 56.52 (U)

Number Sense Mental Math and Reasoning

Remember
Remember to do the operation inside the parentheses first.

You can use number properties to help you add.

Properties of Addition

Commutative (Order) Property	Associative (Grouping) Property
Changing the order of addends does not change the sum. 4 + 9 = 13 9 + 4 = 13	Changing the grouping of addends does not change the sum. 7 + (3 + 8) = 18 (7 + 3) + 8 = 18

Copy and complete. Write >, <, or =. Use the properties to help.

58. $7 + 14 \bullet 15 + 7$ **59.** $4 + (6 + 7) \bullet (4 + 6) + 8$

60. $13 + (7 + 8) \bullet (23 + 7) + 8$ **61.** $10 + 38 \bullet 38 + 9$

62. $7 + 19 \bullet 19 + 6$ **63.** $25 + (5 + 6) \bullet (25 + 5) + 6$

Problem Solving

Analyze Word Problems:
Choose an Operation

You Will Learn

how to choose an operation to write a number sentence

Learn • • • • • • • • • • • • •

In a rating of computer games, the best possible score was 100. The difference between the scores given to Brain Drain and Misty was 9 points. If Brain Drain received a score of 94, what was Misty's score?

Work Together

▶ **Understand**   What do you know?

    What do you need to find out?

▶ **Plan**   What will you do to find out?   Write number sentences and solve.

▶ **Solve**   Write number sentences.   Misty's score is either

        9 more than 94: $n = 94 + 9$
                           $n = 103$

        or

        9 less than 94: $n = 94 - 9$
                           $n = 85$

    What is the answer?   Since the highest possible score was 100, Misty's score is 85.

▶ **Look Back**   How can you check your answer?

(**Talk About It**)

How can both an addition and subtraction sentence fit the story?

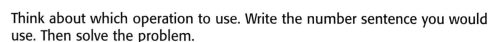

Write the letter of the number sentence you would use.

1. Brain Drain costs $40. Misty costs $17 more than Brain Drain. How much do the games cost together?

   Ⓐ $40 + $40 + $17 = $97   Ⓑ $40 + $17 = $57

   Ⓒ $40 + $17 + $57 = $114

Think about which operation to use. Write the number sentence you would use. Then solve the problem.

2. A game needs a score of at least 81 to be rated Excellent. Kevin gave one game a 73. By how many points did the game miss an Excellent rating?

Problem Solving Practice

Think about which operation to use. Write the number sentence or sentences you would use. Then solve each problem.

3. **Money** The original price of a game that Crystal wanted was $39.95. She waited until the price dropped to $31.50 and then bought it. How much did she save by waiting?

4. **Money** Kelly planned to use her $100 savings to buy a game for $59. She wanted to use the money that was left to buy another game for $45. How much more money will she need?

5. Geneva rated three games that had a total score of 210. Rocket Ride got 79, Alien Blaster III got 68. What score did she give to World Conquest?

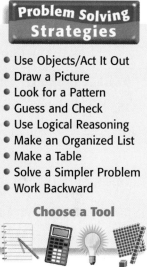

Problem Solving Strategies

- Use Objects/Act It Out
- Draw a Picture
- Look for a Pattern
- Guess and Check
- Use Logical Reasoning
- Make an Organized List
- Make a Table
- Solve a Simpler Problem
- Work Backward

Choose a Tool

6. **Logic** To rate computer games, Brian looked at Santa Fe Trail after trying Blastarama but before New York Mystery. The last game he tried was Mississippi Riverboat. He remembered liking the first game he tried, but could not remember which one it was. Which was the first game Brian rated? What strategy did you use to solve the problem?

7. **Time** It took 5 years for Roy to grow 8 in. He began measuring when he was 7 years old in 1989. Which expression would you use to find how old he was when he stopped measuring?

   Ⓐ 1989 + 8   Ⓑ 8 + 5   Ⓒ 7 + 5   Ⓓ 1989 + 5

PROBLEM SOLVING PRACTICE

SECTION C
Review and Practice

(Lessons 14 and 15) Find each sum or difference. Estimate to check.

1. $\begin{array}{r} 630 \\ + 425 \\ \hline \end{array}$
2. $\begin{array}{r} 962 \\ - 308 \\ \hline \end{array}$
3. $\begin{array}{r} \$25.17 \\ + 7.99 \\ \hline \end{array}$
4. $\begin{array}{r} 621 \\ 243 \\ + 708 \\ \hline \end{array}$
5. $\begin{array}{r} \$7.65 \\ - 3.54 \\ \hline \end{array}$

6. $\begin{array}{r} 3,008 \\ - 876 \\ \hline \end{array}$
7. $\begin{array}{r} 15,391 \\ + 1,589 \\ \hline \end{array}$
8. $\begin{array}{r} 38,672 \\ + 39,005 \\ \hline \end{array}$
9. $\begin{array}{r} 20,000 \\ - 19,889 \\ \hline \end{array}$
10. $\begin{array}{r} 35,007 \\ - 29,999 \\ \hline \end{array}$

 Algebra Readiness Copy and complete.

11. $1{,}250 + n = 3{,}606$
12. $50{,}000 - n = 13{,}999$
13. $n + 12{,}419 = 14{,}985$

14. One survey was sent to 5,935 people. Of these, 2,199 responded. How many people did not respond?

(Lessons 16 and 17) Find each sum.

15. $\begin{array}{r} 2.1 \\ + 8.4 \\ \hline \end{array}$
16. $\begin{array}{r} 3.42 \\ + 9.73 \\ \hline \end{array}$
17. $\begin{array}{r} 3.7 \\ 5.02 \\ + 2.74 \\ \hline \end{array}$
18. $\begin{array}{r} \$1.79 \\ 6.53 \\ + 0.89 \\ \hline \end{array}$
19. $\begin{array}{r} 8.25 \\ 0.9 \\ + 12.62 \\ \hline \end{array}$

20. $3.4 + 6.09 + 8$
21. $1.09 + 6.3 + 12$
22. $0.6 + 0.07 + 3$

(Lessons 16 and 18) Find each difference.

23. $\begin{array}{r} 5.8 \\ - 2.6 \\ \hline \end{array}$
24. $\begin{array}{r} 5.93 \\ - 2.99 \\ \hline \end{array}$
25. $\begin{array}{r} \$3.37 \\ - 2.09 \\ \hline \end{array}$
26. $\begin{array}{r} 8 \\ - 0.68 \\ \hline \end{array}$
27. $\begin{array}{r} 5.75 \\ - 3.9 \\ \hline \end{array}$

(Lesson 19) Choose any strategy to solve each problem.

28. **Science** Hair grows about 0.01 inch daily. Write an addition problem to show how much a hair grows in a week.

29. **Social Studies** It takes 4.5 hr to drive from New York to Washington, D.C. How long does it take to make a round trip?

30. **Literature** Nancy Drew, the popular fictional teenage detective, was first introduced in 1930. New stories continue to be written. How long has she been solving mysteries?

 31. **Journal** Explain how you would find the difference between $5 and $1.75.

Skills Checklist

In this section, you have:

☑ Estimated Sums and Differences

☑ Added and Subtracted Whole Numbers

☑ Explored Adding and Subtracting Decimals

☑ Added and Subtracted Decimals

☑ Solved Problems by Choosing an Operation

REVIEW AND PRACTICE

Choose at least one of the following. Use what you have learned in this chapter.

① Be an Artist

Use 10×10 grid paper and two colored pencils. Show two decimals in hundredths less than 0.50. Show their sum on another sheet of grid paper.

③ Creative Cook

At Home Find cans or boxes whose masses are given in decimals. Make a chart that shows the contents and mass of two or more cans or boxes.

Can	Mass
Corn	0.57 kg
Chocolate Syrup	0.89 kg
Chocolate-Covered Corn	1.46 kg

② Who Am I?

I am a decimal in hundredths. If you double me, my sum is between 0.7 and 0.8. My hundredths digit is not 2, but my double's is. Who am I? Make up your own number puzzle for decimals or large numbers.

④ It Takes Two to Total

Work with a partner. Pick a topic of your choice to access on **www.mathsurf.com/5/ch2**. Choose a topic that will give you large number or decimal data. Write and solve an addition or subtraction problem with your data. Use a calculator if you wish.

⑤ Math Note

Make up a song that tells the steps you use to add and regroup with whole numbers. Make verses for subtraction and decimal addition and subtraction.

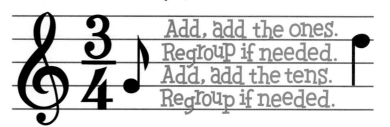

Add, add the ones.
Regroup if needed.
Add, add the tens.
Regroup if needed.

Review/Test

Vocabulary Match each with its meaning.

1. digits
2. period
3. equivalent decimals

   a. symbols: 0, 1, 2, 3, 4, 5, 6, 7, 8, 9
   b. decimals that name the same amount
   c. a group of three digits

(Lessons 2, 4, and 5) Use place value to write the value of each of the following digits in 15,234,678,009.

4. 4
5. 7
6. 5
7. each 0

Copy and complete. Write >, <, or =.

8. 5,103 ● 5,098
9. two billion, 58 million ● 2,580,000

(Lessons 7, 9, 10, and 12) Write each number in decimal form.

10. two hundred fifty and sixteen hundredths
11. three and eight tenths

Copy and complete. Write >, <, or =.

12. 0.16 ● 1.60
13. 1.8 ● 1.08
14. 107.9 ● 107.90

(Lessons 14–18) Find each sum or difference.

15.
$$\begin{array}{r} 8{,}952 \\ + 78{,}635 \\ \hline \end{array}$$

16.
$$\begin{array}{r} 59.86 \\ - 23.91 \\ \hline \end{array}$$

17.
$$\begin{array}{r} 9.1 \\ 5.68 \\ + 13.05 \\ \hline \end{array}$$

18.
$$\begin{array}{r} 86{,}951 \\ - 5{,}639 \\ \hline \end{array}$$

19.
$$\begin{array}{r} \$7.27 \\ - 1.99 \\ \hline \end{array}$$

20.
$$\begin{array}{r} 1{,}508 \\ - 789 \\ \hline \end{array}$$

21.
$$\begin{array}{r} 42.08 \\ + 4.93 \\ \hline \end{array}$$

22.
$$\begin{array}{r} 75{,}111 \\ + 99{,}999 \\ \hline \end{array}$$

(Lessons 1, 3, 6, 8, 11, 13, and 16) Choose any strategy to solve each problem.

23. **Money** If you saved $10 a month, how many months would it take until you had $1,000,000?

24. **Money** Juan has $8.00. Can he buy lunch for $3.99 and then go to the movies for $3.50? Would he have any money left over? Explain.

25. Four books are on a shelf. The mystery is to the left of the biography. The science fiction is to the left of the mystery. The Western is the last book to the right. Give the order from left to right.

Performance Assessment

Suppose your class collected $100 to spend on a holiday meal for 30 senior citizens. How would you spend the $100?

Food Item	Cost	Servings
Turkey	$12.50 each	Serves 10
Soft drinks	$1.99 per pack	6 cans in a pack
Potatoes	$1.59 per bag	10-lb bag serves 10
Squash	$1.69 each	1 squash serves 5
Pumpkin pie	$6.99 each	1 pie serves 10
Salad mix	$7.50 per bag	1 bag serves 30
Green beans	$4.50 per bag	1 bag serves 10
Rolls	$5.00 per pack	1 pack serves 36

1. **Decision Making** Decide which items you will buy. Decide how many of each item.

2. **Recording Data** Make a table like the one shown. Remember that your total can be close to $100, but cannot go over. Some labels to consider for your chart are:
   Item Name   **How Many Needed?**   **Cost of One**   **Total Cost**

3. **Explain Your Thinking** How did you decide which items to buy? How did you decide how many of each item?

4. **Critical Thinking** What would you change in your plan if you wanted to provide a meal for 50 senior citizens and have $150 to spend?

Math Magazine

Place Value Xylophone Lessons

Ancient Romans used letters or symbols as their numeral system.

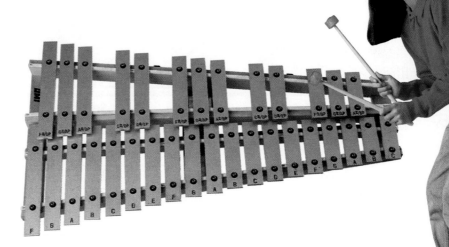

Romans combined seven letters or symbols to represent other numbers. You can do the same!

If the symbol to the right is of equal or lesser value, add its value to the value of the symbol at the left.

If the symbol to the right is of greater value, subtract the left symbol from the right symbol. This usually happens with 4s and 9s.

Roman Numeral	Addition	Standard Form
VI	5 + 1	6
LXII	50 + 10 + 1 + 1	62
CX	100 + 10	110
MD	1,000 + 500	1,500

Roman Numeral	Subtraction	Standard Form
IV	5 − 1	4
XL	50 − 10	40
XC	100 − 10	90
CM	1,000 − 100	900

Try These!

Write the standard number for each Roman numeral and the Roman numeral for each standard number.

1. DCCVI   2. CDXIII   3. MDCXVI   4. CLXXII   5. MDCCLVII

6. 1,545   7. 999   8. 1,842   9. 755   10. 2,720

Roman Challenge!

11. Something is wrong here! Can you move only one toothpick to make these Roman numeral equations true?

12. Where do you find Roman numerals today?

13. Can you finish the sentence in the title using the C, D, and M?

IX + X = XXI

XXIII − VII = XIV

Cumulative Review

Test Prep Strategy: Read Carefully

Watch for tricky problems.

What is the value of the red digit in 8**7**9,030,653?

Ⓐ 700 million Ⓑ 70 million Ⓒ 70 billion Ⓓ 7 billion

Read carefully.
Review periods first:
7 is in the millions.
Review places next: 7 is
in the ten millions place.
So the correct answer is
Ⓑ.

Write the letter of the correct answer. Read carefully. Use any strategy.

Test Prep Strategies

- Read Carefully
- Follow Directions
- Make Smart Choices
- Eliminate Choices
- Work Backward from an Answer

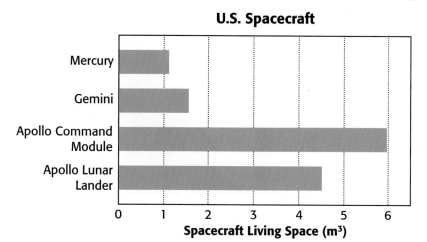

U.S. Spacecraft

Spacecraft Living Space (m³)

1. What was the size of living space in the Mercury spacecraft?

   Ⓐ about 6 m³ Ⓑ about 5 m³

   Ⓒ about 2 m³ Ⓓ about 1 m³

2. Which spacecraft has the greatest amount of living space?

   Ⓐ Mercury Ⓑ Apollo Command

   Ⓒ Gemini Ⓓ Apollo Lunar

3. How many choices are on the menu?

   Ⓐ 3 Ⓑ 4 Ⓒ 17 Ⓓ 21

4. What is the range of the fat grams?

   Ⓐ 9 Ⓑ 35 Ⓒ 37 Ⓓ 7

5. What is the mode of the fat grams?

   Ⓐ 11 Ⓑ 18 and 11 Ⓒ 18 Ⓓ not here

Fat (g) for Menu Choices	
0	4 8 2 9 0
1	1 2 8 4 8 1
2	7 2 1 8
3	7 4

6. Which number is the greatest?

   Ⓐ 38,651,132 Ⓑ 576,999 Ⓒ 22,941,713 Ⓓ 38,651,531

7. Choose the best estimate for 4,988 + 53,455.

   Ⓐ 5,600 Ⓑ 58,000 Ⓒ 103,000 Ⓓ 65,000

REVIEW AND PRACTICE

Chapter 3
Multiplying Whole Numbers and Decimals

SECTION
A

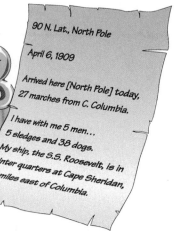

Exploring the North Pole Page 111

Multiplying with Whole Numbers

On April 6, 1909, Admiral Robert Peary and Matthew Henson reached the North Pole, raised the flag of the United States, and left two letters in a bottle. Here is part of a letter written by Peary.

How long ago did the group reach the pole?

90 N. Lat., North Pole

April 6, 1909

Arrived here [North Pole] today, 27 marches from C. Columbia.

I have with me 5 men... 5 sledges and 38 dogs. My ship, the S.S. Roosevelt, is in winter quarters at Cape Sheridan, 90 miles east of Columbia.

Multiplying with Whole Numbers and Decimals

133

Ever dream of owning your own business? The table shows some young business owners, their products, and prices.

Business Owner	Business	Location	Product	Price	Price (10% Increase)
Kiki	Clown	South Daytona, FL	Performance	$125 each	$137.50
Jimmy	Beehives	Austin, TX	Honey	$2 jar	$2.20
Arie	Clothing	Chicago, IL	Sweatshirt	$40 each	$44.00
Ariane	Jewelry	New York, NY	Safety pin jewelry	$26–$40 each	$28.60–$44.00

Ebony Hood is a business woman. Page 133

About how many sweatshirts would Arie need to sell to make as much as Kiki does for one performance?

Multiplying with Decimals

143

Computer use is catching up with phone use. In which country or region is there the most computer use per person?

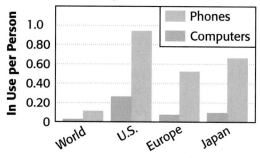

Computers vs. Phones

Famous Flyers Page 143

Surfing the World Wide Web!

Which do you like using better: a computer or a phone? Visit **www.mathsurf.com/5/ch3** to find out more about the technologies people are using.

TEAM PROJECT
ROAD TRIP!

Materials

map, posterboard, ruler, pictures of points of interest, markers

Can you use a map to plan an exciting vacation?

A scale tells you how to find distances on a particular map. This scale shows that 1 inch = 27 miles. Find an area of the United States that interests you. Plan a 6-day trip of about 300 miles each day. Make a poster about this trip.

Make a Plan

- How will you decide where to go?
- How will you record your route?
- What will you put on your poster?
- How will you divide project tasks?

Carry It Out

1. Pick a state or area to visit. Paste a map of this area on posterboard.
2. Pick sights to see. Draw a route that covers about 300 miles per day.
3. Write to the State Board of Tourism or research at the library. Find pictures and write brief descriptions about each place to put on the posterboard.
4. Estimate the daily mileage, and then find the actual mileage. Write both on the map.

Talk About It

- How did your group determine the approximate mileage for each day?

Present the Project

Plan a class presentation and display all the posters. Which trips would you like to take?

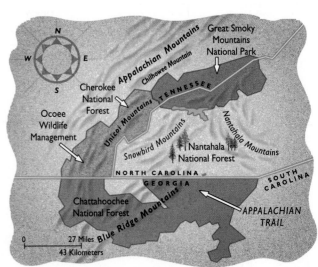

A Multiplying with Whole Numbers

Admiral Robert Peary and his team of explorers reached the North Pole in 1909. Most of the members of the exploration team were Inuit who were experienced in driving dog sleds. How could the team of explorers use multiplication to estimate the distance they could travel in one day?

Skills Checklist

In this section, you will:

☐ Explore Multiplication Patterns and Properties

☐ Estimate Products

☐ Multiply Whole Numbers

☐ Learn About the Distributive Property

☐ Choose a Calculation Method

☐ Explore Patterns with Multiples

☐ Solve Problems by Making Decisions

Estimating Products

Review rounding. Round each number to the place of the underlined digit.

1. <u>5</u>4
2. <u>3</u>59
3. <u>8</u>,701

4. 1<u>0</u>,982
5. <u>3</u>44,499
6. 2<u>2</u>,926

7. <u>3</u>29
8. <u>6</u>6
9. <u>9</u>,992

Exploring Multiplication Patterns and Properties

Problem Solving Connection

Look for a Pattern

Materials

calculator

Vocabulary

multiple
the product of a number and a whole number

multiplication properties
commutative property
associative property

Explore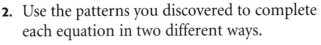

You can use basic multiplication facts and **multiples** of 10 to help you discover multiplication patterns and properties. A number that is the product of 10 and any whole number is a multiple of 10.

Work Together

1. Use a calculator or mental math to find each product. Look for a pattern.

   a. $50 \times 4 \times 2$

   $5 \times 40 \times 2$

   $5 \times 4 \times 20$

   $5 \times 4 \times 2 \times 10$

   b. $50 \times 4 \times 20$

   $5 \times 40 \times 20$

   $500 \times 4 \times 2$

   $5 \times 4 \times 2 \times 100$

   c. $50 \times 400 \times 2$

   $50 \times 40 \times 20$

   $50 \times 4 \times 200$

   $5 \times 4 \times 2 \times 1,000$

2. Use the patterns you discovered to complete each equation in two different ways.

   a. $\blacksquare \times \blacksquare \times 10 = 240$

   b. $3 \times \blacksquare \times \blacksquare = 2,400$

   c. $\blacksquare \times \blacksquare \times \blacksquare = 3,600$

   d. $\blacksquare \times \blacksquare \times \blacksquare = 1,200$

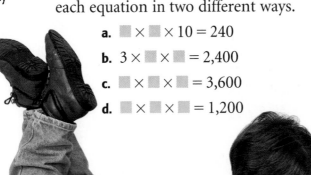

Remember

When finding a multiple of 10 with basic facts like $6 \times 5 = 30$, supply an extra zero.

Talk About It

3. How are the products alike in each of the groups in **1**? Describe any patterns you see.

4. Use what you have learned to tell how to multiply with multiples of 10, 100, or 1,000.

Connect

Properties can help you find some products mentally.

Multiplication Property	Description	Example
Commutative Property	Product is the same regardless of order	$3 \times 7 = 7 \times 3$
Associative Property	Product is the same regardless of grouping	$(3 \times 10) \times 7 = 3 \times (10 \times 7)$

A. $30 \times 50 = (3 \times 10) \times (5 \times 10)$
$\qquad = (3 \times 5) \times (10 \times 10)$
$\qquad = 15 \times 100$
$\qquad = 1,500$

B. $20 \times (73 \times 5) = 20 \times (5 \times 73)$
$\qquad = (20 \times 5) \times 73$
$\qquad = 100 \times 73$
$\qquad = 7,300$

Practice

 Mental Math Find each product. Use mental math.

1. 30×70 **2.** 2×70 **3.** 60×60 **4.** 15×20

5. $15 \times (4 \times 10)$ **6.** $(40 \times 2) \times 20$ **7.** $100 \times (3 \times 20)$ **8.** $(3 \times 5) \times 200$

 Algebra Readiness Copy and complete.

9. $20 \times n = 1,200$ **10.** $50 \times n = 1,500$ **11.** $80 \times n = 24,000$

12. $n \times 70 = 35,000$ **13.** $n \times 90 = 900,000$ **14.** $70 \times n = 21,000$

 Mental Math Find each product. Use mental math and multiplication properties.

15. $(19 \times 25) \times 4$ **16.** $2 \times (68 \times 5)$ **17.** $(2 \times 17) \times 5$ **18.** $(40 \times 25) \times 4$

19. $(40 \times 800) \times 100$ **20.** $(2 \times 33) \times 50$ **21.** $9 \times (200 \times 5)$ **22.** $(3 \times 20) \times (4 \times 5)$

23. How can you use what you learned about multiples of 10 and properties to find $6 \times (7 \times 5)$?

24. Critical Thinking You know that $2 \times 50 \times 300 = 30,000$. Why are there 4 zeros in the product?

25. In the equation $5 \times 8 \times 100 = 4,000$ why is it important to remember $5 \times 8 = 40$?

26. Money How many $20 bills are equal to four $50 bills?

27. Careers A payroll officer writes 30 checks each for the amount shown. How much is the total amount of the checks?

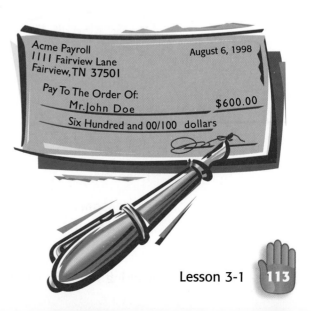

 28. Journal Explain how to find 40×700 by using mental math.

Estimating Products

You Will Learn
how to use rounding
to estimate products

Remember
Number lines can help
you round.
454 is closer
to 500 than
400. 454
rounds to
500.

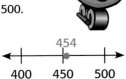

```
        454
|---+----●----+---|
400   450   500
```

Learn

Barry Halper holds the record for
collecting memorabilia from an
all-American sport—baseball.

Barry's Collection
• over 1 million different baseball cards
• 900 uniform jerseys
• nearly 5,000 autographed baseballs
• over 1,000 bats

The numbers shown are estimates.
Use estimates when it is not possible
or necessary to get an exact number.

Memorabilia from the Baseball Hall
of Fame in Cooperstown, New York.

Example 1

You can use rounding to estimate a product.

Suppose Barry buys 28 boxes to store his
baseballs. Each box holds 36 balls. About how
many baseballs can he store? Estimate 28 × 36.

rounds to   **Think:**   3 × 4 = 12

$$28 \longrightarrow 30$$
$$\times 36 \longrightarrow \times 40$$

So, 30 × 40 = 1,200

He can store about 1,200 baseballs.

Example 2

You can also use estimation to check the
reasonableness of an answer.

Estimate to see if 7,161 is a reasonable
product of 217 and 33.

rounds to

$$217 \longrightarrow 200$$
$$\times 33 \longrightarrow \times 30$$
$$\overline{6,000}$$

Since 7,161 is close to 6,000, the answer is
reasonable.

Talk About It

How do basic facts help in estimating products?

Check

Estimate each product.

1. 53 × 4   **2.** 66 × 7   **3.** 28 × 5   **4.** 132 × 16   **5.** 465 × 39

6. Reasoning When you round both factors to a greater number, how
will your estimate compare with the exact answer?

Practice

Skills and Reasoning

Estimate each product.

7. 7×36 **8.** 57×3 **9.** 9×51 **10.** 4×79 **11.** 28×5

12. 37×23 **13.** 54×18 **14.** 62×76 **15.** 93×14 **16.** 72×47

17. 23×126 **18.** 338×59 **19.** 689×32 **20.** 831×39 **21.** 63×455

22. $\begin{array}{r} 42 \\ \times\ 8 \\ \hline \end{array}$ **23.** $\begin{array}{r} 33 \\ \times 58 \\ \hline \end{array}$ **24.** $\begin{array}{r} 19 \\ \times 78 \\ \hline \end{array}$ **25.** $\begin{array}{r} 490 \\ \times\ 32 \\ \hline \end{array}$ **26.** $\begin{array}{r} 841 \\ \times\ 76 \\ \hline \end{array}$

27. Estimate the product of 562 and 23.

28. Give two numbers whose product is about 600.

29. The product of 32 and what number is between 600 and 800?

Problem Solving and Applications

Using Data Use the data on page 114 to answer **30** and **31**.

30. Suppose Barry has 147 boxes for bats. Each holds 12 bats. Does he have enough boxes for his collection? Explain.

31. About how many more baseballs does Barry have than bats?

32. History In 1916, Edd Roush, one of the Cincinnati Reds' greatest hitters, used bats that weighed about 68 oz. About how much would 12 of those bats weigh?

33. Money Sylvia is the treasurer of the baseball club. For a trip she has collected 29 checks of $12.95 each. About how much money has she collected? Explain.

34. Health One way a healthy young person can keep fit is by following a pattern of jogging 3 min and then walking 3 min for a total of 24 min. How many sets of jogging/walking would that be?

35. Journal Explain how to estimate the product of 369×3.

Edd Roush won the batting title in 1917 with a .341 average.

Mixed Review and Test Prep

Find each sum or difference.

36. $\begin{array}{r} 292 \\ + 350 \\ \hline \end{array}$ **37.** $\begin{array}{r} 356 \\ - 220 \\ \hline \end{array}$ **38.** $\begin{array}{r} 623 \\ + 2,310 \\ \hline \end{array}$ **39.** $\begin{array}{r} 963 \\ + 5,060 \\ \hline \end{array}$ **40.** $\begin{array}{r} 468 \\ - 189 \\ \hline \end{array}$

41. Which of the following is standard form for three billion, three hundred three million, thirty three thousand, three?

Ⓐ 3,333,333,333   **Ⓑ** 3,303,033,003   **Ⓒ** 3,333,333   **Ⓓ** 3,033,033,003

Multiplying Whole Numbers

You Will Learn

how to multiply by 1-digit and 2-digit numbers

Learn • • • • • •

The students of Monroe Middle School take an annual hike on the Oregon Trail. This trail was used by settlers traveling west in covered wagons. One kind of wagon had a rear wheel that turned 360 times for every 1 mile traveled.

Students from Monroe Middle School in Green River, Wyoming, hike about 7–8 miles on the Oregon Trail.

Did You Know?

The Oregon Trail ran from Independence, Missouri, to Fort Vancouver, Oregon—a distance of about 2,000 miles.

Example 1

How many times did the wheel turn as the wagon covered 8 miles? Find 8×360.

$$
\begin{array}{r}
\overset{4}{360} \\
\times\ \ 8 \\
\hline
2{,}880
\end{array}
$$

Estimate to check.
$400 \times 8 = 3{,}200$
2,880 is close to 3,200, so the answer is reasonable.

The wheel turned 2,880 times in 8 miles.

Multiplying by a 2-digit number is like multiplying by a 1-digit number.

Example 2

Find the product of 37 and 24.

Step 1	Step 2	Step 3
Multiply the ones. Regroup if necessary.	Multiply the tens. Add the extra tens. Regroup.	Add the products.
$\begin{array}{r}\overset{2}{37}\\ \times 24\\ \hline 148\end{array}$	$\begin{array}{r}\overset{1}{\overset{2}{37}}\\ \times 24\\ \hline 148\\ 740\end{array}$	$\begin{array}{r}\overset{1}{\overset{2}{37}}\\ \times 24\\ \hline 148\\ 740\\ \hline 888\end{array}$

$37 \times 24 = 888$

Example 3

Find the product of 874 and 59.

Step 1	Step 2	Step 3
Multiply ones.	Multiply tens.	Add the products.
$\begin{array}{r} {\scriptstyle 6\ 3} \\ 874 \\ \times\ \ 59 \\ \hline 7866 \end{array}$	$\begin{array}{r} {\scriptstyle 3\ 2} \\ {\scriptstyle 6\ 3} \\ 874 \\ \times\ \ 59 \\ \hline 7866 \\ 43700 \end{array}$	$\begin{array}{r} {\scriptstyle 3\ 2} \\ {\scriptstyle 6\ 3} \\ 874 \\ \times\ \ 59 \\ \hline 7866 \\ 43700 \\ \hline 51,566 \end{array}$

Estimate to check the reasonableness of the answer.

$$\begin{array}{r} 874 \longrightarrow\ \ 900 \\ \times\ 59 \longrightarrow \times\ 60 \\ \hline 54,000 \end{array}$$

51,566 is close to 54,000, so the answer is reasonable.

$874 \times 59 = 51,566$

Talk About It

1. When multiplying by a 2-digit number when is it necessary to regroup?

2. Give an example of a pair of two-digit numbers that requires regrouping when multiplied. Explain how you found your pair of numbers.

Check •

Copy and complete.

1. $\begin{array}{r} 3\ 49 \\ \times\ \ \ 7 \\ \hline 2,\blacksquare\blacksquare 3 \end{array}$

2. $\begin{array}{r} 5\ 06 \\ \times\ \ \ 8 \\ \hline \blacksquare\blacksquare\blacksquare 8 \end{array}$

3. $\begin{array}{r} 3\ 5 \\ \times 1\ 7 \\ \hline 2\ \blacksquare 5 \\ \blacksquare 5\ \blacksquare \\ \hline \blacksquare\blacksquare\blacksquare \end{array}$

4. $\begin{array}{r} 3\ 07 \\ \times\ \ 26 \\ \hline 1\ 8\ \blacksquare 2 \\ 6\ \blacksquare\blacksquare 0 \\ \hline 7,\blacksquare 82 \end{array}$

Find each product. Estimate to show that your answer is reasonable.

5. $\begin{array}{r} 658 \\ \times\ \ \ 3 \end{array}$

6. $\begin{array}{r} 239 \\ \times\ \ \ 4 \end{array}$

7. $\begin{array}{r} 43 \\ \times 52 \end{array}$

8. $\begin{array}{r} 45 \\ \times 39 \end{array}$

9. $\begin{array}{r} 571 \\ \times\ \ 82 \end{array}$

10. 82×36
11. 602×18
12. 375×29
13. 413×28

14. **Reasoning** This jigsaw puzzle has 42 pieces across the top and 26 pieces down the side. Use estimation to decide if the label is correct. Explain.

OVER 1,000 PIECES COVERED WAGON JIGSAW PUZZLE

Skills and Reasoning

Estimate Find each product. Estimate to check.

15. 58 ×62	**16.** 47 ×51	**17.** 820 × 45	**18.** 38 ×16	**19.** 191 × 71

20. 712×8 **21.** 102×24 **22.** 177×3 **23.** 908×9 **24.** 445×5

25. 803 × 6	**26.** 911 × 14	**27.** 14 ×92	**28.** 72 ×66	**29.** 825 × 52
30. 544 × 32	**31.** 807 × 29	**32.** 45 ×92	**33.** 395 × 7	**34.** 298 × 27

35. 26×17 **36.** 416×41 **37.** 97×36 **38.** 211×74 **39.** 84×39

40. Find the product of 69 and 21.   **41.** Find the product of 106 and 52.

42. What is the greatest number of times you would regroup when multiplying two 2-digit factors? Give an example.

Problem Solving and Applications

For **43–46** decide if each problem needs an exact answer or an estimate. Then solve each problem.

43. History Each year from 1840 to 1870, about 17,000 settlers traveled the Oregon Trail. About how many settlers traveled the trail in all?

44. History A wagon could travel about 2 mi/hr on flat ground. About how many miles could a wagon train travel in 3 days if it traveled 8 hr a day?

45. Using Data Use data in the *Did You Know?* on page 116. If a wagon train moving at 2 mi/hr traveled 10 hr a day for 95 days, would it cover the distance of the Oregon Trail?

46. Science The tallest living flowering tree is a mountain ash with a height of 325 ft. The tallest tree ever measured, a Douglas fir, stood 415 ft. How much taller was the Douglas fir than the mountain ash?

Mountain ash

Douglas fir

Problem Solving and GEOGRAPHY

For many early settlers, the Oregon Trail was the passage to the West. Follow their long journey from Independence, Missouri, to Oregon City, Oregon.

OREGON TRAIL

City	Distance (mi)		
	Fort Kearney	Fort Bridger	Fort Boise
Independence, Missouri	285	930	1,268
Rock Creek Station	136	781	1,119
South Pass	1,000	131	465
Whitman Mission	1,220	1,042	221
Oregon City, Oregon	1,392	1,214	393

47. If settlers planned to go from South Pass to Fort Boise and travel 8 hr per day at 3 mi/hr for 20 days, would they arrive at the fort? Explain.

48. Would 5 round trips between Rock Creek Station and Fort Kearney be as many miles as 1 trip from Oregon City to Fort Kearney? Explain.

49. History In the spring of 1864, the Donner family gathered 37 wagons and left Independence, Missouri. Unfortunately, in late August, a snowstorm stranded them at Fort Boise. How far were they from Oregon City?

50. What If You want to be a modern-day explorer and blaze a new trail from your home to Oregon City, Oregon. About how long would the trail be?

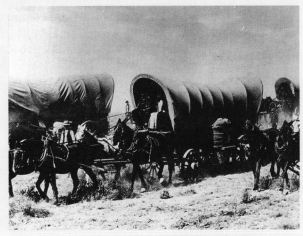

A journey along the Oregon Trail took 6 months.

51. Journal Show and explain the steps used to estimate and find the exact product of 134 and 56.

Mixed Review and Test Prep

Find each product.

52. 20×400 **53.** 60×9 **54.** 30×50 **55.** 620×200 **56.** $9 \times 8 \times 2$

57. 30×200 **58.** 420×60 **59.** 30×70 **60.** 54×200 **61.** $7 \times 6 \times 2$

62. Which number, when rounded to the nearest hundred, equals 600?

   Ⓐ 540   Ⓑ 654   Ⓒ 552   Ⓓ 663   Ⓔ not here

Around the USA Game

Players
two teams, 2–4 players each

Materials
2 number cubes, numbered 1–6

Object
The object of the game is to make multiplication problems whose products are 8,250 or greater.

It is about 8,250 miles around the continental United States from Bangor, Maine, to Seattle, Washington, to San Diego, California, to Key West, Florida, and back to Bangor. Play a game to score 8,250 miles and travel the U.S.A!

How to Play

1. Team leaders roll one number cube. The team with the greater number is Team A and begins play.

2. Team B decides on a number from 20 to 40 and announces it to Team A. Team A rolls both number cubes and uses the two numbers rolled to make a 2-digit number.

3. Team A writes the product of the 2-digit number from the cubes and the number given by Team B. The product is Team A's score, or the number of miles to travel. Record the number of miles your team travels each turn.

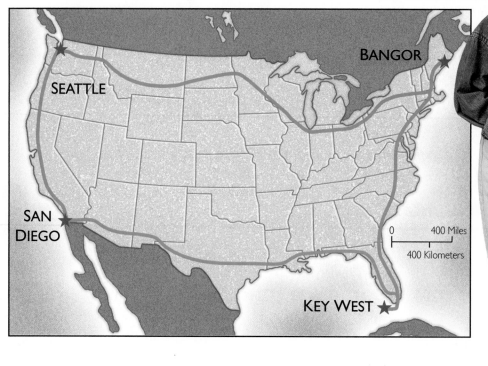

4 Team A announces a number from 20 to 40 and Team B follows the procedure in Step 3.

5 Play continues until at least one team's total score is greater than 8,250, and both teams have taken an equal number of turns.

6 The team that has the score closest to 8,250 wins.

7 If play ends with any team scoring less than 8,250 miles, then that team has to find the approximate location they have reached on the map.

Talk About It

1. How did the number you gave the other team affect the game?

2. How did you decide what number to make from the digits shown on the number cubes?

More Ways to Play

■ Play as before, except that any score ending in 5 or a 0 receives a bonus of 100 points.

■ Use three number cubes to make a 3-digit number. Play to 100,000 miles.

Reasoning

1. Is it always to your team's advantage to select a low number for the other team? Explain.

2. When making your first 2-digit number from your number-cube roll, would you use the greater digit for the tens or ones?

Distributive Property

You Will Learn
how to use the distributive property to multiply mentally

Vocabulary
benchmark numbers
numbers that are simple to work with, such as 10, 50, 100, 500, 1,000, 1,000,000

Learn

Where can you travel straight north and find yourself going south? Robert Peary, Matthew Henson, and four Inuit—Ookeah, Ootah, Egingwah, and Seegloo—did this in 1909. They reached the North Pole.

The distributive property lets you break numbers apart to **benchmarks**. This makes multiplication easier.

Matthew Henson accompanied Robert Peary to the North Pole.

Example 1

If the dog sled teams on one of the Arctic expeditions traveled 19 miles a day for 6 days, how far did they travel?

To find the distance traveled in 6 days, multiply.

6×19

$6 \times 19 = 6 \times (10 + 9)$ ← Break 19 apart.

$= (6 \times 10) + (6 \times 9)$ $19 = 10 + 9$

$= 60 + 54$

$= 114$

$6 \times 19 = 114$

The teams traveled 114 miles in 6 days.

Example 2

You can use addition or subtraction with the distributive property.

5×198 Rewrite 198 as $200 - 2$.

$5 \times 198 = 5 \times (200 - 2)$

$= (5 \times 200) - (5 \times 2)$

$= 1,000 - 10$

$= 990$

$5 \times 198 = 990$

Talk About It

To multiply 72 by 30, which number would you break apart? Explain.

Did You Know?
It took Admiral Robert Peary and Matthew Henson 18 years of repeated expeditions to reach the North Pole.

Check

Use mental math to find each product.

1. 12×97 **2.** 15×99 **3.** 109×9 **4.** 6×511 **5.** 498×3

6. Reasoning Why would you use 100 as a benchmark for 97 and 102? How would you express each?

Practice

Skills and Reasoning

 Mental Math Use mental math to find each product

7. 195×3 **8.** 709×7 **9.** 199×2 **10.** 6×310 **11.** 499×5

12. 203×2 **13.** 408×5 **14.** 7×198 **15.** 908×3 **16.** 7×299

17. 30×98 **18.** 40×101 **19.** 6×98 **20.** 102×13 **21.** 99×69

22. 102×50 **23.** 97×5 **24.** 706×4 **25.** 4×399 **26.** 99×145

27. Find the product of 90 and 15.   **28.** Multiply 399 and 20.

29. Would you use the distributive property to find 5×900? Explain.

Problem Solving and Applications

Use the Data File on page 108 to answer **30** and **31**.

30. History Matthew Henson's journal said that each march lasted 18 to 20 hr. About how many hours of travel did it take to travel from Cape Columbia to the Pole?

31. Critical Thinking The Peary-Henson expedition began in New York on July 6, 1908. How many days did it take them to reach the Pole?

32. Journal Explain how the distributive property works in multiplication.

Mixed Review and Test Prep

 Mental Math Find each answer. Use mental math.

33. $19 + 81 + 27 + 3$ **34.** $400 - 219$ **35.** $2 \times 37 \times 5$ **36.** $56 \div 7$

37. $3,600 \div 60$ **38.** $10 \times 26 \times 10$ **39.** $420 \div 6$ **40.** $14 + 29 + 6$ **41.** $516 - 316$

List the first five non-zero multiples of each number.

42. 2   **43.** 5   **44.** 10   **45.** 6   **46.** 9

47. Money Find the correct change if you bought these two items with a $10 bill.

Ⓐ $6.96   Ⓑ $1.00

Ⓒ $3.00   Ⓓ $3.04

Choosing a Calculation Method

You Will Learn
how to choose a calculation method when multiplying

Materials
calculator

Learn •

Ben and Elizabeth discovered that when Mt. St. Helens erupted, the top of the mountain was gone. In its place was a crater as long as 42 football fields.

Ben and Elizabeth calculated the length of the crater in feet. A football field is 300 ft long. Find 300×42.

Ben's Way

The zeros make it easy, so I'll find the answer using mental math.

$300 \times 40 = 12{,}000$
$300 \times 2 = \underline{+600}$
$12{,}600$

The crater is 12,600 ft long.

Did You Know?
Mt. St. Helens in Washington, erupted on May 18, 1980, after being inactive since 1857.

Elizabeth's Way

These numbers are large. I want the exact answer quickly, so I'll use a calculator.

3 0 0 × 4 2 = [12600]

Talk About It

1. If you had to multiply 2,500 by 20, what method would you use? Explain.

2. Describe how you decide when to use paper and pencil, a calculator, or mental math.

Check

Find each product.

1. 25×32 2. 95×62 3. 200×300 4. 146×827

5. **Reasoning** When is it better to use mental math than a calculator?

Practice

Skills and Reasoning

Choose a tool

Find each product.

6. $\begin{array}{r} 76 \\ \times 95 \\ \hline \end{array}$ 7. $\begin{array}{r} 42 \\ \times 48 \\ \hline \end{array}$ 8. $\begin{array}{r} 29 \\ \times 53 \\ \hline \end{array}$ 9. $\begin{array}{r} 700 \\ \times\ 40 \\ \hline \end{array}$ 10. $\begin{array}{r} 209 \\ \times\ 73 \\ \hline \end{array}$

11. 97×56 12. 400×30 13. 17×40 14. 231×598

15. 280×300 16. 804×125 17. 279×914 18. 196×420

19. Find the product of 652 and 173.   20. Multiply 348 and 63.

21. You and your friend each solve 546 multiplied by 439. Your answer is 539,694. Your friend's is 239,694. Which answer is reasonable? Explain.

22. Estimate 43×267. Is it closer to 8,000 or 12,000? Explain.

Problem Solving and Applications

23. **Using Data** Use the data from *Did You Know?* on page 124. How long had Mt. St. Helens been inactive before the 1980 eruption?

24. **Geography** The highest volcano is Ojos del Salado between Chile and Argentina. It is a little more than 4 mi high. About how many feet high is it?

Math Tip
1 mi = 5,280 ft

25. **Critical Thinking** If Mt. St. Helens erupted 25 times in 20 years, how many times would you expect it to erupt in a century?

Mixed Review and Test Prep

Find the total cost of each order.

26. 2 Fizz Whizzes and 1 Banana Fault Bread

27. 1 Lava Chip Sandwich and 2 Volcanic Shakes

28. 2 Mountain Burgers and 1 Fizz Whizz

29. **Estimation** Choose the best estimate for $8.99 + $13 + $10.03.

Ⓐ $31   Ⓑ $32   Ⓒ 31   Ⓓ 32

Mountain Burger $3.25
Volcanic Fruit Shake $1.50
Fizz Whizz $2.10
Lava Chip Sandwich $1.95
Banana Fault Bread $3.50

Exploring Patterns with Multiples

Problem Solving Connection
Look for a Pattern

Materials
- calendar
- hundred chart
- colored pencils or markers
- calculator

Vocabulary
common multiple
a non-zero number that is a multiple of two or more different numbers

least common multiple (LCM)
the least non-zero number that is a multiple of two or more different numbers

Math Tip
You can use a hundred chart to find least common multiples up to 100.

Explore • • • • • • • • • •

Sarah Ann is busy! She is a soccer player, a flute player, and a tap dancer. She also keeps in touch with her cousins using e-mail on her computer.

Work Together

Sarah Ann e-mails her cousins according to this schedule.

Cousin	Alli, MI	Katie, OH	John, GA
Contact	every 4 days	every 3 days	every 6 days

Sarah Ann is from Waukesha, Wisconsin.

1. Use a calendar to mark off her e-mail dates in October. Start on Oct. 1.
   a. Mark off every 3 days for Katie and every 4 days for Alli.
   b. On which dates will she e-mail both?
2. Now mark off her e-mail to John.
   a. When do all three cousins get e-mail on the same day?
   b. When do just two cousins get e-mail on the same day?
   c. Write all the e-mail dates.
3. Dates with more than one mark show **common multiples**. You can use a hundred chart to find multiples and common multiples.
   a. Find multiples and common multiples for 3, 4, and 6 greater than 30.
   b. Find multiples and common multiples for 3, 5, and 7.

Talk About It

4. Describe patterns you saw as you listed the e-mail dates.
5. If October had 40 days, would all three cousins receive e-mail on the same day again? Do you need a calendar to find that date? Explain.

Connect •

Common multiples can be found by listing the non-zero multiples of each number and then finding those common to each number.

Some multiples of 8 and 12 are:

8, 16, **24,** 32, 40, **48,** …

12, **24,** 36, **48,** 60, 72, …

The **least common multiple (LCM)** of 8 and 12 is 24.

Some multiples of 3 and 9 are:

3, 6, **9,** 12, 15, **18,** …

9, 18, 27 …

The LCM of 3 and 9 is 9.

Practice •

Find the LCM for each pair or set of numbers.

1. 3 and 5	**2.** 8 and 10	**3.** 6 and 9	**4.** 3 and 8	**5.** 4 and 5
6. 7 and 8	**7.** 5 and 7	**8.** 2 and 9	**9.** 10 and 30	**10.** 4 and 6
11. 6 and 8	**12.** 3 and 10	**13.** 7 and 9	**14.** 5 and 8	**15.** 3 and 7
16. 2, 3, and 6	**17.** 4, 5, and 6	**18.** 5, 6, and 10	**19.** 2, 4, and 7	**20.** 2, 3, and 7
21. 2, 6, and 8	**22.** 3, 4, and 12	**23.** 5, 6, and 15	**24.** 2, 3, and 9	**25.** 4, 5, and 8
26. 4, 5, and 10	**27.** 6, 8, and 9	**28.** 2, 3, and 5	**29.** 5, 7, and 10	**30.** 6, 12, and 24

31. Use your calculator to find the LCM for two numbers. Try 36 and 48. Enter ON/AC + 4 8 = = and so on. List the multiples. Do the same for 36. The first multiple that is a multiple for both is the LCM.

32. Make a list of some multiples of 20. Do you need to make a list of multiples of 8 in order to find the LCM of 20 and 8? Explain.

33. Science A spider, an arachnid, has 8 legs. An ant, an insect, has 6 legs. What is the least number of spiders and ants which would give you the same number of legs in each group? How many legs would this be?

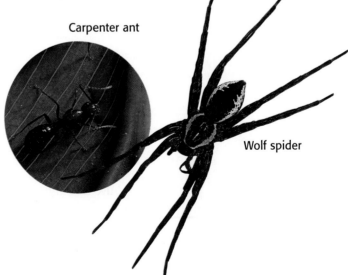

Carpenter ant

Wolf spider

34. Critical Thinking Suppose you want to find the greatest common multiple of 20 and 8. Could you do this? Explain.

35. Journal Explain how you would find the LCM of 4, 6, and 8.

Problem Solving

Decision Making: **Vacation Choices**

You Will Learn
how to use information to make a decision

Explore •

Your family plans to visit Yosemite National Park for one week. You are deciding between camping and staying in a hotel. Which would you choose?

El Capitan, Yosemite National Park, California, 1949, by Ansel Adams

Facts and Data	
Camping	**Hotel**
• There are bears in the area.	• A room costs $75 per night.
• A campsite costs $15 per night.	• If you stay in a hotel, you can only stay 4 nights.
• If you camp, you can stay 7 nights.	• Eating in restaurants for 4 days costs an average of $90 per day.
• Food for a week of camping costs an average of $20 per day.	• The hotel is 10 mi from the park.
• There is little chance of having good weather the whole week.	• The hotel has an indoor pool.

Work Together

▶ **Understand**

1. What are you asked to do?

2. What kind of information do you have to help you?

▶ **Plan and Solve**

3. What is the cost of a campsite for one week?

4. Which is more expensive: a campsite for one week or a hotel for 4 nights? How much more?

5. How much does food for a week of camping cost?

6. Which is more expensive: food for a week of camping or eating out for 4 days? How much more?

7. About how many round trips to and from the park would you make each day if you stayed in the hotel?

8. About how many miles would you drive each day for those trips? For the 4 days?

9. Write a list of reasons why camping might be the better choice.

10. Write a list of reasons why staying in a hotel might be the better choice.

▶ **Make a Decision**

11. What is your decision?

12. How did you make it?

▶ **Present Your Decision**

13. Prepare a presentation to show the class how you made your decision. Use graphs, tables, models, or other visuals to help you.

Technology

Order of Operations

Students held a Nationwide Scavenger Hunt. Their assignment: to bring in 21 postcards from at least 12 different states—or to bring in 15 small souvenirs from at least 8 different states. Students asked friends, relatives, friends' relatives, and relatives' friends— and brought in a tremendous pile of items! But how many items were there in all?

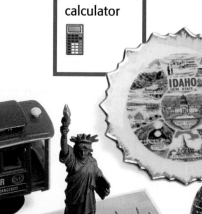

Materials
calculator

Work Together

Use a calculator to find how many items were brought in by the classes.

1. 31 students brought in 6 post cards and 15 souvenirs each.

   $(31 \times 6) + (31 \times 15)$

   When solving problems that require more than one operation, this calculator uses the correct order of operations.

   Enter
   3 1 × 6 +
   3 1 × 1 5 =

   Display
   651

   • It multiplies or divides from left to right.

   • Then it adds or subtracts from left to right.

   The class brought in 651 items.

2 Suppose you wanted to add before you multiply.

	Enter	Display

- If you enter this, you do not get 651. The calculator multiplies before it adds.

$\boxed{6}\boxed{+}\boxed{1}\boxed{5}\boxed{\times}\boxed{3}\boxed{1}\boxed{=}$ → $\boxed{471}$

- To add first, use parentheses. Then multiply to get 651.

$\boxed{(}\boxed{6}\boxed{+}\boxed{1}\boxed{5}\boxed{)}$
$\boxed{\times}\boxed{3}\boxed{1}\boxed{=}$ → $\boxed{651}$

Exercises

Use the calculator and follow the order of operations to answer **1–4**.

1. $14 \times 51 - 10 \times 38$
2. $(3 + 15) \times 4 - 48 \div 6$
3. $7 \times 482 \times 3 + 91$
4. $52 \div 13 + 16 \times (4 - 2)$

Math Tip
- Do what is inside parentheses first.
- Multiply or divide.
- Add or subtract.

Extensions

5. Use the order of operations.

   a. After one week, 14 items had come in from each of 12 states, 8 items had come in from each of 3 states, and 6 states were represented by 1 item each. What was the total number of items collected at this point in the project?

   b. **Reasoning** Write the computations you made for the previous problem using parentheses.

Use parentheses in **6** and **7** to make them true. Show all your work.

6. $12 + 6 \times 7 + 2 = 128$
7. $8 \div 4 + 4 + 12 \div 6 = 3$

Arrange **8** and **9** to make them true. Use parentheses. Show all your work.

8. $75, 2, 9, 3, \times, \div, +, = 43$
9. $7, 5, 4, 2, \times, \times, -, = 18$

131

SECTION A
Review and Practice

Vocabulary Match each with its example.

1. commutative property   **a.** $3 \times (5 + 2) = (3 \times 5) + (3 \times 2)$

2. distributive property   **b.** $4 \times 3 = 3 \times 4$

3. associative property   **c.** 12, 24, 36, 48, ...

4. multiples of 12   **d.** $(2 \times 5) \times 3 = 2 \times (5 \times 3)$

(Lesson 1) Mental Math Find each product. Use mental math and multiplication properties.

5. 3×60 **6.** 50×30 **7.** $20 \times (4 \times 30)$ **8.** $(4 \times 16) \times 25$

(Lesson 2) Estimation Estimate each product.

9. 28×32 **10.** 37×76 **11.** 245×39 **12.** 91×16 **13.** 73×22

14. A can of soup has a mass of 305 g. What is the mass for a case of 48 cans?

(Lessons 3–5) Find each product.

15. $\begin{array}{r} 34 \\ \times\ 23 \\ \hline \end{array}$ **16.** $\begin{array}{r} 15 \\ \times\ 36 \\ \hline \end{array}$ **17.** $\begin{array}{r} 54 \\ \times\ 8 \\ \hline \end{array}$ **18.** $\begin{array}{r} 48 \\ \times\ 69 \\ \hline \end{array}$ **19.** $\begin{array}{r} 62 \\ \times\ 27 \\ \hline \end{array}$

20. $\begin{array}{r} 102 \\ \times\ 27 \\ \hline \end{array}$ **21.** $\begin{array}{r} 115 \\ \times\ 6 \\ \hline \end{array}$ **22.** $\begin{array}{r} 348 \\ \times\ 109 \\ \hline \end{array}$ **23.** $\begin{array}{r} 263 \\ \times\ 324 \\ \hline \end{array}$ **24.** $\begin{array}{r} 143 \\ \times\ 89 \\ \hline \end{array}$

25. 708×6 **26.** 52×14 **27.** 8×399 **28.** 38×22 **29.** 73×51

30. 219×12 **31.** 70×44 **32.** 412×27

33. 386×55 **34.** 109×63 **35.** 39×71

36. 22×471 **37.** 98×13 **38.** 801×34

(Lesson 6) Find the LCM for each set of numbers.

39. 8 and 6   **40.** 22 and 33   **41.** 7 and 9

42. 4, 5, and 7   **43.** 3, 4, and 6   **44.** 2, 9, and 24

45. Journal Explain how the multiplication properties help you multiply.

> ## Skills Checklist
>
> **In this section, you have:**
> - ☑ Explored Multiplication Patterns and Properties
> - ☑ Estimated Products
> - ☑ Multiplied Whole Numbers
> - ☑ Learned About the Distributive Property
> - ☑ Chosen a Calculation Method
> - ☑ Explored Patterns with Multiples
> - ☑ Solved Problems by Making Decisions

B Multiplying with Whole Numbers and Decimals

Running your own business means solving problems every day! Ebony Hood sells pins and scarves. How do you think she uses decimals in her business?

Estimating Decimal Products

Review decimals. Round each number to the place of the underlined digit.

1. 0.59
2. 10.45
3. 9.876
4. 79.991
5. 11.5
6. 3.45
7. 84.62
8. 6.243
9. 39.7

Skills Checklist

In this section, you will:

☐ Explore Decimal Patterns

☐ Estimate Decimal Products

☐ Multiply Whole Numbers and Decimals

☐ Solve Multiple-Step Problems

Exploring Decimal Patterns

Problem Solving Connection

- Look for a Pattern
- Solve a Simpler Problem

Materials

calculator

Explore • • • • • • • • •

You can use multiplication facts and place-value patterns to find the product of a decimal and a power of ten.

$3.751 \times 10 = \blacksquare$

$3.751 \times 100 = \blacksquare$

$3.751 \times 1,000 = \blacksquare$

Work Together

1. Use your calculator.
   Copy and complete each multiplication sentence. Look for patterns.

   a. $2.3 \times 10 = \blacksquare$ **b.** $0.05 \times 10 = \blacksquare$ **c.** $3.751 \times 10 = \blacksquare$

   $2.3 \times 100 = \blacksquare$ $0.05 \times 100 = \blacksquare$ $3.751 \times 100 = \blacksquare$

   $2.3 \times 1,000 = \blacksquare$ $0.05 \times 1,000 = \blacksquare$ $3.751 \times 1,000 = \blacksquare$

Remember

10, 100, and 1,000 are powers of ten.

2. What patterns did you see? Make a rule.

3. Use your rule to complete each multiplication sentence.

   a. $9.6 \times 100 = \blacksquare$ **b.** $4.7 \times 1,000 = \blacksquare$ **c.** $6.3 \times 10 = \blacksquare$

   $2.08 \times 10 = \blacksquare$ $3.28 \times 1,000 = \blacksquare$ $5.06 \times 100 = \blacksquare$

   $327.1 \times 1,000 = \blacksquare$ $251.6 \times 100 = \blacksquare$ $521.9 \times 10 = \blacksquare$

4. Copy each multiplication sentence. Place the decimal point in the product. Write extra zeros if necessary.

   a. $0.24 \times 100 = 2400$ **b.** $3.16 \times 10 = 3160$ **c.** $7.147 \times 100 = 7147$

   $5 \times 1,000 = 5000$ $100 \times 1.6 = 160$ $42.3 \times 1,000 = 423$

Talk About It

5. What rule can you use to mentally find products like those in **1**?

6. Explain why you might need to write extra zeros before placing the decimal in your answer.

Connect •••

Here's a way to use mental math to find the product of a decimal number and a power of ten.

Multiply 62.38 by 10, 100, and 1,000.

$62.38 \times \mathbf{10} = 62.3\,8$
10 has one zero.
Move the decimal point one place to the right.
$62.38 \times \mathbf{10} = 623.8$

$62.38 \times \mathbf{100} = 62.3\,8$
100 has two zeros.
Move the decimal point two places to the right.
$62.38 \times \mathbf{100} = 6,238$

$62.38 \times \mathbf{1,000} = 62.3\,8\,0$
1,000 has three zeros.
Move the decimal point three places to the right. Write an extra zero.
$62.38 \times \mathbf{1,000} = 62,380$

You don't need to show a decimal point at the end of a whole number.

Practice •••

Find each product.

1. 3.8×10
   3.8×100
   $3.8 \times 1,000$

2. 0.09×10
   0.09×100
   $0.09 \times 1,000$

3. 4.367×10
   4.367×100
   $4.367 \times 1,000$

4. 6.02×10
   6.02×100
   $6.02 \times 1,000$

Copy each equation. Place the decimal point in the product. Write extra zeros if necessary.

5. $3.185 \times 10 = 3185$

6. $4.895 \times 100 = 4895$

7. $0.75 \times 1,000 = 75$

8. $675 \times 1,000 = 675$

9. $0.00008 \times 10 = 8$

10. $0.5823 \times 100 = 5823$

 Mental Math Find each product. Use mental math.

11. $1,000 \times 3.42$

12. 100×45.6

13. 8.9×10

14. 10×3.659

15. **Money** New uniforms for the school district's choruses will cost $5,525 including tax. The chorus director plans to collect $35 from each of the 100 chorus members. How much more money will be needed?

16. **Critical Thinking** Multiply 63.81 and 10. What would you have to multiply your answer by so that it has the same product as 63.81×100? The same product as $63.81 \times 1,000$?

17. **Science** Saturn orbits the sun at an average speed of 10 km/sec. The average orbital speed of Earth is 3.1 times as fast as that of Saturn. How fast does Earth orbit the Sun?

Saturn is the second largest planet in our solar system.

18. **Journal** Explain how to multiply 43.95 by 10, 100, and 1,000.

Estimating Decimal Products

You Will Learn

how to use rounding and compatible numbers to estimate products

Vocabulary

compatible numbers
numbers that are easy to work with mentally

Learn

In 1961, President John Fitzgerald Kennedy spoke at a rate of 5.45 words per second in a speech. This was the fastest speaking speed recorded in public life. Seneca read a passage from *Where the Red Fern Grows* to himself. He read 297 words per minute for 3.4 minutes.

You can round numbers or use **compatible numbers** to estimate products.

Seneca is from Saginaw, Michigan.

Example 1

About how many words did President Kennedy speak per minute?

President Kennedy spoke 60×5.45 words per minute.

Think: 5 and 60 are compatible numbers.

$$\begin{array}{ccc} 60 & \longrightarrow & 60 \text{ sec in 1 min} \\ \times\ 5.45 & \longrightarrow & \times\ 5 \text{ words per sec} \\ \hline & & 300 \text{ words per min} \end{array}$$

60×5.45 is about 300.

President Kennedy spoke about 300 words per minute.

Example 2

About how many words did Seneca read in three minutes?

Seneca read 3.4×297 words.

$$\begin{array}{ccc} 297 & \longrightarrow & 300 \text{ words per min} \\ \times\ \ 3.4 & \longrightarrow & \times\ \ 3 \text{ min} \\ \hline & & 900 \text{ words in 3 min} \end{array}$$

297×3.4 is about 900.

Seneca read about 900 words in 3 minutes.

Talk About It

Did You Know?

Few people are able to speak at a rate of 300 words per minute and still be understood.

1. Is 60×5.45 greater or less than 300? Tell how you know.

2. When would you estimate a product?

Check

Estimate each product. Explain what you did.

1. 46.3×57 2. 4.23×8 3. 968×6.47 4. 14×179.2

5. **Reasoning** Compare Seneca's words-per-minute reading speed with President Kennedy's speaking rate. Did the President speak faster than Seneca read? Explain.

Skills and Reasoning

Estimate each product. Explain what you did.

6. 4.2×6 **7.** 8.9×4 **8.** 3.6×7 **9.** 7.1×3

10. 34.6×8 **11.** 45.7×2 **12.** 99.5×6 **13.** 24.6×4

14. 39.2×24 **15.** 98×3.8 **16.** 368.9×26 **17.** 49×2.6

 Mental Math Is each product greater than 150? Write yes or no. Explain.

18. 32.6×5 **19.** 18.89×9 **20.** 25.2×4 **21.** 7×16.99

Mental Math Is each product greater than 1,500? Write yes or no. Explain.

22. 23.5×79 **23.** 149.5×9 **24.** 499.61×2 **25.** 52.75×33

26. Estimate the product of 97.26 and 201.

Problem Solving and Applications

27. Using Data If Seneca continued reading for 9 minutes, about how many words would he likely read?

28. Language Arts The longest entry in the largest English-language dictionary is for the verb *turn*. It contains 5,500 words. About how many minutes would it take Seneca to read this entry?

29. Money One softcover copy of *Sarah, Plain and Tall* costs $3.95. About how much would 5 copies cost?

30. Journal Explain how to round or use compatible numbers to estimate a product. Use an example.

Mixed Review and Test Prep

Find each answer.

31. $\begin{array}{r} 629 \\ \times\ 35 \\ \hline \end{array}$ **32.** $\begin{array}{r} 854 \\ +\ 183 \\ \hline \end{array}$ **33.** $\begin{array}{r} 392 \\ -\ 265 \\ \hline \end{array}$ **34.** $\begin{array}{r} 939 \\ \times\ 13 \\ \hline \end{array}$ **35.** $\begin{array}{r} 317 \\ 84 \\ +\ 192 \\ \hline \end{array}$

36. $540 \div 5$ **37.** 42×29 **38.** $627 \div 3$ **39.** 304×12 **40.** $144 \div 4$

41. Algebra Readiness Which number completes the equation correctly?
$0.17 \times n = 0.17$

Ⓐ 100   Ⓑ 10   Ⓒ 0   Ⓓ 1

Multiplying Whole Numbers and Decimals

You Will Learn
how to multiply a decimal by a whole number

Learn

The Beast, in Cincinnati, Ohio, is the longest roller coaster in the United States. It measures about 1.4 miles.

The Beast is located at Paramount's Kings Island. ® & © 1997 Paramount Parks Inc. All Rights Reserved.

Example

If you rode *The Beast* 20 times, how far would you have traveled?
You can multiply 20 × 1.4 to find the total distance.

Step 1

Multiply as you would with whole numbers.

$$
\begin{array}{r}
1.4 \\
\times\,20 \\
\hline
00 \\
280 \\
\hline
280
\end{array}
$$

Estimate to check.

Round to whole numbers. 20 × 1 = 20

28 is close to 20. The answer is reasonable.

You would travel 28 mi.

Step 2

Count the number of decimal places in both numbers. The total is the number of decimal places in the product.

$$
\begin{array}{r}
1.4 \quad \longleftarrow \quad \text{1 decimal place} \\
\times\,20 \quad \longleftarrow \quad \text{0 decimal places} \\
\hline
28.0 \quad \longleftarrow \quad \text{1 decimal place}
\end{array}
$$

How does multiplying with decimals compare to multiplying with whole numbers?

Did You Know?
The longest roller coaster is in Ripon, England. It is 1.42 mi long.

Check

Find each product.

1. $1.49 × 16   **2.** 44 × 0.11   **3.** 23 × 10.42   **4.** 47.5 × 27   **5.** 31.2 × 36

6. Reasoning How is the product of 2.03 and 5 different from the product of 20.3 and 5 ?

Skills and Reasoning

Find each product.

7. 2.15×8 **8.** 7.05×34 **9.** 6.7×29 **10.** 3.9×42 **11.** 7.35×90

12. $\$14.98 \times 5$ **13.** $\$6.04 \times 28$ **14.** $15 \times \$13.12$ **15.** $29 \times \$3.33$ **16.** $\$18.97 \times 4$

17. 3.14×49 **18.** $\$57.81 \times 7$ **19.** $\$5.95 \times 25$ **20.** 4.1×98 **21.** 6.87×2

Choose the number that is closest to the actual product.

22. $\$4.75 \times 12$ Ⓐ $400   Ⓑ $500   Ⓒ $60

23. $\$7.90 \times 21$ Ⓐ $16   Ⓑ $14   Ⓒ $140

24. 1.003×10 Ⓐ 1   Ⓑ 10   Ⓒ 1000

25. What is the product of 38 and 4.05?   **26.** Multiply $8.03 by 52.

27. Marta says the product of 2 and 3.12 is 62.4. Is she correct? Explain.

Problem Solving and Applications

28. History The *Zippin Pippin* in Memphis, Tennessee, is the oldest operating roller coaster in the United States. In 2015, it will be 100 years old. When was it built?

29. Measurement The world's tallest Ferris wheel is in Yokohama City, Japan, and is 344.5 ft tall. The *Texas Star* in Dallas, Texas, is 212.5 ft tall. How much taller is the one in Yokohama City?

30. Measurement One yard of material is equal to 0.025 bolt. How many yards equal 25 bolts?

The *Texas Star* is the tallest Ferris wheel in the United States.

31. Using Data The *Dragon Khan* in Salou, Spain, has 8 loops! Its track is 0.789 mi long. If you rode this roller coaster 7 times, would you travel a longer or shorter distance than riding *The Beast* 5 times? Use data on page 138.

Mixed Review and Test Prep

Find the LCM of each set of numbers in **32–35.**

32. 5 and 20   **33.** 12 and 18   **34.** 4, 8, and 12   **35.** 3, 5, and 8

36. Find the sum of $2.3 + 2.3 + 2.3 + 2.3 + 2.3 + 2.3 + 2.3 + 2.3 + 2.3$.

37. Which is the standard form for five hundred seven dollars and seven cents?

Ⓐ $507.07   Ⓑ $570.07   Ⓒ $507.70   Ⓓ not here

Problem Solving

Analyze Word Problems:
Multiple-Step Problems

You Will Learn

how to solve
multiple-step
problems

Learn

Some problems require more than one step.
To solve them, write out the steps you
will use.

Ebony Hood sells pins and
scarves. Early in her career
she earned $1,000 in just 4
months. If she sold 80 pins
for $5.00 each, how much did she
earn from selling scarves?

Washington, D.C.

Ebony Hood runs her own business
in Washington, D.C.

Work Together

▶ **Understand**   What question do you need to answer?

                     What information do you have?

▶ **Plan**   How can you find the   Find the amount she earned selling pins.
                     amount she earned   Then subtract that from $1,000.
                     selling scarves?

▶ **Solve**   **Step 1** Find the amount $80 \times \$5.00 = \$400$
                     she earned selling pins:

                     Step 2 Find the amount $\$1,000 - \$400 = \$600$
                     she earned selling scarves:

                                                  Ebony earned $600 selling scarves.

▶ **Look Back**   How can you check your answer?

Talk About It

1. How can you tell from reading a problem that it will take
   more than one step to solve?

2. How do you check a multiple-step problem?

Problem Solving
Understand
Plan
Solve
Look Back

Solve the problem.

1. Shirts in the Seasons Catalog cost $29.95. Sweaters cost $45.50. Shipping is $4.00 per order. Doris ordered 3 shirts and 2 sweaters.

   a. How much will Doris pay for the 3 shirts?

   b. How much will she pay for the 2 sweaters?

   c. How much will it cost Doris to have her order shipped?

   d. How much is her bill?

Problem Solving Practice

Problem Solving Strategies

- Use Objects/Act It Out
- Draw a Picture
- Look for a Pattern
- Guess and Check
- Use Logical Reasoning
- Make an Organized List
- Make a Table
- Solve a Simpler Problem
- Work Backward

Choose a Tool

Solve each problem. Choose any strategy.

2. **Measurement** A clothing manufacturer makes 6 dresses with 18 yd of material. How many yards would be needed to make 10 of the same dresses?

3. **Money** In a store catalog from 1935, a package of 3 shirts cost $8.94. Today 1 shirt similar to those costs $25.50. By how much has the price of 3 shirts increased from 1935 to today?

4. A factory can produce 500 pairs of pants during a 10-hr day. If the factory produces 55 pairs per hour for the first 8 hr, how many are left to produce during the rest of the day?

5. **Science** Clothing can be made from recycled plastic bottles. It takes 7 bottles to make 1 scarf. How many scarves could be made from 56 bottles?

Using Data Use the Data File on page 109 to answer **6** and **7**.

6. **Money** If Kiki, the clown, performs 4 times at her increased price, how much does she make?

7. **Money** Jimmy is selling 3 jars of honey to relatives at his old price and 5 jars of honey to others at his increased price. How much does he make?

8. **Money** If Ariane sells 3 safety pin bracelets at $28.60 each, how much does she get?

This scarf is packaged and sold in the plastic bottle.

Review and Practice

Vocabulary Match each with its example.

1. compatible numbers   **a.** $25 + 175$, 5×20, $360 \div 9$

2. decimal numbers   **b.** 3.2, 6.09, 0.789

(Lesson 8) Find each product.

3. 5.03×10 **4.** 3.45×100 **5.** $1.22 \times 1,000$ **6.** 0.3×100

7. 16.047×100 **8.** $23.6899 \times 1,000$ **9.** 29.0×10 **10.** $0.0086 \times 1,000$

11. Money Nolan has $25 to spend on new clothes. If he buys 10 pair of socks at $1.20 a pair, how much money will he have left to spend?

(Lesson 9) Estimate each product.

12. 40×3.45 **13.** 97×3.3 **14.** 70.3×23 **15.** 86.9×51 **16.** 22.6×21

17. 37×6.71 **18.** 101×56.2 **19.** 2.8×15 **20.** 7.3×21 **21.** 12.4×83

(Lesson 10) Estimation: Use estimation to place the decimal point in each product.

22. $3.16 \times 7 = 2212$ **23.** $6.09 \times 54 = 32886$ **24.** $4.09 \times 68 = 27812$

25. $\$23.78 \times 8 = \$19024$ **26.** $75 \times 3.89 = 29175$ **27.** $5 \times \$19.25 = \$9625$

(Lesson 11) Solve each problem.

28. A 3-lb bag of apples costs $3.57. A 2-lb bag costs $2.58. If you want 6 lb of apples, how should you buy them? Explain.

29. Brenda and Caroline bought a 3.75 lb-bag of dried apricots and a 2.35 lb-bag of almonds. If they divide the 2 bags evenly between themselves, what is the total weight of dried apricots and almonds each girl will have?

30. Money Hazel has two $5 bills to spend on lunch. She buys a sandwich for $2.25, french fries for $0.99, and a soft drink for $0.95. How much money does she have left?

31. Journal Explain how you can decide where to put the decimal in the factor 638 so that $638 \times 100 = 6,380$.

> ## Skills Checklist
>
> **In this section, you have:**
>
> ☑ **Explored Decimal Patterns**
>
> ☑ **Estimated Decimal Products**
>
> ☑ **Multiplied by Whole Numbers and Decimals**
>
> ☑ **Solved Multiple-Step Problems**

Multiplying with Decimals

Harriet Quimby 1911—first female pilot

Bessie Coleman 1921—
first African-American pilot

Women first took to
the skies as pilots in 1911.
How might these pilots
have used multiplication?

Jacqueline Cochran
1953—first female
pilot to break
the sound
barrier

Skills Checklist

In this section, you will:

☐ Explore Decimal
Multiplication

☐ Multiply Decimals By
Decimals

☐ Find High and Low Estimates

☐ Learn About Decimals and
Zeros

☐ Solve Problems by Guessing
and Checking

GET READY!

Multiplying Decimals

Review multiplication. Find each product.

1. 590×9	**2.** $3,804 \times 4$	**3.** 89×56
4. 979×88	**5.** 227×79	**6.** 748×67
7. 301×19	**8.** 835×7	**9.** $3,247 \times 6$
10. 402×21	**11.** $2,045 \times 8$	**12.** 962×78

Exploring Decimal Multiplication

Problem Solving Connection

- Look for a Pattern
- Use Objects/ Act It Out

Materials

- 10 × 10 grid
- red and blue pencils

Explore

You can use decimal squares to show the product of two decimals. A 10 × 10 grid represents one whole.

You can show the product of 0.3 and 0.5 on a 10 × 10 grid.

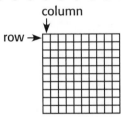

column

row →

Each row is 0.1 of the square.
Each column is 0.1 of the square.

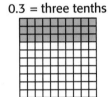

0.5 = five tenths

0.3 = three tenths

0.5 = 0.50 = 50 hundredths   0.3 = 0.30 = 30 hundredths

Work Together

1. Use a 10 × 10 grid to find 0.3 of 0.5.

   a. With your blue pencil, shade 0.5.

   b. With your red pencil, shade 0.3.

   c. How many small squares are shaded both red and blue?

   d. What decimal names the part shaded both red and blue?

2. Use a 10 × 10 grid and colored pencils to solve these:

   a. 0.4 of 0.3   b. 0.2 of 0.6   c. 0.6 of 0.7

   d. 0.3 of 0.6   e. 0.5 of 0.2   f. 0.8 of 0.2

Talk About It

3. How many hundredth squares represent 0.3? 0.5? Explain.

4. What pattern do you see between the total number of decimal places in the factors and the total number of decimal places in the product?

Connect

A 10 × 10 grid can show 0.6 of 0.7.

0.6, six tenths, or 60 hundredths, are shown in red.

0.7, seven tenths, or 70 hundredths, are shown in blue.

There are 42 squares shaded twice. The overlap of red and blue, or purple, shows that 0.6 of 0.7 is 42 hundredths, or 0.42.

Practice

Find each product. You can use 10 × 10 grids to help.

1. 0.5 of 0.2   **2.** 0.8 of 0.3   **3.** 0.9 of 0.5   **4.** 0.4 of 0.7   **5.** 0.4 of 0.4

6. 0.8 of 0.6   **7.** 0.4 of 0.9   **8.** 0.3 of 0.9   **9.** 0.8 of 0.7   **10.** 0.8 of 0.8

11. 0.3 of 0.6   **12.** 0.5 of 0.5   **13.** 0.4 of 0.2   **14.** 0.6 of 0.2   **15.** 0.7 of 0.9

Write a number sentence that describes the shaded areas of each grid.

16.   **17.**   **18.**   **19.**

20. Find the product of 0.9 and 0.9.   **21.** Multiply 0.7 by 0.9.

 22. Algebra Readiness The product is 0.72. One of the factors is 0.9. What is the other factor?

23. Write two numbers whose product is 0.63.

24. Write two numbers whose product is 0.21.

25. Write two numbers whose product is 0.16.

26. Write two numbers whose product is 0.36.

27. Measurement A can of cat food weighs 0.4 lb. Kathy's cat gets 0.5 can of food for breakfast. How much does the cat's breakfast weigh?

28. Two students decide to race. The distance is 0.2 km. When Juan crosses the finish line, Marco has run only 0.9 of the race. How far has Marco run?

 29. Journal Explain how to use a 10 × 10 grid to show the product of 0.7 and 0.5.

Multiplying Decimals by Decimals

You Will Learn

how to multiply decimals by decimals

Did You Know?

The largest sausage had a length of 13.125 mi. It was made in Great Britain in 1988.

Learn • • • • • • • • • •

Maria is helping to plan a class picnic. She has lots of ideas about the food, but one thing is certain—there will be hot dogs! The all-American hot dog has its roots in Germany. The frankfurter from Frankfurt, Germany, is the world's most popular sausage.

Maria lives in Miami, Florida.

Example 1

A hot dog weighs about 1.6 oz and costs about $0.12 per oz. What is the cost of one hot dog?

Step 1	Step 2
Multiply 1.6 by 0.12. Multiply as with whole numbers.	The number of decimal places in the product equals the sum of the decimal places in the factors.

Step 1:

$$
\begin{array}{r}
1.6 \\
\times\, 0.12 \\
\hline
32 \\
160 \\
\hline
192
\end{array}
$$

Step 2:

$$
\begin{array}{r}
1.6 \longleftarrow \text{1 decimal place} \\
\times\, 0.12 \longleftarrow \text{2 decimal places} \\
\hline
32 \\
160 \\
\hline
0.192 \longleftarrow \text{3 decimal places}
\end{array}
$$

Rounded to the nearest cent, the cost of one hot dog is $0.19.

You can use the price per ounce to find the price of a box of granola.

Example 2

Granola costs $0.29 per oz. If it is put in 1.25-oz boxes, what is the cost for each box?

$$
\begin{array}{r}
1.25 \longleftarrow \text{2 decimal places} \\
\times\, 0.29 \longleftarrow \text{2 decimal places} \\
\hline
1125 \\
2500 \\
\hline
0.3625 \longleftarrow \text{4 decimal places}
\end{array}
$$

Estimate to check.

$$
\begin{array}{r}
1.25 \longrightarrow 1 \\
\times\, 0.29 \longrightarrow \times\, 0.30 \\
\hline
\$0.30
\end{array}
$$

Rounded to the nearest cent, the cost of one box of granola is $0.36.

Example 3

You can use estimation to check your placement of the decimal point in the product.

Multiply 4.25 by 2.7.

$$
\begin{array}{r}
4.25 \longleftarrow \text{2 decimal places} \\
\times\ 2.7 \longleftarrow \text{1 decimal place} \\
\hline
2975 \\
8500 \\
\hline
11.475 \longleftarrow \text{3 decimal places}
\end{array}
$$

$4.25 \times 2.7 = 11.475$

Estimate to check.

$$
\begin{array}{r}
4.25 \longrightarrow 4 \\
\times\ 2.7 \longrightarrow \times\ 3 \\
\hline
12
\end{array}
$$

11.475 is close to 12. The answer is reasonable.

Talk About It

1. Give a rule for placing the decimal point in the product.

2. How can you be sure that the decimal point is in the correct place?

3. In Example 1, why was a 0 placed before the decimal?

4. Why is a money product rounded to the nearest hundredth?

Check

Copy each product. Write the decimal point in the correct place.

1.	2.	3.	4.	5.
34.5	12.6	5.07	1.542	15
× 2.5	× 0.4	× 0.3	× 0.6	× 0.08
8625	504	1521	9252	120

6.	7.	8.	9.	10.
28.9	12.69	46.02	9.25	8.19
× 3.6	× 0.08	× 1.2	× 4.7	× 0.20
10404	10152	55224	43475	1638

Find each product. Round to the nearest cent when necessary.

11.	12.	13.	14.	15.
0.4	2.3	$4.25	$3.75	2.054
× 0.8	× 0.7	× 2.7	× 0.29	× 1.36

16.	17.	18.	19.	20.
$6.40	8.021	9.4	$1.50	4.032
× 3.6	× 16	× 0.6	× 0.9	× 6

21. Find the product of 3.9 and 8.12.

22. Find the product of $4.50 and 35.

23. What is $6.35 × 12?

24. What is 3.26 × 2.7?

25. **Reasoning** Which product will have five decimal places?

Ⓐ 1.54 × 6.321   Ⓑ 0.11 × 03.21   Ⓒ 1832.1 × 1.39   Ⓓ 345.8 × 23.1

Skills and Reasoning

Find each product. Round to the nearest cent when necessary.

26. 2.46 × 0.5	**27.** $1.70 × 24	**28.** 1.35 × 7.5	**29.** 2.113 × 3.18	**30.** 6.08 × 3.4
31. 24.3 × 0.94	**32.** 0.65 × 9.1	**33.** $2.30 × 1.23	**34.** $1.58 × 1.4	**35.** 6.37 × 3.9
36. 0.019 × 44.7	**37.** 250 × 0.031	**38.** $16.37 × 0.02	**39.** 2.5 × 2.5	**40.** $10.50 × 7
41. 0.91 × 0.3	**42.** $1.25 × 0.50	**43.** 0.43 × 1.2	**44.** 12.1 × 6.22	**45.** $0.25 × 3.1

46. Find the product of 39.2 and 0.11.

47. Multiply 24.8 by 0.22.

48. Find the product of $8.35 and 20.5. Round to the nearest cent.

49. The product of $3,009 × 60,005$ is 180,555,045. What is the product of $3.009 × 6.0005$?

50. Without doing the multiplication, write how many decimal places are in the product of $3.97 × 4.5$.

Problem Solving and Applications

51. **History** In 1971, a first-class postage stamp pictured Albert Einstein. In 1996, a first-class postage stamp pictured the condor. How much less did the stamp cost in 1971 than in 1996?

52. **Critical Thinking** Is it possible to write the product of $3.5 × 1.2$ with only one number to the right of the decimal point? Explain your answer.

53. **Using Data** Use the data from *Did You Know?* on page 146. An ordinary hot dog is about 0.5 ft. How much longer was the world's largest sausage? (Hint: 1 mi = 5,280 ft)

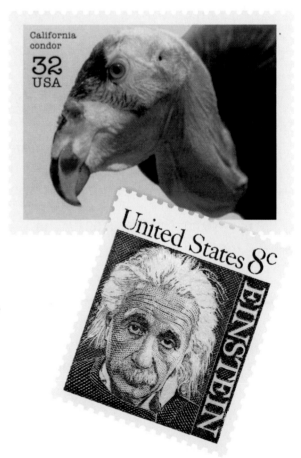

Problem Solving and SCIENCE

The table shows the greatest recorded life spans for selected animals.

Using Data Copy and complete the table using the information given.

The greatest life span for a lake sturgeon is 1.26 times that of a human being.

The greatest life span for a gorilla is 1.51 times that of the oldest bat.

The greatest life span for a chimpanzee times 0.78 equals the greatest life span for a horse.

Record Life Spans	
Animal	**Greatest Recorded Life Span**
Lake Sturgeon	
Human	120.58 yr
Chimpanzee	59.33 yr
Gorilla	
Horse	
Bat	31.42 yr
Slug	1.5 yr

54. — Lake Sturgeon
55. — Gorilla
56. — Horse

Red slug

57. Journal Explain how to multiply 3.8×0.72.

Mixed Review and Test Prep

Copy and complete. Write $<$, $>$, or $=$.

58. $3.08 \bullet 3.80$ **59.** $0.90 \bullet 0.9$ **60.** $0.92 \bullet 0.092$ **61.** $1.09 \bullet 0.109$

62. $1.20 \bullet 1.2$ **63.** $0.203 \bullet 0.230$ **64.** $0.35 \bullet 0.035$ **65.** $0.602 \bullet 0.60$

Find each sum or difference.

66.
$$\begin{array}{r} 93.6 \\ 86.07 \\ + \; 23.9 \\ \hline \end{array}$$

67.
$$\begin{array}{r} 12.9 \\ - \; 5.7 \\ \hline \end{array}$$

68.
$$\begin{array}{r} 0.7 \\ 9.3 \\ + \; 0.07 \\ \hline \end{array}$$

69.
$$\begin{array}{r} 1.06 \\ - \; 0.9 \\ \hline \end{array}$$

70.
$$\begin{array}{r} 8.6 \\ + \; 7.35 \\ \hline \end{array}$$

71. $12.09 + 38.1$ **72.** $48.63 - 10.02$ **73.** $6.7 + 28.9$ **74.** $18.2 - 9.3$ **75.** $90.3 + 45.8$

76. Which number has an 8 in the hundredths place?

   Ⓐ 82.81   Ⓑ 35.28   Ⓒ 835.51   Ⓓ 23.098   Ⓔ 15.638

77. Which number is between 122 and 168?

   Ⓐ 131   Ⓑ 65   Ⓒ 105   Ⓓ 115   Ⓔ 169

STOP and Practice

Find each product.

1.	38 × 43	**2.**	45 × 81	**3.**	92 × 76	**4.**	87 × 95	**5.**	63 × 24
6.	181 × 212	**7.**	471 × 9	**8.**	119 × 305	**9.**	737 × 555	**10.**	211 × 28
11.	6.89 × 1,000	**12.**	73.1 × 100	**13.**	0.009 × 10	**14.**	3.06 × 1,000	**15.**	12.9 × 10
16.	2.6 × 4.4	**17.**	4.2 × 0.6	**18.**	5.3 × 4.5	**19.**	4.09 × 0.19	**20.**	6.24 × 3.04
21.	47 × 0.7	**22.**	2.85 × 0.41	**23.**	4.275 × 0.06	**24.**	3.192 × 0.8	**25.**	5.64 × 19
26.	6.4 × 9	**27.**	0.47 × 1.8	**28.**	6.30 × 80	**29.**	4,352 × 0.07	**30.**	2,605 × 0.2

31. 0.4×0.8 **32.** 0.5×0.7 **33.** 0.1×11 **34.** 0.3×1 **35.** 1.2×0.4

36. 18.1×0.9 **37.** 6.88×5 **38.** 32.24×3 **39.** 3.4×0.7 **40.** 0.52×0.6

41. 3.5×10 **42.** 0.7×100 **43.** $1.23 \times 1,000$ **44.** 1.23×50 **45.** 500×0.7

46. 4.17×3.9 **47.** $\$3.95 \times 1,000$ **48.** 3.785×0.6 **49.** 147×39 **50.** 0.08×0.009

Error Search

Find each product that is not correct. Write it correctly and explain the error.

51.	4.51 × 6.73 ——— 30.0503	**52.**	399 × 26 ——— 10,275	**53.**	3.002 × 8.5 ——— 2.5517	**54.**	0.6 × 0.6 ——— 0.36	**55.**	42.6 × 0.09 ——— 42.69
56.	3.69 × 1.99 ——— 7.3431	**57.**	4.21 × 16 ——— 6,736	**58.**	6.002 × 2.5 ——— 150.05	**59.**	512 × 2.3 ——— 1,177.6	**60.**	8.01 × 6 ——— 48.06

Train Riding Patterns

61. Six good friends often ride the same train. They are all on it today. If they follow this train riding pattern in how many days will they all be on the same train again?

"I ride the train every other day." — Beth

"I ride the train everyday." — Al

"I ride the train every 6 days." — Fred

"I ride the train every 3 days." — Cindy

"I ride the train every 5 days." — Edith

"I ride the train every 4 days" — Dan

Number Sense Estimation and Reasoning

Copy and complete. Write > or <.

62. $24.3 \times 7.8 \bigcirc 2.43 \times 0.78$

63. $1.2 \times 3.6 \bigcirc 0.12 \times 0.36$

64. $700 \times 6.8 \bigcirc 700 \times 68$

65. $2.5 \times 4.0 \bigcirc 250 \times 0.4$

66. $34 \times 11.213 \bigcirc 340 \times 0.11213$

67. $1,000 \times 4.57 \bigcirc 1,000 \times 4.5678$

68. $5,000 \times 2.8 \bigcirc 50 \times 0.28$

69. $2 \times 2.69 \bigcirc 20 \times 0.0269$

70. $3.7 \times 650 \bigcirc 0.37 \times 65,000$

71. $304 \times 6 \bigcirc 3.04 \times 60$

Finding High and Low Estimates

50 USA

Jacqueline
Cochran
Pioneer Pilot

You Will Learn

how to give high and low estimates for a product

Learn

In 1938, Jacqueline Cochran won the Bendix trophy in an air race from Los Angeles, California, to Cleveland, Ohio. She flew for 8.17 hr at 251.3 mi/hr. Estimate the distance she flew.

In 1996, the U.S. Postal Service issued a stamp in Jacqueline Cochran's honor.

Did You Know?

The first licensed woman pilot was Harriet Quimby in 1911. Bessie Coleman became the first African-American international pilot in 1921.

Example 1

Estimate the product of 251.3 and 8.17.

Low Estimate	High Estimate
251.3 ⟶ 200	251.3 ⟶ 300
× 8.17 ⟶ × 8	× 8.17 ⟶ × 9
1,600	2,700

The range for the answer is 1,600 to 2,700.

Harriet
Quimby
Pioneer
Pilot
USAirmail
50

Talk About It

Describe the methods used to get the high and low estimated products.

Check

Between which two numbers will each product be found?

1. 6.25×3.4 Ⓐ 18 and 19   Ⓑ 12 and 18   Ⓒ 18 and 28

2. 8.92×5.2 Ⓐ 40 and 54   Ⓑ 40 and 45   Ⓒ 54 and 63

3. 2.1×9.78 Ⓐ 16 and 20   Ⓑ 18 and 30   Ⓒ 22 and 30

4. 7.91×2.8 Ⓐ 16 and 20   Ⓑ 14 and 24   Ⓒ 24 and 28

5. **Reasoning** Will the product of 3.6×1.9 be closer to 4 or 8?

BLACK HERITAGE

USA
32
BESSIE COLEMAN

Practice

Skills and Reasoning

Between which two numbers will each product be found?

6. 7.6×8.875 Ⓐ 7 and 9   Ⓑ 56 and 72   Ⓒ 76 and 88

7. 9.3×1.63 Ⓐ 1 and 9   Ⓑ 9 and 13   Ⓒ 9 and 20

8. 5.4×0.78 Ⓐ 0 and 6   Ⓑ 5 and 35   Ⓒ 35 and 40

Estimate low and high. Then find each product.

9. 4.5×6 **10.** 43.1×5 **11.** 3.9×8 **12.** 6.7×3

13. 1.99×8 **14.** 2×6.2 **15.** 86.1×4 **16.** 20.6×5.0

17. $\begin{array}{r} 7.6 \\ \times\ 7.3 \\ \hline \end{array}$ **18.** $\begin{array}{r} 4.5 \\ \times\ 5.1 \\ \hline \end{array}$ **19.** $\begin{array}{r} 6.8 \\ \times\ 2.9 \\ \hline \end{array}$ **20.** $\begin{array}{r} 9.7 \\ \times\ 4.7 \\ \hline \end{array}$

21. Estimate low and high. Then find the product of 98.6 and 3.9.

22. What two decimal factors when multiplied result in a product between 30 and 42?

23. How can you use estimation to know that the product of 5.9 and 2.68 is less than 18 without multiplying?

Problem Solving and Applications

24. Science In 1953, Jacqueline Cochran became the first woman to fly faster than the speed of sound. Sound travels at 0.21 mi/sec. About how many miles per hour did she need to fly to break the sound barrier? (Hint: There are 3,600 sec in 1 hr.)

25. Time Your weekly transportation costs are $7.50. What is your annual cost? (Hint: There are 52 weeks in a year.)

 26. Journal Explain how to determine if the product of 6.1 and 8.9 is at least 48.

Mixed Review and Test Prep

 Mental Math Find each product mentally.

27. $3 \times 5 \times 8$ **28.** $2 \times 7 \times 5 \times 3$

29. 37×100 **30.** $2 \times 11 \times 10$

31. Money How much change would you get from $20 if this were your receipt?

   Ⓐ $10.85   Ⓑ $11.85

   Ⓒ $29.15   Ⓓ not here

BUY-RITE
$ 3.99
4.27
0.89

Decimals and Zeros

You Will Learn

how to insert zeros in products with decimals when necessary

Materials

- 10 × 10 grid
- red and blue pencils

Learn • • • • • • • • •

The first all-electronic computer, called ENIAC, was designed in 1945. This computer filled a large room. Today, a computer has parts like a chip that may be less than an inch wide and other parts smaller than the period at the end of this sentence. Now you can carry a computer in a backpack.

Example 1

A computer contains a chip that is 0.4 in. wide. It also contains a part that is 0.2 as wide as the chip. How wide is this part?

Multiply 0.4 by 0.2.

Use a 10 × 10 grid to show the product.

Shade 4 columns red.

Shade 2 rows blue.

The part is 0.08 in. wide.

8 out of 100 squares, 8 hundredths, are shaded twice. So, 0.4 × 0.2 = 8 hundredths or 0.08.

Math Tip

Write zero to the left of the product before placing the decimal point.

Sometimes you have to write zeros after the decimal point to get the right answers.

Example 2

4.9 × 0.002 = ■

Step 1	Step 2
Multiply as you would with whole numbers.	Write zeros to the left of the product to show the correct number of decimal places. Place the decimal point.

Step 1:
$$\begin{array}{r} 4.9 \\ \times\,0.002 \\ \hline 98 \end{array}$$

Step 2:
```
     4.9   ←—— 1 decimal place
 × 0.002   ←—— 3 decimal places
  0.0098   ←—— 4 decimal places
```

Talk About It

Multiply 2.3 and 0.002. Is the product greater or less than 2.3? Is this true whenever you multiply by a number less than 1?

Check

Find each product. Write zeros where needed.

1. 0.6×0.2 **2.** 2.7×0.006 **3.** 4.3×0.009 **4.** 0.06×0.06

5. Reasoning Is the product of 0.03×0.03 the same as the product of 0.3×0.003? Explain.

Practice

Skills and Reasoning

Find each product. Write zeros where needed.

6. 0.03×6 **7.** 0.08×3 **8.** 0.07×0.02 **9.** 0.04×0.003 **10.** 1.4×0.002

11. $\begin{array}{r} 0.007 \\ \times\ 0.003 \\ \hline \end{array}$ **12.** $\begin{array}{r} 0.09 \\ \times\ 0.005 \\ \hline \end{array}$ **13.** $\begin{array}{r} 7.3 \\ \times\ 0.003 \\ \hline \end{array}$ **14.** $\begin{array}{r} 1.2 \\ \times\ 0.08 \\ \hline \end{array}$ **15.** $\begin{array}{r} 23.7 \\ \times\ 0.003 \\ \hline \end{array}$

16. Find the product of 1.20 and 0.31.

17. Is the product of 0.03 and 3.4 greater or less than 3.4? Explain.

18. What multiplication problem is shown in this grid?

Problem Solving and Applications

Using Data Use the Data File on page 109 to answer **19–21.**

19. Social Studies About how many computers are there for every person in the United States?

20. Which country or region has about 1 phone for every 2 people?

21. In the United States, about how many people are there per computer? Use multiplication of compatible numbers to explain.

22. Math History The Greek mathematician Diophantus (3rd century A.D.) used the symbol ↗ to mean subtraction. What is 345.09 ↗ 28.6?

Mixed Review and Test Prep

Estimation Name the low and high estimate for each product.

23. 71.6×5.4 **24.** 6.22×81.3 **25.** 6.7×2.9 **26.** 7.3×2.1

27. Logic Marita is older than Carlos and younger than Beth. Joel is second to the youngest. Which shows the order of their ages from oldest to youngest?

Ⓐ Marita, Carlos, Beth, Joel   Ⓑ Beth, Marita, Carlos, Joel

Ⓒ Beth, Marita, Joel, Carlos   Ⓓ not here

Problem Solving

Analyze Strategies: **Guess and Check**

You Will Learn

how to solve problems using the Guess and Check strategy

Learn

A mountain bike rider pumped the brakes twice to stop at a stop sign 34 ft away. After each pump, the bike traveled the same distance. The bike stopped 12 ft beyond the stop sign. How far did the bike travel after each pump of the brakes?

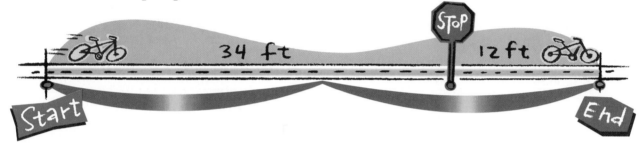

Work Together

▶ **Understand**   What do you know?

What do you need to find out?

▶ **Plan**   How will you find out?   Use the Guess and Check strategy.

▶ **Solve**   Write a number
sentence.

2 brake pumps ⟶ 34 ft to the stop sign

$n + n = 34 + 12$ ⟵ 12 ft past the stop sign

$n + n = 46$

Guess	Check
25	$n + n\ = 46$ $25 + 25 = 50$ Too great!
23	$23 + 23 = 46$ Correct guess!

Reading Tip
Pictures can help you understand a problem.

Make a guess, then check.

Make a second guess. Check the guess.

Write the answer.

The bike traveled 23 ft after each pump.

▶ **Look Back**   Is your answer reasonable? Explain.

When can you use the Guess and Check strategy?

Use the Guess and Check strategy to solve each problem.

Two bike riders compared the weights of their mountain bikes. Together the two bikes weigh 66 lb. The blue bike was 8 lb heavier than the red.

1. What is a reasonable first guess for the weight of the blue bike?

2. The two bikes together weigh 66 lb. Is it possible for the blue bike to weigh 40 lb and the red bike to weigh 26 lb? Explain.

3. How much did each bike weigh?

Problem Solving
Practice •

Problem Solving Strategies

- Use Objects/Act It Out
- Draw a Picture
- Look for a Pattern
- Guess and Check
- Use Logical Reasoning
- Make an Organized List
- Make a Table
- Solve a Simpler Problem
- Work Backward

Choose a Tool

Use Guess and Check or any strategy to help solve each problem.

4. In a 72-mi bike relay, each rider will ride either 8 mi or 4 mi. The same number of riders will ride each distance. How many riders will ride each distance?

5. **Money** Locks cost $18 and reflectors cost $3. The club members spent $120 on a total of 15 items. How many of each item did they buy?

6. **Time** Sara had $225 saved for a mountain bike. She knew she could earn $10 each week from after-school jobs. How many weeks will she have to save to buy a $275 bike?

7. **History** Many early bicycles were designed in the 1800s. The pedal-powered bike was developed 4 years before the High Wheeler. The *draisine* was the first kind of bike to be designed. The safety bicycle was introduced 27 years after the pedal-powered bike. List the bicycles from oldest to newest designs.

8. **Algebra Readiness** The difference between the prices of 2 bikes is $18. The sum of their prices is $258. How much does the less expensive bike cost?

Ⓐ $138   Ⓑ $120   Ⓒ $258   Ⓓ not here

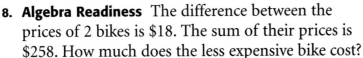

SECTION C
Review and Practice

(Lesson 12) Copy each multiplication sentence. Place a decimal point in each product.

1. $0.7 \times 0.5 = 035$ **2.** $0.3 \times 0.8 = 024$ **3.** $0.12 \times 12 = 144$

4. A file drawer is 0.3 m tall. How tall is a file cabinet with 3 drawers?

(Lesson 13) Find each product. Round to the nearest cent when necessary.

5.	**6.**	**7.**	**8.**	**9.**
16.8	$2.35	0.93	3.017	5.8
$\times\ \ 3.9$	$\times\ \ \ 6.7$	$\times 0.46$	$\times\ \ 2.65$	$\times\ 63$

10. Which costs more: 35 baseball cards at $0.45 each or a box of baseball cards that costs $7.50?

(Lesson 14) Between which two numbers will each product be found?

11. 7.8×5.66 Ⓐ 8 and 6   Ⓑ 35 and 48   Ⓒ 40 and 42

12. 1.99×6.43 Ⓐ 6 and 14   Ⓑ 1 and 6   Ⓒ 2 and 7

13. 10.6×8.9 Ⓐ 10 and 8   Ⓑ 11 and 9   Ⓒ 80 and 99

14. How can you tell if 5.8×9.36 is greater than 43 without finding the actual product?

(Lesson 15) Find each product. Insert zeros where necessary.

15.	**16.**	**17.**	**18.**	**19.**
4.06	0.012	0.53	0.0042	0.0306
$\times 0.009$	$\times\ \ 0.07$	$\times 0.053$	$\times 0.0103$	$\times\ \ 0.002$

(Lesson 16) Solve each problem.

20. Erin ran 18 mi this week. She ran twice as many miles in her neighborhood as on the track at school. How many miles did she run in her neighborhood?

21. Money Marco spent $48 on books and stationery. If he spent 3 times as much on books as on stationery, how much did he spend on stationery?

22. Journal Explain how to determine if the product of 3.2×4.6 is greater than or less than the product of 4.2×3.6.

Skills Checklist

In this section, you have:

☑ Explored Decimal Multiplication

☑ Multiplied Decimals by Decimals

☑ Found High and Low Estimates

☑ Learned About Decimals and Zeros

☑ Solved Problems by Guessing and Checking

YOUR CHOICE

Choose at least one. Use what you have learned in this chapter.

1 Pyramid Patterns

What pattern
do you see
in each?

$11 \times 11 = 121$
$111 \times 111 = 12321$
$1111 \times 1111 = 1234321$
$11111 \times 11111 = 123454321$
$111111 \times 111111 = 12345654321$
$1111111 \times 1111111 = 1234567654321$
$11111111 \times 11111111 = 123456787654321$
$111111111 \times 111111111 = 12345678987654321$

$1 \times 9 + 2 = 11$
$12 \times 9 + 3 = 111$
$123 \times 9 + 4 = 1111$
$1234 \times 9 + 5 = 11111$
$12345 \times 9 + 6 = 111111$
$123456 \times 9 + 7 = 1111111$
$1234567 \times 9 + 8 = 11111111$

2 Rapid Readers

At Home Find a short
poem or excerpt from
a story you like. Ask
at least five friends
or family members
to read it aloud to
you while you time
them. How many words
does each person read per minute?
Record this information in a chart and
share it with people who read for you.

Multiply by the ones,
regroup if you must.
Multiply by the tens,
regroup if you must.
Add the partial products
and you are done.

3 Buying Big

Choose a topic to access on **www.mathsurf.com/5/ch3**
that will give you information about the costs
of different items or services. Then figure
out how much it would cost to
buy these goods or
services in
quantities of
10, 100, and
1,000.

4 Product Poetry

Write a short poem to help you
remember how to multiply by two-digit
numbers, whole numbers and decimals,
or decimals by decimals. Exchange
poems with other members of your class.

REVIEW AND PRACTICE

Chapter 3 • Your Choice **159**

CHAPTER 3
Review/Test

Vocabulary Match each with its example.

1. compatible numbers   **a.** $2 \times (4 + 5) = (2 \times 4) + (2 \times 5)$

2. multiples of 11   **b.** $2 \times 6 = 6 \times 2$

3. commutative property   **c.** $11, 22, 33, 44, \ldots$

4. distributive property   **d.** $25 \times 4, 22 \div 11, 999 + 1$

5. associative property   **e.** $(22 \times 11) \times 6 = 22 \times (11 \times 6)$

(Lessons 1–5) Find each product.

6. 5×300 7. $30 \times (2 \times 40)$ 8. $(5 \times 36) \times 20$ 9. 701×9

10.
$$\begin{array}{r} 278 \\ \times\ \ 82 \\ \hline \end{array}$$

11.
$$\begin{array}{r} 104 \\ \times\ \ 67 \\ \hline \end{array}$$

12.
$$\begin{array}{r} 77 \\ \times 38 \\ \hline \end{array}$$

13.
$$\begin{array}{r} 243 \\ \times 901 \\ \hline \end{array}$$

(Lesson 6) Find the LCM for each set of numbers.

14. 3 and 5   15. 9 and 15   16. 2, 4, and 12

(Lessons 8–10 and 12–15) Find each product. Round to the nearest cent when necessary.

17. 6.38×10 18. $0.1536 \times 1,000$ 19. 0.003×0.004

20.
$$\begin{array}{r} 5.7 \\ \times 3.8 \\ \hline \end{array}$$

21.
$$\begin{array}{r} \$4.56 \\ \times\ \ 2.13 \\ \hline \end{array}$$

22.
$$\begin{array}{r} 0.009 \\ \times\ \ \ \ 8.4 \\ \hline \end{array}$$

23. **Money** If you bought 19 CDs that cost $15.99 each, how much would you pay?

(Lessons 11 and 16) Solve each problem.

24. **Money** The art club for grades 3, 4, and 5 raised $55.65 for a school trip. The third graders raised $12.05; the fourth graders raised two times that amount. The rest was raised by the fifth graders. How much did the fourth graders raise? How much did the fifth graders raise?

25. At one meet, Peter swam in 7 events. He swam in 3 more relays than single races. How many single races did he swim? How many relay races did he swim?

Performance Assessment

The following table shows some nutritional values for several common foods. You need about 45.5 g of protein and 18 mg of iron daily. What are some combinations of these foods that would allow you to meet your needs?

Food	Portion	Protein (g)	Iron (mg)
Apple	1 large	2.4	0.6
Banana	1 large	2.4	1.2
Beef	1 serving	24.7	3.1
Carrot	1 cup	1.2	0.8
Cheese	1 slice	7.1	0.3
Egg	1 medium	6.1	1.3
Milk	1 glass	6.4	0.2
Oatmeal	1 cup	5.4	1.7
Orange	1 medium	1.4	0.6
Tomato	1 large	2.0	1.2
Rice	1 cup	4.2	0.5
Pork	2 slices	19.2	2.0

1. **Decision Making** Choose three foods you like. See how much protein and iron 2.5 portions of these foods would supply.

2. **Recording** Use the foods in the table above to plan breakfast, lunch, and dinner for 1 day. Record the amount of protein and iron in your menu.

3. **Explain Your Thinking** Review your menu. Decide on a way to reach the totals of 45.5 g of protein and 18 mg of iron using decimal numbers of portions of foods you planned. Explain why you decided on your choices and how they supply the right amount of protein and iron.

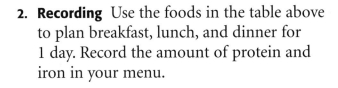

Math Magazine

It's All in Your Mind Thomas Fuller was born in Africa in 1710 and was brought to the United States as a slave when he was about 14 years old. Thomas Fuller had a gift. He could perform difficult mathematical calculations in his head.

70 years, 17 days, 12 hours = 2,210,500,800 seconds

Fuller once demonstrated his unique ability to several members of a British society. He was asked, "If a man has lived for 70 years, 17 days, and 12 hours, how many seconds has he lived?" In less than 2 minutes Fuller calculated that the man had lived for 2,210,500,800 seconds. One member of the society thought he was wrong, until Fuller explained that he had calculated in all the leap years the man had lived.

He was famous throughout the colonies for his gift. This remarkable human calculator died in Boston at the age of 80 years.

We may not be as quick in mental math as Thomas Fuller was. But we can learn to use mental math to calculate or estimate.

Try These!

First, use mental math and give an estimate. Then find the exact answer.

How close were your estimates?

		Estimate	Exact
1.	Number of eggs in 45 dozen		
2.	Numbers of wings and legs on 1,257 chickens		
3.	Number of legs on 27 spiders and 52 ants		
4.	Number of letters in 57 lines of type (each line has 63 letters)		

5. Make up three mental math problems to challenge your classmates.

Cumulative Review

Test Prep Strategy: Make Smart Choices

Use mental math.
Find the product of 29 and 52.
- (A) 158
- (B) 1,018
- (C) 1,508
- (D) 81

Using mental math can save you some time. If you round 29×52 to 30×50 you can mentally estimate the product. $30 \times 50 = 1,500$. With this estimate, you can eliminate answers (A) and (D). Since a low estimate of 29×52 is 1,000, it is unlikely that (B) is the answer. $29 \times 52 = 1,508$, or (C).

Write the letter of the correct answer. Use any strategy.

1. What is the value of 5 in the number 36,576,890?
   - (A) 5 hundred thousand
   - (B) 5 hundred million
   - (C) 5 hundred
   - (D) 5 tens

2. Which is **not** a true statement?
   - (A) $0.4 = 0.40$
   - (B) $0.051 < 0.0501$
   - (C) $0.09 > 0.089$
   - (D) $0.7 = 0.700$

3. Find the sum of $2.35, $1.25, and $4.90.
   - (A) $6.89
   - (B) $85.00
   - (C) $10.35
   - (D) $8.50

4. Find the difference between 9 and 0.03.
   - (A) 0.027
   - (B) 8.97
   - (C) 9.03
   - (D) 8.097
   - (E) not here

5. Complete this statement. $1,357 + n = 4,876$
   - (A) 1,529
   - (B) 8,519
   - (C) 3,519
   - (D) 3,521

6. Find the range of the set: 25, 54, 62, 81, 25.
   - (A) 53
   - (B) 25
   - (C) 54
   - (D) 56

7. Find the LCM of 3, 5, and 12.
   - (A) 3
   - (B) 36
   - (C) 300
   - (D) 60

8. Which statement is equivalent to 8×52?
   - (A) $(8 \times 5) + (8 \times 2)$
   - (B) $(8 \times 50) - (8 \times 2)$
   - (C) $(8 \times 50) + (8 \times 2)$
   - (D) 5×82

9. What is the product of 0.349×100?
   - (A) 3.49
   - (B) 34.9
   - (C) 349
   - (D) 34,900

10. A bag holds 5.8 lb of grass seed. How many pounds do 2.5 bags hold?
    - (A) 14.5 lb
    - (B) 8.3 lb
    - (C) 3.3 lb
    - (D) 1.45 lb

11. What is the product of 0.04 and 0.008?
    - (A) 0.00032
    - (B) 320,000
    - (C) 32
    - (D) 0.0000032

Test Prep Strategies
- Read Carefully
- Follow Directions
- Make Smart Choices
- Eliminate Choices
- Work Backward from an Answer

Chapter 4
Dividing Whole Numbers and Decimals: 1-Digit Divisors

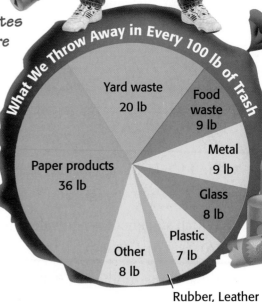

Kids Can Save the Earth

SECTION A

Developing Division Number Sense

What do people in the United States throw away the most? (Hint: You're holding some in your hands!)

Trash-o-saurus!
Page 167

What We Throw Away in Every 100 lb of Trash

Yard waste
20 lb

Food waste
9 lb

Metal
9 lb

Paper products
36 lb

Glass
8 lb

Plastic
7 lb

Other
8 lb

Rubber, Leather
3 lb

Surfing the World Wide Web!

Kids saving the planet! Quick, surf over to **www.mathsurf.com/5/ch4** to find out more about saving the environment. Compare your findings to local efforts in your area.

Dividing

Which three groups have the greatest number of endangered species?

175

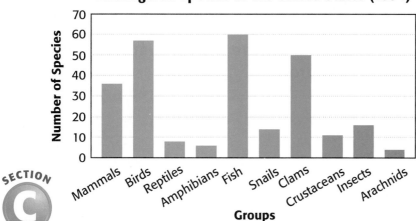

Endangered Species in the United States (1994)

Number of Species / Groups: Mammals, Birds, Reptiles, Amphibians, Fish, Snails, Clams, Crustaceans, Insects, Arachnids

A Force for the Earth
Page 175

Extending Division

Paper bags have been used for over 100 years. Plastic bags were introduced in the early 1980s. Use the information to decide which type bag is better for the environment.

193

Bags	Cost
250 Paper	$55.00
250 Plastic	$22.00

Rate of Decomposition	
Paper	3 months
Plastic	80 years

Customer Preference		
Store	Plastic	Paper
1	70	30
2	60	40
3	84	16

Red worms produce rich soil.
Page 193

TEAM PROJECT
Trash Treasure

You are probably familiar with recycling newspapers, cans, and glass. Choose a product to make from recycled materials. Then decide how to price, advertise, and sell your product.

Materials
scale, art supplies, scissors, poster paper

This soda bottle can now be used as a container for plastic bags.

Make a Plan

- What will you recycle? What will your product be?
- How much material will you collect?
- How much material will be used for each product?

Some stationery is made from recycled maps.

Carry It Out

1. Brainstorm ideas for products you can make. Be realistic. Think about who will buy your product.
2. Decide how much material you will collect. How much material will you need for each product?
3. What is the cost of making your product? How much is that per item?
4. Price your product so that you will make a profit.

Talk About It

- How will you advertise your product? Where will you sell it?
- What will you do with the money you earn? Will you "recycle" it for other environmental products?

Plan a Presentation

Make a poster advertising your product and present your product to the class. Which proposed product would be practical in the real world?

Developing Division Number Sense

This "Trash-o-saurus" sculpture, at the Garbage Museum, is made entirely of garbage!

The Trash-o-saurus weighs 2,000 pounds. If each section of the sculpture weighs 500 pounds, how many sections are there in all?

Estimating Quotients

Review estimating. Estimate each product. Write the factors you used.

1. 73×8
2. 46×11
3. 39×21
4. 703×39
5. 698×82
6. 410×50
7. 297×306
8. 420×13
9. 515×288

Skills Checklist

In this section, you will:

☐ Review the Meaning of Division

☐ Explore Patterns to Divide

☐ Estimate Quotients

Reviewing the Meaning of Division

You Will Learn
the meaning of division

Vocabulary

dividend
a number to be divided

division
tells how many groups or how many in each group

remainder
the number less than the divisor that remains after dividing

divisor
the number by which a dividend is divided

quotient
the number (other than the remainder) that is the result of the division operation

Learn •

Want to learn about recycling? The Children's Garbage Museum is a good place to start. A class of 36 students visited this museum. Touring groups are limited to 9 or 10 students.

Connecticut

This Trash-o-saurus is found at the Children's Garbage Museum in southwestern Connecticut.

Example 1

Can the class be put into 4 equal groups and meet the touring limit?

You can divide to find the number in each group.

$36 \div 4 = 9$ There were 9 students in each group.

The groups met the center's group limit.

You can also divide to find the number of equal groups or a missing factor.

Example 2

Find $18 \div 6$.

Divide to find the number of equal groups.

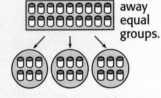

Take away equal groups.

3 equal groups of 6
So, $18 \div 6 = 3$.

Example 3

How many are in each row?

Find n. $15 = 3 \times n$.

Divide to find a missing factor.

$15 \div 3 = n$ 15 cans

$15 \div 3 = 5$

$n = 5$

3 rows

5 cans are in each row.

Did You Know?

The Garbage Museum's Trash-o-saurus is 24 ft long and $11\frac{1}{2}$ ft tall.

Talk About It

In which of the examples above did you divide to find the number of equal groups? Number in each group? Missing factor?

Check

Find each quotient.

1. $36 \div 9$ **2.** $24 \div 3$ **3.** $35 \div 7$ **4.** $42 \div 7$ **5.** $48 \div 6$

6. Reasoning Lena said she could find $144 \div 12$ by subtracting 12s from 144 until zero 12s were left. Do you agree? Explain.

Practice

Skills and Reasoning

Find each quotient.

7. $64 \div 8$ **8.** $32 \div 4$ **9.** $56 \div 8$ **10.** $81 \div 9$ **11.** $56 \div 7$

12. $54 \div 6$ **13.** $45 \div 5$ **14.** $72 \div 9$ **15.** $27 \div 3$ **16.** $28 \div 4$

17. $49 \div 7$ **18.** $36 \div 6$ **19.** $40 \div 8$ **20.** $63 \div 9$ **21.** $24 \div 6$

22. Identify each number in the equations $6 \times 5 = 30$ and $30 \div 5 = 6$ as a factor, a product, a divisor, a dividend, or a quotient.

23. Algebra Readiness If you know that $7 \times 8 = 56$, you also know that $8 \times 7 = 56$. Solve.
   a. $56 \div 7 = n$
   b. $56 \div 8 = n$

24. Critical Thinking Malcolm's father would not tell his age. Instead he gave some clues: "When you divide my age by 7, the quotient is 5. I am older than 30 but younger than 40." What is his age?

Problem Solving and Applications

25. Career Phoebe's uncle works as a separator Monday through Friday at the Recycling Center. Each day he separates the same number of loads of material. If he separates a total of 40 loads, how many loads per day does he separate?

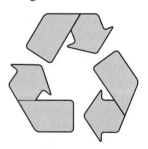

Recycling Symbol

Using Data Use the Data File on page 164 to answer **26** and **27**.

26. If the paper products in 100 lb of trash are packaged equally in 4 large bags, how many pounds are in each bag?

27. Critical Thinking How many pounds of food waste would be in 200 lb of garbage?

Mixed Review and Test Prep

Find each sum or difference.

28. $115 + 90$ **29.** $376 + 489$ **30.** $1,378 - 499$ **31.** $8,001 - 387$ **32.** $5,273 - 727$

33. Algebra Readiness Find the missing addend for $8 + n = 24$.
   Ⓐ 3   Ⓑ 18   Ⓒ 32   Ⓓ 16

Exploring Patterns to Divide

Problem Solving Connection
Look for a Pattern

Materials
calculator

Vocabulary

equation
a number sentence that uses the equals sign to show that two expressions have the same value

$9 + 2 = 11$

Explore •

You can use basic facts and patterns to help you divide.

Work Together

1. Use your calculator to solve each set of division **equations**. Look for a pattern.

   a. $32 \div 4 = \blacksquare$ **b.** $24 \div 6 = \blacksquare$ **c.** $30 \div 5 = \blacksquare$

   $320 \div 4 = \blacksquare$ $240 \div 6 = \blacksquare$ $300 \div 5 = \blacksquare$

   $3,200 \div 4 = \blacksquare$ $2,400 \div 6 = \blacksquare$ $3,000 \div 5 = \blacksquare$

2. Copy and complete. Use patterns to solve the equations mentally.

   a. $56 \div 7 = \blacksquare$ **b.** $24 \div 3 = \blacksquare$

   $560 \div 7 = \blacksquare$ $\blacksquare \div 3 = 80$

   $5,600 \div 7 = \blacksquare$ $2,400 \div \blacksquare = 800$

   c. $81 \div 9 = \blacksquare$ **d.** $63 \div 9 = \blacksquare$

   $810 \div 9 = \blacksquare$ $630 \div 9 = \blacksquare$

   $8,100 \div 9 = \blacksquare$ $6,300 \div 9 = \blacksquare$

   e. $72 \div 8 = \blacksquare$ **f.** $35 \div 7 = \blacksquare$

   $\blacksquare \div 8 = 90$ $\blacksquare \div 7 = 50$

   $7,200 \div \blacksquare = 900$ $3,500 \div \blacksquare = 500$

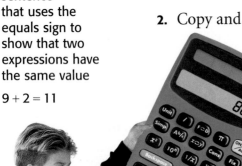

Talk About It

How do basic facts and patterns help you find the answer to $3,200 \div 4$?

Connect

You can use number sense and basic facts to divide multiples of 10.

$32 \div 8 = 4$	$40 \div 5 = 8$	$63 \div 7 = 9$
$320 \div 8 = 40$	$400 \div 5 = 80$	$630 \div 7 = 90$
$3,200 \div 8 = 400$	$4,000 \div 5 = 800$	$6,300 \div 7 = 900$
$32,000 \div 8 = 4,000$	$40,000 \div 5 = 8,000$	$63,000 \div 7 = 9,000$

Practice

Patterns Use number sense and basic facts to divide mentally.

1. $54 \div 9$
2. $540 \div 9$
3. $5,400 \div 9$
4. $54,000 \div 9$
5. $36,000 \div 4$

6. $480 \div 6$
7. $4,500 \div 5$
8. $4,200 \div 7$
9. $4,800 \div 8$
10. $3,000 \div 6$

11. $1,500 \div 5$
12. $28,000 \div 4$
13. $800 \div 2$
14. $9,000 \div 3$
15. $420 \div 7$

 Solve each pair using a calculator. Is the quotient the same or different for each pair? Explain.

16. $20 \div 4$ and $200 \div 40$
17. $1,800 \div 30$ and $18,000 \div 300$

18. $4,200 \div 60$ and $42,000 \div 600$
19. $5,600 \div 70$ and $56,000 \div 700$

 Mental Math Copy and complete.

20. $1,200 \div n = 400$
21. $24,000 \div n = 3,000$
22. $n \div 4 = 800$
23. $2,500 \div n = 500$

24. $n \div 5 = 400$
25. $32,000 \div n = 8,000$
26. $120 \div n = 60$
27. $n \div 3 = 90$

28. $20,000 \div 5 = 4,000$ and $20,000 \div 2 = 10,000$. Explain why there are only 3 zeros in the first quotient and 4 in the second.

29. **Write Your Own Problem** Choose a basic division fact. Write three other division exercises using that fact and patterns.

30. **Science** The world's largest garbage dump, at Fresh Kills, New York, processes 14,000 tons of garbage a day. If the processing takes place in 7 hr, how much garbage is processed per hour?

 31. **Journal** Explain how basic facts and place value help you divide greater numbers, such as $2,700 \div 9$.

Barges transport much of New York City's garbage to Fresh Kills.

Estimating Quotients

Learn • • • • • • • • •

Each morning, Josh gives a recycling report on his school's television system.

At the school, a team of 6 students picked up 257 recyclable cans and bottles. About how many recyclables per student was that? Sometimes you only need to find an estimate. One way to estimate quotients is to substitute numbers that make mental math simpler. These numbers are called **compatible numbers**. Janice and Julio substitute numbers close to 257 to make their mental math simpler.

Josh, from Rogers, Arkansas, uses his puppet to give recycling news.

Janice thinks:
257 ÷ 6 is about
300 ÷ 6
300 ÷ 6 = 50
Each person picked up about 50 cans or bottles.

Julio thinks:
257 ÷ 6 is about
240 ÷ 6
240 ÷ 6 = 40
That was about 40 cans or bottles per person.

Both estimates are reasonable.

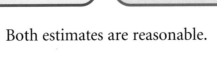
Talk About It

Why did Janice decide 257 is close to 300? Why did Julio choose 240 ÷ 6?

Check •

Estimate each quotient.

1. 710 ÷ 9   **2.** 213 ÷ 7   **3.** 313 ÷ 5   **4.** 251 ÷ 8   **5.** 133 ÷ 7

6. Reasoning Explain whether an estimate for 176 ÷ 3 is greater than or less than the exact answer.

Practice

Skills and Reasoning

Estimate each quotient.

7. $632 \div 8$ **8.** $312 \div 4$ **9.** $762 \div 9$ **10.** $495 \div 6$ **11.** $546 \div 7$

12. $554 \div 6$ **13.** $465 \div 5$ **14.** $536 \div 8$ **15.** $267 \div 3$ **16.** $268 \div 4$

17. $760 \div 8$ **18.** $231 \div 4$ **19.** $343 \div 7$ **20.** $146 \div 4$ **21.** $124 \div 7$

22. $186 \div 2$ **23.** $411 \div 6$ **24.** $243 \div 5$ **25.** $368 \div 9$ **26.** $175 \div 3$

27. Estimate the quotient of $201 \div 9$.

28. Estimate the quotient of $327 \div 7$.

29. You know that $632 \div 8$ is about 80. Is the exact quotient greater than or less than the estimate? Find estimates for $6,320 \div 8$, $63,200 \div 8$, and $63 \div 8$.

30. You know that $413 \div 6$ is about 70. Find estimates for $41 \div 6$ and $41,300 \div 6$.

Problem Solving and Applications

31. Science Supersonic planes like the Concorde, can travel faster than the speed of sound. The speed of sound is about 742 miles per hour. About how far does sound travel in 10 minutes?

32. Money A sculptor made a 15.2-ft sculpture of a supersonic transport plane and was paid $100 per foot. How much money did she receive?

33. Using Data Gina's class collected 253 plastic soda bottles for recycling. Is this enough to make 10 pullovers? Explain. Use the data from *Did You Know?* on page 172.

England and France cooperated to build the Concorde, which made its first flight in 1969.

34. Critical Thinking Is the quotient for $746 \div 9$ greater or less than the quotient for $746 \div 10$? Decide without finding the exact answer. Explain.

Mixed Review and Test Prep

Find each answer.

35. $1,200 - 12$ **36.** 240×3 **37.** $810 + 81 + 8$ **38.** $56 \div 8$ **39.** $2,772 - 349$

40. 120×4 **41.** $32 \div 8$ **42.** $450 - 25$ **43.** $32 + 18 + 5$ **44.** 366×6

45. Which type of graph shows change in data over time?

    Ⓐ line plot   Ⓑ line graph   Ⓒ pictograph   Ⓓ bar graph

SECTION A
Review and Practice

Vocabulary Match each with its example.

1. compatible numbers		**a.** the number 5 in $40 \div 5 = 8$	
2. quotient		**b.** $3 + 5 = 8 - 0$	
3. divisor		**c.** the number 40 in $40 \div 5 = 8$	
4. equation		**d.** the number 8 in $40 \div 5 = 8$	
5. dividend		**e.** combination of numbers that make it simpler to compute with mentally	

 (Lesson 1) Mental Math Find each quotient. Use mental math.

6. $16 \div 2$ **7.** $24 \div 3$ **8.** $40 \div 5$ **9.** $36 \div 4$ **10.** $56 \div 8$

11. $12 \div 3$ **12.** $25 \div 5$ **13.** $49 \div 7$ **14.** $18 \div 9$ **15.** $63 \div 9$

16. Careers Frank manages a baseball team. Each starting team has 9 players. He has 38 players. How many different teams can he make so the greatest number of players get a chance to start?

 (Lesson 2) Mental Math Find each quotient. Use mental math.

17. $1,600 \div 8$ **18.** $35,000 \div 7$ **19.** $180 \div 9$ **20.** $24,000 \div 2$ **21.** $1,500 \div 3$

22. $4,000 \div 5$ **23.** $12,000 \div 3$ **24.** $480 \div 6$ **25.** $3,600 \div 6$ **26.** $18,000 \div 9$

 Algebra Readiness Copy and complete.

27. $18,000 \div n = 2,000$ **28.** $n \div 7 = 300$ **29.** $800 \div n = 200$

30. $n \div 4 = 400$ **31.** $49,000 \div n = 7,000$ **32.** $n \div 8 = 300$

(Lesson 3) Estimate each quotient.

33. $565 \div 8$ **34.** $421 \div 5$ **35.** $635 \div 7$ **36.** $361 \div 4$ **37.** $313 \div 6$

38. $246 \div 6$ **39.** $192 \div 4$ **40.** $280 \div 3$ **41.** $537 \div 9$ **42.** $430 \div 7$

43. $913 \div 30$ **44.** $712 \div 9$ **45.** $238 \div 40$ **46.** $649 \div 8$ **47.** $153 \div 30$

48. Estimation A quilt maker uses 6 ft of thread to stitch 1 quilt square. If a spool of thread has 543 ft of thread, how many squares can he sew?

 49. Journal Explain how knowing the quotient of $72 \div 9$ can help you find the quotient of $72,000 \div 9$.

> **Skills Checklist**
>
> In this section, you have:
> - ☑ Reviewed the Meaning of Division
> - ☑ Explored Patterns to Divide
> - ☑ Estimated Quotients

Dividing

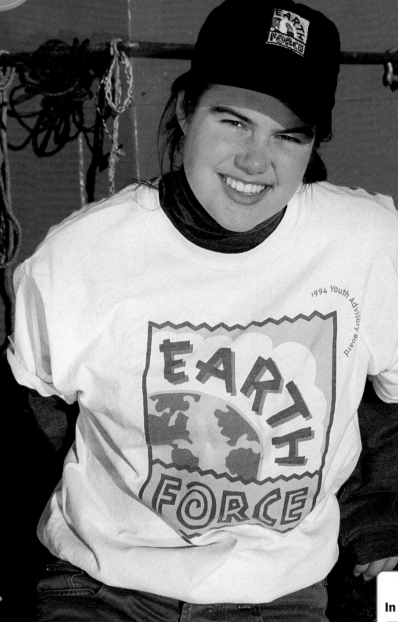

Anna of Freeport, Maine, is a member of the Youth Advisory Panel of Earth Force, a group committed to bettering the environment. What can you do to help the environment where you live? How might division be useful when planning fund-raisers or other group projects?

Skills Checklist

In this section, you will:

☐ Explore Dividing

☐ Divide by 1-Digit Divisors

☐ Solve Problems By Interpreting Remainders

☐ Learn Where to Place the First Digit

☐ Learn Where to Place Zeros in the Quotient

☐ Explore Mean

GET READY!

Dividing By 1-Digit Numbers

Review multiplying. Find each product.

1. 24×6
2. 753×8
3. 672×7
4. 901×5
5. $2,058 \times 9$
6. $4,259 \times 6$
7. $6,827 \times 7$
8. $1,280 \times 4$
9. $13,339 \times 2$

Exploring Dividing

Explore •

If you had $3.75 for lunch money and 2 days to spend equal amounts, how much could you spend each day? You can use play money to find out.

Work Together

1. Use play dollars, dimes, and pennies to find $3.75 ÷ 2.

   a. Show $3.75 as 3 dollars, 7 dimes, and 5 pennies.

   b. Draw two circles. Put an equal number of dollars into each circle. How many extra dollars do you have?

   c. Regroup the extra 1 dollar as 10 dimes. How many dimes do you have?

   d. Put an equal number of dimes in each circle. How many are in each circle?

   e. Regroup the extra 1 dime as 10 pennies. How many pennies do you have?

   f. Put an equal number of pennies in each circle. How much is in each circle? What is the quotient of $3.75 ÷ 2? Are there any pennies left?

Math Tip
You can regroup dollars, dimes, and pennies since they are also based on groups of 10.

2. Divide using money.

   a. $1.54 ÷ 4   **b.** $6.03 ÷ 5   **c.** $2.81 ÷ 9

   d. $5.14 ÷ 3   **e.** $3.29 ÷ 5   **f.** $6.38 ÷ 4

Talk About It

3. How did you decide on the number of groups?

4. How do you know what the dividend is?

Here is a way to record division with money. Find $4.36 ÷ 3.

What You See   **What You Record**

```
      1              ←—— 1 dollar in each group
  3)$4.36
```

```
    − 3             3 dollars shared
      1             1 dollar left
                    Regroup 1 dollar as 10 dimes.
```

```
     1.4            Bring down the dimes.
  3)$4.36           4 dimes in each group
    − 3
     13
    −12             12 dimes shared
      1     ←—— 1 dime left
                    Regroup 1 dime as 10 pennies.
```

```
   $1.45 R1         Bring down the pennies.
  3)$4.36           5 pennies in each group
    − 3
     13
    −12
     16
    −15             15 pennies shared
      1     ←—— 1 is left. Write the remainder.
```

$4.36 divided by 3 is $1.45 R1.

Practice •

Copy and complete. You may use play money to help.

1.
```
   $■.2 2 R■
  6)$7.3 5
    − 6
    ■ 3
   −1 2
    ■ 5
   −■■
     3
```

2.
```
   $■.1 7 R3
  4)$4.7 1
   −■
    ■ 7
   − 4
    3 1
   −■■
    ■
```

3.
```
   $■.4 5 R1
  3)$7.3 6
   − 6
    1 3
   −1■
    1 ■
   − 1 5
      1
```

4.
```
   $■.8 5 R■
  5)$9.2 8
   − 5
    ■ 2
   −4■
    2 ■
   −■■
     3
```

Divide. You may use play money to help.

5. 5)$7.24   6. 7)$8.92   7. 2)$7.25   8. 4)$8.97   9. 6)$9.39

 10. **Journal** Explain why you can use money to show division.

Dividing by 1-Digit Divisors

You Will Learn

how to divide by a
1-digit divisor

Learn

In 1994, the U.S. Department of the Interior listed 640 plant and animal species as being endangered or threatened in the United States.

At one school, three grades decide to work together to research the 640 endangered species. The research is divided among the 3 grades.

	Endangered	Threatened	Total Number
Animals	262	88	350
Plants	378	75	453
Total	640	163	803

Example

How many species does each grade research? Since you want to find the number of species for each of three equal groups, divide. $640 \div 3 = n$

Step 1

Estimate the answer. It will help you decide where to place the first digit in the quotient.

$$\begin{array}{r} 200 \\ \textbf{Think: } 3\overline{)600} \end{array}$$

The first digit goes in the hundreds place. Start by dividing hundreds.

Step 2

Divide the hundreds.

$$\begin{array}{r} 2 \\ 3\overline{)640} \\ -6 \\ \hline 0 \end{array}$$

Divide. $6 \div 3 = 2$
Multiply. $2 \times 3 = 6$
Subtract. $6 - 6 = 0$
Compare. $0 < 3$

Step 3

Bring down the tens. Divide the tens.

$$\begin{array}{r} 21 \\ 3\overline{)640} \\ -6 \\ \hline 04 \\ -3 \\ \hline 1 \end{array}$$

Divide. $4 \div 3 = 1$
Multiply. $1 \times 3 = 3$

Subtract. $4 - 3 = 1$
Compare. $1 < 3$

Step 4

Bring down the ones. Divide the ones. Write remainder.

$$\begin{array}{r} 213 \text{ R}1 \\ 3\overline{)640} \\ -6 \\ \hline 04 \\ -3 \\ \hline 10 \\ -9 \\ \hline 1 \end{array}$$

Divide. $10 \div 3 = 3$
Multiply. $3 \times 3 = 9$
Subtract. $10 - 9 = 1$
Compare. $1 < 3$

Check:

$$\begin{array}{r} 213 \leftarrow \text{quotient} \\ \times \quad 3 \leftarrow \text{divisor} \\ \hline 639 \\ \\ 639 \\ + \quad 1 \leftarrow \text{remainder} \\ \hline 640 \leftarrow \text{dividend} \end{array}$$

The answer is 213 R1.
If the 3 classes wish to research all 640 species, one class must research 214 species and the others 213 each.

Talk About It

Explain how you can use estimation when dividing 683 by 6.

Check

Divide. Use multiplication to check.

1. $98 \div 7$ 2. $4\overline{)485}$ 3. $806 \div 6$ 4. $6\overline{)959}$ 5. $8\overline{)899}$

6. **Reasoning** Explain why you use estimation when dividing 544 by 4.

Practice

Skills and Reasoning

Divide. Use multiplication to check.

7. $2\overline{)285}$ 8. $3\overline{)456}$ 9. $6\overline{)677}$ 10. $8\overline{)955}$ 11. $527 \div 3$

12. $8\overline{)98}$ 13. $7\overline{)819}$ 14. $538 \div 4$ 15. $618 \div 5$ 16. $8\overline{)841}$

17. $837 \div 7$ 18. $3\overline{)648}$ 19. $4\overline{)725}$ 20. $5\overline{)829}$ 21. $3\overline{)987}$

22. Estimate the quotient for $812 \div 9$. What number is in the hundreds place in the quotient?

23. When dividing a 3-digit number by a 1-digit number for what divisors can you get a 2 in the hundreds place in the quotient?

Problem Solving and Applications

Using Data Use the Data File on page 165 to answer **24–26.**

24. **Science** About how many more fish than mammals are endangered?

25. **Critical Thinking** Find 2 endangered groups that when you double the number of species in one group, you get the number in the other.

26. If you wanted to divide the list of endangered animals in half and find their names, about how many names would you need to list?

The lowland gorilla, found in Gabon, Congo, and Zaire in Africa, is an endangered species.

Mixed Review and Test Prep

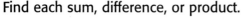

Find each sum, difference, or product.

27. $47.35 − 8.99$ 28. $3.82 + 9.76$ 29. $15.25 × 3$ 30. 1.98 2.03 $+ 0.47$ 31. $12.50 × 4$

32. **Money** Jeff bought a book on endangered animals for $7.98. He gave the cashier a $10 bill. What was his change?

Ⓐ $3.98   Ⓑ $3.02   Ⓒ $2.02   Ⓓ not here

Problem Solving

Analyze Word Problems:
Interpret Remainders

You Will Learn
how to solve
problems using
remainders

Learn • • • • • • • • • • • • • • •

Suppose you go to the
book closet to get math
books for your class of
29 students. The books
are packed 8 to a carton.
How many cartons
do you need?

Work Together

▶ **Understand**	What do you know?	
	What do you need to find out?	

▶ **Plan**	How will you find out what you need to know?	You divide. Write a number sentence. $29 \div 8 = n$

▶ **Solve**   Divide.

$$\begin{array}{r} 3 \text{ R5} \\ 8\overline{)29} \\ -\underline{24} \\ 5 \end{array}$$

What does the remainder
tell you?

You need more
than 3 cartons.

Write the answer.

You need 4 cartons.

**Problem
Solving Hint**

When you divide
to solve a problem,
think about whether
the answer should
be only the quotient,
the next whole-number
quotient, or only
the remainder.

▶ **Look Back**   Is your answer reasonable? Explain.

Talk About It

1. When a problem describes cartons being filled, what
   does the remainder usually represent?

2. What if you were asked how many books you would take
   from the fourth carton? How would you find that answer?

Solve. Use the picture to answer **1–4.**

1. If you needed calculators for 35 students, how many full boxes would you need?

2. How many more calculators would you need?

3. If you opened enough boxes to supply the entire class with calculators, how many boxes would you open?

4. If pairs shared a calculator, how many boxes would you need?

8 calculators

Problem Solving
Practice •

Use any strategy to solve each problem.

5. In the book closet, social studies books are kept in stacks of 4. If each student carries no more than one stack, what is the least number of students needed to carry books for a class of 27?

6. Six students were needed to carry stacks of 4 books to the classroom. What is the greatest number of students who can receive books?

7. In the school lunchroom, students sit at tables for 8. There are 118 students eating lunch. How many tables must be set up?

8. The school sells snacks to the students during lunch. The snacks are packed 6 to a box. If 57 students want to buy snacks, how many boxes must be opened?

9. **Measurement** The school sells 34 lb of cold cuts in a 5-day week. If the cold cuts come in 16-oz packages, how many packages should be available each day?

Problem Solving
Strategies

- Use Objects/Act It Out
- Draw a Picture
- Look for a Pattern
- Guess and Check
- Use Logical Reasoning
- Make an Organized List
- Make a Table
- Solve a Simpler Problem
- Work Backward

Choose a Tool

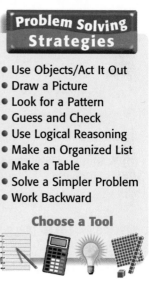

10. **Science** The diagram shows a water molecule which is made up of hydrogen and oxygen atoms. If you had 13 hydrogen atoms, what is the greatest number of water molecules you could have? Would there be any hydrogen left over?

11. **Literature** Roald Dahl is a British writer famous for his imaginative children's stories, including *James and the Giant Peach* and *Charlie and the Chocolate Factory*. A library has 78 copies of his popular children's books. If one shelf can hold 9 books, how many shelves will be needed?

A water molecule is made up of 2 hydrogen atoms and 1 oxygen atom.

PROBLEM SOLVING PRACTICE

Deciding Where to Place the First Digit

You Will Learn
how to estimate to help place the first digit in the quotient

Did You Know?
In one day, people in the United States throw 43,000 tons of food into the garbage.

Learn ● ● ● ● ● ● ● ● ● ● ● ● ● ● ● ●   ● ●

When it comes to garbage, is your family typical? A typical family of four in the United States produces 288 kg (288,000 g) of garbage each month, or 159 lb per person. Four members of one family made a special effort during 1995 to control the amount of garbage they produced. During the month of October, they produced only 211 kg.

Example 1

How much waste was produced by each family member in October?
You can divide 211 by 4.

Step 1	Step 2
Decide where to place the first digit in the quotient.	Divide the tens.

Step 1:

$$\begin{array}{r} 50 \\ 4)\overline{211} \end{array}$$ **Think:** $4)\overline{200}$

Start by dividing tens.

Step 2:

$$\begin{array}{r} 5 \\ 4)\overline{211} \\ -20 \\ \hline 1 \end{array}$$
Divide. $21 \div 4 = 5$
Multiply. $5 \times 4 = 20$
Subtract. $21 - 20 = 1$
Compare. $1 < 4$

Step 3	Step 4
Bring down the ones. Divide the ones.	Record the remainder. Multiply to check.

Step 3:

$$\begin{array}{r} 52 \\ 4)\overline{211} \\ -20 \\ \hline 11 \\ -8 \\ \hline 3 \end{array}$$
Divide. $11 \div 4 = 2$
Multiply. $2 \times 4 = 8$
Subtract. $11 - 8 = 3$
Compare. $3 < 4$

Step 4:

$$\begin{array}{r} 52 \text{ R3} \\ 4)\overline{211} \\ -20 \\ \hline 11 \\ -8 \\ \hline 3 \end{array}$$

Check: 52 ← quotient
$\times4$ ← divisor
$\overline{208}$
$+3$ ← remainder
$\overline{211}$ ← dividend

The answer is 52 R3. Each family member produced about 52 kg of garbage. There were 3 extra kilograms.

Example 2

Divide 107 by 3.

$$\begin{array}{r} 30 \\ 3\overline{)90} \end{array}$$

Estimate. **Think:** 3)90

Start by dividing tens.

$$\begin{array}{r} 35\ R2 \\ 3\overline{)107} \\ -9 \\ \hline 17 \\ -15 \\ \hline 2 \end{array}$$

The answer is 35 R2.

Math Tip

Substitute 90 for 107 to estimate. 90 and 3 are compatible numbers.

Example 3

Divide 459 by 4.

$$\begin{array}{r} 100 \\ 4\overline{)400} \end{array}$$

Estimate. **Think:** 4)400

Start by dividing hundreds.

$$\begin{array}{r} 114\ R3 \\ 4\overline{)459} \\ -4 \\ \hline 05 \\ -4 \\ \hline 19 \\ -16 \\ \hline 3 \end{array}$$

Check: 114 ← quotient
$\times$ 4 ← divisor
456
+ 3 ← remainder
459 ← dividend

The answer is 114 R3.

Talk About It

1. If you divide 400 by 7, how do you decide if you start dividing the hundreds or the tens?

2. What number would you substitute for 374 to divide 374 by 6?

Check

Copy each exercise. Write whether the first digit is in the hundreds or tens place.

1. 6)347
2. 3)474
3. 4)228
4. 6)770
5. 4)295

6. 5)426
7. 2)364
8. 8)520
9. 6)743
10. 3)269

Divide. Check your answer.

11. 5)423
12. 3)379
13. 8)344
14. 7)660
15. 4)435

16. 9)641
17. 6)438
18. 2)537
19. 4)627
20. 6)311

21. **Reasoning** How can you tell before you divide 389 by 4 that the first digit of the quotient is in the tens place?

Skills and Reasoning

Divide. Check your answer.

22. 8)649   **23.** 4)446   **24.** 9)840   **25.** 9)736   **26.** 6)570

27. 6)368   **28.** 5)579   **29.** 8)249   **30.** 3)970   **31.** 4)470

32. 521 ÷ 3   **33.** 719 ÷ 6   **34.** 926 ÷ 7   **35.** 742 ÷ 3   **36.** 725 ÷ 2

37. 526 ÷ 7   **38.** 498 ÷ 9   **39.** 523 ÷ 8   **40.** 645 ÷ 6   **41.** 665 ÷ 4

42. 6)743   **43.** 8)222   **44.** 5)824   **45.** 7)999   **46.** 6)585

47. 4)343   **48.** 6)782   **49.** 9)819   **50.** 3)637   **51.** 8)429

52. Divide 637 by 5.   **53.** Divide 475 by 6.

54. Find 549 divided by 6.   **55.** Find 458 divided by 8.

56. The divisor is 7 and the dividend is 876. Divide.

57. Write a division problem in which the divisor is 5 and there is a 1 in the hundreds place of the quotient.

Problem Solving and Applications

58. A family of five in the Netherlands produces about 2,326 kg of garbage per year. Approximately how much is produced by each family member?

59. **Geography** The Netherlands' total area is 14,373 square miles. The total area of the United States is 3,618,770 square miles. How many more square miles is the United States than the Netherlands?

60. **Using Data** Use the data from *Did You Know?* on page 182. How many days of dumping does 430,000 tons of food represent?

61. **Money** Three classes collected cans and made $207. They agreed to split the money equally. How much did each class get?

62. **Logic** A scout troop collected 240 lb of scrap aluminum for recycling. The recycling center paid them $1 for every 2 lb they collected. Did they earn enough money to buy a tent that costs $150? Explain.

Problem Solving and CAREERS

Using Data Although women's wages for different job types were improving in 1993, women only earned about $\frac{3}{4}$ of what men did. Use this table to answer **63** and **64**.

1993 Median Weekly Earnings		
Job	**Men**	**Women**
Manager	$791	$580
Technician/salesperson	$534	$376
Service worker	$350	$259
Transportation worker	$456	$358
Farmer	$274	$242

63. Give the dollar amount that a male manager earned per day if he worked a 5-day week. Give the dollar amount that a female manager earned per day for a 5-day week.

64. In which job type are men's and women's earnings the closest? The farthest apart?

65. Copy and complete the table. About how many dollars did each earn per day?

Both men and women are finding employment in new areas: women in construction and men in nursing.

Farmer	Median Weekly Earnings	Per Day 5-day Week	Per Day 6-day Week	Per Day 7-day Week
Men	$274			
Women	$242			

66. Journal Make a diagram showing how to determine where the first digit in the quotient goes when dividing a 3-digit dividend by a 1-digit divisor.

Mixed Review and Test Prep

Find each answer.

67. $98 \times 7   **68.** $3.50 + $11.23   **69.** $10.00 - $6.85   **70.** $32 \times 9   **71.** $3.99 + $0.72

 Mental Math Use mental math to find each answer.

72. 307×10 **73.** $90 + 30 + 70 + 10 + 16$ **74.** $56 \div 7$ **75.** $3.00 - $2.49

 Algebra Readiness Solve for *n*.

76. $n \times $3.17 = 3.17 **77.** $n \div 9 = 5$ **78.** $9.29 + n = 9.29$

79. What is the greatest possible remainder when you divide by 7?

Ⓐ 0   Ⓑ 8   Ⓒ 7   Ⓓ 6

Zeros in the Quotient

You Will Learn

how estimation can help place zeros correctly in a quotient

Learn • • • • • • • • • • •

In elementary school, Anna joined the group CAKE (Concerns About Kids' Environment) to help save the earth. They campaigned to ban the use of polystyrene, a type of plastic that does not decompose.

Anna lives in the town of Freeport, Maine.

Example 1

You want to replace polystyrene trays in your school. The new trays are $4 each. How many new trays can you buy for $438?

To find out how many $4 are in $438, divide.

First, estimate. **Think:** $400 \div 4 = 100$

Then start dividing hundreds.

```
   109 R2
4)438
  -4
   03     A zero in the tens place
  -0      shows that there are no
   38     tens.
  -36
    2
```

Use multiplication to check.

$4 \times 109 = 436$ and $436 + 2 = 438$

You can buy 109 new trays. You'll have $2 left over.

Example 2

Divide 632 by 3.

Estimate. **Think:** $600 \div 3 = 200$

Start dividing hundreds.

```
   210 R2
3)632
  -6
   03
  -3
   02
  -0       A zero in the ones place shows
    2      that there are no ones.
```

Use multiplication to check.

```
   210  ← quotient
 ×   3  ← divisor
   630
 +   2  ← remainder
   632  ← dividend
```

632 divided by 3 is 210 R2.

Talk About It

How do you know when to write a zero in the quotient?

Check •

Divide. Multiply to check.

1. 5)551   2. 2)419   3. 3)324   4. 6)662   5. 7)682

6. **Reasoning** How could you use estimation to find the number of zeros in the quotient of $800 \div 2$?

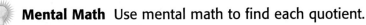
Skills and Reasoning

Divide. Multiply to check.

7. $2\overline{)181}$ **8.** $5\overline{)1,001}$ **9.** $2\overline{)880}$ **10.** $4\overline{)424}$ **11.** $7\overline{)774}$

12. $6\overline{)615}$ **13.** $5\overline{)540}$ **14.** $9\overline{)3,607}$ **15.** $3\overline{)323}$ **16.** $9\overline{)181}$

17. $7\overline{)1,470}$ **18.** $8\overline{)1,742}$ **19.** $3\overline{)919}$ **20.** $6\overline{)1,235}$ **21.** $4\overline{)401}$

Mental Math Use mental math to find each quotient.

22. $140 \div 7$ **23.** $250 \div 5$ **24.** $4,800 \div 8$ **25.** $36,000 \div 9$ **26.** $1,600 \div 4$

27. Divide 526 by 5. **28.** Divide 839 by 4.

29. **Estimation** Are there any zeros in the quotient of $663 \div 3$? How can you tell without finding the quotient?

30. Look at the division problem $4\overline{)3\blacksquare\,\blacksquare}$. Is the quotient greater than 100? How can you tell without dividing?

Problem Solving and Applications

31. **Logic** New cafeteria trays cost twice as much as the old non-biodegradable ones. If the old ones cost $2 each, how many new trays could you get for $441?

32. **Fine Arts** The longest running one-person show was *Comedy in Music* at the Golden Theater in New York City. There were 849 performances in 3 years. How many performances per year was this?

Using Data Use the table to answer **33–35.** Estimate each answer first.

33. How many bus rides can you take for $163?

34. How many vans are needed for 275 people?

35. **Write Your Own Problem** Write a division problem using data from the table.

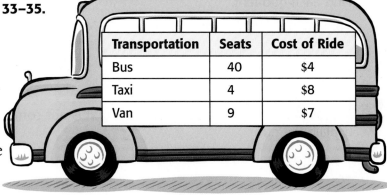

Transportation	Seats	Cost of Ride
Bus	40	$4
Taxi	4	$8
Van	9	$7

Mixed Review and Test Prep

Find each product.

36. 16×37 **37.** 25×438 **38.** 13×498 **39.** 37×42 **40.** 87×357

41. **Algebra Readiness** Which of the following represents the value of n for $n \times 190 = 190,000$?

  A 1,000 **B** 100 **C** 100,000 **D** 10,000

STOP and Practice

Divide.

1. $18 \div 3$ 2. $45 \div 9$ 3. $24 \div 8$ 4. $48 \div 6$ 5. $49 \div 7$

6. $2,400 \div 3$ 7. $3,600 \div 9$ 8. $25,000 \div 5$ 9. $2,000 \div 4$ 10. $900 \div 3$

11. $24,000 \div 6$ 12. $810 \div 9$ 13. $5,400 \div 9$ 14. $72,000 \div 9$ 15. $630 \div 7$

16. $3\overline{)451}$ 17. $8\overline{)93}$ 18. $6\overline{)752}$ 19. $2\overline{)486}$ 20. $7\overline{)787}$

21. $5\overline{)267}$ 22. $4\overline{)237}$ 23. $8\overline{)547}$ 24. $9\overline{)235}$ 25. $3\overline{)117}$

26. $8\overline{)146}$ 27. $4\overline{)341}$ 28. $9\overline{)349}$ 29. $3\overline{)123}$ 30. $5\overline{)347}$

31. $5\overline{)517}$ 32. $8\overline{)244}$ 33. $7\overline{)245}$ 34. $2\overline{)129}$ 35. $3\overline{)181}$

36. $4\overline{)827}$ 37. $5\overline{)652}$ 38. $7\overline{)146}$ 39. $3\overline{)991}$ 40. $4\overline{)436}$

41. $6\overline{)665}$ 42. $2\overline{)819}$ 43. $8\overline{)247}$ 44. $9\overline{)187}$ 45. $5\overline{)539}$

Find each quotient.

46. $2\overline{)574}$ 47. $6\overline{)246}$ 48. $4\overline{)6,120}$ 49. $5\overline{)425}$ 50. $3\overline{)687}$

51. $9\overline{)819}$ 52. $3\overline{)1,359}$ 53. $5\overline{)2,770}$ 54. $4\overline{)540}$ 55. $8\overline{)384}$

Error Search Find each quotient that is not correct. Write it correctly and explain the error.

56. $4\overline{)770}$ quotient $192R2$

57. $3\overline{)107}$ quotient $34R5$

58. $7\overline{)350}$ quotient 500

59. $6\overline{)456}$ quotient 76

60. $9\overline{)279}$ quotient 310

61. $7\overline{)839}$ quotient $119R6$

62. $5\overline{)429}$ quotient $85R5$

63. $2\overline{)642}$ quotient 321

64. $6\overline{)259}$ quotient $430R1$

65. $7\overline{)906}$ quotient $129R3$

66. $3\overline{)427}$ quotient $14R1$

67. $6\overline{)647}$ quotient $107R5$

Sticky Business!

Divide. Match each letter to its answer
in the blank below. Some letters are not used.

The lollipop was named after Lolly Pop.
Who was Lolly Pop?

| 36 R1 | 309 | 36 R1 | 34 R1 | 200 R3 | 40 R4 | 162 R1 |

| 309 | 36 R1 | 162 R1 | 9 R7 | 30 R7 | 200 R3 | 55 R1 | 162 R1 | 60 |

68. $5\overline{)276}$ [R]   **69.** $4\overline{)803}$ [O]   **70.** $8\overline{)79}$ [T]   **71.** $6\overline{)244}$ [U]

72. $307 \div 9$ [M]   **73.** $8\overline{)245}$ [I]   **74.** $2\overline{)618}$ [F]   **75.** $4\overline{)28}$ [N]

76. $5\overline{)811}$ [S]   **77.** $73 \div 2$ [A]   **78.** $244 \div 4$ [P]   **79.** $805 \div 5$ [C]

80. $150 \div 3$ [W]   **81.** $360 \div 6$ [E]   **82.** $3\overline{)902}$ [D]   **83.** $9\overline{)277}$ [H]

Number Sense True or False

Write whether each statement is true or false. Explain your answer.

84. 65 divided by 4 is less than 65.

85. The remainder when 657 is divided by 5 is 7.

86. 0 divided by 6 is 6.

87. 4,679.23 divided by 1 is 4,679.23.

88. 490 divided by 7 is greater than 490 divided by 5.

89. 3,504 is divisible by 2, 3, and 6.

90. The remainder of $432 \div 4$ is greater than 3.

91. 847 cannot be divided equally by 2.

92. 329 divided by 7 is less than 50.

Exploring Mean

Problem Solving Connection
Make a Table

Materials
- yardstick or tape measure
- calculator

Vocabulary

mean
the answer when the sum of a set of numbers is divided by the number of addends

median
middle number of an ordered set of numbers

mode
most common value in a set of data

Remember
To find the median of an even number of data, add the two middle numbers and divide by 2.

Explore •

If you ask several people to estimate a length, each will probably give a different number. You can work with data like this to find an average.

Work Together

What is the length of your classroom in feet?

1. Work with your group to estimate the length.

   a. Have each person in the group estimate the length of your classroom in feet.

   b. List the estimates in a table.

   c. Find the sum of the estimates.

   d. Divide the sum by the number of group members. You may want to use your calculator.

2. You've found your group's **mean** estimate. Now measure the actual length of the room. Compare your mean estimate to the actual length.

Talk About It

3. You can say finding the mean "evens out" the data. Explain.

4. How does your estimate compare to the actual length? How does your group's mean estimate compare to the actual length? What accounts for the difference between your estimate and your group's mean estimate?

This graph gives the prices of 5 magazines.

Magazine Prices per Copy

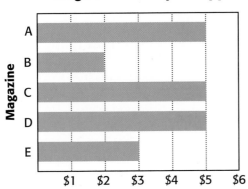

You can find the mean cost of these magazines by dividing their sum by 5.

$5
$2
$5
$5
+ $3
——
$20

$$5)\overline{\$20} = \$4$$

The mean is $4.

Magazine Prices per Copy

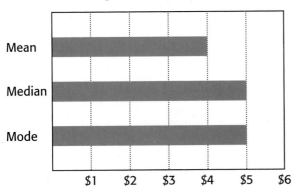

Median: 2, 3, 5, 5, 5
        ↑
    middle number

$5 is the median

Mode:

$5 is the number that appears most. In this example, the median and mode are the same. Often, they are different.

Practice

Find the mean, median, and mode for each set of data.

1. 5, 7, 13, 9, 9, 11   2. 64, 58, 61, 59, 58

3. 198, 203, 241, 255, 211, 199, 198

4. 1,098, 749, 751, 843, 998, 943

5. $27.29, $27.00, $28.01, $27.35, $27.00

6. $0.45, $0.58, $0.68, $0.31, $0.89, $1.05

7. Find the mean, median and mode for the set of data in the bar graph.

8. **Critical Thinking** Can the mode of a set of data ever be the least number? Explain.

9. **What If** You want to find the mean, median, and mode of 42, 43, 44, 45, 46. How could you find them mentally?

10. **Journal** Make up a set of data and find its mean, median, and mode.

Prices of CDs

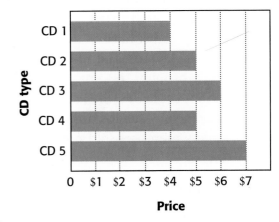

SECTION B
Review and Practice

Vocabulary Match each term with its example or meaning.

1. mean
        a. an operation that tells how many groups or how many are in each group

2. division
        b. the average of a set of numbers

(Lessons 4, 5, 7 and 8) Divide. Multiply to check your answer.

3. $4\overline{)52}$	4. $7\overline{)84}$	5. $642 \div 3$	6. $937 \div 5$	7. $738 \div 4$
8. $9\overline{)819}$	9. $3\overline{)159}$	10. $6\overline{)147}$	11. $6\overline{)426}$	12. $4\overline{)168}$
13. $427 \div 3$	14. $163 \div 5$	15. $916 \div 3$	16. $4{,}817 \div 8$	17. $3{,}185 \div 6$
18. $2{,}918 \div 4$	19. $1{,}256 \div 6$	20. $526 \div 7$	21. $369 \div 3$	22. $145 \div 2$
23. $5\overline{)672}$	24. $7\overline{)6{,}129}$	25. $9\overline{)5{,}640}$	26. $3\overline{)3{,}912}$	27. $7\overline{)2{,}995}$

28. In the art supply closet, there are 10 boxes each containing six sets of watercolor paints. What is the least number of boxes that needs to be opened for a class of 38 students? How many sets of paints will be left over in the open box?

(Lesson 9) Find the mean, median, and mode for each set of data.

29. 16, 23, 23, 38, 20
30. 33, 26, 26, 32, 25, 14
31. 101, 101, 101, 99, 123

32. 4, 9, 20, 13, 9
33. 26, 40, 15, 26, 33
34. 117, 92, 46, 92, 93, 88

35. 129, 129, 150, 131, 126
36. 653, 599, 699, 595, 750, 550

37. 80, 64, 87, 53, 87, 49

38. **Logic** The seven members of Troop 235 sold cookies for a fund raiser. The total number of dollars each brought in were $102, $131, $103, $102, $71, $81, and $124. Find the mean, median, and mode. How many members sold more than the average?

39. **Journal** Explain how you know whether $652 \div 7$ has 2 or 3 digits in its quotient.

Skills Checklist

In this section, you have:

☑ **Explored Dividing**

☑ **Divided by 1-Digit Divisors**

☑ **Solved Problems by Interpreting Remainders**

☑ **Learned Where to Place the First Digit**

☑ **Learned Where to Place Zeros in the Quotient**

☑ **Explored Mean**

REVIEW AND PRACTICE

Extending Division

Wiggling Workers! When Greta wants to improve the environment, she lets worms do all the "dirty" work. Worms eat the garbage and cuttings that Greta feeds them. In return, the worms produce nutrient-rich soil known as compost. How can you use division to find out how long it takes the worms to turn the garbage into compost?

Skills Checklist

In this section, you will:

☐ Explore Products and Quotients

☐ Divide Money

☐ Divide Decimals

☐ Learn About Factors and Divisibility

☐ Explore Prime and Composite Numbers

☐ Solve Problems by Working Backward

GET READY!

Dividing Decimals

Review multiplying decimals. Find each product. Write zeros when necessary.

1. 9.76×1.4 2. 0.75×4.09

3. 11.3×0.39 4. 0.96×0.007

5. 28.98×1.48 6. 4.07×0.3

7. 15.57×1.006 8. 7.067×0.22

Chapter 4
Lesson
10

Exploring Products and Quotients

Problem Solving Connection
Use Logical Reasoning

Explore

You can use clues to help you discover patterns with numbers.

Work Together

Work the example to help you complete each statement.
Write >, <, or =.

1. For multiplication:

a. If both factors are greater than 1, the product is ____ either factor.

$$\begin{array}{r l} 32 & \leftarrow \text{factor } (>1) \\ \times\ 5 & \leftarrow \text{factor } (>1) \\ \hline \blacksquare & \leftarrow \text{product} \end{array}$$

b. If one factor is 1 and the other is greater than 1, the product is ____ the other factor.

$$\begin{array}{r l} 168 & \leftarrow \text{factor } (>1) \\ \times\ \ 1 & \leftarrow \text{factor } (=1) \\ \hline \blacksquare & \leftarrow \text{product} \end{array}$$

Problem Solving Hint
Try solving a few examples with different numbers before you decide how to complete each sentence.

2. For division:

a. When the divisor is 1, the quotient is ____ the dividend.

■ ← quotient
1)28 ← dividend
↑ divisor (=1)

b. When the divisor is greater than 1, the quotient is ____ the dividend.

■ ← quotient
3)39 ← dividend
↑ divisor (>1)

c. If the quotient is 0, the dividend is ____ 0.

0 ← quotient (= 0)
4)■ ← dividend
↑ divisor

d. A remainder is ____ the divisor.

↓ quotient
16R1 ← remainder
4)65 ← dividend
↑ divisor

Talk About It

Can you tell anything about the quotient before you divide 75 by 9? Explain.

Connect

When you multiply, keep these properties in mind.

Multiplication property	Using numbers
Zero property	$0 \times 4 = 0$
One property	$1 \times 4 = 4$
Commutative property	$4 \times 5 = 5 \times 4$
Associative property	$4 \times (5 \times 6) = (4 \times 5) \times 6$

When you divide, keep these patterns in mind.

What you write, using numbers	What you remember, using variables
$0 \div 4 = 0$	$0 \div n = 0$
$4 \div 1 = 4$	$n \div 1 = n$
$4 \div 4 = 1$	$n \div n = 1$

Practice

Patterns Copy and complete. Write >, <, or =.

1. $n \div 3 = 0$ **a.** $n \bullet 3$ **b.** $n \bullet 0$

2. $89{,}501 \times 1 = n$ **a.** $n \bullet 89{,}501$ **b.** $n \bullet 1$

3. $2{,}387 \div 1 = n$ **a.** $n \bullet 2{,}387$ **b.** $n \bullet 1$

4. $46 \times 7 = n$ **a.** $n \bullet 46$ **b.** $n \bullet 7$

5. $147 \div 4 = 36 \text{ R } n$ **a.** $n \bullet 4$ **b.** $n \bullet 147$

6. $48 \div 2 = n$ **a.** $n \bullet 48$ **b.** $n \bullet 2$

7. $35 \times n = 0$ **a.** $n \bullet 0$ **b.** $n \bullet 35$

Math Tip
You cannot divide by zero.

Write whether each equation is true or false. Explain how you know.

8. $8 \times 33 = 33 \times 8$ 9. $33 \div 8 = 8 \div 33$ 10. $1 \times 914 = 914$ 11. $914 \times 1 = 1$

12. $3{,}208 \times 0 = 0$ 13. $0 \times 3{,}208 = 0$ 14. $0 \div 3208 = 3{,}208$ 15. $3{,}208 \div 3{,}208 = 1$

16. $48 \div 1 = 1 \div 48$ 17. $16 \div 16 = 1$ 18. $32 \times 0 = 0$ 19. $0 \times 16 = 412 \times 0$

20. John said he divided 8 into a number and got zero. What is the number? Explain how you know.

21. **Journal** Write examples of three number rules that help you find an answer in multiplication or division.

Dividing Money

Learn

Ben was part of a team that planned
the national Partners for the Planet
Youth Summit in Snowbird, Utah.
He was in charge of the exhibits and
afternoon refreshments at the summit.

Ben is from
South Jordan, Utah.

Example 1

Ben had $75.45 to spend on refreshments for the three-day summit.
How much money could he spend if he spent an equal amount each day?

Divide $75.45 by 3.

Step 1	Step 2	Step 3
Estimate. **Think:**	Divide the tens.	Bring down the ones.
75.45 ÷ 3 is close to 75 ÷ 3. 75 ÷ 3 = 25	The digit in the tens place is 2.	Divide.
There are two digits before the decimal point. Place the decimal point. Start with the tens.	$2 . 3)$75.45 −6 1 1 < 3	$25. 3)$75.45 −6 15 −15 0 0 < 3

Step 4	Step 5	
Bring down the tenths. Divide.	Bring down the hundredths. Divide.	Check.
$25.1 3)$75.45 −6 15 −15 04 −3 1 1 < 3	$25.15 3)$75.45 −6 15 −15 04 −3 15 −15 0 0 < 3	$25.15 ← quotient × 3 ← divisor $75.45 ← dividend

Ben could spend $25.15 each day.

Remember
To separate dollars from cents in the quotient, place the decimal point directly above where it is in the dividend.

Example 2

A press kit is a packet of information with facts about a group or special event.

How much did each of six students have to contribute to help pay for the copies?

$6.42 ÷ 6 = n$

$$
\begin{array}{r}
\$1.07 \\
6)\overline{\$6.42} \\
-6 \\
\hline
04 \\
-0 \\
\hline
42 \\
-42 \\
\hline
0
\end{array}
$$

Each student contributed $1.07.

Example 3

You can use a calculator to divide money.

The mailing cost of the kits was $22.01.

Use a calculator to find out how much each of the six students spent on postage.

Round your answer to the nearest cent.

[2] [2] [.] [0] [1] [÷] [6] [=]

3.6683333

The answer is between $3.66 and $3.67.

The **8** shows that it is closer to $3.67.

Each student spent $3.67 on postage.

Talk About It

1. How do you decide where to place the decimal point?

2. Why is it important to place the decimal point correctly when dividing money?

Check

1. $7)\overline{\$61.29}$
   a. Estimate the answer.
   c. Divide $61.29 by 7.
   b. Will the quotient be greater or less than your estimate? Explain.
   d. Round your answer to the nearest cent.

Find each quotient.

2. $5)\overline{\$85.00}$ 3. $4)\overline{\$37.44}$ 4. $6)\overline{\$12.06}$ 5. $7)\overline{\$88.20}$

6. $3)\overline{\$9.57}$ 7. $2)\overline{\$96.40}$ 8. $8)\overline{\$180.80}$ 9. $5)\overline{\$65.90}$

10. $4)\overline{\$56.04}$ 11. $5)\overline{\$172.10}$ 12. $9)\overline{\$16.83}$ 13. $8)\overline{\$7.52}$

14. $6)\overline{\$89.58}$ 15. $3)\overline{\$59.61}$ 16. $7)\overline{\$138.95}$ 17. $4)\overline{\$25.00}$

Use a calculator to divide. Round to the nearest cent.

18. $3)\overline{\$28.90}$ 19. $8)\overline{\$166.66}$ 20. $4)\overline{\$55.18}$ 21. $7)\overline{\$39.12}$

22. $9)\overline{\$100.15}$ 23. $4)\overline{\$12.99}$ 24. $8)\overline{\$48.20}$ 25. $6)\overline{\$179.97}$

26. **Reasoning** For $4.56 ÷ 6, will the quotient be more or less than $1? Explain how you know.

Skills and Reasoning

Find each quotient. Multiply to check.

27. 5)$120.00   **28.** 3)$27.00   **29.** 7)$14.00   **30.** 9)$162.00   **31.** 3)$63

32. 3)$3.03   **33.** 5)$16.85   **34.** 4)$24.16   **35.** 3)$99.99   **36.** 2)$55.12

37. 5)$101.50   **38.** 6)$374.10   **39.** 8)$410.48   **40.** 4)$625.16   **41.** 3)$255.27

42. 2)$51.78   **43.** 8)$100.56   **44.** 4)$99.00   **45.** 5)$344.30   **46.** 6)$511.68

Use a calculator to divide. Round to the nearest cent.

47. $4.73 ÷ 4   **48.** $13.94 ÷ 5   **49.** $33.05 ÷ 2   **50.** $60.66 ÷ 8   **51.** $87.93 ÷ 6

52. 3)$662.15   **53.** 7)$2,018.50   **54.** 6)$960.17   **55.** 9)$567.22   **56.** 5)$999.99

57. For $35.21 ÷ 2, $6.35 ÷ 6, and $307.55 ÷ 7, are any of the quotients less than a dollar? How can you tell?

Problem Solving and Applications

58. **Patterns** Use patterns to find each missing number.

  a. If $6.50 ÷ 5 = $1.30, then $65.00 ÷ 5 = n.

  b. If $27.16 ÷ 4 = $6.79, then $271.60 ÷ 4 = n.

  c. If $47.58 ÷ 2 = $23.79, then n ÷ 2 = $237.90.

  d. If $99.36 ÷ 3 = $33.12, then n ÷ 3 = $331.20.

  e. If $17.71 ÷ 7 = $2.53, then n ÷ 7 = $25.30.

  f. Explain the patterns that helped you find the missing numbers for **a.–e.**

Using Data Use the Data File on page 165 for **59–61.**

59. **Science** How many more months does it take plastic to decompose than paper? (Hint: Find the number of months in 80 years first.)

60. How many times longer than paper bags does it take plastic bags to decompose?

61. How much would 125 plastic bags cost? 125 paper bags?

62. **History** Plastic was first developed when a manufacturer in New England offered $10,000 to anyone who could find a cheap substitute for ivory. In 1869 John Wesley Hyatt, from Albany, New York, won the prize by inventing a plastic product called celluloid. How long ago did Hyatt develop the first celluloid?

These objects are some of the first products that were made with celluloid.

Problem Solving and LITERATURE

Science fiction author Isaac Asimov's short story "A Feeling of Power" deals with a future society in which people cannot calculate. Only calculators and computers can calculate. In the story, Aub, the technician, uses paper and pencil to solve some problems like these, to the amazement of the leaders of the society.

Divide or multiply.

63. 17×23 **64.** $27 \div 8$

65. $\$4.60 \div 5$ **66.** $\$3.80 \div 4$

67. Why do you think "A Feeling of Power" is a good title for this story?

Isaac Asimov, a Russian-born American biochemist and writer, published his 300th book in 1984.

Mixed Review and Test Prep

STAY SHARP!

Find each sum or difference.

68.	**69.**	**70.**	**71.**	**72.**
$2.67 + 5.41	$5.01 + 9.99	$188.50 − 45.25	$329.83 + 6.29	$955.12 − 67.50

73.	**74.**	**75.**	**76.**	**77.**
$18.29 + 6.25	$208.25 − 82.99	$67.19 + 78.82	$42.90 − 9.65	$119.60 − 22.75

Find each product or quotient.

78. 67×0.54 **79.** $12.8 \div 4$ **80.** $56.34 \div 6$ **81.** 0.2×0.4 **82.** 1.56×100

83. 29×1.8 **84.** $18.4 \div 8$ **85.** 1.2×0.89 **86.** $66.24 \div 9$ **87.** 0.82×13

88. Money Four zebra finches sell for $23.96. How much does each bird cost?

89. Science The long jaw of the American alligator is filled with about 80 teeth. It keeps its teeth sharp by losing teeth that wear down. In 30 to 35 years, an alligator can go through up to 3,000 teeth! About how many times does an alligator replace each set of 80 teeth during that time?

Ⓐ about 100 times   Ⓑ about 38 times

Ⓒ about 400 times   Ⓓ about 300 times

American alligator (*Alligator mississipiensis*)

Dizviding Decimals

You Will Learn

how to divide
decimals to
thousandths

Learn

Greta knows how to turn garbage into dirt!
She puts table scraps in her worm bin.
Wiggly red worms eat the garbage and make
a rich, dark soil that is great for gardens.

Greta from Middleville,
New York, and her dad
built an indoor worm bin
that looks like a window seat.

Example 1

Suppose Greta wants to divide 9.2 pounds of garbage equally among
the 4 sections of the worm bin.

Find $9.2 \div 4$. Estimate:
$$4\overline{)8} = 2$$

Step 1

Divide the ones.

$$\begin{array}{r} 2 \\ 4\overline{)9.2} \\ -8 \\ \hline 1 \end{array}$$

Step 2

Place the decimal point. Divide the tenths.

$$\begin{array}{r} 2.3 \\ 4\overline{)9.2} \\ -8 \\ \hline 12 \\ -12 \\ \hline 0 \end{array}$$

Multiply to check.
2.3 ← quotient
$\times$ 4 ← divisor
9.2 ← dividend

$9.2 \div 4 = 2.3$ Greta should put 2.3 pounds of garbage in each section.

Other Examples

A. Find $12.96 \div 3$.

$$\begin{array}{r} 4.32 \\ 3\overline{)12.96} \\ -12 \\ \hline 09 \\ -9 \\ \hline 06 \\ -06 \\ \hline 0 \end{array}$$

Check:
$$\begin{array}{r} 4.32 \\ \times\ 3 \\ \hline 12.96 \end{array}$$

B. Find $3.055 \div 5$.

$$\begin{array}{r} 0.611 \\ 5\overline{)3.055} \\ -30 \\ \hline 05 \\ -5 \\ \hline 05 \\ -5 \\ \hline 0 \end{array}$$

Check:
$$\begin{array}{r} 0.611 \\ \times\ 5 \\ \hline 3.055 \end{array}$$

Math Tip

Be sure to place the
decimal point
directly over the
decimal point in the
dividend.

Talk About It

To divide 21.671 by 4, how would you check to make sure that the
decimal point in the quotient is in the right place?

Check

Find each quotient.

1. $2\overline{)2.248}$ 2. $9\overline{)8.136}$ 3. $4\overline{)17.224}$ 4. $8\overline{)24.992}$ 5. $6\overline{)31.206}$

6. **Reasoning** How can you use estimates to check that $8.925 \div 5 = 1.785$ is reasonable?

Practice

Skills and Reasoning

Find each quotient.

7. $5\overline{)24.305}$ 8. $6\overline{)29.346}$ 9. $7\overline{)14.119}$ 10. $4\overline{)45.204}$ 11. $5\overline{)13.320}$

12. $9\overline{)19.017}$ 13. $8\overline{)25.776}$ 14. $5\overline{)6.120}$ 15. $6\overline{)18.702}$ 16. $3\overline{)24.162}$

17. $3\overline{)24.729}$ 18. $2\overline{)16.422}$ 19. $7\overline{)17.948}$ 20. $4\overline{)21.684}$ 21. $8\overline{)8.392}$

 Geometry Find the length of the side of each square.

22.  perimeter = 8.252 cm   23. perimeter = 15.244 cm   24. perimeter = 26.352 m   25.  perimeter = 41.264 m

26. Is $75.234 \div 8 = 24.406$ a reasonable answer? Explain why or why not.

Problem Solving and Applications

 27. **Geometry** A square fence has a perimeter of 10.248 m. How long is each side?

28. **Money** Greta's uncle buys "red wiggler" worms for the compost box. They cost $25.14 per pound. How much do 3 lb of worms cost?

29. **Science** It takes 2 kg of worms to eat a kilogram of garbage. If Greta put 5.257 kg of garbage in the compost box, how many kg of worms will be needed? Round your answer to the nearest whole number.

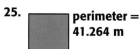

Red worms turn food scraps into compost.

Mixed Review and Test Prep

Find each answer.

30. $\$123.25 \times 7$ 31. $\$38.97 + \$4.89 + \$3.12$ 32. $36,007 - 4,289$

Estimation Estimate each product.

33. 32×5 34. 63×4 35. 99×7 36. 233×2

 37. **Algebra Readiness** It takes 2 kg of worms to eat 1 kg of garbage. Which rule shows the relationship of kg of worms to kg of garbage?

Ⓐ $n + 2$ Ⓑ $n - 2$ Ⓒ $2 \times n$ Ⓓ $n \div 2$ Ⓔ not here

Factors and Divisibility

You Will Learn
how to find the
factors of a number

Vocabulary
factor
any number that
divides another
number with a
remainder of 0

divisible
can be divided by
another number
without leaving a
remainder

Learn • • • • • • • • • • • • • •

What kind of a farm raises crops with
wings? A butterfly farm! On this kind of
farm, caterpillars turn into butterflies. Jars
of 3 or 6 caterpillars can be ordered to make
a farm. If 12 students each want to raise his
or her own butterfly, how many jars should
they order?

Laura, from Glenview, Illinois, studies
and raises Monarch butterflies.

Look for **factor** pairs of 12 that have 3 or 6 as a member of the pair.

1   2   3   4   6   12

The factors 3 and 4 tell you that the students can order 4 jars of
3 caterpillars. The factors 6 and 2 tell you that the students can order
2 jars of 6 caterpillars.

Math Tip
Divisibility rules give
ways to
tell when
one
number
is divisible
by
another.

Divisibility rules help you find the factors of a number.

Divisibility Rules	
Number	**Divisible by**
is even	2
ends in 5 or 0	5
ends in 0	10
has digits whose sum is divisible by 3	3
is divisible by 2 and 3	6

Example

Is 6 a factor of 210?
210 is an even number, so it is divisible by 2.
The digits add up to 3, so it is also divisible by 3.
Therefore, it must also be divisible by 6.
6 is a factor of 210.

How can you find the factors of 96?

Check

Find the factors for each number.

1. 14   **2.** 35   **3.** 40   **4.** 24   **5.** 66

6. Reasoning What two numbers are always factors of a number?

Practice

Skills and Reasoning

Find the factors for each number.

7. 15   **8.** 18   **9.** 26   **10.** 16   **11.** 50   **12.** 19   **13.** 56

14. 39   **15.** 42   **16.** 80   **17.** 64   **18.** 27   **19.** 72   **20.** 13

21. 36   **22.** 25   **23.** 63   **24.** 21   **25.** 12   **26.** 22   **27.** 20

28. What are the factors of 75?   **29.** Is 6 a factor of 246? Explain how you know.

Problem Solving and Applications

30. Luis has a butterfly farm at his school in Costa Rica. Luis and his class sell chrysalises to animal parks. Use factors to figure out how many containers Luis's class will need to send 600 chrysalises. (A container holds 10 or 12 chrysalises.)

31. Time An animal park orders butterflies from many butterfly farms for one of its exhibits. The park replaces its 3,000 butterflies every two weeks. About how many butterflies does it order in one month?

32. Science In warm regions, it takes 4 weeks for a caterpillar to change into a butterfly. In colder climates, this change can take two years. How many times as long does it take a caterpillar to change into a butterfly in colder climates than in warmer climates?

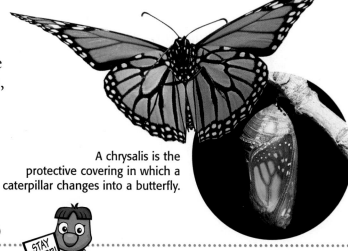

A chrysalis is the protective covering in which a caterpillar changes into a butterfly.

Mixed Review and Test Prep

Find each quotient.

33. $3\overline{)25.251}$ **34.** $51.660 \div 5$ **35.** $7\overline{)44.464}$ **36.** $63.936 \div 3$ **37.** $4\overline{)301.048}$

38. $89.552 \div 8$ **39.** $62.236 \div 2$ **40.** $533.972 \div 5$ **41.** $288.160 \div 4$ **42.** $32.088 \div 8$

43. Which digit is in the hundredths place of 327.056?

    Ⓐ 6   Ⓑ 3   Ⓒ 0   Ⓓ 5

Exploring Prime and Composite Numbers

Explore • • • • • • • • • • • • •

Eratosthenes (*ehr uh TAHS thuh neez*) was a mathematician from Cyrene (now known as Libya) who lived about 2,200 years ago. He studied **prime numbers**. The number 3 is an example of a prime number. It has only two factors, 1 and 3.

Composite numbers have more than two factors. An example of a composite number is 8. Its factors are 1, 2, 4, and 8.

Cyrene was the capital of ancient Cyrenaica.

1×8 • • • • • • • • 2×4 • • • • (two rows)

You tell whether a number is prime by testing possible factors. There are no other factors for 7 besides 7 and 1. So, 7 is a prime number.

1×7 • • • • • • •

Eratosthenes' Sieve is a process that "strains" out composite numbers and leaves prime numbers behind. Use it to find the prime numbers between 1 and 100.

Work Together

1. Use a hundred chart. Follow the directions to cross out composite numbers and circle prime numbers.

   1 2 3 4 5 6 7 8 9 10 11 12 13 14 15 16 17 18 19 20 21 22

   a. Cross out 1. It has only 1 factor.

   b. Circle 2, the least prime number. Cross out all numbers divisible by 2.

   c. Repeat this step with 3, the next prime number.

2. Continue this process until you reach 100.

3. List all of the circled numbers. There should be 25.

Talk About It

What pattern can you see in the list of prime numbers?

Connect

A **prime** number has exactly two different factors, itself and 1.

13 is a prime number. Its factors are 1 and 13. It has only one rectangular array.

1×13 • • • • • • • • • • • • •

A **composite** number has more than two factors.

12 is a composite number. It has more than 1 rectangular array.

Math Tip
You can write 12 as
$3 \times 2 \times 2$ or 3×2^2.

1×12

• • • • • • • • • • • •

2×6

• • • • • •
• • • • • •

3×4

• • • •
• • • •
• • • •

A factor tree shows 12 written as the product of prime factors.

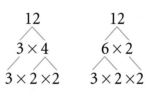

$$12 = 3 \times 2 \times 2$$

Practice

Write whether each number is prime or composite.

1. 91   **2.** 65   **3.** 37   **4.** 89   **5.** 42

6. 27   **7.** 11   **8.** 24   **9.** 39   **10.** 71

Use factor trees to find the prime factors of each number.

11. 15   **12.** 27   **13.** 30   **14.** 48   **15.** 75

16. 45   **17.** 63   **18.** 16   **19.** 56   **20.** 36

x **Algebra Readiness** Look for patterns. Write the missing numbers.

21. 1, ▓, 4, ▓, 16   **22.** 1, 2, ▓, ▓, 16, 32   **23.** 1, ▓, 25   **24.** 1, 2, 11, 22, 111, ▓

25. 3, 5, 15, 5, 75, 5, ▓   **26.** ▓, 2, 3, ▓, 6, ▓, 12, 16, 24, 36, ▓, 72, 144

27. Can a whole number ending in zero be prime? Explain.

28. Logic Explain why 2 is the only even prime number.

29. Critical Thinking Do you think there are more prime numbers between 100 and 200 or between 200 and 300? Why?

30. Journal Explain the steps you would use to find all the prime numbers between 100 and 120.

"Don't Block Me In Game"

Players
4 players

Materials
- gameboard like the one shown
- number cube
- 50 number cards: 17 with a 2-digit number, 17 with a 3-digit number, 16 with a 3-digit amount of money
- sets of 15 colored markers, a different color for each player
- game piece for each player

Object
The object of the game is to place the most markers on the board while preventing other players from placing their markers.

How to Play

1 Mix the number cards and place them face down in the center of the game board.

2 Players toss a number cube to see who goes first. The player with the greatest number showing begins play. Each player begins play at a different corner of the board and proceeds clockwise around the board.

3 The player tosses the number cube and moves his or her game piece that number of squares. The player then draws a number card and reads the number. The player should divide the number on the card by the number on the square on which he or she has landed.

4 If the player divides correctly, he or she may place a marker on any unoccupied square on the board. If the quotient has a prime number remainder, the player can place another marker.

5 If a player lands on a square where there is a marker, he or she loses a turn.

6 Play continues until one player uses all his or her markers, or until there are no more plays possible. The player with the most markers on the board wins.

Talk About It

1. How did you decide where to place your markers?

2. Did your ideas about placing the markers change during the game? How?

More Ways to Play

■ If a quotient is a 3-digit number, the player gets to place an additional marker. An additional marker is still given for prime number remainders.

■ Use multiplication instead of division. If the last digit of the product is prime, the player gets to place an additional marker.

Reasoning

1. Where do you think you should start placing markers to best block the other players? Why?

2. Where do you think you should start placing markers to allow yourself the best chance of not landing on one of your own markers? Why?

Problem Solving

Analyze Strategies: **Work Backward**

You Will Learn
how to solve problems by working backward from an answer

Learn

Suppose a friend has been playing a board game in which each player begins with a certain number of points. She tells you that she doubled her points on her first turn, she lost 22 points on her second turn, she made 15 points on her third turn, and she ended the game with 33 points. Can you tell how many points she had when she started?

Work Together

▶ **Understand**
What do you know?

What are you asked to find?

▶ **Plan**
How will you find the answer?

Start with 33 points and work backward.

Each step backward will help undo the problem.

▶ **Solve**
Remember, to undo a step, do the opposite of it. Begin with ending points. Undo each step to solve the problem.

Write the answer.

Ending Point: 33

(undo + 15) $33 - 15 = 18$
(undo − 22) $18 + 22 = 40$
(undo ×2) $40 \div 2 = 20$

Your friend had 20 points when she began.

▶ **Look Back**
How can you check your answer?

Another Example

After a heavy snowstorm, Steven took his shovel and went looking for work. After his first job, he had twice the amount of money he had when he left home. After his second job, he doubled his money again. When he got home, he had $24. How much money did he have when he left to look for work?

n is the amount of money he had when he left.

$$n \rightarrow 2 \times n \rightarrow 2 \times 2 \times n \rightarrow \$24$$

Work from the back of the problem to the front.

What You Read	What You Do
a. Steven had $24 when he got home.	Write $24 to begin.
b. He doubled his money during the second job.	$24 ÷ 2 = $12 (undo doubling)
c. He doubled his money during the first job.	$12 ÷ 2 = $6 (undo doubling)

Steven had $6 when he left the house.

Talk About It

1. How do you know when to start solving the problem from the end?

2. How can you keep track of the actions in a problem when you work backward?

Check

Problem Solving
Understand
Plan
Solve
Look Back

1. The national bestseller *Super Marino* was selling fast. After only 3 hours, half of the store's copies were gone. During the next hour, another 12 books were sold. From then until the time the store closed, half of the remaining copies were bought. At closing, there were only 15 copies left.

   a. How many books were in the store at closing?

   b. What operation undoes dividing a number of books by two?

   c. What operation undoes subtracting 12 books?

   d. How many copies of the book were in the store when it opened that day?

2. **Time** Maria began her homework early enough to finish by 8:00 P.M., knowing that dinner would take 1 hour. The picture shows how long she must work on each subject. At what time did Maria begin her assignments?

Problem Solving Strategies

- Use Objects/Act It Out
- Draw a Picture
- Look for a Pattern
- Guess and Check
- Use Logical Reasoning
- Make an Organized List
- Make a Table
- Solve a Simpler Problem
- Work Backward

Choose a Tool

Apply the Strategy

Work backward to solve each problem.

3. Tim kept track of his weekly expenses. At the end of a week, he knew he had $1.75 of his allowance left. He had bought 3 packs of baseball cards for $0.95 each, one pack of basketball cards for $1.50, and one drink each day after school for $0.85 each. How much did Tim have at the beginning of the week?

4. A full trash can weighs 21 lb. Kevin collected trash while cleaning his yard. He first put in 8 lb, then noticed one of his favorite books in the can! He rescued the book, which weighed 3 lb. He filled the can up with another 12 lb of trash. How much does the empty can weigh?

5. The tag shows that the price has been lowered twice: What was the original price?

$\frac{1}{2}$ OFF
$\frac{1}{2}$ OFF
$20.00

Choose a Strategy

Use any strategy to solve each problem.

6. Maria, Kevin, and Tina went to buy videos. They bought a western, a cartoon, and a mystery. Maria did not buy a mystery. Kevin bought a western. What kind of video did Tina buy?

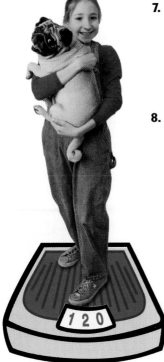

7. Raymond and his two sisters each contributed the same amount of money to buy a paint set for their mother. They still needed to ask their father for $14. If they paid $36.50 for the gift, how much did Raymond and each of his sisters contribute toward the gift?

8. Laurel needs to give medicine to her dog. In order to give the correct amount of medicine, she must weigh the dog. She gets on the scale holding the dog. If Laurel weighs 50 lb more than the dog, how much do they each weigh? Tell what strategy you used.

Problem Solving and SCIENCE

You may be wearing plastic soda bottles right now! Some polyester sweaters are made from recycled plastic bottles. The plastic is first turned into fiber and then into sweaters.

This pullover was made from plastic bottles.

Facts about Recycled Plastic
a. It takes 25 one-liter bottles to make a sweater.
b. One company expected to recycle about 250,000,000 bottles in 1996.
c. One estimate is that enough energy can be saved by using these bottles to power a large city for a year.

Write which fact above you need to answer **9–12.** Then answer each question.

9. If you have 38 bottles to recycle, how many more do you need for 3 sweaters?

10. A recycling company collects bottles in large bags. Each bag can hold 120 bottles. How many sweaters can be made from the bottles in a full bag?

11. If a collection bag contains 87 bottles, how many would be left after all are used for sweaters?

12. At the end of 1996, the recycling company found that it had recycled 20,000,000 more bottles than expected. What was the company's actual number of recycled bottles for 1996?

13. Journal Make up a story about shopping in which you know the amount you end up with and have to find the beginning amount. Then write a step-by-step diagram to fit the story.

Mixed Review and Test Prep

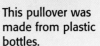

Find each difference.

14.	**15.**	**16.**	**17.**	**18.**
45	61	55	102	133
− 19	− 34	− 29	− 86	− 57

19. 81 − 39   **20.** 48 − 21   **21.** 56 − 27   **22.** 83 − 57   **23.** 75 − 48

24. In a pictograph, each picture of a child stands for 10 children. How many children do $3\frac{1}{2}$ pictures stand for?

Ⓐ 3   Ⓑ 350   Ⓒ 35   Ⓓ $3\frac{1}{2}$ Ⓔ not here

SECTION C
Review and Practice

Vocabulary Match each with its meaning.

1. factor

    a. whole number with exactly two different factors

2. prime number

    b. any number that divides another number with a remainder of 0.

3. composite number

    c. whole number greater than 1 that is not prime

(Lesson 10) Copy and complete.

4. $n \div 8 = 0$ 5. $83,105 \times n = 83,105$ 6. $65 \div n = 65$ 7. $285 \div n = 1$

(Lesson 11) Find each quotient.

8. $4\overline{)\$180.00}$ 9. $8\overline{)\$24.08}$ 10. $6\overline{)\$18.66}$ 11. $\$347.13 \div 7$ 12. $\$635.20 \div 5$

13. **Money** Rajiv earns $31.50 for 6 hours of work. How much does he earn per hour?

(Lesson 12) Find each quotient.

14. $2\overline{)2.528}$ 15. $4\overline{)10.452}$ 16. $6\overline{)14.364}$ 17. $7\overline{)25.123}$ 18. $3\overline{)3.345}$

19. **Measurement** A square carpet has a perimeter of 38.248 ft. How long is each side?

(Lesson 13) Find all the factors for each number.

20. 35   21. 22   22. 11   23. 36   24. 88

25. Name six ways to get a product of 60 using two whole number factors.

(Lesson 14) Write whether each number is prime or composite.

26. 110   27. 11   28. 207   29. 93   30. 19

Use factor trees to find the prime factors of each number.

31. 16   32. 33   33. 125   34. 24   35. 38

(Lesson 15) Work backward to solve.

36. Amanda decided to spend some of the money she had earned from babysitting. She bought 2 used books for $0.95 each and 2 for $1.25 each. She spent $5.31 on supplies for her science project and treated herself to a slice of pizza and a drink for $2.50 total. She had $2.84 left. How much did Amanda have when she began?

37. **Journal** Explain why 7 is prime and why 8 is composite.

Skills Checklist

In this section, you have:

- ☑ Explored Products and Quotients
- ☑ Divided Money
- ☑ Divided Decimals
- ☑ Learned About Factors and Divisibility
- ☑ Explored Prime and Composite Numbers
- ☑ Solved Problems by Working Backward

YOUR CHOICE

Choose at least one. Use what you have learned in this chapter.

① Time to Divide

Pick out photos or articles from newspapers or magazines. Write division problems with information from the articles. Post them on the bulletin board for your classmates to solve.

② Shopping for Sense

At Home
Accompany a family member or friend to a grocery or shopping center. Compare the prices on goods sold as multiples, such as VCR tapes, snack packs, or school supplies. Use division to find out the cost of each individual item if sold separately. Compare that price to the price of an individual item.

③ Eco-Math

Pick a topic of your choice to access on **www.mathsurf.com/5/ch4**. Choose an ecology topic that will give you information expressed as a decimal or dollar amount. Write and solve a division problem based on your data. Check.

④ Dividing Your Time

Keep a diary of what you do with your time in school every day for one week. Record how much time you spend on each of the activities in the table. Are there any ways you could make better use of your time? Develop a schedule that divides your school day into blocks of time and plan what you want to get done each day.

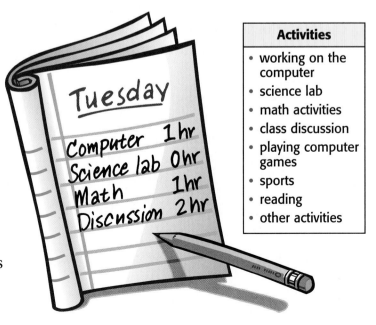

Activities
• working on the computer
• science lab
• math activities
• class discussion
• playing computer games
• sports
• reading
• other activities

CHAPTER 4
Review/Test

Vocabulary Match each with its example or meaning.

1. quotient   **a.** the average of a set of numbers

2. divisor   **b.** the number 6 in $42 \div 6 = 7$

3. dividend   **c.** the number 42 in $42 \div 6 = 7$

4. mean   **d.** whole number with exactly two different factors

5. prime number   **e.** the number 7 in $42 \div 6 = 7$

(Lessons 1, 3, 5, 7, and 8) Divide.

6. $2\overline{)72}$ 7. $5\overline{)85}$ 8. $6\overline{)728}$ 9. $3\overline{)652}$ 10. $4\overline{)135}$

11. $7\overline{)394}$ 12. $8\overline{)2,407}$ 13. $6\overline{)658}$ 14. $7\overline{)625}$ 15. $8\overline{)1,632}$

(Lessons 11 and 12) Divide.

16. $3\overline{)\$45.69}$ 17. $4\overline{)\$5.08}$ 18. $8\overline{)\$496.24}$ 19. $9\overline{)\$18.27}$ 20. $3\overline{)30.069}$

21. $176.904 \div 8$ 22. $50.697 \div 9$ 23. $4.624 \div 4$ 24. $17.28 \div 4$ 25. $65.808 \div 8$

(Lesson 13) List all the factors of each number.

26. 33   27. 100   28. 13   29. 45

(Lessons 2, 4, 9, 10, and 14) Solve.

30. The girls' volleyball team earned $86 washing cars. They want to give an equal amount of money to 5 different charities. How much money will each charity receive? Will there be any money left?

31. Sam has kept a record of his paychecks for the past 6 months. He has earned $16.25, $23.52, $18.35, $16.25, $25, and $14.63. What is the mean of these paychecks?

32. **Money** Jessy has two jobs. On Saturday she works at an ice-cream parlor for 9 hr and earns $6 per hr. On Sunday she works at the grocery store for 6 hr and earns $9 per hr. Which job earns her more money per day? Explain.

33. Betsy needs $18 to buy her class yearbook. She figures she would have to work for 2 hr if she got paid $9 per hr to earn the $18. Name two other ways she could work to earn $18.

Performance Assessment

Write ten division problems using these ten numbers as dividends.
Your problems must meet the following requirements:

Use These Dividends

> ### Rules for Dividing
>
> **a.** The divisor must be a digit from 2 to 9.
>
> **b.** Two problems must have no remainder.
>
> **c.** Two problems must have a remainder less than 4.
>
> **d.** One problem must have a 0 in the tenths place in the quotient.
>
> **e.** Three problems must have three digits in the quotient.
>
> **f.** Two problems must have quotients less than the divisor.

2,360
54,724
635
892
781
2.01
3.258
45.65
1.156
6.003

1. **Decision Making** Decide how you are going to approach the task of writing division problems that fit the requirements. Reread each rule to make sure you understand the task.

2. **Recording** Write the problems and solve them. Check that the problem meets the specific requirements. Next to the problem, write which of the above requirements is met (**a–f**).

3. **Explain Your Thinking** Pick two of your examples and explain how you decided on their divisors. Discuss the strategies you used to create problems that meet the requirements.

4. **Critical Thinking** Could some of your problems fulfill more than one of the requirements in **b–f**? Could one problem meet all of **a–f**?

Quotient
?
Divisor ?)54,724

Math Magazine

The Daily Recycler

MAN TIED TO JUNK TIRE RECYCLING

Dennis LaShier of Greenfield, Massachusetts, has discovered a use for worn-out tires. He makes them into neckties.

The ties are called "Rubber-Necker Ties" and are made completely from old tires. They are available in several different styles: blackwall, whitewall, raised white letters, and custom letters.

GARBAGE DUMP EXPLODES!

A park in Virginia Beach, Virginia, has exploded into one of the most popular family outing spots around.

The park, Mount Trashmore, is built on top of garbage. The trash is covered by a layer of soil, grass, and trees.

NEW USES FOR OLD MONEY!

A company in Illinois is now recycling money! The company has introduced greenback pencils. Each pencil is made from an average of $7.33 of old, used, shredded United States currency. They even come in a variety of colored leads!

Try These!

1. Research an unusual way in which trash is being recycled. Look in a newspaper or a library for information. Find out how much recycled material goes into each product.

2. Make up four division problems from the information you have found. Trade problems and information with classmates, and solve them.

Test Prep Strategy: Follow Directions

- **Watch for words like *not*.**
- **Answer the question asked.**

Which of the following division problems does **not** have a zero in the tens place of its quotient?

Ⓐ 2)356   Ⓑ 3)328   Ⓒ 5)2,518   Ⓓ 9)3,682

Did you notice the word *not* in the directions? In Ⓑ, Ⓒ, and Ⓓ, your first division step has no remainder and the next digit is less than the divisor, so there is a 0 in the tens place. The answer is Ⓐ.

Write the letter of the correct answer. Choose any strategy.

1. Saul's 8 library books are 7 days overdue. The fine for overdue books is $0.05 per day for each book. How much does Saul owe?
   Ⓐ $0.35   Ⓑ $2.80   Ⓒ $0.40   Ⓓ $28.00

2. 32 boys and 40 girls sign up for swimming lessons. If 8 children are put into each class, how many classes will there need to be?
   Ⓐ 4   Ⓑ 5   Ⓒ 45   Ⓓ not here

3. Which of these numbers is **not** between 0.4 and 0.5?
   Ⓐ 0.4555   Ⓑ 0.468   Ⓒ 0.046   Ⓓ 0.499

4. Which of these numbers is **not** a prime number?
   Ⓐ 2   Ⓑ 7   Ⓒ 9   Ⓓ 11

5. Earl checked the prices of a box of 24 crayons at 5 stores. He recorded the prices as $0.99, $0.89, $1.59, $1.19, $0.89. What is the median price?
   Ⓐ $0.99   Ⓑ $1.11   Ⓒ $0.89   Ⓓ $0.70

6. Which has a quotient greater than 60?
   Ⓐ 8)415   Ⓑ 5)119   Ⓒ 9)299   Ⓓ 6)578

7. Find the standard form for 50,000,000 + 300,000 + 4,000 + 60 + 9.
   Ⓐ 50,304,069   Ⓑ 50,300,469   Ⓒ 50,304,690   Ⓓ 534,690

8. Find the mean for: 113.5, 108.21, 162.53, 99.07, 52.01, 79.74.
   Ⓐ 110.52   Ⓑ 99.07   Ⓒ 108.21   Ⓓ 102.51   Ⓔ 12.51

9. Which of these numbers is divisible by 6?
   Ⓐ 732   Ⓑ 568   Ⓒ 1,246   Ⓓ 580   Ⓔ not here

Test Prep Strategies

- Read Carefully
- Follow Directions
- Make Smart Choices
- Eliminate Choices
- Work Backward from an Answer

Chapter 5
2-Digit Divisors: Whole Numbers and Decimals

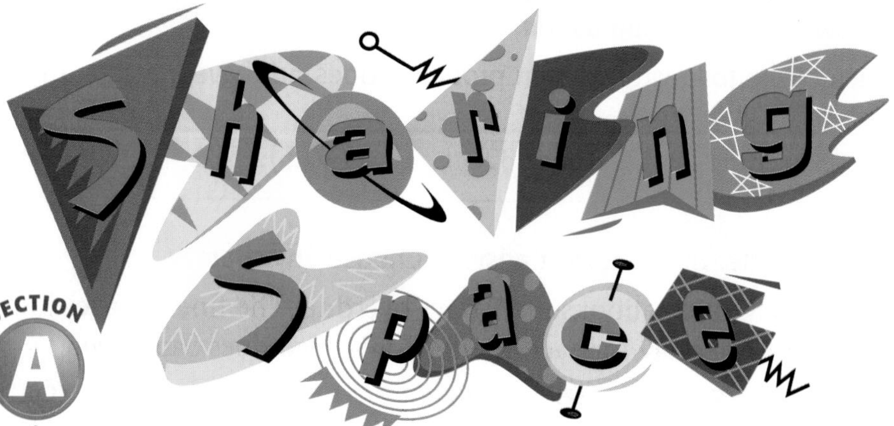

Sharing Space

SECTION A

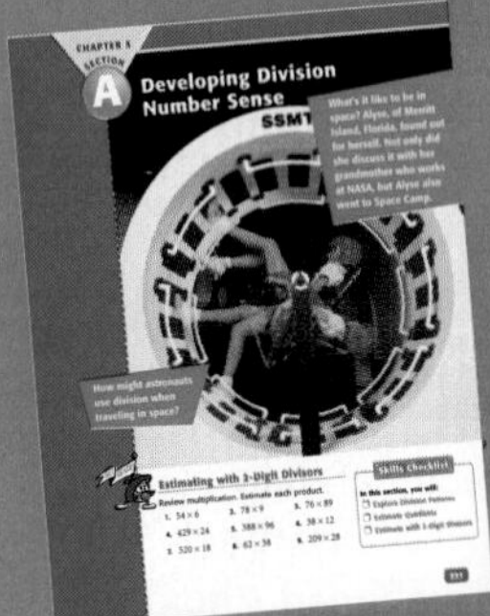

**Visiting NASA
Page 221**

Developing Division Number Sense

221

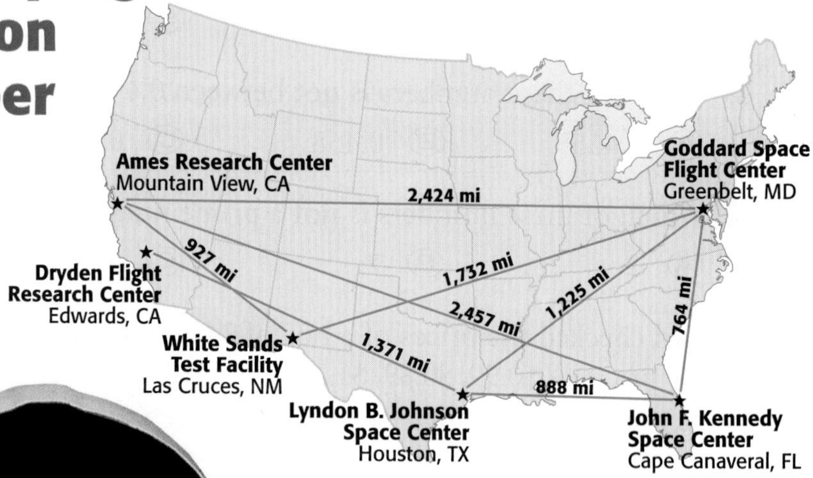

Ames Research Center
Mountain View, CA

Goddard Space Flight Center
Greenbelt, MD

Dryden Flight Research Center
Edwards, CA

White Sands Test Facility
Las Cruces, NM

Lyndon B. Johnson Space Center
Houston, TX

John F. Kennedy Space Center
Cape Canaveral, FL

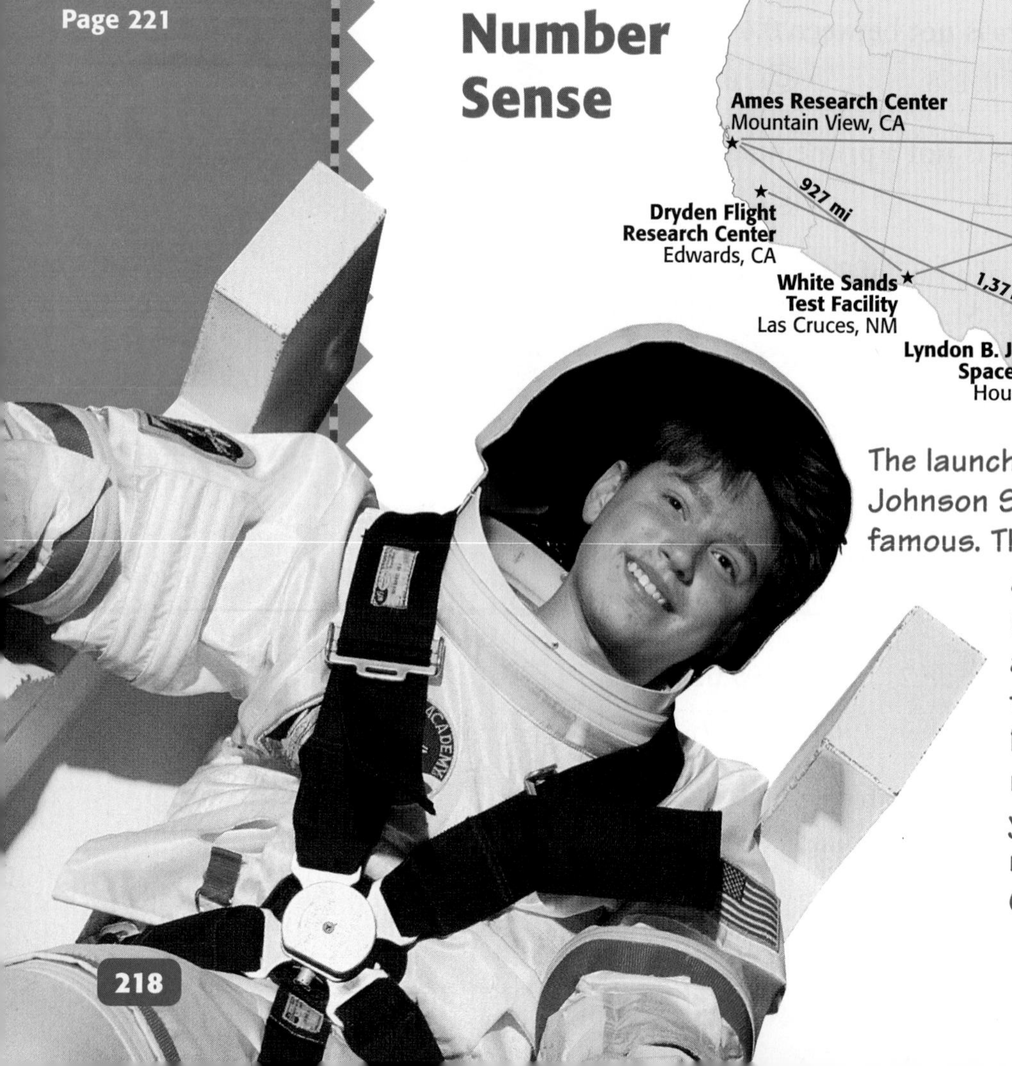

2,424 mi
927 mi
1,732 mi
2,457 mi
1,225 mi
764 mi
1,371 mi
888 mi

The launchings from Lyndon B. Johnson Space Center are world famous. The National Aeronautics and Space Administration (NASA) has space centers across the U. S. If you were traveling from Dryden Research Center, how many miles per day would you need to travel to reach Johnson Space Center in 3 days?

SECTION B

Dividing

**Moon Rocks
Page 229**

229

From the Wright Brothers' 1903 hop to orbiting in space, dreams of flying farther and faster have become reality. How many minutes was the first transatlantic flight?

Historic Flights			
Flight	**Date**	**Distance**	**Duration**
First successful powered flight	Dec. 17, 1903	120 ft	12 sec
First transatlantic airplane flight	May 27, 1919	4,717 mi	53 hr 58 min
First piloted space flight	April 12, 1961	25,395 mi	87 min
First American space flight orbiting the Earth	Feb. 20, 1962	81,000 mi	5 hr

Surfing the World Wide Web!

Soar over to **www.mathsurf.com/5/ch5** to find out more about these events. Which three inventions do you think contributed to the creation of our current flying machines?

SECTION C

Extending Division

249

**Shoot for the Stars
Page 249**

Most planets in our solar system are orbited by at least one moon.

How many small moons are in our solar system?

Moons in Our Solar System		
Planet	**Number of Large Moons**	**Number of Small Moons**
Earth	1	0
Mars	0	2
Jupiter	4	12
Saturn	1	17
Uranus	4	11
Neptune	1	7
Pluto	1	0

TEAM PROJECT
Home Away From Home

Living in outer space may seem like science fiction to most of us, but it is just another day at work for the astronauts of the Russian *Mir* orbiting space station. Design your own space station for a crew of 4 astronauts.

Make a Plan

- What will you need to consider in your design?
- How will you show all the parts of your space station?

Mir space station

Carry It Out

1. Decide on the shape of your space station. Choose a 3-digit number greater than 500 for the total area of the station.

2. In this space, you will create 9 areas for the astronauts to live and work. Follow these guidelines:

   a. Divide the station into two equal sections.
   b. In one, divide the section into three equal spaces for work, exercise, and storage.
   c. Divide the other section into two equal spaces.
   d. Divide one of these spaces by 2 to create a kitchen and a bathroom.
   e. Divide the other space into four equal sleeping quarters for the astronauts.

3. Determine the area of each space and label it.

Talk About It

- Review your plan. Is there anything missing from your design?

Present the Project

Plan a class presentation where all the teams' plans are displayed. Do you see anything that might not work well? Explain your reasoning.

A Developing Division Number Sense

SSMT

What's it like to be in space? Alyse, of Merritt Island, Florida, found out for herself. Not only did she discuss it with her grandmother who works at NASA, but Alyse also went to Space Camp.

How might astronauts use division when traveling in space?

Estimating with 2-Digit Divisors

Review multiplication. Estimate each product.

1. 54×6
2. 78×9
3. 76×89
4. 429×24
5. 388×96
6. 38×12
7. 520×18
8. 62×38
9. 209×28

Skills Checklist

In this section, you will:

☐ Explore Division Patterns

☐ Estimate Quotients

☐ Estimate with 2-Digit Divisors

Exploring Division Patterns

Problem Solving Connection
Look for Patterns

Materials
calculator

Vocabulary
quotient
the number (other than the remainder) that is the result of the division operation

Explore •

What you know about basic facts and multiples of 10 will help you divide mentally to find the **quotient**.

Work Together

1. Use a calculator or mental math to find each quotient. Look for patterns.

   a. 24 ÷ 6
   240 ÷ 6
   2,400 ÷ 6

   b. 40 ÷ 8
   400 ÷ 8
   4,000 ÷ 8

   c. 36 ÷ 9
   360 ÷ 9
   3,600 ÷ 9

   d. 7,200 ÷ 9
   7,200 ÷ 90
   7,200 ÷ 900

   e. 28,000 ÷ 7
   28,000 ÷ 70
   28,000 ÷ 700

   f. 1,800 ÷ 3
   1,800 ÷ 30
   1,800 ÷ 300

2. Use patterns to find each quotient mentally.

   a. 270 ÷ 30
   b. 4,200 ÷ 70
   c. 6,400 ÷ 800

   d. 1,400 ÷ 20
   e. 81,000 ÷ 90
   f. 20,000 ÷ 500

Remember
You can use multiples of 10 and basic facts to multiply greater numbers.

Talk About It

3. Describe the patterns you found.

4. How do basic facts help you divide mentally? Give an example.

Connect

You can use number sense and basic facts to divide with multiples of 10.

You see	$720 \div 90 =$	$4{,}500 \div 90 =$	$56{,}000 \div 700 =$
You think	$72 \div 9 = 8$	$45 \div 9 = 5$	$56 \div 7 = 8$
You write	$720 \div 90 = 8$	$4{,}500 \div 90 = 50$	$56{,}000 \div 700 = 80$

Practice

 Mental Math Find each quotient. Use mental math.

1. $3{,}000 \div 60$
2. $3{,}200 \div 40$
3. $4{,}500 \div 50$
4. $14{,}000 \div 70$

5. $4{,}500 \div 500$
6. $540 \div 90$
7. $7{,}200 \div 900$
8. $2{,}700 \div 9$

9. $4{,}800 \div 800$
10. $3{,}500 \div 70$
11. $4{,}000 \div 50$
12. $160 \div 20$

13. $28{,}000 \div 40$
14. $21{,}000 \div 700$
15. $40{,}000 \div 200$
16. $2{,}500 \div 500$

17. How is dividing 560 by 80 like dividing 5,600 by 800?

Algebra Readiness Solve for n.

18. $1{,}200 \div n = 20$
19. $24{,}000 \div n = 30$
20. $1{,}600 \div n = 40$

21. $n \div 400 = 80$
22. $n \div 70 = 700$
23. $n \div 30 = 900$

For each pair, write whether the quotient is the same or different. Explain.

24. $20 \div 4$ and $200 \div 40$
25. $180 \div 30$ and $18{,}000 \div 300$

26. $4{,}200 \div 60$ and $42{,}000 \div 600$
27. $5{,}600 \div 70$ and $56{,}000 \div 70$

28. How would you find $36{,}000 \div 900$?

29. **Health** A person burns about 60 calories per hour while resting in bed. The average American eats 3,600 calories in one day.

   a. How many hours would the average American have to stay in bed to burn 3,600 calories?

   b. Explain why a person resting in bed would not burn up 3,600 calories in a day.

30. **Using Data** Copy and complete.

Outdoor Seats for Space Launch	Sections	Seats per Section	Rows	Seats per Row
36,000	40		200	
48,000	60		300	

The shuttle *Atlantis* prepares for take off at the Kennedy Space Center, Florida.

 31. **Journal** Write directions for finding $32{,}000 \div 80$.

Lesson 5-1 **223**

Estimating Quotients: High and Low

Learn

The fastest circumnavigation of the earth, a distance of 23,069 mi, on a commercial flight took slightly more than 44 hr.

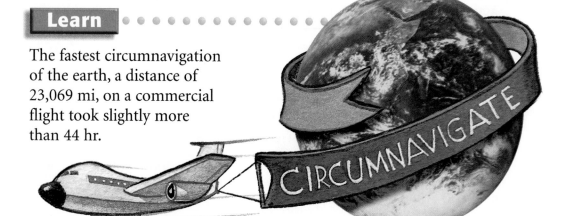

Example

Find a high and low estimate for the average speed in miles per hour.

To find the average speed in miles per hour you can divide the miles by the hours.

Estimate $23{,}069 \div 44$.

Use 20,000 to get a low estimate.

$20{,}000 \div 40$

Think: $20 \div 4 = 5$

So, $20{,}000 \div 40 = 500$.

500 mi/hr is a low estimate.

Use 24,000 to get a high estimate.

$24{,}000 \div 40$

Think: $24 \div 4 = 6$

So, $24{,}000 \div 40 = 600$.

600 mi/hr is a high estimate.

Talk About It

Without dividing, how could you tell that the estimate of 500 mi/hr would be a low estimate?

Did You Know?

A minimum distance of 22,858.8 miles (the distance of the Tropic of Cancer or Capricorn) must be flown for circumnavigation.

Check

Estimate each quotient. Give a high and low estimate.

1. 198 astronauts ÷ 30 classes

2. 691 phone calls ÷ 90 workers

3. $503 ÷ 20 winners

4. 2,297 visitors ÷ 40 days

5. **Reasoning** How does changing only the dividend in a problem change the estimated quotient? Give an example.

Practice

Skills and Reasoning

Estimate each quotient. Give a high and low estimate.

6. 12,578 ÷ 50   **7.** $38,123 ÷ 40   **8.** 5,022 ÷ 60   **9.** 3,258 ÷ 50

10. $19,792 ÷ 60   **11.** 4,989 ÷ 80   **12.** 64,621 ÷ 90   **13.** 2,336 ÷ 70

14. 1,776 ÷ 20   **15.** 5,300 ÷ 80   **16.** 5,280 ÷ 50   **17.** 2,000 ÷ 30

18. How is estimating the quotient of 7,840 and 80 similar to estimating the quotient of 784,000 and 800?

Problem Solving and Applications

19. Geography Use the data in the *Did You Know?* on page 224. How many circumnavigations would you need to make if you wanted to travel at least 100,000 miles?

20. Logic An elevator at an airport can safely carry 12 people, or a maximum of 2,500 pounds. Estimate how many pounds each person could weigh for the elevator to operate safely. Would it be better to give a low or high estimate for the number of pounds? Explain.

21. Time Each year more than 80 million greeting cards are mailed each day between Thanksgiving and the New Year. Estimate how many million cards are mailed during this time. (Hint: There are about 5 weeks between Thanksgiving and January 1.)

22. Science The planet Jupiter's diameter is about 11 times that of Earth's. What is the diameter of Earth?

about 88,000 mi

Jupiter is the fifth planet in our solar system.

 Algebra Readiness Give two numbers that make each sentence true.

23. 912 ÷ n is about 20.   **24.** n ÷ 58 is about 30.

25. 420 ÷ n is between 6 and 7.   **26.** n ÷ 64 is between 10 and 20.

Mixed Review and Test Prep

Divide.

27. 99 ÷ 3   **28.** 91 ÷ 8   **29.** 58 ÷ 4   **30.** 712 ÷ 5   **31.** 324 ÷ 6

32. What is the mean for 100, 90, 80, 40, and 70?

Ⓐ 5   Ⓑ 76   Ⓒ 80   Ⓓ 95

Estimating with 2-Digit Divisors

Learn • • • • • • • • • •

Alyse, from Merritt Island, Florida, is very interested in training to be an astronaut. At age 12, she attended NASA's Space Camp in Titusville, Florida. At this camp, students of all ages learn about space exploration.

Alyse hopes to one day travel in space!

Example

Suppose that during one summer, a total of 572 students in 26 equal groups attended Space Camp. About how many students were in each group?

To find the number of students in each group, divide.

$572 \div 26$

Use compatible numbers and basic facts. 600 and 30 are compatible numbers because 6 is divisible by 3.

$600 \div 30 = 20$

About 20 students were in each group.

Talk About It

1. How do basic facts help when estimating?

2. How do multiples of 10 help when estimating?

Did You Know?

In 1996, Shannon Lucid set a record for the longest space flight by a U.S. citizen—188 days in space.

Check •

Estimate each quotient. Use compatible numbers.

1. $\$206 \div 23$
2. $829 \div 43$
3. $3,674 \div 66$
4. $462 \div 93$
5. $570 \div 78$
6. $1,536 \div 34$
7. $\$638 \div 78$
8. $\$308 \div 65$

9. **Reasoning** Do you think the exact answer to 2,712 divided by 52 is more or less than 50? Explain.

Practice

Skills and Reasoning

Estimate each quotient. Use compatible numbers.

10. $632 \div 19$ **11.** $786 \div 43$ **12.** $475 \div 89$ **13.** $2,189 \div 23$

14. $9,836 \div 18$ **15.** $\$18,066 \div 92$ **16.** $\$817 \div 20$ **17.** $723 \div 80$

18. $618 \div 29$ **19.** $\$4,290 \div 74$ **20.** $165 \div 38$ **21.** $13,000 \div 44$

22. $\$528 \div 63$ **23.** $470 \div 55$ **24.** $\$13,016 \div 26$ **25.** $789 \div 78$

26. Estimate the quotient of $999 \div 47$. Is the exact quotient greater than or less than your estimate?

27. Which quotient is greater: $6,413 \div 16$ or $6,413 \div 17$?

28. Which quotient is greater: $2,159 \div 81$ or $2,459 \div 81$?

Problem Solving and Applications

29. Time The Ames Research Center schedules 120 min of fun-filled activities for students. If each session takes 30 min, how many sessions are there? Is your answer exact or an estimate?

30. Using Data Use the data in *Did You Know?* on page 226. About how many months did Shannon Lucid stay in space? Explain how you found your answer.

31. Using Data Use the Data File on page 218. If you drove between the John F. Kennedy Space Center in Florida and the Ames Research Center in California at 58 mi/hr, about how long would it take you to make the trip? Explain how you found your answer.

Ames Research Center

John F. Kennedy Space Center

 Algebra Readiness Give one number that makes each sentence true.

32. $n \div 18$ is about 20. **33.** $n \div 34$ is about 50.

34. $75 \div n$ is between 3 and 4. **35.** $798 \div n$ is between 10 and 20.

Mixed Review and Test Prep

Find each quotient or product.

36. $246 \div 6$ **37.** $729 \div 9$ **38.** 345×27 **39.** 632×18 **40.** $114 \div 3$

41. Round 63.453 to the nearest tenth.

(A) 63 (B) 63.4 (C) 63.5 (D) 63.45

Review and Practice

Vocabulary Choose the correct word to make a true statement.

1. In the problem $18 \div 3 = 6$ the 3 is the _____.
   - (A) divisor
   - (B) dividend
   - (C) quotient

(Lesson 1) Mental Math Find each quotient. Use mental math.

2. $4,200 \div 70$ 3. $45,000 \div 90$ 4. $320 \div 80$ 5. $30,000 \div 60$

6. $5,600 \div 70$ 7. $6,400 \div 800$ 8. $630,000 \div 900$ 9. $1,200 \div 20$

10. $1,600 \div 400$ 11. $2,800 \div 70$ 12. $15,000 \div 500$ 13. $350,000 \div 7,000$

14. Are the quotients for $500 \div 50$ and $50,000 \div 500$ the same or different? Explain.

15. Are the quotients for $320,000 \div 400$ and $320 \div 4$ the same or different? Explain.

(Lesson 2) Estimate each quotient. Give a high and low estimate.

16. $13,452 \div 20$ 17. $5,678 \div 70$ 18. $2,001 \div 20$ 19. $\$11,873 \div 40$

20. $5,122 \div 50$ 21. $36,901 \div 60$ 22. $82,456 \div 90$ 23. $3,012 \div 30$

24. $4,352 \div 70$ 25. $1,750 \div 40$ 26. $64,090 \div 80$ 27. $90,022 \div 90$

(Lesson 3) Estimate each quotient by using compatible numbers.

28. $54,123 \div 62$ 29. $998 \div 12$ 30. $3,535 \div 71$ 31. $\$46,792 \div 92$

32. $\$591 \div 31$ 33. $73,892 \div 89$ 34. $438 \div 19$ 35. $175 \div 38$

36. $\$8,065 \div 93$ 37. $332,097 \div 432$ 38. $\$445 \div 9$ 39. $35,920 \div 570$

40. One museum tour lasts 125 min. If this tour stops at 31 points of interest, on average, about how many minutes are spent at each point?

41. Which quotient is greater: $5,768 \div 81$ or $5,768 \div 79$?

42. A theater made $1,512 in ticket sales over the weekend.

   a. If 432 tickets were sold, was the average cost of each ticket more or less than $4?

   b. **Journal** Explain when it would be better to overestimate the cost of each ticket.

Skills Checklist

In this section, you have:

☑ **Explored Division Patterns**

☑ **Estimated Quotients**

☑ **Estimated with 2-Digit Divisors**

B Dividing

Kevin loves to collect all sorts of rocks, both near his home in St. Louis, Missouri, and whenever he goes on a trip. Think about how many rocks he could collect with a vehicle like the Surveyor 3 which was used to collect rocks on the moon!

How might Kevin use division when sorting through his rock collection?

Skills Checklist

In this section, you will:

- ❏ Divide by 2-Digit Divisors
- ❏ Divide Greater Numbers
- ❏ Choose a Calculation Method
- ❏ Learn About Zeros in the Quotient
- ❏ Explore Algebra by Using Expressions
- ❏ Solve Problems by Using Objects or Acting It Out

GET READY!

Dividing Greater Numbers

Review subtracting. Find each difference.

1. $79 - 46$	**2.** $83 - 29$	**3.** $123 - 78$
4. $369 - 273$	**5.** $837 - 479$	**6.** $413 - 82$
7. $462 - 88$	**8.** $502 - 126$	**9.** $48 - 39$

Dividing by 2-Digit Divisors

You Will Learn
how to divide with 2-digit divisors

Learn • • • • • • • •

Kevin collects rocks on Earth. *Surveyor 3*, a lunar exploration vehicle, collects rocks on the moon. It has a scoop and claw that place rock samples in front of its camera.

Kevin from St. Louis, Missouri, has over 500 rocks in his collection.

The *Surveyor 3* mission was launched on April 17, 1967.

Remember
Estimate before you divide.

Example 1

If the Surveyor collected and recorded 131 rock samples during a 21-hr period, how many rocks did it collect and photograph per hour on average?

To separate into equal groups per hour, you divide. $131 \div 21 = n$

Step 1	Step 2
Estimation can help you decide where to place the first digit.	Divide ones.

Step 1

Estimation can help you decide where to place the first digit.

Estimate: $21\overline{)131}$

Think: 6
$20\overline{)120}$

Start dividing ones.

You can use multiplication to check.

$$
\begin{array}{r}
21 \leftarrow \text{divisor} \\
\times\ 6 \leftarrow \text{quotient} \\
\hline
126 \\
+\ \ 5 \leftarrow \text{remainder} \\
\hline
131 \leftarrow \text{dividend}
\end{array}
$$

Surveyor 3 collected and recorded more than 6 moon rocks per hour.

Step 2

Divide ones.

$$
\begin{array}{r}
6\ \text{R5} \\
21\overline{)131} \\
-126 \\
\hline
5
\end{array}
$$

Divide.
Multiply. $6 \times 21 = 126$
Subtract. $131 - 126 = 5$
Compare. $5 < 21$
Write the remainder.

Sometimes your first estimate doesn't work, and you need to try again.

Example 2

One time, 161 soil samples were sent in equal groups to 23 labs. How many soil samples were sent to each lab? To find the number of samples, divide. $161 \div 23 = n$

Step 1

Estimate: $23\overline{)161}$

Think: $20\overline{)160}^{8}$

Start dividing ones.

Step 2

Divide ones.

$$23\overline{)161}^{8}$$
$$-184$$

Multiply.
Sometimes when you multiply, you find that the estimate is too high.

Use a lower estimate. Try 7.

Step 3

Divide ones.

$$23\overline{)161}^{7}$$
$$-161$$
$$0$$

Divide.
Multiply. $7 \times 23 = 161$
Subtract. $161 - 161 = 0$
Compare. $0 < 23$

7 soil samples were sent to each lab.

Check:
$$\begin{array}{r} 23 \\ \times\ 7 \\ \hline 161 \end{array}$$

Math Tip
You can use multiplication to check.

Talk About It

1. How could you tell that your answers in Examples 1 and 2 would not have any tens?

2. What do you do if your first estimate is too high?

Check

Copy and complete.

1. $42\overline{)231}^{5\ R\ \blacksquare}$

2. $64\overline{)286}^{4\ R\ \blacksquare}$

3. $39\overline{)360}^{9\ R\ \blacksquare}$

4. $55\overline{)353}^{6\ R\ \blacksquare}$

5. $25\overline{)159}^{6\ R\ \blacksquare}$

6. $57\overline{)402}^{7\ R\ \blacksquare}$

7. $72\overline{)524}^{7\ R\ \blacksquare}$

8. $19\overline{)120}^{6\ R\ \blacksquare}$

Divide.

9. $21\overline{)189}$
10. $27\overline{)242}$
11. $83\overline{)447}$
12. $15\overline{)120}$

13. $53\overline{)457}$
14. $24\overline{)216}$
15. $93\overline{)852}$
16. $45\overline{)360}$

17. $88 \div 2$
18. $378 \div 62$
19. $528 \div 88$
20. $737 \div 82$

21. $163 \div 40$
22. $456 \div 82$
23. $168 \div 24$
24. $365 \div 65$

25. **Reasoning** What is the least dividend that could be divided by 42 and have a 2-digit quotient?

Skills and Reasoning

Copy and complete.

26. 5 R ▨
    15)84

27. 8 R ▨
    31)269

28. 7 R ▨
    28)198

29. 8 R ▨
    48)429

Divide.

30. 39)97

31. 51)472

32. 11)88

33. 53)107

34. 42)120

35. 25)178

36. 92)400

37. 50)200

38. 93)669

39. 23)79

40. 42)295

41. 94)532

42. 46)211

43. 38)266

44. 65)319

45. 34)172

46. 60)343

47. 61)360

48. 95)688

49. 12)103

50. 27)206

51. 84)465

52. 53)259

53. 94)842

54. 89)224

55. 86 ÷ 4

56. 225 ÷ 25

57. 438 ÷ 54

58. 118 ÷ 35

59. 488 ÷ 73

60. 242 ÷ 7

61. 117 ÷ 50

62. 297 ÷ 54

63. 315 ÷ 63

64. 114 ÷ 37

65. 2 R ▨
    41)8▨
    − ▨▨
    ———
    5

66. 5 R ▨
    54)2▨8
    − ▨7▨
    ———
    ▨

67. ▨
    25)2▨5
    − ▨2▨
    ———
    ▨

68. 3 R ▨
    37)▨14
    − 11▨
    ———
    ▨

69. What is 472 divided by 59?

70. What is 672 ÷ 85?

71. Divide 326 by 45.

72. Divide 273 by 91.

73. Can a remainder be greater than a divisor? Explain.

Problem Solving and Applications

74. **Critical Thinking** Alicia solved 339 ÷ 41 and checked her work. Did Alicia solve the problem correctly? Explain.

```
  7 R52    Check:    41
41)339              x  7
 -287               ———
 ————               287
  52              + 52
                  ————
                   339
```

75. If Kevin spent about 20 hr one summer collecting 180 rocks, about how many rocks did he collect per hour?

Marble

Limestone

76. Kevin needs to put 420 rocks into boxes. If he wants to put 20 rocks in each box, how many boxes will he need?

Granite

Slate

Problem Solving and SCIENCE

Using Data The table below shows how many times some birds flap their wings on the average in 20 sec. Most birds flap really fast. Most people can only flap their arms about 40 times in 20 sec.

Bird	Flaps (20 sec)
Heron	40
Pigeon	120
Starling	140
Chickadee	540
Hummingbird	1,400

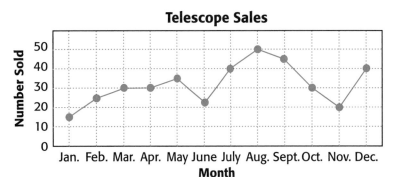

Great Blue Heron

77. How many flaps per second are there for each?

   a. heron   **b.** pigeon   **c.** starling

   d. chickadee   **e.** hummingbird

78. Critical Thinking The hummingbird flaps its wings 10 times as fast as which bird?

79. Make a bar graph to show flaps per second for each bird.

80. Write Your Own Problem Use the data about birds to write a question that can be answered by using division.

 81. Journal Explain how you know when an estimate is too high or low.

Mixed Review and Test Prep

Using Data Use the line graph for **82–86.**

82. How many telescopes were sold in January?

83. How many telescopes were sold in November?

84. During which month were the most sales made?

85. During which three months were the sales the same?

Telescope Sales

86. How many more telescopes were sold in December than in January?

87. Which of the following is the same as 20.3×10?

   Ⓐ 0.203×10 **Ⓑ** 2.03×100 **Ⓒ** $20.3 \times 1,000$ **Ⓓ** 203×100

Dividing Greater Numbers

The *Pioneer 10* space probe was launched March 2, 1972.

You Will Learn

how to divide greater numbers with a 2-digit divisor

Learn ● ● ● ● ● ●

Pioneer 10 was the first space probe to reach the planet Jupiter. To find out how fast a space probe can travel, you will need to know how to divide greater numbers.

Example 1

Pioneer 10 took 21 months to travel 391 million miles to Jupiter.

How many million miles did *Pioneer 10* travel each month?

To find how many miles traveled during each month, divide. $391 \div 21 = n$

Step 1

Decide where to place the first digit.

Estimate: $21\overline{)391}$

Think: $20\overline{)400}$ with 20 above

Start by dividing tens.

Remember

Begin by estimating the quotient.

Step 2

Divide tens.

$$\begin{array}{r} 1 \\ 21\overline{)391} \\ -21 \\ \hline 18 \end{array}$$

Multiply. $1 \times 21 = 21$
Subtract. $39 - 21 = 18$
Compare. $18 < 21$

Step 3

Bring down ones.
Divide ones.

$$\begin{array}{r} 18 \text{ R}13 \\ 21\overline{)391} \\ -21 \\ \hline 181 \\ -168 \\ \hline 13 \end{array}$$

Multiply. $8 \times 21 = 168$
Subtract. $181 - 168 = 13$
Compare. $13 < 21$

Write the remainder.

Check.

$$\begin{array}{r} 21 \leftarrow \text{divisor} \\ \times 18 \leftarrow \text{quotient} \\ \hline 168 \\ 210 \\ \hline 378 \\ + 13 \leftarrow \text{remainder} \\ \hline 391 \leftarrow \text{dividend} \end{array}$$

Pioneer 10 traveled more than 18 million miles per month.

Example 2

When dividing greater numbers, sometimes you have to place the first digit in the hundreds.

Find 9,475 ÷ 28.

Step 1	Step 2
Decide where to place the first digit.	Divide.

Step 1

Decide where to place the first digit.

Estimate: 28)9,475

            300
Think: 30)9,000

Start by dividing hundreds.

9,475 divided by 28 is 338 R11.

Step 2

Divide.

```
        338 R11    Check:      338  ← quotient
  28)9,475                   ×  28  ← divisor
    − 8 4                      2704
      107                      6760
    −  84                      9464
      235                    +   11  ← remainder
    − 224                     9,475  ← dividend
       11
```

Talk About It

If you divide 4,300 by 71, where would you place the first digit in the quotient?

Check

Copy and complete.

```
        2 1 R▧▧▧           2▧ R▧            3▧              4▧ R▧
1. 45)9 8 0        2. 27)6 7 8       3. 97)3,2 9 8     4. 72)3,3 9 0
   − 9 0              − 5 4             ▧▧▧1               2 8▧
   ▧ 0              ▧▧8             3 8▧              5 1▧
   − 4 5              − 1 3 5           − ▧▧8              − ▧▧4
     3 5                  3               0                  ▧
```

Divide. Check your answer.

5. 435 ÷ 15   6. 280 ÷ 15   7. 7,840 ÷ 39   8. 1,025 ÷ 82

9. 25)621   10. 44)968   11. 21)687   12. 56)2,072

Estimate. Use your number sense to choose the best answer.

13. 396 ÷ 20 is   Ⓐ less than 2   Ⓑ less than 20   Ⓒ more than 20

14. What is 394 divided by 28?   15. What is 2,150 ÷ 95?

16. What is 456 divided by 18?   17. What is 1,260 ÷ 11?

18. **Reasoning** Which is wrong, the problem or the check? Explain.

```
            41 R35        41
  57)2,372             × 57
   − 228               287
      92               205
    − 57             2,337
      35
```

Skills and Reasoning

Divide. Check your answer.

19. $18\overline{)72}$ **20.** $24\overline{)720}$ **21.** $45\overline{)855}$ **22.** $75\overline{)3,750}$ **23.** $58\overline{)820}$

24. $17\overline{)85}$ **25.** $19\overline{)981}$ **26.** $67\overline{)938}$ **27.** $82\overline{)5,814}$ **28.** $47\overline{)1,315}$

29. $40\overline{)815}$ **30.** $28\overline{)592}$ **31.** $32\overline{)877}$ **32.** $23\overline{)2,805}$ **33.** $35\overline{)2,501}$

34. $96 \div 16$ **35.** $840 \div 42$ **36.** $641 \div 53$ **37.** $1,320 \div 66$ **38.** $5,910 \div 64$

39. $97 \div 46$ **40.** $740 \div 37$ **41.** $580 \div 32$ **42.** $7,466 \div 47$ **43.** $3,012 \div 27$

Estimate. Use your number sense to select the best answer for **44–46.**

44. $650 \div 40$ is   Ⓐ less than 16   Ⓑ more than 16   Ⓒ exactly 16

45. $2,250 \div 70$ is   Ⓐ less than 3   Ⓑ less than 30   Ⓒ more than 30

46. $9,321 \div 50$ is   Ⓐ less than 100   Ⓑ more than 200   Ⓒ between 100 and 200

47. Find the answer of 907 divided by 31.

48. 952 divided by 56 is what number?

49. If your divisor is 54 what is the greatest possible remainder you could have?

50. **Science** It took 21 months for *Pioneer 10* to reach Jupiter. How many years and months was that?

Problem Solving and Applications

51. Countries other than the United States placed about 8,400 objects in space in 40 years. About how many is this on the average per year?

52. One month 648 students in 36 equal groups toured a NASA exhibit. How many students were in each group?

53. **Money** This table shows ticket prices for The Red or Blue Tour at Cape Canaveral in 1996. What combination of tickets could you buy for exactly $20?

54. **Time** Tours start at 9:30 A.M. and depart every 15 min until 2 hr before dusk. If dusk is at 5:15 P.M., how many tours are there?

Adults	$7.00
Children Ages 3–11	$4.00

Problem Solving and HISTORY

The first powered flight took place near Kitty Hawk, North Carolina on Dec. 17, 1903. During this flight, Orville and Wilbur Wright flew 120 feet in 12 seconds. Other American fliers helped to advance the science of aviation. On July 4, 1908, Glenn Curtiss flew the *June Bug* a distance of 5,090 feet in about 2 minutes.

55. On average, how many feet per second did the Wright Brothers' airplane fly?

56. About how many feet per minute did the *June Bug* fly?

Using Data Use the Data File on page 219 to answer **57** and **58**.

57. Critical Thinking Which flight flew the greatest number of miles per minute?

58. About how many miles per hour did the first American flight orbiting Earth go?

Orville and Wilbur Wright on their first flight.

 59. Journal Write a step-by-step plan for dividing a 3-digit number by a 2-digit number such as 329 ÷ 45. Include how to treat overestimates and underestimates.

Mixed Review and Test Prep

Find each product or difference.

60.	**61.**	**62.**	**63.**	**64.**
329 × 27	2,619 − 408	$6.24 × 49	$26.30 − 11.57	$100.00 − 57.32

65.	**66.**	**67.**	**68.**	**69.**
$9.15 × 41	486 − 79	$36.95 − 12.66	413 × 52	5.02 × 12

Estimate each product or difference.

70.	**71.**	**72.**	**73.**	**74.**
428 × 92	3,601 − 1,019	$7.57 × 39	391 × 11	$247.51 − 98.36

75. Time How many seconds are in an hour?

Ⓐ 1   Ⓑ 60   Ⓒ 1,290   Ⓓ 3,600

Dividing: Choosing a Calculation Method

The space shuttle *Atlantis* was first launched at the Kennedy Space Center in 1985.

You Will Learn

how to choose a calculation method when dividing

Materials

calculator

Learn • • • • • • • • • • • • • • • •

Every 30 days the Visitor Center at Kennedy Space Center Florida, sells about 4,500 bus tickets to transport visitors to see the Space Shuttle launch pad. How many tickets does the Visitor Center sell daily?

Here are three methods that you can choose from to solve a problem. The size and kind of numbers you are working with will help you choose a calculation method.

To find the number of tickets sold daily, you divide.

Calculation Methods

- Paper and Pencil
- Calculator
- Mental Math

Michael, Brooke, and Stefanie each use a different way to find 4,500 ÷ 30.

Michael uses paper and pencil.

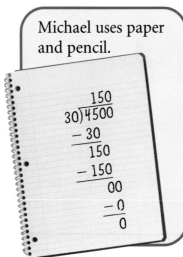

Brooke uses a calculator.

Brooke enters:

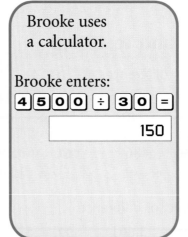

Stefanie uses mental math.

Since the divisor is 30, I can do this in my head: $45 \div 3 = 15$, so, $4{,}500 \div 30 = 150$.

Math Tip

Some math problems can be solved faster mentally than by using a calculator.

They all check their answers by multiplication: $30 \times 150 = 4{,}500$. All are correct. About 150 tickets are sold daily.

 **Talk About It**

What are some cases in which mental math is faster and easier than pencil and paper?

Check

Divide and check. Explain what method you used and why.

1. 490 ÷ 7   **2.** 236 ÷ 7   **3.** 500 ÷ 25   **4.** 1,135 ÷ 6

5. Reasoning When do you use pencil and paper or a calculator to divide?

Practice

Skills and Reasoning

Choose a tool

Divide and check. Explain what calculation method you used and why.

6. 20)‾40‾   **7.** 12)‾168‾   **8.** 20)‾187‾   **9.** 8)‾640‾

10. 10)‾100‾   **11.** 14)‾42,000‾   **12.** 60)‾360‾   **13.** 72)‾8,712‾

14. 902 ÷ 630   **15.** 365 ÷ 47   **16.** 381 ÷ 4   **17.** 810 ÷ 90

18. 55)‾4,440‾   **19.** 30)‾286‾   **20.** 40)‾360‾   **21.** 40)‾48,000‾

22. 16)‾256‾   **23.** 30)‾180‾   **24.** 26)‾760‾   **25.** 26)‾754‾

26. 23)‾828‾   **27.** 40)‾320‾   **28.** 54)‾378‾   **29.** 61)‾586‾

30. 560 ÷ 7   **31.** 9,820 ÷ 24   **32.** 615 ÷ 53   **33.** 472 ÷ 60

34. 300 ÷ 5   **35.** 588 ÷ 84   **36.** 24,000 ÷ 12   **37.** 28,063 ÷ 70

Problem Solving and Applications

38. Science The distance of the stars is measured in light years. A light year is how far light travels in one year. Light travels 186,000 miles in one second.

  a. How far does light travel in one minute?

  b. In an hour?

  c. In a day?

39. Critical Thinking Divide by 10 on your calculator and the number after the decimal point is the remainder. Is this so when dividing by other numbers? Explain.

This spiral galaxy is NGC 2997.

Mixed Review and Test Prep

Find each answer.

40. 643 × 81   **41.** 54,069 + 8,984   **42.** 8,040 − 4,765   **43.** 325 × 13

Compare.

44. 80,000 ● 68,000   Ⓐ >   Ⓑ <   Ⓒ =

EARN YOUR WINGS GAME

Players
2 teams

Materials
- scorecards
- 4 number cubes, each numbered 1–6
- 2 blank spinners

Object
Create division problems that have remainders 0 through 9.

How to Play

1. Each player makes a scorecard.

0	1	2	3	4	5	6	7	8	9

2. Each team makes a spinner with 10 numbers from 20 to 99.

3. Players determine who will start by rolling a number cube. The player who rolls the least number goes first. Players take turns clockwise around the table.

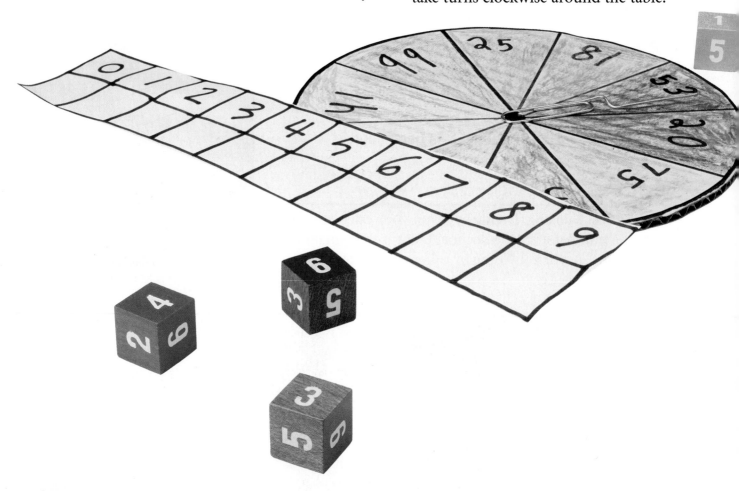

4 Player 1 rolls 4 number cubes and spins the spinner.

5 Player 1 creates and solves a division problem by first making a four-digit number from the numbers on the number cubes and then divides this number by the two-digit numbers on the spinner. Digits on the number cubes may be used in any order.

4,361 ÷ 53 or 3,614 ÷ 53 or 6,134 ÷ 53

6 If a player creates a problem whose quotient includes a remainder of 0–9, the remainder is recorded. Players find the total of their remainders after 20 minutes of play. The player with the least total wins and earns wings.

Talk About It

Did your playing strategy change during the game?

More Ways to Play

■ Change the rules so that the player with the greatest total for the remainders wins.

■ Extend the scorecard. Play for remainders from 0 to 20.

Reasoning

1. When were you more likely to get a remainder from 0 to 9? Explain your reasoning.

2. How would your strategy change if you were playing for the greatest total of remainders?

Zeros in the Quotient

You Will Learn

how to divide whole numbers with zeros in the quotient

Learn ● ● ● ● ● ● ● ● ● ● ● ● ● ● ● ● ● ● ●

In 1964, the *Ranger 7* lunar probe took 4,316 photographs of the moon's surface.

Example 1

If 42 scientists were assigned to study an equal number of these photos, how many did each scientist study?

Since the total is separated into equal groups, divide 4,316 by 42.

Step 1	**Step 2**
Decide where to place the first digit.	Divide hundreds.
Estimate: $42\overline{)4{,}316}$	$\begin{array}{r} 1 \\ 42\overline{)4{,}316} \\ -4\,2 \\ \hline 1 \end{array}$
Think: $4{,}000 \div 40 = 100$	
Start by dividing hundreds.	

Step 3	**Step 4**
Bring down the tens. Divide tens.	Bring down the ones. Divide ones.
$\begin{array}{r} 10 \\ 42\overline{)4{,}316} \\ -4\,2 \\ \hline 11 \\ -\,0 \\ \hline 11 \end{array}$ You cannot divide 11 (tens) into 42 parts and get a whole number so write 0 in the quotient.	$\begin{array}{r} 102\text{ R32} \\ 42\overline{)4{,}316} \\ -4\,2 \\ \hline 11 \\ -\,0 \\ \hline 116 \\ -\,84 \\ \hline 32 \end{array}$

Each scientist studied 102 photographs. There were 32 photographs left to be studied.

Other Examples

A. $\begin{array}{r} 370\text{ R8} \\ 66\overline{)24{,}428} \\ -19\,8 \\ \hline 4\,62 \\ -4\,62 \\ \hline 08 \\ -\,0 \\ \hline 8 \end{array}$ Check: $\begin{array}{r} 370 \\ \times\ 66 \\ \hline 24{,}420 \\ +\quad 8 \\ \hline 24{,}428 \end{array}$

B. $\begin{array}{r} 600\text{ R21} \\ 23\overline{)13{,}821} \\ -13\,8 \\ \hline 02 \\ -\,0 \\ \hline 21 \\ -\,0 \\ \hline 21 \end{array}$ Check: $\begin{array}{r} 600 \\ \times\ 23 \\ \hline 13{,}800 \\ +\quad 21 \\ \hline 13{,}821 \end{array}$

Talk About It

How does estimation help you know $3{,}604 \div 34 = 16$ is not correct?

Check

Divide and check.

1. $74\overline{)7,844}$
2. $42\overline{)4,306}$
3. $49\overline{)10,045}$
4. $62\overline{)52,135}$

5. $52,250 \div 58$
6. $6,537 \div 32$
7. $38\overline{)15,890}$
8. $29\overline{)9,422}$

9. **Reasoning** Which calculation method would you choose to divide 36,036 by 36? Why? What is the quotient?

Practice

Skills and Reasoning

Divide and check.

10. $41\overline{)423}$
11. $12\overline{)708}$
12. $49\overline{)9,960}$
13. $29\overline{)8,971}$

14. $48\overline{)9,851}$
15. $49\overline{)10,058}$
16. $89\overline{)9,889}$
17. $74\overline{)33,364}$

18. $9,020 \div 22$
19. $26,850 \div 66$
20. $8,413 \div 40$
21. $14,230 \div 75$

Use number sense to decide whether each answer is reasonable. Explain.

22. $32\overline{)22,528}$ quotient 74
23. $25\overline{)7,600}$ quotient 304
24. $58\overline{)32,456}$ quotient 55
25. $46\overline{)38,429}$ quotient 835

Problem Solving and Applications

26. Suppose after a shuttle launch a newspaper printed 9,476 papers. If these papers are delivered to 46 stores, what is the average number of papers delivered to each store?

27. **What If** The NASA switchboard received 2,180 phone calls in 20 minutes. This is about how many phone calls per minute?

28. **Science** The *Saturn V* moon rocket is 365 ft long. Would ten of them lined up end to end cover a mile? (Hint: A mile is 5,280 ft.) Explain.

Saturn V moon rocket

Mixed Review and Test Prep

Find each quotient or product.

29. $20\overline{)260}$
30. $8\overline{)640}$
31. $6\overline{)1,248}$
32. $5\overline{)305}$
33. $16\overline{)208}$

34. $\begin{array}{r} 375 \\ \times\ 19 \\ \hline \end{array}$
35. $\begin{array}{r} 498 \\ \times\ 37 \\ \hline \end{array}$
36. $\begin{array}{r} 87 \\ \times 93 \\ \hline \end{array}$
37. $\begin{array}{r} \$4.59 \\ \times\ \ 23 \\ \hline \end{array}$
38. $\begin{array}{r} 48 \\ \times 31 \\ \hline \end{array}$

39. **Estimation** Choose the best estimate for $\$48.98 \times 25$.

Ⓐ $2   Ⓑ $1,250   Ⓒ $125.00   Ⓓ $12.50   Ⓔ not here

Exploring Algebra: Using Expressions

Problem Solving Connection

Use Logical Reasoning

Vocabulary

algebraic expression
an expression that contains a variable

evaluate
find the number an algebraic expression names

Explore

3, 2, 1, Blast off! How can you represent the length of each of these model rocket ships?

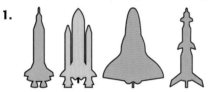

The total length can be found by adding.

$3 + 7$ tells how many inches in all. $4 + n$ tells how many inches in all.

An expression such as $4 + n$ that contains a variable is an **algebraic expression**.

Work Together

Choose the correct algebraic expression for each.

1.

4 spacecraft with n astronauts in each

$n + 4$ $4 \times n$ $n \div 4$

2.
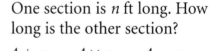
The launch pad is 4 ft long. One section is n ft long. How long is the other section?

$4 + n$ $4 \times n$ $4 - n$

3.

Two astronauts share n space meals

$n - 2$ $n \div 2$ $n \times 2$

4. 3 rows of space stamps with n stamps in each row

$3 \times n$ $n + 3$ $n \div 3$

Talk About It

What algebraic expression can you use to represent 8 groups of n students each?

Connect

You can **evaluate** an algebraic expression by replacing the variable with a number and doing the computation.

If 6 toy rockets are in a pack, how many rockets are in n packs?

Evaluate $6 \times n$.

For $n = 3$	For $n = 7$	For $n = 32$
$6 \times n = 6 \times 3$	$6 \times n = 6 \times 7$	$6 \times n = 6 \times 32$
$6 \times n = 18$	$6 \times n = 42$	$6 \times n = 192$
18 rockets	42 rockets	192 rockets

Math Tip
$6 \times n = 6n$

Practice

Evaluate each expression for $n = 9$ and $n = 10$.

1. $n + 25$ 2. $4 \times n$ 3. $n \div n$ 4. $n - 4$ 5. $n + 17$

6. $101 + n$ 7. $12 \times n$ 8. $37 - n$ 9. $40 - n$ 10. $n + n$

11. $n + 10$ 12. $60 \div n$ 13. $20 - n$ 14. $n \times 2$ 15. $n \times n$

16. $20 \div n$ 17. $12 - n$ 18. $n \div 1$ 19. $n - 3$ 20. $n + 8$

Copy and complete.

21.

n	$n + 7$
5	
8	
15	
22	

22.

n	$n \div 3$
9	
15	
24	
36	

23.

n	$n - 11$
21	
35	
48	
62	

24.

n	$n \times 8$
0	
2	
4	
6	

25. If $n = 7$, what is $5 \times n$?   26. If $n = 8$, what is $n \div 4$?

27. If $n = 3$, what is $27 \div n$?   28. If $n = 10$, what is $5 \times n$?

Write the algebraic expression for **29–31**.

29. Erika is 12. Write her age n years ago.

30. A scientist uses 7 g of one chemical and n g of another to make a compound. What is the total number of grams she uses?

31. **Science** The *Juno II* rocket is n meters tall. The *Titan II* rocket is 10 m taller. How tall is the *Titan II* rocket?

 32. **Journal** Explain how to evaluate an expression when you know the value of the variable.

Juno II   *Titan II*

Problem Solving

Analyze Strategies: Use Objects/Act It Out

You Will Learn

how to solve a problem by using objects and acting it out

Learn •

You and your team have just been hired to design a modular apartment building for the first colony on the moon. Each of the apartments will be built separately and will then be put together on the moon.

You want your design to be in the shape of a staircase. The tallest part will have 6 section apartments. How many apartments will be in the building?

The *Habitat* modular complex in Montreal, Canada, was designed by Moshe Safdie.

Work Together

▶ **Understand**   What do you know?

What do you need to find out?

▶ **Plan**   How will you find the answer?   Use cubes to represent apartments.

▶ **Solve**   Use cubes to build the building.

Count the cubes to find the number of apartments.   There will be 21 apartments in the building.

▶ **Look Back**   How can you check your answer?

1. Why would you want to use objects instead of drawing a picture?

2. For what kinds of problems does the Use Objects/Act It Out strategy make sense?

Use objects to solve each problem.

You decide to try a design in which the building is in the shape of a cube. Each side of the cube will be 3 apartments long. Use cubes to make a model.

1. How many apartments will be on the first floor?

2. How many floors high will the building be?

3. How many apartments will there be in the building in all?

4. You realize that the design cannot be used because there are some apartments with no windows. How many apartments in the building have no windows?

Problem Solving Practice ••••••••••••••••••••••••••••••

Problem Solving Strategies

- Use Objects/Act It Out
- Draw a Picture
- Look for a Pattern
- Guess and Check
- Use Logical Reasoning
- Make an Organized List
- Make a Table
- Solve a Simpler Problem
- Work Backward

Choose a Tool

Use any strategy to solve each problem.

5. In the apartment house you designed above in the shape of a cube, each outside wall in each apartment has one window. How many apartments would have a total of

  a. only one window?   b. two windows?

6. You want to design an apartment house with 15 apartments so that the greatest possible number of walls have windows. How will you design the building? How many windows will there be if each outside wall has one window?

7. Another building design you decide to try is in the shape of a staircase. You want this building to have 12 floors. When you start to build your model, you run out of cubes after completing floors 1–7. How many more cubes will you need to complete your model?

8. You want to build a fence in the shape of a square around the building. Each side of the square will have 10 fence posts. How many posts will be needed?

9. An apartment house has 28 one-bedroom apartments, 18 two-bedroom apartments, and 12 three-bedroom apartments. How many apartments are there?

10. Mr. Zarra used 2.5 gal of paint to repaint each kitchen in one of the apartments in the building he manages. The building has 9 floors and each floor has 6 apartments. How many gallons of paint did Mr. Zarra use to paint all the kitchens?

PROBLEM SOLVING PRACTICE

SECTION B
Review and Practice

(Lessons 4 and 5) Divide.

1. $23\overline{)135}$ 2. $41\overline{)365}$ 3. $61\overline{)411}$ 4. $33\overline{)233}$

5. $63\overline{)597}$ 6. $55\overline{)116}$ 7. $78\overline{)492}$ 8. $94\overline{)682}$

9. $49\overline{)441}$ 10. $17\overline{)136}$ 11. $12\overline{)10,800}$ 12. $32\overline{)19,237}$

13. $35\overline{)241}$ 14. $21\overline{)834}$ 15. $45\overline{)1,519}$ 16. $64\overline{)14,290}$

(Lesson 6) Divide and check. Explain which method you used and why.

17. $20\overline{)2,400}$ 18. $13\overline{)546}$ 19. $37\overline{)879}$ 20. $4,000 \div 500$

21. $36,036 \div 6$ 22. $7,273 \div 72$ 23. $482 \div 7$ 24. $360 \div 9$

(Lesson 7) Divide and check.

25. $18\overline{)1836}$ 26. $25\overline{)7,700}$ 27. $36\overline{)32,508}$ 28. $63\overline{)31,564}$

29. $24\overline{)14,597}$ 30. $19\overline{)10,070}$ 31. $16\overline{)8,154}$ 32. $23\overline{)9,292}$

33. $38\overline{)25,999}$ 34. $42\overline{)5,208}$ 35. $90\overline{)10,912}$ 36. $36\overline{)4,512}$

(Lesson 8) Solve each.

37. Cartons of eggs are packaged 8 to a box. If 832 cartons of eggs were packaged, how many boxes were needed?

38. In one month 11 students earned 265 bonus points in math. Is it possible that they each received the same number of points? Explain your answer.

39. 28 students collected 12,374 soda can tabs. If some of the students collected one more tab each than the rest of the students, how many collected 441 and how many collected 442 tabs?

40. While recycling, some students found that they could fit 45 bottles in one garbage bag. Would 5,000 bottles fit in 100 bags? Explain.

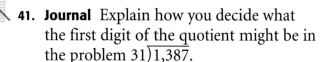

41. **Journal** Explain how you decide what the first digit of the quotient might be in the problem $31\overline{)1,387}$.

> ## Skills Checklist
>
> **In this section, you have:**
>
> ☑ **Divided by 2-Digit Divisors**
>
> ☑ **Divided Greater Numbers**
>
> ☑ **Learned About Choosing a Calculation Method**
>
> ☑ **Learned About Zeros in the Quotient**
>
> ☑ **Explored Algebra by Using Expressions**
>
> ☑ **Solved Problems by Using Objects or Acting It Out**

REVIEW AND PRACTICE

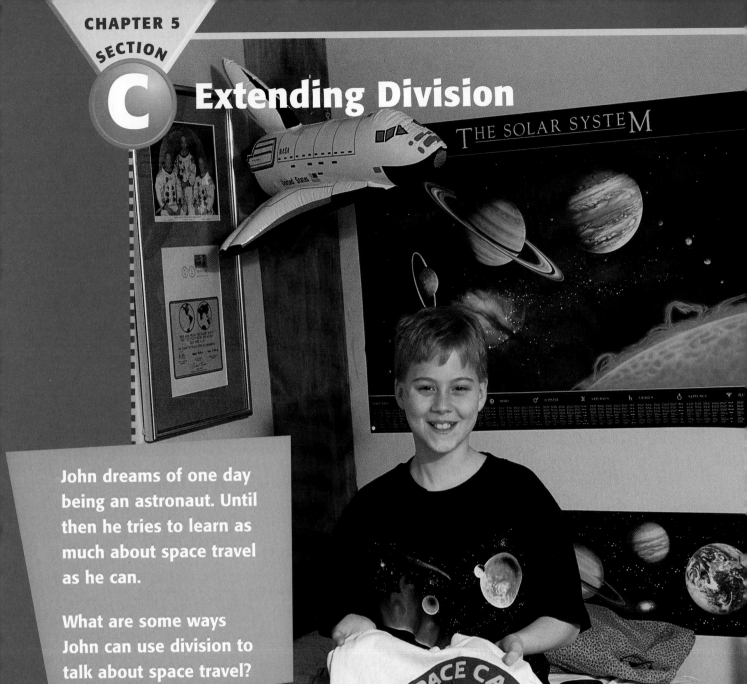

Extending Division

THE SOLAR SYSTEM

John dreams of one day being an astronaut. Until then he tries to learn as much about space travel as he can.

What are some ways John can use division to talk about space travel?

U.S. SPACE CAMP CALIFORNIA

GET READY!

Dividing Money

Review dividing decimals. Divide and check.

1. $4.46 ÷ 2
2. $6.15 ÷ 3
3. $31.25 ÷ 5
4. $31.44 ÷ 4
5. $0.36 ÷ 9
6. $22.30 ÷ 5
7. $20.40 ÷ 4
8. $33.50 ÷ 5
9. $0.36 ÷ 6
10. $19.20 ÷ 4
11. $0.84 ÷ 3
12. $13.22 ÷ 2

Skills Checklist

In this section, you will:

☐ Divide Money

☐ Solve Problems by Making Decisions

☐ Explore Decimal Patterns in Division

Dividing Money

Learn • • • • • • • • • • • •

Because he is interested in space travel, John has tried many things astronauts do. He has even tasted space ice cream. Not many people have had space ice cream, but many people have used the flavored powder astronauts use to make nutritious drinks in space.

John from Acton, Massachusetts, has attended Space Camp.

Massachusetts

Example

A container holds 18 oz of drink mix and costs $6.48. How much does the mix cost per ounce?

Since each ounce costs the same amount, you can divide to find the cost per ounce. $6.48 ÷ 18 = n

Step 1	Step 2
Place the decimal point in the quotient directly above the decimal point in the dividend.	Estimate.
$$18\overline{)\$6.48}$$ (with decimal point placed above)	**Think:** $$\begin{array}{r} \$0.30 \\ 20\overline{)\$6.00} \end{array}$$ Start dividing tenths.

Step 3	Step 4
Divide tenths.	Bring down hundredths. Divide.
$$\begin{array}{r} \$0.3 \\ 18\overline{)\$6.48} \\ -5\,4 \\ \hline 1\,0 \end{array}$$ Divide. Multiply. Subtract. Compare.	$$\begin{array}{r} \$0.36 \\ 18\overline{)\$6.48} \\ -5\,4 \\ \hline 108 \\ -108 \\ \hline 0 \end{array}$$ Divide. Multiply. Subtract. Check: $$\begin{array}{r} \$0.36 \\ \times\quad 18 \\ \hline 2\,88 \\ 3\,60 \\ \hline \$6.48 \end{array}$$

Each ounce of drink mix costs $0.36, or 36 cents.

(**Talk About It**)

How does dividing money differ from dividing whole numbers?

Check

Divide and check.

1. $15)\overline{\$9.30}$ **2.** $80)\overline{\$74.40}$ **3.** $34)\overline{\$36.38}$ **4.** $11)\overline{\$12.54}$

5. Reasoning Use estimation to find the error. $\$57.96 \div 23 = \$25.17$

Practice

Skills and Reasoning

Divide and check.

6. $50)\overline{\$125.00}$ **7.** $17)\overline{\$6.80}$ **8.** $16)\overline{\$8.00}$ **9.** $12)\overline{\$5.64}$

10. $\$8.40 \div 21$ **11.** $\$99.16 \div 37$ **12.** $\$464.00 \div 80$ **13.** $\$66.90 \div 30$

Estimation Use your number sense to choose the best answer.

14. $\$7.30 \div 80$ is   **(A)** less than $0.09.   **(B)** more than $0.09.

Estimate to decide whether each quotient in **15–18** is more or less than $1.00.

15. $23)\overline{\$40.00}$ **16.** $23)\overline{\$22.00}$ **17.** $9)\overline{\$9.09}$ **18.** $12)\overline{\$10.99}$

19. Find the quotient of $\$733.20 \div 60$.

 20. Mental Math If you have $225.50 to share with 50 people, how much should each person get?

Problem Solving Hint

When you want to find a cost per unit, use division.

Problem Solving and Applications

21. A box of 24 yo-yos costs $35.28. One costs $1.79. What is the savings for each yo-yo if you buy a box?

22. How much would 6 containers of powdered space drink at $6.36 each cost?

Using Data Use the Data File on page 219 to answer **23** and **24**.

23. Which planet has three times as many small moons as large moons?

24. Is the number of Neptune's moons greater than the mean number of moons in the solar system? Explain.

The planet Saturn and some of its moons

Mixed Review and Test Prep

Write the word name for each.

25. $5,034,060,000   **26.** $590,300,006   **27.** $456,020,015

28. Find the standard form for $70,000,000,000 + 707,000,000 + 70,000 + 700$.

   (A) 7,707,070,700   **(B)** 70,707,700,700   **(C)** 70,707,070,700   **(D)** 70,070,707,700

Problem Solving

Decision Making:
Planning a Class Trip

You Will Learn

how to make
decisions to plan
a class trip

Explore • • • • • • • • • • • • •

Suppose your teacher would like
to take the class on a trip to
Washington, D.C., to visit the
National Air and Space Museum.
You need to decide how to use
the time you will have once
you are there.

Facts and Data

• The museum is open from 10:00 A.M. to 5:30 P.M.

• The bus trip from your school to Washington, D.C., takes about
2 hr 30 min. A bus can pick up your class at school as early as
8:00 A.M.

• The bus must be back at school no later than 5:00 P.M.

• Some of the more popular exhibits that you will want to visit are:

Milestones of Flight	Rocketry
Skylab Space Station	Computers in Space
"Where Next, Columbus?"	Large Screen Movie

• Admission to the museum is free. The charge for the movie is
$3.25 per student and $4.00 per adult.

• The movie lasts about 35 min.

The National Air and
Space Museum
displays many
artifacts related to
aviation and space
travel.

Work Together

▶ **Understand**

1. What is the earliest you can be at the museum?

2. What is the latest you can leave?

3. Is $85 enough for 25 students to see the movie?

4. What if your teacher and 3 parents also attend the movie?

5. Which exhibits would you most want to see?

▶ **Plan and Solve**

6. What other activities do you need to consider when making your schedule?

7. If you estimate it takes about 30 min to go through each exhibit that you want to see, what is the greatest number you will be able to see? Assume that for each exhibit you also will have to wait in line about 10 min.

8. Given other activities and time spent in line, what is a realistic estimate of the number of exhibits you can see?

▶ **Make a Decision**

9. Make a list of everything you think will happen between the time you leave school in the morning and the time you must be back on the bus.

10. Write a schedule using 15-minute time periods.

8:00 A.M.
Leave from school

__:__ A.M.
Arrive at museum

__:__ A.M.
First exhibit

▶ **Present Your Decision**

11. Share your schedule with your class.

12. Did you leave enough time to do all the things you included? How did you check to be sure?

Exploring Decimal Patterns in Division

Explore • • • • •

Problem Solving Connection

Look for a Pattern

Materials

calculator

You used patterns to divide whole numbers. Patterns also can be used to divide decimals by 10, 100, and 1,000.

Work Together

1. Use your calculator to divide. Look for patterns.

   a. $425.7 \div 10$
   $425.7 \div 100$
   $425.7 \div 1,000$

   b. $63.8 \div 10$
   $63.8 \div 100$
   $63.8 \div 1,000$

   c. $9.1 \div 10$
   $9.1 \div 100$
   $9.1 \div 1,000$

2. Find each quotient. Use the patterns you found above.

   a. $82.82 \div 10$
   $82.82 \div 100$
   $82.82 \div 1,000$

   b. $445.6 \div 10$
   $445.6 \div 100$
   $445.6 \div 1,000$

   c. $6.98 \div 10$
   $6.98 \div 100$
   $6.98 \div 1,000$

3. Use 10, 100, or 1,000 to complete each.

   a. $35.4 \div \blacksquare = 3.54$
   b. $900.1 \div \blacksquare = 9.001$
   c. $8,100 \div \blacksquare = 8.1$

Remember

When you multiply numbers by 10, you move the decimal point one place-value position to the right.

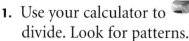 **Talk About It**

4. How is dividing by 10, 100, and 1,000 alike for whole numbers and decimals?

5. What happens to the position of the decimal point when you divide by 10? 100? 1,000?

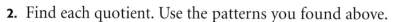

Connect

When dividing by 10, 100, or 1,000, move the decimal point one place to the left for each zero in the divisor.

$43.6 \div 10 = 43.6$	$43.6 \div 100 = 043.6$	$43.6 \div 1,000 = 0.0436$
1 zero in divisor	2 zeros in divisor	3 zeros in divisor
Move decimal 1 place.	Move decimal 2 places.	Move decimal 3 places.

Math Tip
Insert a zero to get 3 places.

Practice

Mental Math Find each quotient. Use mental math.

1. $601.4 \div 10$ **2.** $53.71 \div 100$ **3.** $\$149 \div 100$ **4.** $937 \div 1,000$

5. $11.9 \div 100$ **6.** $167 \div 1,000$ **7.** $138.2 \div 1,000$ **8.** $4.78 \div 100$

9. $\$830 \div 1,000$ **10.** $\$19.90 \div 100$ **11.** $423.7 \div 100$ **12.** $8.5 \div 1,000$

13. $60.7 \div 10$ **14.** $2,814 \div 100$ **15.** $7.56 \div 100$ **16.** $\$3.50 \div 10$

Algebra Readiness Use 10, 100, or 1,000 to complete each.

17. $9.8 \div n = 0.098$ **18.** $14.9 \div n = 1.49$ **19.** $\$75 \div n = \$0.75$ **20.** $366 \div n = 0.366$

Choose a word or number to complete **21** and **22.**

21. If you divide 85.1 by 100, the place value of 8 in the quotient is _____.

22. Dividing 5.6 by 10 gives the same result as dividing 56 by _____.

10	tenths
100	hundredths
1,000	thousandths

23. There are 100 paper clips packed in one box and 10 boxes in one carton. How many cartons would be used to package 30,000 paper clips?

24. **Science** A specimen is 3.5 cm wide when viewed under a microscope that increases the size 10 times. What is the actual width of the specimen?

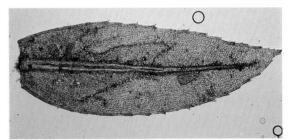

Specimen of Mnium leaf

25. **Social Studies** The Nina Tower, a 100-story skyscraper in Hong Kong, is 1,535 ft tall. If all stories are the same height, how tall is one story?

26. **Journal** Write a rule for dividing a decimal by 10, 100, or 1,000. Give an example.

STOP and Practice

Divide.

1. $13\overline{)\$36.53}$ 2. $12\overline{)766}$ 3. $8\overline{)\$717.04}$ 4. $26\overline{)415}$

5. $27\overline{)14,890}$ 6. $64\overline{)9,403}$ 7. $76\overline{)1,470}$ 8. $13\overline{)1,098}$

9. $13\overline{)12,012}$ 10. $14\overline{)\$8,505.98}$ 11. $8\overline{)915}$ 12. $89\overline{)12,600}$

13. $69\overline{)1,270}$ 14. $81\overline{)21,109}$ 15. $3\overline{)913}$ 16. $46\overline{)1,915}$

17. $\$255.99 \div 7$ 18. $1,215 \div 4$ 19. $99 \div 13$ 20. $\$40.14 \div 3$

21. $\$412 \div 50$ 22. $763 \div 61$ 23. $1,970 \div 36$ 24. $651 \div 28$

25. $603 \div 28$ 26. $\$47.96 \div 11$ 27. $\$1,025.97 \div 33$ 28. $816 \div 57$

29. $89 \div 5$ 30. $315 \div 11$ 31. $297 \div 38$ 32. $436 \div 27$

33. $67\overline{)465}$ 34. $51\overline{)259}$ 35. $59\overline{)688}$ 36. $83\overline{)250}$

37. $11\overline{)2,211}$ 38. $22\overline{)11,197}$ 39. $5\overline{)4,036}$ 40. $38\overline{)182}$

41. $43\overline{)\$110.08}$ 42. $78\overline{)\$97.50}$ 43. $16\overline{)\$37.28}$ 44. $43\overline{)\$102.77}$

45. $11\overline{)\$16.39}$ 46. $9\overline{)\$1.53}$ 47. $31\overline{)\$97.65}$ 48. $26\overline{)\$88.92}$

Error Search

Find each quotient that is not correct. Write it correctly and explain the error.

49. $15\overline{)3030}^{\,22}$ 50. $60\overline{)54,000}^{\,90}$ 51. $12\overline{)\$62.76}^{\,\$5.23}$ 52. $8\overline{)\$84.40}^{\,\$15.50}$

53. $100\overline{)2,000}^{\,200}$ 54. $48\overline{)\$300.48}^{\,\$60.26}$ 55. $18\overline{)\$148.50}^{\,\$8.25}$ 56. $28\overline{)448}^{\,16}$

57. $39\overline{)858}^{\,12}$ 58. $45\overline{)2,835}^{\,63}$ 59. $65\overline{)\$131.30}^{\,\$2.20}$ 60. $51\overline{)2,448}^{\,48}$

Drenched in Division!!

Divide. Use only the quotients that have remainders to solve the riddle. Some letters are not used.

Why was the scientist's head wet?

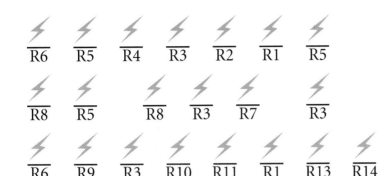

$\dfrac{}{\text{R6}}$ $\dfrac{}{\text{R5}}$ $\dfrac{}{\text{R4}}$ $\dfrac{}{\text{R3}}$ $\dfrac{}{\text{R2}}$ $\dfrac{}{\text{R1}}$ $\dfrac{}{\text{R5}}$

$\dfrac{}{\text{R8}}$ $\dfrac{}{\text{R5}}$ $\dfrac{}{\text{R8}}$ $\dfrac{}{\text{R3}}$ $\dfrac{}{\text{R7}}$ $\dfrac{}{\text{R3}}$

$\dfrac{}{\text{R6}}$ $\dfrac{}{\text{R9}}$ $\dfrac{}{\text{R3}}$ $\dfrac{}{\text{R10}}$ $\dfrac{}{\text{R11}}$ $\dfrac{}{\text{R1}}$ $\dfrac{}{\text{R13}}$ $\dfrac{}{\text{R14}}$ $\dfrac{}{\text{R9}}$ $\dfrac{}{\text{R15}}$

61. $16\overline{)1{,}119}$ [M]   **62.** $45\overline{)4{,}905}$ [P]   **63.** $8\overline{)849}$ [S]

64. $32\overline{)327}$ [D]   **65.** $19\overline{)\$361}$ [F]   **66.** $61\overline{)1{,}536}$ [N]

67. $34\overline{)3{,}473}$ [E]   **68.** $5\overline{)2{,}025}$ [G]   **69.** $9\overline{)8{,}293}$ [C]

70. $11\overline{)615}$ [I]   **71.** $84\overline{)3{,}037}$ [T]   **72.** $44\overline{)26{,}408}$ [H]

73. $23\overline{)3{,}499}$ [A]   **74.** $13\overline{)6{,}259}$ [B]   **75.** $82\overline{)20{,}746}$ [L]

76. $17\overline{)3{,}970}$ [R]   **77.** $15\overline{)9{,}317}$ [U]   **78.** $91\overline{)18{,}487}$ [O]

Number Sense Estimation and Reasoning

Copy and complete. Write >, <, or =.

79. $\$1.63 \div 15$ ● $\$6.84 \div 18$ **80.** $\$38 \div 13$ ● $\$76 \div 26$

81. $\$99.13 \div 11$ ● $\$88.99 \div 10$ **82.** $\$16.62 \div 10$ ● $\$32.32 \div 20$

83. $\$142 \div 50$ ● $\$288 \div 100$ **84.** $\$456.89 \div 1{,}000$ ● $\$3{,}678 \div 100$

85. $\$268.50 \div 30$ ● $\$412.90 \div 60$ **86.** $\$450.07 \div 15$ ● $\$317.25 \div 10$

87. $\$12.89 \div 10$ ● $\$128.90 \div 100$ **88.** $\$302.12 \div 80$ ● $\$4{,}715.14 \div 400$

89. $\$14.73 \div 14$ ● $\$40.38 \div 43$ **90.** $\$1{,}410 \div 200$ ● $\$705 \div 100$

91. $\$18.50 \div 20$ ● $\$1.85 \div 2$ **92.** $\$55.10 \div 12$ ● $\$71.07 \div 11$

93. $\$430.12 \div 29$ ● $\$43.12 \div 29$ **94.** $\$1{,}171 \div 400$ ● $\$598.07 \div 10$

Technology

Finding the Mean

Apollo 9 was the first piloted flight of the lunar module.

On May 25, 1961, President John F. Kennedy issued a challenge to the whole United States. His goal: for the United States to send an astronaut to the moon within a decade. This challenge created the Apollo program, which sent the *Apollo 11* spacecraft to the moon in 1969. However, *Apollo 11* was just one of many Apollo missions. How can you use the data below to compare the missions?

Materials

DataWonder! or other graphing software

Work Together

Use your software to organize and graph this data.

Duration of Flight		
Mission		Hours
1	Apollo 8 (1968)	147
2	Apollo 11 (1969)	195
3	Apollo 15 (1971)	295
4	Apollo 17 (1972)	302

1 Open a **Full Data Table**. Create a table like the one shown of some of the Apollo missions and their durations.

2 Graph the data.

- Pull down the **Graphs** menu and select **Show Graph**.

Graphs	
Show Graph	⌘G
Choose Scale...	⌘H
Vertical Bar	
Line Graph	
Pictograph	
Histogram	
Scattergram	
Circle Graph	
Horizontal Bar	
Stem and Leaf	
Box Plot	

Suppose you wanted to compare the missions by checking them against the mean number of days the missions lasted. This information is not found easily using the graph. But the program offers another way to find it.

3 Find the duration of each flight in days.

- To the right of the first column heading, type in two new headings: *Number of Hours in a Day* and *Length of Flight in Days*

- Type the number *24* in each cell in the *Number of Hours in a Day* column.

- To find the number of days each mission lasted, divide the number of hours in each mission by the number of hours in a day. First, pull down the **Calculate** menu and select **Divide.** Select the length in hours of the Apollo 8 mission. Then select the number of hours in a day. Press return. Finally, click Insert Result and select the length of flight in days cell for the *Apollo 8* mission. Repeat this process for each mission.

(4) Find the mean number of days the missions lasted.

- Type *Mean* below *Apollo 17 (1972).*

- Pull down the **Calculate** menu and select **Mean.**

- To select the length-in-days cells for the four missions in your table, hold down the shift key. Press Return.

- Click Insert Result and select the length-in-days cells for the **Mean** row.

- Put your Data Table in your Report.

Exercises

Answer **1–3** in your Report window. **Print Report** when you are finished.

1. What is the mean duration in days for the four Apollo missions in your Data Table?

2. Which missions were shorter than the mean duration? Which were longer?

3. By how much was the longest mission longer than the mean?

Extensions

Create a new Full Data Table like the one below. Then answer **4–6** in your Report window. **Print Report** when you are finished.

David Scott emerging from *Apollo 9.*

4. What is the mean number of hours for the 5 missions shown above? Create a **Mean** row for this data table, then put the data table in your Report.

5. How much shorter was the shortest mission than the mean?

6. Look at the data from both data tables. What generalizations can you make about the Apollo program?

Duration of Flight		
Mission		Hours
1	Apollo 7 (1968)	260
2	Apollo 9 (1969)	241
3	Apollo 10 (1969)	192
4	Apollo 12 (1969)	245
5	Apollo 16 (1972)	265

Calculate

Random Data...

Add	⌘+
Subtract	⌘−
Multiply	⌘M
Divide	⌘/
Mean	
Median	
Mode	
Maximum	
Minimum	
Quartile	

Sort By Row
Sort By Column

SECTION C
Review and Practice

(Lesson 10) Find each quotient.

1. $40\overline{)\$321.60}$
2. $13\overline{)\$6.50}$
3. $15\overline{)\$30.00}$
4. $43\overline{)\$74.82}$

5. $39\overline{)\$86.58}$
6. $50\overline{)\$74.00}$
7. $78\overline{)\$88.14}$
8. $36\overline{)\$83.88}$

9. $23\overline{)\$48.53}$
10. $37\overline{)\$99.16}$
11. $30\overline{)\$27.90}$
12. $20\overline{)\$135.00}$

13. $\$123.15 \div 15$
14. $\$561 \div 60$
15. $\$28.35 \div 21$
16. $\$95.55 \div 65$

(Lesson 12) Mental Math Find each quotient. Use mental math.

17. $43.81 \div 10$
18. $135 \div 10$
19. $19.99 \div 10$
20. $68.25 \div 100$

21. $1,385.6 \div 1,000$
22. $5.4 \div 1,000$
23. $8.39 \div 100$
24. $430.8 \div 10$

25. $0.18 \div 10$
26. $432.1 \div 1,000$
27. $5.9 \div 100$
28. $677.2 \div 1,000$

Find each quotient.

29. $\$17.00 \div 100$
30. $\$26.00 \div 100$
31. $\$562 \div 10$
32. $\$2,350 \div 1,000$

33. $\$40.00 \div 10$
34. $\$926 \div 100$
35. $\$64.30 \div 10$
36. $\$817 \div 100$

37. $\$4,025 \div 100$
38. $\$551 \div 10$
39. $\$89.30 \div 10$
40. $\$290 \div 1,000$

(Lesson 11) Use any strategy to solve each problem.

41. Kim has been offered two jobs. One job pays $68.00 for every 16 hours worked. The other pays $99.75 for every 21 hours worked. Which job would pay more per hour?

42. 100 students are going on a field trip. Which would be cheaper per person: charter 2 buses that hold 50 students each for $125 per bus or 3 buses that hold 34 students each for $98.35 per bus?

43. Would it be cheaper per can to buy 20 jars of paint for $63.00 or 34 jars of paint for $75.00?

44. In 11 days Janice saved 274 stamps. In 33 days Andy saved 495 stamps. Who saved more stamps per day?

45. Which would cost less per day, a 10-day trip for $565 or an 8-day trip for $500?

46. **Journal** Explain how you would decide if $7.10 \div 90$ is less than or greater than $0.08.

> ### Skills Checklist
> **In this section, you have:**
> ☑ Divided Money
> ☑ Solved Problems By Making Decisions
> ☑ Explored Decimal Patterns in Division

REVIEW AND PRACTICE

YOUR CHOICE

Choose at least one. Use what you have learned in this chapter.

1 Air Time

At Home Spend 30 minutes listening to music on the radio with a family member. Record how long each song lasts in seconds. Also record the length of each commercial. How much time was spent on commercials? What was the average length of one commercial? How many commercials could be played in 30 minutes? How many songs?

2 Mail Order Math

Find a catalog for a mail order company. Check **www.mathsurf.com/5/ch5** for ideas. Choose items from the catalog, recording the price of each. Make sure the number of items you choose is a two-digit number. Add your choices to find the total cost. Then divide the total cost by the number of items to find the average cost per item. Remember to round the answer to the nearest cent.

3 Surprise!

Plan a surprise party for a friend. Find the total cost for the items you will need– food, drink, decorations, and so on. Suppose 6 friends say they will chip in to help you pay for the party. How much money should each person pay?

4 X Marks the Spot

Complete these problems.

$$\begin{array}{r} 2X \\ 27\overline{)XXX} \\ -\underline{XX} \\ X43 \\ -\underline{2XX} \\ 0 \end{array}$$

$$\begin{array}{r} 1XX \\ 32\overline{)X,XXX} \\ -\underline{XX} \\ XX9 \\ -\underline{XXX} \\ 96 \\ -\underline{XX} \\ 0 \end{array}$$

Write your own missing number division problem for a partner to solve.

CHAPTER 5
Review/Test

Vocabulary Match each word with its example.

1. dividend   **a.** the 4 in the problem $124 \div 31 = 4$

2. divisor   **b.** the 16 in the problem $48 \div 16 = 3$

3. quotient   **c.** the 245 in the problem $245 \div 5 = 49$

 (Lessons 1, 7, and 12) Mental Math Use mental math to divide.

4. $5,600 \div 7$ 5. $81,000 \div 90$ 6. $240 \div 30$

7. $70\overline{)490,490}$ 8. $6\overline{)3,637}$ 9. $500\overline{)3,500}$

10. $3.2 \div 1,000$ 11. $5.06 \div 100$ 12. $0.12 \div 10$

(Lessons 2 and 3) Estimation Estimate each quotient. Identify whether your estimate is more or less than the actual quotient.

13. $6,520 \div 71$ 14. $\$368 \div 42$ 15. $461,891 \div 49$

16. $63\overline{)4,943}$ 17. $69\overline{)215}$ 18. $88\overline{)1,961}$

19. $25\overline{)\$1,576}$ 20. $19\overline{)\$448}$ 21. $33\overline{)899}$

(Lessons 4, 5, 6, and 10) Divide.

22. $24\overline{)145}$ 23. $81\overline{)405}$ 24. $38\overline{)112}$

25. $21\overline{)18,942}$ 26. $33\overline{)6,866}$ 27. $83\overline{)1,244}$

28. $13\overline{)\$66.56}$ 29. $43\overline{)\$392.16}$ 30. $51\overline{)\$57.63}$

(Lessons 8 and 9) Solve.

31. If marbles are sold in bags of 50 and there are 23 bags in each carton, how many cartons will be needed for 3,450 marbles?

32. On a recent field trip a class of 24 students each got a complete lunch for a total of $71.76 at a restaurant. If they had stopped at the restaurant across the street they could have bought a complete lunch that cost $3.19 per student. Did they get the better deal? Explain.

33. Which is the cheaper cost per energy bar: 5 energy bars for $2.25 or 8 energy bars for $2.80? Explain.

CHAPTER 5
Performance Assessment

An office building with 81 offices is being completed. The structure is built, but now the inside work must be done. It has been estimated that there are 88,800 hr of labor that will need to be done by the electricians, carpenters, painters, plumbers, and interior decorators. Your job is to decide how to divide up the hours per job and per worker.

These are your guidelines:

- You must employ a total of between 200 and 300 people.

- Each worker will work only 40 hr per week.

- You want the building completed in 12 weeks.

	Total Number of Hours of Work	Number of People Assigned	Number of Hours Worked Per Person	Number of Weeks Required to Complete Job
Electricians	24,000			
Carpenters	19,000			
Painters	10,000			
Plumbers	22,000			
Interior Decorators	13,800			
		Total: between 200–300		

1. **Decision Making** Decide how many people you want to put on each job. Keep a running total of your number of workers to be sure you are in the range of 200 to 300.

2. **Recording Data** Copy and complete a chart like the one shown. Make sure the work can be completed in 12 weeks.

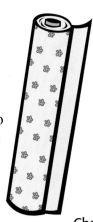

3. **Explain Your Thinking** How did you decide to allot workers for each job? Do you think certain jobs might take more hours to complete? If so, did you hire more people for those jobs?

4. **Critical Thinking** If you wanted the entire building complete in six weeks, what could you do?

Math Magazine

Reporting for Duty
So You Want to Be an Astronaut?

The word **astronaut** means *star sailor* in Latin. But there's much more involved than just sailing between stars.

NASA reviews applications from about 4,000 people for the only 20 or so positions available every two years. Those selected are experienced in math and their chosen scientific field. All have at least a college education and years of work experience. Astronauts must be people who can work as a team and have a great deal of self-motivation. In addition, they must be at least 58.5 inches tall and in excellent physical and mental health.

Mae C. Jemison, Pioneer

Mae C. Jemison was born in Alabama and grew up in Chicago. In college she studied engineering and Afro-American Studies. She went on to medical school and became a doctor. She spent 1.5 years in the Peace Corps, serving in Africa.

Dr. Jemison was accepted into the astronaut program the second time she applied. After 5 years, she became the first African-American woman to travel in space. In 1992, Dr. Jemison was a crew member on Spacelab J, where she conducted experiments in life sciences. She was in space for a total of 190 hr and 31 min.

Try These!

1. Check out **www.mathsurf.com/5/ch5** to learn more about careers related to space.

2. Must an astronaut be more than 5 feet tall? Remember 12 in. = 1 ft. Explain. Give your answer in feet and inches.

3. To the nearest hour, Dr. Jemison was in space for 191 hr. About how many days was this?

Cumulative Review

Test Prep Strategy: Eliminate Choices

Estimate the quotient.

What is the answer when 861 is divided by 9?

    Ⓐ 195 R3   Ⓑ 105 R6   Ⓒ 75 R6   Ⓓ 95 R6

Since 9 does not divide into 8, the first digit in the quotient is not in the hundreds place. This eliminates choices Ⓐ and Ⓑ. 9 does divide into 86 9 times,

therefore Ⓓ is the only possible solution.

Write the letter of the correct answer. Choose any strategy.

1. Find the quotient of 1,854 divided by 18.

    Ⓐ 103   Ⓑ 13   Ⓒ 1,003   Ⓓ 130

2. What is the remainder when 136 is divided by 23?

    Ⓐ 0   Ⓑ 2   Ⓒ 5   Ⓓ 21

3. If the data 23, 15, 28, 23, 36, 18, 35 was put into a stem-and-leaf plot, what numbers would make up the stem?

    Ⓐ 3, 5, 6, 8   Ⓑ 1, 2, 3
    Ⓒ 15, 18, 23, 28, 35, 36   Ⓓ not here

4. What is the sum of 1.308 and 62.1?

    Ⓐ 1.929   Ⓑ 7.518   Ⓒ 63.408   Ⓓ 62.2308

5. Jim is three times as old as Kara. Which could **not** possibly be Jim's and Kara's ages?

    Ⓐ 27, 9   Ⓑ 11, 8   Ⓒ 3, 1   Ⓓ 15, 5

6. Which are not factors of 210?

    Ⓐ 10, 21   Ⓑ 30, 7   Ⓒ 35, 6   Ⓓ not here

7. How many more trees were sold in 1996 than in 1995?

    Ⓐ 2   Ⓑ 50   Ⓒ 25   Ⓓ 1

8. How many trees were sold all together in the three years represented?

    Ⓐ 15   Ⓑ 275   Ⓒ 1,375   Ⓓ 375

9. What must be added to 28.3 to equal 34?

    Ⓐ 5.7   Ⓑ 6.3   Ⓒ 62.3   Ⓓ 5.3

10. What place value does 8 have in the product of 0.163 and 0.05?

    Ⓐ thousands   Ⓑ thousandths   Ⓒ tens   Ⓓ tenths

Test Prep Strategies

- Read Carefully
- Follow Directions
- Make Smart Choices
- Work Backward from an Answer
- Eliminate Choices

Christi's Tree Farm

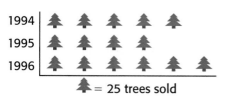

🌲 = 25 trees sold

REVIEW AND PRACTICE

Chapter 6
Geometry

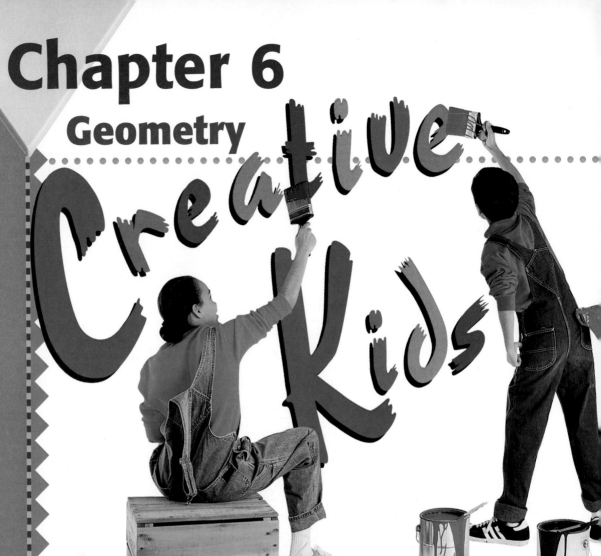

Creative Kids

SECTION
Ⓐ

Exploring Angles and Polygons 269

One of Houston's best-known theaters is the Nina Vance Alley Theatre. Name a street near this theater.

DOWNTOWN HOUSTON ⬈N

FRANKLIN
CONGRESS
WESTON
PRAIRIE
TEXAS
CAPITOL
RUSK
WALKER
McKINNEY
LAMAR
DALLAS
POLK

BAGBY · BRAZOS · SMITH · LOUISIANA · MILAM · TRAVIS · MAIN · FANNIN · SAN JACINTO · CAROLINE · AUSTIN

KEY TO NUMBERED SIGHTS

① ALLEY THEATRE
② CITY HALL
③ SAM HOUSTON PARK
④ SAM HOUSTON COLISEUM
⑤ PILLOT HOUSE
⑥ THE LONG ROW
⑦ OLD COTTON EXCHANGE
⑧ TRANQUILITY PARK
⑨ CONVENTION & VISITORS CENTER
⑩ MUSIC HALL
⑪ ALBERT THOMAS SPACE HALL OF FAME
⑫ JONES HALL FOR PERFORMING ARTS
⑬ OLD MARKET SQUARE

Analyzing Polygons

Quilting in the United States began during colonial days. What polygons have been sewn together to make the patch from the pieced quilt?

Navajo
Weaving
Page 283

Types of Quilts		
Quilting Method	**Description**	**Example**
Pieced Quilt	scraps of cloth sewn into design	
Story Quilt	scenes that tell a story	
Appliquéd Quilt	cutout designs sewn onto a large piece of cloth	
Crazy Quilt	randomly placed pieces of many sizes, colors, and shapes	

Surfing the World Wide Web!

How do you like to be creative? Do you draw, paint, make necklaces, or build models? Check out **www.mathsurf.com/5/ch6** to find out how other students use their creativity. Create a table to organize your data about these creative activities.

TEAM PROJECT
That's a Wrap

Materials
small piece of cardboard, scissors, tape, large sheet of paper, crayons or markers

A tessellation is a repeating shape that completely covers an area. One of the most famous artists to use tessellations was M.C. Escher (1898–1972). Make a sheet of wrapping paper using a tessellation.

M.C. Escher's "Symmetry Drawing E73" © 1998 Cordon Art–Baarn–Holland. All rights reserved.

Make a Plan

- What polygon will you use to make your tessellation?

- What shape will you try to make?

Carry It Out

1. Draw and cut out a cardboard pattern of a quadrilateral or a triangle.

2. Color one side of your polygon so you remember not to flip any pieces. Change your polygon. Here are two choices.

   a. Cut off a piece of the polygon. Slide the piece to the side directly opposite from the cut. Tape the piece.

    a.

   b. Cut off a piece of the polygon. Rotate the piece around one point. Tape the piece in place.

   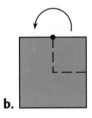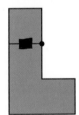

3. Trace the new shape on the paper. Fit the shapes together as you trace. Color the finished wrapping paper.

   b.

Talk About It

- Was changing the polygon easier or more difficult than you expected? How?

- Did your tessellation work the first time you tried it? If not, what happened?

Present the Project

Plan a class presentation of wrapping papers. Examine each team's new shape. Can you guess what polygon was changed to this shape?

Exploring Angles and Polygons

The *tinikling* is a traditional dance from the Philippines that uses bamboo poles.

Why might an understanding of lines and angles help keep the dancers from getting their feet caught in the poles?

Classifying Triangles

Review patterns. Give the next three numbers.

1. 1, 3, 5, 7, 9, ▪, ▪, ▪

2. 15, 30, 45, 60, 75, ▪, ▪, ▪

3. 3, 4, 4, 5, 6, 6 ▪, ▪, ▪

4. 180, 150, 120, ▪, ▪, ▪

Skills Checklist

In this section, you will:

☐ **Learn About Lines and Angles**

☐ **Explore Measuring Angles**

☐ **Learn About Triangles**

☐ **Learn About Quadrilaterals**

☐ **Solve Problems by Solving a Simpler Problem**

Lines and Angles

You Will Learn
how to show and name lines and angles

Vocabulary
line
a straight path that goes on forever in both directions

ray
part of a line having only one endpoint

angle
two rays having the same endpoint

Types of Lines
parallel
intersecting
perpendicular

endpoint
a point at the end of a ray

vertex
the point that two rays of an angle have in common

Learn • • • • • • • • •

Carlos from Santa Clara, California, enjoys dancing the *tinikling*, a folk dance from the Philippines. The poles used in the *tinikling*, like many objects in our world, remind us of **lines** and **angles**.

These poles are held parallel to one another.

Line *MN* is named by two points and this symbol: $\overleftrightarrow{MN}$.

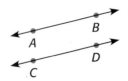 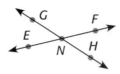

$\overleftrightarrow{AB}$ and $\overleftrightarrow{CD}$ are **parallel**. They never cross, even if they are extended.

$\overleftrightarrow{EF}$ and $\overleftrightarrow{GH}$ are **intersecting**. They cross each other at point *N*.

$\overleftrightarrow{IJ}$ and $\overleftrightarrow{KL}$ are **perpendicular**. They form square corners where they cross.

Part of a line is a **ray**. A ray extends in only one direction.

Ray *AB* ($\overrightarrow{AB}$) starts at *A* and goes on in the direction of *B*.

Ray *BA* ($\overrightarrow{BA}$) starts at *B* and goes on in the direction of *A*.

An angle is formed by two rays that have the same **endpoint**.

The sides of the angle are $\overrightarrow{QP}$ and $\overrightarrow{QR}$.

The **vertex** is the endpoint of the rays, *Q*.

Names for this angle are $\angle Q$, $\angle PQR$, or $\angle RQP$. Its interior and exterior are shown.

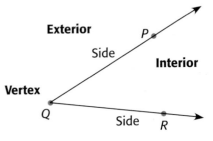

Math Tip
You can use the symbol $\angle$ instead of writing the word *angle*.

Talk About It

Are all intersecting lines perpendicular? Explain.

Check

Write the name for each.

1.

2.

3.

4.

5. **Reasoning** One side of $\angle XYZ$ is $\overrightarrow{YZ}$. Name its other side.

Practice

Skills and Reasoning

Write the name for each.

6.

7.

8.

9.

Name each in the figure at the right.

10. perpendicular lines

11. parallel lines

12. an angle that has L as its vertex

13. the rays that form $\angle N$

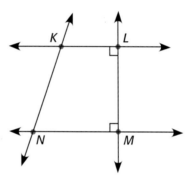

Problem Solving and Applications

Using Data Use the Data File on page 266 to answer **14–16.**

14. Which street looks like it is parallel to Polk?
   Ⓐ Travis   Ⓑ Smith   Ⓒ McKinney   Ⓓ not here

15. Which street looks like it is perpendicular to Capitol?
   Ⓐ Congress   Ⓑ Texas   Ⓒ Austin   Ⓓ not here

16. Describe two ways to get from the Jones Hall for Performing Arts to Tranquility Park.

Mixed Review and Test Prep

Divide.

17. $4{,}327 \div 32$ **18.** $9{,}876 \div 48$ **19.** $\$72.48 \div 16$ **20.** $\$426.24 \div 24$

21. Choose the best estimate for $2{,}498 \div 51$.
   Ⓐ 5   Ⓑ 500   Ⓒ 50   Ⓓ 40

Lesson 6-1   **271**

Exploring Measuring Angles

Materials
- protractors
- scissors

Vocabulary

protractor
an instrument used to measure the size of an angle

degree (°)
a unit of measure for angles

Types of Angles
acute
right
obtuse
straight

Problem Solving Hint

To measure an angle, you may need to trace it and extend its sides.

Explore •

You can use a **protractor** to find the size, or measure, of an angle. An angle is measured in **degrees** (°).

To Measure an Angle

Place the protractor's arrow on the angle's vertex.

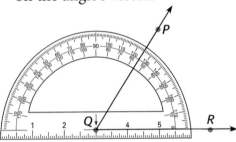

Place the 0° mark on one side of the angle. Read the measure where the other side of the angle intersects the protractor.

∠PQR has a measure of 55°.

To Draw an Angle of 140°

Draw $\overleftrightarrow{SU}$. Place a point on the line. Label it *T*. Place the protractor's arrow on *T*. Align the straight edge on $\overleftrightarrow{SU}$. Place a point at 140°. Label it *W*. Use a straight edge to draw $\overleftrightarrow{TW}$.

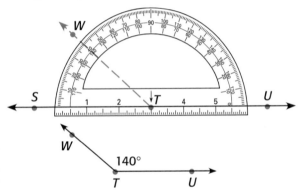

∠WTU has a measure of 140°.

Work Together

1. Trace each angle and extend its sides. Use a protractor to measure.

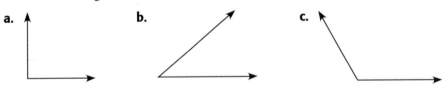

2. Use a protractor to draw an angle with each measure.
   a. 150°   **b.** 35°   **c.** 180°   **d.** 90°   **e.** 45°

3. Cut out the angles you drew. Sort them into three groups according to size.

Talk About It

How did you decide how to group the angles? Explain.

Angles can be classified by the way their measures compare to 90°.

∠PQR is an **acute** angle. Its measure is less than 90°.

∠LMN is a **right** angle. Its measure is 90°.

∠DEF is an **obtuse** angle. Its measure is greater than 90° and less than 180°.

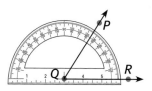

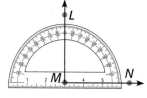

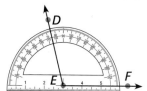

A **straight** angle measures 180°. ∠STU is a straight angle.

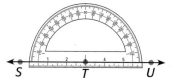

Practice •

Measurement Classify each angle as acute, right, or obtuse. Trace each angle and extend its sides. Then measure each with a protractor.

1.

2.

3.

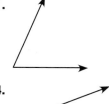

4.

5.

6.

7.

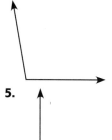

Estimation Choose the best estimate of each angle's measure. Then use a protractor to check your estimate.

8.

9.

10.

Ⓐ 10°

Ⓑ 45°

Ⓒ 90°

Ⓐ 75°

Ⓑ 90°

Ⓒ 170°

Ⓐ 50°

Ⓑ 95°

Ⓒ 180°

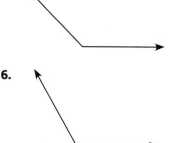

11. **Science** The cells in a honeycomb each form a hexagon. Classify the angles in this honeycomb cell as acute, obtuse, or right. Explain.

12. **Journal** Without using a protractor, draw an angle that is close to 30° and an angle that is close to 135°. Explain how you made your drawings.

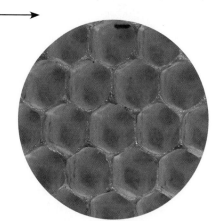

Honeycombs are made of wax.

Triangles

You Will Learn

how to classify triangles

Vocabulary

polygon
a plane, closed figure formed by line segments

line segment
a part of a line that has two end points

Triangles Classified by the Measure of Their Sides
equilateral
isosceles
scalene

Triangles Classified by the Measure of Their Angles
right
acute
obtuse

Learn • • • • • • • • • • • • • • • • • • •

Triangles in space! Greg, from Everett, Washington, just visited the Space Needle in Seattle with his class. When he described this structure to a friend, he said he could see many triangles in it.

Triangles are three-sided **polygons**. Each side is a **line segment**. They are named by their vertices. Triangle *ABC* is formed with line segments $\overline{AB}$, $\overline{BC}$, and $\overline{CA}$.

You can classify triangles by the lengths of their sides.

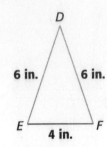

The 607 ft Space Needle was built for the 1962 World's Fair.

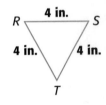

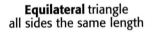

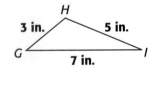

Equilateral triangle
all sides the same length

Isosceles triangle
at least two sides the same length

Scalene triangle
no sides the same length

Remember

An open figure does not have all sides connected.

You can also classify triangles by the measures of their angles.

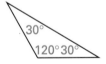

Right triangle
one right angle

Acute triangle
all angles less than 90°

Obtuse triangle
one angle greater than 90°

(**Talk About It**)

Could a triangle be both right and isosceles? Explain.

Check

1. Classify triangle *HIJ* by its sides.

5 in. 5 in.
H 5 in. J

2. Classify triangle *XYZ* by its angles.

Y
X Z

3. **Reasoning** Sabine said that a triangle was isosceles. Could it also be equilateral? Scalene? Equilateral and scalene? Explain.

Practice

Skills and Reasoning

Classify each triangle as equilateral, isosceles, or scalene.

4.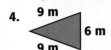
9 m
6 m
9 m

5.

6.
YIELD

Classify each triangle as acute, right, or obtuse.

7.
22° 140° 18°

8.

9.

10. Marsha drew a triangle with a 20° angle. Could it be right? Acute? Obtuse? Explain.

Problem Solving and Applications

11. **Collecting Data** Investigate the sums of the measures of the angles of a triangle.

    a. Use a ruler to draw a large triangle on a separate sheet of paper. Cut out the triangle. Measure the angles of the triangle. What is their sum?

    b. Tear off each angle of the triangle. Place all angles together at one point. What figure do they make?

    c. Draw two more triangles. Repeat steps **a.** and **b.**

    d. **Logic** What can you now conclude about the sum of the measures of the angles of any triangle?

    e. Use your conclusion to find the missing angle measure. Then check it with a protractor by tracing the missing angle and extending the sides.

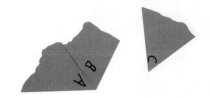

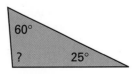
60°
? 25°

Mixed Review and Test Prep

STAY SHARP!

Find each product.

12. 927 × 52

13. 4,038 × 76

14. $24.99 × 37

15. $58.06 × 72

16. Which number is prime?

    Ⓐ 6   Ⓑ 23   Ⓒ 15   Ⓓ 27

Quadrilaterals

Learn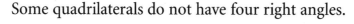

These Miao children, internationally
known as Hmong, are from the
Guizhou province in south central
China. Their rectangular-shaped
shoulder shawls are worn at one of the
many festivals they celebrate each year.

Some of the shapes in Miao patterns
are **quadrilaterals**, polygons with four
sides.

There are about 8 million
Hmong (mawng) worldwide.

Square
all sides the same length,
four right angles

Rectangle
opposite sides parallel
and the same length,
four right angles

Some quadrilaterals do not have four right angles.

Parallelogram
two pairs of parallel sides

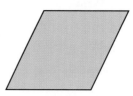

Rhombus
two pairs of parallel sides,
all sides the same length

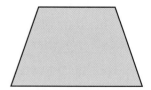

Trapezoid
only one pair of
parallel sides

Talk About It

Is it true that a square is a rectangle and a rhombus? Explain.

Check

Write the name that best describes each figure.

1.   2.   3.   4.

5. **Reasoning** Kevin was making a design using only parallelograms. Could Kevin use a square or a rhombus in his design? Explain.

Practice

Skills and Reasoning

Write the name that best describes each figure.

6.   7.   8.   9.

10.   11.  12.  13.

14. Latisha is making a design using a quadrilateral that has four equal sides and four same-sized angles. What shape is she using?

15. You are making a design using a quadrilateral with 2 pairs of parallel sides but no right angles. What shape could you use?

Problem Solving and Applications

Patterns Suppose you are asked to tile a floor. Trace each set of tiles and use them to design a pattern to tile the floor.

16.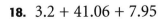

17.

Mixed Review and Test Prep

Find each sum.

18. 3.2 + 41.06 + 7.95   19. $63.40 + $7.15 + $9.80   20. 0.28 + 3.9 + 84.1

21. **Algebra Readiness** Find n.

$7 \times (9 \times 6) = (7 \times n) \times 6$ Ⓐ 6   Ⓑ 7   Ⓒ 9   Ⓓ 54

Problem Solving

Analyze Strategies:
Solve a Simpler Problem

You Will Learn

how solving a simpler problem can help you solve more difficult problems

Learn

Marc has had his own greeting card company since he was 6 years old.

Suppose Marc and 7 of his artist co-workers have a meeting. As they arrive, each one hands a sample of his or her work to each of the other artists.

How many greeting cards will be passed around?

Marc lives in Windsor, Ontario, in Canada.

Work Together

▶ **Understand**

What information do you have?

What are you trying to find?

▶ **Plan**

How will you find out the number of cards?

Solve a simpler problem similar to this one.

▶ **Solve**

Solve the simpler problem.

Start with 2 artists.
2 cards would be passed.

Continue with 3 artists.
6 cards would be passed.

Use a table to organize the data.

Find a pattern and complete the table.

Artists	2	3	4	5	6	7	8
Cards	2	6	12	20	30	42	56
Pattern	2×1	3×2	4×3	5×4	6×5	7×6	8×7

What is the answer?

There will be 56 greeting cards passed around.

▶ **Look Back**

What other strategy could you have used?

Another Example

If 8 artists are assigned to work in pairs,
how many different pairs of artists are possible?

Solve a similar simpler problem.
Use letters to represent artists.

2 artists: A, B   A —— B   1 pair

3 artists: A, B, C   A —— B   3 pairs
                              \ /
                               C

4 artists: A, B, C, D   A —— B   6 pairs
                             | ⨉ |
                             C —— D

Artists	2	3	4	5	6	7	8
Number of Pairs	1	3	6	10	15	21	28

+ 2   + 3   + 4   + 5   + 6   + 7

28 pairs of artists are possible.

Talk About It

1. In the example above, how did the table make the problem easier to solve?

2. How can solving a simpler problem help you solve a more difficult one?

Check

Problem Solving
Understand
Plan
Solve
Look Back

1. During a work period, 5 artists sit along one side of a
rectangular work bench. How many different ways can 5
artists be arranged along one side? Solve a simpler problem.
Use letters to represent artists.

   a. If only 2 artists are at the bench, how many arrangements are
   possible?

   b. With 3 artists, how many different arrangements can there be?

   c. With 4 artists, how many different arrangements are possible?

   d. In how many different ways can 5 artists be arranged along one
   side of the bench?

   e. Copy and complete the table.

Artists	2	3	4	5	6
Arrangements	2	6			

Apply the Strategy

Solve a simpler problem.

2. Diane makes greeting cards in unusual shapes. She makes 1 cut in a sheet of paper to get 2 pieces. With 2 cuts, she gets 4 pieces. With 3 cuts, she gets 7 pieces. What is the greatest number of pieces she can get by making 6 cuts?

3. Time Mr. Perez teaches his 30 students a new skill in art class. He will teach it to 2 students. Then each of them will teach 2 others and so on. It takes 10 min to learn the skill. No one will teach it more than once. How long will it take for all 30 students to learn the skill?

4. When a quilt is completed, each row will contain 6 of these designs. There will be a total of 9 rows. How many pieces of each size rectangle will be used?

Problem Solving Strategies
- Use Objects/Act It Out
- Draw a Picture
- Look for a Pattern
- Guess and Check
- Use Logical Reasoning
- Make an Organized List
- Make a Table
- Solve a Simpler Problem
- Work Backward

Choose a Tool

Choose a Strategy

Use any strategy to solve each problem.

5. Marc pays his artists $0.25 per card. He sells them for $1.00 and donates $0.10 of every sale to charity. If he sells 500 cards, how much will he keep?

6. An art school buys 8 jars of paint per carton. What is the least number of cartons they could buy to have 66 jars of paint?

7. Time A group of student artists finished a project at 4:00 P.M. on a Saturday. They worked for 2 hr before taking a 15-min break. They then worked for another $1\frac{1}{2}$ hr before lunch. After a 30-min lunch break, they worked $2\frac{1}{2}$ hr until the project was completed. At what time did they begin?

8. a. What choices could you make from this menu so that you had a sandwich, a drink, and a snack and spent exactly $5.00?

b. How much money would you need to buy any one choice of a sandwich, a drink, and a snack?

9. Money Two greeting cards together cost $3.00. The difference between their costs is $0.30. What is the cost of each card?

10. Jerome puts 8 colored markers in a box. He can fit 5 boxes on each shelf. If he has 200 markers in all, how many shelves will he fill?

MENU

SANDWICHES
HAM............$3.50
CHEESE............$3.00
TUNA............$2.50
PEANUT BUTTER....$2.25

SNACKS
APPLE............$0.75
BANANA............$0.90
YOGURT............$1.00

DRINKS
MILK............LARGE $1.50 SMALL $1.00
JUICE............$1.75
COCOA............$1.80

Problem Solving and HEALTH

Worthwhile exercise does not have to put a strain on your body. Each exercise below will burn about 150 calories.

- Washing a car for 45 min
- Playing volleyball for 45 min
- Fast dancing for 30 min
- Shoveling snow for 15 min
- Bicycling 4 mi in 15 min
- Gardening for 30 min
- Walking $1\frac{1}{2}$ mi in 35 min
- Raking leaves for 30 min
- Wheeling oneself in a wheelchair for 30 min

Using Data Use the data to answer 11–14.

11. How many calories would you burn washing cars for $1\frac{1}{2}$ hr?

12. For how long must you garden to burn the same number of calories as washing cars for $1\frac{1}{2}$ hr?

13. How many calories would you burn by bicycling 12 mi in 45 min?

14. Which burns more calories: fast dancing for 1 hr or bicycling 12 mi in 45 min? How many more?

15. **Journal** How do you decide when to use the Solve a Simpler Problem strategy?

Mixed Review and Test Prep

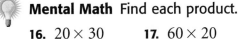

Mental Math Find each product.

16. 20×30	**17.** 60×20	**18.** 70×30	**19.** 20×80	**20.** 40×50
21. 35×6	**22.** 61×7	**23.** 47×8	**24.** 59×4	**25.** 25×5

Find each sum.

26.	27.	28.	29.	30.
$3.75	354	37	111	145
0.95	453	989	333	37
+ 4.10	+ 534	+ 22	+ 555	+ 456

31. Stanley was 8 years old in 1992. How old will he be in the year 2010?

    Ⓐ 18   Ⓑ 26   Ⓒ 16   Ⓓ 20   Ⓔ not here

SECTION A
Review and Practice

Vocabulary Copy and complete with the correct word from the list.

1. A ____ is a unit used to describe the measure of an angle.
2. When two rays share an endpoint they form an ____ .
3. A ____ is a straight path that goes on forever in both directions.
4. An instrument used to measure angles is called a ____ .
5. A polygon with four sides is called a ____ .

(Lesson 1) Name each in the figure at the right.

6. an angle that has $\overrightarrow{EF}$ as one of its sides
7. a pair of parallel lines
8. a pair of perpendicular lines
9. a pair of intersecting lines

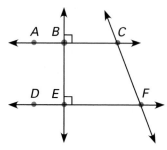

(Lesson 2) Trace and find the measure of each angle.

10.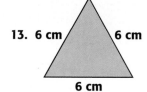

11.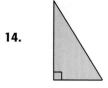

12.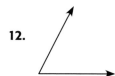

(Lessons 3 and 4) Match each figure with all the names that describe it.

13.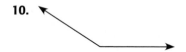
6 cm 6 cm
6 cm

14.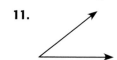

Word List	
acute triangle	right triangle
parallelogram	trapezoid
scalene triangle	rectangle
equilateral triangle	

15.

16.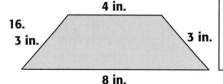
4 in.
3 in.   3 in.
8 in.

(Lesson 5) Solve.

17. For a meeting, 16 square tables will be pushed together to make a long table. Each table seats one person on each side. How many people can sit at the long table?

18. **Journal** Draw a square. Draw a rhombus that is not a square. Compare the two figures. How are they alike? Different?

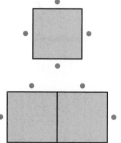

Skills Checklist

In this section, you have:

☑ Learned About Lines and Angles

☑ Explored Measuring Angles

☑ Learned About Triangles

☑ Learned About Quadrilaterals

☑ Solved Problems by Solving a Simpler Problem

REVIEW AND PRACTICE

Analyzing Polygons

Janice Maktina arranges a display of blankets at The Wheelwright Museum of The American Indian, Sante Fe, New Mexico. Describe how geometry and polygons are shown in the weaving.

GET READY!

Identifying Similar Polygons

Review finding patterns. Find the missing numbers.

1. A	3	4	5	
B		16	20	24

2. A	1	2		4
B	2	4	6	

3. A	2		6	8
B		12	18	24

4. A	1		5	7
B	6	18		42

Skills Checklist

In this section, you will:

☐ Learn About Similar and Congruent Polygons

☐ Explore Congruence and Motions

☐ Explore Line Symmetry

☐ Solve Problems by Making Decisions

Similar and Congruent Polygons

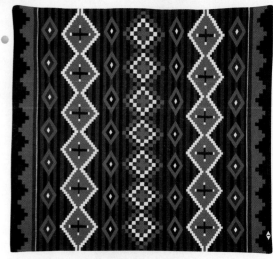

You Will Learn

how to recognize similar and congruent polygons

Vocabulary

similar polygons
polygons that have the same shape

congruent polygons
polygons that have the same size and shape

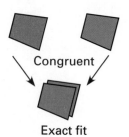

Congruent

Exact fit

Learn ● ● ● ● ● ● ● ● ● ● ● ●

This traditional revival style Navajo weaving is by Nina Beno. It contains a variety of polygons.

Similar polygons have the same shape but may or may not be the same size. The sides may or may not have the same length.

Similar Polygons	Nonsimilar Polygons

Congruent polygons have the same size and shape. They have sides of the same length and angles of the same measure.

Talk About It

Are all squares similar? Congruent? Explain.

Check ●

Math Tip

If two polygons are congruent, you can slide one on top of the other so they fit together exactly.

1. Which polygon is similar to ?

  Ⓐ   Ⓑ

2. Which polygon is congruent to ?

  Ⓐ   Ⓑ

3. Reasoning Are congruent figures always similar? Explain.

Skills and Reasoning

4. Which is similar to 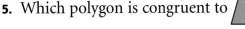 ? **5.** Which polygon is congruent to ?

Ⓐ  Ⓑ   Ⓐ  Ⓑ

6. Can two similar figures be congruent? Give an example to explain your answer.

Problem Solving and Applications

Use the figure to answer **7–12**.

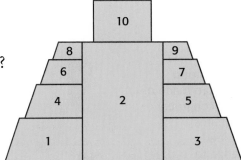

7. Which quadrilateral in the pyramid is congruent to 1?

8. Find two quadrilaterals that are similar to 4.

9. Which quadrilateral is similar to 2?

10. There are seven quadrilaterals that are similar to 6. Name them.

11. How many pairs of congruent quadrilaterals are there?

12. Write Your Own Problem Use the pyramid to write a problem about quadrilaterals, polygons, similar figures, or congruent figures.

Using Data Use the Data File on page 267 to answer **13**.

13. History Because cloth was scarce in colonial America, quilters used scraps of linen and wool to make quilts. They created designs by sewing triangular scraps into patterns.

　a. Look closely at the pattern of the pieced quilt design. What type of triangle do you see?

　b. Find the total number of small triangles in one pieced quilt square.

　c. Which triangles are congruent?

Mixed Review and Test Prep

Find each sum or difference.

14. $1,388 + 479 + 205$ **15.** $3,007 - 2,889$ **16.** $1,348 + 792$ **17.** $4,090 - 2,777$

18. Mental Math Without solving the problem, what is $274 \div 12$?

　Ⓐ 22 R10 　Ⓑ 220 R12 　Ⓒ 2 R34 　Ⓓ 21 R22

Exploring Congruence and Motions

Problem Solving Connection

- Draw a Picture
- Use Objects/ Act It Out

Materials

grid paper

Vocabulary

pentomino
a figure made of five congruent squares joined edge to edge

Explore

Each square in a **pentomino** must share a side with its neighbor.

These figures are not pentominoes because their sides do not line up.

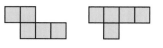 

Pentominoes   Not Pentominoes

You can flip, turn, and slide pentominoes to see if they are congruent.

  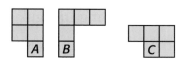

Flip   Turn   Slide   Line Up

Remember

Congruent figures are exactly the same size and shape.

Work Together

Pentominoes *A*, *B*, and *C* are shown.

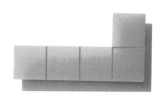

1. Draw *A*, *B*, and *C* on grid paper. Cut out each.

   a. Use slides, flips, and turns to test whether pentominoes *A*, *B*, and *C* are congruent.

   b. How many non-congruent, or different, pentominoes are shown?

2. Draw and cut out a new pentomino.

   a. Trace it on grid paper.

   b. Have your partner sketch a slide, flip, and turn of the pentomino.

   c. Test whether each sketch is congruent to your pentomino. Repeat with other pentominoes.

Talk About It

How do you know which pentominoes are congruent?

Connect

You can use slides, flips, and turns to show if figures are congruent. Use this chart to help visualize the motions you use to test for congruence.

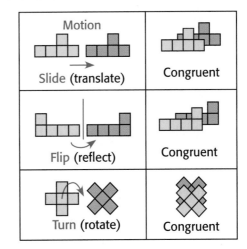

Motion	
Slide (translate)	Congruent
Flip (reflect)	Congruent
Turn (rotate)	Congruent

Practice

For each pentomino, write whether you would flip, turn, or slide the figures to show that they are congruent.

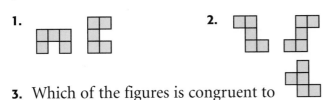

1.

2.

3. Which of the figures is congruent to  ?

   Ⓐ   Ⓑ   Ⓒ   Ⓓ

4. Which of the figures is **not** congruent to ⬚⬚⬚ ?

   Ⓐ   Ⓑ   Ⓒ   Ⓓ

5. Which of the figures shows ⬚ flipped?

   Ⓐ   Ⓑ   Ⓒ   Ⓓ

6. Draw two pentominoes that are congruent to this pentomino.

7. **Critical Thinking** What happens when you flip a pentomino and then flip it again in the same direction?

8. **What If** There are figures that are just like pentominoes except they are made of only four squares. How many of these figures could you draw that are all different from one another? Draw them.

9. **Journal** Explain how to use flips, turns, and slides to test whether two figures are congruent.

Exploring Line Symmetry

Problem Solving Connection

Look for a Pattern

Materials

grid paper

Vocabulary

line of symmetry
a line on which a figure can be folded so that the two parts fit exactly

Explore • • • • • • • • • • • • • •

Many artistic objects from around the world are symmetric. A **line of symmetry** separates a figure into two congruent parts. Figures may have more than one line of symmetry.

Gabon
Bakwele mask,
from Zaire, Africa

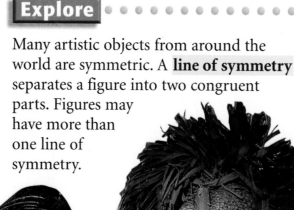

Seneca
corn husk mask

Lwalwa mask
from Zaire, Africa

19th
century
Japanese
mask

Some figures have no lines of symmetry.

Work Together

1. Copy each figure onto grid paper. Draw all lines of symmetry.

   a.   **b.**

2. Copy each figure onto grid paper. Use the line of symmetry to complete the drawing.

   a.   **b.**

3. You can use grid paper to create your own designs.

   a. Draw a design with one line of symmetry.

   b. Draw a design with two or more lines of symmetry.

(**Talk About It**)

When you are shown half of a drawing and the line of symmetry, would you flip, slide, or turn your half to make the second half? Explain.

Connect

How many lines of symmetry does this figure have?

You can check by tracing the outline.

Fold the figure along the possible lines of symmetry.

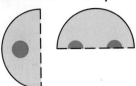

If the two sides match exactly, your fold line is a line of symmetry.

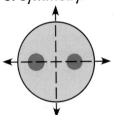

This figure has two lines of symmetry.

Practice

Trace the figure. Draw all lines of symmetry.

1.

2.

3.

Trace the figure. Use the line of symmetry to complete the figure.

4.

5.

6.

Use flips, turns, or slides. Is each pair of figures congruent? Explain.

7.

8.

9.

10. These figures are called hexominoes. How many lines of symmetry does each hexomino have?

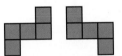

11. Draw three hexominoes that have no lines of symmetry.

12. Describe how you could use a mirror to see if a figure has a line of symmetry.

 13. Journal Explain how you know whether a figure is symmetric.

Problem Solving

Decision Making: Choose a Geometry Project

You Will Learn

how to decide which geometry project you would choose

Explore •

You must complete a geometry project by the end of the week. There are four projects from which you can choose. You can either work alone or with a partner.

Partner Projects

- **Polygon Mobile** Make a mobile including all the polygons from this chapter. Include some similar and some congruent figures. Be sure your mobile is balanced to hang correctly.

- **Gator Grabber** Make a movie flip book that shows an alligator opening its mouth from a 30° angle through to 180° and back again. Your book should have at least 20 pages.

Individual Projects

- **Symmetry and Art** Identify two works of art such as baskets, sculptures, or jewelry. One should have a line of symmetry and the other none. Name the work of art and the artist. Describe the symmetry or non-symmetry.

- **Mask** Make a paper mask that has absolutely no symmetry.

Other Facts and Data
The Symmetry and Art project will require time to find examples of art in newspapers, magazines, or books.
You can only work on the project after school and before dinner.

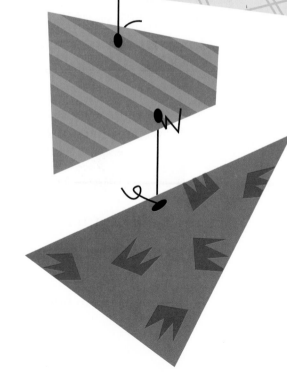

Work Together

▶ **Understand**

To make a good decision, you have to consider the details of a project. Here are a few things you should consider before choosing a geometry project.

1. Do you work better by yourself or with a partner?

2. How much time do you have to work on the project?

3. Do you have or can you get the materials you will need?

4. How will you use any of the finished projects?

5. Which project would you enjoy completing?

▶ **Plan and Solve**

6. Write an estimate of the time (in minutes) each step will take.

7. Write an estimate of the total time (in minutes) each project will take.

8. Divide the time you will need for each project equally among the number of days allowed for the project.

▶ **Make a Decision**

9. Copy and complete the table to help you make your decision. Which project will work best for you?

Considerations					
Project	**Alone/ Partner**	**Time**	**Materials**	**Use**	**Fun**
Polygon Mobile					
Gator Grabber					
Symmetry and Art					
Mask					

▶ **Present Your Decision**

10. Tell the class which project you chose.

11. Explain the reasons for your decision.

Claes Oldenburg's *Clothespin* is located in Philadelphia, Pennsylvania and stands 45 ft high!

Review and Practice

Vocabulary Match each with its meaning.

1. line of symmetry
2. congruent polygons
3. similar polygons
4. pentominoes

a. same shape and size
b. separates a figure into two congruent parts
c. same shape, not necessarily same size
d. five congruent squares joined side to side

(Lesson 6) Use the figure to answer **5–8**.

5. Which triangle is congruent to triangle *ACH*?
6. Which triangle looks similar to triangle *ABH*?
7. Is polygon *ABDC* similar to *CDSR*? Explain.
8. Are triangles *ACD* and *BDC* congruent? Explain.

(Lesson 7) Use the figures to answer **9–11**.

a.   b.   c.   d.   e.   f.

9. Which figures are pentominoes?
10. Which of the figures are congruent?
11. Which figures are congruent to this pentomino?

(Lesson 8) Trace each figure. Draw all lines of symmetry.

12.    13.    14. 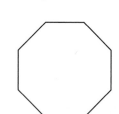   15.

16. Sandra said that squares and rectangles have the same number of lines of symmetry. Is she correct? Explain.

17. **Journal** Draw a pentomino that has one line of symmetry. Explain how you decided where that line should be drawn.

Skills Checklist

In this section, you have:

☑ **Learned About Similar and Congruent Polygons**

☑ **Explored Congruence and Motions**

☑ **Explored Line Symmetry**

☑ **Solved Problems by Making Decisions**

YOUR CHOICE

Choose at least one. Use what you have learned in this chapter.

1 Shape Search

Go on an art search to **www.mathsurf.com/5/ch6** and look for works of art that contain polygons. Make a list of these works of art and the polygons you found. Draw an example of each type of polygon next to each name. Compare your list with those of other students.

2 Polygon Border

You can use polygons to design a bulletin board border. On a sheet of graph paper, draw the outline of a bulletin board. Then use a ruler to create a pattern of parallelograms, rhombuses, and trapezoids around its border. Color each type of polygon a different color.

3 Facts About Faces

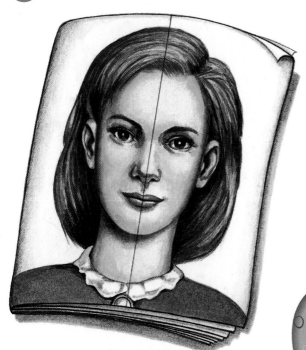

At Home Find magazine or newspaper advertisements which feature people's faces. Fold each ad to see if there is a line of symmetry from the top to the bottom of the face. How closely does each side of a human face match?

4 Amazing Mosaic

Quick! What's your favorite thing in the whole world? Your pet iguana? Your hacky sack? Your bike? A CD? Identify the major shape or shapes that make up this object. Trace each shape on a different color of construction paper, cut them out, and reassemble. Which shape did you use most often? Compare your drawings with those of your classmates.

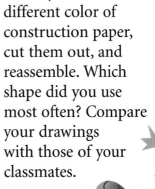

Review/Test

(Lessons 1, 3, 4 and 7) Choose a term that best decribes each figure.

1.

2.

parallel lines	perpendicular lines
ray	right angle
obtuse angle	acute angle
trapezoid	parallelogram
line segment	pentomino

3.

4.

5.

6.

7.

8.

9.

10.

(Lesson 3) Classify each triangle by its angles and by its sides.

11.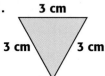
3 cm, 3 cm, 3 cm

12.
5 in., 5 in.

13.
6 m, 7 m, 5 m

(Lesson 5) Choose any strategy to solve.

14. Suppose you design a tile floor using this pattern. To cover the floor you must repeat the pattern 8 times in each row for 11 rows. How many triangular tiles will you need?

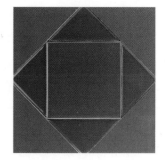

(Lesson 6) Write whether each pair of figures is similar, congruent, both similar and congruent, or neither.

15. A   B

16. A   B

17. A   B

(Lessons 2, 7, and 8) Follow the directions to draw each figure.

18. Use your protractor to draw a 35° angle.

19. Draw a pentomino and then draw it flipped.

20. Copy this figure and draw all the lines of symmetry.

CHAPTER 6
Performance Assessment

Beautiful window designs are often made with polygons. The window pictured has similar and congruent figures and symmetry that create amazing geometric designs.

Use what you have learned in this chapter to create your own design for a window.

Your window design must include:

- polygons
- triangles and quadrilaterals
- at least one pair of similar polygons
- at least one pair of congruent polygons
- at least one line of symmetry
- at least one obtuse angle

Palau de la Musica by Siqui Sanchez in Barcelona, Spain.

1. **Decision Making** Decide on the shape and size of your window. Decide whether your design will include a specific pattern. If so, does your pattern fit within the shape and size of the window? What tools will you need to create your design? You may want to draw your design on grid paper and use markers or pencils to color the panes.

2. **Planning** There are several elements that must be included in your design. How will you know if you have included them all? You can copy the list above and use it as a checklist. How will you check congruent and similar polygons? Lines of symmetry?

3. **Critical Thinking** Which element do you think will be the most difficult to include in your design? How will you make sure it's part of your design? What part of creating the design will be the easiest?

Math Magazine

Dance of Symmetry

In 1980 the small town of Wolcott, Vermont, began a children's fine arts center in an old railroad station. Although it has been a financial struggle for the town residents, the Wolcott Children's Ballet now has 50 dancers and a well-respected director.

The troupe travels throughout northern Vermont performing at schools, town halls, and with the Vermont Symphony Orchestra.

Classical ballet has five basic positions which are taught from the first lesson. All other steps are based on one of these five.

First position   Second position   Third position   Fourth position   Fifth position

Which of the five basic positions have line symmetry?

Try These!

1. Look at the gymnast. Does this position have line symmetry? Explain.

2. Look through magazines and books or go to **www.mathsurf.com/5/ch6** to find other examples of dance or sport activities that have line symmetry.

Jaier Lynch won a silver medal on the parallel bars for the U.S. team at the 1996 Summer Olympics.

Test Prep Strategy: Read Carefully

Watch for extra information.

A Girl Scout troop must sell 1,000 candy bars in order to afford to go to camp. The camp is 86 miles away. There are 20 girls in the troop. So far they have sold 826 bars. How many more candy bars do they need to sell?

   Ⓐ 500   Ⓑ 174   Ⓒ 9   Ⓓ 280

How far away the camp is or how many are going to camp is not necessary information.
1,000 − 826 is Ⓑ 174.

Write the letter of the correct answer. Choose any strategy to help.

1. Which figure is similar to polygon *ABCD*?

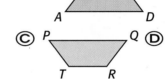

  Ⓐ 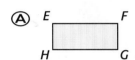   Ⓑ   Ⓒ   Ⓓ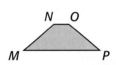

2. Name all the factors of 20.

  Ⓐ 1, 2, 4, 5, 10, 20   Ⓑ 4, 10, 20   Ⓒ 1 and 20   Ⓓ not here

3. What is 108 divided by 12?

  Ⓐ 3   Ⓑ 5   Ⓒ 8   Ⓓ 9

4. Which division problem has a quotient with a zero in the tens place?

  Ⓐ 335 ÷ 3   Ⓑ 275 ÷ 3   Ⓒ 315 ÷ 3   Ⓓ 524 ÷ 3

5. Mr. Rodriguez's class is hoping to make $300 at their car wash. In order to reach their goal, how many people must each donate $6 to have their cars washed?

  Ⓐ 12   Ⓑ 55   Ⓒ 5   Ⓓ 50

6. If the following numbers were in order, where would 0.3 be placed?

  0.285   0.4   0.365   0.036   0.2

  Ⓐ between 0.036 and 0.285   Ⓑ between 0.285 and 0.365
  Ⓒ between 0.365 and 0.4   Ⓓ before all the numbers

7. Wally spent $2.95, $3.05, $1.85, $1.55, and $3.65 on lunches. He started the week with a $20 bill. Find the mean cost for his lunches.

  Ⓐ $6.95   Ⓑ $2.95   Ⓒ $2.61   Ⓓ not here

8. Choose the best estimate for 211×37.

  Ⓐ 800   Ⓑ 60,000   Ⓒ 600   Ⓓ 8,000

Test Prep Strategies

- Read Carefully
- Follow Directions
- Make Smart Choices
- Eliminate Choices
- Work Backward from an Answer

REVIEW AND PRACTICE

Chapter 7
Fractions and Mixed Numbers

WATER, WATER, EVERYWHERE!

In the Swim
Page 301

SECTION A

Understanding Fractions

301

Which food or foods in the table have the greatest water content? The least?

Water Content of Some Popular Foods			
Whole egg (raw)	$\frac{3}{4}$	Banana	$\frac{3}{4}$
Skim milk	$\frac{9}{10}$	Cantaloupe	$\frac{9}{10}$
Cream cheese	$\frac{1}{2}$	Grape	$\frac{4}{5}$
Cottage cheese	$\frac{4}{5}$	Raisin	$\frac{1}{5}$
Swiss cheese	$\frac{2}{5}$	Prune	$\frac{3}{10}$
Potato (raw)	$\frac{4}{5}$	Plum	$\frac{9}{10}$

Surfing the World Wide Web!

Which of the foods listed do you like the most? The least? Find out more about different foods by checking out **www.mathsurf.com/5/ch7**. Use the data you find to report students' three most and least favorites.

Extending Fraction Understanding

321

Your body is 70% water, but the water in living things makes up a very small part of the active or moving fresh water on the earth. What percent of the active water is found in living things?

Where the Fresh Water Is

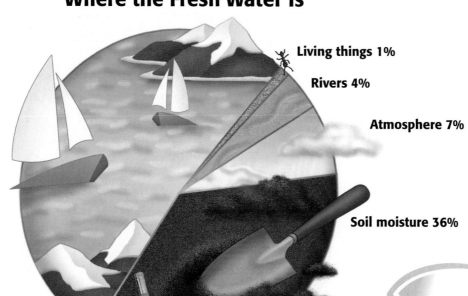

Living things 1%

Rivers 4%

Atmosphere 7%

Soil moisture 36%

Lakes 52%

Surveys
Page 321

TEAM PROJECT
Raindrops keep fallin'

Rain gauges are used to measure the amount of rainfall in a given period. Make your own rain gauge.

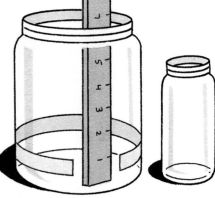

Make a Plan

- Where will you place your rain gauge?
- How will you record and report your data?

Carry It Out

1. Make the rain gauge.

   a. Measure and mark 1 inch on a large jar. Fill the jar with water to that mark. Then pour the water into a small narrow jar.

   b. Use the water level in the small jar to mark 1 inch on a strip of paper. Divide it into fourths and eighths. Repeat the marks for another inch.

   c. Empty the jar and attach the paper ruler. Put a funnel in the top.

2. Place the rain gauge securely in an open area.

3. Record the measurement after each rainfall, or every 24 hours. Empty the jar after each recording. You might make a graph of your data.

Talk About It

- Why did you use two jars to measure the water?

Present the Project

Plan a class presentation of the rain gauges and the data you recorded. Compare the gauges and the measuring strips. Are they alike?

Understanding Fractions

Eric started swimming when he was 6 years old. Since then, he has won 200 awards. About $\frac{1}{3}$ of these are first-place awards.

How could you use fractions to describe the awards that are not first place?

GET READY!

Working with Fractions

Review factors. Find the factors of each number.

1. 8   **2.** 12   **3.** 24   **4.** 10   **5.** 7

Copy and complete the patterns.

6. 3, 6, 9, ▪, ▪, 18   **7.** 4, 8, ▪, 16, ▪, ▪

8. 5, ▪, ▪, 20, 25, ▪   **9.** 6, ▪, ▪, 24, 30

301

Wholes and Parts

Learn • • • • • • • •

Eric is a champion swimmer
from Palo Alto, California.
He swims in a regulation
pool, which has 8 lanes.

Eric spends up to 2 hours a day
in the pool while training.

Example 1

What **fraction** can you use to describe
the lane in which Eric swims?

The region has 8 equal-sized lanes,
1 of the 8 lanes for each swimmer.
Say: "one eighth"

Write: $\dfrac{1}{8}$ ⟵ **numerator**
⟵ **denominator**

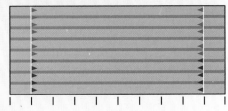

Eric uses $\dfrac{1}{8}$ of the pool, or region. The other swimmers use $\dfrac{7}{8}$.

You can also use fractions to describe parts of sets or segments.

Example 2

What part of the set of flags on the flag line is red?

$\dfrac{7}{12}$ ← flags are red
← flags in the whole set

$\dfrac{7}{12}$ of the flags are red.

Did You Know?

The flag lines warn
backstroke
swimmers
that they are
5 m from the
pool wall.

Example 3

What fraction names where the second flag line is?
The length of the pool is divided into 10 segments.

$\dfrac{9}{10}$ ← segments from the left
← segments in all

$\dfrac{9}{10}$ from the left names where the second flag line is.

Talk About It

Does the numerator of a fraction show the same thing for regions, sets,
and segments? The denominator? Explain.

Check

Write the fraction that names the shaded part of each.

1.

2.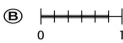

3.

4.

5. Which shows the fraction five sixths?

   Ⓐ  Ⓑ

6. **Reasoning** This drawing shows $\frac{7}{8}$ of a large Sicilian pizza. Describe the shape that represents the whole pizza.

   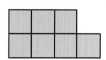

Practice

Skills and Reasoning

7. Write the fraction that names the shaded part.

   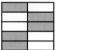

8. Write the fraction that names the circles in the set.

9. Which shading shows two thirds?

   Ⓐ

   Ⓑ

10. **Estimation** Estimate the fraction of the figure that is shaded.

    Ⓐ $\frac{1}{4}$ Ⓑ $\frac{1}{8}$ Ⓒ $\frac{1}{2}$

11. You and your friend each won first place in $\frac{1}{4}$ of your races. You won 3 firsts and your friend won 4 firsts. Explain how this could be.

Problem Solving and Applications

Using Data Use the table to answer 12.

12. What fraction names the part of all the medals that are **a.** gold? **b.** silver and bronze?

1996 U.S. Swim Team Olympic Medals		
Gold	Silver	Bronze
13	11	2

Language Arts Write what fraction of each word is vowels.

13. towel   14. question   15. bit   16. algebra   17. truth

Mixed Review and Test Prep

Find each sum or difference.

18.   37.8   19.   52.7   20.   0.9   21.   81.5   22.   3.9
    + 9.6   − 3.8   +5.38   − 4.3   +6.1

23. **Geometry** Which of the following figures is congruent to ?

    Ⓐ   Ⓑ   Ⓒ   Ⓓ

Lesson 7-1   **303**

Exploring Equivalent Fractions

Problem Solving Connection
Look for a Pattern

Materials
fraction strips

Vocabulary
equivalent fractions
fractions that name the same amount

Explore •

A fraction has many different names.

Remember

The numerator shows the number of equal parts considered. The denominator shows the number of equal parts in all.

Work Together

Use your fraction strips to help you answer these questions.

1. Find fraction strips that name the same amount as $\frac{1}{2}$.

   a. How many $\frac{1}{4}$ strips do you need?

   b. Can you use $\frac{1}{3}$ strips? What other strips can you use?

   c. Write all the fractions that match the $\frac{1}{2}$ strip.

2. Find as many fractions as possible that name the same amount as:

   a. $\frac{1}{4}$ **b.** $\frac{2}{3}$ **c.** $\frac{3}{4}$ **d.** $\frac{3}{6}$ **e.** $\frac{4}{12}$

Talk About It

As you use more strips to make a whole, what happens to their size? Explain.

Connect

Fractions that name the same amount are called **equivalent fractions**.

Each picture is shaded to show a fraction equivalent to $\frac{1}{2}$ of the whole amount.

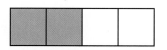

$\frac{2}{4}$ $\frac{3}{6}$ $\frac{4}{8}$ $\frac{5}{10}$

Practice

1. Which picture shows a fraction equivalent to $\frac{1}{3}$?

      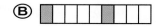

Write two fractions that name the shaded part.

2.   3.   4.   5.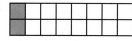

6.   7. 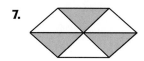   8.   9.

10. Write a fraction for the shaded part of each picture. Which fractions are equivalent to $\frac{2}{5}$?

a.   b. 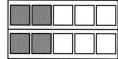   c. 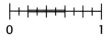   d.

11. Pat said she ate $\frac{1}{2}$ of a pizza. Amir said he ate more since he ate $\frac{4}{8}$ of the same-size pizza. Is Amir correct? Explain.

12. Draw a picture to show 4 of 16 sections of a swimming pool. Write two fractions that describe the picture.

 13. **Journal** Explain how you can use fraction strips to find fractions equivalent to $\frac{2}{3}$.

Patterns with Equivalent Fractions

Learn • • • • • • • • • • • • • • • • •

Cadaro has a collection of colorful fish. His favorite fish are gold.

Write two equivalent fractions for the part of the set that is gold. 4 of the 8 fish are gold.

gold → $\frac{4}{8} = \frac{1}{2}$
in all →

Cadaro is from Baton Rouge, Louisiana.

You can use shaded regions to show fractions equivalent to $\frac{1}{2}$.

$\frac{1}{2}$ $\frac{2}{4}$ $\frac{3}{6}$ $\frac{4}{8}$

You can multiply or divide the numerator and denominator by the same non-zero number to get equivalent fractions.

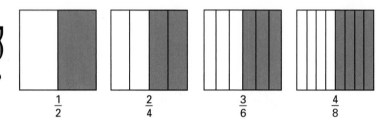

$$\frac{1}{2} = \frac{2}{4} \qquad \frac{1}{2} = \frac{3}{6} \qquad \frac{4}{8} = \frac{1}{2} \qquad \frac{3}{6} = \frac{1}{2}$$

(**Talk About It**)

Describe patterns you see in fractions equivalent to $\frac{1}{2}$.

Check •

Find equivalent fractions with a denominator of 12.

1. $\frac{1}{4}$ **2.** $\frac{2}{3}$ **3.** $\frac{4}{24}$ **4.** $\frac{12}{36}$ **5.** $\frac{10}{24}$

6. Reasoning How can both the numerator and the denominator of a fraction increase and yet the fraction names the same amount?

Skills and Reasoning

Find equivalent fractions with a denominator of 6.

7. $\frac{2}{3}$ **8.** $\frac{10}{12}$ **9.** $\frac{8}{24}$ **10.** $\frac{3}{18}$ **11.** $\frac{1}{2}$

Write the fractions in the box equivalent to each fraction below.

12. $\frac{1}{2}$ **13.** $\frac{1}{3}$ **14.** $\frac{3}{4}$

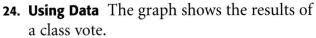

$\frac{2}{4}$	$\frac{6}{8}$	$\frac{4}{12}$	$\frac{12}{16}$	$\frac{2}{6}$	$\frac{3}{9}$	$\frac{4}{8}$	$\frac{9}{12}$	$\frac{3}{6}$

Copy and complete.

15. $\frac{6}{8} = \frac{\blacksquare}{4}$ **16.** $\frac{5}{6} = \frac{\blacksquare}{12}$ **17.** $\frac{7}{8} = \frac{14}{\blacksquare}$ **18.** $\frac{12}{24} = \frac{\blacksquare}{2}$

Write whether each pair is equivalent. Explain how you decided.

19. $\frac{8}{12}$ and $\frac{2}{3}$ **20.** $\frac{3}{4}$ and $\frac{6}{8}$ **21.** $\frac{1}{4}$ and $\frac{4}{12}$

22. Two quarters of a water polo match are complete. Now it is half time. Explain how this could be.

Problem Solving and Applications

23. **Time** A clock shows that $\frac{5}{60}$ and $\frac{1}{12}$ are equivalent fractions. Explain.

24. **Using Data** The graph shows the results of a class vote.
    a. What fraction of the voters like red fish?
    b. What fraction like blue fish?
    c. Compare these fractions.
    d. **Write your own problem** about this graph.

Favorite Sea Creatures

Mixed Review and Test Prep

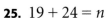

 Algebra Readiness Copy and complete.

25. $19 + 24 = n$ **26.** $72 - n = 53$ **27.** $n + 45 = 63$ **28.** $101 + n = 175$

 Mental Math Find each product.

29. 9×8 **30.** 9×80 **31.** 0.9×8 **32.** 0.09×8

33. What is the middle number in an ordered set of data called?

     Ⓐ range   Ⓑ median   Ⓒ mode   Ⓓ stem

Greatest Common Factor

Vocabulary

common factor
a number that is a factor of two or more different numbers

greatest common factor (GCF)
the greatest number that is a factor of each of two or more numbers

Remember
A number is a factor of another number if it divides the number with a remainder of zero.

Learn

A group of 18 scientists and 24 photographers are scuba diving to study a coral reef. The group must split up equally into same-sized teams and take turns diving. There should be as many teams as possible.

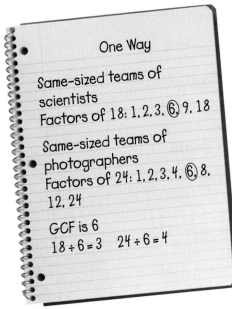

One Way

Same-sized teams of scientists
Factors of 18: 1, 2, 3, ⑥, 9, 18

Same-sized teams of photographers
Factors of 24: 1, 2, 3, 4, ⑥, 8, 12, 24

GCF is 6
18 ÷ 6 = 3   24 ÷ 6 = 4

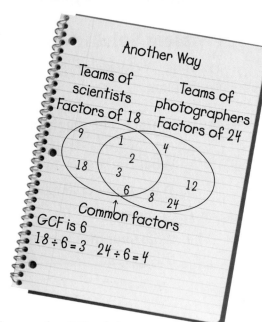

Another Way

Teams of scientists
Factors of 18

Teams of photographers
Factors of 24

9   1   4
18   2
     3   12
     6   8   24
Common factors
GCF is 6
18 ÷ 6 = 3   24 ÷ 6 = 4

There should be 6 teams of 3 scientists and 4 photographers.

Talk About It

What number is a factor of every whole number? Explain.

Check

Find the common factors and the greatest common factor for each pair.

1. 6 and 8   **2.** 9 and 18   **3.** 12 and 30   **4.** 7 and 8

5. Find the greatest common factor of 12, 24, and 36.

6. Reasoning If 15 is a factor of a number, what other numbers must also be factors?

Practice

Skills and Reasoning

Find the common factors and the greatest common factor for each pair.

7. 8 and 12   **8.** 4 and 6   **9.** 10 and 15   **10.** 6 and 18

11. 9 and 3   **12.** 18 and 27   **13.** 16 and 20   **14.** 20 and 30

15. 12 and 24   **16.** 9 and 30   **17.** 10 and 45   **18.** 16 and 24

19. Find the greatest common factor of 8, 16, and 24.

20. Find the factors and the common factors of 6 and 15.

21. Could 10 be the greatest common factor of 35 and 40? Explain.

22. The common factors of two numbers are 1 and 3. The two numbers could be 9 and 21 or 3 and 6. Explain how.

Problem Solving and Applications

23. Patterns A scientist has 36 photos of reef fish that she wants to arrange in equal rows and columns to frame. How many photo arrangements can be made?

24. Science A scientist is setting up some study tanks. She has collected 12 identical fish and 15 identical plants. She wants all tanks to be alike and contain as many fish and plants as possible. What is the greatest number of tanks she can set up?

Mixed Review and Test Prep

Copy and complete.

25. $\frac{2}{4} = \frac{4}{\blacksquare}$ **26.** $\frac{1}{\blacksquare} = \frac{2}{12}$ **27.** $\frac{4}{12} = \frac{\blacksquare}{3}$ **28.** $\frac{2}{5} = \frac{\blacksquare}{10}$ **29.** $\frac{\blacksquare}{3} = \frac{8}{12}$

Find equivalent fractions.

30. $\frac{20}{40}$ **31.** $\frac{8}{12}$ **32.** $\frac{8}{16}$ **33.** $\frac{2}{8}$ **34.** $\frac{6}{16}$

 Algebra Readiness Copy and complete.

35. $5 \times n = 30$ **36.** $3 \times n = 12$ **37.** $n \times 4 = 20$ **38.** $n \times 3 = 21$

39. Which number correctly completes the number sentence $\frac{3}{7} = \frac{\blacksquare}{14}$?

     Ⓐ 7   Ⓑ 10   Ⓒ 6   Ⓓ 11

Simplest Form

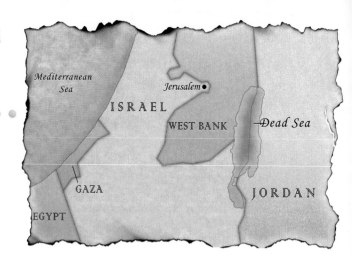

Mediterranean
Sea

Jerusalem •

ISRAEL

WEST BANK

—Dead Sea

GAZA

JORDAN

EGYPT

You Will Learn
how to find the simplest form of a fraction

Vocabulary
simplest form
when the greatest common factor (GCF) of the numerator and denominator is 1

Learn • • • • • • • • •

Did you ever wonder where the Dead Sea got its name? It's so salty that no fish can live in it. The Dead Sea is $\frac{24}{100}$, or $\frac{6}{25}$, salt. $\frac{6}{25}$ is in simplest form.

A fraction is in its **simplest form** if the greatest common factor (GCF) of the numerator and the denominator is 1.

You can find the simplest form of $\frac{18}{24}$ in more than one way.

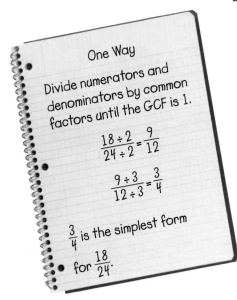

One Way

Divide numerators and denominators by common factors until the GCF is 1.

$$\frac{18 \div 2}{24 \div 2} = \frac{9}{12}$$

$$\frac{9 \div 3}{12 \div 3} = \frac{3}{4}$$

$\frac{3}{4}$ is the simplest form for $\frac{18}{24}$.

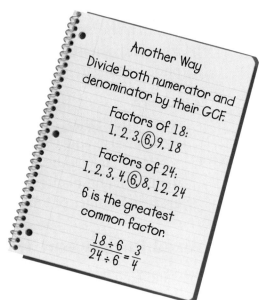

Another Way

Divide both numerator and denominator by their GCF.

Factors of 18:
1, 2, 3, ⑥ 9, 18

Factors of 24:
1, 2, 3, 4, ⑥ 8, 12, 24

6 is the greatest common factor.

$$\frac{18 \div 6}{24 \div 6} = \frac{3}{4}$$

Did You Know?
The shore around the Dead Sea is 1,310 feet below sea level.

Talk About It

Which method is a short cut? Explain.

Check •

Find the simplest form for each fraction.

1. $\frac{12}{16}$ 2. $\frac{6}{8}$ 3. $\frac{4}{10}$ 4. $\frac{10}{15}$ 5. $\frac{8}{12}$

6. **Reasoning** Explain why all fractions with a numerator of 1 are in simplest form.

Skills and Reasoning

Find the simplest form for each fraction.

7. $\frac{10}{12}$ 8. $\frac{10}{20}$ 9. $\frac{3}{5}$ 10. $\frac{16}{24}$ 11. $\frac{5}{6}$ 12. $\frac{2}{8}$

13. $\frac{14}{16}$ 14. $\frac{15}{20}$ 15. $\frac{10}{16}$ 16. $\frac{5}{12}$ 17. $\frac{7}{14}$ 18. $\frac{8}{10}$

19. $\frac{20}{30}$ 20. $\frac{12}{21}$ 21. $\frac{8}{12}$ 22. $\frac{10}{25}$ 23. $\frac{3}{18}$ 24. $\frac{3}{7}$

Write whether each fraction is in simplest form. If it is not, find the simplest form.

25. $\frac{3}{9}$ 26. $\frac{2}{7}$ 27. $\frac{2}{14}$ 28. $\frac{3}{8}$ 29. $\frac{4}{15}$ 30. $\frac{12}{16}$

31. $\frac{4}{32}$ 32. $\frac{3}{10}$ 33. $\frac{6}{16}$ 34. $\frac{2}{9}$ 35. $\frac{5}{24}$ 36. $\frac{3}{15}$

37. Explain why a fraction whose numerator is 2 and whose denominator is an odd number is in simplest form.

Problem Solving and Applications

38. **Science** The water in the Pacific Ocean is about $\frac{4}{100}$ salt. What is this fraction in simplest form?

39. **Geography** There are 50 states in the United States. Only Florida, Alabama, Mississippi, Louisiana, and Texas border the shore of the Gulf of Mexico.

   a. What fraction of all states is this? What is the fraction in simplest form?

   b. **Critical Thinking** When might you prefer to use a fraction that is not in simplest form, such as $\frac{5}{50}$?

 40. **Journal** Explain how to find the simplest form for $\frac{16}{24}$.

Mixed Review and Test Prep

Find each product.

41. 317
   $\times\ 7$

42. 425
   $\times\ 8$

43. 97
   $\times\ 6$

44. 99
   $\times\ 3$

45. 289
   $\times\ 7$

46. Which is the standard form for one hundred seven thousandths?

   Ⓐ 107,000   Ⓑ 0.170   Ⓒ 0.107   Ⓓ 0.0107

Technology

Simplifying Fractions on a Calculator

It's time to train for the great brain vs. calculator contest. You learned to simplify fractions by using common factors. Do you think you could do it faster on your calculator?

Work Together

Here is how to simplify a fraction on the calculator. See how fast it goes.

1 Enter the fraction $\frac{6}{12}$ by entering 6 $\boxed{/}$ 12.

2 Next press the $\boxed{\text{Simp}}$ key followed by $\boxed{=}$. What do you get? By what number did the calculator divide both the numerator and denominator?

3 Besides $\frac{3}{6}$, what else do you see on the display?

4 Press the $\boxed{\text{Simp}}$ key and $\boxed{=}$ again. What do you get? By what number did the calculator divide the numerator and denominator?

5 Press the $\boxed{\text{Simp}}$ keys and $\boxed{=}$ again. What happens? Why does this happen? Does N/D → n/d appear? Explain.

6 Name the factors that the calculator used to divide.

7 Do you think it is easier to simplify by calculator or in your head?

Math Tip
N/D → n/d means that the fraction is not yet in its simplest form.

Exercises

Use your calculator to simplify. Show each result.

1. $\dfrac{8}{12}$ **2.** $\dfrac{8}{24}$ **3.** $\dfrac{25}{75}$ **4.** $\dfrac{9}{36}$ **5.** $\dfrac{4}{20}$

Use your calculator to simplify each fraction. Give the factors the calculator uses in order, as well as the simplest form.

6. $\dfrac{4}{100}$ **7.** $\dfrac{12}{48}$ **8.** $\dfrac{4}{64}$ **9.** $\dfrac{4}{12}$ **10.** $\dfrac{4}{8}$

Extensions

11. And here's the contest!

- Work with a partner. Decide on five fractions you want to simplify.

- List the fractions on two sheets of paper.

- One of you will use the calculator. The other will use her or his brain.

- Start together. Use a timer if you wish.

- Now change roles and select new fractions.

12. Reasoning Do you think that it is always most efficient to use technology? Explain.

13. Math History How do you think calculators have changed over time? See if you can find a calculator from the 1960s or an article about one. What functions did it have? How large was it? How heavy? What did it cost? Compare your information with your classmates' information.

14. Journal How will you decide when to simplify a fraction using a calculator?

Exploring Comparing and Ordering Fractions

Problem Solving Connection
Look for a Pattern

Materials
fraction strips

Vocabulary
common denominators
denominators that are the same

Explore •

How do you decide if one fraction is greater than another?

Work Together

You can use fraction strips to help you compare and order fractions.

Remember
> means greater than

< means less than

1. Which is greater, $\frac{2}{6}$ or $\frac{1}{2}$? Take a $\frac{1}{2}$ strip. Line up two $\frac{1}{6}$ strips under it.

2. Decide whether each fraction is greater than or less than $\frac{1}{2}$.

   a. $\frac{2}{5}$ b. $\frac{5}{8}$ c. $\frac{3}{4}$ d. $\frac{3}{8}$

3. Compare and tell which fraction is greater. Use < or >.

   a. $\frac{1}{3}$ ● $\frac{1}{6}$ b. $\frac{1}{12}$ ● $\frac{1}{4}$ c. $\frac{1}{6}$ ● $\frac{1}{8}$

   d. When numerators are 1, which is the greater fraction?

4. Compare and tell which fraction is greater.

   a. $\frac{2}{8}$ ● $\frac{2}{12}$ b. $\frac{5}{6}$ ● $\frac{5}{8}$ c. $\frac{2}{12}$ ● $\frac{2}{3}$

   d. When numerators are the same, which is the greater fraction?

5. Compare and tell which fraction is greater. Use < or >.

   a. $\frac{2}{3}$ ● $\frac{1}{3}$ b. $\frac{7}{12}$ ● $\frac{11}{12}$ c. $\frac{4}{4}$ ● $\frac{3}{4}$

   d. When denominators are the same, which is the greater fraction?

6. Order these fractions from least to greatest: $\frac{1}{4}, \frac{2}{3}, \frac{3}{8}, \frac{5}{6}, \frac{1}{12}$.

Talk About It

Tell how you used patterns to compare fractions.

Comparing Fractions			
Fraction Type	**Test**	**Comparison**	**Example**
Numerators of 1	Check denominators	Fraction with lesser denominator is greater	$\frac{1}{3} > \frac{1}{5}$
Same numerators	Check denominators	Fraction with lesser denominator is greater	$\frac{2}{3} > \frac{2}{7}$
Same denominators	Check numerators	Fraction with greater numerator is greater	$\frac{4}{5} > \frac{2}{5}$

When 2 fractions have the same denominator, we say they have a **common denominator**.

Practice •

Compare each pair of fractions. You may use fraction strips or draw pictures. Copy and complete. Write >, <, or =.

1. $\frac{1}{2}$ ● $\frac{1}{4}$ 2. $\frac{2}{3}$ ● $\frac{1}{3}$ 3. $\frac{1}{2}$ ● $\frac{7}{8}$ 4. $\frac{5}{8}$ ● $\frac{2}{3}$ 5. $\frac{6}{7}$ ● $\frac{2}{3}$

6. $\frac{3}{4}$ ● $\frac{5}{8}$ 7. $\frac{1}{2}$ ● $\frac{7}{14}$ 8. $\frac{2}{4}$ ● $\frac{3}{4}$ 9. $\frac{7}{8}$ ● $\frac{5}{6}$ 10. $\frac{3}{9}$ ● $\frac{1}{3}$

11. $\frac{1}{8}$ ● $\frac{1}{12}$ 12. $\frac{1}{2}$ ● $\frac{4}{8}$ 13. $\frac{1}{6}$ ● $\frac{1}{3}$ 14. $\frac{5}{6}$ ● $\frac{3}{6}$ 15. $\frac{4}{7}$ ● $\frac{4}{9}$

16. Use fraction strips. Order these fractions from least to greatest.

   $\frac{3}{4}$ $\frac{2}{3}$ $\frac{1}{6}$ $\frac{7}{12}$ $\frac{5}{8}$

17. Use fraction strips. Order these fractions from greatest to least.

   $\frac{1}{3}$ $\frac{5}{6}$ $\frac{1}{4}$ $\frac{11}{12}$ $\frac{7}{8}$

18. **Critical Thinking** Is $\frac{1}{17}$ greater than or less than $\frac{1}{7}$? Explain.

19. André swam $\frac{3}{6}$ the length of the pool. Susan swam $\frac{7}{8}$ the length of the same pool. Who swam farther?

20. **a.** For $\frac{5}{6}$, enter 5 ÷ 6 and write the decimal.

   b. For $\frac{5}{8}$, enter 5 ÷ 8 and write the decimal.

   c. Use the decimals to compare the fractions. Write your answer.

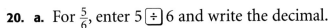

21. **Journal** Explain how to compare two fractions with

   a. the same denominators   **b.** the same numerators

Comparing and Ordering Fractions

You Will Learn

how to use common denominators to compare and order fractions

Learn • • • • • • • • • • • • • • • • • •

Did you know that a banana is $\frac{3}{4}$ water?
Grapes are $\frac{5}{6}$ water.

Which kind of fruit is made up of more water?

Compare $\frac{3}{4}$ and $\frac{5}{6}$. Find a common denominator to compare.

Remember

Common multiples for two numbers are multiples for both numbers.

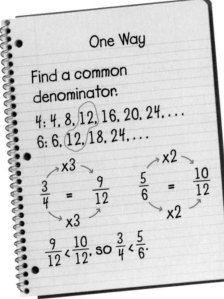

One Way

Find a common denominator.

4: 4, 8, 12, 16, 20, 24, ...
6: 6, 12, 18, 24, ...

$$\frac{3}{4} \overset{\times 3}{\underset{\times 3}{=}} \frac{9}{12} \qquad \frac{5}{6} \overset{\times 2}{\underset{\times 2}{=}} \frac{10}{12}$$

$\frac{9}{12} < \frac{10}{12}$, so $\frac{3}{4} < \frac{5}{6}$.

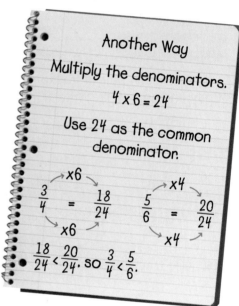

Another Way

Multiply the denominators.
$4 \times 6 = 24$

Use 24 as the common denominator.

$$\frac{3}{4} \overset{\times 6}{\underset{\times 6}{=}} \frac{18}{24} \qquad \frac{5}{6} \overset{\times 4}{\underset{\times 4}{=}} \frac{20}{24}$$

$\frac{18}{24} < \frac{20}{24}$, so $\frac{3}{4} < \frac{5}{6}$.

Grapes contain more water than bananas.

You can use a common denominator to order fractions.

Example

Compare $\frac{2}{3}$, $\frac{3}{4}$, and $\frac{7}{12}$. Write in order from least to greatest.

$$\frac{2}{3} \overset{\times 4}{\underset{\times 4}{=}} \frac{8}{12} \qquad \frac{3}{4} \overset{\times 3}{\underset{\times 3}{=}} \frac{9}{12}$$

$\frac{7}{12} < \frac{8}{12}$ and $\frac{8}{12} < \frac{9}{12}$, so $\frac{7}{12} < \frac{2}{3} < \frac{3}{4}$.

Talk About It

Why is using fractions with common denominators like solving a simpler problem?

Check

Copy and complete. Write >,<, or =.

1. $\frac{1}{2}$ ● $\frac{3}{5}$ **2.** $\frac{5}{6}$ ● $\frac{6}{7}$ **3.** $\frac{9}{12}$ ● $\frac{3}{4}$ **4.** $\frac{2}{3}$ ● $\frac{5}{8}$ **5.** $\frac{3}{10}$ ● $\frac{3}{8}$

6. Compare $\frac{1}{3}$, $\frac{1}{4}$, and $\frac{1}{5}$. Write them in order from least to greatest.

7. Reasoning Explain how you know $\frac{2}{3}$ is greater than $\frac{2}{5}$.

Practice

Skills and Reasoning

Copy and complete. Write >,<, or =.

8. $\frac{1}{4}$ ● $\frac{1}{3}$ **9.** $\frac{3}{5}$ ● $\frac{5}{6}$ **10.** $\frac{3}{4}$ ● $\frac{3}{5}$ **11.** $\frac{5}{7}$ ● $\frac{7}{8}$ **12.** $\frac{3}{4}$ ● $\frac{7}{10}$

13. $\frac{4}{10}$ ● $\frac{9}{20}$ **14.** $\frac{2}{6}$ ● $\frac{6}{18}$ **15.** $\frac{4}{9}$ ● $\frac{7}{8}$ **16.** $\frac{9}{12}$ ● $\frac{2}{3}$ **17.** $\frac{6}{9}$ ● $\frac{2}{3}$

18. $\frac{1}{5}$ ● $\frac{1}{15}$ **19.** $\frac{2}{3}$ ● $\frac{3}{5}$ **20.** $\frac{1}{4}$ ● $\frac{3}{8}$ **21.** $\frac{1}{5}$ ● $\frac{2}{10}$ **22.** $\frac{6}{10}$ ● $\frac{59}{100}$

Compare the fractions. Write them in order from least to greatest.

23. $\frac{1}{4}$, $\frac{3}{8}$, $\frac{2}{3}$ **24.** $\frac{7}{8}$, $\frac{2}{5}$, $\frac{2}{3}$ **25.** $\frac{5}{12}$, $\frac{3}{5}$, $\frac{2}{3}$ **26.** $\frac{2}{3}$, $\frac{3}{7}$, $\frac{7}{8}$ **27.** $\frac{5}{9}$, $\frac{1}{2}$, $\frac{4}{7}$

28. Explain how you can tell whether $\frac{3}{7}$ or $\frac{3}{8}$ is greater.

Problem Solving and Applications

Using Data Use the Data File on page 298 to answer **29–31.** Which has the greater fraction of water?

29. a prune or a plum   **30.** a potato or a banana   **31.** cream, cottage, or Swiss cheese

32. Science The human body is $\frac{7}{10}$ water. Is the human body more than $\frac{3}{4}$ water? Explain.

Mixed Review and Test Prep

Divide.

33. $3\overline{)618}$ **34.** $6\overline{)965}$ **35.** $50\overline{)250}$

36. What is the favorite fruit of these students?

ⓐ apples

ⓑ bananas

ⓒ plums

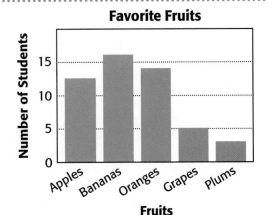

Favorite Fruits

Problem Solving

Analyze Strategies: **Make a Table**

Learn •

Some sneakers are pumped with air each time they are worn. The gas cartridges for the pump cost about $3 and can be used about 15 times.

If you plan to wear your sneakers to school 90 times this year, how much will it cost to fill them with the pump?

This gas cartridge and pump are used to fill sneakers with air.

Work Together

▶ **Understand**   What do you know?

What do you need to find out?

▶ **Plan**   Make a table to see a pattern.

Find the cost of 90 uses.

Cost	$3
Number of uses	15

▶ **Solve**   Use patterns to complete the table.

Continue until you reach the answer.

What is the answer?

Cost	$3	$6	$9	$12	$15	$18
Number of uses	15	30	45	60	75	90

The cost of 90 uses is $18.

Reading Tip
You can get data from your table.

▶ **Look Back**   How can you check?

(**Talk About It**)

Describe how patterns were used to solve the problem.

Check

Use a table to solve each problem.

A survey of sneaker wearers found that 7 out of 10 wore their sneakers for less than one year. The survey included 80 students.

1. If only 10 students had been asked, how many should have said that they use their sneakers for one year or less?

2. How many students were asked about their sneakers?

3. Copy and complete the table. How many wore their sneakers less than 1 year?

Total number surveyed	10	20	30	40	50	60	70	80
Those using sneakers for less than 1 year	7	14	21					

Problem Solving Practice

Use a table or any strategy to solve each problem.

4. Some sneakers light up! They have 3 small bulbs in each shoe or 6 in each pair. How many bulbs are needed to light up 25 pairs of sneakers?

5. Two out of every 5 students who wear sneakers say that they help pay for each new pair. Out of 50 wearers, how many help pay for their sneakers?

6. A sporting-goods store uses 3 storage shelves for every 20 pairs of basketball shoes. If 160 pairs are to be stored, how many shelves are needed?

7. **Money** A friend bought a pair of sneakers for $51. If you buy a $95 pair on sale for $78, how much more do you pay than your friend?

8. **Money** Alex came home from shopping with $12. At his last stop, he paid $15 for a T-shirt and $7.50 for 3 pairs of socks. Before that he had bought a pair of basketball shoes for $51.50. How much money did Alex take with him when he left home?

9. One company sells sneakers with lights that will flash for between 6 and 8 months. What is the least number of pairs you should buy if you want 2 years' worth of these sneakers? Explain.

10. In one store, sneakers with pumps cost $5 more than sneakers with lights and $22 more than sneakers with air in the soles. If the air-soled sneakers are $49, how much are sneakers with pumps?

　Ⓐ $86　　Ⓑ $71　　Ⓒ $64　　Ⓓ $37　　Ⓔ not here

Problem Solving Strategies

- Use Objects/Act It Out
- Draw a Picture
- Look for a Pattern
- Guess and Check
- Use Logical Reasoning
- Make an Organized List
- Make a Table
- Solve a Simpler Problem
- Work Backward

Choose a Tool

PROBLEM SOLVING PRACTICE

Review and Practice

Vocabulary Complete each sentence with a word or words from the list.

numerator	denominator	equivalent fractions
greatest common factor (GCF)	simplest form	

1. Fractions that name the same region, part of a set, or part of a segment are called _____.

2. The _____ is the top number in a fraction.

3. The _____ is the bottom number in a fraction.

4. A fraction is in _____ when the greatest common factor of the numerator and denominator is 1.

5. The greatest number that is a factor of each of two numbers is called the _____.

(Lessons 1 and 5) Write the fraction that names each shaded part. Then write it in simplest form.

6. 7.  8.  9.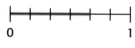

(Lessons 2 and 3) Copy and complete.

10. $\frac{2}{3} = \frac{\blacksquare}{6} = \frac{8}{\blacksquare} = \frac{16}{\blacksquare}$ 11. $\frac{12}{36} = \frac{\blacksquare}{18} = \frac{4}{\blacksquare} = \frac{\blacksquare}{9}$

(Lesson 4) Find the greatest common factor for each pair.

12. 12 and 18   13. 3 and 4   14. 2 and 9   15. 6 and 10

(Lessons 6 and 7) Write each set of fractions in order from least to greatest.

16. $\frac{1}{2}, \frac{1}{3}, \frac{1}{4}$ 17. $\frac{2}{3}, \frac{5}{8}, \frac{3}{4}$ 18. $\frac{8}{9}, \frac{5}{6}, \frac{3}{4}$

(Lesson 8) Solve. You may make a table to help.

19. It costs $4 for 5 tubes of oil paint. If your art class needs 40 tubes for a project, how much will they cost?

20. **Journal** Would you prefer using fractions strips or equivalent fractions to compare $\frac{5}{6}$ and $\frac{3}{8}$? Explain.

Skills Checklist

In this section, you have:

☑ Learned About Wholes and Parts

☑ Explored Equivalent Fractions

☑ Used Patterns and Found Equivalent Fractions

☑ Found the Greatest Common Factor

☑ Found the Simplest Form

☑ Compared and Ordered Fractions

☑ Solved Problems by Making a Table

REVIEW AND PRACTICE

B Extending Fraction Understanding

April collects data about sea mammals, since she is interested in marine biology. How might you use fractions, decimals, and percents to represent data?

Skills Checklist

In this section, you will:

☐ Explore Mixed Numbers

☐ Write Improper Fractions and Mixed Numbers

☐ Explore Comparing and Ordering Mixed Numbers

☐ Learn About Percents

☐ Connect Fractions, Decimals, and Percents

☐ Solve Problems by Making Decisions

GET READY!

Relating Fractions, Decimals, and Percents

Review decimals. Write the word name for each decimal.

1. 4.24   **2.** 48.903   **3.** 0.32   **4.** 8.004

Write each in standard form.

5. three tenths   **6.** seventeen hundredths

7. one and one hundred four thousandths

Exploring Mixed Numbers

Problem Solving Connection
Use Objects/
Act It Out

Materials
fraction strips

Vocabulary
mixed number
a number that has a whole-number part and a fraction part

improper fraction
a fraction greater than or equal to one

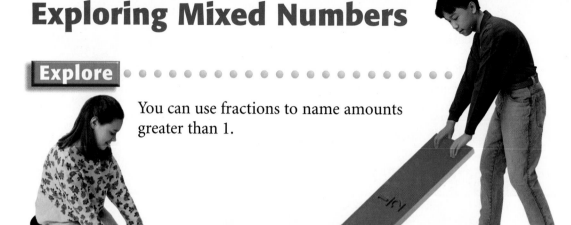

Explore

You can use fractions to name amounts greater than 1.

Work Together

Use fraction strips or draw pictures to help.

1. Find how many halves are the same as 2 wholes and 1 half.

   a. Use two 1 strips and a $\frac{1}{2}$ strip to show 2 wholes and 1 half.

   b. How many $\frac{1}{2}$ strips are needed to match 2 wholes and 1 half?

   c. What fraction names the same amount as 2 wholes and 1 half?
   2 wholes and 1 half → $\frac{\blacksquare}{2}$

2. Find a fraction that names the same region as:

   a. 1 whole and 3 fourths. → $\frac{\blacksquare}{4}$ b. 3 wholes and 2 thirds. → $\frac{\blacksquare}{3}$

3. How many wholes and thirds are the same as $\frac{8}{3}$? Use the fewest strips possible to match all 8 of the $\frac{1}{3}$ strips.

   $\frac{8}{3}$ = ■ wholes and ■ thirds

4. Find each.

   a. Number of wholes and halves that are the same as $\frac{7}{2}$

   b. Number of wholes that are the same as $\frac{8}{4}$

Remember
It takes four $\frac{1}{4}$ strips to equal 1 whole.
It takes three $\frac{1}{3}$ strips to equal 1 whole.

Talk About It

How can you tell that $\frac{8}{4}$ is another name for 2?

Connect

A whole number and a fraction make up a **mixed number**.
$3\frac{1}{4}$ is called a mixed number.

A fraction greater than or equal to 1 is called an **improper fraction**.
$\frac{5}{5}$ and $\frac{13}{4}$ are improper fractions.

$\frac{5}{5}$ and 1 name an equal amount.	$3\frac{1}{4}$ and $\frac{13}{4}$ name an equal amount.
$\frac{1}{5}$ $\frac{1}{5}$ $\frac{1}{5}$ $\frac{1}{5}$ $\frac{1}{5}$ $\rightarrow$ $\frac{5}{5}=1$	 1 1 1 $\frac{1}{4}$ $\rightarrow$ $3+\frac{1}{4}=3\frac{1}{4}$  $\frac{4}{4}$ $\frac{4}{4}$ $\frac{4}{4}$ $\frac{1}{4}$ $\rightarrow$ $\frac{13}{4}$

Practice

Write the mixed or whole number and the improper fraction that name the shaded part of each.

1.   **2.**   **3.**

4.   **5.**    **6.**
```
0          1          2
```

Make a drawing that shows each fraction.

7. $2\frac{1}{3}$ **8.** $\frac{9}{5}$ **9.** $\frac{6}{2}$ **10.** $1\frac{5}{8}$ **11.** $\frac{4}{4}$

Health It is recommended that people drink 2 qt of water each day to keep their bodies working properly. An average glass of water is $\frac{1}{4}$ qt.

12. This is what Caleb drank one day. Did he drink the recommended amount? Explain.

13. This is what Sarah drank one day. Did she drink the recommended amount? Explain.

14. Journal Explain how to write the mixed number and improper fraction that name the shaded part.

Mixed Numbers

You Will Learn

how to write improper fractions as mixed numbers and mixed numbers as improper fractions

Learn

Many people like to drink "sports drinks" when they are dehydrated. Water is better for you. If you drink 9 qt of water in a week, how many gallons of water do you drink? A quart is $\frac{1}{4}$ of a gallon. Write 9 qt as $\frac{9}{4}$ gal.

You can write improper fractions as mixed numbers and mixed numbers as improper fractions.

Example 1

Write $\frac{9}{4}$ as a mixed number.

Divide the numerator by the denominator.

$$\frac{9}{4} \rightarrow 4\overline{)9} \begin{array}{r} 2\ R1 \\ -8 \\ \hline 1 \end{array}$$

Write the quotient as the whole number.

Write the remainder as the numerator.

The divisor is the denominator.

$2\ R1 \rightarrow 2\frac{1}{4}$ $\frac{9}{4} = 2\frac{1}{4}$

If you drink $\frac{9}{4}$ gal, you drink $2\frac{1}{4}$ gal.

Example 2

Write $3\frac{2}{5}$ as an improper fraction.

Multiply the denominator by 3.

Add the numerator.

$(5 \times 3) + 2 = 17$

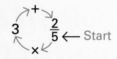

Write the sum as the numerator. $\rightarrow 17$

The denominator stays the same. $\rightarrow \overline{5}$

$3\frac{2}{5} = \frac{17}{5}$

Talk About It

Did You Know?

The widest waterfall in the world is Khône Falls in Laos. It is $6\frac{7}{10}$ mi wide.

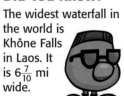

1. Suppose you get zero as the remainder when you divide a numerator by a denominator. What does this tell you?

2. What operations do you use to write $2\frac{2}{3}$ as an improper fraction? To write $\frac{5}{4}$ as a mixed number? How are these operations related?

Check

Write each improper fraction as a mixed number in simplest form or as a whole number. Write each mixed number as an improper fraction.

1. $\frac{5}{3}$ 2. $\frac{11}{5}$ 3. $\frac{12}{8}$ 4. $1\frac{1}{2}$ 5. $2\frac{5}{6}$ 6. $3\frac{2}{3}$

7. **Reasoning** If you have 14 quarters, do you have $4.00? Explain.

Practice

Skills and Reasoning

Write each improper fraction as a mixed number in simplest form or as a whole number.

8. $\dfrac{28}{4}$ 9. $\dfrac{16}{2}$ 10. $\dfrac{17}{4}$ 11. $\dfrac{15}{3}$ 12. $\dfrac{17}{10}$

13. $\dfrac{10}{3}$ 14. $\dfrac{24}{10}$ 15. $\dfrac{24}{6}$ 16. $\dfrac{25}{8}$ 17. $\dfrac{32}{6}$

Write each mixed number as an improper fraction.

18. $7\dfrac{3}{10}$ 19. $2\dfrac{1}{5}$ 20. $4\dfrac{3}{5}$ 21. $2\dfrac{3}{4}$ 22. $5\dfrac{1}{3}$

23. $8\dfrac{1}{8}$ 24. $1\dfrac{4}{7}$ 25. $6\dfrac{2}{5}$ 26. $1\dfrac{3}{8}$ 27. $7\dfrac{7}{8}$

 Algebra Readiness Copy and complete.

28. $4 = \dfrac{n}{5}$ 29. $3 = \dfrac{n}{3}$ 30. $5 = \dfrac{n}{2}$ 31. $1 = \dfrac{n}{4}$

32. Tony needs $\dfrac{1}{2}$ gal of water for each of his tropical fish. His fish tank holds 24 gal. If Tony has 50 fish, is his tank big enough? Explain.

Problem Solving and Applications

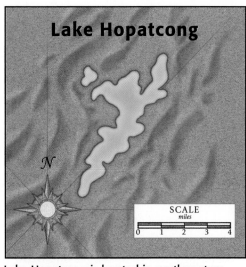

Lake Hopatcong is located in northwestern New Jersey.

33. **Using Data** Use the data in *Did You Know?* on page 324. Write the width of the Khône Falls as an improper fraction.

On this map, $\dfrac{1}{4}$ in. represents 1 mi. Use the scale to answer **34** and **35**.

34. **Geography** On the map, Lake Hopatcong is $1\dfrac{3}{4}$ in. long. How long is the lake in miles?

35. Lake Sparta, not shown here, is 4 mi from Lake Hopatcong. What map distance would this be?

Mixed Review and Test Prep

Copy and complete. Write <, >, or =.

36. $\dfrac{2}{3} \bullet \dfrac{2}{5}$ 37. $\dfrac{1}{2} \bullet \dfrac{2}{3}$ 38. $\dfrac{3}{8} \bullet \dfrac{6}{16}$ 39. $\dfrac{5}{8} \bullet \dfrac{3}{5}$ 40. $\dfrac{5}{6} \bullet \dfrac{5}{8}$

41. Which number is equal to 1.70?

　Ⓐ 1.070   Ⓑ 1.7   Ⓒ 1.07   Ⓓ $1\dfrac{1}{7}$

Exploring Comparing and Ordering Mixed Numbers

Problem Solving Connection

- Use Objects/ Act It Out
- Look for a Pattern

Materials

fraction strips

Explore •

How can you compare and order amounts greater than 1 that include fraction parts?

Work Together

1. Use fraction strips to find out how $3\frac{3}{8}$ compares to 3, to $3\frac{1}{2}$, and to 4.

   a. Does $3\frac{3}{8}$ fall between 3 and $3\frac{1}{2}$ or between $3\frac{1}{2}$ and 4? How do you know?

   b. Complete each statement.

      $3\frac{3}{8}$ is $\frac{\blacksquare}{8}$ away from 3.

      $3\frac{3}{8}$ is $\frac{\blacksquare}{8}$ away from $3\frac{1}{2}$.

   c. Is $3\frac{3}{8}$ closer to 3 or to $3\frac{1}{2}$? Explain.

2. Find out how you can write $3\frac{3}{8}$, $3\frac{1}{3}$, $4\frac{1}{5}$, and $\frac{16}{5}$ in order. Use fraction strips to help, if you wish.

   a. Write $\frac{16}{5}$ as a mixed number to make your work easier.

   b. Which number is greatest? How do you know?

   c. Which number is least? How do you know?

   d. What two numbers are left? Of these, which is less? How do you know?

   e. Write $3\frac{3}{8}$, $3\frac{1}{3}$, $4\frac{1}{5}$, $\frac{16}{5}$ in order from least to greatest.

Talk About It

How would you compare two improper fractions such as $\frac{26}{3}$ and $\frac{19}{9}$?

Connect •

Order $2\frac{5}{8}$, $1\frac{3}{4}$, and $2\frac{3}{4}$ from least to greatest.

What You See	What You Know	What You Write
Different whole number parts $2\frac{5}{8}$ $1\frac{3}{4}$	Mixed number with greater whole number is greater.	$2\frac{5}{8} > 1\frac{3}{4}$
Same whole number parts $2\frac{5}{8}$ $2\frac{3}{4}$	Mixed number with greater fraction is greater.	$2\frac{5}{8} < 2\frac{3}{4}$

The mixed numbers $1\frac{3}{4}$, $2\frac{5}{8}$, and $2\frac{3}{4}$ are in order from least to greatest.

Practice •

Give a mixed number for the shaded part of each picture. Use > or < to compare each pair of mixed numbers.

1.   **2.**   **3.**

Compare. Use > or <.

4. $4\frac{2}{3}$ ● $4\frac{5}{6}$ **5.** $5\frac{1}{2}$ ● $3\frac{7}{8}$ **6.** $1\frac{2}{5}$ ● $1\frac{3}{8}$ **7.** $2\frac{1}{4}$ ● $\frac{19}{8}$

Write in order from least to greatest.

8. $3\frac{3}{4}$, $3\frac{1}{6}$, $\frac{5}{2}$, $2\frac{4}{5}$ **9.** $\frac{13}{8}$, $1\frac{7}{8}$, $\frac{7}{4}$, $1\frac{2}{3}$

Literature The famous author Mark Twain wrote a short story about a frog-jumping contest in Calaveras County, California.

Match each jump with the appropriate frog on the graph.

10. $6\frac{1}{4}$ ft   **11.** $6\frac{5}{8}$ ft   **12.** $5\frac{1}{2}$ ft

13. $6\frac{1}{3}$ ft   **14.** $5\frac{3}{8}$ ft   **15.** $5\frac{2}{3}$ ft

16. Journal Explain how to compare $\frac{17}{4}$ and $4\frac{5}{8}$.

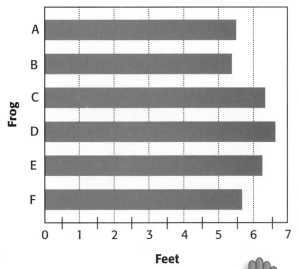

Frog Jumping Distances

Understanding Percent

You Will Learn

how to use percents to name amounts less than or equal to 1

Vocabulary

percent
a way to compare a number with one hundred

Learn

In a recent survey, 100 students were asked which household chore they liked the least. The list shows which jobs the students mentioned.

How can you name the part of those surveyed who liked washing dishes the least?

Did You Know?
Percent means per 100. It comes from the Latin *per centum*.

Mia wrote a fraction to describe the part. $\frac{31}{100}$

Donnell used a **percent**. Percent means per hundred or out of 100. % is a symbol for percent. 31%

José thought of the number of students as 31 out of 100.

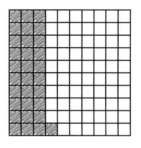

0.31

Chores we Like the Least
Washing dishes 31
Laundry 20
Yard work 19
Cleaning room 17
Babysitting 13

Talk About It

Look at the grid shown above. What fraction and percent name the unshaded part?

Check

Write the hundredths fraction and the percent shaded in each picture.

1.   2.   3.

4. **Reasoning** Doing laundry was the chore least liked by 20 of the 100 students. Use a grid to show the percent who named laundry.

Skills and Reasoning

Write the hundredths fraction and the percent shaded in each picture.

5. 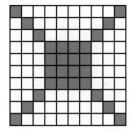 **6.** 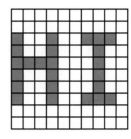 **7.**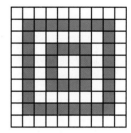

Write each as a percent.

8. 66 out of 100   **9.** $\frac{50}{100}$ **10.** 7 out of 100   **11.** $\frac{48}{100}$

Write each as a hundredths fraction.

12. 16%   **13.** 5%   **14.** 59%   **15.** 70%   **16.** 100%

For each set, decide which does **not** belong.

17. Ⓐ 6 out of 100   Ⓑ 60%   Ⓒ $\frac{6}{100}$ Ⓓ 6%

18. Ⓐ 29%   Ⓑ 29 out of 100   Ⓒ 2 out of 9   Ⓓ $\frac{29}{100}$

Estimation Estimate the percent of each figure that is shaded.

19.   **20.**   **21.**

Problem Solving and Applications

22. Collecting Data Survey your class to find the least popular chore.

Using Data Use the Data File on page 299 to answer **23** and **24**.

23. Where is the most active water found?

24. Write a fraction for the amount of active water found in

   a. rivers   **b.** lakes   **c.** soil   **d.** atmosphere   **e.** living things

Mixed Review and Test Prep

Copy and complete. Write >, <, or =.

25. $4\frac{4}{5} \bullet 5\frac{8}{10}$ **26.** $2\frac{2}{3} \bullet \frac{8}{3}$ **27.** $7\frac{3}{5} \bullet 6\frac{2}{3}$ **28.** $3\frac{5}{8} \bullet 3\frac{5}{6}$

29. Which number is standard form for eighty-one hundredths?

   Ⓐ 81   Ⓑ 0.081   Ⓒ 8.100   Ⓓ 0.81

Connecting Fractions, Decimals, and Percents

You Will Learn

how to write percents as fractions and decimals, and fractions and decimals as percents

Remember

Percent means per hundred or out of 100.

Learn

April went on a field trip to see water mammals. She decided to count and classify the first 100 sea mammals she saw. She used a 10 × 10 grid to record her findings. What part of the water mammals that she saw were whales?

April from Sugar Mill, Florida, is interested in marine biology.

W	M	D	D	D	D	M	M	D	D
M	M	W	W	D	D	M	M	D	D
D	D	D	D	D	D	D	M	M	D
M	M	M	D	W	D	M	D	D	D
W	M	M	M	D	D	D	D	D	D
D	M	D	D	D	M	M	M	M	D
D	D	M	D	D	D	D	D	M	D
D	D	D	D	W	D	M	M	M	W
M	D	W	D	M	D	M	D	D	M
D	M	M	D	D	D	D	D	W	D

W = whale
D = dolphin
M = manatee

$\dfrac{9}{100}$ ← whales
  ← mammals

You can think of $\frac{9}{100}$ in other ways.

9%   9 out of 100   9 hundredths

Of the water mammals April saw, 9%, $\frac{9}{100}$, or 0.09 of them were whales.

Example 1

Write the fraction, decimal, and percent that name the shaded region.

$\dfrac{47}{100}$ ← parts shaded
← parts in the whole

$\dfrac{47}{100} = 0.47$ **47** hundredths

$\dfrac{47}{100} = 0.47 = 47\%$ **47** shaded parts
out of 100 parts

If you know the percent that is shaded, you can also write the fraction and decimal that describe the part that is shaded.

Example 2

In a 10×10 grid, 22% of the squares are shaded.

Write the fraction and decimal that name the shaded part.

22%   **22** shaded parts out of 100 equal parts

$22\% = \dfrac{22}{100}$ ← parts shaded
← parts in the whole

$22\% = \dfrac{22}{100} = 0.22$, or **22** hundredths

Talk About It

1. How can you write $\dfrac{97}{100}$ as a percent? Explain.

2. How can you write 0.04 as a percent? Explain.

3. How can you write 83% as a fraction? Explain.

4. How can you write 55% as a decimal? Explain.

Check

Copy and complete.

1. $27\% = 0.2\blacksquare = \dfrac{\blacksquare}{100}$ 2. $\dfrac{4}{100} = 0.\blacksquare = \blacksquare\%$ 3. $0.09 = \dfrac{\blacksquare}{100} = \blacksquare\%$

Write each as a percent.

4. 0.15   5. $\dfrac{33}{100}$ 6. 0.07   7. $\dfrac{88}{100}$ 8. 0.99

Write each as a fraction and a decimal.

9. 25%   10. 60%   11. 2%   12. 75%   13. 10%

14. **Reasoning** How can you tell if a percent names an amount greater than or less than $\frac{1}{2}$?

Skills and Reasoning

Write a fraction, a decimal, and a percent that name each shaded part.

15.   **16.**   **17.**

Write each as a percent.

18. 3 out of 100   **19.** 79 out of 100   **20.** 21 out of 100   **21.** 80 out of 100

22. $\frac{37}{100}$ **23.** 0.45   **24.** 0.01   **25.** $\frac{70}{100}$ **26.** $\frac{53}{100}$

27. 0.50   **28.** $\frac{3}{100}$ **29.** 0.22   **30.** $\frac{96}{100}$ **31.** 0.02

Write each as a fraction and a decimal.

32. 2%   **33.** 49%   **34.** 95%   **35.** 9%   **36.** 30%   **37.** 22%

38. 91%   **39.** 17%   **40.** 4%   **41.** 20%   **42.** 68%   **43.** 5%

44. Which is greater: 0.08 or 80%?   **45.** Which is less: $\frac{1}{4}$ or 40%?

Problem Solving and Applications

Use the table to decide whether each statement is true or false. If false, explain why.

46. Less than 60% of the passengers were teens or adults.

47. Of the passengers, $\frac{36}{100}$ were children or teens.

48. More than $\frac{1}{4}$ of the passengers were teens.

49. More than 0.5 of the passengers were adults or senior citizens.

Passengers on Whale Watch Cruise	
Children	24%
Teens	12%
Adults	48%
Senior Citizens	16%

Using Data Use the Data File on page 299 to answer **50** and **51**.

50. Science Write the amount of water found in your body as a percent, decimal, and fraction.

51. Write the amount of water found in the atmosphere as a percent, decimal, and fraction.

Problem Solving and SCIENCE

Have you ever felt hotter than the temperature indicates? Maybe it's the humidity. The temperature-humidity index (THI) graph below shows that, as temperature and relative humidity increase, people feel more uncomfortable. The higher the THI reading, the more uncomfortable people feel.

"It's not the heat, it's the humidity."

TEMPERATURE 85° F
HUMIDITY 80%

Use the THI graph to answer 52–54.

52. At 85° F, at what relative humidity will people be put in danger?

53. Look at the forecast above. How would this weather make most people feel?

54. Write Your Own Problem Choose a THI reading. Explain whether most people would be comfortable. List some of the air temperatures and relative humidities which could give that THI.

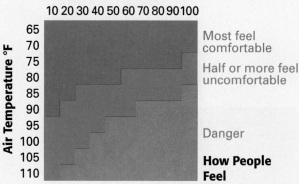

Relative Humidity (%)
10 20 30 40 50 60 70 80 90 100

Air Temperature °F: 65, 70, 75, 80, 85, 90, 95, 100, 105, 110

Most feel comfortable

Half or more feel uncomfortable

Danger

How People Feel

55. Journal Explain how to write $\frac{32}{100}$ and 0.32 as a percent.

Mixed Review and Test Prep

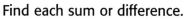

STAY SHARP!

Find each sum or difference.

56.	**57.**	**58.**	**59.**	**60.**
5,387	137	6,877	4,358	3,999
− 4,989	498	− 308	+ 5,687	+ 2,999
	+ 3,207			

Write each fraction in simplest form.

61. $\frac{9}{12}$ **62.** $\frac{20}{25}$ **63.** $\frac{6}{9}$ **64.** $\frac{6}{5}$ **65.** $\frac{12}{16}$ **66.** $\frac{10}{2}$ **67.** $\frac{7}{7}$

68. This set of mixed numbers is in order from least to greatest. Identify the missing number. $1\frac{1}{6}$, $1\frac{5}{9}$, ■, $2\frac{2}{5}$

Ⓐ $1\frac{1}{3}$ Ⓑ $2\frac{1}{2}$ Ⓒ $\frac{13}{9}$ Ⓓ $\frac{13}{6}$

Problem Solving

Decision Making: Comparing Survey Results

Explore

Suppose you read a magazine article that stated 3 out of 10 young people think jellyfish are scarier than sharks. The article showed a circle graph with results of the survey. You wonder if your class feels the same way. You can survey your classmates and make a table of your results. Then you can compare your results with those of the article.

Which Creature is Scarier?

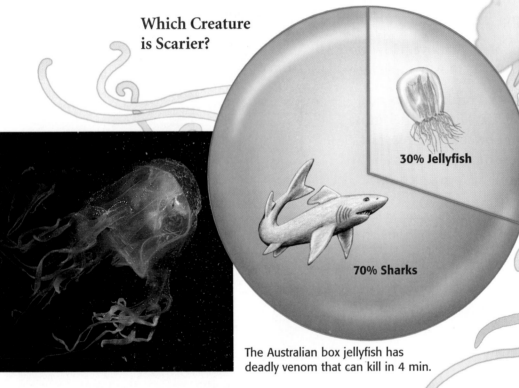

30% Jellyfish

70% Sharks

The Australian box jellyfish has deadly venom that can kill in 4 min.

Work Together

▶ **Understand**

1. What do you know?

2. What are you asked to do?

3. How will you organize your data so that you can compare it?

▶ **Plan and Solve**

4. What question will you ask your classmates?

5. What will you do if someone answers that he or she doesn't know or that both jellyfish and sharks are scary?

6. What will your table look like? What labels will it have?

7. Make your table.

Which Creature is Scarier?				
Creature	**Student Votes**	**Fraction**	**Decimal**	**Percent**
Sharks				
Jellyfish				
Total				

8. How can you compare your data with the data from the magazine?

9. Does your class feel the same way as the people surveyed by the magazine? Explain.

▶ **Present Your Decision**

10. Tell how your class data compares to that in the magazine.

11. Explain why you found a percent.

12. Use Data Wonder or other graphing software to make a circle graph of your data.

13. Find out more about scary sea creatures. Slither over to **www.mathsurf.com/5/ch7**.

Great White Sharks usually swim alone.

PROBLEM SOLVING PRACTICE

Technology

Connecting Fractions, Decimals, and Percents

It's a decimal! It's a fraction! No, it's a percent! What kinds of numbers do you usually work with on a calculator? Most people work with decimals. You can also work with fractions and percents.

Work Together

You can use a calculator to change among fractions, decimals, and percents.

1 To change a fraction to a decimal:

	Enter	Display
Enter the fraction $\frac{3}{4}$.	3 / 4	3/4
Press the FↃD key.	FↃD	0.75

2 To change a decimal to a fraction:

	Enter	Display
Enter the decimal 0.75.	0 . 7 5	0.75
Press the FↃD key.	FↃD	N/D→n/d 75/100
Press the Simp and = keys to simplify.	Simp =	N/D→n/d 15/20
The fraction is still not in simplest form. Press the Simp and = keys again.	Simp =	3/4

Try it yourself. Use $\frac{6}{10}$.

Remember
N/D→n/d means that the fraction is not yet in simplest form.

3 To change a percent to a decimal:

	Enter	Display
Enter 38%.	3 8 %	0.38

4 **To change a percent to a fraction:**

	Enter	Display
Enter 38%.	③ ⑧ %	0.38
Press the FↃD key.	FↃD	N/D→n/d 38/100
Press the Simp and = keys to simplify.	Simp =	19/50

Try it yourself. Use 44%.

Exercises

1. Use your calculator to complete the following table.

Fraction	Decimal	Percent
$\frac{7}{10}$		
$\frac{1}{4}$		
$\frac{4}{5}$	0.8	
$\frac{3}{10}$		

2. How do you know on a calculator when a fraction is in simplest terms?

3. Do you think it is easier to change fractions, decimals, and percents on the calculator or in your head?

Extensions

4. How could you change 38 out of 100 to a percent without the % key?

5. Enter a 2-place decimal. Convert to a fraction. Enter a 3-place decimal. Convert to a fraction. Enter a 4-place decimal. Convert to a fraction. Try a 5-place decimal. What do you notice?

Review and Practice

Vocabulary Match each with its example.

1. mixed number   2. improper fraction   3. percent

a. $\dfrac{19}{8}$ b. 35%   c. $3\dfrac{4}{5}$

(Lesson 9) Write the mixed or whole number and the improper fraction that name each shaded part.

4.    5. 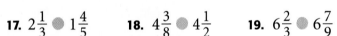   6.

(Lesson 10) Write each improper fraction as a mixed number in simplest form or as a whole number. Write each mixed number as an improper fraction.

7. $\dfrac{28}{16}$ 8. $\dfrac{13}{2}$ 9. $\dfrac{21}{14}$ 10. $\dfrac{27}{9}$ 11. $\dfrac{34}{15}$

12. $6\dfrac{3}{5}$ 13. $3\dfrac{5}{8}$ 14. $2\dfrac{2}{3}$ 15. $9\dfrac{1}{4}$ 16. $13\dfrac{2}{7}$

(Lesson 11) Copy and complete. Write >, <, or =.

17. $2\dfrac{1}{3}$ ● $1\dfrac{4}{5}$ 18. $4\dfrac{3}{8}$ ● $4\dfrac{1}{2}$ 19. $6\dfrac{2}{3}$ ● $6\dfrac{7}{9}$

(Lessons 12–14)

Using Data Use the circle graph to answer **20–22**.

20. What fraction of the people enrolled are children?

21. What percent enrolled are adults or senior citizens?

22. Are more than 0.3 of those enrolled teens?

(Lessons 12 and 13) Write each as a percent.

23. 33 out of 100   24. $\dfrac{20}{100}$

25. 60 out of 100   26. $\dfrac{100}{100}$

Write each as a hundredths fraction and as a decimal.

27. 3%   28. 18%   29. 99%   30. 52%

31. **Journal** Explain how you can write 18 out of 100 as a percent, a fraction in simplest form, and a decimal.

People Enrolled in David's Karate School

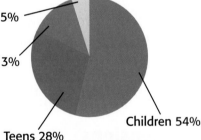

Senior citizens 5%
Adults 13%
Teens 28%
Children 54%

Skills Checklist

In this section, you have:

☑ Explored Mixed Numbers

☑ Written Improper Fractions and Mixed Numbers

☑ Explored Comparing and Ordering Mixed Numbers

☑ Learned About Percents

☑ Connected Fractions, Decimals, and Percents

☑ Solved Problems by Making Decisions

REVIEW AND PRACTICE

YOUR CHOICE

Choose at least one of the following. Use what you have learned in this chapter.

① Snack Attack

At Home Make a list and conduct a survey of what snacks your friends and family members like the most. Then find what fraction of those you surveyed prefer to munch on each food. Compare your figures with those of others. Is there one favorite snack food in your surveys?

Snack Food	Number Who Chose It	Fraction
Total		
Favorite		

② Music to Your Ears

An orchestra is divided into four major sections. First, find the total number of people who are in this orchestra. Next, find what fraction each part of the orchestra is of the total. Give your answers as decimals and percents.

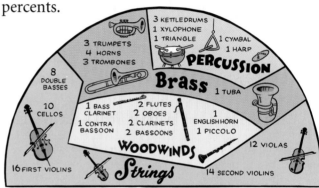

3 KETTLE DRUMS
1 XYLOPHONE
1 TRIANGLE
1 CYMBAL
1 HARP
3 TRUMPETS
4 HORNS
3 TROMBONES
PERCUSSION
8 DOUBLE BASSES
Brass
1 TUBA
10 CELLOS
1 BASS CLARINET
1 CONTRA BASSOON
2 FLUTES
2 OBOES
2 CLARINETS
2 BASSOONS
1 ENGLISH HORN
1 PICCOLO
12 VIOLAS
WOODWINDS
16 FIRST VIOLINS
Strings
14 SECOND VIOLINS

A SYMPHONY ORCHESTRA

③ Fishin' the Net

Snorkle over to **www.mathsurf.com/5/ch7** to find data about fresh-water fish that you can represent as fractions. Write these fractions as decimals and percents.

④ Describing Letters

You can break words into fractional or decimal parts or describe them with percents. Copy and complete this table. Add your own words.

Word	Vowels	Letters	Vowels / Letters	Decimal Equivalent	%
Water	2	5	$\frac{2}{5}$		40%
Aquarium	5	8	$\frac{5}{8}$	0.625	

CHAPTER 7
Review/Test

Vocabulary Match each with its meaning.

1. mixed number
2. percent
3. improper fraction
4. greatest common factor
5. denominator
6. numerator

a. number of equal parts considered
b. the greatest number that is a factor of each of two numbers
c. a number that has a whole number part and a fraction part
d. per hundred
e. number of equal parts in all
f. a fraction with a numerator greater than or equal to the denominator

(Lessons 1–7) Copy and complete.

7. $\frac{5}{8} = \frac{\blacksquare}{24} = \frac{25}{\blacksquare} = \frac{\blacksquare}{56}$

8. $\frac{27}{54} = \frac{\blacksquare}{6} = \frac{9}{\blacksquare}$

9. $\frac{3}{4} = \frac{\blacksquare}{16} = \frac{18}{\blacksquare}$

10. $\frac{56}{63} = \frac{40}{\blacksquare} = \frac{\blacksquare}{9}$

Write each fraction in simplest form.

11. $\frac{20}{40}$

12. $\frac{8}{24}$

13. $\frac{8}{32}$

14. $\frac{16}{48}$

15. $\frac{15}{27}$

Write the fractions in order from least to greatest.

16. $\frac{2}{3}, \frac{5}{6}, \frac{9}{12}$

17. $\frac{2}{3}, \frac{2}{6}, \frac{2}{4}$

18. $\frac{4}{9}, \frac{1}{3}, \frac{12}{13}$

19. $\frac{5}{12}, \frac{3}{4}, \frac{2}{7}$

(Lessons 5, 9, 10, and 13) Write each improper fraction as a mixed number in simplest form or as a whole number.

20. $\frac{32}{6}$

21. $\frac{23}{3}$

22. $\frac{13}{5}$

23. $\frac{24}{4}$

24. $\frac{19}{2}$

(Lessons 5, 12, and 13) Write each as a percent, a fraction in simplest form, and as a decimal.

25. 22 out of 100

26. 15 out of 100

27. 34 out of 100

28. 67 out of 100

(Lesson 8) **Measurement** Copy and complete.

29.
feet	1	2		5	10
inches	12		36		

30.
yards	1		5
inches	36	72	

Write two equivalent fractions for **31** and **32**.

31. What fraction of a yard is 1 inch?

32. What fraction of a yard is 1 foot?

(Lessons 2, 6, 9, and 11) Solve.

33. A cracker breaks into six sections. Sheila eats $3\frac{1}{3}$ crackers. Marshal eats $3\frac{2}{6}$ crackers. Who eats more? How many sections do each of them eat?

CHAPTER 7
Performance Assessment

Your art class is doing an art project. You have been given a 10×10 grid on which to make a design. These are the rules you must follow:

- You can use only red, blue, green, and yellow.
- You must color at least $\frac{4}{5}$ of the squares.
- Red must be on a total of at least 3% of the squares. Green must be on a total of at least 3% of the squares. Blue and yellow together must be a total of at least 0.5 of the squares.

1. **Decision Making** Decide what design you would like to make. Decide how many squares of each color you will use. Remember that there are 100 squares on the grid and you must follow the rules.

2. **Recording Data** Copy and complete this chart.

Color	Number of Squares	Fractional Part of Grid (in lowest terms)	Decimal Equivalent	Percent of Grid
Red				
Green				
Blue				
Yellow				
Blank squares				

3. **Explain Your Thinking** How did you decide how many squares of each color to use? How did you know what fractional part of the grid that was? How did you decide what decimal part of the grid each color was? How did you get the percent for those amounts?

4. **Critical Thinking** What is the greatest percent of blank squares you could have in your drawing? Explain.

5. **Analyze Your Data** What do you notice about the sum of your decimals and the sum of your percents? What would you expect the sum of your fractions to be?

REVIEW/TEST

Math Magazine

Going Round in Circles

There were 78 final events at the 1996 Summer Olympics that involved water sports.

The breakdown of events was:
40%—swimming
30%—rowing and yachting
20%—canoeing or kayaking
10%—other (water polo, diving, synchronized swimming)

A circle graph would allow you to compare percents quickly. One way to make a circle graph is to place 100 beads on a string, all the same distance apart. When you make a circle with the string, each bead represents 1% of the circle.

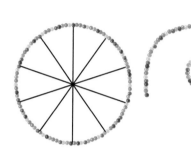

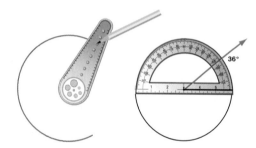

You can also use a compass and a protractor. Make a circle with the compass, then measure with the protractor. Every 36° represents 10% of the circle.

Computers now do much of the work for us—and in wonderful colors, too! But they still need us to tell them what to do.

Try These!

1. Choose one of the methods above to make your own circle graph. Graph the data about the Olympics at the top of the page. Color your graph.

2. Compare your graph with a graph made using a different method.

Cumulative Review

Test Prep Strategy: Eliminate Choices
Estimate.
A box of 25 frames costs $256.25. If each costs the same amount, how much does each cost?

Ⓐ $1.25   Ⓑ $100.25   Ⓒ $102.50   Ⓓ $10.25   Ⓔ $10.10

First eliminate unreasonable answers. Estimate: $1 times 25 is only $25. $100 times 25 is $2,500. Therefore eliminate answers Ⓐ, Ⓑ, and Ⓒ. This leaves only choices Ⓓ and Ⓔ. Divide to find the answer, Ⓓ $10.25.

Write the letter of the correct answer. Eliminate choices or use any strategy.

1. Find the area of a rectangle that is 5.6 cm wide by 9.3 cm long.

   Ⓐ 510.8 cm^2 Ⓑ 14.9 cm^2 Ⓒ 52.08 cm^2 Ⓓ not here

2. Which fraction does not represent hitting 12 out of 28 pitches?

   Ⓐ $\frac{4}{9}$ Ⓑ $\frac{12}{28}$ Ⓒ $\frac{3}{7}$ Ⓓ $\frac{6}{14}$ Ⓔ not here

3. A car trip is two thousand three hundred ninety-six miles. What would the mileage be if you continued for two hundred thirty-two miles?

   Ⓐ 2,528   Ⓑ 2,020,428   Ⓒ 250,128   Ⓓ 2,628

4. Which list shows 6.05, 6.5, 6.15, 6.005 in order from least to greatest?

   Ⓐ 6.05, 6.5, 6.005, 6.15   Ⓑ 6.005, 6.05, 6.15, 6.5
   Ⓒ 6.5, 6.15, 6.05, 6.005   Ⓓ 6.005, 6.05, 6.5, 6.15

5. How many lines of symmetry does a square have?

   Ⓐ 1   Ⓑ 2   Ⓒ 3   Ⓓ 4   Ⓔ 0

6. Which of the following is the answer for 7,345 ÷ 24?

   Ⓐ 36 R1   Ⓑ 306   Ⓒ 306 R1   Ⓓ 360 R1

7. What is the range of these scores: 89, 93, 65, 82, and 93?

   Ⓐ 93   Ⓑ 84   Ⓒ 89   Ⓓ 28   Ⓔ 38

8. Which list shows $\frac{2}{3}, \frac{5}{12}, \frac{3}{8}$, and $\frac{1}{2}$ in order from least to greatest?

   Ⓐ $\frac{3}{8}, \frac{5}{12}, \frac{1}{2}, \frac{2}{3}$ Ⓑ $\frac{1}{2}, \frac{2}{3}, \frac{3}{8}, \frac{5}{12}$ Ⓒ $\frac{1}{2}, \frac{2}{3}, \frac{5}{12}, \frac{3}{8}$ Ⓓ $\frac{3}{8}, \frac{1}{2}, \frac{5}{12}, \frac{2}{3}$

9. Which of the following shows three ways to represent 45 out of 100?

   Ⓐ $\frac{45}{100}$, 4,500, 0.045   Ⓑ 0.45, $\frac{45}{100}, \frac{9}{10}$ Ⓒ 0.45, $\frac{45}{100}, \frac{9}{20}$ Ⓓ not here

10. Which of the following best describes a triangle with a 90° angle and two sides of equal length?

   Ⓐ scalene right   Ⓑ isosceles right   Ⓒ equilateral obtuse   Ⓓ pentomino

---

Test Prep Strategies

- Read Carefully
- Follow Directions
- Make Smart Choices
- Eliminate Choices
- Work Backward from an Answer

Chapter 8
Fraction Operations and Customary Linear Measurement

SECTION **A**

Fraction Action with Hobbies

Rain, Rain
Page 347

Adding and Subtracting Fractions

Monica likes to record weather data. This circle graph displays data for April. The circle graph shows the part of one April that was rainy, cloudy, snowy, or sunny. Would your umbrella or sunglasses get more use?

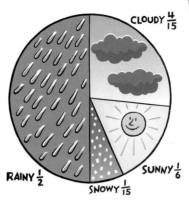

CLOUDY $\frac{4}{15}$

RAINY $\frac{1}{2}$

SNOWY $\frac{1}{15}$

SUNNY $\frac{1}{6}$

347

Surfing the World Wide Web!

Surfing the World Wide Web! What is the weather usually like in your area for April? Put on your raincoat, grab your umbrella, and check out the weather at **www.mathsurf.com/5/ch8**. Use *DataWonder!* or other graphing software to make a circle graph to show the information you find.

Adding and Subtracting Mixed Numbers

367

Which train route seems the most direct?

Travel Times from Orlando, FL, to Seattle, WA				
	Time			
Part of Trip	**Trip A**	**Trip B**	**Trip C**	**Trip D**
First Segment	$19\frac{1}{3}$ hr	$18\frac{2}{3}$ hr	$63\frac{1}{5}$ hr	$35\frac{2}{3}$ hr
Change Trains	$6\frac{1}{3}$ hr	$2\frac{2}{3}$ hr	$3\frac{5}{12}$ hr	$2\frac{5}{12}$ hr
Second Segment	$19\frac{5}{6}$ hr	19 hr	$34\frac{2}{3}$ hr	$30\frac{1}{2}$ hr
Change Trains	$6\frac{1}{6}$ hr	$6\frac{1}{2}$ hr		$2\frac{1}{6}$ hr
Third Segment	$45\frac{1}{4}$ hr	$45\frac{1}{4}$ hr		$45\frac{1}{4}$ hr

Spicy Cooking
Page 367

Using Customary Linear Measurements

387

How many leaps does an antelope make to go 100 ft?

Leaps and Bounds			
Animal	**Feet**	**Inches**	**Yards**
Jumping mouse	12	144	4
Antelope	20	240	$6\frac{2}{3}$
Cottontail rabbit	8	96	$2\frac{2}{3}$
Impala	33	396	11
Jack rabbit	$17\frac{1}{2}$	210	$5\frac{5}{6}$

L-o-o-o-ng Jumping
Page 387

TEAM PROJECT
CRITTER RIDDLE

Can you solve this riddle?

What do you get if you mix $\frac{3}{5}$ of a <u>chick</u>, $\frac{2}{3}$ of a <u>cat</u>, and $\frac{1}{2}$ of a <u>goat</u>?

Answer: Chicago

Can you make your own critter riddle? Try to make 3 riddles!

Make a Plan

- How will your team create a riddle?
- What fractions will your riddle use?
- Who will record your team's ideas and final riddles?
- How will you illustrate the fractional parts of your critter?

Carry It Out

1. Write a list of animals you might use in your riddle. You can use different names for the same animal, such as *rabbit* and *bunny*.

2. Brainstorm which letters from the names of the animals will fit together to make another word. You can use the name of a city, a vegetable, a sport, or anything else you'd like.

3. Draw or paint a picture of your new animal using parts of the animals in the riddle. Write the riddle below the picture. Write the answer on the back of your picture.

Talk About It

- Did you find a method for making a riddle that worked every time? Explain why or why not.
- What was the most challenging part of the project?

Present the Project

- Plan a class presentation of the riddles.
- Did any teams create the same riddle? Why do you think this happened?

A Adding and Subtracting Fractions

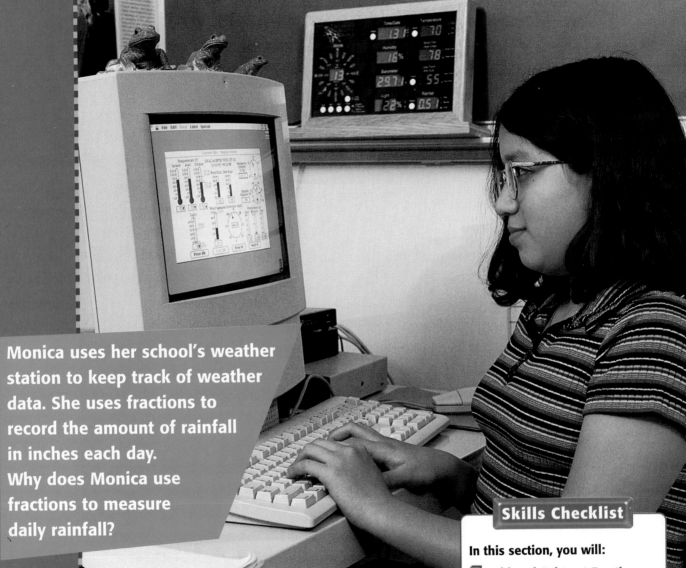

Monica uses her school's weather station to keep track of weather data. She uses fractions to record the amount of rainfall in inches each day. Why does Monica use fractions to measure daily rainfall?

Skills Checklist

In this section, you will:

☐ Add and Subtract Fractions with Like Denominators

☐ Explore Adding and Subtracting Fractions

☐ Find the Least Common Denominator

☐ Add and Subtract Fractions with Unlike Denominators

☐ Solve Problems with Too Much or Too Little Information

GET READY!

Adding and Subtracting Fractions

Review factors. List the factors of each number. Then give the greatest common factor.

1. 4 and 12
2. 24 and 16
3. 8 and 10
4. 18 and 27
5. 20 and 40
6. 21 and 24
7. 9 and 36
8. 2 and 10
9. 5 and 15

Adding and Subtracting Fractions with Like Denominators

You Will Learn
how to add and subtract fractions with like denominators

Materials
fraction strips

Math Tip
Add the numerators. Write the sum over the denominator.

 **Learn** •

Monica wants to be a meteorologist. She records the amount of rainfall every day. She often uses a table like this:

Day	Sunday	Monday	Tuesday
Rainfall (in.)	$\frac{3}{8}$	$\frac{1}{8}$	$\frac{7}{8}$

Monica's school in Denton, Texas, has its own weather station.

Example 1
How much rain fell on Sunday and Monday?
$$\frac{3}{8}+\frac{1}{8}=n$$
$$\frac{3}{8}+\frac{1}{8}=\frac{4}{8}$$
Since $\frac{4}{8}=\frac{1}{2}$, Monica reported that $\frac{1}{2}$ in. of rain fell on these two days.

You can subtract fractions to find differences. You can add fractions to find sums of two or more addends.

Example 2
Find $\frac{3}{8}-\frac{1}{8}$.

$$\frac{3}{8}$$
$$-\frac{1}{8}$$
$$\overline{\frac{2}{8}}=\frac{1}{4}$$

Simplify.

Example 3
Find $\frac{3}{8}+\frac{1}{8}+\frac{7}{8}$.
$$\frac{3}{8}+\frac{1}{8}+\frac{7}{8}=\frac{11}{8}$$
$$\frac{11}{8}=1\frac{3}{8}$$

Talk About It
Why add only numerators when adding fractions with like denominators?

Check •

Find each sum or difference. Simplify.

1. $\frac{1}{6}+\frac{4}{6}$ **2.** $\frac{3}{4}-\frac{1}{4}$ **3.** $\frac{2}{3}+\frac{2}{3}$ **4.** $\frac{11}{12}-\frac{6}{12}$

5. Reasoning Can the sum of two fractions equal 1? Explain.

Skills and Reasoning

Find each sum or difference. Simplify.

6. $\frac{1}{10} + \frac{4}{10}$ **7.** $\frac{7}{8} - \frac{2}{8}$ **8.** $\frac{1}{12} + \frac{11}{12}$ **9.** $\frac{5}{6} - \frac{1}{6}$ **10.** $\frac{4}{5} - \frac{1}{5}$

11. $\begin{array}{r} \frac{1}{3} \\ + \frac{1}{3} \\ \hline \end{array}$ **12.** $\begin{array}{r} \frac{5}{8} \\ + \frac{7}{8} \\ \hline \end{array}$ **13.** $\begin{array}{r} \frac{9}{10} \\ - \frac{3}{10} \\ \hline \end{array}$ **14.** $\begin{array}{r} \frac{7}{16} \\ + \frac{5}{16} \\ \hline \end{array}$ **15.** $\begin{array}{r} \frac{9}{10} \\ - \frac{4}{10} \\ \hline \end{array}$

16. $\begin{array}{r} \frac{10}{12} \\ + \frac{7}{12} \\ \hline \end{array}$ **17.** $\begin{array}{r} \frac{3}{5} \\ + \frac{2}{5} \\ \hline \end{array}$ **18.** $\begin{array}{r} \frac{3}{4} \\ - \frac{2}{4} \\ \hline \end{array}$ **19.** $\begin{array}{r} \frac{8}{9} \\ + \frac{4}{9} \\ \hline \end{array}$ **20.** $\begin{array}{r} \frac{4}{6} \\ - \frac{4}{6} \\ \hline \end{array}$

21. $\frac{5}{8} + \frac{5}{8}$ **22.** $\frac{8}{9} - \frac{5}{9}$ **23.** $\frac{2}{3} - \frac{1}{3}$ **24.** $\frac{4}{8} + \frac{5}{8}$ **25.** $\frac{5}{16} - \frac{1}{16}$

26. $\frac{1}{10} + \frac{3}{10} + \frac{5}{10}$ **27.** $\frac{1}{4} + \frac{1}{4} + \frac{3}{4}$ **28.** $\frac{2}{3} + \frac{2}{3} + \frac{1}{3}$ **29.** $\frac{1}{8} + \frac{3}{8} + \frac{5}{8}$

30. Find the sum of $\frac{2}{7}$ and $\frac{3}{7}$. **31.** Find the difference of $\frac{3}{8}$ and $\frac{2}{8}$.

32. Why does $\frac{5}{12} + \frac{3}{12} = \frac{3}{12} + \frac{5}{12}$? **33.** What is $\frac{1}{5} + \frac{2}{5}$?

Problem Solving and Applications

34. Algebra Readiness What number must be subtracted from $\frac{5}{8}$ to get a difference of $\frac{1}{8}$?

Using Data Use the Data File on page 344 to answer **35** and **36**.

35. What part of April had snowy or cloudy days?

36. How many days were rainy? Snowy or cloudy? Sunny?

37. Critical Thinking In a survey, $\frac{37}{100}$ voters planned to vote for candidate A, $\frac{43}{100}$ planned to vote for candidate B, and the rest were undecided. What fraction of the voters was undecided?

Cumulus clouds can rise to great heights and develop into clouds that bring thunderstorms.

Mixed Review and Test Prep

Multiply or divide.

38. 238×57 **39.** $419 \div 7$ **40.** $1{,}099 \times 7$ **41.** $8\overline{)394}$ **42.** $219 \div 3$

43. What is the mean of these heights: 53 in., 54 in., 59 in., 59 in., 55 in.?

 Ⓐ 53 in. **Ⓑ** 55 in. **Ⓒ** 59 in. **Ⓓ** 54 in. **Ⓔ** not here

Exploring Adding Fractions

Problem Solving Connection

Use Objects/
Act It Out

Materials

fraction strips

Explore •

You can add fractions that have unlike denominators.

Work Together

Use fraction strips to find
equivalent fractions before
you add.

1. Find the sum of $\frac{1}{4}$ and $\frac{3}{8}$.

2. Find the sum of $\frac{1}{3}$ and $\frac{5}{6}$.

3. Find each sum. You may use fraction strips or draw pictures to help.

    a. $\frac{3}{4} + \frac{1}{8}$ **b.** $\frac{1}{5} + \frac{3}{10}$ **c.** $\frac{2}{3} + \frac{5}{6}$ **d.** $\frac{1}{2} + \frac{3}{4}$ **e.** $\frac{1}{3} + \frac{1}{2}$

Math Tip

To add fractions with
unlike denominators,
change them to like
denominators and solve
a simpler problem.

Talk About It

What fraction equivalent to $\frac{1}{2}$ can you use to add $\frac{1}{2}$ and $\frac{1}{4}$?
To add $\frac{1}{2}$ and $\frac{1}{6}$? To add $\frac{1}{2}$ and $\frac{5}{8}$?

Connect

To add fractions with unlike denominators, first find equivalent fractions that have a like denominator.

$\frac{1}{4} + \frac{5}{8} = n$

↓

$\frac{2}{8} + \frac{5}{8} = \frac{7}{8}$

$\frac{1}{6} + \frac{1}{3} + \frac{1}{12} = n$

↓   ↓

$\frac{2}{12} + \frac{4}{12} + \frac{1}{12} = \frac{7}{12}$

Practice

Find each sum.

1. $\frac{3}{8} + \frac{1}{2}$

2. $\frac{1}{3} + \frac{1}{6}$

3. $\frac{3}{4} + \frac{1}{8}$

4. $\frac{1}{12} + \frac{1}{2}$

Find each sum. You may use fraction strips or draw pictures to help.

5. $\frac{1}{10} + \frac{1}{5}$ **6.** $\frac{1}{2} + \frac{3}{10}$ **7.** $\frac{1}{3} + \frac{5}{12}$ **8.** $\frac{3}{16} + \frac{3}{4}$ **9.** $\frac{3}{8} + \frac{1}{4}$

10. $\frac{5}{8} + \frac{3}{4}$ **11.** $\frac{3}{5} + \frac{7}{10}$ **12.** $\frac{2}{3} + \frac{5}{6}$ **13.** $\frac{1}{2} + \frac{3}{4}$ **14.** $\frac{1}{6} + \frac{2}{9}$

15. $\frac{1}{8} + \frac{1}{4} + \frac{1}{2}$ **16.** $\frac{1}{3} + \frac{3}{4} + \frac{1}{12}$ **17.** $\frac{5}{6} + \frac{1}{4} + \frac{5}{12}$ **18.** $\frac{3}{8} + \frac{3}{4} + \frac{1}{2}$

19. Find the sum of $\frac{2}{3}$ and $\frac{1}{6}$.

20. Find the sum of $\frac{1}{5}$ and $\frac{3}{10}$.

21. Measurement Draw a ruler to show that $\frac{5}{8}$ in. plus $\frac{3}{4}$ in. is equal to $1\frac{3}{8}$ in.

22. Estimation Following city streets, about how far is it from the corner of Ferry St. and Russell St. to the corner of St. Aubin Ave. and Warren Ave.?

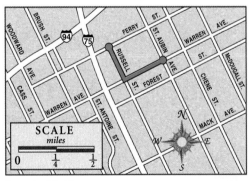

Detroit, Michigan

23. Ed added $\frac{1}{3}$ and $\frac{1}{6}$ and got $\frac{2}{9}$. What mistake did he make?

24. Journal Explain how you might add $\frac{1}{4}$ and $\frac{1}{3}$.

Least Common Denominator

You Will Learn

how to find the least common denominator (LCD) for two or more fractions

Vocabulary

least common denominator (LCD) the least common multiple of the denominators of two or more fractions

Learn

Suppose you want to make balsawood gliders. The instructions call for one piece of wood $\frac{3}{4}$ ft long and another piece $\frac{2}{3}$ ft long. You would need to add fractions with unlike denominators to find out how much balsa is needed. You would need to find a common denominator.

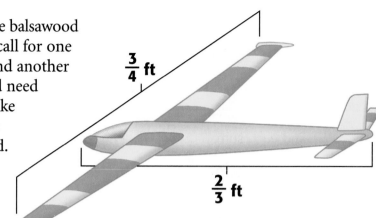

$\frac{3}{4}$ ft

$\frac{2}{3}$ ft

Example 1

Find a common denominator for $\frac{3}{4}$ and $\frac{2}{3}$.

First, find the non-zero multiples of each denominator.

Multiples of 4: 4, 8, 12, 16, 20, 24...

Multiples of 3: 3, 6, 9, 12, 15, 18, 21, 24...

So, 12 is the **least common denominator** (LCD) of $\frac{3}{4}$ and $\frac{2}{3}$.

Fourths and thirds can be renamed as twelfths.

Example 2

Find the least common denominator for $\frac{7}{8}$ and $\frac{5}{12}$.

Multiples of 8: 8, 16, 24, 32, 40...

Multiples of 12: 12, 24, 36, 48, 60...

The LCD is 24.

Talk About It

The denominator of one fraction is a factor of the denominator of a second fraction. What is the LCD of the two fractions? Explain.

Math Tip

12 and 24 are common multiples of 4 and 3.

Check

Find the LCD for each pair of fractions.

1. $\frac{1}{3}$ and $\frac{1}{5}$ **2.** $\frac{3}{4}$ and $\frac{2}{5}$ **3.** $\frac{5}{6}$ and $\frac{1}{7}$ **4.** $\frac{1}{8}$ and $\frac{5}{12}$

5. Reasoning Why is 24 the LCD for $\frac{1}{8}$ and $\frac{5}{12}$?

Practice •

Skills and Reasoning

Find the LCD for each pair of fractions.

6. $\frac{4}{5}$ and $\frac{1}{2}$ **7.** $\frac{2}{3}$ and $\frac{4}{5}$ **8.** $\frac{5}{6}$ and $\frac{2}{9}$ **9.** $\frac{3}{4}$ and $\frac{1}{5}$

10. $\frac{2}{3}$ and $\frac{1}{10}$ **11.** $\frac{3}{8}$ and $\frac{1}{4}$ **12.** $\frac{5}{8}$ and $\frac{2}{3}$ **13.** $\frac{5}{6}$ and $\frac{3}{10}$

14. $\frac{3}{4}$ and $\frac{1}{10}$ **15.** $\frac{2}{3}$ and $\frac{4}{9}$ **16.** $\frac{3}{8}$ and $\frac{7}{12}$ **17.** $\frac{3}{7}$ and $\frac{4}{5}$

18. $\frac{2}{3}$ and $\frac{1}{4}$ **19.** $\frac{3}{5}$ and $\frac{2}{15}$ **20.** $\frac{1}{6}$ and $\frac{3}{8}$ **21.** $\frac{1}{3}$ and $\frac{2}{7}$

22. Why is the LCD for $\frac{5}{6}$ and $\frac{2}{3}$ **not** the product of 6 and 3?

23. If you know that the least common multiple (LCM) of 2 and 7 is 14, what do you know about the least common denominator (LCD) of $\frac{1}{2}$ and $\frac{3}{7}$?

Problem Solving and Applications

24. Time Sally spends $\frac{1}{2}$ hr practicing the flute each day. She also spends $\frac{1}{3}$ hr exercising. What is the least common denominator of these fractions?

25. Math History The Sumerians were the first to divide a circle into 360 parts. If 240 parts are shaded, what fraction of the circle is shaded?

26. Critical Thinking Eric said he can always find the least common denominator for two fractions with different denominators by multiplying the denominators. Erika said that's not always true. Who is correct? Explain.

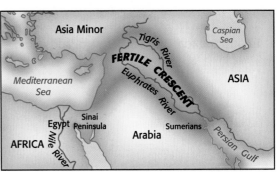

The Fertile Crescent is an historical region that borders the desert of Syria in Asia. There the Sumerians developed one of the world's first great civilizations about 5,500 years ago. Other great ancient cultures developed later in this region.

Mixed Review and Test Prep

Find each product.

27. 17
× 7

28. 107
× 7

29. 177
× 7

30. 1,177
× 7

31. 1,077
× 7

Money Find each sum.

32. $4.95 + $3.98   **33.** $0.43 + $29.00   **34.** $13.59 + $7.08   **35.** $6.23 + $16.09

36. Which of the following is the least common multiple of 9 and 15?

Ⓐ 135   Ⓑ 15   Ⓒ 16   Ⓓ 45

Adding Fractions

You Will Learn

how to add fractions with unlike denominators

Did You Know?

Bunraku, Japanese puppet theater, was organized in the early 1800s and uses nearly life-size puppets.

Learn • • • • • • • • • • •

Who wears a clothing size that is a fraction? Many puppets do! You can use fractions to help you make hand puppets.

To make the face for one puppet, you need $\frac{1}{2}$ yd of yarn to create the eyebrows and hair and $\frac{1}{3}$ yd to make the moustache. How much yarn do you need for the puppet's face?

Example 1

Step 1

To find the total amount of yarn, add $\frac{1}{2}$ and $\frac{1}{3}$.

$$\frac{1}{2} + \frac{1}{3} = n$$

| $\frac{1}{2}$ | $\frac{1}{3}$ |

Find a common denominator for $\frac{1}{2}$ and $\frac{1}{3}$.

Multiples of 2: 2, 4, 6, 8, 10, 12, . . .
Multiples of 3: 3, 6, 9, 12, 15, 18, . . .

The least common denominator (LCD) for $\frac{1}{2}$ and $\frac{1}{3}$ is 6.

Step 2

Write the equivalent fractions with 6 as the denominator.

$$\frac{1}{2} = \frac{3}{6}$$
$$+\frac{1}{3} = +\frac{2}{6}$$

| $\frac{1}{2}$ | → | $\frac{1}{6}$ | $\frac{1}{6}$ | $\frac{1}{6}$ |
| $\frac{1}{3}$ | → | $\frac{1}{6}$ | $\frac{1}{6}$ |

Step 3

Add the equivalent fractions.

$$\frac{1}{2} = \frac{3}{6}$$
$$+\frac{1}{3} = +\frac{2}{6}$$
$$\overline{\quad\quad\; \frac{5}{6}}$$

You need $\frac{5}{6}$ yd of yarn for the puppet's face.

When you add fractions, sometimes the sum is greater than 1. You write the answer as a mixed number in simplest form.

Example 2

Add $\frac{3}{4}$ and $\frac{5}{6}$. Simplify.

Step 1	Step 2	Step 3
Find the LCD of $\frac{3}{4}$ and $\frac{5}{6}$. Multiples of 4: 4, 8, 12, 16, 20 Multiples of 6: 6, 12, 18, 24 The LCD of $\frac{3}{4}$ and $\frac{5}{6}$ is 12. So, $\frac{3}{4} + \frac{5}{6} = 1\frac{7}{12}$.	Find the equivalent fractions. **Think:** **Think:** $\frac{3}{4} \xrightarrow[\times 3]{\times 3} \frac{9}{12}$ $\frac{5}{6} \xrightarrow[\times 2]{\times 2} \frac{10}{12}$	Add the equivalent fractions. Simplify. $\frac{9}{12} + \frac{10}{12} = \frac{19}{12} = 1\frac{7}{12}$

The steps are the same when you add three or more fractions.

Example 3

Find $\frac{1}{2} + \frac{1}{3} + \frac{1}{6}$. Simplify.

Step 1	Step 2	Step 3
Find a common denominator. Multiples of 2: 2, 4, 6, 8, . . . Multiples of 3: 3, 6, 9, 12, . . . Multiples of 6: 6, 12, 18, . . . The LCD of the three fractions is 6. So, $\frac{1}{2} + \frac{1}{3} + \frac{1}{6} = 1$.	Find the equivalent fractions. $\frac{1}{2} = \frac{3}{6}$ $\frac{1}{3} = \frac{2}{6}$ $\frac{1}{6} = \frac{1}{6}$	Add the equivalent fractions. Simplify. $\frac{3}{6} + \frac{2}{6} + \frac{1}{6} = \frac{6}{6}$ $\frac{6}{6} = 1$

Talk About It

In the examples, you found least common denominators. Do you think other common denominators would work? Explain.

Check

Find each sum. Simplify.

1. $\frac{2}{9} + \frac{1}{3}$ 2. $\frac{1}{4} + \frac{2}{3}$ 3. $\frac{4}{5} + \frac{2}{3}$ 4. $\frac{5}{8} + \frac{2}{3} + \frac{5}{6}$ 5. $\frac{1}{4} + \frac{2}{5} + \frac{3}{10}$

6. $\frac{2}{5}$ 7. $\frac{1}{2}$ 8. $\frac{1}{2}$ 9. $\frac{1}{6}$ 10. $\frac{3}{4}$
   $+\frac{1}{3}$ $+\frac{2}{7}$ $+\frac{1}{5}$ $+\frac{3}{4}$ $+\frac{1}{6}$

11. **Reasoning** Without adding, how can you tell if the sum of $\frac{1}{5}$ and $\frac{1}{4}$ is greater than or less than 1?

Skills and Reasoning

Find each sum. Simplify.

12. $\frac{3}{4} + \frac{2}{5}$
13. $\frac{9}{10} + \frac{1}{4}$
14. $\frac{7}{12} + \frac{1}{3}$
15. $\frac{1}{2} + \frac{3}{10}$
16. $\frac{1}{4} + \frac{1}{8}$

17. $\begin{array}{r} \frac{5}{8} \\ + \frac{7}{12} \\ \hline \end{array}$
18. $\begin{array}{r} \frac{4}{5} \\ + \frac{4}{10} \\ \hline \end{array}$
19. $\begin{array}{r} \frac{1}{4} \\ + \frac{5}{12} \\ \hline \end{array}$
20. $\begin{array}{r} \frac{1}{6} \\ + \frac{2}{9} \\ \hline \end{array}$
21. $\begin{array}{r} \frac{1}{10} \\ + \frac{1}{2} \\ \hline \end{array}$

22. $\begin{array}{r} \frac{1}{5} \\ + \frac{1}{3} \\ \hline \end{array}$
23. $\begin{array}{r} \frac{2}{5} \\ + \frac{1}{4} \\ \hline \end{array}$
24. $\begin{array}{r} \frac{1}{6} \\ + \frac{3}{4} \\ \hline \end{array}$
25. $\begin{array}{r} \frac{3}{4} \\ + \frac{5}{8} \\ \hline \end{array}$
26. $\begin{array}{r} \frac{3}{5} \\ + \frac{3}{8} \\ \hline \end{array}$

27. $\frac{1}{2} + \frac{5}{8} + \frac{1}{4}$
28. $\frac{3}{5} + \frac{1}{3} + \frac{5}{6}$
29. $\frac{7}{10} + \frac{1}{5} + \frac{1}{10}$
30. $\frac{1}{2} + \frac{1}{4} + \frac{1}{5}$

31. Find the sum of $\frac{1}{3}$ and $\frac{2}{5}$.
32. Add $\frac{2}{3}$ and $\frac{7}{9}$.
33. Add $\frac{4}{5}$ and $\frac{1}{6}$.

 34. Mental Math Find $\frac{1}{2} + \frac{2}{4} + \frac{3}{6} + \frac{4}{8} + \frac{5}{10}$.

35. Do you get the same sum when you use 12 rather than 6 as a common denominator for the fractions $\frac{2}{3}$ and $\frac{1}{2}$? Explain.

36. Can you always use the product of the denominators as a common denominator? Explain.

Problem Solving and Applications

37. For one puppet costume you need $\frac{2}{9}$ yd of cotton for pants and $\frac{1}{2}$ yd for a matching coat. How much cotton do you need for the costume?

38. Using Data Use the *Did You Know?* on page 354. Which fraction would better describe how the *bunraku* puppet's size and a person's size relate: $\frac{1}{4}$ or $\frac{7}{8}$? Explain.

39. Science A patio door is made of two panes of safety glass, each $\frac{3}{16}$ in. thick. There is $\frac{3}{8}$ in. of air space between the two panes. How thick is the patio door?

40. Measurement In a science experiment, Plant A grew $\frac{3}{4}$ in. one week and $\frac{5}{8}$ in. the next week. How many inches did it grow during the two weeks?

Glass   Air   Glass

$\frac{3}{16}$ in. $\frac{3}{8}$ in. $\frac{3}{16}$ in.

Problem Solving and LITERATURE

Folktales are a type of oral literature found in most cultures. Stories are passed from one generation to the next.

41. In a Nigerian folktale, a farmer had 19 cows. He planned to share them with his 3 children as follows:

• The first child gets $\frac{1}{2}$.   • The second child gets $\frac{1}{4}$.   • The third child gets $\frac{1}{5}$.

a. What is the least common denominator for these fractions?

b. Find the sum for $\frac{1}{2} + \frac{1}{4} + \frac{1}{5}$.

c. Since there were 19 cows, is 19 a common denominator for the fractions $\frac{1}{2}$, $\frac{1}{4}$, and $\frac{1}{5}$? Explain.

d. The farmer's wife borrowed 1 cow from a neighbor so that there were 20 cows. Once she did this, she could find the number of cows for each child. How many cows did each child get?

e. Was the farmer's wife able to return the cow? Explain.

42. **Journal** Write the steps you use to add two fractions with unlike denominators.

Mixed Review and Test Prep

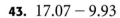

Find each sum or difference.

43. $17.07 - 9.93$ **44.** $13.1 + 0.05 + 0.6$ **45.** $8.9 - 3.05$ **46.** $4.92 + 16.1$

Find each product.

47. $\begin{array}{r} 13.2 \\ \times\ 0.7 \\ \hline \end{array}$ **48.** $\begin{array}{r} \$15.29 \\ \times\quad 35 \\ \hline \end{array}$ **49.** $\begin{array}{r} 0.46 \\ \times\ 7 \\ \hline \end{array}$ **50.** $\begin{array}{r} 4.09 \\ \times\ 1.3 \\ \hline \end{array}$

51. Which of the following is the mode for this data?

8, 9, 9, 11, 11, 11, 13, 14, 15, 16, 17, 18

Ⓐ 10   Ⓑ 12.7   Ⓒ 12   Ⓓ 11   Ⓔ not here

Exploring Subtracting Fractions

Problem Solving Connection

- Use Objects/ Act It Out

- Solve a Simpler Problem

Materials

fraction strips

Explore •

You can subtract fractions that have unlike denominators.

Work Together

Use fraction strips to find equivalent fractions before you subtract.

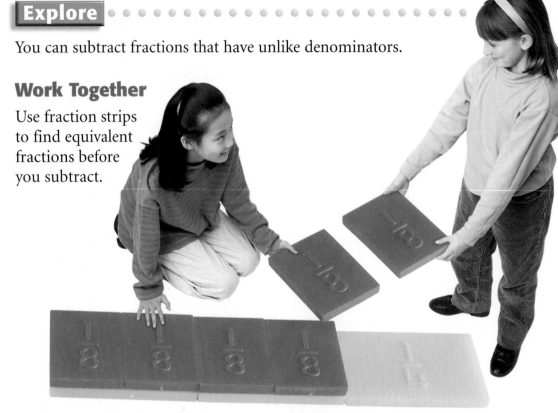

Math Tip

To subtract fractions with unlike denominators, change them to like denominators and solve a simpler problem.

1. Find the difference of $\frac{3}{4}$ and $\frac{1}{8}$.

2. Find the difference of $\frac{1}{2}$ and $\frac{1}{6}$.

3. Find each difference. You may use fraction strips or drawings to help.

   a. $\frac{2}{3} - \frac{1}{6}$ b. $\frac{4}{5} - \frac{3}{10}$ c. $\frac{5}{6} - \frac{1}{12}$ d. $\frac{4}{5} - \frac{1}{2}$ e. $\frac{5}{6} - \frac{3}{4}$

Talk About It

4. What fraction equivalent to $\frac{5}{8}$ would you use to subtract $\frac{3}{16}$ from $\frac{5}{8}$?

5. What fraction equivalent to $\frac{3}{4}$ would you use to subtract $\frac{1}{8}$ from $\frac{3}{4}$?

Connect ●

To subtract fractions with unlike denominators, first find equivalent fractions that have common denominators. Simplify if needed.

$$\frac{1}{2} - \frac{3}{10} = n$$

$$\frac{5}{10} - \frac{3}{10} = \frac{2}{10}$$

$$\frac{2}{10} = \frac{1}{5}$$

$$\frac{1}{3} - \frac{1}{6} = n$$

$$\frac{2}{6} - \frac{1}{6} = \frac{1}{6}$$

Practice ●

Find each difference. Simplify.

1. $\frac{3}{4} - \frac{5}{8}$

2. $\frac{5}{8} - \frac{1}{4}$

3. $\frac{5}{12} - \frac{1}{6}$

4. $\frac{5}{6} - \frac{1}{3}$

Find each difference. You may use fraction strips or draw pictures to help.

5. $\frac{3}{5} - \frac{1}{10}$

6. $\frac{5}{10} - \frac{1}{5}$

7. $\frac{7}{8} - \frac{1}{4}$

8. $\frac{5}{6} - \frac{1}{3}$

9. $\frac{5}{6} - \frac{1}{2}$

10. $\frac{7}{10} - \frac{2}{5}$

11. $\frac{7}{8} - \frac{1}{2}$

12. $\frac{11}{12} - \frac{3}{4}$

13. $\frac{3}{4} - \frac{1}{2}$

14. $\frac{1}{2} - \frac{1}{8}$

15. Find the difference of $\frac{1}{2}$ and $\frac{3}{10}$.

16. Critical Thinking What needs to be added to the following rule for subtracting fractions with unlike denominators? To subtract fractions, subtract the numerators.

Mantle: $\frac{9}{20}$ ft ——
Outer core: $\frac{7}{20}$ ft ——
Inner core: $\frac{1}{5}$ ft ——

Science This is a model of Earth with a section cut out to show the inner regions. The dimensions for the widths of the inner regions are shown. Use the model to answer **17** and **18**.

17. Geometry What is the total radius? Hint: Add the width of the inner core, outer core, and mantle.

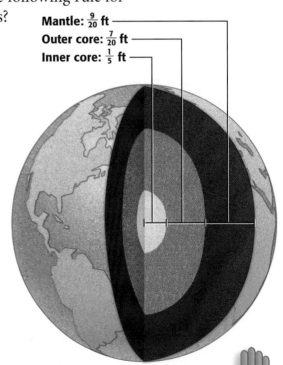

18. How much wider than the inner core is the outer core?

19. Journal Explain how to use equivalent fractions to subtract fractions with unlike denominators. Use an example.

Subtracting Fractions

You Will Learn

how to subtract fractions with unlike denominators

Learn • • • • • • • • • • • • •

Paul's hobby keeps him hopping! He raises rabbits. He uses a table to figure out how much to feed them.

Weight of Rabbit	Amount of Food
8–10 lb	$\frac{1}{2}$ c
11–15 lb	$\frac{3}{4}$ c

Paul raises his rabbits in Lafayette, Indiana.

Example 1

How much more does Paul feed his 12-lb rabbit than his 9-lb rabbit?
Since you want to compare the amounts, subtract. $\frac{3}{4} - \frac{1}{2} = n$

Step 1	Step 2	Step 3
Find a common denominator.	Write equivalent fractions.	Subtract.

Step 1

The LCM of 2 and 4 is 4.
So, the least common denominator for $\frac{3}{4}$ and $\frac{1}{2}$ is 4.

Step 2

$$\frac{3}{4} = \frac{3}{4}$$
$$-\frac{1}{2} = -\frac{2}{4}$$

Step 3

$$\frac{3}{4} = \frac{3}{4}$$
$$-\frac{1}{2} = -\frac{2}{4}$$
$$\frac{1}{4}$$

The 12-lb rabbit gets $\frac{1}{4}$ c more pellets.

Example 2

Find the difference of $\frac{4}{5}$ and $\frac{3}{4}$. Simplify.

$$\frac{4}{5} = \frac{16}{20} \qquad \frac{3}{4} = \frac{15}{20} \qquad \frac{16}{20} - \frac{15}{20} = \frac{1}{20}$$

The answer is in simplest form.

Remember

To subtract fractions with like denominators, subtract the numerators. Write the difference over the common denominator.

Talk About It

How is finding $\frac{1}{2} + \frac{1}{3}$ like finding $\frac{1}{2} - \frac{1}{3}$? How is it different?

Check •

Find each difference. Simplify.

1. $\frac{7}{12} - \frac{3}{8}$ 2. $\frac{5}{6} - \frac{1}{4}$ 3. $\frac{7}{8} - \frac{1}{3}$ 4. $\frac{1}{2} - \frac{1}{5}$ 5. $\frac{1}{3} - \frac{1}{9}$

6. **Reasoning** Which answer will be greater: $\frac{3}{4} - \frac{1}{3}$ or $\frac{3}{4} - \frac{1}{2}$? Explain.

Skills and Reasoning

Find each difference. Simplify.

7. $\dfrac{9}{10} - \dfrac{1}{4}$ **8.** $\dfrac{2}{3} - \dfrac{1}{8}$ **9.** $\dfrac{1}{3} - \dfrac{1}{4}$ **10.** $\dfrac{1}{2} - \dfrac{1}{6}$ **11.** $\dfrac{1}{4} - \dfrac{1}{8}$

12. $\dfrac{7}{10} - \dfrac{1}{3}$ **13.** $\dfrac{8}{10} - \dfrac{3}{4}$ **14.** $\dfrac{5}{6} - \dfrac{3}{4}$ **15.** $\dfrac{2}{5} - \dfrac{3}{10}$ **16.** $\dfrac{5}{8} - \dfrac{1}{3}$

17. $\begin{array}{r} \frac{11}{12} \\ -\frac{7}{8} \\ \hline \end{array}$ **18.** $\begin{array}{r} \frac{4}{5} \\ -\frac{1}{2} \\ \hline \end{array}$ **19.** $\begin{array}{r} \frac{3}{4} \\ -\frac{1}{6} \\ \hline \end{array}$ **20.** $\begin{array}{r} \frac{7}{12} \\ -\frac{1}{2} \\ \hline \end{array}$ **21.** $\begin{array}{r} \frac{9}{10} \\ -\frac{3}{4} \\ \hline \end{array}$

22. $\begin{array}{r} \frac{9}{10} \\ -\frac{1}{2} \\ \hline \end{array}$ **23.** $\begin{array}{r} \frac{7}{9} \\ -\frac{3}{4} \\ \hline \end{array}$ **24.** $\begin{array}{r} \frac{2}{5} \\ -\frac{1}{10} \\ \hline \end{array}$ **25.** $\begin{array}{r} \frac{5}{6} \\ -\frac{7}{12} \\ \hline \end{array}$ **26.** $\begin{array}{r} \frac{4}{5} \\ -\frac{2}{3} \\ \hline \end{array}$

27. Find the difference between $\dfrac{4}{5}$ and $\dfrac{1}{3}$.

28. If $\dfrac{1}{2}$ is subtracted from $\dfrac{4}{5}$, will the difference be greater or less than $\dfrac{1}{2}$?

Problem Solving and Applications

29. A recipe called for $\dfrac{3}{4}$ c of shredded carrots. Chad had $\dfrac{1}{8}$ c. How much more should he shred?

30. Time On Monday, a comet was visible for $\dfrac{5}{6}$ hr. Three days later, it was visible for only $\dfrac{3}{4}$ hr. For how many fewer minutes was the comet visible on Thursday?

31. Collecting Data Find out what fraction of a news program is really news. Time the length of the news and commercials for a 30 min news program. Round to the nearest minute.

   a. What fraction of the program was the news?

   b. What fraction of the program was commercials?

   c. Which portion of the program was longer? How much longer?

32. One literature collection is $\dfrac{1}{8}$ fiction. Another is $\dfrac{3}{4}$ fiction. How much more of the second collection is fiction than of the first?

Mixed Review and Test Prep

Find each sum or difference.

33. $0.75 - 0.06$ **34.** $0.7 + 0.09 + 0.13$ **35.** $1.09 - 0.3$ **36.** $\$4.50 + \$1.25$

37. Which of the following is the decimal for three hundredths?

   Ⓐ 0.03   Ⓑ 0.3   Ⓒ 0.003   Ⓓ 0.300

STOP and Practice

Find each sum or difference. Simplify.

1. $\dfrac{3}{8}$ $-\dfrac{1}{8}$

2. $\dfrac{2}{3}$ $+\dfrac{2}{3}$

3. $\dfrac{6}{7}$ $+\dfrac{2}{3}$

4. $\dfrac{9}{11}$ $-\dfrac{3}{22}$

5. $\dfrac{11}{12}$ $-\dfrac{3}{4}$

6. $\dfrac{7}{12}$ $-\dfrac{1}{3}$

7. $\dfrac{7}{8}$ $-\dfrac{3}{8}$

8. $\dfrac{3}{4}$ $+\dfrac{2}{5}$

9. $\dfrac{4}{9}$ $+\dfrac{1}{6}$

10. $\dfrac{8}{9}$ $-\dfrac{4}{5}$

11. $\dfrac{5}{20}$ $+\dfrac{2}{5}$

12. $\dfrac{2}{9}$ $+\dfrac{2}{3}$

13. $\dfrac{1}{2}$ $-\dfrac{1}{3}$

14. $\dfrac{5}{6}$ $+\dfrac{1}{3}$

15. $\dfrac{1}{8}$ $+\dfrac{3}{10}$

16. $\dfrac{3}{4}$ $-\dfrac{3}{8}$

17. $\dfrac{7}{9}$ $-\dfrac{1}{6}$

18. $\dfrac{6}{7}$ $+\dfrac{1}{7}$

19. $\dfrac{7}{8}$ $-\dfrac{4}{5}$

20. $\dfrac{8}{9}$ $+\dfrac{1}{3}$

21. $\dfrac{3}{4}$ $-\dfrac{2}{3}$

22. $\dfrac{1}{3}$ $+\dfrac{7}{9}$

23. $\dfrac{3}{8}$ $-\dfrac{1}{10}$

24. $\dfrac{1}{5}$ $-\dfrac{1}{6}$

25. $\dfrac{2}{5}$ $+\dfrac{3}{7}$

26. $\dfrac{6}{7}$ $-\dfrac{4}{9}$

27. $\dfrac{1}{6}$ $+\dfrac{7}{8}$

28. $\dfrac{5}{9}$ $-\dfrac{1}{3}$

29. $\dfrac{5}{8}$ $-\dfrac{1}{2}$

30. $\dfrac{3}{4}$ $+\dfrac{2}{5}$

31. $\dfrac{2}{3}+\dfrac{4}{5}+\dfrac{1}{2}$

32. $\dfrac{3}{8}+\dfrac{1}{4}+\dfrac{5}{6}$

33. $\dfrac{2}{3}+\dfrac{3}{10}+\dfrac{3}{5}$

34. $\dfrac{4}{5}+\dfrac{1}{3}+\dfrac{7}{15}$

35. $\dfrac{1}{6}+\dfrac{5}{12}+\dfrac{1}{4}$

Error Search

Find each sum or difference that is not correct. Write it correctly and explain the error.

36. $\dfrac{3}{5}$ $-\dfrac{1}{6}$ $\dfrac{13}{30}$

37. $\dfrac{1}{5}$ $+\dfrac{3}{8}$ $\dfrac{4}{13}$

38. $\dfrac{7}{8}$ $-\dfrac{3}{4}$ $1\dfrac{5}{8}$

39. $\dfrac{5}{8}$ $-\dfrac{2}{7}$ $\dfrac{3}{7}$

40. $\dfrac{3}{8}$ $+\dfrac{1}{6}$ $\dfrac{13}{24}$

41. $\dfrac{2}{3}$ $-\dfrac{2}{7}$ $\dfrac{20}{21}$

Seeing Double?

Find each sum or difference. Simplify. To solve the riddle, match each letter to its answer in the blank below. Some letters are not used.

How can you tell if you have poison ivy or poison oak?

Poison Oak

Poison Ivy

42. $\frac{1}{3} + \frac{3}{4}$ (L)

43. $\frac{4}{5} - \frac{2}{5}$ (I)

44. $\frac{1}{8} + \frac{3}{8}$ (D)

45. $\frac{5}{8} - \frac{1}{3}$ (Y)

46. $\frac{1}{2} + \frac{1}{3} + \frac{5}{6}$ (C)

47. $\frac{5}{8} - \frac{1}{4}$ (O)

48. $\frac{7}{8} + \frac{3}{4}$ (')

49. $\frac{5}{6} - \frac{2}{3}$ (E)

50. $\frac{1}{5} + \frac{7}{10}$ (S)

51. $\frac{3}{10} + \frac{3}{4}$ (U)

52. $\frac{2}{9} - \frac{1}{12}$ (G)

53. $\frac{1}{5} + \frac{3}{4}$ (T)

54. $\frac{5}{9} - \frac{2}{5}$ (H)

55. $\frac{1}{4} + \frac{3}{5} + \frac{3}{10}$ (N)

56. $\frac{1}{5} - \frac{1}{8}$ (A)

57. $\frac{1}{2} + \frac{2}{3} + \frac{2}{5}$ (W)

$\frac{7}{24}$ $\frac{3}{8}$ $1\frac{1}{20}$ $1\frac{2}{3}$ $\frac{3}{40}$ $1\frac{3}{20}$ $1\frac{5}{8}$ $\frac{19}{20}$ $\frac{3}{40}$ $1\frac{1}{12}$ $1\frac{17}{30}$ $\frac{3}{40}$ $\frac{7}{24}$ $\frac{9}{10}$

$\frac{19}{20}$ $\frac{1}{6}$ $1\frac{1}{12}$ $1\frac{1}{12}$ $1\frac{17}{30}$ $\frac{7}{45}$ $\frac{2}{5}$ $1\frac{2}{3}$ $\frac{7}{45}$ $\frac{2}{5}$ $\frac{19}{20}$ $1\frac{2}{3}$ $\frac{7}{45}$

$\frac{2}{5}$ $\frac{9}{10}$ $1\frac{17}{30}$ $\frac{7}{45}$ $\frac{2}{5}$ $1\frac{2}{3}$ $\frac{7}{45}$

Number Sense Pattern Hunt

Look for patterns. Copy and write the next three numbers.

58. $\frac{1}{2}, \frac{1}{4}, \frac{1}{6}, \frac{1}{8}$, ▪, ▪, ▪

59. $\frac{1}{2}, \frac{2}{3}, \frac{3}{4}, \frac{4}{5}$, ▪, ▪, ▪

60. $3\frac{11}{12}, 3\frac{7}{12}, 3\frac{1}{4}, 2\frac{11}{12}, 2\frac{7}{12}$, ▪, ▪, ▪

Problem Solving

Analyze Word Problems:
Too Much or Too Little Information

You Will Learn

how to find out if you have enough or too much information to solve a word problem

Learn · · · · · · · · · · ·

People spend their free time doing a wide range of activities. In 1992, $\frac{3}{10}$ of the adults in the United States visited art museums, $\frac{1}{5}$ went to see musical plays, and $\frac{1}{8}$ attended concerts. Think about the musical events. What fraction more attended musical plays?

Work Together

▶ **Understand**

What do you know?

What do you need to find out?

▶ **Plan**

What information do you need?

fractions of adults who attended musical events

Is there any extra information?

the fraction of adults who visited art museums

▶ **Solve**

To compare, subtract.

$$\frac{1}{5} = \frac{8}{40}$$
$$-\frac{1}{8} = -\frac{5}{40}$$
$$\frac{3}{40}$$

Reading Tip
Once you decide what you need, ignore the other information.

Write your answer.

$\frac{3}{40}$ more adults went to musical plays than to concerts.

▶ **Look Back**

Does your answer make sense?

Talk About It

1. How did you decide what information you needed?

2. How did you decide on the correct operation?

Write if each problem has too much or too little information. Solve, if possible, or write what is needed to solve.

1. To host the Olympics, a site has to win 45 of the 89 votes cast by members of the International Olympic Committee (IOC). For the 1996 Olympics, 11 U.S. cities other than Atlanta wanted to be the site. How many votes did each of the sites receive?

2. Suppose $\frac{1}{2}$ of all adults attended a sporting event in 1992. $\frac{1}{3}$ visited a historical park, and $\frac{1}{20}$ attended a ballet. What is the difference in the fraction who visited a historical park and attended a sporting event?

Problem Solving
Practice •

Problem Solving Strategies

- Use Objects/Act It Out
- Draw a Picture
- Look for a Pattern
- Guess and Check
- Use Logical Reasoning
- Make an Organized List
- Make a Table
- Solve a Simpler Problem
- Work Backward

Choose a Tool

Write if each problem has too much or too little information. Solve, if possible, or write what is needed to solve.

3. Suppose $\frac{1}{4}$ of all people in the United States jog on a regular basis and $\frac{1}{8}$ of the remaining population walk. How many people walk?

4. Julio walks $\frac{2}{3}$ mi every day. Maggie walks $\frac{5}{8}$ mi every day and runs $1\frac{1}{2}$ mi every other day. How much farther does Julio walk than Maggie?

5. The number of people who use a computer at home is increasing faster than the number of people watching videos. If 2,000,000 more people use a computer, how many more people will be watching videos?

Use the data in the table for **6** and **7**.

6. How many more countries were represented in the Summer Olympics of 1996 than in the Winter Olympics of 1994?

7. For the Atlanta Olympics, the Organizing Committee ordered 22,000 lb of pasta and 70,000 gal of milk. How many gallons of water were needed to cook the pasta if all of it were cooked?

	1994 Winter Olympics	1996 Summer Olympics
Athletes	More than 2,000	More than 10,000
Countries	64	197

8. The Olympic torch traveled across the United States. More than 10,000 people each carried it a short distance. About how far did each person carry the torch, on average?

PROBLEM SOLVING PRACTICE

SECTION A
Review and Practice

Vocabulary Write true or false. Explain.

1. The least common denominator (LCD) is the least common multiple of two numerators.

(Lesson 1) Find each sum or difference. Simplify.

2. $\dfrac{2}{3}$
$+\dfrac{1}{3}$

3. $\dfrac{6}{7}$
$-\dfrac{3}{7}$

4. $\dfrac{4}{9}$
$+\dfrac{3}{9}$

5. $\dfrac{11}{13}$
$-\dfrac{9}{13}$

6. $\dfrac{4}{8}$
$-\dfrac{2}{8}$

7. What is the sum of $\dfrac{3}{5}$ and $\dfrac{1}{5}$?

8. What number must be added to $\dfrac{4}{9}$ to get 1?

(Lessons 2–4) Find each sum. Simplify.

9. $\dfrac{1}{6} + \dfrac{2}{3}$

10. $\dfrac{3}{5} + \dfrac{4}{10}$

11. $\dfrac{1}{2} + \dfrac{7}{8}$

12. $\dfrac{2}{9} + \dfrac{1}{6}$

13. $\dfrac{2}{3} + \dfrac{5}{6}$

14. $\dfrac{1}{5} + \dfrac{2}{3}$

15. $\dfrac{3}{8} + \dfrac{1}{3}$

16. $\dfrac{2}{5} + \dfrac{2}{3}$

17. Marcia ran $\dfrac{1}{3}$ mi on Monday, $\dfrac{3}{4}$ mi on Tuesday, and $\dfrac{3}{4}$ mi on Wednesday. What was the total number of miles she ran?

(Lessons 5 and 6) Find each difference. Simplify.

18. $\dfrac{5}{8}$
$-\dfrac{1}{4}$

19. $\dfrac{8}{9}$
$-\dfrac{2}{3}$

20. $\dfrac{2}{3}$
$-\dfrac{1}{6}$

21. $\dfrac{9}{10}$
$-\dfrac{4}{5}$

22. $\dfrac{5}{6}$
$-\dfrac{1}{4}$

23. $\dfrac{2}{3}$
$-\dfrac{5}{9}$

24. $\dfrac{7}{8}$
$-\dfrac{2}{3}$

25. $\dfrac{7}{10}$
$-\dfrac{1}{2}$

26. $\dfrac{7}{9}$
$-\dfrac{1}{3}$

27. $\dfrac{3}{4}$
$-\dfrac{1}{5}$

(Lessons 7) Solve.

28. **Time** On Friday, Stephan practiced the piano for $\dfrac{3}{4}$ hr. On Saturday, he practiced $\dfrac{1}{2}$ hr. On Sunday, he practiced for $\dfrac{1}{4}$ hr longer than both days combined. How many fewer minutes did he practice on Saturday than Friday?

29. **Journal** Write the steps you would use to subtract $\dfrac{2}{3}$ from $\dfrac{4}{5}$.

> ### Skills Checklist
>
> In this section, you have:
>
> ☑ Added and Subtracted Fractions with Like Denominators
>
> ☑ Explored Adding and Subtracting Fractions
>
> ☑ Found the Least Common Denominator
>
> ☑ Added and Subtracted Fractions with Unlike Denominators
>
> ☑ Solved Problems with Too Much or Too Little Information

B Adding and Subtracting Mixed Numbers

Ralph loves to cook! For his favorite recipes, he often mixes many different spices.

How are mixed numbers used in cooking?

Adding and Subtracting Mixed Numbers

Review fraction operations. Find each sum or difference. Simplify.

1. $\frac{2}{6} + \frac{3}{6}$

2. $\frac{9}{16} + \frac{3}{8}$

3. $\frac{3}{8} + \frac{1}{6}$

4. $\frac{3}{8} - \frac{1}{8}$

5. $\frac{7}{10} - \frac{1}{2}$

6. $\frac{5}{6} - \frac{3}{4}$

Skills Checklist

In this section, you will:

☐ **Explore Adding and Subtracting Mixed Numbers**

☐ **Estimate Sums and Differences**

☐ **Add and Subtract Mixed Numbers**

☐ **Solve Problems by Working Backward/Drawing a Picture**

Exploring Adding and Subtracting Mixed Numbers

Problem Solving Connection

Use Objects/
Act It Out

Explore •

You can add and subtract mixed numbers. Use what you've learned about adding and subtracting fractions to help you.

Materials

fraction strips

Work Together

1. Use fraction strips to help you find $2\frac{1}{4} + 1\frac{1}{4}$.

   a. Show $2\frac{1}{4} + 1\frac{1}{4}$.

   b. Combine the $\frac{1}{4}$ strips.

   c. Combine the 1 strips.

   d. Simplify. Exchange the two $\frac{1}{4}$ strips for a $\frac{1}{2}$ strip.

$$
\begin{array}{r}
2\frac{1}{4} \\
+\ 1\frac{1}{4} \\
\hline
3\frac{2}{4} = 3\frac{1}{2}
\end{array}
$$

Think:

$\frac{1}{4} + \frac{1}{4} = \frac{2}{4}$

$2 + 1 = 3$

Remember

A mixed number is made up of a whole number and a fraction.

2. Use fraction strips to help you find $2\frac{1}{2} - 1\frac{1}{4}$.

3. Find each answer. Use fractions strips or drawings to help. Simplify.

   a. $3\frac{1}{3} + 1\frac{1}{3}$ **b.** $6\frac{3}{4} - 5\frac{1}{2}$ **c.** $7\frac{1}{8} + 4\frac{1}{2}$ **d.** $4\frac{2}{3} - 1\frac{1}{6}$

Talk About It

When adding $2\frac{1}{4}$ and $1\frac{1}{4}$, how did you exchange strips?

Connect

Sometimes you may need to rename.

$$3\frac{1}{2} = 3\frac{2}{4}$$
$$+1\frac{3}{4} = +1\frac{3}{4}$$
$$4\frac{5}{4} = 4 + 1\frac{1}{4}$$
$$= 5\frac{1}{4}$$

$$4 = 3\frac{5}{5}$$
$$-1\frac{3}{5} = -1\frac{3}{5}$$
$$2\frac{2}{5}$$

Math Tip

Think:

Rename: $\frac{5}{4} = 1 + \frac{1}{4}$

Rename: $4 = 3\frac{5}{5}$

Practice

Find each sum or difference. Use fraction strips or drawings to help. Simplify.

1. $3\frac{1}{2} = \blacksquare\frac{\blacksquare}{6}$
$-1\frac{1}{6} = -1\frac{1}{\blacksquare}$
$\frac{\blacksquare}{6} = 2\frac{1}{\blacksquare}$

2. $2\frac{3}{4} = \blacksquare\frac{3}{\blacksquare}$
$-1\frac{1}{2} = -1\frac{\blacksquare}{4}$
$\frac{\blacksquare}{4}$

3. $4\frac{1}{2} = 4\frac{\blacksquare}{6}$
$-2\frac{1}{6} = -\blacksquare\frac{1}{\blacksquare}$
$\frac{2}{\blacksquare} = 2\frac{1}{\blacksquare}$

4. $2\frac{3}{4}$
$-1\frac{1}{4}$

5. $2\frac{1}{3}$
$+1\frac{2}{3}$

6. 4
$-2\frac{1}{2}$

7. $3\frac{1}{4}$
$+2\frac{1}{4}$

8. $3\frac{2}{3}$
$-1\frac{1}{3}$

9. $1\frac{3}{4} + 2\frac{1}{3}$

10. $5\frac{3}{4} - 2\frac{1}{8}$

11. $6\frac{1}{2} + 2\frac{7}{8}$

12. $5\frac{1}{2} - 2\frac{1}{4}$

13. $2 + 1\frac{1}{2}$

14. $3 - 1\frac{1}{2}$

15. $5\frac{5}{6} + 4\frac{1}{2}$

16. $4\frac{3}{4} - 2\frac{1}{5}$

17. $9\frac{4}{5} - 2\frac{1}{2}$

18. $8\frac{1}{6} - 1\frac{1}{8}$

19. $6 - \frac{3}{5}$

20. $4\frac{7}{8} + 4\frac{1}{2}$

21. Find the sum of $3\frac{3}{4}$ and $2\frac{3}{4}$.

22. Find the difference of $3\frac{3}{4}$ and $2\frac{1}{4}$.

23. Measurement How much longer is the pencil than the crayon? Look at the objects shown.

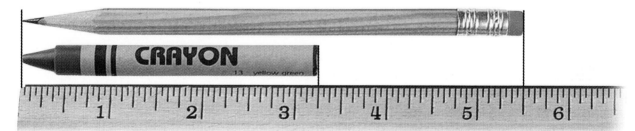

24. Science A slide of an onion root is $1\frac{7}{8}$ in. long. A slide of a leaf cross-section is $\frac{3}{4}$ in. long. How much longer is the onion root slide?

25. Journal Explain how you would use fraction strips to find $1\frac{3}{4} - \frac{1}{2}$.

Estimating Sums and Differences

You Will Learn

how to estimate sums and differences of mixed numbers

Learn

The HO model trains are about $\frac{1}{87}$ the size of a real train. The N model trains are about $\frac{1}{160}$ the size.

Sizes of Model Trains				
	Engine	**Box Car**	**Flat Car**	**Caboose**
N Model	$3\frac{3}{5}$ in.	$3\frac{2}{3}$ in.	$3\frac{1}{3}$ in.	$2\frac{3}{5}$ in.
HO Model	$6\frac{3}{4}$ in.	$6\frac{7}{10}$ in.	$5\frac{1}{2}$ in.	$4\frac{3}{4}$ in.

Example 1

Estimate the length of an N model train with an engine, box car, and flat car.

To estimate the length, round to the nearest inch.

$$
\begin{array}{rcl}
3\frac{3}{5} & \longrightarrow & 4 \\
3\frac{2}{3} & \longrightarrow & 4 \\
+\,3\frac{1}{3} & \longrightarrow & +3 \\
\hline
& & 11
\end{array}
$$

An N model train with an engine, box car, and flat car is about 11 in. long.

Example 2

Estimate $6\frac{3}{8}$ in. $- 4\frac{1}{16}$ in.
You can round to the nearest $\frac{1}{2}$ inch.

$$
\begin{array}{rcl}
6\frac{3}{8} & \longrightarrow & 6\frac{1}{2} \\
-4\frac{1}{16} & \longrightarrow & -4 \\
\hline
& & 2\frac{1}{2}
\end{array}
$$

$6\frac{3}{8}$ in. $- 4\frac{1}{16}$ in. is about $2\frac{1}{2}$ in.

Talk About It

When might you use the method shown in Example 1?

Did You Know?

The smallest model railroad engine measures $\frac{5}{16}$ of an inch and runs on a $4\frac{1}{2}$ volt battery.

Check

Estimate each sum or difference.

1. $3\frac{2}{3} + 1\frac{1}{4}$
2. $7\frac{3}{4} - 6\frac{1}{8}$
3. $5\frac{7}{8} + 1\frac{4}{5}$
4. $5 - 3\frac{1}{2}$
5. $4\frac{1}{3} + 3\frac{1}{8}$

6. Reasoning Is it easier to round $4\frac{5}{6}$ to the nearest whole number or to the nearest half? Explain.

Practice

Skills and Reasoning

Estimate each sum or difference.

7. $7\frac{1}{2} + 3\frac{1}{4}$ **8.** $3\frac{2}{3} - 1\frac{1}{4}$ **9.** $4\frac{5}{8} - 1\frac{1}{3}$ **10.** $6\frac{2}{5} + 2\frac{3}{4}$ **11.** $6\frac{2}{3} - 1\frac{1}{4}$

12. $\begin{aligned} 9\frac{7}{10} \\ +\ 4\frac{2}{3} \\ \hline \end{aligned}$ **13.** $\begin{aligned} 6\frac{3}{8} \\ -\ 2\frac{1}{2} \\ \hline \end{aligned}$ **14.** $\begin{aligned} 8\frac{1}{3} \\ -\ 7\frac{4}{5} \\ \hline \end{aligned}$ **15.** $\begin{aligned} 5\frac{1}{2} \\ -\ 5\frac{1}{3} \\ \hline \end{aligned}$ **16.** $\begin{aligned} 4\frac{1}{8} \\ +\ 6\frac{2}{3} \\ \hline \end{aligned}$

17. $5\frac{1}{4} + 5\frac{1}{5} + 2$ **18.** $1\frac{1}{2} + 2\frac{1}{3} + 3\frac{7}{12}$ **19.** $6\frac{2}{3} + 3\frac{1}{4} + 7\frac{4}{5}$ **20.** $3\frac{1}{3} + 5\frac{3}{4} + 1\frac{8}{11}$

21. $4\frac{1}{4} + 2\frac{2}{3}$ **22.** $1\frac{3}{4} + \frac{5}{6}$ **23.** $3\frac{1}{2} + 3\frac{1}{3} + 3\frac{2}{3}$ **24.** $6\frac{2}{5} + 2\frac{2}{9}$

25. Estimate the difference between $5\frac{1}{2}$ and $3\frac{7}{8}$.

26. Why does rounding mixed numbers to the nearest $\frac{1}{2}$ make sense?

Problem Solving and Applications

Using Data Use the data on page 370 for **27** and **28**.

27. Estimate, to the nearest $\frac{1}{2}$-inch, the length of an HO train that is made up of an engine, a box car, a flat car, and a caboose.

28. To the nearest $\frac{1}{2}$-inch, how much longer is an HO train than an N train?

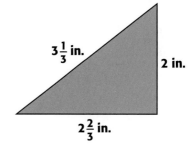

3$\frac{1}{3}$ in.   2 in.

2$\frac{2}{3}$ in.

 29. Geometry Estimate the distance around the triangle to the nearest inch.

30. Logic What is the sum of 23.75 and 18.5? Without writing a new problem, give the sum of $23\frac{3}{4}$ and $18\frac{1}{2}$. Explain.

Mixed Review and Test Prep

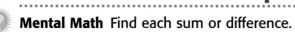

Mental Math Find each sum or difference.

31. $6.25 + 2.75$ **32.** $5.5 - 4$ **33.** $1.5 + 8.5$ **34.** $5 - 2.75$

Money Find each answer.

35. $\$18.95 \times 4$ **36.** $\$7.60 + \$2.19 + \$8.45$ **37.** $\$22.52 \div 4$ **38.** $\$20.75 - \$0.85$

 39. Algebra Readiness Which number completes this number sentence?
$4.75 - n = 2.5$

Ⓐ 7.25   Ⓑ 2.5   Ⓒ 2.25   Ⓓ 2   Ⓔ not here

Adding and Subtracting Mixed Numbers

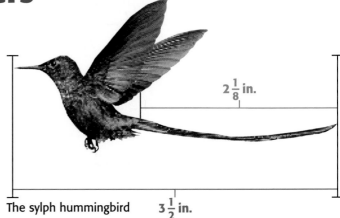

$2\frac{1}{8}$ in.

The sylph hummingbird $3\frac{1}{2}$ in.

You Will Learn

how to add and subtract mixed numbers

Learn • • • • • • • •

Birdwatching is a popular hobby. The world record for birdwatching is held by Phoebe Snetsinger, who has recorded over 7,772 of the 9,700 known species of birds.

Did You Know?

At $2\frac{6}{25}$ in. long, the bee hummingbird of Cuba and the Isle of Pines is the world's smallest bird.

Example 1

The sylph hummingbird is found in the Andes Mountains of South America.

How long is the bird without its tail? To compare, subtract. $3\frac{1}{2} - 2\frac{1}{8} = n$.

Step 1

Find the LCD.

$3\frac{1}{2}$

$-2\frac{1}{8}$ The LCD is **8**.

Step 2

Find equivalent fractions

$3\frac{1}{2} = 3\frac{4}{8}$

$-2\frac{1}{8} = -2\frac{1}{8}$

Step 3

Subtract the fractions.

$3\frac{1}{2} = 3\frac{4}{8}$

$-2\frac{1}{8} = -2\frac{1}{8}$

$\frac{3}{8}$

Step 4

Subtract the whole numbers.

$3\frac{1}{2} = 3\frac{4}{8}$

$-2\frac{1}{8} = -2\frac{1}{8}$

$1\frac{3}{8}$

The bird is $1\frac{3}{8}$ in. long from bill tip to base of tail.

Other Examples

A. $4\frac{1}{2} = 4\frac{3}{6}$

$+5\frac{1}{3} = +5\frac{2}{6}$

$9\frac{5}{6}$

B. $8\frac{1}{2} = 8\frac{2}{4}$

$-\frac{1}{4} = -\frac{1}{4}$

$8\frac{1}{4}$

Talk About It

How is adding mixed numbers like adding fractions?

Find each sum or difference. Simplify.

1. $3\frac{1}{3} + 2\frac{1}{6}$ **2.** $6\frac{3}{4} - 1\frac{1}{2}$ **3.** $1\frac{1}{6} + 1\frac{1}{4}$ **4.** $2\frac{7}{10} + 3$ **5.** $5\frac{2}{3} - \frac{1}{2}$

6. Reasoning When adding or subtracting mixed numbers, how can you tell if your answer is reasonable?

Skills and Reasoning

Find each sum or difference. Simplify.

7. $\begin{array}{r} 2\frac{1}{3} \\ -1\frac{1}{4} \\ \hline \end{array}$ **8.** $\begin{array}{r} 4\frac{1}{2} \\ +1\frac{1}{6} \\ \hline \end{array}$ **9.** $\begin{array}{r} 3\frac{7}{8} \\ -1\frac{3}{4} \\ \hline \end{array}$ **10.** $\begin{array}{r} 4\frac{2}{5} \\ +1\frac{1}{10} \\ \hline \end{array}$ **11.** $\begin{array}{r} 5\frac{2}{3} \\ -4\frac{1}{5} \\ \hline \end{array}$

12. $1\frac{5}{6} - 1\frac{4}{5}$ **13.** $1\frac{3}{4} + 5$ **14.** $7\frac{2}{3} - 3$ **15.** $6\frac{1}{10} + \frac{3}{5}$

16. $\frac{5}{8} + 2\frac{1}{4}$ **17.** $6\frac{1}{2} - \frac{1}{3}$ **18.** $8\frac{5}{6} - 1\frac{2}{3}$ **19.** $4\frac{5}{12} + \frac{1}{6}$

20. $3\frac{1}{3} + 4\frac{1}{8}$ **21.** $2\frac{7}{8} - \frac{3}{4}$ **22.** $6\frac{1}{5} + 2\frac{3}{10}$ **23.** $5\frac{7}{9} - 1\frac{3}{18}$

24. Find the sum of $6\frac{7}{8}$ and $2\frac{1}{4}$.   **25.** Find the difference of $4\frac{4}{7}$ and $2\frac{1}{3}$.

26. When you add the fraction parts of mixed numbers and get an improper fraction, what do you do?

Problem Solving and Applications

27. Science The rufous hummingbird is $3\frac{3}{4}$ in. long. The ruby-throated hummingbird is $3\frac{1}{3}$ in. How much longer is the rufous hummingbird?

Rufous hummingbird (western United States)

28. Algebra Readiness What must be added to $6\frac{3}{8}$ to get a sum of 7?

Ruby-Throated hummingbird (eastern United States)

Mixed Review and Test Prep

Estimation Estimate each sum or difference.

29. $4.8 + 3.1$ **30.** $7.9 - 3.3$ **31.** $18.7 - 3.4$ **32.** $2.9 + 3.7$

33. Algebra Readiness Which of the following is the missing factor?
$5 \times n = 85$

   Ⓐ 17   Ⓑ 15   Ⓒ 27   Ⓓ 13   Ⓔ not here

Adding Mixed Numbers

Ralph was born in Philadelphia, Pennsylvania.

You Will Learn
how to add mixed numbers with renaming

Learn • • • • • • • • • • • • • • • • • •

Put some spice in your life like Ralph does! To make his cooking more flavorful, he uses many spices.

Example 1

Ralph bought the spices shown. How many ounces did he buy?

Find $4\frac{1}{4} + 1\frac{7}{8} + 2\frac{1}{2}$.

$1\frac{7}{8}$ oz

$2\frac{1}{2}$ oz

$4\frac{1}{4}$ oz

Step 1	Step 2	Step 3
Find the LCD. The LCD is 8.	Add the fractions.	Add the whole numbers.
Write equivalent fractions.	$$4\frac{1}{4} = 4\frac{2}{8}$$	$$4\frac{1}{4} = 4\frac{2}{8}$$
$$4\frac{1}{4} = 4\frac{2}{8}$$	$$1\frac{7}{8} = 1\frac{7}{8}$$	$$1\frac{7}{8} = 1\frac{7}{8}$$
$$1\frac{7}{8} = 1\frac{7}{8}$$	$$+2\frac{1}{2} = +2\frac{4}{8}$$	$$+2\frac{1}{2} = +2\frac{4}{8}$$
$$+2\frac{1}{2} = +2\frac{4}{8}$$	$$\frac{13}{8}$$	Simplify. $7\frac{13}{8} = 7 + 1 + \frac{5}{8}$
		$= 8\frac{5}{8}$

Ralph bought $8\frac{5}{8}$ oz of spices.

Other Examples

A.
$$2\frac{1}{3} = 2\frac{4}{12}$$
$$3\frac{1}{2} = 3\frac{6}{12}$$
$$+1\frac{3}{4} = +1\frac{9}{12}$$
$$6\frac{19}{12} = 7\frac{7}{12}$$

Estimate to check.
2 + 4 + 2 = 8
So, the answer is reasonable.

B. Find $\frac{7}{8} + 1\frac{1}{3} + 1\frac{1}{8}$ mentally.
Combine fractions with a common denominator.

$$\frac{7}{8} + 1\frac{1}{3} + 1\frac{1}{8} = 2 + 1\frac{1}{3} = 3\frac{1}{3}$$

How would you write a sum of $14\frac{8}{6}$ in simplest form?

Check

Find each sum. Simplify, if possible.

1. $2\frac{1}{5} + 1\frac{1}{2} + 1\frac{3}{10}$

2. $5\frac{1}{4} + 2\frac{1}{2} + 3\frac{3}{4}$

3. $3\frac{7}{8} + 2\frac{3}{4} + 1\frac{1}{2}$

4. **Reasoning** How would you use mental math to find $1\frac{1}{3} + 6\frac{1}{2} + 3\frac{2}{3} + 4\frac{1}{2}$?

Practice

Skills and Reasoning

Find each sum. Simplify, if possible.

5.
$$\begin{array}{r} 2\frac{2}{3} \\ 1\frac{1}{2} \\ +3\frac{2}{3} \\ \hline \end{array}$$

6.
$$\begin{array}{r} 4\frac{1}{4} \\ 1\frac{3}{4} \\ +2\frac{1}{2} \\ \hline \end{array}$$

7.
$$\begin{array}{r} 1\frac{1}{5} \\ 2\frac{3}{10} \\ +3\frac{3}{5} \\ \hline \end{array}$$

8.
$$\begin{array}{r} 4\frac{1}{3} \\ 3\frac{2}{3} \\ +8\frac{2}{3} \\ \hline \end{array}$$

9.
$$\begin{array}{r} 6\frac{1}{2} \\ 1\frac{7}{8} \\ +\ \frac{3}{4} \\ \hline \end{array}$$

10. $6 + 3\frac{1}{4} + 5\frac{9}{10}$

11. $\frac{4}{5} + 3\frac{1}{10} + 2\frac{1}{5}$

12. $7\frac{1}{8} + 3\frac{3}{10} + \frac{4}{5}$

13. $2\frac{3}{7} + 19\frac{1}{4} + 4\frac{4}{7}$

14. $\frac{2}{3} + 4\frac{1}{5} + 6\frac{2}{3}$

15. $6\frac{1}{4} + 2\frac{1}{8} + 1\frac{3}{4}$

16. Add $7\frac{1}{4}$, $6\frac{7}{8}$, and $5\frac{1}{3}$.

17. Add $5\frac{2}{3}$, $2\frac{1}{4}$, and $1\frac{5}{6}$.

18. When you add several whole numbers, you can look for tens to make addition easier. How can you combine numbers to add $5\frac{1}{3} + \frac{5}{8} + 2\frac{2}{3}$?

Problem Solving and Applications

Using Data Use the Data File on page 345 to answer **19–21**.

19. **Estimation** Estimate the total travel time for each trip. Which is the longest?

20. What is the total travel time for trip D?

21. **Critical Thinking** Use the data to give a reasonable estimate for a trip from Orlando to Seattle without stopping or changing trains.

Mixed Review and Test Prep

Write each percent as a fraction in simplest form.

22. 20%   23. 75%   24. 30%   25. 80%   26. 78%

27. What is the range of these test scores?

| 72 | 65 | 84 | 77 | 88 | 70 | 90 | 84 |

Ⓐ 78.75   Ⓑ 84   Ⓒ 25   Ⓓ 90

Subtracting Mixed Numbers

You Will Learn

how to subtract mixed numbers using renaming

Learn • • • • • • • • • • •

Laurie grows prize winning pumpkins. She wonders if the length of their vines is related to the size of the pumpkins.

Did You Know?

The world's largest grapevine was planted in 1842 in Carpintería, CA. It produced more than $9\frac{9}{10}$ tons of grapes in some years.

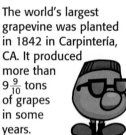

Laurie is from Alta, Iowa.

Vine	Length (ft)
A	$9\frac{1}{4}$
B	5
C	$4\frac{1}{4}$
D	$6\frac{1}{2}$

Example 1

How much longer is vine A than vine D?

Since you want to compare the lengths, subtract $6\frac{1}{2}$ from $9\frac{1}{4}$.

Step 1

Write the fractions with a common denominator. The LCD is 4.

$$9\frac{1}{4} = 9\frac{1}{4}$$
$$-6\frac{1}{2} = -6\frac{2}{4}$$

Step 2

Rename if needed.

$$9\frac{1}{4} = 8\frac{5}{4}$$
$$-6\frac{1}{2} = -6\frac{2}{4}$$

Think: $9\frac{1}{4} = 8 + 1 + \frac{1}{4}$
$$= 8 + \frac{4}{4} + \frac{1}{4}$$
$$= 8\frac{5}{4}$$

Step 3

Subtract the fractions.

$$9\frac{1}{4} = 8\frac{5}{4}$$
$$-6\frac{1}{2} = -6\frac{2}{4}$$
$$\frac{3}{4}$$

Vine A is $2\frac{3}{4}$ ft longer than vine D.

Step 4

Subtract the whole numbers.

$$9\frac{1}{4} = 8\frac{5}{4}$$
$$-6\frac{1}{2} = -6\frac{2}{4}$$
$$2\frac{3}{4}$$

Example 2

How much longer is vine B than vine C?

$$
\begin{array}{rcl}
5 & = & 4\frac{4}{4} \\
-4\frac{1}{4} & = & -4\frac{1}{4} \\
\hline
& & \frac{3}{4}
\end{array}
$$

Vine B is $\frac{3}{4}$ ft longer than vine C.

Example 3

Another vine is $3\frac{2}{3}$ ft long. How much longer is vine C?

$$
\begin{array}{rclclcl}
4\frac{1}{4} & = & 4\frac{3}{12} & = & 3\frac{15}{12} \\
-3\frac{2}{3} & = & -3\frac{8}{12} & = & -3\frac{8}{12} \\
\hline
& & & & \frac{7}{12}
\end{array}
$$

Vine C is $\frac{7}{12}$ ft longer.

Talk About It

1. In Example 1, how is renaming used to write $9\frac{1}{4}$ as $8\frac{5}{4}$?

2. In Example 2, how is renaming used to subtract $4\frac{1}{4}$ from 5?

Check

Copy and complete. Simplify.

1.
$$
\begin{array}{rclclcl}
4\frac{1}{4} & = & 4\frac{3}{12} & = & 3\frac{\blacksquare}{12} \\
-2\frac{1}{3} & = & -2\frac{4}{12} & = & -2\frac{4}{12} \\
\hline
& & & & 1\frac{\blacksquare}{12}
\end{array}
$$

2.
$$
\begin{array}{rcl}
5 & = & \blacksquare\frac{8}{8} \\
-2\frac{3}{8} & = & -2\frac{3}{8} \\
\hline
& & \blacksquare\frac{5}{8}
\end{array}
$$

3.
$$
\begin{array}{rcl}
3\frac{3}{4} & = & 3\frac{\blacksquare}{\blacksquare} \\
-2\frac{1}{8} & = & -2\frac{1}{8} \\
\hline
& & 1\frac{\blacksquare}{\blacksquare}
\end{array}
$$

Find each difference. Simplify.

4. $\begin{array}{r} 6\frac{1}{3} \\ -2\frac{1}{2} \\ \hline \end{array}$

5. $\begin{array}{r} 4\frac{2}{5} \\ -1\frac{3}{4} \\ \hline \end{array}$

6. $\begin{array}{r} 4 \\ -1\frac{1}{3} \\ \hline \end{array}$

7. $\begin{array}{r} 1\frac{1}{8} \\ -\frac{5}{8} \\ \hline \end{array}$

8. $\begin{array}{r} 6\frac{1}{6} \\ -4\frac{1}{3} \\ \hline \end{array}$

9. $\begin{array}{r} 4\frac{2}{3} \\ -2\frac{3}{4} \\ \hline \end{array}$

10. $3\frac{3}{8} - 1\frac{1}{2}$

11. $6 - \frac{3}{4}$

12. $18\frac{1}{4} - 2\frac{5}{6}$

13. $20 - 15\frac{1}{4}$

14. $5\frac{1}{3} - \frac{9}{10}$

15. $4\frac{3}{5} - 2\frac{1}{3}$

16. $5 - 2\frac{1}{2}$

17. $6\frac{7}{8} - 3\frac{3}{8}$

18. $1\frac{1}{2} - \frac{1}{8}$

19. $2\frac{3}{4} - 1\frac{1}{2}$

20. Find the difference of $7\frac{1}{2}$ and $2\frac{1}{16}$.

21. Subtract $2\frac{3}{4}$ from $4\frac{1}{6}$.

22. What is $8\frac{1}{2} - 2\frac{1}{3}$?

23. What is $3\frac{7}{8} - 1\frac{2}{3}$?

24. **Reasoning** When do you need to rename from a whole number when subtracting mixed numbers?

Skills and Reasoning

Find each difference. Simplify.

25. $7\frac{2}{3}$
$-3\frac{3}{4}$

26. $6\frac{1}{4}$
$-2\frac{7}{8}$

27. $8\frac{1}{2}$
$-3\frac{2}{3}$

28. $7\frac{1}{4}$
$-6\frac{1}{2}$

29. $4\frac{1}{5}$
$-2\frac{3}{5}$

30. 5
$-1\frac{1}{6}$

31. 4
$-1\frac{3}{4}$

32. $17\frac{1}{10}$
$-15\frac{1}{2}$

33. $6\frac{2}{3}$
$-\frac{4}{5}$

34. $24\frac{2}{3}$
$-12\frac{1}{8}$

35. $6\frac{1}{9}$
$-1\frac{2}{3}$

36. $5\frac{9}{10}$
$-\frac{3}{8}$

37. $2\frac{1}{4}$
$-1\frac{1}{2}$

38. $4\frac{6}{7}$
$-3\frac{1}{4}$

39. $14\frac{2}{9}$
$-10\frac{5}{6}$

40. $14-6\frac{1}{5}$
41. $12\frac{3}{4}-\frac{7}{8}$
42. $4\frac{1}{9}-1\frac{2}{3}$
43. $9\frac{11}{12}-4\frac{5}{9}$

44. $6\frac{1}{3}-1\frac{1}{2}$
45. $2\frac{3}{10}-\frac{2}{5}$
46. $7-1\frac{2}{3}$
47. $16\frac{3}{8}-2\frac{1}{2}$

48. $10-5\frac{3}{4}$
49. $17\frac{2}{5}-13\frac{7}{10}$
50. $11-9\frac{1}{12}$
51. $4\frac{1}{5}-3\frac{3}{10}$

52. Find the difference of $12\frac{1}{5}$ and $2\frac{1}{4}$.
53. What is $12\frac{1}{8}-4\frac{2}{3}$?

54. Estimation What is $3\frac{3}{4}-2\frac{4}{5}$ to the nearest whole number?

55. Sandra added $\frac{2}{3}$ to both 10 and $5\frac{1}{3}$ when subtracting $10-5\frac{1}{3}$. Explain.

Problem Solving and Applications

56. Using Data Use the information in *Did You Know?* on page 376. How many more tons of grapes would the vine need to produce to reach 10 tons?

57. Collecting Data Measure the length of a pencil and a piece of chalk to the nearest $\frac{1}{8}$ inch. Which is longer? By how much?

58. Shawn drank $2\frac{1}{3}$ cups of fruit shake. Debra drank $2\frac{3}{8}$ cups. How many cups did they drink in all?

59. Fine Arts In a kind of Japanese flower arrangement called *moribana*, the size of the flowers and the bowl are related. According to the rules, if the middle-height flower is $8\frac{2}{3}$ in. tall, the shortest flower must be $4\frac{1}{3}$ in. tall. How much shorter than the middle-height flower is the shortest flower?

Problem Solving and MATH HISTORY

The ancient Egyptians used fractions at least as early as 1600 B.C. But they used only unit fractions, fractions with a numerator of 1. The only exception was the fraction $\frac{2}{3}$. Fractions like $\frac{3}{4}$ or $\frac{5}{6}$ were not used. Instead, each was written as a sum of other fractions, each with a numerator of 1.

The Sphinx is located in Giza, Egypt. It is thought to have been built about 4,500 years ago.

60. Use the Egyptian system of fractions to complete the table.

Modern Fraction	Egyptian Fraction
$\frac{3}{4}$	$\frac{1}{2} + \frac{1}{4}$
$\frac{5}{6}$	$\frac{1}{2} + \frac{1}{3}$
$\frac{3}{8}$	$\frac{1}{4} + \frac{1}{8}$
$\frac{7}{8}$	$\frac{1}{2} + \frac{1}{4} + \frac{1}{8}$

Modern Fraction	Egyptian Fraction
$\frac{7}{12}$	$\frac{1}{2} + \frac{1}{12}$
$\frac{5}{8}$	
$\frac{11}{12}$	
$\frac{7}{16}$	

61. What modern fraction is equal to this Egyptian fraction: $\frac{1}{4} + \frac{1}{3} + \frac{1}{5}$?

62. Write Your Own Problem Choose two modern fractions from the table. Find the Egyptian fractions for them and add.

63. Journal Write step-by-step instructions for finding the difference of $3\frac{1}{6}$ and $2\frac{3}{4}$.

Mixed Review and Test Prep

Find each answer. Simplify.

64. $6\frac{2}{5} + 5\frac{9}{10}$ **65.** $1\frac{3}{4} + 2\frac{5}{6}$ **66.** $6\frac{5}{8} - \frac{2}{3}$ **67.** $10\frac{1}{3} - 2\frac{11}{12}$

68. Geometry Trace this triangle. Draw its lines of symmetry.

Find each answer.

69. $744 \div 6$ **70.** 85×90 **71.** $\$20 - \$12.79$ **72.** $4.2 + 1.08$

73. Which shows the order from greatest to least?

0.7   0.07   7.0   0.007   7.07

Ⓐ 0.007, 0.07, 0.7, 7.0, 7.07   Ⓑ 7.07, 7.0, 0.7, 0.07, 0.007
Ⓒ 7.0, 7.07, 0.7, 0.07, 0.007   Ⓓ 7.07, 7.0, 0.07, 0.7, 0.007

THE ADD-TO-3 GAME

Players
2 teams of 4 players each

Materials
2 bean bags

masking tape

fraction cards: $\frac{1}{2}$, $\frac{2}{3}$, $\frac{3}{4}$, $\frac{4}{5}$, $\frac{5}{6}$, $\frac{6}{7}$, $\frac{7}{8}$, $\frac{8}{9}$, $\frac{9}{10}$

Object
The object of the game is to add team scores to get a total as close to 3 as possible.

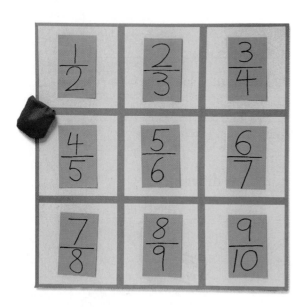

How to Play

1. Make a playing field on the floor. Use masking tape to make a grid 3 squares wide and 3 squares deep. Each square side should be about 1 ft. Tape a fraction card at the center of each square.

2. Teams toss a bean bag at the fraction cards. The team with the greatest fraction goes first.

3. A member of Team 1 faces backward about a foot from the playing field and tosses the bean bag over his or her shoulder. A score is made when a bean bag lands entirely in a square. If the bean bag is touching a line, the player tosses again. Player records her or his score.

4. Each Team 1 member tosses and records.

5. Each Team 2 member tosses and records.

6. Repeat Steps 4 and 5.

7. Each team reviews its 8 scores and selects 4 whose total is as close to 3 as possible. The closer-to-3 team wins.

1. Did you have a team plan about which squares to aim for? Describe it.

2. Did facing away from the playing field make the game more difficult? Explain.

More Ways to Play

■ Add all 8 team scores. The team with the greater total score wins.

■ Use 4 of the 8 scores. Add 2 sets of 2 scores. Subtract the lesser total from the greater. Try to get a final score of zero. The team closer to 0 wins.

Reasoning

1. Suppose your team has scores of $\frac{4}{5}$, $\frac{5}{6}$, and $\frac{1}{2}$. What fraction would you hope to get?

2. Suppose your team had scores of $\frac{3}{4}$, $\frac{2}{3}$, $\frac{7}{8}$, $\frac{4}{5}$, $\frac{1}{2}$, $\frac{8}{9}$, and $\frac{6}{7}$. Which 4 scores would you choose? Explain your reasoning.

Problem Solving

Compare Strategies: Work Backward/Draw a Picture

Learn •

Tina asked 15 people: "What's your favorite hobby?" She recorded the responses but forgot to record the number of girls and boys who gave each response.

Favorite Hobby	
Inline skating	卌 卌
Drawing	卌

She spoke with 7 girls and 8 boys. The same number of girls as boys chose inline skating as their favorite hobby. How many girls chose drawing as their favorite hobby?

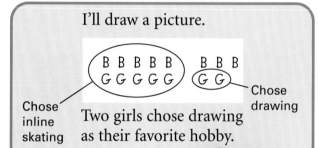

I'll draw a picture.

Chose inline skating

Chose drawing

Two girls chose drawing as their favorite hobby.

I'll work backward.

10 people chose inline skating.

5 were girls and 5 were boys.

Tina spoke with 7 girls.

$7 - 5 = 2$

So, two girls chose drawing as their favorite hobby.

Talk About It

1. When do you think working backward is a good strategy to use?

2. When could you draw a picture to help you understand a problem?

3. How can you check your solution to this problem?

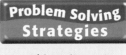

Work backward or draw a picture to solve the problem.

1. A group of skaters collected money to help clean the park. They divided the money into three equal parts. One part was used to buy plastic collection bags, one part was used for rakes, and $42.50 of the last part was used for seed. Of the last part, they had $8.00 left. How much did they collect?

Problem Solving
Practice

Work backward or use any strategy to solve each problem.

2. **Time** Reuben is going out but has promised he would be home by 5:30 P.M. It takes him 20 min to skate over to his friend's house. He will stay there for 2 hr. On the way home, he always stops for a snack, so the return trip takes 30 min. If Reuben is to keep his promise, by what time must he leave home?

violins   viola   cello

Problem Solving Strategies

- Use Objects/Act It Out
- Draw a Picture
- Look for a Pattern
- Guess and Check
- Use Logical Reasoning
- Make an Organized List
- Make a Table
- Solve a Simpler Problem
- Work Backward

Choose a Tool

3. Keith, Barb, and Jill made fruit punch for a small party. Keith poured 32 oz of his punch into Barb's pitcher. When Jill added her punch to the pitcher it doubled the amount that was already there. Keith, Barb, and Jill drank 48 oz. There were 80 oz left for other guests. How much fruit punch did each one make?

4. **Music** A string quartet usually consists of 2 violins, a viola, and a cello. William, Sandra, Kelly, and Andre are performing in a quartet. William and Sandra play different instruments. Andre plays the largest instrument. Sandra and Kelly also play different instruments. Who plays each instrument?

5. **Measurement** Look at the odometer on Mr. Ruiz's car. Before he picked up his daughter Sharon from the park and drove her 5 mi to her friend's house, it read 17,196 miles. Then Mr. Ruiz returned to the park, picked up his son Tony, and drove home. How far does the Ruiz family live from the park?

6. **Journal** When will you use the Work Backward strategy? Can you always use the Draw a Picture strategy instead?

Technology

Operations with Fractions and Mixed Numbers

You can be a big time operator on the calculator. You already know how to enter and simplify fractions. You can also perform operations with mixed numbers.

Materials

calculator

Work Together

A To add or subtract fractions enter the first fraction, the operation, the second fraction, and the $\boxed{=}$.

Problem   **Display**

$\dfrac{7}{8} + \dfrac{2}{3}$ **7** $\boxed{/}$ **8** $\boxed{+}$ **2** $\boxed{/}$ **3** $\boxed{=}$ **37/24**

B To change an improper fraction to a mixed number use $\boxed{\text{Ab/c}}$.

The **u** tells you it is a mixed number: $1\frac{13}{24}$

$\boxed{\text{1u 13/24}}$

C To add or subtract mixed numbers, you need another key. Use the $\boxed{\text{Unit}}$ to show the whole number part of the mixed number.

Remember to use $\boxed{\text{Simp}}$ to simplify answers when N/D → n/d shows in the display.

Problem   **Display**

$4\frac{1}{3} - 2\frac{3}{4}$ 4 $\boxed{\text{Unit}}$ 1 $\boxed{/}$ 3 $\boxed{-}$ 2 $\boxed{\text{Unit}}$ 3 $\boxed{/}$ 4 $\boxed{=}$ $\boxed{\text{1u 7/12}}$

$2\frac{5}{6} + 3\frac{2}{3}$ 2 $\boxed{\text{Unit}}$ 5 $\boxed{/}$ 6 $\boxed{+}$ 3 $\boxed{\text{Unit}}$ 2 $\boxed{/}$ 3 $\boxed{=}$ $\boxed{\text{5u 9/6}}$

$\boxed{\text{Ab/c}}$ $\boxed{\text{N/D → n/d   6u 3/6}}$

$\boxed{\text{Simp}}$ $\boxed{=}$ $\boxed{\text{6u 1/2}}$

Exercises

Find each sum or difference. Use $\boxed{\text{Ab/c}}$ to change an improper fraction to a mixed number.

1. $\dfrac{2}{3} - \dfrac{1}{4}$ 2. $\dfrac{5}{6} + \dfrac{1}{4}$ 3. $\dfrac{4}{5} - \dfrac{2}{3}$ 4. $7\dfrac{1}{2} - 4\dfrac{2}{3}$ 5. $6\dfrac{3}{4} + 1\dfrac{5}{8}$ 6. $7 - 2\dfrac{5}{6}$

Extensions

You also can change fractions and mixed numbers to decimals and add or subtract them. First change mixed numbers to improper fractions.

You'll need to use these keys too.

$\boxed{\text{M+}}$ Adds display to calculator's memory.

$\boxed{\text{M−}}$ Subtracts display from calculator's memory.

$\boxed{\text{MR}}$ Recalls total in memory.

$\boxed{\text{ON/AC}}$ Clears the memory before starting a new problem.

Here's how.

	Problem		**Display**

A. $1\dfrac{3}{4} + \dfrac{4}{5}$ 1 $\boxed{\text{Unit}}$ 3 $\boxed{/}$ 4 $\boxed{\text{F}\supset\text{D}}$ $\boxed{1.75}$

$\boxed{\text{M+}}$

4 $\boxed{/}$ 5 $\boxed{\text{F}\supset\text{D}}$ $\boxed{0.8}$

$\boxed{\text{M+}}$

$\boxed{\text{MR}}$ $\boxed{2.55}$

$\boxed{\text{F}\supset\text{D}}$ $\boxed{\text{N/D} \rightarrow \text{n/d} \quad 2u\ 55/100}$

$\boxed{\text{Simp}}\ \boxed{=}$ $\boxed{2u\ 11/20}$

B. $1\dfrac{4}{5} - \dfrac{1}{4}$ 1 $\boxed{\text{Unit}}$ 4 $\boxed{/}$ 5 $\boxed{\text{F}\supset\text{D}}$ $\boxed{1.8}$

$\boxed{\text{M+}}$

1 $\boxed{/}$ 4 $\boxed{\text{F}\supset\text{D}}$ $\boxed{0.25}$

$\boxed{\text{M−}}$

Math Tip

You can only use this method for decimals that end in the hundredths place.

$\boxed{\text{MR}}$ $\boxed{1.55}$

$\boxed{\text{F}\supset\text{D}}$ $\boxed{\text{N/D} \rightarrow \text{n/d} \quad 1u\ 55/100}$

$\boxed{\text{Simp}}\ \boxed{=}$ $\boxed{1u\ 11/20}$

Unit   /   F⊃D   π   ON/A

Simp   Ab/c   x⊃y   Cons   F

SECTION B
Review and Practice

(Lesson 8) Find each sum or difference. Simplify.

1. $2\frac{4}{5}$
   $+\ 3\frac{3}{5}$
   _____

2. $6\frac{3}{4}$
   $-\ 4\frac{1}{4}$
   _____

3. $5\frac{2}{3}$
   $-\ 1$
   _____

4. 8
   $+\ 3\frac{7}{8}$
   _____

5. $4\frac{3}{8}$
   $+\ 6\frac{5}{8}$
   _____

6. $3\frac{1}{6} + 4\frac{5}{6}$

7. $15 - 14\frac{1}{8}$

8. $12 + \frac{1}{12}$

9. $3\frac{1}{2} - 1\frac{1}{4}$

10. Mr. Ortiz bought $1\frac{3}{4}$ lb of corn, $2\frac{1}{4}$ lb of beans, and $4\frac{3}{4}$ lb of onions. How many pounds of produce did he buy in all?

(Lessons 9–11) Find each sum or difference. Simplify.

11. $4\frac{2}{3}$
    $-\ 1\frac{1}{4}$
    _____

12. $3\frac{1}{2}$
    $+\ 2\frac{5}{6}$
    _____

13. $5\frac{8}{9}$
    $-\ 3\frac{2}{3}$
    _____

14. $3\frac{1}{5}$
    $+\ 3\frac{3}{10}$
    _____

15. $6\frac{9}{10}$
    $-\ 4\frac{3}{20}$
    _____

16. $3\frac{4}{5}$
    $1\frac{1}{2}$
    $+\ 2\frac{7}{10}$
    _____

17. $4\frac{1}{4}$
    $3\frac{4}{5}$
    $+\ 1\frac{3}{4}$
    _____

18. $3\frac{5}{8}$
    $2\frac{5}{24}$
    $+\ \frac{7}{8}$
    _____

19. $12\frac{4}{7}$
    $8\frac{1}{7}$
    $+\ 3\frac{11}{21}$
    _____

20. 8
    $2\frac{3}{5}$
    $+\ 5\frac{9}{10}$
    _____

(Lesson 12) Find each difference. Simplify.

21. $5\frac{1}{8}$
    $-\ 2\frac{5}{8}$
    _____

22. $4\frac{3}{10}$
    $-\ 2\frac{5}{6}$
    _____

23. 6
    $-\ \frac{6}{7}$
    _____

24. $23\frac{1}{3} - 11\frac{4}{9}$

25. $15\frac{1}{5} - \frac{3}{10}$

26. $8\frac{5}{8} - 2\frac{5}{6}$

(Lesson 13) Solve.

27. Kristina wanted to change her skate brake after 200 mi of skating. She went 55 mi in August, 10 mi more than that in July, and twice as far in June as in July. Did she go over 200 mi in the three months? If so, by how much?

28. **Journal** Explain how $12\frac{5}{8}$ can be written as $11\frac{13}{8}$.

> ### Skills Checklist
>
> **In this section, you have:**
> - ☑ Explored Adding and Subtracting Mixed Numbers
> - ☑ Estimated Sums and Differences
> - ☑ Added and Subtracted Mixed Numbers
> - ☑ Solved Problems By Working Backward/Drawing a Picture

Using Customary Linear Measurements

How far can you jump? Laura's best long jump distance is more than 16 ft!

What other customary linear units might you use to find the length of a long jump?

Skills Checklist

GET READY!

Adding and Subtracting Lengths

Review adding and subtracting mixed numbers. Find each sum or difference. Simplify.

1. $3\frac{5}{8} - \frac{1}{8}$

2. $2\frac{5}{7} + \frac{3}{7}$

3. $6\frac{1}{8} - 1\frac{3}{8}$

4. $9 - \frac{5}{6}$

5. $14\frac{2}{3} + \frac{5}{6}$

6. $39\frac{2}{9} + \frac{2}{3} + 9\frac{5}{6}$

In this section, you will:

☐ Measure Length Using Fractional Parts of an Inch

☐ Change Among Units of Feet, Yards, and Miles

☐ Solve Problems by Deciding if You Need an Exact Answer or an Estimate

Linear Measure

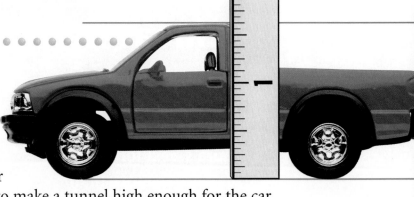

Learn

Collecting model cars is a popular hobby. Collectors often make model roadways, bridges, and tunnels for their cars. If you wanted to make a tunnel high enough for the car shown, you would need to measure its height.

Example

You could measure the height of the car to the nearest inch, $\frac{1}{2}$ inch, $\frac{1}{4}$ inch, and $\frac{1}{8}$ inch.

a. To the nearest inch   2 in.   **b.** To the nearest $\frac{1}{2}$ inch $1\frac{1}{2}$ in.

c. To the nearest $\frac{1}{4}$ inch $1\frac{3}{4}$ in.   **d.** To the nearest $\frac{1}{8}$ inch $1\frac{5}{8}$ in.

In order to be safe you probably would build your tunnel 2 in. high.

Measurements with smaller units are more accurate. $1\frac{5}{8}$ is the most accurate measure of the car height.

Talk About It

1. Could the car fit through a tunnel $1\frac{3}{4}$ in. tall? Explain.

2. Should you start at the end of a ruler to measure? Explain.

Did You Know?

The smallest motorized scale model car was 0.001 of the size of the actual car and measured less than $\frac{19}{100}$ in. long.

Check

1. Copy and complete. Measure the length of your book cover.

Measurement to the nearest:	Inch	$\frac{1}{2}$ inch	$\frac{1}{4}$ inch	$\frac{1}{8}$ inch
Length				

Use your ruler to draw a line segment for each length.

2. $1\frac{1}{2}$ in.   **3.** $4\frac{3}{4}$ in.   **4.** $2\frac{5}{8}$ in.   **5.** $6\frac{7}{8}$ in.

6. Reasoning Is measurement more accurate to the nearest $\frac{1}{8}$ or $\frac{1}{4}$ inch?

Practice

Skills and Reasoning

Find the length to the nearest $\frac{1}{4}$ inch.

7.

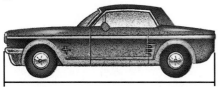

8.

Find the length to the nearest $\frac{1}{8}$ inch.

9.

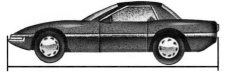

10.

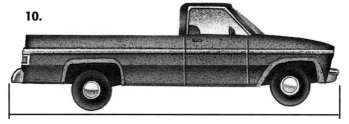

11. If you buy a new model car that is $4\frac{3}{4}$ in. long to the nearest $\frac{1}{8}$ inch, does this mean that it is exactly $4\frac{3}{4}$ in. long? Explain.

Use your ruler to draw a line segment for each length.

12. $2\frac{3}{4}$ in.   **13.** $5\frac{3}{8}$ in.   **14.** $4\frac{1}{2}$ in.   **15.** $3\frac{1}{8}$ in.

Problem Solving and Applications

16. Estimation If Patrick has a car $6\frac{7}{8}$ in. long, how long, to the nearest inch, must the tunnel be in order to be 3 times as long as the car?

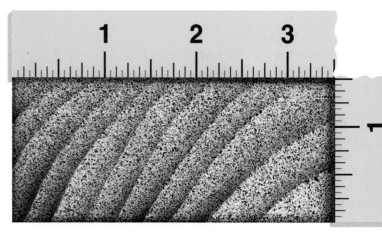

17. Career Clara uses 2-by-4s to build frames for houses. She has discovered that 2-by-4s are not really 2 in. by 4 in. Using the diagram, what are the true dimensions to the nearest $\frac{1}{8}$ inch?

Mixed Review and Test Prep

Find each product or quotient.

18. $108 \div 12$ **19.** $1,760 \times 36$ **20.** 12×15 **21.** $5,280 \div 3$

22. Which of the following is the range for this set of data?
13, 15, 15, 12, 18, 17, 14, 14, 14

Ⓐ 6   Ⓑ 14   Ⓒ 14.7   Ⓓ 9

Feet, Yards, and Miles

Learn • • • • • • • • • • • • •

Laura has participated in track and field events for several years. Each year, she jumps higher and farther.

At a meet of young athletes, these distances were recorded:

	First Try	Second Try
High Jump	43 in.	4 ft 3 in.
Long Jump	2 yd 1 ft	7 ft

Which tries were better?

You will need to change units to compare.

Laura is from Waco, Texas.

Example 1

For the high jump, change 43 in. to feet.

To change lesser units to greater units, divide. 12 in. = 1 ft

$$\begin{array}{r} 3 \text{ feet} \\ 12\overline{)43} \\ -36 \\ \hline 7 \text{ extra inches} \end{array}$$

43 in. = 3 ft 7 in. So, compare.

The second try, at 4 ft 3 in., is a better jump.

Example 2

For the long jump, change 2 yd 1 ft to feet.

To change greater units to lesser units, multiply.

1 yd = 3 ft

2 yd = 6 ft

2 yd 1 ft = 6 ft + 1 ft = 7 ft

2 yd 1 ft = 7 ft. So, compare.

The first and second tries are the same.

Talk About It

How do you decide which operation to use when you change from one unit to another? Explain.

Check •

Copy and complete.

1. 7 yd = ▇ ft
2. 16 in. = ▇ ft ▇ in.
3. 3 mi = ▇ yd
4. 6 mi 400 yd = ▇ yd

5. **Reasoning** There is a familiar phrase: Give an inch and they'll take a mile. How many inches would it be to take a mile?

Practice

Skills and Reasoning

Copy and complete.

6. 15 yd = ▨ ft

7. 4 mi = ▨ ft

8. 168 in. = ▨ ft

9. 6 mi = ▨ yd

10. 144 in. = ▨ ft

11. 10,560 ft = ▨ mi

12. 73 in. = ▨ ft ▨ in.

13. 15 ft 4 in. = ▨ in.

14. 5 ft 2 in. = ▨ in.

15. 4 yd 1 ft = ▨ ft

16. 42 in. = ▨ ft ▨ in.

17. 21,120 yd = ▨ mi

18. Your best high jump is 4 ft 10 in. Suppose your friend's best high jump is 59 in. Who has the better record?

19. Patterns Copy and complete.

a.	**Number of feet**	3	6	9		15
b.	**Number of yards**	1			4	

c. To change feet to yards, divide the number of feet by _____.

d. To change yards to feet, _____ the number of yards by 3.

Problem Solving and Applications

Using Data Use the Data File on page 345 to answer **20–22**.

20. Science How much farther does a jack rabbit jump than a cottontail? Give your answer in yards and in feet.

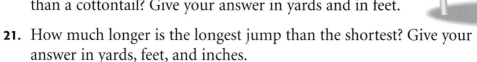

21. How much longer is the longest jump than the shortest? Give your answer in yards, feet, and inches.

22. A large kangaroo can cover a distance of 25 ft in a single leap. How many yards and feet would that be?

Mixed Review and Test Prep

Use your ruler to draw a line segment for each length.

23. $3\frac{1}{8}$ in.

24. $2\frac{1}{2}$ in.

25. $1\frac{1}{4}$ in.

26. $4\frac{5}{8}$ in.

Solve **27** and **28**. Give the operation used.

27. Each inline skate has 4 wheels. How many wheels are on 4 pairs?

28. You have 36 fish. You want to put the same number of fish in each of 3 tanks. How many fish should you put in each tank?

29. Algebra Readiness Which of the following expressions shows the number of minutes in 7 hr?

Ⓐ $7 \times 24 \times 60$ Ⓑ 7×60 Ⓒ $7 + 60$ Ⓓ $60 \div 7$ Ⓔ not here

Problem Solving

Analyze Word Problems: **Exact or Estimate?**

You Will Learn

how to solve problems by making decisions about whether an exact answer or an estimate is needed

Learn • • • • • • • • • • • • • • • •

Kate built her own inline skating ramp. She used boards that cost $3.00 each to build the base. If each board is 8 feet long, could Kate pay for the boards to make the base with $6.00?

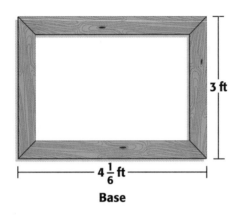

3 ft

$4\frac{1}{6}$ ft

Base

Kate lives and skates in Cincinnati, Ohio.

Work Together

▶ **Understand**   What do you know?

What do you need to know?

▶ **Plan**   How will you find your answer?   Estimate to see if $6 is enough.

▶ **Solve**   About how much wood does Kate need?   Estimate the perimeter of the base: 3 ft + 3 ft = 6 ft. $4\frac{1}{6}$ ft + $4\frac{1}{6}$ ft < 10 ft. Kate needs less than 16 ft. That's about 2 boards.

Write your answer. $2 \times \$3 = \$6$

Kate will be able to make the base for $6.

▶ **Look Back**   How can you check your answer?

Talk About It

What helps you decide whether you need an exact answer or an estimate?

Problem
Solving
Understand
Plan
Solve
Look Back

Decide whether you need an exact answer or an estimate. Solve.
Use the information on page 392.

1. If Kate wanted to make a second base 5 ft wide and $11\frac{2}{3}$ ft long, could she buy enough boards for it with $12.00? Explain your answer.

2. If Kate didn't want to spend more than $12.00 on boards, what is the greatest perimeter she could make?

Problem Solving Practice •

Problem Solving Strategies

- Use Objects/Act It Out
- Draw a Picture
- Look for a Pattern
- Guess and Check
- Use Logical Reasoning
- Make an Organized List
- Make a Table
- Solve a Simpler Problem
- Work Backward

Choose a Tool

Decide whether you need an exact answer or estimate. Solve.

3. Kate usually skates an hour a day. On weekends she skates an extra half hour each day. About how many hours does she skate in a month?

4. **Time** Joe starts eating breakfast at 7:30 A.M. He wants to be at school by 8:15 A.M. School is about a $\frac{1}{4}$-hr walk away. About how long does he have for breakfast?

5. Between allowance and jobs, Yvonne has saved $175 for a $220 mountain bike. Her father will lend her the rest but expects her to repay him at the rate of $5 per week. How many months will it take Yvonne to repay the loan?

6. A restaurant lists the calories and fat content for each item sold. You order a chicken sandwich and fries and eat everything. If the sandwich has 440 calories and the fries have 350, have you stayed below 750 calories for lunch?

7. **Time** Bryan got to school at 8:05 A.M. It took him $\frac{1}{4}$ hr to walk from home, $\frac{1}{4}$ hr to look at some magazines along the way, and $\frac{1}{2}$ hr to eat breakfast. What time did he sit down to eat? Tell what strategy you used.

8. **Geography** Jason and his mother are driving from Pittsburgh, Pennsylvania to Houston, Texas. Their car gets 20 mi/gal and the gas tank has a capacity of 20 gal. How many times will the gas tank have to be filled to make the trip?

PROBLEM SOLVING PRACTICE

Review and Practice

(Lesson 14) Find each length to the nearest $\frac{1}{8}$-inch.

1.

2.

3.

4.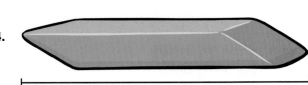

Use your ruler to draw a line segment for each length.

5. $1\frac{3}{8}$ in. **6.** $3\frac{1}{2}$ in. **7.** $2\frac{7}{8}$ in. **8.** $4\frac{1}{4}$ in. **9.** $2\frac{3}{4}$ in.

10. Joseph was printing a For Sale sign on an 11 in. long sheet of paper. He wanted to have a $1\frac{1}{4}$ in. margin on each side. How much room does that leave for the words?

(Lesson 15) Copy and complete.

11. 48 in. = ■ ft

12. 3 mi = ■ ft

13. 93 ft = ■ yd

14. 137 ft = ■ yd ■ ft

15. 2 mi 320 ft = ■ ft

16. 3 mi = ■ yd

17. 16,892 yd = ■ mi ■ yd

18. 128 ft 4 in. = ■ yd ■ ft ■ in.

19. How many yards must be added to 2 mi 18 yd to make 3 miles?

20. Using Data Use the table. Which field is longer? By how many yards?

Sports Fields

Sport	Length
Soccer	330 ft
Football	100 yd

(Lesson 16) Decide whether you need an exact answer or an estimate. Solve.

21. $1\frac{3}{4}$ yd of material cost Wendy \$6.50. She gave the cashier a \$10 bill. The cashier gave her \$4.50 back. Did the cashier give Wendy the correct change?

22. Jim can walk 1 mi in 20 min. His school is $1\frac{1}{8}$ mi from home. About how long does it take him to walk to school?

23. Journal Explain how you know where $2\frac{5}{8}$ in. is on this ruler.

Skills Checklist

In this section, you have:

☑ **Measured Length Using Fractional Parts of an Inch**

☑ **Changed Among Units of Feet, Yards, and Miles**

☑ **Solved Problems by Deciding if You Need an Exact Answer or an Estimate**

REVIEW AND PRACTICE

YOUR CHOICE

Choose at least one. Use what you have learned in this chapter.

1 Measure for Measure

Most sheets of paper—copy paper, notebook paper, ruled paper—measure $8\frac{1}{2}$ inches in width. Use paper to estimate the length of the objects below. Check with a ruler. How close were you?

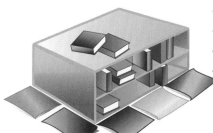

- A table
- A doorway
- Your desktop
- Your shoes

2 Make New Friends, But Keep the Old

At Home Make a list of the ages of the pets of four friends or family members. If your dog is 5 years old and has 2 months before its next birthday, its age would be $5\frac{10}{12}$ or $5\frac{5}{6}$. Add the ages on your list and compare your total to those of other classmates. Who listed the oldest pets? Youngest pets?

Pet	Age
Tinker	$6\frac{1}{4}$
Milo	$1\frac{7}{12}$
Shadow	$10\frac{2}{3}$

3 Hold that Note!

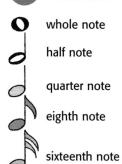

- whole note
- half note
- quarter note
- eighth note
- sixteenth note

A musical note tells the length or duration of a particular tone relative to a whole note. Use the chart to find the musical equivalent for fractions and mixed numbers. Add and subtract mixed numbers shown as musical notes.

4 Take a Long Trip

72 miles

Choose a topic to access on **www.mathsurf.com/5/ch8** that will give you distances between cities. Then challenge yourself to express these distances in inches. Do you think this would ever be useful information?

Review/Test

Vocabulary Write true or false.

1. The least common denominator (LCD) of $\frac{3}{8}$ and $\frac{3}{4}$ is 4.

(Lessons 1, 2, 3, 4, and 6) Find each sum or difference. Simplify.

2. $\begin{array}{r} \frac{3}{4} \\ -\frac{1}{4} \\ \hline \end{array}$
3. $\begin{array}{r} \frac{8}{9} \\ +\frac{1}{9} \\ \hline \end{array}$
4. $\begin{array}{r} \frac{3}{7} \\ +\frac{3}{14} \\ \hline \end{array}$
5. $\begin{array}{r} \frac{5}{8} \\ -\frac{1}{4} \\ \hline \end{array}$
6. $\begin{array}{r} \frac{3}{2} \\ -\frac{1}{6} \\ \hline \end{array}$

(Lessons 9–12) Find each sum or difference. Simplify.

7. $\begin{array}{r} 6\frac{1}{3} \\ +3\frac{2}{3} \\ \hline \end{array}$
8. $\begin{array}{r} 5\frac{7}{8} \\ -2\frac{5}{8} \\ \hline \end{array}$
9. $\begin{array}{r} 9 \\ -3\frac{4}{7} \\ \hline \end{array}$
10. $\begin{array}{r} 16\frac{3}{7} \\ +21\frac{4}{21} \\ \hline \end{array}$
11. $\begin{array}{r} 10\frac{1}{2} \\ -2\frac{1}{8} \\ \hline \end{array}$

12. $2\frac{1}{8} - 1\frac{1}{3}$
13. $5\frac{2}{9} + 6\frac{1}{6}$
14. $23 + 2\frac{4}{9}$
15. $6\frac{4}{5} - 1\frac{1}{2}$

(Lesson 14) Use your ruler to draw a line segment for each length.

16. $2\frac{1}{2}$ in.
17. $3\frac{5}{8}$ in.
18. $1\frac{3}{4}$ in.
19. $2\frac{1}{8}$ in.

(Lesson 15) Copy and complete.

20. 72 in. = ▮ ft
21. 4 mi 100 yd = ▮ yd
22. ▮ yd = 66 ft

(Lessons 2, 5, 7, 8, 13, and 16) Solve each problem.

23. Of the 18 dogs available for adoption, two weigh more than 8 lb. The three youngest puppies weigh $1\frac{1}{2}$ lb, $1\frac{3}{8}$ lb, and $1\frac{3}{4}$ lb. What is the total weight of the three youngest puppies?

24. Mike jogged $4\frac{1}{2}$ mi in about 45 min Monday. Yesterday he jogged $6\frac{1}{8}$ mi in about 60 min. Mike jogged again today. If he ran 15 mi altogether, how many miles did he run today?

25. Becca needs two pieces of rope, each $10\frac{1}{2}$ yd long, to make a swing. She found a rope that was $22\frac{3}{4}$ yd long. Does she have enough rope to make the swing? Explain.

Performance Assessment

You get to plan a trip. The map shows some distances between several cities along the Mississippi River. You can travel between any of the cities, however, you are limited in the total distance you travel each day.

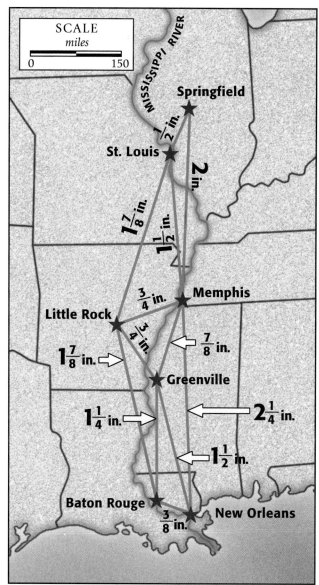

Day	Distance Allowed (in.)
Monday	$3\frac{1}{2}$
Tuesday	$2\frac{1}{4}$
Wednesday	4
Thursday	$\frac{3}{8}$
Friday	$3\frac{5}{8}$
Saturday	$1\frac{1}{8}$

1. **Decision Making** Decide which city is your starting point for each day. Decide which cities you want to visit. Will you make this a round trip? Make sure that you don't travel more than the allowed distance each day.

2. **Recording Data** Make a table like the one shown. List the cities to which you travel in the order in which you visit them. Compare your daily total with the distance allowed. Tell how many more inches you could have gone each day.

Day	Cities Visited	Distance (in.)	Total

3. **Explain Your Thinking** How did you decide which cities to visit? Did the distance between the cities affect your decision making? Explain.

4. **Analyze Your Data** How far did you travel in all? How far could you have gone if you traveled the exact distance allowed each day? What is the difference between that distance and the actual distance traveled?

Math Magazine

Do You Have the Time? There are 24 main time zones in the world (plus a few extra odd zones). The 24 zones were based on the 24 hours it takes for the Earth to make one complete revolution.

The table shows some countries and how their time differs from the Greenwich Mean Time.

← Greenwich Mean Time

International Date Line

If it is 3:00 GMT, what time is it in Botswana?
3:00 + 2 = 5:00

Country	Time from GMT
Afghanistan	$+4\frac{1}{2}$ hr
Australia (western)	$+4\frac{1}{2}$ hr
Botswana	$+2$ hr
Chatham Island	$+12\frac{3}{4}$ hr
Greenland	-3 hr
Honduras	-6 hr
India	$+5\frac{1}{2}$ hr
Marquesas Islands	$-9\frac{1}{2}$ hr
Nepal	$+5\frac{3}{4}$ hr
Samoa	-11 hr
U.S. (central)	-6 hr

Try These!

1. Locate all the countries listed in the chart on a world map or globe.

2. What is the difference between GMT and your time zone?

3. While Angela is having breakfast in Dallas, Texas, at 7 A.M. central time, are her grandparents in Honduras having breakfast or dinner? Explain.

4. When a person who lives on Chatham Island goes to bed at 10:00 P.M., what time is it in

   a. Greenwich?   **b.** the Marquesas Islands?

Test Prep Strategy: Work Backward from an Answer

Replace the missing number with each choice.
Jasmine has $3\frac{1}{4}$ c of flour. Her recipe for samosas calls for $2\frac{3}{8}$ c of flour. How much flour will be left?

    Ⓐ $1\frac{1}{4}$ c   Ⓑ $1\frac{1}{2}$ c   Ⓒ $1\frac{3}{8}$ c   Ⓓ $\frac{7}{8}$ c

---

To work backward add each of the choices to $2\frac{3}{8}$ to find which equals $3\frac{1}{4}$. Start with common denominators:

Ⓒ $1\frac{3}{8} + 2\frac{3}{8} = 3\frac{6}{8}$ or $3\frac{3}{4}$, no

Ⓓ $\frac{7}{8} + 2\frac{3}{8} = 2\frac{10}{8}$ or $3\frac{1}{4}$, yes

Adding $\frac{7}{8}$ to $2\frac{3}{8}$ gives you $2\frac{10}{8}$ or $3\frac{2}{8}$ which simplifies to $3\frac{1}{4}$. Therefore, Ⓓ is the correct answer.

Test Prep Strategies

- Read Carefully
- Follow Directions
- Make Smart Choices
- Eliminate Choices
- Work Backward from an Answer

Write the letter of the correct answer. Work backward from an answer or choose any strategy to help.

1. Which number is between $3\frac{9}{16}$ and $4\frac{3}{8}$?

  Ⓐ $3\frac{1}{2}$ Ⓑ $4\frac{1}{2}$ Ⓒ $3\frac{7}{8}$ Ⓓ $2\frac{3}{8}$

2. Which figure is congruent to the figure shown?

  Ⓐ   Ⓑ   Ⓒ   Ⓓ

3. The restaurant bill for 59 soccer players came to $472.00. How much does each player owe?

  Ⓐ $8.00   Ⓑ $10   Ⓒ $5.50   Ⓓ $80   Ⓔ not here

4. The largest blue whale ever found was 30 yd 8 in. in length. How long is that in feet and inches?

  Ⓐ 92 ft   Ⓑ 90 ft 24 in.   Ⓒ 10 ft 8 in.   Ⓓ 90 ft 8 in.

5. This stem-and-leaf plot represents the ages of 13 people. What was the median age?

  Ⓐ 31   Ⓑ 13   Ⓒ 3   Ⓓ 27

```
0 | 8 8 9
1 | 2 3 3
3 | 1 3 5 7
4 | 0 0 1
```

6. Which number has a quotient of 2.3 when divided by 6?

  Ⓐ 121.8   Ⓑ 12.18   Ⓒ 13.8   Ⓓ 345

7. Which of the following is the measurement of angle ABC to the nearest degree?

  Ⓐ 75 degrees   Ⓑ 105 degrees

  Ⓒ 90 degrees   Ⓓ 135 degrees

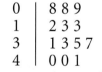

8. There were 3 pizzas. Noah and friends ate $1\frac{5}{8}$ pizzas. Sue and friends ate $1\frac{5}{16}$ pizzas. How much was left?

  Ⓐ $\frac{1}{16}$ pizza   Ⓑ no pizza   Ⓒ $\frac{1}{2}$ pizza   Ⓓ $\frac{3}{8}$ pizza

Chapter 9
Fractions and Multiplication

Food Around The **WORLD**

Puffy, Sweet Treats!
Page 403

403

Developing Fraction Multiplication Sense

Japanese *bento* boxes are often divided into sections for different foods. This *bento* box is divided into 5 sections. Which food takes up the largest section?

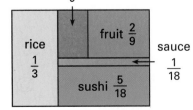

vegetable salad $\frac{1}{9}$

| rice $\frac{1}{3}$ | fruit $\frac{2}{9}$ |
| | sushi $\frac{5}{18}$ |

sauce $\frac{1}{18}$

Extending Multiplication

Food products are important to the economy of India. The chief crops are rice, grains, sugar cane, spices, tea, and cashews.

The map of India below shows some information about farming in India. India's area is a little more than 1 million mi². About how much is covered by farms?

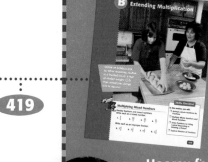

419

Hooray for Challah Page 419

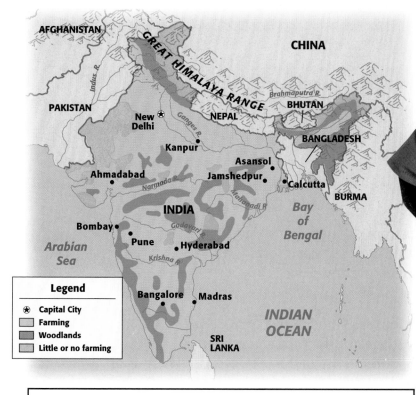

Farming Facts

Farms cover $\frac{1}{2}$ the area of India

About $\frac{7}{10}$ of the population earn their living by farming.

About $\frac{1}{3}$ of the farms are less than $\frac{1}{2}$ acre.

About $\frac{2}{3}$ of the farmers own their land.

About $\frac{4}{5}$ of the farmland is used for grains, vegetables and rice.

Surfing the World Wide Web!

What is your favorite type of food? Find out more about foods from around the world at **www.mathsurf.com/5/ch9**.

TEAM PROJECT
Yummy, Yummy Recipes!

Materials
folder or colored paper for booklet, old magazines, scissors, paste

Everyone has favorite foods. Plan a cookbook that includes recipes for your favorite foods and shows the diversity of the foods you and your classmates like.

Make a Plan

- Whom will you ask to contribute a recipe?
- How will you represent different tastes?
- How will you organize and present your collection of recipes?

Carry It Out

1. Ask students from different grades and classes to name their favorite foods. Make a list of their answers.

2. Review the list and select a good variety.

3. Find recipes for these foods. Give two versions of each recipe, first for a family of 4 and a second for a class of 32.

4. Make a book including both versions of the recipes. Illustrate the book.

Talk About It

- Which recipes do you think you would like to try?
- Describe how you revised recipes for different-sized groups.
- What fractions and mixed numbers are represented in the recipes? What uncommon fractions are in your recipes?

Present the Project

Plan a class presentation and display of all cookbooks. Which recipes show many fractions and/or mixed numbers?

Developing Fraction Multiplication Sense

Sopaipillas (So-pa-pee-yas) are sweet treats common in Mexico and the southwestern United States. How might you use fractions when making sopaipillas?

Skills Checklist

In this section, you will:

☐ **Explore Multiplying Whole Numbers by Fractions**

☐ **Multiply with Fractions**

☐ **Estimate Products**

☐ **Explore Multiplying Fractions by Fractions**

☐ **Multiply Fractions**

☐ **Solve Problems by Overestimating and Underestimating**

GET READY!

Multiplying with Fractions

Review division facts. Find each quotient.

1. $18 \div 3$ 2. $16 \div 4$ 3. $54 \div 6$

4. $40 \div 5$ 5. $80 \div 10$ 6. $36 \div 4$

7. $48 \div 8$ 8. $72 \div 9$ 9. $42 \div 7$

10. $35 \div 5$ 11. $81 \div 9$ 12. $36 \div 6$

Exploring Multiplication of Whole Numbers by Fractions

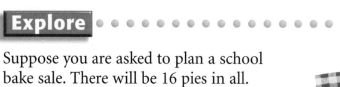

Problem Solving Connection

Use Objects/ Act It Out

Materials

counters

Explore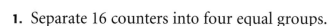

Suppose you are asked to plan a school bake sale. There will be 16 pies in all. Of these, $\frac{3}{4}$ of the pies will be sweet potato pies, a Southern specialty. How many sweet potato pies will there be?

Work Together

See how counters can help you multiply a whole number by a fraction.

1. Separate 16 counters into four equal groups.

   a. Find $\frac{1}{4}$ of 16.   **b.** Find $\frac{2}{4}$, or $\frac{1}{2}$, of 16.

   c. Find $\frac{3}{4}$ of 16.   **d.** How many sweet potato pies will there be?

Math Tip

When a non-zero whole number is multiplied by a fraction less than 1, the product is less than the whole number.

2. Use counters to find each answer.

   a. $\frac{1}{3}$ of 12   **b.** $\frac{2}{3}$ of 12   **c.** $\frac{1}{7}$ of 21   **d.** $\frac{2}{7}$ of 21

   e. $\frac{3}{5}$ of 20   **f.** $\frac{4}{5}$ of 20   **g.** $\frac{3}{8}$ of 24   **h.** $\frac{5}{9}$ of 27

Talk About It

3. Describe how you could use $\frac{1}{4}$ of 12 to find $\frac{3}{4}$ of 12.

4. How could you find $\frac{3}{8}$ of 16? Explain your answer.

Connect •

You can use division to find a fraction of a number.

 $\frac{1}{8}$ of 24 gives the same result as dividing 24 by 8.

$24 \div 8 = 3$

So, $\frac{1}{8}$ of 24 is 3.

Find $\frac{3}{8}$ of 24.

Think:

$\frac{3}{8}$ is three times as much as $\frac{1}{8}$.

$3 \times 3 = 9$, so $\frac{3}{8}$ of 24 is 9.

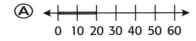 **Practice** •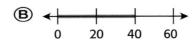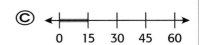

Find each product. You may use counters to help.

1. $\frac{1}{3}$ of 15   **2.** $\frac{1}{5}$ of 20   **3.** $\frac{1}{4}$ of 8   **4.** $\frac{2}{5}$ of 35   **5.** $\frac{4}{5}$ of 20

6. $\frac{2}{3}$ of 21   **7.** $\frac{3}{4}$ of 20   **8.** $\frac{5}{8}$ of 32   **9.** $\frac{5}{6}$ of 36   **10.** $\frac{3}{8}$ of 24

11. Find four-fifths of thirty.   **12.** Find three-eighths of sixteen.

13. Which of the number lines below show $\frac{1}{4}$ of 60?

Ⓐ 0 10 20 30 40 50 60   Ⓑ 0 20 40 60   Ⓒ 0 15 30 45 60

14. Use the number line to help find the answer. If 90 people came to the bake sale and two-thirds of them bought something at the sale, how many people made purchases?

0 10 20 30 40 50 60 70 80 90

15. **Time** A school bake sale lasted 5 hr. The students sold 100 items. On average, how many items were sold each hour?

Using Data Use the recipe to answer **16** and **17**.

16. One-half of the filling is needed for a smaller pie tin. How many sweet potatoes will be needed?

17. **Measurement** A student chef measured 2 tbsp of butter for a small pie $\frac{1}{4}$ the size of this recipe. Did the chef measure the right amount? Explain.

18. **Journal** Explain how finding $\frac{1}{6}$ of 36 can help you find $\frac{5}{6}$ of 36.

PIES

SWEET POTATO PIE

Filling for one pie:
4 medium sized sweet potatoes
4 tbsp softened butter
$\frac{3}{4}$ c dark-brown sugar
$\frac{1}{3}$ c light corn syrup
$\frac{1}{3}$ c milk
2 tsp lemon peel
pinch salt, ground nutmeg

Multiplying with Fractions

You Will Learn

how to multiply a whole number by a fraction mentally

Vocabulary

unit fraction
a fraction that has 1 as the numerator

Learn • • • • • • • • • • • • • • •

In Japan, students don't brown bag it for lunch, they box it instead. When *O-hiru* (lunch time) comes, many open up their *bento* boxes. These boxes contain food and a set of chopsticks—all neatly packed in separate compartments.

Example 1

There are 36 students in the science club. Thursday, $\frac{1}{3}$ of them are going on a field trip. How many *bento* boxes will be needed for their lunches?

Find $\frac{1}{3}$ of 36.

You can use division to figure it out mentally.

Divide by three. **Think:** $36 \div 3 = 12$

So, $\frac{1}{3} \times 36 = 12$.

12 boxes are needed for lunches.

Example 2

You can also use mental math to multiply non-unit fractions by whole numbers.

What is $\frac{2}{3}$ of 12? **Think:** $12 \div 3 = 4$

$\frac{1}{3}$ of 12 is 4.

$2 \times 4 = 8$

So, $\frac{2}{3} \times 12 = 8$.

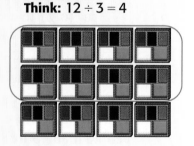

Talk About It

1. How could you use division to find $\frac{1}{4}$ of 20?

2. How does finding $\frac{1}{3}$ of a number help you find what $\frac{2}{3}$ of a number is?

Math Tip
The fraction $\frac{1}{3}$ is a unit fraction.

Check •

Find each product. Use mental math.

1. $\frac{1}{5}$ of 20   2. $\frac{2}{3}$ of 15   3. $\frac{4}{7}$ of 21   4. $\frac{1}{6}$ of 18   5. $\frac{3}{4}$ of 12

6. **Reasoning** If $\frac{2}{3}$ of a number is 10, what is the number? Explain how you figured out the number.

Practice

Skills and Reasoning

 Mental Math Find each product. Use mental math.

7. $\frac{1}{10}$ of 30　　**8.** $\frac{1}{5}$ of 30　　**9.** $\frac{3}{4}$ of 28　　**10.** $\frac{2}{5}$ of 25　　**11.** $\frac{3}{8}$ of 40

12. $\frac{3}{7}$ of 14　　**13.** $\frac{2}{3}$ of 21　　**14.** $\frac{5}{6}$ of 60　　**15.** $\frac{1}{4}$ of 16　　**16.** $\frac{4}{5}$ of 25

17. $\frac{3}{10}$ of 50　　**18.** $\frac{2}{7}$ of 28　　**19.** $\frac{5}{9}$ of 45　　**20.** $\frac{1}{6}$ of 54　　**21.** $\frac{2}{9}$ of 27

22. Multiply one-fourth and forty.　　**23.** Multiply one-third and eighteen.

24. Patterns Copy and complete the table. Use patterns to help you find each product.

$\frac{1}{8}$ of 16	2	$\frac{3}{8}$ of 16		$\frac{5}{8}$ of 16		$\frac{7}{8}$ of 16	
$\frac{2}{8}$ of 16	4	$\frac{4}{8}$ of 16		$\frac{6}{8}$ of 16		$\frac{8}{8}$ of 16	

25. How could you use the product of $\frac{1}{4}$ and 400 to find the product of $\frac{1}{8}$ and 400?

Problem Solving and Applications

 Algebra Readiness Copy and complete each table. Write a rule for each one using variables.

26.

n	4	6	10	20
	2	3		

27.

n	4	8	16	32
	3	6		

Using Data Use the Data File on page 400 for **28.**

28. The size of the *bento* box is 18 square units.

    a. How many square units does the rice cover?

    b. How many square units does the vegetable salad cover?

    c. How many square units does the sushi cover?

29. Geography Japan has about 200 volcanoes. 50 of them are active. What fraction of Japan's volcanoes are active? What percent?

This sushi is made from salmon eggs wrapped in seaweed.

Mixed Review and Test Prep

Round to the nearest whole number.

30. $\frac{3}{4}$　　**31.** $3\frac{5}{8}$　　**32.** $1\frac{1}{16}$　　**33.** $5\frac{3}{7}$　　**34.** $7\frac{3}{5}$　　**35.** $6\frac{2}{9}$

 36. Geometry Which of the following shows a right angle?

    Ⓐ   Ⓑ   Ⓒ   Ⓓ

PRACTICE AND APPLY

Estimating Products

Learn • • • • • • • • • • • •

Joey is baking sopaipillas, crisp puffy breads popular in Mexico and the southwestern United States. Served dipped in honey, these sweet treats can be eaten with dinner or as a dessert.

A recipe for sopaipillas requires $1\frac{3}{4}$ c of sifted flour. About how much flour is needed to make 5 times a recipe of sopaipillas?

Joey from Tad, West Virginia, enjoys sports and cooking.

Example 1

One way to estimate fraction products is to round mixed numbers to the nearest whole number.

Find $5 \times 1\frac{3}{4}$.

Estimate. $1\frac{3}{4}$ is close to 2.

$5 \times 2 = 10$

So, $5 \times 1\frac{3}{4}$ is about 10.

A little less than 10 cups is required.

Example 2

Another way to estimate fraction products is to use compatible numbers.

Find $\frac{3}{8} \times 26$.

Estimate. 8 is not a factor of 26.

But 8 is a factor of 24 and 24 is close to 26.

$\frac{3}{8} \times 24$ is easier to multiply mentally.

$\frac{1}{8} \times 24 = 3$ and $\frac{3}{8} \times 24 = 9$.

So, $\frac{3}{8}$ of 26 is about 9.

You can also estimate by replacing a fraction with a benchmark.

Remember

Benchmarks are numbers like $\frac{1}{2}$, 1, $1\frac{1}{2}$, and 2.

Sopaipillas are a tasty treat!

Example 3

Find $\frac{5}{8}$ of 30.   Estimate. $\frac{5}{8}$ is close to $\frac{1}{2}$.

$\frac{1}{2}$ of 30 is 15.

So, $\frac{5}{8}$ of 30 is about 15.

Talk About It

To estimate $\frac{2}{5} \times 26$, would you use $\frac{2}{5} \times 25$ or $\frac{2}{5} \times 24$? Explain.

Use rounding, benchmarks, or compatible numbers to estimate each product.

1. $\frac{8}{9} \times 6$ 2. $\frac{4}{5} \times 12$ 3. $2\frac{1}{8} \times 7$ 4. $\frac{1}{6} \times 35$ 5. $\frac{3}{7} \times 10$

6. **Reasoning** How could finding $\frac{1}{8}$ of 40 help you estimate $\frac{7}{8}$ of 39?

Practice •

Skills and Reasoning

Use rounding, benchmarks, or compatible numbers to estimate the products.

7. $\frac{3}{4} \times 41$ 8. $1\frac{5}{11} \times 20$ 9. $9\frac{1}{8} \times 11$ 10. $\frac{1}{5} \times 37$ 11. $\frac{2}{7} \times 48$

12. $\frac{5}{8} \times 31$ 13. $\frac{1}{4} \times 15$ 14. $5\frac{6}{7} \times 10$ 15. $\frac{1}{6} \times 35$ 16. $\frac{3}{8} \times 20$

17. $1\frac{2}{3} \times 32$ 18. $2\frac{3}{5} \times 16$ 19. $\frac{4}{7} \times 48$ 20. $\frac{5}{9} \times 61$ 21. $3\frac{4}{9} \times 75$

22. **Reasoning** Estimate the product of $\frac{2}{3}$ and 29. Describe your method.

Use rounding, benchmarks, or compatible numbers to estimate each product. Write the letter of the estimate that is closer to the actual product.

23. $\frac{1}{4} \times 13$ Ⓐ more than 3   Ⓑ less than 3

24. $2\frac{7}{8} \times 15$ Ⓐ more than 45   Ⓑ less than 45

25. $\frac{1}{5} \times 21$ Ⓐ more than 4   Ⓑ less than 4

Problem Solving and Applications

26. **Measurement** Suppose you needed to measure 2 c of flour for a recipe. You can only find the $\frac{1}{4}$-c measuring cup. If you fill it 7 times, will you have measured 2 c of flour? Explain.

27. If $\frac{1}{8}$ of a batch of sopaipillas dough makes 6 triangles, how many triangles will the rest make?

28. **Write Your Own Problem** Write a multiplication problem with fractions. Choose a method for estimation. Tell why you chose the method.

Sopaipillas are made by cutting dough into triangular pieces.

Mixed Review and Test Prep

Patterns Find each product. Describe the patterns.

29. 375×19 30. 3.75×19 31. 37.5×0.19 32. 3.75×1.9

33. Which of the following is the product of 836 and 0.1?

Ⓐ 836   Ⓑ 8.36   Ⓒ 0.836   Ⓓ 83.6

Exploring Multiplication of Fractions by Fractions

Problem Solving Connection

- Look for a Pattern
- Use Objects/ Act It Out

Materials

- paper squares
- blue, red pencils

Explore

How can you find a fraction of a fraction?

Work Together

You can find a fraction of a fraction by paper folding and shading.

1. Use paper folding to find $\frac{1}{2}$ of $\frac{1}{4}$.

   a. Fold a square of paper vertically down the center. What fraction of the whole piece is each section?

   b. Fold the paper once more vertically to get four equal sections. What fraction is each section?

   c. Now fold the paper in half horizontally. How many sections are there? What fraction of the square is each small section?

2. Use your folded paper.

   a. Shade $\frac{3}{4}$ red vertically.   b. Shade $\frac{1}{2}$ blue horizontally.

   c. The purple section shows $\frac{1}{2}$ of $\frac{3}{4}$. What is $\frac{1}{2}$ of $\frac{3}{4}$?

3. Fold a new square of paper to find $\frac{1}{2}$ of $\frac{1}{2}$.

4. Use paper folds to find each answer.

   a. $\frac{3}{4}$ of $\frac{1}{8}$ b. $\frac{1}{4}$ of $\frac{7}{8}$ c. $\frac{3}{4}$ of $\frac{3}{8}$ d. $\frac{1}{4}$ of $\frac{3}{8}$

Talk About It

5. In the illustration for **1c** above, what fraction of the whole do two sections make?

6. Explain how you could use paper folding to find $\frac{1}{3}$ of $\frac{1}{5}$.

Connect

$\frac{3}{8} \times \frac{1}{2}$ means $\frac{3}{8}$ of $\frac{1}{2}$. The drawings show $\frac{3}{8} \times \frac{1}{2} = \frac{3}{16}$.

$\frac{3}{8}$ $\frac{1}{2}$ $\frac{3}{8} \times \frac{1}{2}$ $\frac{3}{16}$

Practice

1. Which of the drawings below shows $\frac{1}{6} \times \frac{1}{3}$?

Ⓐ   Ⓑ   Ⓒ   Ⓓ

Use each drawing to help you complete each sentence.

2. $\frac{1}{2}$ is shaded. $\frac{1}{3}$ of $\frac{1}{2}$ is ▦.   3. $\frac{3}{8}$ is shaded. $\frac{1}{3}$ of $\frac{3}{8}$ is ▦.   4. $\frac{2}{5}$ is shaded. $\frac{1}{4}$ of $\frac{2}{5}$ is ▦.

          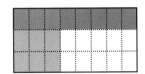

Draw pictures or use paper folding to find each product.

5. What is $\frac{1}{3}$ of $\frac{1}{6}$?   6. What is $\frac{2}{3}$ of $\frac{1}{6}$?   7. What is $\frac{3}{4}$ of $\frac{1}{3}$?

8. $\frac{1}{2} \times \frac{1}{2}$ 9. $\frac{1}{2} \times \frac{1}{3}$ 10. $\frac{2}{3} \times \frac{1}{3}$ 11. $\frac{1}{4} \times \frac{1}{3}$ 12. $\frac{2}{3} \times \frac{1}{4}$

13. $\frac{1}{4} \times \frac{1}{8}$ 14. $\frac{1}{4} \times \frac{1}{2}$ 15. $\frac{1}{4} \times \frac{3}{4}$ 16. $\frac{1}{2} \times \frac{3}{8}$ 17. $\frac{2}{3} \times \frac{3}{4}$

18. Sheila's mother has reserved $\frac{1}{2}$ of the seats in a restaurant for Sheila's party. $\frac{1}{8}$ of those seats will be needed for family, the rest for Sheila and her friends. What fraction of the restaurant's seats will be used by the family? Use paper folding to solve.

19. **Fine Arts** Origami figures often start from a 6-in. paper square. If you fold a 6-in. square horizontally in thirds, what are the dimensions of each section?

 20. **Journal** If you multiply two fractions less than 1, is their product greater than or less than each of the original fractions? Explain.

Origami is a traditional Japanese art of paper folding.

Multiplying Fractions

You Will Learn
how to multiply
fractions

Learn • • • • • •

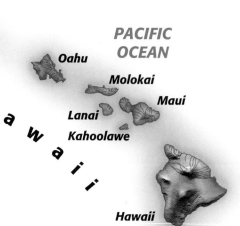

Kauai

Nihau

Oahu

PACIFIC
OCEAN

Molokai

Maui

Lanai

Kahoolawe

Hawaii

Hawaii

Hawaii has many local delicacies
including guavas, passion fruit,
and macadamia nuts. Tom, Tino,
and Clara each got $\frac{1}{3}$ of a $\frac{3}{4}$-lb bag of
macadamia nuts. How much did each
share weigh? To find $\frac{1}{3}$ of $\frac{3}{4}$ lb, multiply.

Example 1

$\frac{1}{3} \times \frac{3}{4} = n$

Step 1	Step 2	Step 3
Multiply the numerators.	Multiply the denominators.	Simplify.
$\frac{1}{3} \times \frac{3}{4} = \frac{1 \times 3}{3 \times 4} = \frac{3}{}$	$\frac{1 \times 3}{3 \times 4} = \frac{3}{12}$	$\frac{1 \times 3}{3 \times 4} = \frac{3}{12} = \frac{1}{4}$

So, $\frac{1}{3} \times \frac{3}{4} = \frac{1}{4}$.

Each share weighed $\frac{1}{4}$ pound.

If the numerator and the denominator have a common factor, you
can simplify before you multiply.

Example 2

$\frac{2}{3} \times \frac{5}{8} = n$

Step 1	Step 2	Step 3
Divide common factors.	Multiply the numerators.	Multiply the denominators.
$\frac{2}{3} \times \frac{5}{8} = \frac{\overset{1}{2} \times 5}{3 \times \underset{4}{8}}$	$\frac{\overset{1}{2} \times 5}{3 \times \underset{4}{8}} = \frac{5}{}$	$\frac{\overset{1}{2} \times 5}{3 \times \underset{4}{8}} = \frac{5}{12}$

So, $\frac{2}{3} \times \frac{5}{8} = \frac{5}{12}$.

Talk About It

1. Compare both ways of multiplying fractions.

2. How is dividing the common factors like dividing by 1?

Remember
To simplify a fraction divide
the numerator and denom-
inator by a common factor.

Check

Find each product. Simplify.

1. $\frac{2}{3} \times \frac{3}{5}$ 2. $\frac{1}{8} \times \frac{3}{4}$ 3. $\frac{3}{10} \times \frac{5}{6}$ 4. $\frac{3}{3} \times \frac{2}{5}$ 5. $\frac{1}{2} \times \frac{7}{8}$

6. **Reasoning** What is true about the products of $\frac{3}{3} \times \frac{4}{5}$, $\frac{4}{4} \times \frac{4}{5}$, and $\frac{5}{5} \times \frac{4}{5}$? Explain.

Practice

Skills and Reasoning

Find each product. Simplify.

7. What is $\frac{1}{2}$ of $\frac{1}{8}$?   8. What is $\frac{7}{8}$ of $\frac{2}{2}$?   9. What is $\frac{1}{3}$ of $\frac{5}{8}$?

10. $\frac{3}{10} \times \frac{2}{5}$ 11. $\frac{2}{3} \times \frac{3}{8}$ 12. $\frac{7}{10} \times \frac{4}{5}$ 13. $\frac{1}{2} \times \frac{4}{7}$ 14. $\frac{1}{5} \times \frac{5}{6}$

15. $\frac{3}{4} \times \frac{3}{7}$ 16. $\frac{1}{8} \times \frac{9}{10}$ 17. $\frac{1}{8} \times \frac{3}{8}$ 18. $\frac{9}{10} \times \frac{1}{3}$ 19. $\frac{1}{7} \times \frac{2}{3}$

20. What is the product of $\frac{3}{4}$ and $\frac{9}{9}$?   21. Multiply $\frac{5}{6}$ and $\frac{3}{4}$.

22. **Algebra Readiness** $\frac{2}{3}$ is multiplied by a fraction and the product is $\frac{4}{9}$. What is the fraction?

23. If $\frac{7}{8}$ is multiplied by $\frac{4}{5}$, will the product be greater than either of the two fractions being multiplied? Explain.

Problem Solving and Applications

24. Clara found a recipe for Macadamia Wedges that uses $\frac{3}{4}$ c of macadamia nuts. If she only wants to make half a batch, how many cups of macadamia nuts should she use?

25. **Critical Thinking** Guava and passion fruit juice costs $8.95 a can. There are 12 cans in a case. Would $100 be enough to buy a case? Explain.

26. A scientist had $\frac{3}{4}$ of a bottle of a solution. She used $\frac{1}{6}$ of the solution in an experiment. How much of the bottle did she use?

Passion fruit and macadamia nuts

Mixed Review and Test Prep

Find each product.

27. 3.4   28. 18.04   29. 0.03   30. 11.2   31. 12
    $\times 0.5$ $\times\ \ \ 7$ $\times\ \ \ 9$ $\times 0.51$ $\times 0.7$

32. Which of the following decimals is equal to $\frac{51}{100}$?

   (A) 5.1   (B) 0.051   (C) 0.51   (D) 51.00

STOP and Practice

Find each product. Simplify.

1. $\frac{2}{3}$ of 18   2. $\frac{1}{5}$ of 25   3. $\frac{1}{6}$ of 48   4. $\frac{1}{2}$ of 48   5. $\frac{1}{5}$ of 15

6. $\frac{2}{3}$ of 27   7. $\frac{3}{4}$ of 28   8. $\frac{5}{8}$ of 64   9. $\frac{7}{8}$ of 64   10. $\frac{5}{7}$ of 42

11. $\frac{1}{4} \times 36$ 12. $\frac{2}{5} \times 30$ 13. $\frac{2}{8} \times 24$ 14. $\frac{3}{10} \times 40$ 15. $\frac{1}{7} \times 28$

16. $\frac{3}{4} \times 80$ 17. $\frac{5}{10} \times 50$ 18. $\frac{7}{8} \times 16$ 19. $\frac{3}{8} \times 56$ 20. $\frac{2}{3} \times 27$

21. $\frac{3}{4} \times 4$ 22. $\frac{3}{5} \times 5$ 23. $\frac{3}{4} \times 8$ 24. $\frac{3}{5} \times 10$ 25. $\frac{4}{5} \times 40$

26. $\frac{4}{5} \times 5$ 27. $\frac{7}{8} \times 24$ 28. $\frac{2}{3} \times 9$ 29. $\frac{2}{5} \times 15$ 30. $\frac{8}{9} \times 72$

31. $\frac{4}{5} \times \frac{5}{12}$ 32. $\frac{2}{3} \times \frac{9}{24}$ 33. $\frac{3}{5} \times \frac{15}{24}$ 34. $\frac{7}{10} \times \frac{5}{12}$ 35. $\frac{5}{6} \times \frac{12}{15}$

36. $\frac{1}{6} \times \frac{2}{3}$ 37. $\frac{3}{8} \times \frac{9}{10}$ 38. $\frac{5}{6} \times \frac{3}{20}$ 39. $\frac{1}{5} \times \frac{5}{12}$ 40. $\frac{7}{10} \times \frac{5}{8}$

41. $\frac{3}{4} \times \frac{4}{15}$ 42. $\frac{3}{4} \times \frac{3}{36}$ 43. $\frac{5}{8} \times \frac{7}{20}$ 44. $\frac{4}{5} \times \frac{7}{8}$ 45. $\frac{2}{7} \times \frac{11}{20}$

46. $\frac{1}{12} \times \frac{3}{8}$ 47. $\frac{2}{5} \times \frac{1}{24}$ 48. $\frac{3}{16} \times \frac{3}{4}$ 49. $\frac{5}{8} \times \frac{2}{3}$ 50. $\frac{3}{5} \times \frac{1}{6}$

51. $\frac{1}{5} \times \frac{1}{3}$ 52. $\frac{3}{4} \times \frac{2}{5}$ 53. $\frac{1}{3} \times \frac{9}{24}$ 54. $\frac{7}{12} \times \frac{3}{10}$ 55. $\frac{4}{9} \times \frac{18}{28}$

Error Search

Find each product that is not correct. Write it correctly and explain the error.

56. $\frac{2}{5} \times \frac{3}{8} = \frac{3}{20}$ 57. $\frac{2}{3} \times 15 = 30$ 58. $\frac{3}{4} \times \frac{1}{4} = \frac{3}{1}$ 59. $\frac{2}{9} \times \frac{1}{2} = \frac{3}{18}$

60. $\frac{1}{2} \times \frac{4}{7} = \frac{2}{7}$ 61. $\frac{1}{2} \times \frac{2}{3} = \frac{2}{5}$ 62. $\frac{2}{10} \times \frac{5}{8} = \frac{1}{8}$ 63. $\frac{6}{7} \times \frac{1}{3} = \frac{7}{21}$

64. $\frac{3}{5} \times \frac{5}{8} = \frac{3}{8}$ 65. $\frac{1}{3} \times \frac{1}{3} = \frac{2}{9}$ 66. $\frac{1}{8} \times \frac{1}{4} = \frac{1}{12}$ 67. $\frac{1}{8} \times \frac{2}{5} = \frac{1}{20}$

Fraction Scramble!

How good is your mental math? Can you find the problems whose products all equal $\frac{1}{4}$? Choose problems to solve that you think have a product of $\frac{1}{4}$. Keep solving problems until you are sure you have found all the $\frac{1}{4}$s. Then unscramble the letters to find a hidden word.

$\frac{1}{2} \times \frac{1}{2}$	$\frac{2}{3} \times 9$	$\frac{1}{8} \times \frac{4}{5}$	$\frac{2}{5} \times \frac{5}{8}$
A	D	P	F
$\frac{1}{2} \times \frac{2}{3}$	$\frac{3}{8} \times \frac{2}{3}$	$\frac{1}{8} \times \frac{2}{3}$	$\frac{8}{12} \times \frac{3}{64}$
Q	C	E	M
$\frac{1}{2} \times 8$	$\frac{1}{4} \times 16$	$\frac{3}{4} \times \frac{1}{3}$	$\frac{1}{4} \times \frac{1}{4}$
B	S	R	L
$\frac{1}{2} \times \frac{5}{24}$	$\frac{5}{8} \times \frac{2}{5}$	$\frac{2}{5} \times \frac{15}{24}$	$\frac{7}{24} \times \frac{6}{7}$
U	I	N	O
$\frac{9}{32} \times \frac{8}{9}$	$\frac{3}{5} \times \frac{5}{24}$	$\frac{3}{8} \times 16$	$\frac{2}{3} \times \frac{3}{7}$
T	W	V	G

"BRPTF!"

68. How many products of $\frac{1}{4}$ did you find? What word did you find?

Number Sense Pattern Hunt

Look for patterns. Copy and complete.

69. $\frac{1}{3}, \frac{1}{6}, \frac{1}{12}, \blacksquare, \blacksquare, \blacksquare$

70. $\frac{2}{3}, 1, 1\frac{1}{3}, \blacksquare, \blacksquare, \blacksquare$

71. $\frac{1}{2}, \frac{3}{4}, \frac{5}{6}, \blacksquare, \blacksquare, \blacksquare$

72. $\frac{1}{2}, \frac{1}{4}, \frac{1}{8}, \blacksquare, \blacksquare, \blacksquare$

73. $\frac{32}{3}, \frac{30}{3}, \frac{28}{3}, \blacksquare, \blacksquare, \blacksquare$

74. $\frac{1}{2}, 1, 1\frac{1}{2}, \blacksquare, \blacksquare, \blacksquare$

75. $\frac{13}{5}, \frac{12}{5}, \frac{11}{5}, \blacksquare, \blacksquare, \blacksquare$

76. $1, \frac{2}{3}, \frac{4}{9}, \blacksquare, \blacksquare, \blacksquare$

77. $\frac{1}{4}, \frac{3}{4}, 1\frac{1}{4}, \blacksquare, \blacksquare, \blacksquare$

Problem Solving

Analyze Word Problems: Overestimating and Underestimating

You Will Learn

when to use overestimating or underestimating to solve word problems

Reading Tip

You will understand the problem better if you know the meanings of all the words.

Learn • • • • • • • • • •

The owner of Super Soups Factory is ordering ingredients. She knows she will make about 100 batches of black bean soup before she can order again. How many pounds of black beans should she order?

Since the owner doesn't need to know the exact amount, she can estimate. Should she overestimate or underestimate?

SOUPS

BLACK BEAN SOUP

$1\frac{3}{4}$ lb black beans
$\frac{1}{2}$ tsp oregano
$\frac{1}{2}$ cup chopped onions
$\frac{1}{2}$ tsp hot pepper flakes
2 cloves crushed garlic
1 tsp salt
8 cups water
(makes 1 batch)

Work Together

▶ **Understand**   What do you know?

What do you need to find out?

▶ **Plan**   How can you begin?   Overestimate so that the owner has enough black beans.
Round $1\frac{3}{4}$ lb to 2.

▶ **Solve**   Multiply. $2 \times 100 = 200$

What's the answer?   She needs about 200 lb of black beans.

▶ **Look Back**   Why does overestimation make sense in this case?

If you are saving for a gift, why might it be better to underestimate your earnings from your after school job?

Overestimate or underestimate to solve the problem.

1. A carton holds 350 cans of soup. Groups of cans are coming down the assembly line in the following amounts: 89, 74, 56, and 48. Will there be room in the carton for 28 more cans?

   a. Can the problem be solved with an estimate or does it require an exact answer?

   b. Should you overestimate or underestimate to solve the problem? Why?

   c. Do the 28 cans fit?

   d. If there are 40 cans instead of 28, will they still all fit in the carton? How do you know?

Problem Solving
Practice •

Problem Solving Strategies

- Use Objects/Act It Out
- Draw a Picture
- Look for a Pattern
- Guess and Check
- Use Logical Reasoning
- Make an Organized List
- Make a Table
- Solve a Simpler Problem
- Work Backward

Choose a Tool

Estimate to solve **2–4.** Write whether you overestimated or underestimated. Explain your reasoning.

2. The soup factory gives visiting students folders with information about the business. There are 540 folders left for the last week of the school year. Three schools are scheduled to bring 195, 184, and 176 students. Are there enough folders?

3. Susan is making fruit punch for a party. She has invited 15 people and expects each person to drink $3\frac{1}{2}$ cups. How many cups of punch does she need?

4. **Time** A chef is making soup before the diner opens at 9 A.M. It takes him $\frac{3}{4}$ hr to make one batch of soup. It is 6:00 A.M. Will he have enough time to make 7 batches of soup before opening?

Solve. Write what strategy you used.

5. An industrial vegetable slicer doubles the number of times it slices every minute. One minute after the slicer begins, it has sliced 2 times; after two minutes 4 slices, after 3 minutes 8 slices, and so on. How many minutes after the slicer begins will it slice at least 30 times per minute?

Review and Practice

Vocabulary Rewrite each statement correctly.

1. If the numerators and denominators of two fractions have a common <u>multiple</u>, you can simplify before you multiply.

2. Factors are numbers that are combined by <u>addition</u> to give a number called the product.

(Lessons 1 and 2) Find each product.

3. $\frac{1}{6}$ of 42   4. $\frac{1}{3}$ of 27   5. $\frac{1}{5}$ of 50   6. $\frac{1}{8}$ of 56   7. $\frac{1}{4}$ of 24

8. $\frac{2}{5} \times 25$ 9. $\frac{3}{4} \times 32$ 10. $\frac{7}{10} \times 20$ 11. $\frac{3}{4} \times 36$ 12. $\frac{2}{5}$ of 20

13. Find three-eighths of sixty-four.   14. Find two-thirds of twenty seven.

15. On Tuesday, 35 students bought hot lunches. Three-fifths of them bought milk. How many students bought milk?

16. If $\frac{1}{6}$ of a recipe makes 6 muffins, how many muffins will the remaining mix make?

(Lesson 3) Estimate each product. Use rounding, benchmarks, or compatible numbers.

17. $\frac{2}{3} \times 16$ 18. $1\frac{5}{9} \times 21$ 19. $2\frac{1}{8} \times 25$ 20. $\frac{8}{9} \times 73$ 21. $\frac{3}{7} \times 50$

(Lessons 4 and 5) Find each product.

22. $\frac{1}{4} \times \frac{1}{3}$ 23. $\frac{2}{3} \times \frac{1}{8}$ 24. $\frac{3}{4} \times \frac{5}{12}$ 25. $\frac{3}{5} \times \frac{7}{8}$ 26. $\frac{2}{5} \times \frac{10}{12}$

27. $\frac{1}{10} \times \frac{5}{12}$ 28. $\frac{1}{4} \times \frac{3}{8}$ 29. $\frac{9}{10} \times \frac{4}{5}$ 30. $\frac{3}{10} \times \frac{5}{8}$ 31. $\frac{7}{12} \times \frac{3}{8}$

Copy and complete.

32. $\frac{1}{2}$ of $\frac{1}{3}$ = ▨   33. $\frac{1}{3}$ of $\frac{2}{3}$ = ▨

34. Two friends are sharing a $\frac{2}{3}$-lb bag of peanuts. If each one gets the same amount, how much will each portion weigh?

(Lesson 6) Solve.

35. Estelle is making hats out of colored paper for a party she is having. Each hat takes $2\frac{3}{4}$ sheets of paper. If she has 80 sheets, does she have enough for 25 guests? Decide whether you will overestimate or underestimate and then solve.

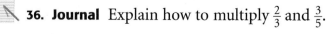

36. **Journal** Explain how to multiply $\frac{2}{3}$ and $\frac{3}{5}$.

> **Skills Checklist**
>
> In this section, you have:
> ☑ Explored Multiplying Whole Numbers by Fractions
> ☑ Multiplied With Fractions
> ☑ Estimated Products
> ☑ Explored Multiplying Fractions by Fractions
> ☑ Multiplied Fractions
> ☑ Solved Problems by Over- and Underestimating

Extending Multiplication

Served on holidays and on other occasions, challah is a braided bread. A loaf of challah weighs $1\frac{3}{8}$ lb. How would you change this to ounces?

Skills Checklist

In this section, you will:

☐ Multiply Whole Numbers by Fractions

☐ Multiply Whole Numbers and Mixed Numbers

☐ Solve Problems by Using Logical Reasoning or Drawing a Picture

☐ Explore Division of Fractions

GET READY!

Multiplying Mixed Numbers

Review fractions and mixed numbers.
Write each as a mixed number.

1. $\frac{5}{2}$ **2.** $\frac{10}{3}$ **3.** $\frac{23}{5}$ **4.** $\frac{31}{7}$

Write each as an improper fraction.

5. $3\frac{4}{5}$ **6.** $5\frac{2}{3}$ **7.** $4\frac{2}{7}$ **8.** $2\frac{5}{9}$

Multiplying Whole Numbers by Fractions

You Will Learn

how to multiply fractions and whole numbers

Learn • • • • • • •

Raymond and his family are West Indian. They like to make and eat West Indian dishes like chicken curry and rice. Chicken curry smells delicious as it cooks!

Raymond from Brooklyn, New York uses spices and many different ingredients to make curries.

Raymond is making 5 times the recipe of chicken curry for a family reunion. He needs a $\frac{1}{4}$-in. piece of fresh ginger for one batch. How much will he need for 5 batches?

Did You Know?

Some West Indian dishes contain over 12 different kinds of spices.

One Way

Find $5 \times \frac{1}{4}$.

Solve the problem using a number line. Mark off $\frac{1}{4}$ five times.

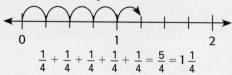

$\frac{1}{4} + \frac{1}{4} + \frac{1}{4} + \frac{1}{4} + \frac{1}{4} = \frac{5}{4} = 1\frac{1}{4}$

Another Way

To find the total amount of ginger, find the product of 5 and $\frac{1}{4}$.

$5 \times \frac{1}{4} = n$

Think: $5 = \frac{5}{1}$

$\frac{5}{1} \times \frac{1}{4} = \frac{5 \times 1}{1 \times 4} = \frac{5}{4} = 1\frac{1}{4}$

Raymond needs $1\frac{1}{4}$ in. of fresh ginger.

Ginger is a tangy spice used to flavor baked goods and beverages.

Talk About It

1. How does the number line show $\frac{5}{4}$?

2. How does the number line show $5 \times \frac{1}{4}$?

Check

Copy and complete.

1. $4 \times \dfrac{2}{3} = \dfrac{\blacksquare}{1} \times \dfrac{2}{3} = \dfrac{\blacksquare \times 2}{1 \times 3} = \dfrac{\blacksquare}{3} = 2\dfrac{2}{3}$

2. $\dfrac{1}{2} \times 6 = \dfrac{\blacksquare}{2} \times \dfrac{6}{1} = \dfrac{\blacksquare \times 6}{2 \times 1} = \dfrac{6}{2} = 3$

3. **Reasoning** Is $\dfrac{4}{5} \times 7$ the same as $7 \times \dfrac{4}{5}$? Explain.

Practice

Skills and Reasoning

Copy and complete.

4. $2 \times \dfrac{7}{8} = \dfrac{2}{1} \times \dfrac{\blacksquare}{8} = \dfrac{2 \times \blacksquare}{1 \times 8} = \dfrac{\blacksquare}{8} = 1\dfrac{6}{8} = 1\dfrac{3}{4}$

5. $\dfrac{4}{5} \times 4 = \dfrac{\blacksquare}{5} \times \dfrac{4}{1} = \dfrac{\blacksquare \times 4}{5 \times 1} = \dfrac{\blacksquare}{5} = \blacksquare$

Find each product.

6. $9 \times \dfrac{4}{3}$

7. $7 \times \dfrac{2}{5}$

8. $8 \times \dfrac{5}{6}$

9. $56 \times \dfrac{2}{7}$

10. $72 \times \dfrac{1}{2}$

11. $\dfrac{5}{2} \times 11$

12. $\dfrac{2}{3} \times 60$

13. $\dfrac{4}{7} \times 42$

14. $\dfrac{3}{2} \times 32$

15. $\dfrac{9}{8} \times 72$

16. Explain how you can find the product of 3 and $\dfrac{5}{8}$.

17. Complete. $9 \times \dfrac{2}{3} = 6$, so $\dfrac{2}{3} \times 9 = \blacksquare$.

18. Lea says that she knows all the answers to the following problems are whole numbers even without solving them. Explain how she knows.

$\dfrac{7}{8} \times 816$ $\qquad$ $\dfrac{3}{10} \times 450$ $\qquad$ $\dfrac{11}{13} \times 390$

Problem Solving and Applications

19. Six family members each ate $\dfrac{7}{8}$ cup of chicken curry. How much chicken curry was eaten?

Using Data Use the Data File on page 401 for **20** and **21**.

20. **Geography** The population of India is about 900 million. About how many people earn their living by farming?

21. Farms cover about 600,000 mi². About how much land is used for grains, vegetables, and rice?

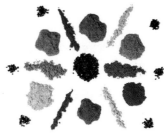

Curry is a mix of spices, such as turmeric and cumin.

Mixed Review and Test Prep

Divide.

22. $7\overline{)934}$

23. $21\overline{)235}$

24. $35\overline{)241}$

25. $12\overline{)817}$

26. $17\overline{)402}$

27. Which of the following is the remainder for $717 \div 7$?

Ⓐ 17 $\qquad$ Ⓑ 10 $\qquad$ Ⓒ 3 $\qquad$ Ⓓ 13 $\qquad$ Ⓔ not here

Multiplying Whole Numbers and Mixed Numbers

You Will Learn

how to multiply whole numbers and mixed numbers

Math Tip

You can use what you know about multiplying fractions to multiply mixed numbers.

 Learn • • •  • • • • • •

Katy from Tucson, Arizona, makes her own challah bread to give to her relatives for family feasts.

Katy and her mother prepare challah, an egg-twist bread.

If each loaf weighs $1\frac{3}{8}$ lb, would 3 loaves weigh more or less than 5 lb?

Example 1

You can multiply a mixed number by a whole number.

Multiply $3 \times 1\frac{3}{8}$.

Step 1	Step 2	Step 3
Rewrite $1\frac{3}{8}$ as an improper fraction.	Multiply.	Simplify the answer.
$1\frac{3}{8} = \frac{11}{8}$	$\frac{3}{1} \times \frac{11}{8} = \frac{33}{8}$	$\frac{33}{8} = 4\frac{1}{8}$

3 loaves weigh $4\frac{1}{8}$ lb, which is less than 5 lb.

You can also multiply a mixed number by a mixed number.

Example 2

What is $2\frac{1}{5} \times 3\frac{1}{3}$?

Step 1	Step 2	Step 3
Rewrite as improper fractions.	Simplify factors.	Multiply.
$2\frac{1}{5} \times 3\frac{1}{3} = \frac{11}{5} \times \frac{10}{3}$	$\frac{11}{5} \times \frac{10}{3} = \frac{11 \times \overset{2}{\cancel{10}}}{\cancel{5} \times 3}$	$\frac{11 \times \overset{2}{\cancel{10}}}{\cancel{5} \times 3} = \frac{22}{3} = 7\frac{1}{3}$
So, $2\frac{1}{5} \times 3\frac{1}{3} = 7\frac{1}{3}$.	_{1}	_{1}

Talk About It

If you multiply $\frac{3}{4}$ by $2\frac{1}{8}$, will the product be more than $2\frac{1}{8}$? Explain.

Check

Copy and complete.

1. $1\frac{1}{3} \times 6 = \frac{\blacksquare}{3} \times 6$

2. $14 \times 3\frac{3}{4} = 14 \times \frac{\blacksquare}{4}$

3. $2\frac{1}{3} \times 4\frac{3}{8} = \frac{\blacksquare}{3} \times \frac{\blacksquare}{4}$

4. Reasoning How could you use 15 to estimate $\frac{1}{3} \times 14\frac{1}{3}$? Explain.

Practice

Skills and Reasoning

Copy and complete.

5. $6\frac{4}{5} \times 2 = \frac{\blacksquare}{5} \times 2$

6. $3 \times 3\frac{1}{8} = 3 \times \frac{\blacksquare}{8}$

7. $5\frac{3}{4} \times 6\frac{1}{4} = \frac{\blacksquare}{4} \times \frac{\blacksquare}{4}$

Find each product. Simplify.

8. $4\frac{3}{7} \times 2$

9. $5 \times 7\frac{1}{2}$

10. $1\frac{1}{8} \times 11$

11. $3\frac{3}{4} \times 2$

12. $2\frac{4}{7} \times 4$

13. $6 \times 2\frac{1}{2}$

14. $10 \times 5\frac{3}{5}$

15. $4\frac{1}{2} \times 5$

16. $\frac{1}{5} \times 5\frac{2}{5}$

17. $2\frac{1}{4} \times \frac{4}{9}$

18. $2\frac{1}{2} \times \frac{5}{6}$

19. $9\frac{1}{10} \times \frac{1}{10}$

20. $1\frac{1}{3} \times 2\frac{1}{3}$

21. $3\frac{1}{2} \times 2\frac{2}{3}$

22. $\frac{1}{8} \times 7\frac{5}{6}$

23. Find the product of $2\frac{1}{8}$ and $2\frac{2}{3}$.

24. Multiply $5\frac{1}{5}$ and $2\frac{1}{2}$.

Problem Solving and Applications

25. Measurement If 1 lb of berries makes $2\frac{3}{4}$ c of jam, how much jam can be made from 6 lb? Use estimation to check.

26. Fine Arts A movie theater is showing the classic horror film *Frankenstein*. The film is $1\frac{1}{3}$ hr long. If the theater schedules 4 daily showings, what is the total number of hours the film will be shown each day?

James Whale's
Frankenstein (1930)
starring Boris Karloff

Mixed Review and Test Prep

Find each sum.

27. $\frac{1}{5} + \frac{4}{5}$

28. $3\frac{1}{3} + 2\frac{1}{2}$

29. $\frac{4}{9} + \frac{1}{3}$

30. $\frac{2}{7} + \frac{1}{3}$

31. $\frac{2}{5} + 2\frac{3}{4}$

Find each product.

32. 0.25×0.5

33. 0.75×0.1

34. 0.2×0.7

35. 0.5×0.8

36. The product of 0.5 and 0.5 is the same as the product of:

(A) 0.5×0.05

(B) 5×0.5

(C) 0.1×0.5

(D) 0.25×0.5

(E) not here

FRACTION of a CHANCE GAME

Players
2 teams of 2–4 players

Materials
- spinner
- paper clip
- counter for each team
- posterboard
- crayons or paints

Object
The object of the game is to make multiplication problems whose products total 200.

How to Play

1 Make a gameboard and spinner like those shown.

2 Team leaders spin to see which team goes first. The team that spins the lesser number is Team A and will go first.

3 Teams A and B place counters on starting places at opposite ends of the gameboard. Team A spins the spinner. Team A then makes and solves a multiplication problem using the number on the spinner and one of the mixed numbers in the space just ahead of Team A's counter.

4. If Team A gets a correct answer, the product is added to its total.
   If Team A gets an incorrect answer, it must then multiply the number on the spinner by the mixed number it did not use in Step 3.
   If this answer is correct, the product is added to Team A's total.
   If the answer is incorrect, no points are added to the total.
   Team A's counter is then advanced 1 space. It is now Team B's turn.

5. Play alternates after each spin until both teams have crossed the game board.

6. Each team's products are then totaled. Include only the correct answers. The team whose total is closest to 200, either over 200 or under 200, wins.

Talk About It

1. What advantage is there to keeping a running total of products during the game?

2. Was there a point during the game when you changed from choosing the greater mixed number to choosing the lesser mixed number?

More Ways to Play

- Play to 500 points. Each team reaches the opposite end of the gameboard and returns. The first team to get to 500 or more points wins the game.

- Start with 800 points. Subtract each product. The team with the most points after moving across the board once wins the game.

Reasoning

1. When did you select the greater mixed number in the space? When did you select the lesser mixed number?

2. Explain how you could go over 200 and still win the game.

3. How would your strategies change if you were playing the 800-point subtraction version of Fraction of a Chance Game? Would you choose greater or lesser mixed numbers? Explain.

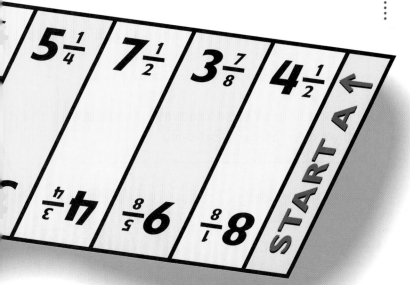

$5\frac{1}{4}$ $7\frac{1}{2}$ $3\frac{7}{8}$ $4\frac{1}{2}$ START A

$7\frac{3}{4}$ $6\frac{5}{8}$ $8\frac{1}{8}$

Problem Solving

Compare Strategies: Logical Reasoning/ Draw a Picture

You Will Learn

how to use logical reasoning or draw a picture to solve problems

Learn •

Cathy, Donna, Hal, and Rob love bagels. They each have a favorite. Which bagel is each person's favorite?

Clues

1. Cathy's friend only likes sesame.
2. Donna likes either onion or plain.
3. Hal and Cathy dislike plain.
4. Rob only likes onion.

One Way

Use logical reasoning and what you learn directly from clues 1–4.

	Cathy	**Donna**	**Hal**	**Rob**
plain	no	yes	no	no
sesame	no	no	yes	no
raisin	yes	no	no	no
onion	no	no	no	yes

1. If Cathy's friend likes sesame, Cathy does not. Write *no* for sesame under Cathy.
2. Donna does not like sesame or raisin. Write *no* for sesame and raisin under Donna.
3. Hal and Cathy dislike plain. Write *no* for plain under Hal and Cathy.
4. Write *yes* for onion for Rob.

Then you can write *no* for plain, sesame and raisin under Rob and *no* for Cathy, Donna, and Hal across from onion. So, Donna must like plain. Cathy must like raisin. That leaves sesame for Hal.

Another Way

Draw colored arrows, red for *yes* and blue for *no*.

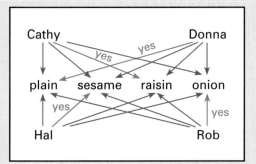

1. Draw a blue arrow from Cathy to sesame.
2. Draw a blue arrow from Donna to sesame and raisin.
3. Draw blue arrows from Hal and Cathy to plain.
4. Draw a red arrow from Rob to onion.

Draw blue arrows from Rob to all other bagels and blue arrows from Cathy, Donna and Hal to onion. Donna must have a red arrow to plain. Cathy must have a red arrow to raisin and Hal must have a red arrow to sesame.

Talk About It

Compare both ways of solving this problem.

Check

Use logical reasoning to solve the problem.

1. Anna, Gary, Mark, and Tina are from Alabama, Georgia, Mississippi, and Tennessee. None comes from a state that begins with the same letter as his or her name. Neither Anna nor Tina is from Georgia. Gary is from Tennessee.

Which person comes from each state?

	AL	GA	MS	TN
Anna				
Gary				
Mark				
Tina				

Gary lives Here!

Problem Solving Practice

Use logical reasoning or any strategy to solve each problem.

2. **Logic** Ivan always answers in riddles. Daniella asked him what his address is on Chestnut Street. Ivan answered "It's a 3-digit number. The digit in the tens place is twice the digit in the ones place. The digit in the hundreds place is 3 times as great as the tens digit." What is Ivan's address?

3. **Time** Chantelle gets home from school each day at 4:40 P.M. On her way home she first walks to her friend's home. This takes 15 minutes. After chatting for 15 min, she walks to the library in 10 min. She stays there 45 min, doing her homework. The walk home from the library takes 15 min. What time does she leave school? What strategy did you use to solve this problem?

School
Friend's house
Library
Chantelle's house

4. **Write Your Own Problem** Write a problem using the data shown in the table.

5. **Journal** When you can use either logical reasoning or draw a picture, which do you prefer? Give your reasons.

Problem Solving Strategies

- Use Objects/Act It Out
- Draw a Picture
- Look for a Pattern
- Guess and Check
- Use Logical Reasoning
- Make an Organized List
- Make a Table
- Solve a Simpler Problem
- Work Backward

Choose a Tool

Pizza Toppings				
	Cheese	Mushroom	Sausage	Broccoli
Ali	yes	no	no	no
Ben	no	no	yes	no
Cass	no	no	no	yes
Dee	no	yes	no	no

Exploring Division of Fractions

Problem Solving Connection

Look for a Pattern

Materials

fraction strips

Explore •

A giant sandwich is known by many different names. To some it's a hero, to others a grinder, poor boy, or submarine. Philadelphians call it a hoagie. This jumbo hoagie is too big for one person to eat!

Work Together

Did You Know?

The longest loaf of bread, baked in Guadalajara, Mexico, on January 6, 1991, measured $3,491\frac{3}{4}$ ft, or $\frac{2}{3}$ mi.

Each hoagie is cut into fourths. How many fourths are there if three hoagies are cut into fourths?

1. Use fraction strips to see how many $\frac{1}{4}$s are in 3.

   a. How many $\frac{1}{4}$ pieces are in one whole?

   b. How many $\frac{1}{4}$ pieces are in two wholes?

   c. How many $\frac{1}{4}$ pieces are in three wholes?

2. If there were 10 hoagies divided into $\frac{1}{4}$s, how many portions would there be?

3. Party hoagies can be divided into twelfths. How many portions would three of these sandwiches provide?

4. Copy and complete.

Fraction	Number in 1 hoagie	Number in 3 hoagies	Number in 10 hoagies
$\frac{1}{2}$	2		
$\frac{1}{5}$		15	
			100

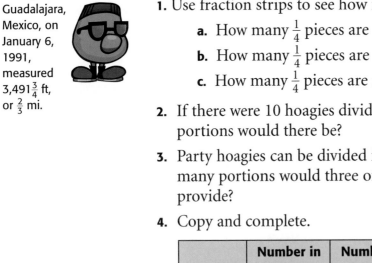

Talk About It

How is dividing 3 by $\frac{1}{4}$ different from multiplying 3 by $\frac{1}{4}$?

Connect

How many $\frac{1}{4}$s are there in 3?

$3 \div \frac{1}{4} = n$

The drawing shows there are twelve $\frac{1}{4}$s in 3.
So, $3 \div \frac{1}{4} = 12$.

Practice

1. How many $\frac{1}{3}$s are in 3?

2. How many $\frac{1}{2}$s are in 4?

Use fraction strips or draw pictures to find each quotient.

3. $2 \div \frac{1}{2}$

How many $\frac{1}{2}$s are in 2?

4. $4 \div \frac{1}{4}$

How many $\frac{1}{4}$s are in 4?

5. $2 \div \frac{1}{6}$

How many $\frac{1}{6}$s are in 2?

6. $4 \div \frac{1}{10}$

How many $\frac{1}{10}$s are in 4?

Find each quotient.

7. $6 \div \frac{1}{8}$ **8.** $2 \div \frac{1}{5}$ **9.** $7 \div \frac{1}{2}$ **10.** $2 \div \frac{1}{11}$ **11.** $4 \div \frac{1}{7}$

12. $13 \div \frac{1}{4}$ **13.** $5 \div \frac{1}{5}$ **14.** $3 \div \frac{1}{3}$ **15.** $10 \div \frac{1}{2}$ **16.** $8 \div \frac{1}{4}$

17. $5 \div \frac{1}{3}$ **18.** $4 \div \frac{1}{6}$ **19.** $12 \div \frac{1}{3}$ **20.** $15 \div \frac{1}{3}$ **21.** $11 \div \frac{1}{3}$

22. At the Surf City Sub Shop, each pound of Swiss cheese is divided into $\frac{1}{8}$-lb portions for sandwiches. How many portions does Surf City get from a 5-lb cheese?

23. Time What fraction of an hour is ten minutes? Explain how you can use division by a fraction to figure out how many ten-minute periods there are in a day.

24. Music Write a division statement that solves this problem: Three measures of music in $\frac{4}{4}$ time are all half notes. If each measure equals one whole note, how many half notes are there in 3 measures?

Notes in $\frac{4}{4}$ Time		
Symbol	Name	Beats
o	whole	4
♩	half	2

25. Measurement To convert a temperature from Celsius to Fahrenheit, divide by $\frac{1}{9}$, then divide by 5, then add 32. $24°C = 75.2°F$. What is the temperature in Fahrenheit at $6°C$?

26. Journal Describe what happens when you divide 8 by $\frac{1}{2}$. Use pictures.

Review and Practice

(Lessons 7 and 8) Find each product. Simplify.

1. $\frac{2}{3} \times 6$ **2.** $\frac{3}{4} \times 4$ **3.** $\frac{7}{10} \times 40$ **4.** $5 \times \frac{4}{5}$ **5.** $10 \times \frac{9}{10}$

6. $\frac{1}{8} \times 7$ **7.** $2 \times \frac{2}{3}$ **8.** $\frac{2}{5} \times 5$ **9.** $3 \times \frac{5}{12}$ **10.** $\frac{2}{7} \times 8$

11. $4\frac{1}{2} \times 8$ **12.** $1\frac{5}{6} \times \frac{2}{5}$ **13.** $2\frac{1}{2} \times 1\frac{1}{3}$ **14.** $\frac{3}{5} \times 3\frac{2}{3}$ **15.** $4\frac{1}{3} \times 1\frac{1}{2}$

16. $2\frac{1}{2} \times 3\frac{2}{3}$ **17.** $\frac{3}{5} \times 1\frac{2}{3}$ **18.** $\frac{1}{6} \times 7\frac{1}{2}$ **19.** $10\frac{1}{4} \times 12$ **20.** $5\frac{5}{7} \times 2\frac{1}{8}$

21. A recipe calls for $\frac{3}{8}$ lb of butter. If you make half the recipe, how much butter do you need?

(Lesson 9) Solve each problem.

22. Logic Ivan wants to double a recipe to six servings. Three servings contain 3 cups of flour, 1 cup of sugar, and $\frac{1}{4}$ cup of raisins. How many cups total will he use?

23. Time May has to leave home by 8:00 A.M. It is 7:15 A.M. now. She has to eat, pack her bag, feed the dog, and call her friend. The call will take 10 min, feeding the dog takes 5 min, packing takes 20 min, and eating takes 20 min. Will she leave on time?

(Lesson 10) Find each quotient.

24. How many $\frac{1}{2}$s are in 5?   **25.** How many $\frac{1}{4}$s are in 4?

26. How many $\frac{1}{5}$s are in 7?   **27.** How many $\frac{1}{6}$s are in 12?

28. $9 \div \frac{1}{3}$ **29.** $2 \div \frac{1}{3}$ **30.** $3 \div \frac{1}{8}$

31. $5 \div \frac{1}{3}$ **32.** $6 \div \frac{1}{7}$ **33.** $11 \div \frac{1}{2}$

34. $6 \div \frac{1}{4}$ **35.** $15 \div \frac{1}{5}$ **36.** $10 \div \frac{1}{8}$

37. Journal Use a number line or a drawing to explain how to multiply $\frac{1}{3} \times 4$.

Skills Checklist

In this section, you have:

☑ **Multiplied Whole Numbers by Fractions**

☑ **Multiplied Whole Numbers and Mixed Numbers**

☑ **Solved Problems by Using Logical Reasoning or Drawing a Picture**

☑ **Explored Division of Fractions**

REVIEW AND PRACTICE

Choose at least one. Use what you have learned in this chapter.

① Friendly Fixings

At Home Look through a cookbook. Pick a recipe that you would like to make. Copy the list of ingredients. Then revise the list of ingredients so you make the recipe for a different number of people.

BAKLAVA - Serves 6 People

Ingredients:
  500 grams of filo pastry
  300 grams of unsalted butter
  2 cups chopped walnuts
Syrup:
  500 grams of sugar
  $\frac{1}{2}$ liter of water
  Juice of $\frac{1}{2}$ lemon

BAKLAVA

③ Figuring With Fractions

Get cooking on **www.mathsurf.com/5/ch9**. Choose a recipe that has fractions and mixed numbers. Write and solve a multiplication problem with your data.

② Fabulous Fashions

There is a special play coming up and you have been asked to design the costumes! Create some sketches for the types of clothing worn by the characters in the play. Then use the table below to figure out about how much fabric you would need if you were to make the costumes for 5 characters.

Clothing	Fabric (yd)
dress shirt	$1\frac{1}{2}$
skirt	$1\frac{1}{4}$
men's suit	$4\frac{3}{4}$
dress	$3\frac{1}{4}$
T-shirt	$\frac{3}{4}$
pants or jeans	$2\frac{1}{2}$

④ Food for Thought

Two sisters visited their uncle, a strawberry farmer. He told them that they could pick as many berries to take home as they wanted, as long as they didn't take more than 10 baskets. After a little while the farmer came out to the fields to see how they were doing. "How many baskets have you got?" he asked. The girls told him that if they had twice as many baskets as they did then, plus half as many baskets as they did then, they would be at the limit. How many baskets did they have?

Review/Test

(**Lessons 1–5, 7, and 8**) Find each product. Simplify.

1. $40 \times \frac{1}{5}$ **2.** $36 \times \frac{1}{4}$ **3.** $21 \times \frac{1}{3}$ **4.** $54 \times \frac{1}{6}$ **5.** $35 \times \frac{1}{5}$

6. $56 \times \frac{1}{8}$ **7.** $18 \times \frac{1}{2}$ **8.** $18 \times \frac{1}{3}$ **9.** $16 \times \frac{1}{4}$ **10.** $48 \times \frac{1}{6}$

11. $12 \times \frac{3}{4}$ **12.** $20 \times \frac{2}{5}$ **13.** $18 \times \frac{3}{5}$ **14.** $18 \times \frac{5}{6}$ **15.** $21 \times \frac{5}{6}$

16. $32 \times \frac{3}{8}$ **17.** $64 \times \frac{3}{8}$ **18.** $63 \times \frac{2}{3}$ **19.** $17 \times \frac{2}{3}$ **20.** $15 \times \frac{5}{12}$

21. $9\frac{4}{5} \times 30$ **22.** $1\frac{1}{5} \times 40$ **23.** $8 \times 1\frac{2}{3}$ **24.** $6 \times 2\frac{7}{8}$ **25.** $7 \times 1\frac{3}{8}$

26. $\frac{3}{5} \times \frac{5}{8}$ **27.** $\frac{1}{6} \times \frac{9}{10}$ **28.** $\frac{3}{8} \times \frac{5}{36}$ **29.** $\frac{3}{4} \times 2\frac{1}{2}$ **30.** $3\frac{1}{5} \times \frac{5}{8}$

31. $10\frac{1}{2} \times 1\frac{3}{5}$ **32.** $3\frac{1}{3} \times 5\frac{2}{5}$ **33.** $4\frac{2}{3} \times 3$ **34.** $\frac{1}{6} \times 2\frac{3}{4}$ **35.** $\frac{3}{10} \times \frac{1}{6}$

36. What is $\frac{1}{4}$ of 12?   **37.** What is $\frac{2}{5}$ of 10?   **38.** What is $\frac{3}{8}$ of 48?

39. Find the product of $\frac{1}{3}$ and $\frac{3}{80}$.   **40.** Find the product of $1\frac{2}{9}$ and $2\frac{2}{5}$.

41. Find the product of $1\frac{1}{4}$ and $3\frac{1}{5}$.   **42.** Find the product of $\frac{3}{8}$ and $2\frac{2}{3}$.

(**Lessons 6 and 9**) Solve each problem.

43. If $\frac{1}{3}$ of a pack of tissues is 8 tissues, how many tissues are in the pack?

44. How many minutes are in three-fifths of an hour?

45. A box contains 24 pairs of socks that are either blue, black, or white. If $\frac{1}{3}$ are blue and $\frac{1}{6}$ are black, then how many pairs are white?

46. A recipe for pancakes serves 10–12 people. If there are five people in your family, what should you do to the recipe?

(**Lesson 10**) Find each quotient.

47. $8 \div \frac{1}{2}$ **48.** $9 \div \frac{1}{3}$ **49.** $7 \div \frac{1}{8}$ **50.** $8 \div \frac{1}{4}$

Performance Assessment

Suppose you want to make a frame to hold these recycling bins. Your family is tired of the bins blowing around outside. Choose the materials you will purchase to build the frame as inexpensively as possible.

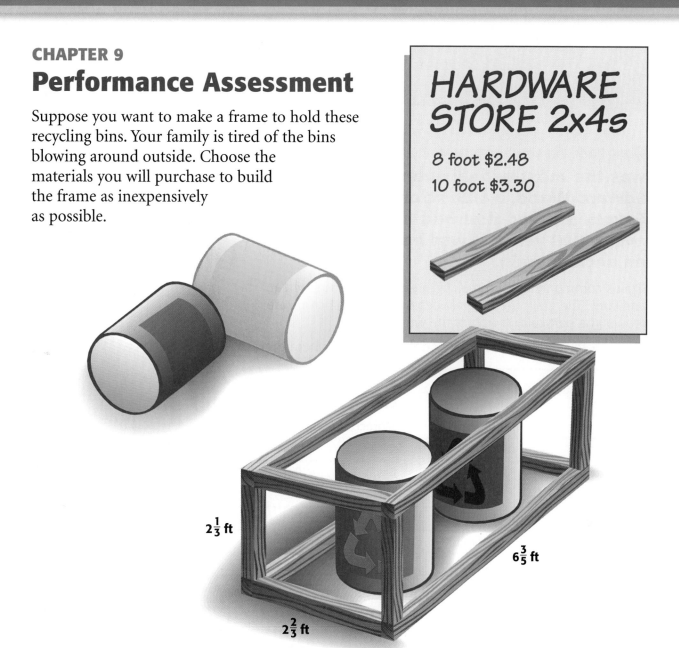

HARDWARE STORE 2x4s

8 foot $2.48

10 foot $3.30

$2\frac{1}{3}$ ft

$6\frac{3}{5}$ ft

$2\frac{2}{3}$ ft

1. **Decision Making** You need 2 × 4s for the frame. What's the total length of 2 × 4s you will need? Will you buy 8 ft or 10 ft 2 × 4s, or a combination of the two?

2. **Recording Data** Make a table showing the items you will purchase and the quantity and cost of each item.

3. **Explain Your Thinking** How did you make your choices? How are you sure you have the most inexpensive option?

4. **Critical Thinking** If 12 ft 2 × 4s cost $4.19, could you make the frame any less expensively? Explain.

Math Magazine

Bread, the Staff of Life Bread is and was the most widely eaten food in the world. Edward Wood, a U.S. scientist, re-created an Egyptian bread that had not been made for over 4,000 years! It was based on emmer, an ancient grain.

Grains commonly used in making bread include rice, wheat, and corn. The grain used largely depends on what crops are grown in a particular region of the world.

Here are some different breads and the countries where they originated.

Country	Bread	Country	Bread
Russia	Bliny	China	Mantou
Mongolia	Boortsog	Morocco	Milles Troues
Israel	Burekas	Japan	Mochi
France	Crepes	Egypt	Pancakes
Australia	Damper	Greece	Pitas
Ethiopia	Dabo	India	Roti
Argentina	Galleta Criolla	Mexico	Tortilla
Jordan	Khobz	Norway	Lefse

How many of these breads have you heard of? How many have you tasted?

Try These!

Find the amount of each ingredient you would need to serve:

a. 24 to 30 people
b. 4 to 5 people

Can you find other breads not listed here? Find out more about the bread eaten in a country of your choice. No loafing—start at www.mathsurf.com/5/ch9.

Raisin-Pecan-Ginger Bread (Caribbean)

$1\frac{1}{4}$ c   flour
1 c   whole wheat flour
$2\frac{1}{2}$ tsp baking powder
$\frac{1}{2}$ tsp   baking soda
$1\frac{1}{4}$ tsp ground ginger
$\frac{2}{3}$ c   raisins

$\frac{1}{4}$ c   chopped pecans
$1\frac{1}{2}$ c   plain yogurt
$\frac{1}{3}$ c   brown sugar
3   egg whites
2 tbsp   vegetable oil
$1\frac{1}{2}$ tsp vanilla extract
1 tsp   orange extract

Serves 8 to 10 people.

Test Prep Strategy: Read Carefully

Answer the question asked.

Kiram bought three boards each $2\frac{3}{4}$ ft long. How long is half of one of these boards?

   Ⓐ $8\frac{1}{4}$ ft   Ⓑ $\frac{1}{2}$ ft   Ⓒ $4\frac{1}{8}$ ft   Ⓓ $1\frac{3}{8}$ ft

Be careful! You might quickly answer the question: How many feet are in the three boards all together? Take time to read the entire problem. Find $\frac{1}{2}$ of $2\frac{3}{4}$. The solution is $\frac{1}{2} \times 2\frac{3}{4}$, or Ⓓ $1\frac{3}{8}$ ft.

Write the letter of the correct answer. Choose any strategy.

1. Which statement is true?

   Ⓐ $6.34 > 6.304$ Ⓑ $6.304 > 6.340$

   Ⓒ $6.340 > 6.34$ Ⓓ $6.304 = 6.340$

2. Find the median of the set: 8, 9, 4, 6.

   Ⓐ 8   Ⓑ 6   Ⓒ 9   Ⓓ 7

3. Which product is the same as the product of 4.04×10?

   Ⓐ 40.4×10 Ⓑ 0.0404×100 Ⓒ 0.404×100 Ⓓ $0.404 \times 1,000$

4. Which has a remainder of 6?

   Ⓐ $2\overline{)631}$ Ⓑ $4\overline{)325}$ Ⓒ $5\overline{)164}$ Ⓓ $8\overline{)134}$

5. Which number is composite?

   Ⓐ 2   Ⓑ 119   Ⓒ 11   Ⓓ 113

6. Which has the same quotient as 8.06 divided by 100?

   Ⓐ $0.806 \div 10$ Ⓑ $806 \div 1,000$ Ⓒ $8.06 \div 10$ Ⓓ not here

7. Which angle is about 135 degrees?

   Ⓐ   Ⓑ   Ⓒ   Ⓓ

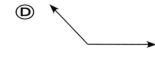

8. Which statement is **not** true?

   Ⓐ $1\frac{1}{2} > \frac{4}{3}$ Ⓑ $\frac{1}{3} < \frac{1}{8}$ Ⓒ $\frac{3}{4} = \frac{6}{8}$ Ⓓ $1 > \frac{4}{5}$

9. Brandon lives $\frac{3}{4}$ mi from school. On Wednesday and Friday he walked to and from school. How many miles did he walk on Friday?

   Ⓐ $1\frac{1}{2}$ mi   Ⓑ $\frac{3}{4}$ mi   Ⓒ 6 mi   Ⓓ 3 mi

Chapter 10
Length, Perimeter, and Area

ANIMALS AND YOU

S-s-snakes!
Page 439

SECTION A

Using Linear Metric Measurement

439

What units of measure does this table include?

How would you figure out which snake is the longest?

Snake	Length
Garter snake	4.6–13.1 dm
Indian cobra	0.6–1.5 m
Water snake	55.7–134.7 cm
Anaconda	5.5–7.6 m
Timber rattlesnake	8.9–18.9 dm

436

Exploring Perimeter and Area

449

The table below shows some rectangular dog pens you can build with 36 ft of fencing. Which one would you build? Explain.

Length (ft)	Width (ft)	Perimeter (ft)	Area (ft²)
17	1	36	17
15	3	36	45
13	5	36	65
11	7	36	77
9	9	36	81

Organic Gardening
Page 449

Finding Area and Perimeter

463

A great deal of time and money goes into restoring carousels. Which is the most common carousel animal?

Carousel	Location	Animals	Diameter (ft)
The Cottage Grove Carousel	Cottage Grove, Oregon	22 horses, 2 rabbits, 2 pigs, 2 zebras, 1 dog, 1 rooster, 2 chariots	36
The Crossroads Village Carousel	Leavenworth, Kansas	36 horses, 1 dragon chariot, 4 kiddies' ponies with mother's benches	40
The Glen Echo Carousel	Glen Echo Park, Maryland	40 horses, 4 rabbits, 4 ostriches, 1 giraffe, 1 deer, 1 lion, 1 tiger	48

Dogs Who Dine Out
Page 463

Surfing the World Wide Web!

To find out more about carousels in the United States, circle back to **www.mathsurf.com/5/ch10**. Which carousel is nearest to you?

Materials

cardboard, ruler, scissors, crayons (optional)

Tangrams and tangram puzzles originated in China. A tangram set is made from one square cut into seven pieces as shown. When the pieces are rearranged, they can form many designs including animal shapes.

Use tangrams to make other animals. Be sure to use all the pieces for each design. Challenge other teams to solve the puzzles.

Make a Plan

- How will you measure to make your tangram pieces?
- Which animals will you make?

Carry It Out

1. Make a set of tangrams.

    a. Cut out a cardboard square.

    b. Mark the pieces as shown here.

    c. Cut out the tangram shapes.

2. Make 3 different animal shapes. Use all the tangram pieces.

3. Record the solutions by tracing the outlines on a separate piece of paper.

Talk About It

- Name the tangram pieces using geometric terms.
- Describe how you made the different animals.

Present the Project

Plan a class presentation of the tangram puzzles. Display all the tangram animals on the bulletin board. Did any groups make the same animal? Did these animals have exactly the same shapes?

A Using Linear Metric Measurement

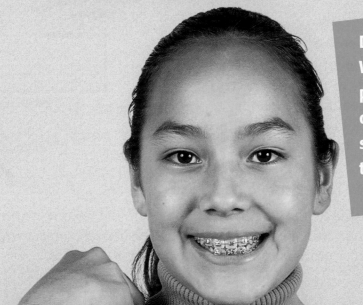

Do you like snakes? Would you like one as a pet? Jenny is very proud of the school's pet garter snake. It is kept in a terrarium in a classroom.

How can you use metric measurements to tell how long the school's snake is?

Changing Centimeters, Meters, and Decimals

Review multiplication. Find each product.

1. 10×4.27 2. 0.0879×100

3. 9.7×100 4. $1,000 \times 0.024$

5. $0.02 \times 1,000$ 6. 0.09×10

Skills Checklist

In this section, you will:

☐ Explore Estimating and Measuring Length

☐ Learn About Millimeters, Centimeters, Meters, and Decimals

Exploring Estimating and Measuring Length

Problem Solving Connection

Use Objects/
Act It Out

Materials

metric ruler or
measuring tape

Vocabulary

centimeter (cm)
one hundredth of a
meter

decimeter (dm)
one tenth of a meter

meter (m)
a unit of measure, a
little more than a
yard long

kilometer (km)
one thousand meters

Explore • • • • • • • • • • • • • • •

You can estimate the lengths of
objects in **centimeters (cm)**.
One centimeter is about
the width of your little finger
or the length of an ant.

This ant's body measures about 1 cm.

This grasshopper's
body measures
about 5 cm.

Work Together

1. Estimate the length of each object to the nearest centimeter. Record
your estimates on paper. Then measure each object with a metric
ruler or measuring tape to check your estimates.

   a.   b.

2. Copy and complete the table.

   a. Choose five classroom objects
   to measure in centimeters.

   b. Estimate the length of each object.

   c. Measure each object to check your estimates.

Object	Estimate	Actual (cm)

Did You Know?

The metric system was
created by a group of
French scientists
in the 1790s.

Talk About It

3. How did you decide which
objects to measure?

4. How did you estimate
the length of an object?

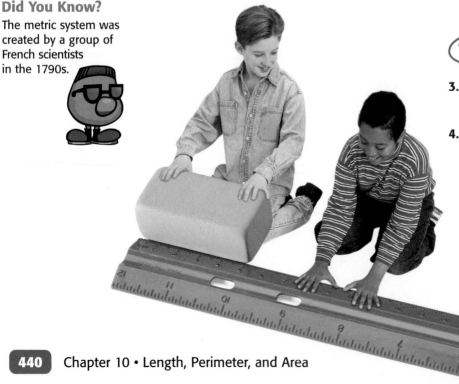

Connect

You can use different metric units to describe length.

10 centimeters (cm) = 1 **decimeter (dm)**   100 centimeters (cm) = 1 meter (m)

10 decimeters (dm) = 1 **meter (m)**   1,000 meters (m) = 1 **kilometer (km)**

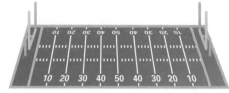

A cassette tape is about 1 dm long.

A bat is about 1 m long.

Nine football fields are about 1 km long.

Since a kilometer is a very large unit, it would not be appropriate to measure a cassette tape or a baseball bat in kilometers.

Practice

Choose the most appropriate unit of measure to estimate the length or height of each. Write cm, dm, or m.

1.
2.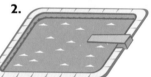
3.
4.

Choose the most appropriate unit of measure to estimate the length or height of each. Write m or km.

5.
6.
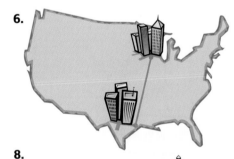

7.
8.

9. **Journal** Explain how you chose the most appropriate units of measure for 1–8.

Millimeters

Learn • • • • • • • • • • •

Jenny's school has a pet garter snake. At birth, the snake was 96 **millimeters (mm)** long. A millimeter is a very small unit of measure. A flea, for example, measures about 1 mm.

Jenny and the snake are from Oakland, California.

The metric system, like our place-value system, is based on groups of ten. To change units of measure, you can use multiplication or division.

meter	decimeter	centimeter	millimeter

1 m = 10 dm   1 dm = 10 cm   1 cm = 10 mm

Example 1

The garter snake is now 5 dm long. How many millimeters is this?

5 dm = ▧ mm

10 mm = 1 cm and 10 cm = 1 dm

1 dm = 10 × 10 mm = 100 mm

5 × 100 = 500

So, 5 dm = 500 mm.

The snake is 500 mm long.

Example 2

4,000 mm = ▧ m

1 m = 100 cm and 1 cm = 10 mm

1 m = 100 × 10 mm = 1,000 mm

4,000 ÷ 1,000 = 4

So, 4,000 mm = 4 m.

Talk About It

Remember

Place value helps you multiply.

8 × **10** = **8**0

8 × **100** = **8**00

Do you multiply or divide to change 3 cm to millimeters? Explain.

Check •

Copy and complete.

1. 3 cm = ▧ mm   2. 70 cm = ▧ mm

3. 40 mm = ▧ cm   4. 800 mm = ▧ dm

5. **Reasoning** Is a 5-cm lizard longer or shorter than 5 mm? Explain.

Practice

Skills and Reasoning

Copy and complete.

6. 4 cm = ■ mm   **7.** 9 dm = ■ mm   **8.** 500 cm = ■ m   **9.** 200 cm = ■ dm

10. 30 mm = ■ cm   **11.** 7 m = ■ mm   **12.** 20 cm = ■ mm   **13.** 6,000 mm = ■ m

14. 9 m = ■ cm   **15.** 800 dm = ■ m   **16.** 600 mm = ■ dm   **17.** 40 cm = ■ mm

18. Science The largest lizard is the Komodo dragon, which lives in Indonesia. It can grow to 30 dm in length. Is this longer or shorter than 5 m? Explain.

The Komodo dragon belongs to the oldest group of lizards.

Problem Solving and Applications

Using Data Use the Data File on page 436 to answer **19–21**.

19. Which snake can grow to a greater length, a garter snake or a water snake?

20. Which snake is at least three times as long as the longest timber rattlesnake?

21. Give the names of the snakes in order from the shortest to the longest.

22. Science A human can run short distances at about 20 km/hr. The fastest snakes move at about $\frac{1}{4}$ of this speed. At about what speed do the fastest snakes move?

Mixed Review and Test Prep

Choose the most appropriate unit of measure to estimate the length or height of each. Write cm, dm, m, or km.

23. goldfish   **24.** soccer field   **25.** pencil   **26.** house

Mental Math Find each product or quotient.

27. $326.2 \div 100$ **28.** $48.95 \div 10$ **29.** $5.9 \div 10$ **30.** $42.5 \div 100$

31. 3.27
       $\times\ \ 10$

32.   100
       $\times 5.9$

33. 1,000
       $\times\ \ 2.5$

34. 23.97
       $\times\ \ \ \ 10$

35. Which of the following is the answer for $835 \div 7$?

Ⓐ 105   Ⓑ 119 R2   Ⓒ 119   Ⓓ 19 R2

Centimeters, Meters, and Decimals

You Will Learn

how to express meters and centimeters as decimal equivalents of each other

Learn

Height or length is often measured in centimeters. You can use the fact that 1 m = 100 cm to write the measurement in meters, too.

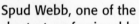

| meter | decimeter | centimeter | millimeter |

Example 1

Kareem Abdul-Jabbar, a long-time leading scorer in professional basketball, is 218 cm tall. What is his height in meters?

218 cm = ▓ m

218 cm
↓
2 m 18 cm

218 cm = 2.18 m

Kareem Abdul-Jabbar is 2.18 m tall.

Think: 100 cm = 1 m

1 cm = 0.01 m

So, 18 cm = 0.18 m

Example 2

If a measurement is expressed in meters, you can also express it in centimeters.

Spud Webb, one of the shortest professional basketball players, is 1.70 m tall. What is his height in centimeters?

1.70 m = ▓ cm

1.70 m
↓
1 m 70 cm

1.70 m = 170 cm

Spud Webb is 170 cm tall.

Think: 0.01 m = 1 cm

So, 0.70 m = 70 cm

Talk About It

1. How many meters are in 345 cm? Explain.

2. How many centimeters are in 5.95 m? Explain.

Check

Copy and complete.

1. 927 cm = ▓ m
2. 7.38 m = ▓ cm
3. 402.6 cm = ▓ m

4. 3.60 m = ▓ cm
5. 480 cm = ▓ m
6. 2.2 m = ▓ cm

7. **Reasoning** Emily is 1.40 m tall. Julie said she is taller because she is 138 cm tall. Is Julie correct? Explain.

Practice

Skills and Reasoning

Copy and complete.

8. 0.25 m = ▧ cm   **9.** 607 cm = ▧ m   **10.** 8.20 m = ▧ cm   **11.** 562 cm = ▧ m

Write each measurement, first in centimeters only and then in meters only.

12. 9 m 25 cm   **13.** 3 m 60 cm   **14.** 4 m 4 cm   **15.** 7 m 38 cm

Science Choose the taller animal. Heights given are to the shoulder.

16. Ⓐ an African elephant 2.99 m tall

Ⓑ an Asian elephant 244 cm tall

17. Ⓐ a llama 1.05 m tall

Ⓑ a horse 150 cm tall

African elephant

Asian elephant

Problem Solving and Applications

18. Science The blue whale can grow to a length of 30 m. The height of how many 150 cm horses would equal the length of one blue whale?

19. Patterns Copy and complete. Look for patterns.

cm	374		509		16
m		2.68		3.50	

20. Critical Thinking
Complete each statement.

a. To write a measurement expressed in meters as centimeters, multiply by _____ or move the decimal point _____.

b. To write a measurement expressed in centimeters as meters, divide by _____ or move the decimal point _____.

Mixed Review and Test Prep

Copy and complete.

21. 8 m = ▧ mm   **22.** 40 mm = ▧ cm   **23.** 60 cm = ▧ dm   **24.** 5 cm = ▧ mm

Ⓧ **Algebra Readiness** Find the value of *n* for each.

25. $3,600 \div 90 = n$ **26.** $560 \div n = 8$ **27.** $4,000 \div 80 = n$ **28.** $n \div 70 = 90$

29. Money Which of the following is the correct change for $20.00 − $9.99?

Ⓐ $4.39   Ⓑ $1.01   Ⓒ $10.10   Ⓓ $9.01   Ⓔ not here

Millimeters, Centimeters, and Decimals

These birdhouses were made for birds at the Zooland Animal Park.

You Will Learn

how to use decimals when working with centimeters, millimeters, and meters

Learn

It's for the birds! Allan and his classmates from Mobile, Alabama, made birdhouses for the birds at a local park.

The roof of each bird-house measured about 203 mm. How many centimeters is this?

meter	decimeter	centimeter	millimeter

← ÷ 10 — ÷ 10 — ÷ 10 —

Example 1

You can use the fact that 1 mm = 0.1 cm to write smaller measurements in centimeters.

203 mm = ▨ cm

   203 mm
     ↓
20 cm 3 mm

  20.3 cm

203 mm = 20.3 cm

The roof of the birdhouse is 20.3 cm.

Think: 10 mm = 1 cm
1 mm = 0.1 cm
So, 3 mm = 0.3 cm.

Example 2

You can use the fact that 0.1 cm = 1 mm to write larger measurements in mm.

11.4 cm = ▨ mm

   11.4 cm
     ↓
110 mm 4 mm

  114 mm

11.4 cm = 114 mm

Think: 1 cm = 10 mm
0.1 cm = 1 mm
So, 0.4 cm = 4 mm.

Talk About It

How can you tell the number of centimeters and of millimeters in 9.3 cm?

Math Tip

To change to a smaller unit, multiply.

To change to a larger unit, divide.

Check

Copy and complete.

1. 24 mm = ▨ cm   **2.** 3.6 cm = ▨ mm   **3.** 105 mm = ▨ cm

4. 5.0 cm = ▨ mm   **5.** 115 mm = ▨ cm   **6.** 9.8 cm = ▨ mm

7. Reasoning Nina said her pet parakeet was 9.2 mm tall. Could she be correct? Explain.

Practice

Skills and Reasoning

Copy and complete.

8. 4.3 cm = ☐ mm   **9.** 90 mm = ☐ cm   **10.** 2.87 m = ☐ cm   **11.** 148 mm = ☐ cm

12. 64 cm = ☐ m   **13.** 4 mm = ☐ cm   **14.** 12.1 cm = ☐ mm   **15.** 1.90 m = ☐ cm

16. 52 cm = ☐ mm   **17.** 3.1 m = ☐ cm   **18.** 1,437 cm = ☐ m   **19.** 421.5 cm = ☐ mm

20. Which length is longest?

ⓐ 35 mm   ⓑ 3.5 cm   ⓒ 3.50 m   ⓓ 40 mm

21. Which length is shortest?

ⓐ 1.14 m   ⓑ 750 mm   ⓒ 102 cm   ⓓ 600 mm

Problem Solving and Applications

Using Data Use the data to answer **22–25**.

Type of Egg	Length
Goldfinch	1.7 cm
Hummingbird	13 mm
Auk	11 cm
Cuckoo	3.5 cm
Robin	27 mm

Cuckoos lay their eggs in the nests of other birds and abandon their young.

Auks often make their nests in rocky territory.

22. Which is longer, a cuckoo egg or a hummingbird egg?

23. Which is shorter, a hummingbird egg or a goldfinch egg?

24. Write the list in order from shortest to longest eggs.

25. About how many times as long as a robin egg is an auk egg?

Mixed Review and Test Prep

STAY SHARP!

Find each product.

26. $4 \times \frac{2}{5}$ **27.** $\frac{2}{3} \times \frac{3}{4}$ **28.** $\frac{3}{8} \times 2\frac{1}{2}$ **29.** $1\frac{5}{6} \times \frac{3}{5}$ **30.** $2\frac{3}{8} \times 3$

 Algebra Readiness Copy and complete.

31. $6 \times (2 + 3) = (6 \times \blacksquare) + (6 \times \blacksquare)$ **32.** $4 \times (8 + 7) = (\blacksquare \times 8) + (\blacksquare \times 7)$

33. **Critical Thinking** Choose the correct answer. When you multiply two fractions that are both less than 1, the product is

ⓐ less than 1.   ⓑ less than the first fraction.

ⓒ less than the second fraction.   ⓓ all of these.

SECTION A
Review and Practice

Vocabulary Match each with its meaning.

1. centimeter
   a. one tenth of a meter
2. kilometer
   b. a unit of measure, a little more than a yard
3. meter
   c. one hundredth of a meter
4. millimeter
   d. one thousandth of a meter
5. decimeter
   e. one thousand meters

(Lesson 1) Choose the most appropriate unit of measure to estimate the length or height of each. Write mm, cm, dm, m, or km.

6. length of a hammer
7. length of a car
8. distance between cities
9. length of your finger
10. height of a house
11. length of a tick

(Lesson 2) Copy and complete.

12. 3 m = ▨ cm
13. 800 cm = ▨ m
14. 200 mm = ▨ cm
15. 7 dm = ▨ mm
16. 60 mm = ▨ cm
17. 6,000 mm = ▨ m
18. 5 m = ▨ dm
19. 8 dm = ▨ cm
20. 5 km = ▨ m
21. 100 mm = ▨ dm
22. 8 cm = ▨ mm
23. 70 km = ▨ m
24. 20 m = ▨ cm
25. 40 dm = ▨ mm
26. 9 km = ▨ m
27. 30 dm = ▨ m

(Lesson 3) Write each measurement in centimeters and then in meters.

28. 8 m 36 cm
29. 9 m 50 cm
30. 3 m 25 cm
31. 1 m 32 cm
32. 18 m 1 cm

(Lesson 4) Copy and complete.

33. 0.38 m = ▨ cm
34. 819 cm = ▨ m
35. 2.3 m = ▨ cm
36. 3.92 m = ▨ cm
37. 10.2 cm = ▨ m
38. 4.8 m = ▨ cm
39. 99.9 cm = ▨ m
40. 621 cm = ▨ m
41. 23.9 cm = ▨ m
42. 8.2 m = ▨ cm

43. **Journal** Explain why it is important to know how to change from one unit of measure to another. Use a real life situation as an example in your explanation.

Skills Checklist

In this section, you have:

☑ Explored Estimating and Measuring Length

☑ Learned About Millimeters, Centimeters, Meters, and Decimals

Exploring Perimeter and Area

Leigh wanted to grow an organic garden. When she told her grandfather, he agreed to give her some of his garden space.

How might measuring length be important when planning a garden?

Converting Units to Find Perimeter

Review multiplying mixed numbers.
Find each product. Simplify.

1. $2 \times 2\frac{3}{4}$ **2.** $4\frac{4}{5} \times 6$ **3.** $3\frac{1}{2} \times 7\frac{1}{2}$

4. $2\frac{1}{3} \times 4\frac{2}{3}$ **5.** $5\frac{1}{2} \times 1\frac{3}{8}$ **6.** $2\frac{4}{9} \times 3\frac{1}{3}$

Exploring Perimeter of Polygons

Explore

The distance around all the sides of a sheet of paper is its **perimeter**. The measure of its surface is its **area**.

Work Together

1. Measure and record the distance around a sheet of notebook paper to the nearest centimeter.

2. Cut the sheet of paper into 4 pieces using straight cuts. Tape the pieces together to form a new polygon. Make sure there are no gaps or overlaps.

3. Measure and record the perimeter of the new polygon you made.

Talk About It

4. Did the area of the paper change? Explain.

5. Did the perimeter of the paper change? Explain.

6. How could you make the perimeter of the paper still greater?

Connect

The **perimeter** of a polygon is the distance around the polygon.

You can find the perimeter of any polygon by adding the lengths of all its sides.

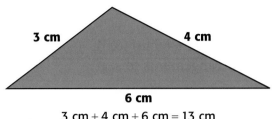

3 cm + 4 cm + 6 cm = 13 cm
Perimeter = 13 cm

You can find the perimeter of a **regular polygon** by multiplying the length of one side by the number of sides.

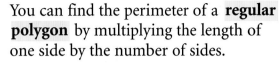
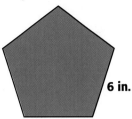

6 in. × 5 = 30 in.
Perimeter = 30 in.

Practice

Find each perimeter.

1.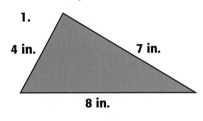
4 in. 7 in. 8 in.

2.
4 cm

3.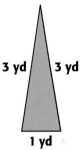
3 yd 3 yd 1 yd

4.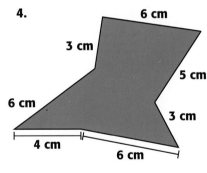
6 cm 3 cm 5 cm 6 cm 3 cm 4 cm 6 cm

5.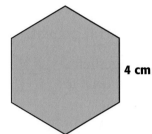
2 in. 3 in. 5 in. 5 in. 2 in. 7 in.

6.
2 ft

7. a regular octagon with sides 5 in.

8. a triangle with sides of 6 m, 10 m, and 12 m

9. a pentagon with sides of 4 cm, 5 cm, 4 cm, 6 cm, and 6 cm

10. an equilateral triangle with sides of 7 dm

11. a rectangle with sides of 3 m and 8 m

12. a pentagon with sides of 4 in., 8 in., 9 in., 5 in., and 5 in.

13. a triangle with sides of 5 dm, 7 dm, and 7 dm

14. a square with sides of 4 cm

15. **Journal** Explain how you would find the perimeter of your classroom. What unit of measure would you use?

Exploring Perimeter of Rectangles

Problem Solving Connection

- Draw a Picture
- Look for a Pattern
- Make a Table

Materials

- grid paper
- scissors

Problem Solving Hint

Organizing and recording your work in a table can help you find patterns.

Explore •

The Scrumptious Snack Bar uses small square tables for 4. They are put together in rectangular arrangements to seat groups of 5 or more.

Work Together

1. Find all possible table arrangements for a group of 12 people.

   a. Draw each arrangement on grid paper.

   b. Cut out each arrangement.

   c. Put the arrangements in order from least to greatest in area.

   d. Record the length, width, area, and perimeter of each table arrangement.

length (units)	width (units)	area (square units)	perimeter (units)
5	1	5	12

2. Find and record all possible table arrangements for a group of 16 people.

Talk About It

3. How is the perimeter of a rectangle related to its length and width?

4. How are the perimeter and area of rectangles related?

Connect

You can use a formula to help you find the perimeter of a rectangle.

The perimeter (*P*) of a rectangle equals 2 times the sum of the length (*l*) and the width (*w*).

$P = 2 \times (l + w)$

$P = 2 \times (10 + 5)$

$P = 2 \times 15$

$P = 30$ cm

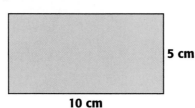

5 cm

10 cm

You can also use the Distributive Property:

$P = 2 \times l + 2 \times w$

$P = (2 \times 10) + (2 \times 5)$

$P = 20 + 10$

$P = 30$ cm

Practice

Find the perimeter of each rectangle.

1.

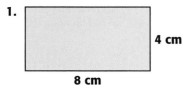

4 cm

8 cm

2.

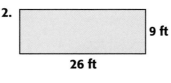

9 ft

26 ft

3.

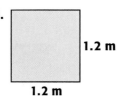

1.2 m

1.2 m

4. $l = 12$ ft
$w = 20$ ft

5. $l = 37$ mi
$w = 50$ mi

6. $l = 1.85$ cm
$w = 2.50$ cm

7. a square with sides of 14 in.

Estimation Estimate the perimeter of each rectangle.

8.

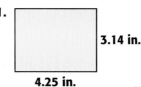

84 ft

289 ft

9.

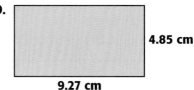

4.85 cm

9.27 cm

10.

2.61 m

7.8 m

11.

3.14 in.

4.25 in.

12. The tables for a banquet are arranged in a rectangular shape to seat 15 people along two sides and 18 people along two sides. How many people can be seated?

13. **Fine Arts** The WPA poster shown is on display at the Rochester Art Mart Exhibition. Its measures are 2 ft by 1 ft 2 in. What is its perimeter?

14. **Journal** Explain how to use a formula to find the perimeter of a rectangle 8 in. long and 10 in. wide.

The WPA founded in 1935 created jobs for builders and artists.

Converting Units to Find Perimeter

You Will Learn

how to find the perimeter of a rectangle when measurements are given in mixed units

Learn ● ● ● ● ● ● ● ● ● ●

To the bat house! Bill Holden and his students built bat houses to attract bats to the banks of the Mississippi River. The bats help control the mosquito population.

Each bat house was made from a board 8 in. wide, and 6 ft 2 in. long. What is the perimeter of this board?

Bill Holden and his students are from the Webster Open School in Minneapolis, Minnesota.

8 in.

6 ft 2 in.

A brown bat may eat half its weight in insects in one night.

Here are two ways to find the perimeter.

Remember

12 in. = 1 ft

36 in. = 1 yd

3 ft = 1 yd

One Way

$P = 2 \times (l + w)$

Add the length and width.

$$\begin{array}{r} 6 \text{ ft } 2 \text{ in.} \\ + \quad 8 \text{ in.} \\ \hline 6 \text{ ft } 10 \text{ in.} \end{array}$$

Multiply by 2.

$$\begin{array}{r} 6 \text{ ft } 10 \text{ in.} \\ \times 2 \\ \hline 12 \text{ ft } 20 \text{ in.} \end{array}$$

Change 20 in. to 1 ft 8 in.

12 ft 20 in. = 13 ft 8 in.

Perimeter = 13 ft 8 in.

Another Way

Change the measurements to inches before using the formula. Then change the perimeter back to feet and inches.

length: 6 ft 2 in. $= (6 \times 12) + 2$

$= 72 + 2$

$= 74$ in.

$P = 2 \times (l + w)$

$= 2 \times (74 + 8)$

$= 2 \times 82$

$= 164$ in.

$164 \div 12 = 13$ R8

164 in. = 13 ft 8 in.

Perimeter = 13 ft 8 in.

Little Brown Bat

You can also find the perimeter of a rectangle using fractions.

Example 2

Find the perimeter of a rectangle that is 2 yd 2 ft long and 1 yd 2 ft wide.

Step 1	Step 2	Step 3
Change the measurements.	Add the length and width.	Multiply by 2.

length	width
2 yd 2 ft = ▢ yd	1 yd 2 ft = ▢ yd
3 ft = 1 yd	
1 ft = $\frac{1}{3}$ yd	
2 ft = $\frac{2}{3}$ yd	
2 yd 2 ft = $2\frac{2}{3}$ yd	1 yd 2 ft = $1\frac{2}{3}$ yd

Step 2

$$2\frac{2}{3} \text{ yd}$$
$$+ 1\frac{2}{3} \text{ yd}$$
$$3\frac{4}{3} \text{ yd} = 4\frac{1}{3} \text{ yd}$$

Step 3

$$2 \times 4\frac{1}{3} \text{ yd} = 8\frac{2}{3} \text{ yd}$$
$$8\frac{2}{3} \text{ yd} = 8 \text{ yd 2 ft}$$

The perimeter is 8 yd 2 ft.

Talk About It

1. Describe how the methods on page 454 are alike. How are they different?

2. How could you have solved Example 2 using feet?

Check

Find each sum.

1. 6 ft + 8 ft 7 in.   2. 3 yd 1 ft + 5 yd 2 ft   3. 3 yd 2 ft + 1 yd 2 ft

Estimation Find each perimeter. Use estimation to check.

4.

5.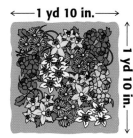

6. **Reasoning** Juan built a square frame. One of its sides is 2 ft 3 in. Does he have enough information to find its perimeter? Explain.

Skills and Reasoning

Find each sum.

7. 4 yd + 6 yd 2 ft   **8.** 2 yd 29 in. + 4 yd 7 in.   **9.** 3 ft 10 in. + 4 ft 2 in.

10. 2 yd 1 ft + 3 yd 2 ft   **11.** 1 ft 9 in. + 3 ft 8 in.   **12.** 6 yd 2 ft + 1 yd 2 ft

Find each product.

13. 2 × (3 ft 8 in.)   **14.** 4 × (6 yd 10 in.)   **15.** 3 × (3 yd 2 ft)

16. Find the perimeter of a dog run 20 ft 7 in. by 8 ft 3 in.   **17.** Find the perimeter of a hamster cage 1 ft 3 in. by 2 ft 5 in.

Find each perimeter.

18. a rectangular plot of farmland 1 mi 2,000 ft long and 2 mi 1,000 ft wide

19. a square window with sides of 2 ft 9 in.

20. a rectangular fountain 4 ft 10 in. long and 5 ft 1 in. wide

21. Which rectangle has the greater perimeter? Explain how you know.

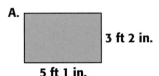

A.   3 ft 2 in.   5 ft 1 in.

B.   4 ft 7 in.   4 ft 9 in.

22. Marcus said the perimeter of a rectangle 3 ft 2 in. by 5 ft 11 in. is 9 ft 1 in. Is Marcus correct? Explain.

Problem Solving and Applications

23. **Using Data** Use the drawing of a bird sanctuary to help you solve each problem.

     a. There is a walkway that goes completely around the perimeter of the sanctuary. What is the length of the walkway?

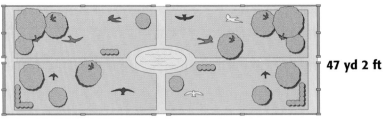

47 yd 2 ft

151 yd 2 ft

     b. The sanctuary is enclosed by a fence that has a 15 ft opening on 2 sides and a 7 ft opening on 2 sides. What is the length of the fence?

24. **Money** The cost of visiting a bird sanctuary is $2.50 per person. If an average of 400 people visit the sanctuary per day, how much is collected per 7-day week?

Problem Solving and CAREERS

An architect designs and draws plans for different kinds of buildings, including houses. An interior decorator helps people choose wall, floor, and window coverings for their homes or offices.

Maryland

Architect Patricia Hayes Parker, from Maryland, uses computers to develop scale models and diagrams.

Using Data Use the floor plan to find the perimeter of each room.

25. living room   26. dining room

27. kitchen   28. den

Wallpaper border comes in 15 ft rolls. How many rolls are needed to create a border around the ceiling in each room shown?

29. living room   30. dining room

31. kitchen   32. den

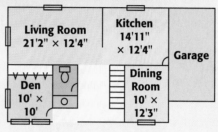

Living Room 21'2" × 12'4"	Kitchen 14'11" × 12'4" / Garage
Den 10' × 10'	Dining Room 10' × 12'3"

Architects write the dimensions of a space using symbols. For instance, 21'2" × 12'4" means a length of 21 ft 2 in. by a width of 12 ft 4 in.

33. **Journal** Explain which method you prefer for finding the perimeter.

Mixed Review and Test Prep

Algebra Readiness Copy and complete.

34. $600 \times n = 1,200$ 35. $3 \times n = 15,000$ 36. $72,000 \div n = 9,000$ 37. $n \div 5 = 400$

Using Data Use the mileage table to answer **38–40.**

	Albuquerque, NM	Atlanta, GA	Boston, MA	Charlotte, NC
Albuquerque, NM		1,409	2,236	1,665
Atlanta, GA	1,409		1,044	238
Boston, MA	2,236	1,044		864
Charlotte, NC	1,665	238	864	

38. How many miles is it round trip from Charlotte to Boston?

39. **What If** You live in Atlanta. You drive to Boston, then on to Charlotte, and straight back to Atlanta. How many miles did you travel?

40. **Time** Traveling at an average speed of 50 mi/hr, about how many hours would it take to drive from Atlanta to Albuquerque?

41. Choose the correct answer. $2\frac{1}{2} \times 3\frac{3}{4}$

Ⓐ $9\frac{3}{8}$ Ⓑ $\frac{2}{3}$ Ⓒ $6\frac{3}{8}$ Ⓓ $6\frac{1}{4}$ Ⓔ not here

Exploring Area of a Rectangle

Problem Solving Connection

■ Draw a Picture

■ Look for a Pattern

■ Make a Table

Materials
grid paper

Explore • • • • • • • • • • • • •

When Leigh was in sixth grade, she grew vegetables in a garden free from pesticides and herbicides.

Suppose you were going to plant a rectangular garden that covered 24 square feet. What might it look like?

Leigh lives in Wheaton, Maryland.

Maryland

Work Together

1. On grid paper, draw all possible outlines of your garden. Let each square represent 1 square foot (ft^2). Use whole squares only.

2. Record all possible measurements in a table.

3. Look for patterns in your table.

Length	Width	Area
6 ft	4 ft	24 ft²

Remember

Area is the measure of the surface of a region in square units.

Talk About It

4. How are all the rectangles you drew the same? Different?

5. What pattern is there in the length, width, and area of each rectangle?

6. If you know a rectangle's area, can you find its perimeter? Explain.

Rectangle	Square
You can use this formula to find the area of a rectangle. **Area = length × width** $A = l \times w$ $A = 10 \times 5$ $A = 50$ cm^2 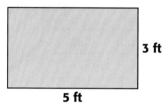 5 cm 10 cm	There is a special formula for the area of a square. $A = s \times s = s^2$ $A = s^2$ $A = 5^2$ $A = 25$ cm^2 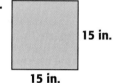 5 cm 5 cm

Math Tip

You can write square centimeters as cm^2.

Practice ●

Find the area of each rectangle or square.

1.
3 ft
5 ft

2.
15 in.
15 in.

3. $s = 28$ ft

4. $l = 9$ in.
$w = 7$ in.

5. $l = 2$ m
$w = 6.3$ m

6. $s = 12$ yd

7. $l = 8$ yd
$w = 4$ yd

8. $s = 6$ mi

9. $s = 12$ cm

10. $l = 1.5$ dm
$w = 7$ dm

11. $l = 3$ ft
$w = 8$ ft

12. $s = 7$ in.

13. $l = 5.4$ yd
$w = 10$ yd

14. $s = 4.5$ m

 15. Algebra Readiness A rectangle has an area of 125 cm^2 and a width of 5 cm. What is its length?

 16. Using Data Use the Data File on page 437.

    a. Geometry Which pen has the greatest area? The least area?

    b. Which shape has the greatest area?

17. What If You are building a pen with 40 ft of fencing. What length and width gives you the greatest area? What shape is this pen?

18. How many feet of fence would you need to build a dog pen 20 ft by 10 ft?

 19. Journal Make a sketch of a rectangular garden you might plant. Label its length and width. Explain how to find its area.

Problem Solving

Decision Making: **Choose a Pet**

Explore •

You Will Learn

how to use facts and data to help you make a decision

Your family has agreed to allow you to get a pet. You love both dogs and cats, but must choose only one. There are many things you need to think about before you decide.

You have to consider:

- the amount of money each pet will cost once you have it.

- the amount of time you will need to spend with each pet.

- the amount of space each pet will need.

Facts and Data		
Things to Think About	**Dog**	**Cat**
Daily cost of food	$1.50	$1.00
Monthly cost of other items	$5.00	$6.00
Minimum daily time needed for care	10 min morning 20 min evening	15 min
Space required	4 ft by 2 ft bed in shape of rectangle	2 ft by 3 ft litter box
Expected life span	12 yr	18 yr

Both pets are free.

Your family will take care of large expenses and give you some money each week for your pet. You will have to pay the rest of the weekly expenses from money you earn.

The responsibility for taking care of the pet will be yours.

You must leave for school no later than 7:45 A.M. You get home at 3:30 P.M.

Work Together

▶ **Understand**

1. What decision do you have to make?

2. What information do you have to help you decide?

3. What other things are important to you in making this decision?

▶ **Plan and Solve**

4. What is the difference in monthly costs between the two pets? (Use 4 7-day weeks as 1 month.)

5. If your parents give you $5 each week, how much will you need to contribute each month?

6. What is the difference in time needed each week for the two pets?

7. What is the difference in the amount of space taken up by a dog's bed and a cat's litter box? Is the difference important?

8. Do you think you will have to spend more time some weeks than others taking care of your pet? Explain.

9. What is the latest you could take your dog out for a walk each morning?

▶ **Make a Decision**

10. List the factors you considered in order of their importance to you. Begin with the most important.

11. Is the decision you made in line with the factors you think are important?

12. Write an explanation of how having a pet will change your daily schedule.

▶ **Present Your Decision**

13. Tell the class your decision and your reasons for making it.

14. What was the most difficult part of making a decision?

PROBLEM SOLVING PRACTICE

Review and Practice

Vocabulary Change one word in each statement to make the statement true.

1. To find the area of a polygon you must add the lengths of all its sides.

2. The perimeter of a polygon is measured in square units.

(Lessons 5–7) Find each perimeter.

3.
5 in.   4 in.
8 in.

4.
12 cm

5.   8 mm
3 mm

6.   11 ft
5 ft

7.
$\frac{1}{2}$ in.

8.   12 ft 5 in.
6 ft 8 in.

9.   4 yd 2 ft
3 yd 2 ft

10.   8 yd 1 ft
6 yd 1 ft

(Lesson 8) Find each area.

11.
$7\frac{3}{8}$ in.
4 in.

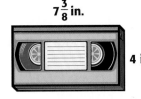

12.
$6\frac{1}{2}$ ft
$9\frac{1}{3}$ ft

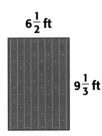

13.   4.1 cm

14. A builder wants to build on an area of 400 ft². What length and width could give that area?

15. Christine is planning to build a treehouse. She has a piece of plywood measuring 4 ft by 8 ft. If she uses this wood as the floor, what will the area of the treehouse floor be?

16. Sunset Park has a rectangular sandbox measuring 12 ft by 9 ft. Rolling Meadow Park has a rectangular sandbox that is 10 ft by 11 ft. Which park has the larger sandbox?

17. **Journal** Is the area of a 12 in. × 6 in. rectangle equal to 6 ft² or $\frac{1}{2}$ ft²? Explain how you know.

Skills Checklist

In this section, you have:

☑ Explored Perimeter of Polygons

☑ Explored Perimeter of Rectangles

☑ Converted Units to Find Perimeter

☑ Explored Area of Rectangles

☑ Solved Problems by Making Decisions

Finding Area and Perimeter

Some restaurants now have dogs as their diners. It's OK for a dog to eat at the table! Look at the picture. If you placed another table next to the one shown, how many pooches could party?

Skills Checklist

In this section, you will:

☐ **Explore Area of Triangles**

☐ **Explore Area of Other Polygons**

☐ **Explore Area of Parallelograms**

☐ **Explore Algebra by Balancing Equations**

☐ **Solve Problems by Looking for a Pattern**

☐ **Explore Circumference**

Finding Area and Perimeter

Review multiplication and addition.
Find each product or sum.

1. 17×3 2. $\frac{1}{2} \times 78$ 3. 8×19

4. $12 + 8 + 12 + 8$ 5. $15 + 13 + 15 + 13$

6. $4 + 8 + 4 + 8$ 7. $5 + 3 + 5 + 3$

Exploring Area of Right Triangles

Problem Solving Connection

■ Use Objects/ Act It Out

■ Look for a Pattern

■ Make a Table

Materials

■ geoboard

■ rubber bands

■ dot paper

Vocabulary

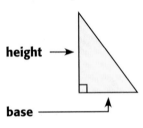

height →

base

Explore •

How can you use what you know about the area of rectangles to find the area of right triangles?

Right triangle

Right angle →

Work Together

1. Make a rectangle on a geoboard.

2. Form two triangles within the rectangle by stretching a rubber band from one corner of the rectangle to another.

3. Check that the two triangles are the same size.

4. How does the size of the triangles compare with the size of the rectangles?

5. Record your findings in a table.

Length of rectangle (units)	Width of rectangle (units)	Area of rectangle (units²)	Area of each triangle (units²)

6. Repeat Steps 1–5. Make two different-sized rectangles.

Remember
Dividing by 2 is the same as multiplying by $\frac{1}{2}$.

Talk About It

7. Use your table to compare the length and width of each rectangle with the area of its triangles. Describe any pattern you see.

8. How would you find the area of the shaded triangle?

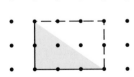

Connect

You can use the **base** and **height** to find the area of a right triangle.

Area of a Rectangle

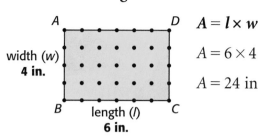

$A = l \times w$

$A = 6 \times 4$

$A = 24 \text{ in}^2$

The area is 24 in².

Area of a Right Triangle

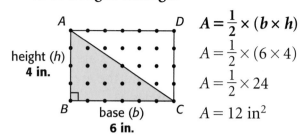

$A = \frac{1}{2} \times (b \times h)$

$A = \frac{1}{2} \times (6 \times 4)$

$A = \frac{1}{2} \times 24$

$A = 12 \text{ in}^2$

The area is 12 in².

The area of triangle *ABC* is half the area of rectangle *ABCD*.

Practice

Find the area of each shaded triangle. Use dot paper or a geoboard to help.

1.

2.

3.

4.

5.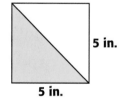

5 in.
5 in.

6.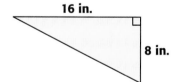

12 ft
20 ft

7.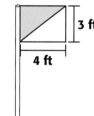

3 ft
4 ft

8.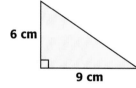

6 cm
9 cm

9.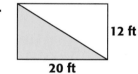

16 in.
8 in.

10.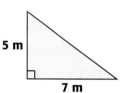

5 m
7 m

11. **What If** A triangle has a base of 4 in. and an area of 12 in². Would all right triangles with a base of 4 in. have the same area? Explain.

12. **Math History** Egyptians made right triangles by stretching an evenly knotted rope. What is the area of this right triangle?

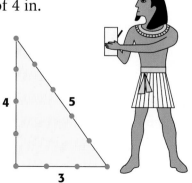

4   5

3

13. **Journal** Explain how you would find the area of a right triangle with a base of 7 ft and a height of 4 ft.

Exploring Area of Triangles

Problem Solving Connection

Use Objects/ Act It Out

Materials

- grid paper
- colored marker or pencil
- scissors

Remember

Perpendicular line segments form right angles where they meet.

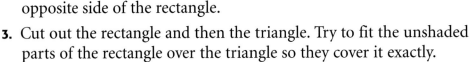
Explore

Not all triangles are right triangles. You can find the area of other kinds of triangles.

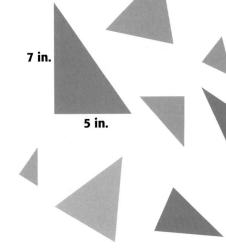

7 in.

5 in.

Work Together

1. Draw a rectangle on grid paper.

2. Draw and shade a triangle inside the rectangle. Make one side of the rectangle the triangle's base. The triangle should come to a point somewhere on the opposite side of the rectangle.

3. Cut out the rectangle and then the triangle. Try to fit the unshaded parts of the rectangle over the triangle so they cover it exactly.

4. Draw two new rectangles, one smaller and one larger than the original. Follow Steps 2–3 again.

Talk About It

5. How does the area of each triangle you drew compare to the area of its rectangle? How do you know?

6. How could you find the area of any triangle?

Connect

You can use the formula $A = \frac{1}{2} \times (b \times h)$ to find the area of any triangle.

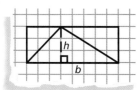

$A = \frac{1}{2} \times (b \times h)$

$A = \frac{1}{2} \times (7 \times 4)$

$A = \frac{1}{2} \times (28)$

$A = 14 \text{ in}^2$

The area is 14 in².

Math Tip
The height is always perpendicular to the base.

$A = \frac{1}{2} \times (b \times h)$

$A = \frac{1}{2} \times (3 \times 10)$

$A = \frac{1}{2} \times 30$

$A = 15 \text{ cm}^2$

The area is 15 cm².

Practice

Find each area.

1.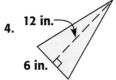

2.

3.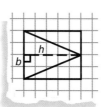

4.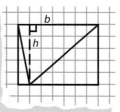

5.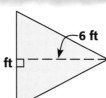

6.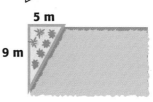

7.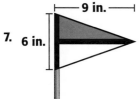

8.

9.

10. **Mental Math** Find the area of a triangle with a base of 6 in. and a height of 4 in.

11. Triangle A has a base of 5 ft and a height of 6 ft. Triangle B has a base of 7 ft and a height of 4 ft. Which triangle has the greater area?

12. **Social Studies** The Washington Monument was completed in 1884 in Washington, D.C., to honor George Washington. To the nearest foot, it is 555 ft tall. The top of the monument forms a small pyramid. What is the area of each triangular face of the pyramid?

13. **Journal** Make a sketch of a triangle that has an area of 8 in². Label the length of the base and height. Explain how you know the area is 8 in².

Exploring Area of Other Polygons

Problem Solving Connection

Use Objects/
Act It Out

Materials

■ geoboard

■ rubber bands

■ dot paper

Explore •

You can use a geoboard to find the area of other figures.

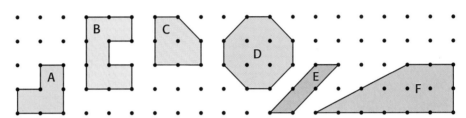

Area = 1 square unit

Area = $\frac{1}{2}$ square unit

Work Together

1. Find the area of each polygon.

a. Copy each figure on your geoboard.

b. Find the number of square units each figure covers.

2. Make figures with the areas listed below. Draw each on dot paper.

a. 10 square units

b. 6 square units

c. 8 square units

Problem Solving Hint

To help find the area of some polygons on a geoboard, try building rectangles around them.

Talk About It

3. How did you find the areas of the figures with square corners?

4. How did you find the areas of the triangles?

Connect

To find the area of a figure, you can trace the figure on dot paper and count the square units it covers.

The area of this polygon is 4 square units.

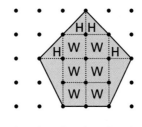

This pentagon covers 6 whole squares and 4 half squares. 4 halves make 2 wholes. The 2 remaining pieces each form a whole. So, the area of this pentagon is 10 square units.

Practice

Find each area.

1.

2.

3.

4.

5.

6.

7.

8.

9. Order the figures from least to greatest area.

10. Order the figures from greatest to least area.

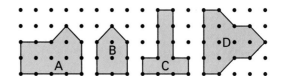

On dot paper, draw a figure with each area.

11. 4 square units

12. 6 square units

13. $1\frac{1}{2}$ square units

14. 3 square units

15. $5\frac{1}{2}$ square units

16. 7 square units

17. **Journal** On dot paper, draw two figures. Make one drawing with only square corners. Explain how to find the area of each polygon.

Exploring Area of Parallelograms

Problem Solving Connection

- Use Objects/ Act It Out

- Look for a Pattern

Materials

- grid paper

- scissors

Explore •

Some parallelograms are also rectangles. How can you use what you know about the area of a rectangle to find the area of any parallelogram?

Work Together

1. Copy parallelogram A with the dotted line on grid paper.

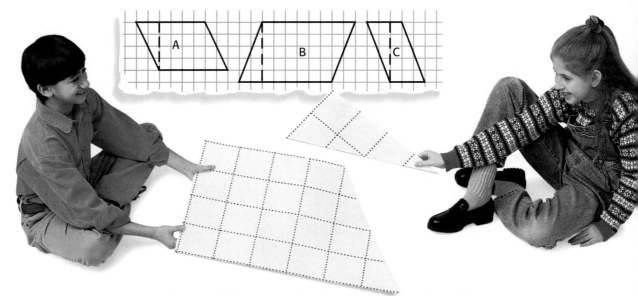

2. Cut out the parallelogram. Then cut along the dotted line.

3. Move the triangular piece to the other side of the larger piece to make a new quadrilateral. What new figure did you make?

4. What is the area of the new figure?

5. Repeat Steps 1–4 for parallelograms B and C.

Remember

A parallelogram is a quadrilateral whose opposite sides are parallel and of equal lengths.

Talk About It

6. How do the length and width of each figure you made compare to the base and height of the parallelogram you started with? How do you know?

7. How does the area of each figure you made compare to the area of the parallelogram you started with? How do you know?

8. How could you find the area of this parallelogram?

Connect

You can use a formula to find the area of any parallelogram.

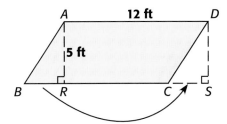

Slide $\triangle ABR$ to $\triangle DCS$
Area of rectangle $ARSD$
$A = 12 \times 5$
$A = 60$ ft^2

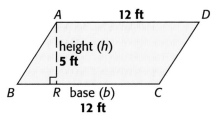

You can use this formula
to find area:
$A = b \times h$
$A = 12 \times 5$
$A = 60$ ft^2

Practice

Find each area.

1.
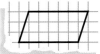

2.

3.
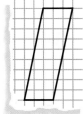

4.
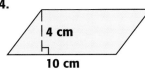
4 cm
10 cm

5.

20 in.
12 in.

6.
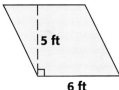
5 ft
6 ft

 Algebra Readiness Find each missing base or height.

7.
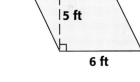
h
8 m
$A = 16$ m^2

8.
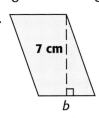
7 cm
b
$A = 35$ cm^2

9.
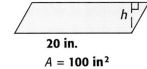
h
20 in.
$A = 100$ in^2

10. Parallelogram A has a base of 15 ft and a height of 12 ft. Parallelogram B has a base of 14 ft and a height of 13 ft. Which parallelogram has the lesser area?

11. Yin found that the area of a parallelogram with a base of 10 in. and a height of 12 in. was 22 in^2. Explain what mistake she made and give the correct area.

 12. **Journal** Draw and label a parallelogram that has a base of 4 cm and a height of 3 cm. Draw and label another parallelogram that has a base of 5 cm and a height of 2 cm. Explain which parallelogram has the greater area. How do you know?

Exploring Algebra: Balancing Equations

Explore • • • • • • • • • • • • • • • •

An equation balances when the value of the left side equals the value of the right side. You can use an equation workmat and counters to show the values.

Work Together

1. Make an equation workmat.

2. Work with your partner to show $n + 3 = 12$.

   a. One person places counters on the right side of the mat. That person places the same number of counters on the left side, hiding some of the counters in an envelope.

   b. The partner guesses how many counters are in the envelope.

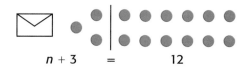

$$n + 3 \quad = \quad 12$$

Math Tip

When you have two envelopes, divide the counters into two equal groups.

3. Work with your partner to show $n + n$ or $2 \times n = 10$.

4. Take turns solving the following equations for n. Keep a record of your work.

   a. $n + 5 = 13$ b. $6 + n = 11$ c. $n + n = 16$

   d. $2 \times n = 22$ e. $n + n = 18$ f. $2 \times n = 26$

$$\begin{aligned} n + n \\ \text{or} \\ 2 \times n \end{aligned} \quad = \quad 10$$

Talk About It

How did you decide on the number of counters in the envelopes for the two types of equations? What operations did you use?

Connect ●

You can write equations to show what is happening when you find the number of counters in an envelope.

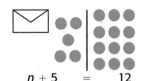 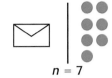   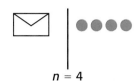

$n + 5$ =   12 $n = 7$ $2 \times n$ =   8 $n = 4$

Find the value of n.
Subtract 5 from both sides.
$n + 5 - 5 = 12 - 5$
            $n = 7$
Check. $7 + 5 = 12$
7 is the correct value for n.

Find the value of n.
Divide both sides by 2.
$(2 \times n) \div 2 = 8 \div 2$
                $n = 4$
Check. $2 \times 4 = 8$
4 is the correct value for n.

Practice ●

Use counters to find the number of counters in each envelope.

1.

$7 + n$ =   15

2.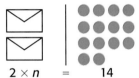

$2 \times n$ =   14

3.

9   = $4 + n$

4.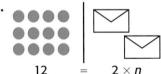

12   = $2 \times n$

5.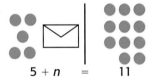

$5 + n$ =   11

6.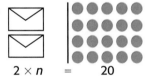

$2 \times n$ =   20

Match each equation with its model. Then find the value of n.

7. $n + 7 = 21$

8. $2 \times n = 16$

9. $n + 3 = 11$

10. $2 \times n = 26$

a.

b.

c.

d.

11. Write Your Own Problem Write an equation using the variable n. Have a partner find the value of n.

12. Critical Thinking Use counters or draw a picture to show $(2 \times n) + 5 = 13$.

13. Journal Describe how you can find the value of n using counters for $2 \times n = 14$.

Problem Solving

Analyze Strategies:
Look for a Pattern

You Will Learn

how to solve problems using a pattern

Learn • • • • • • • • • •

Misha's restaurant serves very special clients—dogs! People can bring their pooch pals for treats they love to eat.

Sandy called ahead to make a reservation for her dog Belle and 9 of Belle's friends. Misha wants to put tables in a long row. How many tables will he need to line up?

Work Together

▶ **Understand**

What information do you have?

What do you need to find?

▶ **Plan**

How can you organize your information?

Make a data table and look for a pattern in the numbers.

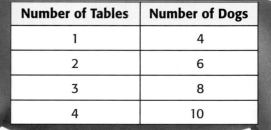

▶ **Solve**

Continue the pattern to see how many tables are needed for 10 dogs. Write the answer.

Number of Tables	Number of Dogs
1	4
2	6
3	8
4	10

4 tables are needed for 10 dogs.

▶ **Look Back**

How can you check your answer?

Talk About It

1. Describe the pattern you see in your list.

2. How does making an organized list help you solve the problem?

Check

Look for a pattern to solve the problem.

1. The City Cafe has tables like the one shown here. How many people can be seated if 5 tables are placed end to end?

   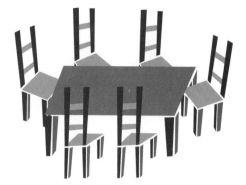

   a. How many people can be seated at 1 table?

   b. How many people can be seated if 2 tables are connected end to end? 3 tables?

   c. Make an organized list of the information you have so far. Is there a pattern?

   d. Continue the pattern. How many people can be seated at 7 tables?

Problem Solving Practice

Look for a pattern or use any strategy to help solve each problem.

2. The school lunchroom has tables that seat 8 students. How many students can be seated if 6 tables are put end to end?

   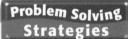

3. **Estimation** City Cafe uses about 35 loaves of bread daily. About how many loaves should they order for the week if they are closed Monday? Should they overestimate or underestimate?

4. **Time** Misha asks people with reservations to arrive at least 15 min early. The Jacobsons have a reservation for 7:00 P.M. It takes them 30 min to travel to the restaurant. If they need 1 hr 30 min to get ready to leave, what is the latest they should start to get ready?

5. **Geography** A number of interesting places to visit in Philadelphia are located along the Benjamin Franklin Parkway. City Hall is about 1.25 mi southwest of the Philadelphia Museum of Art. The Franklin Institute and the Free Library, located around Logan Circle, are 0.5 mi northeast of City Hall. How far is it from Logan Circle to the Museum of Art?

Problem Solving Strategies

- Use Objects/Act It Out
- Draw a Picture
- Look for a Pattern
- Guess and Check
- Use Logical Reasoning
- Make an Organized List
- Make a Table
- Solve a Simpler Problem
- Work Backward

Choose a Tool

PROBLEM SOLVING PRACTICE

The Philadelphia Museum of Art contains over 500,000 works of art.

Exploring Circumference

Problem Solving Connection

- Use Objects/ Act It Out
- Look for a Pattern
- Make a Table

Materials

- compass
- string
- metric ruler or metric measuring tape

Vocabulary

Circle Terms
diameter
circumference
chord
radius

Did You Know?

The original Ferris wheel was built in 1893. Its diameter was 250 ft, and it could carry 2,160 passengers at a time!

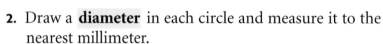

Explore • • • • • • • • • • • • • •

You have learned how to find the distance around, or perimeter of, polygons. You can also find the distance around, or the **circumference** of a circle.

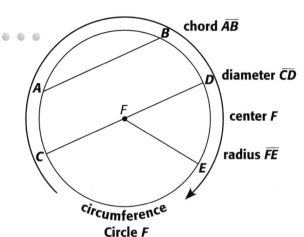

chord $\overline{AB}$
diameter $\overline{CD}$
center F
radius $\overline{FE}$
circumference
Circle F

Work Together

1. Use a compass to draw several different-sized circles.

2. Draw a **diameter** in each circle and measure it to the nearest millimeter.

3. Place a string around each circle. Measure the string to the nearest millimeter to find the circumference.

4. Record your measurements in a table. Look for a pattern.

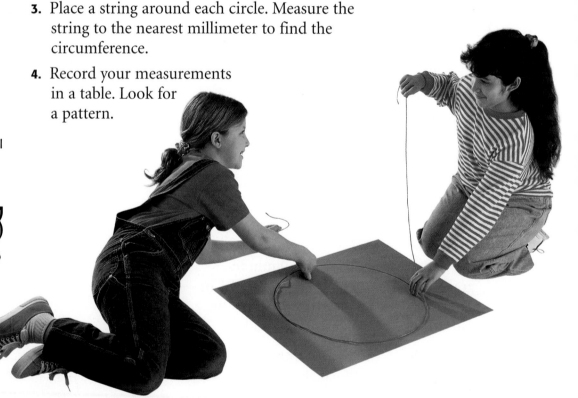

Talk About It

5. What pattern, if any, did you find in your table?

6. Estimate the distance around this circle. Explain your thinking.

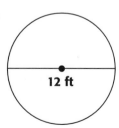

12 ft

Connect

The circumference of a circle is greater than its diameter. It is always the same number of times as great. This number is called *pi* and is represented by the symbol π. ($\pi \approx 3.14$) You can find the circumference by multiplying π times the diameter. ($C = \pi \times d$)

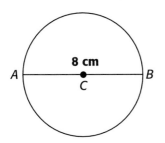

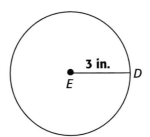

$C = \pi \times d$
$= 3.14 \times 8$
$= 25.12$ cm

The circumference is 25.12 cm.

$C = 2 \times \pi \times r$
$= 2 \times 3.14 \times 3$
$= 18.84$ in.

The circumference is 18.84 in.

Math Tip
The length of the diameter is 2 times the radius, so $d = 2 \times r$.

Practice

Find each circumference. Use 3.14 for π.

1.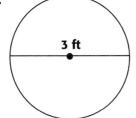
3 ft

2.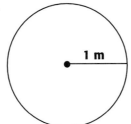
1 m

3.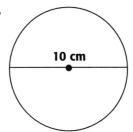
10 cm

4. $d = 6$ cm   5. $r = 4$ ft   6. $d = 1$ in.   7. $r = 10$ mm

Find each diameter to the nearest hundredth. Use 3.14 for π.

8. $C = 20$ ft   9. $C = 6$ cm   10. $C = 40$ mm   11. $C = 17$ in.

Find each radius to the nearest hundredth. Use 3.14 for π.

12. $C = 50$ m   13. $C = 9$ in.   14. $C = 62$ mm   15. $C = 4$ ft

Using Data Use the Data File on page 437 to answer **16** and **17**.

16. **Mental Math** Without calculating, write which carousel has the greatest circumference. How do you know?

17. Find the circumference of each carousel. Order them from least to greatest.

18. **Journal** Suppose you set your compass opening at 2 in. and drew a circle. Explain how you would find the circumference of the circle.

The Glen Echo Park carousel is located in Rock Hall, Maryland.

SECTION C
Review and Practice

Vocabulary Match each with its example.

1. $\overline{RW}$
2. $\overline{AB}$
3. $\overline{FE}$
4. $\overline{CD}$
5. $\overline{ST}$

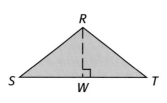

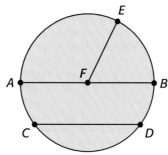

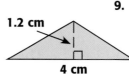

Word List	
base	height
chord	radius
diameter	

(Lessons 10–13) Find the area of each figure.

6.

7.

8.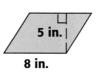
1.2 cm
4 cm

9.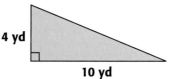
4 yd
10 yd

10.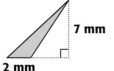
7 mm
2 mm

11. 10 ft
24 ft

12. 5 in.
8 in.

13.
13 m 7 m

(Lesson 14) Find the value of *n*. You may use counters to help.

14.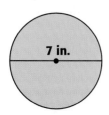
$n + 5 = 10$

15.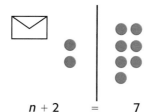
$n + 2 = 7$

16.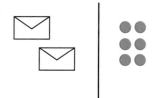
$n \times 2 = 6$

(Lesson 16) Find each circumference. Use 3.14 for π.

17. 7 in.

18. 9 yd

(Lesson 15) Use the drawing to answer **19**.

19. **Journal** Explain how you can use patterns to find how many tables you would need to seat 50 people.

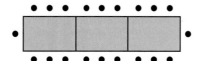

REVIEW AND PRACTICE

YOUR CHOICE

Choose at least one. Use what you have learned in this chapter.

1 Tangram Tables

Make at least 4 rectangular tables using tangram pieces. Trace the tables onto dot paper. Find the area and perimeter of each table. If one person needs one unit of space at the edge of the table, how many people can sit around each table?

2 Interior Designs

At Home Work with a member of your family to create a floor plan for the rooms of a floor of your house or apartment. Measure each wall at its base and record the length. Make a sketch of each room and find the area and perimeter of each floor.

3 Desk Diagram

Draw a diagram of your desk. Measure each dimension to the nearest inch and label it in your drawing. What's the area of your desktop?

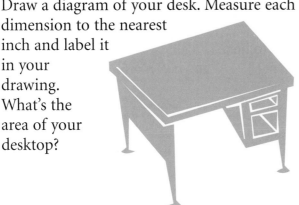

4 Millimeters, Centimeters, and Meters

Just how long is a giraffe's neck? An elephant's trunk? Find out more about an animal that interests you. Start prowling at **www.mathsurf.com/5/ch10**. Look for data expressed in meters. Then change it into millimeters and centimeters.

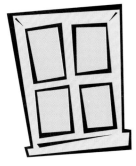

5 Triangles, Circles, and Squares . . . Oh My!

Search your classroom for different shapes, such as squares, rectangles, triangles, circles, and other polygons. Use what you have learned to measure the perimeter, area, and/or circumference of these different shapes.

CHAPTER 10
Review/Test

Vocabulary Choose the word that best fits each statement.

1. The (circumference, chord) of a circle is the distance around a circle.

2. The (perimeter, height) of a triangle is perpendicular to its base.

(Lessons 1–4) Copy and complete.

3. 8 m = ■ cm   **4.** 12 mm = ■ cm   **5.** 235 cm = ■ m   **6.** 8 m 13 cm = ■ m

(Lessons 5–7) Find the perimeter of each polygon.

7.  2 yd 1 ft / 1 yd ½ ft

8. 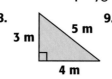 3 m, 5 m, 4 m

9. 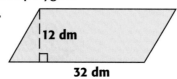 2 ft 2 ft / 6 ft 6 ft

10. 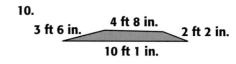 3 ft 6 in. / 4 ft 8 in. / 2 ft 2 in. / 10 ft 1 in.

11. a rectangle with a length of 15 cm and a width of 8 cm

12. a square whose sides have a length of 12 feet

(Lessons 8, 10–13) Find the area of each polygon.

13. 5 m / 16 m

14. 12 dm / 32 dm

15.

16. Find the area of a right triangle with a 12 ft base and a height of 6.5 ft.

(Lesson 14) Find the value of *n*. You may use counters to help.

17. $n + 3 = 11$ **18.** $n + 12 = 21$ **19.** $2 \times n = 14$ **20.** $n + n = 6$

(Lesson 15) Use the drawing to answer **21.**

21. A restaurant manager is planning the seating arrangements for a banquet. She can seat 6 people at one table. She plans to pull tables together end to end. How many tables will she need to seat 25 people?

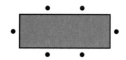

(Lesson 16) Find the circumference of each circle. Use 3.14 for π.

22. 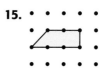 3 cm

23. 8 dm

24. 4.8 in.

25. A gardener wants to put a circular border of flowers around his flag pole. He wants the flowers 2.3 ft from the pole. About how many feet will the border of flowers be?

Performance Assessment

Use what you've learned about squares, rectangles, triangles, parallelograms, circles, and other polygons to design some furniture and other home needs for a pet of your choice. How about a new blanket and bed for a dog? An improved litter box for a kitty? A fancy water dish for a turtle? The possibilities are endless!

1. **Decision Making** Decide what item you want to design for a pet. Decide what shapes you will use in your design and what measurements they should be.

2. **Recording** Make a list showing shape, dimensions, area, and perimeter of your item. Make a drawing of your design. You may wish to use grid paper or dot paper to help represent your dimensions, like the cat pillow design shown.

3. **Explain Your Thinking** How did you decide on an item? Why did you choose the shapes and sizes you did? How did you decide on a unit of measure?

4. **Critical Thinking** How do you know that the dimensions you selected are reasonable?

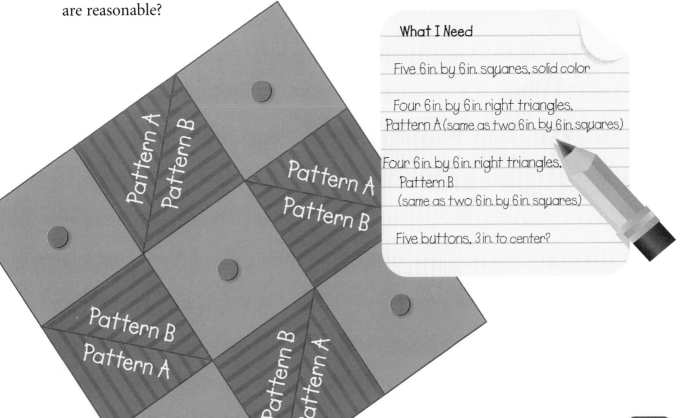

What I Need

Five 6 in. by 6 in. squares, solid color

Four 6 in. by 6 in. right triangles, Pattern A (same as two 6 in. by 6 in. squares)

Four 6 in. by 6 in. right triangles, Pattern B (same as two 6 in. by 6 in. squares)

Five buttons, 3 in. to center?

Math Magazine

Elbow Room Animals travel over great distances for food, water, and shelter. You probably know that many birds migrate from north to south when the weather gets colder. Most animals do not travel far, but roam over a somewhat smaller area.

Animal	Area Covered (mi²)
Black Bear	8–15
Eagle	20–60
Elephant	100
Gorilla	2–15
Gray Wolf	100–260
Grizzly Bear	10–12
Jaguar	7–176
Lion	15–100
Tiger	25–250

Wild animals, especially those native to areas where the weather changes little, generally roam over an area where the boundaries might be mountains, rivers, lakes, or valleys. The table shows how much territory each animal covers.

Exactly how far each individual animal will travel depends on the availability of food and water, the number of enemies also occupying that area, and the weather.

Try These!

1. Look at the table. Which animal or animals might cover this area?

```
┌─────────────────────────────┐ 3 mi
└─────────────────────────────┘
        50 mi
```

2. Select two animals from the table. Draw a rectangle that shows an area each one might cover.

Test Prep Strategy: Work Backward From an Answer

Replace missing number with each choice.

The area of a triangle is 25 cm². If the base is 5, what is the height of the triangle?

Ⓐ 5 cm Ⓑ 8 cm Ⓒ 9 cm Ⓓ 10 cm

You know that $\frac{1}{2} \times$ (base × height) gives the area. Sometimes working backward from an answer is faster. Take each choice and try it in the formula until you get the area of 25 cm². $\frac{1}{2} \times$ (5 × height). The only choice that works is 10 cm, or Ⓓ.

Write the letter of the correct answer. Use any strategy.

1. Elias, Sally, and Jerome bought a raffle ticket together and won. How much will each of them get if the prize was $198?

   Ⓐ $66 Ⓑ $56 Ⓒ $103 Ⓓ $6.60

2. Which is not a true statement?

   Ⓐ $3.8 \times 100 > 380 \div 100$ Ⓑ $5.2 \div 1,000 = 0.052 \div 10$
   Ⓒ $16.5 \div 2 < 18 \div 3$ Ⓓ $7.6 \times 10 < 7,600 \div 10$

3. The height of a triangle is twice as great as its base. If the base is 8 m, what is the area of the triangle?

   Ⓐ 4 m² Ⓑ 16 cm² Ⓒ 64 m² Ⓓ 16 m²

4. The circumference of a circle is 18.84 feet. What is the diameter of the circle? Use 3.14 for π.

   Ⓐ 1 ft Ⓑ 3 ft Ⓒ 6 ft Ⓓ not here

5. How much change would you receive from a twenty-dollar bill if you owed $18.65?

   Ⓐ $2.45 Ⓑ $1.35 Ⓒ $10.35 Ⓓ $20.45

6. What is the perimeter of a backyard with sides measuring 8 yd 2 ft, 20 yd 1 ft, 16 yd 2 ft, and 32 yd?

   Ⓐ 77 yd Ⓑ 77 yd 2 ft Ⓒ 81 yd Ⓓ 77 ft

7. Josh's test grades in history are 75 and 80. What grade must he get on his next test so that his average is an 85?

   Ⓐ 80 Ⓑ 90 Ⓒ 95 Ⓓ 100

8. Which number is not divisible by 3?

   Ⓐ 36 Ⓑ 111 Ⓒ 123 Ⓓ 46

Test Prep Strategies

- Read Carefully
- Follow Directions
- Make Smart Choices
- Eliminate Choices
- Work Backward From an Answer

Chapter 11
Measurement

THINGS TO BUILD

SECTION **A**

**Mayan
Monument
Page 487**

Understanding Solids and Shapes

Pyramids come in many shapes! They are named by the shape of their bases.

What geometric figures do you see in the pyramid to the left?

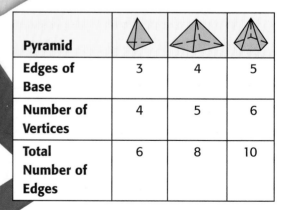

Pyramid			
Edges of Base	3	4	5
Number of Vertices	4	5	6
Total Number of Edges	6	8	10

487

Understanding Weight, Mass, and Temperature

The first known thermometer was invented by Italian astronomer Galileo in 1593. In 1714, German physicist Gabriel Fahrenheit developed the more accurate mercury thermometer.

Which is warmer: room temperature or body temperature?

SECTION

C

Celsius	Fahrenheit
Water boils 100°C	Water boils 212°F
Body temperature 37°C	Body temperature 98.6°F
Room temperature 22.2°C	Room temperature 72°F
Water freezes 0°C	Water freezes 32°F

499

Soap Box Derby
Page 499

507

A Measurable Difference
Page 507

Understanding Volume and Capacity

A shipping service makes boxes in the sizes shown in the table. Which could you use to ship a 16 in. × 16 in. × 12 in. treasure box you made?

	Box Dimensions (in.)		
	Length	**Width**	**Height**
Box A	12	12	12
Box B	18	12	12
Box C	22	18	12

Surfing the World Wide Web!

What do you like to make or build? Find out more information about the things people build and construct at **www.mathsurf.com/5/ch11**.

TEAM PROJECT
TURN UP THE VOLUME

Materials
Power Solids (prism, pyramid, cone, cylinder, sphere), rice, or sand

Just visit the freezer section of a grocery store and you'll see containers in many different shapes. Which of the shapes has the greatest volume? Unusual shapes can make it difficult to tell, but if you know the volumes of regular solids you can use them to compare and estimate.

Make a Plan

- How will you measure and compare the volumes of the solids?
- How will you determine if special relationships between volumes exist?

Carry It Out

1. Use rice to measure the volume of each Power Solid.

2. Order the solids from least to greatest volume.

3. What is true about the areas of the bases of the prism and the pyramid? The heights?

4. What is true about the areas of the bases of the cone and the cylinder? The heights?

5. Estimate the number of pyramids full of rice it will take to fill the prism. Estimate the number of cones of rice it will take to fill the cylinder.

6. Compare the volumes.

    a. prism and pyramid   **b.** cone and cylinder

Talk About It

- Do any volumes of the solids show a special relationship? Explain.
- Why is it important to compare solids with the same bases?

Present the Project

Plan a class presentation of the results. Did all teams order the solids in the same way? If not, why? What, if any, relationships among volumes did teams notice?

A Understanding Solids and Shapes

The Maya built huge pyramids with temples on top like this one in Tikal, Guatemala.

What geometric shapes can you find in this pyramid?

GET READY!

Exploring Surface Area

Review area of polygons. Find each area.

1. a rectangle with $l = 4$ yd and $w = 3$ yd

2. a triangle with $h = 12$ cm and $b = 8$ cm

3. a parallelogram with $b = 4\frac{1}{2}$ ft and $h = 3\frac{1}{3}$ ft

Skills Checklist

In this section, you will:

☐ Explore Solids

☐ Explore Patterns with Solids

☐ Explore Nets

☐ Explore Surface Area

☐ Solve Problems by Making Decisions

Exploring Solids

Explore • • • • • • • •

Solid geometric figures are everywhere around us. Two examples are the **pyramid** and the **prism**.

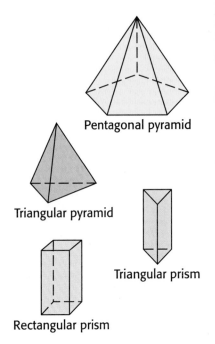

Pentagonal pyramid

Triangular pyramid

Triangular prism

Rectangular prism

Mayan pyramid in Guatemala. Built in A.D. 500.

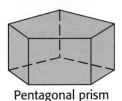

Rectangular pyramid

Pentagonal prism

Work Together

Use Power Solids to explore prisms and pyramids.

1. Choose a Power Solid. Suppose your Power Solid is a large building.

   a. Draw how it would look if you were seeing it from above.

   b. Draw your view of the building as you'd see it from the front.

   c. Draw side views of the building as you walk around it.

2. Repeat steps **a**, **b**, and **c** above with a different solid. How did each view change?

Talk About It

3. Describe the Power Solids you explored by the shapes of their faces.

4. How are pyramids different from prisms?

Connect

Base

Face

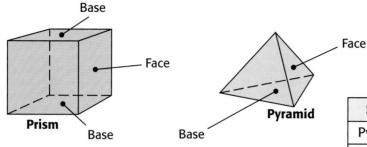

Prism

Base

Base

Face

Base

Pyramid

Math Tip

A pyramid comes to a point or vertex.

Solid	Base	Face
Pyramid	1	Triangular
Prism	2 congruent	Rectangular

Practice

Write the name of the solid suggested in each photograph.

1.

2.

3.

4.

5.

6.

Decide if each statement is true *always*, *sometimes*, or *never*.

7. Each side face of a pyramid is a triangle.

8. The base of a pentagonal prism has 4 sides.

9. The top of a solid is congruent to its base.

10. The side faces of a prism are squares.

11. A solid with rectangular side faces and triangular bases is a triangular prism.

12. A hexagonal prism comes to a point.

13. **What If** You have to tell someone over the phone what a pyramid looks like. What would you say?

14. **Critical Thinking** Which would collect more snow on its roof: a house in the shape of a prism or a pyramid? Explain.

15. **Journal** Draw a line down the middle of a page in your journal. On the left, write two ways in which prisms and pyramids are different. On the right, write two ways in which prisms and pyramids are the same.

Exploring Patterns with Solids

Problem Solving Connection

■ Use Objects/ Act It Out

■ Look for a Pattern

Materials
Power Solids

Vocabulary
edge
a line segment where two faces meet

vertex
a point where two or more edges meet; plural is vertices

types of lines
parallel
skew

Explore ●

Some geometric solids have **edges** and **vertices**.

This figure has 18 edges and 12 vertices.

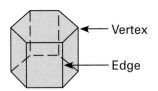
← Vertex

← Edge

Work Together

1. Copy and complete the table. Count all faces including the 2 bases of each figure.

Name of Solid	Triangular prism	Rectangular prism	Pentagonal prism	Hexagonal prism	Heptagonal prism	Octagonal prism
Number of Faces	5					
Number of Vertices	6					
Number of Edges	9					

2. Look for patterns. Write a rule to show how the number of faces, vertices, and edges are related. Hint: How does the sum of faces and vertices compare to the number of edges?

3. Predict how many faces and vertices you would find in a prism with a 9-sided base.

4. Explain how you made your prediction.

Connect

For any prism, the following rule is true:

number of faces + number of vertices = number of edges + 2

For a cube: 6 +   8   =   12   + 2

$$14 = 14$$

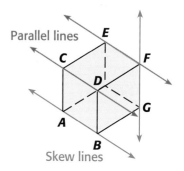

$\overleftrightarrow{EF}$ and $\overleftrightarrow{CD}$ are **parallel** .

$\overleftrightarrow{AB}$ and $\overleftrightarrow{FG}$ are **skew**.

Practice

1. **Algebra Readiness** Copy and complete the table for each prism.

Number of Edges of One Base	3			
Number of Vertices				
Total Number of Edges				

   a. Write a rule for prisms that relates the number of edges of one base and the number of vertices.

   b. Write a rule for prisms that relates the number of edges of one base and the total number of edges.

2. **Patterns** Suppose you wanted to draw a prism with one base that had 20 edges. How many vertices would the prism have?

Using Data Use the Data File on page 484 to answer **3–6.**

3. Write a rule for pyramids that relates the number of edges of the base and the number of vertices.

4. Write a rule for pyramids that relates the number of edges of the base and the total number of edges.

5. Write a rule to show how the number of base edges and the number of vertices are related to the total number of edges in a pyramid.

6. **Critical Thinking** A pyramid has a total number of 24 edges. How many edges does its base have?

7. **Estimation** Suppose you had two containers with the same base and height—one a prism, the other a pyramid. Which container would hold more liquid? Explain.

8. **Journal** This solid is neither a pyramid nor a prism. Each side face is a trapezoid. Write a rule to show how the number of faces including bases, vertices, and edges are related in such a solid. Describe how you discovered the rule.

Exploring Nets

Problem Solving Connection

Use Objects/
Act It Out

Materials

■ dot paper

■ scissors

Vocabulary

net
a pattern that can be
cut out and folded to
make a solid

Explore •

You can make a box to hold some of your small items.
Here is a **net** for a cube-shaped box. The diagram
shows how you can fold the net into a cube.

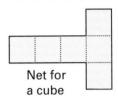

Net for
a cube

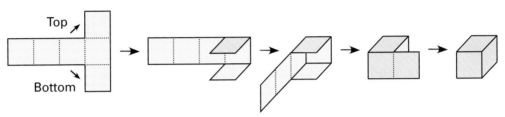

Work Together

There are other nets you can make out of 6 squares. Will all of them fold
into cubes? To find out, draw A and B on dot paper and cut them out.

1. Which of these
   designs is a
   net for a cube?

2. In all, there are 12 different nets
   that can be folded into cubes.
   Find 6 or more of these nets.
   Record the nets on dot paper.
   Make sure that all your nets
   are different. Circle the
   nets that make cubes.

(**Talk About It**)

Explain how you
knew that the nets
you discovered
were different from
ones you already found.

Connect

A net is a pattern that can be folded to make a solid.

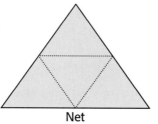

Net

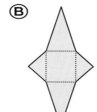

Triangular pyramid

Practice

1. Which design forms a net for a square pyramid? Explain.

   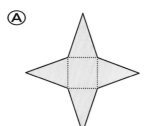

   Ⓐ   Ⓑ

2. Which design forms a net for a rectangular prism? Explain.

   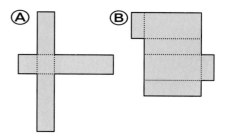

   Ⓐ   Ⓑ

3. Which design forms a net for a hexagonal pyramid? Explain.

   Ⓐ   Ⓑ

4. Which design forms a net for a pentagonal prism? Explain.

   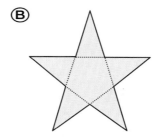

   Ⓐ   Ⓑ

5. Design a net for a prism. Write letters *T* and *B* on two faces of the net so that when the net is folded the *T* will be on the top and the *B* will be on the bottom.

6. **History** The Great Pyramid at Giza, Egypt, built for Cheops in 2600 B.C., is a square pyramid. Design a net for this pyramid.

7. **Critical Thinking** What is the least number of faces you could use to make a net? What kind of figure would your net make?

8. **Journal** Explain how you can tell if a certain net would make a prism or pyramid.

Three of the largest and best-preserved pyramids are located at Giza. The Great Pyramid is shown in the center.

Exploring Surface Area

**Problem Solving
Connection**

Draw a Picture

Materials

dot paper

Vocabulary

surface area
total area of all
faces of a solid

Explore • • • • • • • • • •

Which box will need
more paint?

The box with the greater
surface area will need
more paint. The surface
area of any solid is the sum
of the areas of all of its faces.

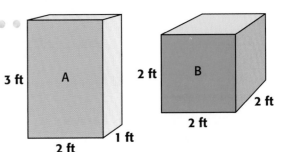

3 ft   A   2 ft   B   2 ft

2 ft   1 ft   2 ft

Work Together

Remember
For a rectangle,
$A = l \times w$.

1. One way to find the surface
   area is to take the figure apart
   and find the area of each face.

   a. Draw each face of box A
      on dot paper.

   b. Find the area of each face.

   c. What is the surface area of
      box A?

2. A second way to find the
   surface area is to make a net.

   a. Draw a net for box B on
      dot paper.

   b. Find the area of each part
      of the net.

   c. What is the surface area of
      box B?

Talk About It

3. Which of the two boxes has a greater surface area? Tell how you know.

4. Explain how to find the surface area of any rectangular prism.

Connect •

Use this formula to find the surface area of any rectangular prism.

surface area = (2 × front area) + (2 × side area) + (2 × top area)

surface area = (2 × 32) + (2 × 36) + (2 × 72)
     = 64 + 72 + 144
     = 280 cm²

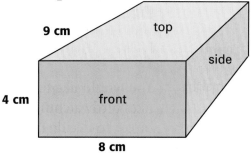

9 cm   top
   side
4 cm   front
8 cm

Practice •

 Measurement Find the surface area of each figure. You may use a calculator.

1.
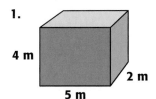
4 m
2 m
5 m

2.
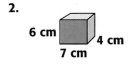
6 cm
4 cm
7 cm

3.
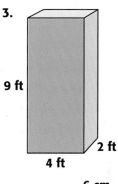
9 ft
2 ft
4 ft

4.

2.5 cm   3.4 cm
1.0 cm

5.

3.5 in.   9 in.
13.5 in.

6.
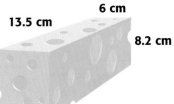
13.5 cm   6 cm
8.2 cm

7. What is the surface area of a box 4 in. long, 8 in. wide, and 6 in. high?

8. What is the surface area of an ice chest 3 ft long, 2 ft wide, and 2 ft high?

9. **Critical Thinking** You split a rectangular block of wood in half. Does the total surface area increase, decrease, or stay the same? Explain.

10. A 10-gallon can of paint covers 3,000 ft² to 4,000 ft². How many cans will you need to paint the outside walls of a building that is 15 ft wide, 20 ft long, and 50 ft high?

 11. **Algebra Readiness** Write a formula for the surface area of a cube. Hint: What is the area of each face of the cube?

 12. **Journal** Describe two ways you can find the surface area of a box.

Problem Solving

Decision Making: **Build a Birdhouse**

You Will Learn

how to solve problems by making decisions

Explore •

You would like to build at least three birdhouses for a friend who really likes birdwatching. You have $26 to spend on wood. Use the information below to decide if you can build the birdhouses.

Facts and Data

The diagrams show different pieces of the birdhouse.

The pine wood comes in boards that are 8 ft long and 12 in. wide.

The cost of the wood is $10.00 per board, or $1.50 for each foot when the board is less than a full 8 ft.

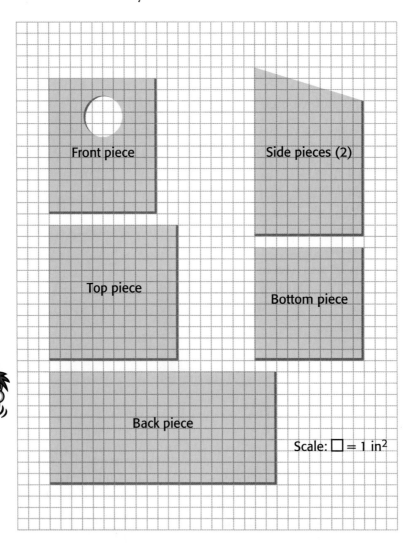

Problem Solving Hint

You can use the scale to find the dimensions of each piece.

Work Together

▶ **Understand**

1. What are you trying to do?

2. How will the diagrams help you to reach your goal?

▶ **Plan and Solve**

3. Into what geometric figures will the board be cut?

4. How much wood can you afford?

5. How many inches long is one board?

6. What length of wood will you need for:

   a. the two sides?   **b.** the back?

   c. the front?   **d.** the bottom?

   e. the top?

7. How many inches will be left from the first board after cutting the wood for one birdhouse?

8. How can you make the best use of the leftover wood?

▶ **Make a Decision**

9. Can you make at least 3 birdhouses from the wood you can buy? Explain.

▶ **Present Your Decision**

10. Describe to the class how you would get the most use out of the wood that you have.

11. Compare your group's decision on how to use the boards with another group's decision.

Review and Practice

Vocabulary Match each term with its meaning.

<table>
<tr><td></td><td></td><td colspan="2">

Word List

</td></tr>
<tr><td></td><td></td><td>three</td><td>nine</td></tr>
<tr><td></td><td></td><td>rectangles</td><td>thirty</td></tr>
<tr><td></td><td></td><td>triangle</td><td>prism</td></tr>
<tr><td></td><td></td><td colspan="2">rectangular solid</td></tr>
</table>

1. edge	**a.**	total area of all faces of a solid
2. vertex	**b.**	point where two or more edges meet
3. surface area	**c.**	a line segment where two faces meet

(Lessons 1 and 2) Choose the word from the list that best completes each sentence.

4. The side faces of a prism are _____.

5. A prism with triangular bases has _____ side faces

6. A solid with rectangular side faces and a square base is a _____.

7. Each side face of a pyramid is a _____.

8. A prism with a 15-sided base would have _____ vertices.

9. A pyramid with an 8-sided base would have _____ vertices.

(Lesson 3) Name the solid each net makes.

10.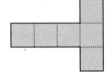

11.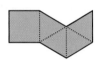

12.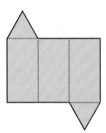

(Lesson 4) Find the surface area of each figure.

13.
3.5 in.
3.5 in.
3.5 in.

14.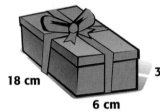
18 cm
3 cm
6 cm

15.
2 ft
3 ft
1 ft

16. 40 ft
10 ft
8 ft

17. **Journal** Explain how to find the surface area of a rectangular solid whose measurements are 4 m × 6 m × 3 m.

Skills Checklist

In this section, you have:

☑ **Explored Solids**

☑ **Explored Patterns with Solids**

☑ **Explored Nets**

☑ **Explored Surface Area**

☑ **Solved Problems by Making Decisions**

B Understanding Weight, Mass, and Temperature

Tim is the 1996 champion of the Masters Division of the All-American Soap Box Derby. The regulation weight for cars in his division is 240 pounds.

Why do you think there are rules about what these cars can weigh?

Changing Among Ounces, Pounds, and Tons

Review whole numbers. Multiply or divide.

1. 15×12
2. 137×36
3. 207×18
4. $48 \div 12$
5. $625 \div 25$
6. $1,488 \div 19$
7. 94×17
8. $80 \div 16$
9. $176 \div 22$

Skills Checklist

In this section, you will:

☐ Change Among Ounces, Pounds, and Tons

☐ Change Between Grams and Kilograms

☐ Learn About Temperature

Ounces, Pounds, and Tons

You Will Learn
how to change among ounces, pounds, and tons

Vocabulary

ounce (oz)
a unit of weight

pound (lb)
a unit of weight equal to 16 oz

ton (T)
a unit of weight equal to 2,000 lb

Learn

"From an envelope to a truckload." That is the advertising slogan of a delivery service in Brooklyn, New York. They've shipped everything from a light rose to a heavy piano.

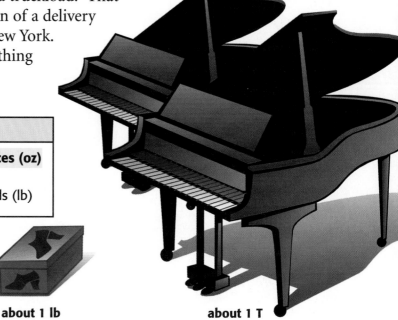

Key Facts
1 **pound (lb)** = 16 **ounces (oz)**
1 **ton (T)** = 2,000 pounds (lb)

about 1 oz   about 1 lb   about 1 T

To change from one unit to another, you need to multiply or divide.

Example 1

Suppose a farmer in New Jersey wanted to ship a 7-T tractor. Find its weight in pounds.

$$7 \text{ T} = \blacksquare \text{ lb}$$

When changing from greater to lesser units, multiply.

$$1 \text{ T} = 2,000 \text{ lb}$$
$$7 \times 2,000 = 14,000$$
$$7 \text{ T} = 14,000 \text{ lb}$$

The tractor weighs 14,000 lb.

Example 2

$$35 \text{ oz} = \blacksquare \text{ lb} \ \blacksquare \text{ oz}$$

When changing from lesser to greater units, divide.

$$16 \text{ oz} = 1 \text{ lb}$$

$$\begin{array}{r} 2 \text{ R3} \\ 16\overline{)35} \\ -32 \\ \hline 3 \end{array}$$

So, 35 oz = 2 lb 3 oz.

35 oz is a little more than 2×16 or 32 oz, so the answer is reasonable.

Math Tip
You can also write 35 oz as $2\frac{3}{16}$ lb.

Talk About It

How do you know if you should multiply or divide when changing pounds to ounces?

Check

Copy and complete. Check the reasonableness of your answer.

1. 7 lb = ■ oz   **2.** 160 oz = ■ lb   **3.** 3 T = ■ lb   **4.** 8,000 lb = ■ T   **5.** 36 lb = ■ oz

6. Reasoning Which is less: 3 lb or 50 oz? Explain.

Practice

Skills and Reasoning

Copy and complete. Check the reasonableness of your answer.

7. 96 oz = ■ lb   **8.** 3 T = ■ lb   **9.** 50 oz = ■ lb ■ oz   **10.** 200 oz = ■ lb ■ oz

11. 8 T = ■ lb   **12.** 73 oz = ■ lb ■ oz   **13.** 16 T 40 lb = ■ lb   **14.** 151 oz = ■ lb ■ oz

15. 13 lb = ■ oz   **16.** 20,000 lb = ■ T   **17.** 44 oz = ■ lb ■ oz   **18.** 7 T 100 lb = ■ lb

19. Which is greater, 5 lb or 84 oz? Explain.

20. Estimation Estimate the number of tons in 24,793 lb.

Problem Solving and Applications

Using Data Use the table to answer **21** and **22**.

21. Estimation About how many pounds did the Port of South Louisiana ship in 1993?

22. Social Studies San Juan, Puerto Rico, shipped 14 million tons in 1993. Is that greater or less than the amount Houston shipped?

23. Journal Write a rule for changing ounces to pounds and pounds to ounces. When do you divide? Multiply?

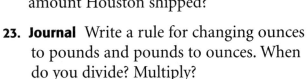

4 Busiest U.S. Ports in 1993	
Port	**Tons Shipped**
Port of South Louisiana	193,796,104
Houston, TX	141,476,979
New York, NY and NJ	116,735,760
Valdez, AK	85,722,337

Mixed Review and Test Prep

Geometry Use the figure to answer **24** and **25**.

24. What is the name of this solid?

25. What is the surface area of the solid?

26. Patterns Which numbers come next in the pattern?
16, 32, 48, 64, 80, ■, ■

Ⓐ 96, 102   Ⓑ 96, 112   Ⓒ 96, 122   Ⓓ 96, 132

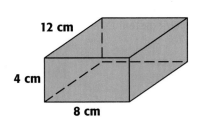

12 cm
4 cm
8 cm

Grams and Kilograms

You Will Learn
how to change between grams and kilograms

Vocabulary
gram (g)
a unit of mass

kilogram (kg)
a unit of mass equal to 1,000 g

Learn

Ready, set, go! At the age of 12, Tim won the All-American Soap Box Derby Championship. A regulation soap box derby car must be at least 33 cm wide, between 36–74 cm high, and no longer than 213 cm.

A regulation derby car can have a mass of no more than 558,800 g.

Key Facts
1,000 **grams (g)** = 1 **kilogram (kg)**

Tim Scrofano is from Conneaut, Ohio.

Example 1
Find the mass of a regulation derby car in kilograms.

558,800 g = ▮ kg

To change from a lesser unit to a greater unit, divide.

1,000 g = 1 kg

558,800 ÷ 1,000 = 558.800 = 558.8

558,800 g = 558.8 kg

The mass of the car is 558.8 kg.

Example 2
2.7 kg = ▮ g

To change from a greater unit to a lesser unit, multiply.

1 kg = 1,000 g

$2.7 \times 1,000 = 2.700 = 2,700$

2.7 kg = 2,700 g

Check: 2,700 g = 2,000 g + 700 g
            = 2 kg + 0.7 kg = 2.7 kg

Talk About It

How can you use place value and the powers of 10 (10, 100, 1,000) to help you change kilograms to grams?

Did You Know?
The metric system has a ton unit.

1 metric ton = 1,000 kilograms

Check

Mental Math Use mental math to change to kilograms or grams.

1. 4 kg = ▮ g   **2.** 3,400 g = ▮ kg   **3.** 7.27 kg = ▮ g   **4.** 9,340 g = ▮ kg

5. Reasoning Would you multiply or divide to change from

   a. grams to kilograms?   **b.** kilogram to grams?

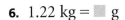

Skills and Reasoning

Mental Math Use mental math to change to kilograms or grams.

6. 1.22 kg = ■ g
7. 890 g = ■ kg
8. 0.37 kg = ■ g
9. 28 g = ■ kg

10. 35 g = ■ kg
11. 3.03 kg = ■ g
12. 27,444.4 g = ■ kg
13. 0.003 kg = ■ g

14. 8 g = ■ kg
15. 48.23 kg = ■ g
16. 209.8 g = ■ kg
17. 13.6 kg = ■ g

18. How many kilograms?
19. How many grams?
20. How many kilograms?

105 g

541.2 kg

160 g

21. **Money** Small nails cost $0.84 kg. If you need 500 g of nails to build a soap box car, how much money will you need for nails?

Problem Solving and Applications

22. Mike bought some fruit to make a salad: a 170-g banana, a 0.8-kg melon, a 395-g box of berries, and a 0.18-kg peach. Which item has the greatest mass? Which has greater mass, the banana or the peach?

23. **Critical Thinking** Bananas cost $0.98 kg. About how many 170-g bananas could you buy for a dollar?

24. **Science** Refer to the *Did You Know?* on page 502. The 3-story Hotel Fairmount of San Antonio, Texas, was moved 5 blocks. It had a mass of 1,454,545 kg. How many metric tons is this?

25. **Collecting Data** Find two items in your classroom: one with a mass of about 1 g and one with a mass of about 1 kg.

It took 36 dollies and 6 days to move the Hotel Fairmount to its new location.

Mixed Review and Test Prep

Find each product or quotient.

26. $43.29 ÷ 12
27. 159.6 × 100
28. $20.15 × 15
29. 236.7 ÷ 10

30. **Estimation** Which of the following has a mass of about 100 grams?

Ⓐ a paper clip   Ⓑ a chair   Ⓒ a stick of butter   Ⓓ a hammer

PRACTICE AND APPLY

Temperature

Maya is from Detroit, Michigan.

You Will Learn

how to read temperatures on a thermometer and calculate changes in temperature

Vocabulary

Celsius (°C)
temperature scale in which water boils at 100°C and freezes at 0°C

Fahrenheit (°F)
temperature scale in which water boils at 212°F and freezes at 32°F

Learn • • • • • • •

Maya used a thermometer to test the body temperature of an iguana against the temperature in the classroom. She wanted to know how well the iguana adapted to temperature changes. She read both the degrees **Celsius** (°C) and degrees **Fahrenheit** (°F) every day for four days.

Example 1

Find the difference between the classroom temperature and the iguana's temperature.

Classroom temperature   Iguana's temperature

Maya read each temperature on both scales. Then she subtracted to find each difference:

Difference °F: 70°F − 66°F = 4°F

Difference °C: 21°C − 19°C = 2°C

The iguana's temperature was lower, or cooler, than the temperature in the classroom.

Example 2

You can find a change in temperature by finding the difference between high and low temperatures.

If you measured a high temperature of 3°C and a low temperature of −10°C, what was the change in temperature? Hint: Use the thermometer like a number line.

There was a 13°C change in temperature.

Math Tip

Negative numbers are numbers that are less than zero.

Talk About It

If the temperature during the day reached a high of 70°F, but it dropped to 55°F that night, how would you find the change in temperature?

Check ●

Write each temperature in Celsius and Fahrenheit.

1.
2.
3.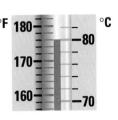

Find each change in temperature.

4. 12°F to 56°F   5. 5°C to 41°C   6. 2°F to 101°F   7. 0°C to 31°C

8. **Reasoning** Look at **2** above. Is 46°C warmer than 112°F? Explain.

Practice ●

Skills and Reasoning

Write each temperature in Celsius and Fahrenheit.

9.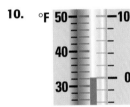
10.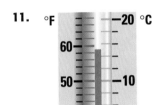
11.

Use the thermometer to find each change in temperature.

12. 22°C to 31°C 13. 46°F to 8°F 14. 18°F to −4°F 15. 21°C to −11°C

16. Which increase would feel warmer: 10°C or 10°F? Explain.

Problem Solving and Applications

Using Data Use the Data File on page 485 to answer **17** and **18**.

17. **Science** What is the difference in degrees Celsius between water freezing and water boiling? In Fahrenheit?

18. **Science** What is the difference in degrees Fahrenheit between room temperature and body temperature?

19. **Write Your Own Problem** Use the Celsius or Fahrenheit scale to write your own problem about temperature.

Mixed Review and Test Prep

 Mental Math Copy and complete.

20. 7.35 kg = ▥ g   21. 686.4 g = ▥ kg   22. 0.56 kg = ▥ g   23. 28.44 g = ▥ kg

24. Choose the greatest fraction.

Ⓐ $\frac{8}{9}$ Ⓑ $\frac{18}{19}$ Ⓒ $\frac{28}{29}$ Ⓓ $\frac{38}{39}$

Review and Practice

Vocabulary Use a word from the list to complete each sentence. Not all words will be used.

Word List
ounce
pound
ton
gram
kilogram
Celsius
Fahrenheit

1. Zero degrees on the _____ scale is the same as 32° on the _____ scale.

2. A _____ is a unit of mass equal to 1,000 g.

3. A _____ is a unit of weight equal to 16 oz.

4. A _____ is a unit of weight equal to 2,000 lb.

(Lesson 6) Copy and complete.

5. 14 lb = ▦ oz
6. 10,000 lb = ▦ T
7. 60 oz = ▦ lb ▦ oz
8. 2 lb 9 oz = ▦ oz

9. 8,024 lb = ▦ T ▦ lb
10. 26,000 oz = ▦ lb
11. 1 T 360 lb = ▦ lb
12. 4 lb 12 oz = ▦ oz

13. 16 T = ▦ lb
14. 105 oz = ▦ lb ▦ oz
15. 8,500 lb = ▦ T
16. 6 lb = ▦ oz

(Lesson 7) **Mental Math** Copy and complete.

17. 3.5 kg = ▦ g
18. 420 g = ▦ kg
19. 0.73 kg = ▦ g
20. 35 g = ▦ kg

21. 63.009 kg = ▦ g
22. 54,219 g = ▦ kg
23. 25.17 kg = ▦ g
24. 3 kg = ▦ g

25. 28,662 g = ▦ kg
26. 4.2 kg = ▦ g
27. 319 g = ▦ kg
28. 5,420 g = ▦ kg

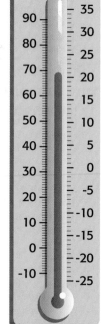

(Lesson 8) Use the thermometer to find each change in temperature.

29. 13°F to 25°F
30. 1°C to 39°C
31. −15°C to 10°C

32. 25°C to −5°C
33. −9°C to 22°C
34. 32°F to 88°F

35. 7°C to 29°C
36. −10°F to 2°F
37. 4°F to 69°F

38. 50°C to 23°C
39. 82°F to −1°F
40. −8°C to 18°C

41. On one particular day it was 71°F in Miami, Florida, and −2°F in Bangor, Maine. What was the difference in temperature between these two cities?

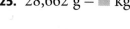

42. **Journal** If you are outside in shorts and the temperature is 30°, is it 30°C or 30°F? Explain.

> **Skills Checklist**
>
> **In this section, you have:**
>
> ☑ **Changed Among Ounces, Pounds, and Tons**
>
> ☑ **Changed Between Grams and Kilograms**
>
> ☑ **Learned About Temperature**

Understanding Volume and Capacity

How could you use a measuring cup if you could not see the markings on the side? Tova invented a cup with raised markings on the inside so anyone can use it to measure!

What are some of the fractions you might find listed on the side of a measuring cup?

TOVA ANN LEIGH
8TH GRADE
Regional Winner
1989

Skills Checklist

In this section, you will:

- ☐ Explore Volume
- ☐ Learn About Customary and Metric Units of Capacity
- ☐ Connect Units of Volume, Mass, and Capacity
- ☐ Solve Problems by Comparing Strategies: Solve a Simpler Problem/Draw a Picture

GET READY!

Connecting Volume, Weight, and Capacity

Review operations. Find the value of each expression.

1. $(7 \times 8) + 4$
2. $(4 + 12) \div 8$
3. $\frac{1}{2} \times (4 \times 6)$
4. $(7.5 \times 0.008) + 7.5$
5. $\left(2\frac{1}{4} \times 5\frac{1}{3}\right) - 4\frac{5}{12}$
6. $(9 \times 2.5) - 16$

Exploring Volume

Problem Solving Connection
Use Objects/
Act It Out

Materials
- unit cubes
- small box

Vocabulary
volume
the number of cubic units in a solid

Math Tip
When finding volume, you can use the commutative property to multiply in any order.

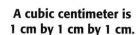 **Explore** •

Volume is measured in cubic units. Two common units of volume are the cubic centimeter (cm³) and the cubic inch (in³). Volume is found using three dimensions: length, width, and height.

 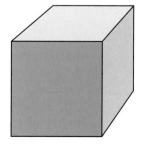

A cubic unit is
1 unit by 1 unit by 1 unit.

A cubic centimeter is
1 cm by 1 cm by 1 cm.

A cubic inch is
1 in. by 1 in. by 1 in.

Work Together

Estimate the volume of a rectangular prism.

1. Use unit cubes to help you estimate the volume of a small box.

   a. Estimate the number of cubes needed for the bottom layer.

   b. Estimate the number of layers.

   c. Estimate the number of cubes needed to fill the whole box.

   d. Use cubes to check your estimate.

Find the volume of a rectangular prism.

2. Use unit cubes to make a rectangular prism that is 4 cubes wide, 6 cubes long, and 2 cubes high. What is the volume of the prism?

3. Make a rectangular prism of different dimensions with the same number of cubes as the one above. Give its length, width, and height.

Talk About It

How is finding area similar to finding volume? How is it different?

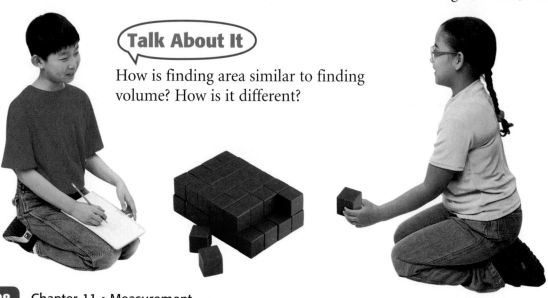

Connect

The **volume** of a solid figure is the number of cubic units that it contains.
You can find the volume of a rectangular prism in more than one way.

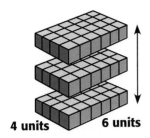

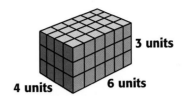

Find the volume of one layer.
$4 \times 6 = 24$
Multiply by the number of layers.
$3 \times 24 = 72$
The volume is 72 cubic units.

Use the formula for volume.
Volume = length × width × height
$V = l \times w \times h$
$V = 6 \times 4 \times 3 = 72$
The volume is 72 cubic units.

Practice

Find each volume.

1.

2.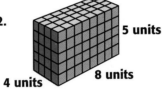

3.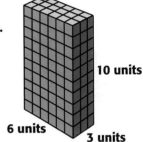

Copy and complete.

4. $l = 17$ cm
$w = 9$ cm
$h = 8$ cm
$V = \blacksquare$ cm^3

5. $l = 7$ in.
$w = 12.5$ in.
$h = 4$ in.
$V = \blacksquare$ in^3

6. $l = 20$ ft
$w = 8$ ft
$h = \blacksquare$ ft
$V = 1,600$ ft^3

7. Estimation Use mental math to estimate the volume of a box whose
dimensions are 19 cm × 10 cm × 11 cm. Hint: Use rounding.

Using Data Use the Data File on page 485 to answer **8** and **9**.

8. Which packing box has the greatest
volume? How can you find out?

9. How much greater is the volume of
the largest box than the smallest box?

10. Critical Thinking Explain how a box
with a base 4 ft by 3 ft could hold
more than one with base 5 ft by 4 ft.

11. Sandra plans to build a doghouse
that will be 3 ft wide, 4 ft high, and
3 ft long. What will its volume be?

12. Jennifer and Cortez made a fort. The
fort was 4 ft wide and 5 ft long. It
had a volume of 100 ft^3. How high
were the walls?

 13. Journal Give all possible whole
number dimensions of a 12 in^2
rectangle and 12 in^3 rectangular
prism. Explain your reasoning.

Customary Units of Capacity

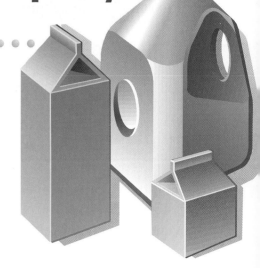

You Will Learn
how to change among customary units of capacity

Vocabulary

capacity
the volume of a space figure given as a liquid measurement

Learn

Sometimes you need to change from one unit of **capacity** to another.

Units of Capacity
1 tablespoon (tbsp) = $\frac{1}{2}$ fluid ounce (fl oz)
1 fl oz = 2 tbsp
1 cup (c) = 8 fl oz
1 pint (pt) = 2 c
1 quart (qt) = 2 pt
1gallon (gal) = 4 qt

Nadra and Charlie are organizing their club's camping trip. The club's leader says they need 2 gal of milk. Charlie bought 6 qt. Is that enough milk? Nadra and Charlie decided to find out using different methods.

Math Tip

Ounces are used to measure both weight and capacity.

For weight,
16 oz = 1 lb.

For capacity,
8 oz = 1 cup.

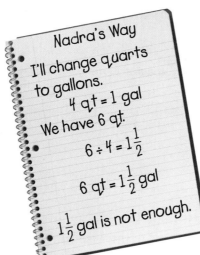

Nadra's Way
I'll change quarts to gallons.
4 qt = 1 gal
We have 6 qt.
$6 \div 4 = 1\frac{1}{2}$
$6 \text{ qt} = 1\frac{1}{2} \text{ gal}$
$1\frac{1}{2}$ gal is not enough.

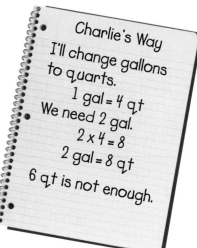

Charlie's Way
I'll change gallons to quarts.
1 gal = 4 qt
We need 2 gal.
$2 \times 4 = 8$
2 gal = 8 qt
6 qt is not enough.

Talk About It

How many cups are equal to 6 qt? Explain.

Check

Copy and complete.

1. 3 qt = ■ c   2. 11 c = ■ fl oz   3. 10 tbsp = ■ fl oz   4. 12 pt = ■ gal

5. **Reasoning** Could you fit the contents of three $11\frac{1}{2}$-fl oz jars into two 1-pt containers? Explain.

Practice

Skills and Reasoning

Measurement Copy and complete.

6. $\frac{1}{2}$ pt = ▨ c

7. 24 fl oz = ▨ c

8. $5\frac{1}{2}$ gal = ▨ pt

9. 3 qt = ▨ c

Use the drawings to answer 10–15.

10. ▨ c of mayonnaise

11. ▨ pt of apple cider

12. ▨ tbsp of vinegar

13. ▨ c of barbecue sauce

14. ▨ qt of milk

15. ▨ fl oz of syrup

16. Science An elephant's trunk can hold $1\frac{1}{2}$ gal of water. How many cups of water is that equivalent to?

17. Carole says a 3-gal container has a greater capacity than twenty 1-pt containers. Is she right? Explain.

Problem Solving and Applications

Using Data Use the packing list to answer **18** and **19**.

18. Diane has 2 qt of orange juice. How many more quarts does she need to buy?

19. If 8 campers are going on the trip, how many cups of lemonade are there for each?

20. Tom is carrying water in a pitcher to fill the birdbath in his front yard. If the birdbath holds 2 gal of water and the pitcher holds 1 qt, how many trips will Tom have to make to fill up the birdbath?

CAMPING TRIP DRINKS
ORANGE JUICE $1\frac{1}{2}$ gal
APPLE JUICE 1 gal
LEMONADE 2 gal
MILK 2 gal

Mixed Review and Test Prep

Find each product.

21. 307 × 27

22. 499 × 53

23. 1,708 × 29

24. 2,333 × 17

25. 5,609 × 48

26. Geometry Which figure has a volume of 48 in³?

Ⓐ 10 in. 20 in. 18 in.

Ⓑ 3 in. 8 in. 2 in.

Ⓒ 4 in. 12 in.

Ⓓ 3 in. 6 in. 3 in.

Metric Units of Capacity

Massachusetts

Learn • • • • • • • • • • • •

Braille is a writing system that allows visually impaired people to read by feeling raised dots. When Tova was 14, she invented a Braille measuring cup called the "Braille Pail." Braille markings inside the cup allow people who cannot see to measure amounts.

Tova is from Pepperell, Massachusetts. Tova's Braille Pail was a winning entry in her school's Invent America contest.

A measuring cup can show customary or metric units. In the metric system, you usually measure capacity using **milliliters** (mL) and **liters** (L).

A liter is a little more than a quart.

1 L = 1,000 mL

A half-gallon of milk is almost 2 L.

A gallon of gas is a little less than 4 L.

A milliliter is about 20 drops of water.

1 mL = 0.001 L

A small bottle of vanilla holds about 60 mL.

A soda can holds 355 mL.

Example 1
350 mL = ■ L
To change milliliters to liters, divide by 1,000.
350 ÷ 1,000 = 0.35
350 mL = 0.35 L

Example 2
4.5 L = ■ mL
To change liters to milliliters, multiply by 1,000.
4.5 × 1,000 = 4,500
4.5 L = 4,500 mL

Talk About It

1. Would you multiply or divide to change 2,400 mL to liters? Explain.

2. Which do you think would be more likely to be measured in milliliters: cold medicine or gasoline? Explain.

Check

Copy and complete.

1. 3,000 mL = ▨ L   2. 35 mL = ▨ L   3. 1.3 L = ▨ mL   4. 750 mL = ▨ L

5. **Reasoning** If you were filling a 1-L container by pouring liquid from a
125-mL measuring cup, would you have to fill it 10 times? Explain.

Practice

Skills and Reasoning

Mental Math Copy and complete.

6. 4,000 mL = ▨ L   7. 250 mL = ▨ L   8. 8 L = ▨ mL   9. 4.15 L = ▨ mL

10. 0.3 L = ▨ mL   11. 2.85 L = ▨ mL   12. 960 mL = ▨ L   13. 30 mL = ▨ L

Use the pictures to solve 14–17.

14. ▨ mL of almond extract

15. ▨ L of oil

16. ▨ mL of orange juice

17. ▨ L of liquid soap

946 mL   **1.5 L**   **2,000 mL**   **0.118 L**

Problem Solving and Applications

18. Chuck is making a loaf of wheat bread.
The recipe calls for 250 mL of milk. He
has a 1 L container of milk. How much
of the container should he use?

19. A frosting recipe calls for 350 mL of
water. Kim filled her 0.5 L Braille
measuring cup to the top. How many
fewer milliliters of water does she need?

20. **Time** Jeanette built an automatic plant-watering device. It releases
25 mL of water an hour. If the device holds 2.5 L of water, can it go
a week without needing to be refilled? Explain.

21. An experiment calls for 50 mL of water and 250 mL of iodine
solution. How many liters is the combined mixture?

Mixed Review and Test Prep

Find each answer. Simplify.

22. $\frac{1}{4} + \frac{1}{3}$ 23. $3\frac{1}{2} + \frac{5}{8}$ 24. $\frac{7}{8} - \frac{2}{3}$ 25. $3\frac{1}{8} - 1\frac{2}{3}$ 26. $\frac{1}{2} + \frac{3}{8}$

27. $\frac{2}{3} \times \frac{4}{5}$ 28. $1\frac{3}{4} \times \frac{2}{3}$ 29. $7 \div \frac{1}{4}$ 30. $8 \div \frac{1}{3}$ 31. $\frac{4}{5} \times \frac{1}{6}$

32. **Mental Math** Find the quotient of $\frac{7}{3}$ and $\frac{3}{3}$.

   Ⓐ 21   Ⓑ 7   Ⓒ $\frac{7}{9}$ Ⓓ $2\frac{1}{3}$ Ⓔ not here

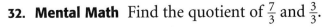

Connecting Volume, Mass, and Capacity

You Will Learn

how to connect units of volume, capacity, and mass

Learn •

You want to build an aquarium stand that can support a mass of 35 kg. The aquarium has a mass of 5 kg. If you fill the aquarium with water 5 cm from the top, will it be too heavy for the stand?

In the metric system, units of volume, mass, and capacity are connected.

1 cm³ holds 1 mL of water.
1 mL of water has a mass of 1 g.

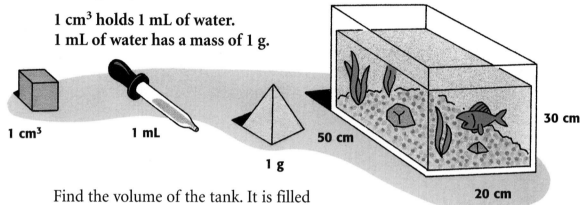

1 cm³   1 mL   1 g   50 cm   30 cm   20 cm

Remember

The formula for volume is $V = l \times w \times h$.

Find the volume of the tank. It is filled to 5 cm from the top, so use 25 cm for h.

$V = 50 \text{ cm} \times 20 \text{ cm} \times 25 \text{ cm} = 25{,}000 \text{ cm}^3$

25,000 cm³ holds **25,000 mL** of water and has a mass of **25,000 g.** Change grams to kilograms:
$25{,}000 \text{ g} = 25 \text{ kg}$

The mass of the aquarium (5 kg) and the water (25 kg) combined is 30 kg. Compare: 30 kg < 35 kg. So, the stand will support the filled aquarium.

Talk About It

How is the relationship between grams and kilograms like the relationship between milliliters and liters?

Check •

Write the number for each ▇.

1. A 2,000 cm³ container holds ▇ L.   **2.** 1 L of water has a mass of ▇ g.

3. **Reasoning** Cory says she used a metric kitchen scale to figure out how many liters of water an unmarked pitcher could hold. Explain what she did.

Practice

Skills and Reasoning

Write the number for each ▨.

4. 1,200 mL water would fill a ▨ cm³ container.

5. 1.4 kg of water would fill a ▨ mL container.

6. 0.86 L of water has a mass of ▨ kg.

7. A 475 cm³ container can hold ▨ L.

8. Copy and complete the table.

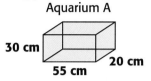
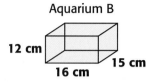
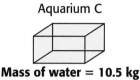

Aquarium A   30 cm   20 cm   55 cm

Aquarium B   12 cm   15 cm   16 cm

Aquarium C   Mass of water = 10.5 kg

	Volume (cm³)	Amount of Water (L)	Amount of Water (mL)	Mass of Water (kg)	Mass of Water (g)
Aquarium A	33,000			33	
Aquarium B		2.88			
Aquarium C					10,500

9. If you know the mass of the water a rectangular container can hold, can you figure out its volume and its dimensions? Explain.

Problem Solving and Applications

10. **Science** Black phantom tetras need at least an 18-in. depth of water. Each tetra needs 20 in² of surface area at the top of the water. What is the volume of the smallest aquarium you could use to house 20 tetras?

11. **Algebra Readiness** The water that fills a rectangular container has a mass of 1.35 kg. The container has a width of 10 cm and length of 9 cm. What is the height of the container?

Two male phantom black tetras (megahamphodus megalopterus)

Mixed Review and Test Prep

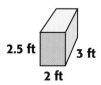

Copy and complete.

12. $\frac{2}{3} = \frac{▨}{18}$ 13. $\frac{1}{3} = \frac{▨}{21}$ 14. $\frac{9}{12} = \frac{▨}{4}$ 15. $\frac{3}{8} = \frac{▨}{80}$ 16. $\frac{3}{16} = \frac{6}{▨}$

17. **Geometry** Which of the following shows the surface area of the box?

Ⓐ 7.5 ft²   Ⓑ 15 ft²   Ⓒ 37 ft²

Ⓓ 56.25 ft²   Ⓔ not here

2.5 ft   3 ft   2 ft

Problem Solving

Compare Strategies:
Solve a Simpler Problem/Draw a Picture

You Will Learn

how to solve problems by solving a simpler problem and drawing a picture

Reading Tip

The information you are given and what you are asked to find will help you decide what strategy to use.

Learn • • • • • • • • • • • • •

Steven and Callie are going to build a model of an ancient pyramid as part of a report. The top row will have only one block. The next row down will have 4 blocks, then 9, and so on. When it is finished, the pyramid will have 6 rows. They want to know how many blocks they will need in all.

The Ziggurat of Ur, Iraq

**Callie's Way
Solve a Simpler Problem**

If the pyramid has only 2 rows, there will be $(1 \times 1) + (2 \times 2)$, or 5 blocks. For 3 rows, there will be $(1 \times 1) + (2 \times 2) + (3 \times 3)$, or 14 blocks. So, for 6 rows, there will be $(1 \times 1) + (2 \times 2) + (3 \times 3) + (4 \times 4) + (5 \times 5) + (6 \times 6)$, or 91 blocks.

**Steven's Way
Draw a Picture**

$1 + 4 + 9 + 16 + 25 + 36 = 91$

Steven and Callie both found that they would need 91 blocks.

Talk About It

1. Which way of solving the problem do you think has more chances for making a mistake? Why?

2. How many simpler problems did Callie solve? Why do you think she solved more than one?

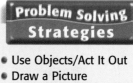

Use Solve a Simpler Problem or Draw a Picture to solve.

1. When Steven and Callie hand their report to their teacher, she will give them one copy of each report handed in by the other 9 teams in the class. If each team gets copies of all the other teams' reports, how many copies must she make in all?

   a. If there were 2 teams in the class, how many copies would she have to make?

   b. How many copies would be needed for 3 teams?

   c. How many for 4 teams?

   d. How many for 5 teams?

   e. Describe the pattern you see.

Problem Solving Practice •

Use any strategy to solve each problem.

2. Safia decorated the cover of her report with the pattern shown at the right. How many squares of any size are there in her pattern?

3. For their report, Steven and Callie had a photograph of statues standing in rows of 4. The first row had statues 1–4, the next had 5–8, and so on. In which row was the 75th statue?

4. When they gave their report, Carlos and Jermaine held it open to show a 2-page map. The sum of the page numbers that they were showing was 29. What pages were they holding open?

5. Carlos and Jermaine gave their report before Nicole and Jessica, but after Steven and Callie. Shawn and Amber were the first to report. Which of the four groups was last?

6. **Time** Each of the 10 teams was allowed 5 min to give their report. There were 2 min between reports for the next team to set up. Could all teams finish in 1 hr if they all took the full 5 min? How did you decide?

7. The teacher made a book of all 10 reports. There were 145 pages in all. She numbered each page. How many digits did she have to write in all? Explain.

8. **Journal** How are the Solve a Simpler Problem strategy and the Draw a Picture strategy similar?

Problem Solving Strategies

- Use Objects/Act It Out
- Draw a Picture
- Look for a Pattern
- Guess and Check
- Use Logical Reasoning
- Make an Organized List
- Make a Table
- Solve a Simpler Problem
- Work Backward

Choose a Tool

PROBLEM SOLVING PRACTICE

SECTION C
Review and Practice

Vocabulary Fill in the blank with the correct word in parentheses.

1. The volume of a space figure given as a liquid measurement is known as _____ . (mass or capacity)

2. In _____ units, you measure capacity using fluid ounces. (customary or metric)

(Lesson 9) Find each volume.

3.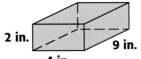
2 in. 9 in. 4 in.

4.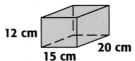
12 cm 20 cm 15 cm

5.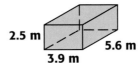
2.5 m 5.6 m 3.9 m

(Lessons 10 and 11) Copy and complete.

6. 32 fl oz = ▦ c

7. $3\frac{1}{2}$ gal = ▦ pt

8. 6 tbsp = ▦ fl oz

9. 3 c = ▦ tbsp

10. 16 fl oz = ▦ qt

11. 8 L = ▦ mL

(Lesson 12) Copy and complete. Use the information below the table.

12.

	Volume (cm³)	Amount of Water (L)	Amount of Water (mL)	Mass of Water (kg)	Mass of Water (g)
Container A					
Container B					
Container C					
Container D				3.5	

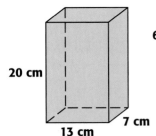
20 cm 7 cm 13 cm
Container A

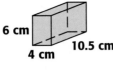
6 cm 10.5 cm 4 cm
Container B

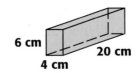
6 cm 20 cm 4 cm
Container C

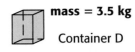
mass = 3.5 kg
Container D

(Lesson 13) Solve.

13. Roya is building a pyramid. The top row has 1 block, the 2nd row has 2 blocks, the third has 4 blocks, and the fourth row has 8 blocks. If the blocks are counted from the top, in which row will you find the 100th block?

14. **Journal** Explain how you can solve problems by solving a simpler problem.

> ### Skills Checklist
>
> **In this section, you have:**
>
> ☑ **Explored Volume**
>
> ☑ **Learned About Customary and Metric Units of Capacity**
>
> ☑ **Connected Units of Volume, Mass, and Capacity**
>
> ☑ **Solved Problems by Comparing Strategies: Solve a Simpler Problem/Draw a Picture**

YOUR CHOICE

Choose at least one. Use what you have learned in this chapter.

① Prisms and Pyramids

Create your own decorated prisms and pyramids. Use what you have learned about nets to design a solid. Trace your net on lightweight cardboard. Color patterns on the surface area. Then fold and tape.

② Changing Ounces to Pounds

Pick a topic of your choice to access on **www.mathsurf.com/5/ch11**. Choose a topic that will give you data expressed as ounces. Write and solve a problem which will require you to change the data into pounds.

③ Weighing In

Look at the items shown in a grocery ad. Record which items are sold in customary units, which are sold in metric units, and which are sold in both customary and metric units. Do you see any patterns between the kinds of items and how they are labeled? Explain.

④ Water Music

At Home Find six same-sized drinking glasses. Use a grease pencil to mark six equal parts on each glass. Pour water to the first mark on a glass. Then add $\frac{1}{6}$ more water to each glass than the glass before. Tap the glasses lightly and carefully with a pencil. What is the connection between the volume of water in the glass and the sound that the glass produces? Can you use the glasses to play a simple tune?

⑤ Decorative Wrapping

Find a small box to gift wrap. Calculate the surface area of the box to determine the amount of gift wrap needed. Design enough wrapping paper to cover the package. Then wrap your package. Decorate with a ribbon if you wish.

Review/Test

(Lessons 1–4) Name each solid and find its surface area.

1.

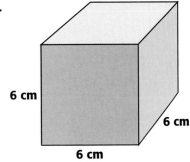

6 cm

6 cm

6 cm

2.

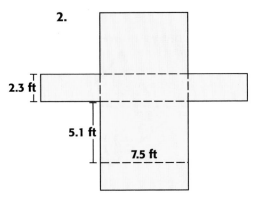

2.3 ft

5.1 ft

7.5 ft

(Lessons 6 and 7) Copy and complete.

3. 16,009 lb = ■ T ■ lb

4. 3 lb 7 oz = ■ oz

5. 50 oz = ■ lb ■ oz

6. 6.92 kg = ■ g

7. 47 g = ■ kg

8. 0.09 kg = ■ g

(Lesson 8) Find each change in temperature.

9. $10°F$ to $48°F$

10. $41°C$ to $15°C$

11. $52°F$ to $23°F$

12. $13°C$ to $3°C$

(Lessons 10 and 11) Copy and complete.

13. 40 fl oz = ■ c

14. ■ pt = 1 gal 3 qt

15. 16 tbsp = ■ fl oz

16. 5 mL = ■ L

17. 0.05 L = ■ mL

18. 2,769 mL = ■ L

(Lesson 12) Copy and complete.

	Volume, Capacity, and Mass	Aquarium
19.	Volume (cm³)	
20.	Amount of Water (L)	
21.	Amount of Water (mL)	
22.	Mass of Water (kg)	
23.	Mass of Water (g)	

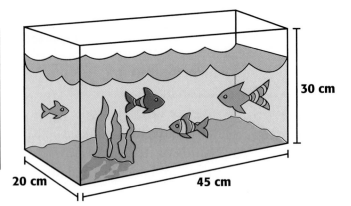

30 cm

20 cm

45 cm

(Lesson 13) Use any strategy to solve.

24. If students lined up in rows of 5, in which row would you find the 32nd student?

25. Billie is building a large cube from smaller ones. If each edge of the large cube will be made up of 4 smaller cubes, how many cubes in all will Billie need?

Performance Assessment

Packaging can be deceptive. Many shapes and sizes of containers are used to package products. Some containers are designed to appear to hold more than they actually do. You are going to design two such packages. Here are the requirements:

- Both packages must have the same volume.

- The dimensions of the packages must be different.

- Use grid paper to make nets for each of your packages.

- Cut out your nets and fold them into the packages.

1. **Decision Making** Decide on a volume to use. Find two different sets of dimensions that will give that volume. Remember, the net for each package must fit on a piece of grid paper. Name one package A and the other B.

2. **Explain Your Thinking** How did you choose your dimensions? Did the size of the grid paper affect your choice of a volume? Your choice in dimensions?

3. **Record Your Data** Copy and complete the table for the two packages you made. You will need to measure your finished packages in both customary and metric units in order to complete the table.

	Dimensions in Metric Units (cm)	Dimensions in Customary Units	Volume in Metric Units	Volume in Customary Units
Package A				
Package B				

4. **Critical Thinking** Which of your packages makes you think it holds more? Can you think of any product in a grocery store that is packaged in different-sized packages that have the same volume? Do the units of measure used on the labels make you think the package holds more or less? Explain.

Math Magazine

Is It Live, or Is It CAD?

If you have been to the movies recently, you have probably seen CAD in action. CAD stands for Computer Assisted Design. CADs are computer software programs that allow you to see different views of 3-dimensional objects. For instance, an architect can turn a picture of a building to see what it would look like from the back or side.

CADs also allow you to add or change detail on a figure. If the architect wants to change the design of a window, it can be done quickly and easily with CAD.

CAD and Movies

If you have ever seen films that use special effects like *Jurassic Park,* you already know what CAD can do.

While filming *Jurassic Park,* the actors had to act afraid of dinosaurs that weren't there. The dinosaurs were created using CAD and added to the original film. In the final movie, it looked as though the dinosaurs were really chasing the actors.

Materials
centimeter or unit cubes

> ### Try These!
> Look at the stacks of cubes below. Draw pictures to show what you think each stack looks like from the left side, the right side, the back, the top, and the bottom.

1.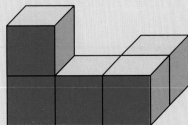

2.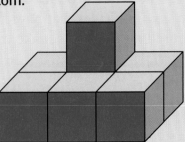

3. Use cubes to make the stacks shown above. Examine them from each side, top, and bottom. Compare the views with your drawings.

4. Use 8 cubes to make a new stack and draw a picture of it from the front view. Challenge a friend to draw the other 5 views.

Cumulative Review

Test Prep Strategy: Make Smart Choices

Use logical reasoning.

The volume of a rectangular solid is 165 ft³. If two of its sides measure 5 feet and 11 feet, what would be the third dimension?

Ⓐ 30 ft   Ⓑ 10 ft   Ⓒ 3 ft   Ⓓ 500 ft

STAY SHARP! You know that volume equals $l \times w \times h$. Multiply 5×11 to get 55. 55×10 is 550, which is too much, therefore the answer must be less than 10. The only choice then is Ⓒ, 3 ft. Check: $5 \times 11 \times 3 = 165$.

Write the letter of the correct answer. Choose any strategy.

1. Find the median of these temperatures: 25°C, 34°C, 25°C, 14°C, 17°C, 16°C.

   Ⓐ 21°C   Ⓑ 25°C   Ⓒ 21.8°C   Ⓓ 20°C

2. Which set of numbers is in order from least to greatest?

   Ⓐ 0.028, 0.0201, 0.02   Ⓑ 0.0201, 0.028, 0.02

   Ⓒ 0.02, 0.028, 0.0201   Ⓓ 0.02, 0.0201, 0.028

3. Yesterday's low temperature was 0°F. Tomorrow's predicted low temperature is 36°F. What is the difference between yesterday's low and tomorrow's predicted low temperature?

   Ⓐ 26°C   Ⓑ 12°F   Ⓒ 4°F   Ⓓ 36°F

4. What is the area of a parallelogram with $b = 15$ cm and $h = 8$ cm?

   Ⓐ 60 cm²   Ⓑ 120 cm²   Ⓒ 60 cm   Ⓓ not here

5. Name this triangle by its angles.

   Ⓐ equilateral   Ⓑ acute   Ⓒ obtuse   Ⓓ right

6. What are the next three numbers in this pattern: $\frac{1}{5}, \frac{2}{10}, \frac{3}{15}, \blacksquare, \blacksquare, \blacksquare$?

   Ⓐ $\frac{4}{45}, \frac{5}{90}, \frac{6}{180}$ Ⓑ $\frac{2}{5}, \frac{3}{10}, \frac{4}{15}$ Ⓒ $\frac{1}{20}, \frac{2}{25}, \frac{3}{30}$ Ⓓ $\frac{4}{20}, \frac{5}{25}, \frac{6}{30}$

7. Peg bought a pair of inline skates for $65.98. The next day they were 25% off. To the nearest cent, how much could she have saved?

   Ⓐ $49.49   Ⓑ $0.25   Ⓒ $16.50   Ⓓ $25.00

8. A candy bar cost $0.45. How much change would you get back if you used a $5-bill to pay for 7 of these candy bars?

   Ⓐ $1.85   Ⓑ $3.15   Ⓒ $2.15   Ⓓ not here

9. Which is not equivalent to the product of $1\frac{2}{3}$ and $3\frac{3}{5}$?

   Ⓐ $\frac{18}{3}$ Ⓑ $\frac{90}{15}$ Ⓒ 6   Ⓓ $4\frac{19}{15}$

Test Prep Strategies

- Read Carefully
- Follow Directions
- Make Smart Choices
- Eliminate Choices
- Work Backward from an Answer

Chapter 12
Ratio, Percent, and Probability

SECTION
A

Swimmer and Doll Maker
Page 527

Ratio and Proportion

527

This table shows Nikki McCray's free-throw record for the first five games of the 1996 season and Grant Hill's free-throw record for the first four games. Which person's record do you think is closer to 50%? Explain.

	Nikki McCray of the Columbus Quest	Grant Hill of the Detroit Pistons
Free Throws Attempted	34	23
Free Throws Made	28	17

SECTION B

Percent

537

The bar graph shows the percent of people in the United States over the age of 7 who participated in sports activities in 1993. How many activities had more participation by females than males?

Artist in Action
Page 537

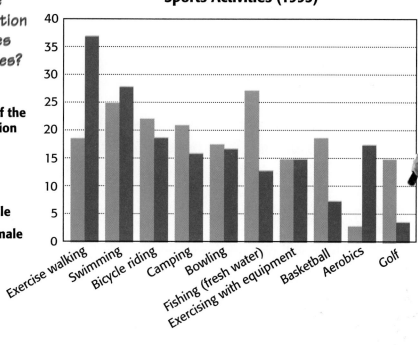

Participation in Ten Most Popular Sports Activities (1993)

Percent of the Population

| | Male |
| | Female |

(Exercise walking, Swimming, Bicycle riding, Camping, Bowling, Fishing (fresh water), Exercising with equipment, Basketball, Aerobics, Golf)

Surfing the World Wide Web!

What sport or game do you enjoy most? Find out more about sports activities at **www.mathsurf.com/5/ch12**.

SECTION C

Probability

545

In 1996, minor league baseball players played for major league baseball players 395 times. If each minor league substitution was for a different major league player, how many major league players never used substitutes?

Major League Baseball Players	Minor League Baseball Players
1,120	5,800

Carnival Games
Page 545

525

TEAM PROJECT
Think Big

Materials

grid paper, ruler, crayons or markers, scissors

African Americans have been making quilts in the United States since the late eighteenth century. Many quilts like the one shown are based on African designs. Draw a pattern and enlarge it so that you could use it to make a quilt.

Make a Plan

- What design will you use for your project?
- How will you enlarge the pattern?

a.

Carry It Out

1. Choose one of these patterns or create one of your own.
2. Make a 2-in. square on grid paper. Copy the pattern onto it.
3. Color and cut out the enlarged pattern.

Talk About It

- What percent of the large pattern is the small pattern?
- If you need 2 yd of purple cloth to make a quilt the sample size, how much purple cloth would you need to make the large quilt?

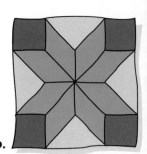

b.

Present the Project

Plan a class presentation of the large patterns. As a class project, make more of the large patterns. Tape the patterns together and display the quilt.

c.

Ratio and Proportion

Liz is an active person. When she's not cutting through the water at the swim center, she's making porcelain dolls. How might Liz use fractions to help make a schedule for a busy week?

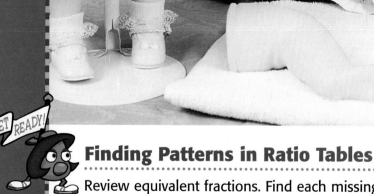

GET READY!

Finding Patterns in Ratio Tables

Review equivalent fractions. Find each missing numerator or denominator.

1. $\frac{1}{2} = \frac{\blacksquare}{4}$ **2.** $\frac{1}{3} = \frac{3}{\blacksquare}$ **3.** $\frac{3}{4} = \frac{6}{\blacksquare}$ **4.** $\frac{2}{5} = \frac{8}{\blacksquare}$

5. $\frac{5}{6} = \frac{\blacksquare}{18}$ **6.** $\frac{3}{7} = \frac{12}{\blacksquare}$ **7.** $\frac{5}{8} = \frac{\blacksquare}{24}$ **8.** $\frac{4}{5} = \frac{16}{\blacksquare}$

Skills Checklist

In this section, you will:

☐ **Learn About Ratios**

☐ **Learn About Patterns in Ratio Tables**

☐ **Explore Equal Ratios**

☐ **Solve Problems by Making Decisions**

Ratios

You Will Learn
how to write and
simplify ratios

Vocabulary
ratio
a pair of numbers
used to compare
quantities

Learn • • • • • •

A ball game from
New Guinea is played
with 4 players. The
players use 5 balls,
4 hoops, and 1 rope.

You can use **ratios** to compare two quantities.

Example 1

Express the number of balls compared to the
number of hoops as a ratio.

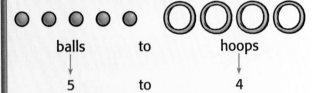

balls	to	hoops
5	to	4

You can express ratios in several ways:

in words	5 to 4
with a colon	5:4
as a fraction	$\frac{5}{4}$

Example 2

Simplify the ratio 24 to 16.

Write 24:16 as a fraction and simplify.

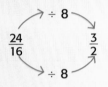

$$\frac{24}{16} \quad \frac{3}{2}$$
÷ 8

3 to 2 is the ratio
24 to 16 in simplest form.

A ratio is not written
as a mixed number.

Math Tip
Order is important
in ratios. 3:2 is not
the same as 2:3.

Talk About It

How is a ratio like a fraction? How is it different?

Check •

Use the New Guinea game. Write each ratio in three ways. Simplify.

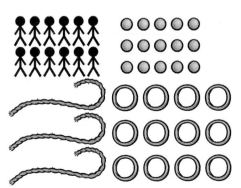

		Ratio			Ratio Simplified		
	Number of	▦ to ▦	▦ : ▦	$\frac{▦}{▦}$	▦ to ▦	▦ : ▦	$\frac{▦}{▦}$
1.	hoops to ropes	12 to 3				4:1	
2.	ropes to players			$\frac{3}{12}$			$\frac{1}{4}$

3. **Reasoning** A different game is played with a
ball-to-player ratio of 1:3. If there are 12 players,
how many balls will be needed? How do you know?

Practice

Skills and Reasoning

Write each ratio in three ways. Simplify.

4. balls to clubs

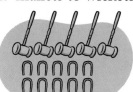

5. tires to tricycle

6. hoop to basketballs

7. mallets to wickets

8. birdies to racquets

9. wheels to skates

10. Which shows the ratio 2:3? 4:3?

a.

b.

c.

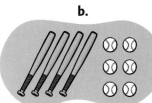

11. Write three different ratios for the picture. Explain what each ratio compares.

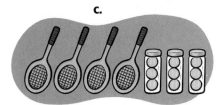

Problem Solving and Applications

12. Money A can of tennis balls is now on sale. What is the ratio of balls to dollars? What is the ball-to-dollar ratio at the regular price?

13. Collecting Data Take a class survey to find out how many of your classmates like soccer, basketball, volleyball, or swimming. Then write your results as ratios comparing the number who like each sport to the whole class.

14. What If You invent your own four-player game using 20 counters and 3 number cubes. Describe your game using ratios.

Mixed Review and Test Prep

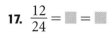

Name two equivalent fractions for each fraction.

15. $\frac{3}{4} = \blacksquare = \blacksquare$ **16.** $\frac{7}{12} = \blacksquare = \blacksquare$ **17.** $\frac{12}{24} = \blacksquare = \blacksquare$

 18. Geometry Which of the following shows the volume of the figure?

Ⓐ 530 cm³   Ⓑ 5,304 cm³   Ⓒ 398 cm³   Ⓓ 3,980 cm³

13 cm, 17 cm, 24 cm

Patterns in Ratio Tables

Learn

Softball, anyone? Courtney's and Taylor's team
won a softball championship. The team often
practices throwing in pairs. That's a ratio of:

$\dfrac{1 \text{ softball}}{2 \text{ players}}$

Courtney and Taylor play
softball in Bethlehem, Pennsylvania.

Math Tip
What you know
about equivalent
fractions will help
you work with
equal ratios.

Example 1
How many softballs will be needed by 10 players? A table of equal ratios can help.

		(1×2)	(1×3)	(1×4)	(1×5)
Softballs	1	2	3	4	5
Players	2	4	6	8	10
		(2×2)	(2×3)	(2×4)	(2×5)

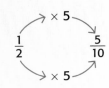

The ratio is 5:10. So, there are 5 softballs for 10 players.

You can also divide to find **equal ratios**.

Example 2
There are 8 teams with 72 players. Use equal ratios to find the number on 1 team.

$\dfrac{\text{teams}}{\text{players}} = \dfrac{8}{72} = \dfrac{1}{\blacksquare}$

		$(8 \div 2)$	$(8 \div 4)$	$(8 \div 8)$
Teams	8	4	2	1
Players	72	36	18	9
		$(72 \div 2)$	$(72 \div 4)$	$(72 \div 8)$

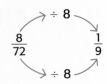

The ratio is 1:9. So, each team has 9 players.

A statement that two ratios are equal is called a **proportion**.

$\dfrac{1}{2} = \dfrac{5}{10}$ is a proportion. $\dfrac{8}{72} = \dfrac{1}{9}$ is a proportion.

How can ratio tables be used to find equal ratios?

Check

Soccer balls	3		9	12	
Players	5	10		20	

1. Copy and complete the ratio table to find equal ratios.

2. **Reasoning** A ratio table includes $\frac{9}{12}$. Name another ratio in the table.

Practice

Skills and Reasoning

Copy and complete each ratio table.

3.

6	12			30
7		21	35	

4.

4	8	12		
	18		36	45

5. In a game, each player gets 5 number cards. Make a ratio table that shows how many cards for 3, 4, 5, and 6 players.

6. A table of equal ratios includes $\frac{15}{40}$.

   a. Name another ratio in the table.

   b. Write a proportion for these ratios.

Problem Solving and Applications

7. Kyle says the ratio of players to pucks at hockey practice is $\frac{12}{5}$. How many pucks would there be for 36 players?

8. **Critical Thinking** The ratio of teaspoons to tablespoons is 3 to 1. If a recipe for 4 people calls for 6 tsp of sugar, how many tablespoons of sugar would you need for 12 people?

9. **Language Arts** The words *dealer, wooden,* and *eleven* have a vowel-to-consonant ratio of 3 to 3. List 6 other words with equal ratios.

10. **Write Your Own Problem** Choose a vowel-to-consonant ratio and find three words for it.

11. **Algebra Readiness** What must n be to make this equation true? $\frac{7}{8} = \frac{(7 \times n)}{48}$

12. **Using Data** Use the Data File on page 524. Whose free throw statistics are better: McCray's or Hill's? Explain.

Mixed Review and Test Prep

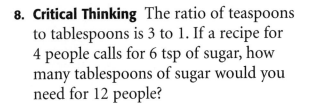

Write each fraction in simplest form.

13. $\frac{15}{36}$ 14. $\frac{7}{49}$ 15. $\frac{32}{40}$ 16. $\frac{27}{18}$ 17. $\frac{44}{12}$

18. **Measurement** Which of the following shows a height of 3 ft 5 in.?

   Ⓐ 14 in.   Ⓑ 36 in.   Ⓒ 40 in.   Ⓓ 41 in.   Ⓔ not here

Exploring Equal Ratios

Problem Solving Connection

■ Make a Table

■ Look for a Pattern

Materials
grid paper

Vocabulary
coordinates
an ordered number pair used in graphing

Explore • • • • • • • • • • •

Liz keeps herself busy. She enjoys making porcelain dolls and their clothes. She also swims each week.

Liz is from Marcus, Iowa.

Work Together

Liz swims one day a week. She works on her dolls three days a week.

1. What is the ratio of doll-making days to swimming days in one week?

2. Copy and complete the ratio table that shows this ratio up to 6 weeks. Show each ratio as an ordered pair.

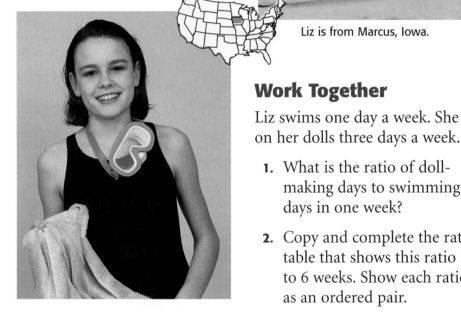

Ratio of Doll-Making Days to Swimming Days						
Week	1	2	3	4	5	6
Doll-Making	3	6		12		
Swimming	1					
Ordered Pairs	(3,1)					

3. Create a graph and plot the **coordinates** in the ratio table. What will you label each axis on this graph?

Did You Know?
Fred Newton swam the longest distance on record in 1930. He swam 1,826 mi down the Mississippi River.

Talk About It

4. What happens when ordered pairs for equal ratios are graphed? What kind of pattern do you see?

5. Explain why the ratios $\frac{3}{2}$, $\frac{6}{4}$, $\frac{9}{6}$, $\frac{12}{8}$, and $\frac{15}{10}$ would lie on the same line if they were graphed.

Connect

This graph shows the ordered pairs for the equal ratios $\frac{1}{2}$, $\frac{2}{4}$, $\frac{4}{8}$, $\frac{6}{12}$, and $\frac{8}{16}$. They lie on the same line.

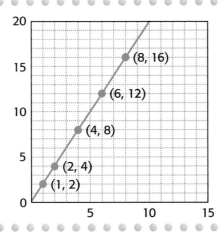

Math Tip

The ordered pairs for equal ratios lie on the same line.

Practice

Use grid paper. Graph the coordinates from each ratio table.

1.

1	7	9	12	14
2	14	18	24	28

2.

2	6	10	14	20
3	9	15	21	30

3.

1	2	3	4	5
4	8	12	16	20

4.

3	6	9	12	15
4	8	12	16	20

5.

2	4	6	8	10
5	10	15	20	25

6. Science When lightning strikes, the number of seconds before you hear thunder can help you tell how far away the lightning is. If lightning strikes 1 mi away, you will hear thunder 5 sec later. This ratio of distance to time is $\frac{1}{5}$. Make a graph that shows the distance/time ratios for lightning that is 3, 5, 7, 9, and 11 mi away.

7. Using Data Copy the graph of equal ratios below. Plot three more equal ratios.

8. Collecting Data Survey your friends and family about how many hours a day they spend playing a sport or game. Create ratios comparing these numbers to the numbers of hours in a day. Then graph the ratios. Do they lie on a straight line? What does your graph show you about your survey results?

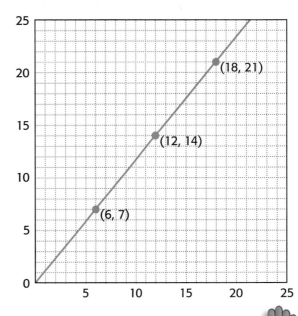

9. Journal Create a ratio that compares the hours you spend at school on a given day to the total number of hours you are awake. Then find five other ratios that equal this one. Make a graph that shows these ratios.

Problem Solving

Decision Making: **Scale Drawing**

You Will Learn

how to solve problems by making decisions about scale drawings

Materials

grid paper

Vocabulary

scale
a ratio that shows the relationship between a scale drawing and the actual object

Explore •

Your team has won first prize in the Little League tournament: play a game at a major league stadium! You decide to make a **scale** drawing of the playing field on grid paper to use in discussing the big game.

You want your drawing to be in proportion to the actual baseball field. This means the dimensions of your drawing and the actual field will be equal ratios.

You will need to consider how you will decide on a scale for your drawing and how many feet each square on the grid paper will represent.

Problem Solving Hint

Equal ratios can be found by dividing all the dimensions by the same number.

Dodger Stadium, Los Angeles, California

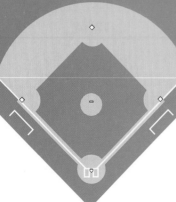

Facts and Data
• Each side of the baseball diamond is 90 feet.
• The distance along the left field foul line is 330 feet.
• The distance along the right field foul line is 330 feet.
• The lines connecting the bases and home plate are called base lines.
• The area enclosed by the bases and home plate is called the infield.
• The area beyond the base lines is called the outfield.
• The pitcher's mound is in the center of the infield.

Work Together

▶ **Understand**

1. What do you know?

2. What do you need to decide?

3. How can you use your understanding of equal ratios to help you make decisions?

4. What are the greatest dimensions you must represent? The least?

▶ **Plan and Solve**

5. How many feet will each square on your grid paper represent?

6. How many squares will each foul line be? Each base line?

7. Do you notice any patterns in the baseball field's dimensions? If so, what are they?

8. Give a proportion you could use to relate a real baseball diamond to your drawing.

▶ **Make a Decision**

9. How did you decide on a scale?

10. Can you make a larger scale drawing on your grid paper? A smaller scale drawing?

▶ **Present Your Decision**

11. Share your scale drawing with others. Explain your scale and the proportion you used.

PROBLEM SOLVING PRACTICE

Review and Practice

Vocabulary Match each with its meaning.

1. ratio   **a.** ratios that give the same comparison

2. equal ratios   **b.** statement that two ratios are equal

3. proportion   **c.** a pair of numbers used to compare quantities

(Lesson 1) Write each ratio in three ways. Simplify.

4. baseballs to mitts   5. flowers to vase

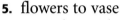

6. A bag of six jump ropes is on sale for $8.00. What is the ratio of ropes to dollars? What is the rope-to-dollar ratio at the regular price of $10.00?

(Lesson 2) Copy and complete each ratio table.

7.

5	15	25		45
9		45	63	

8.

3		12	18	
7	14	28		56

9. For a test, the teacher gave 3 pencils to each student who did not have them. Make a ratio table that shows how many pencils would be given out in all if there were 3, 4, 5, 6, or 7 students needing pencils.

(Lesson 3) Use grid paper. Graph the ordered pairs from each ratio table.

10.

1	2	3	4	5
2	4	6	8	10
(1, 2)	(2, 4)	(3, 6)	(4, 8)	(5, 10)

11.

2	4	6	8	10
3	6	9	12	15
(2, 3)	(4, 6)	(6, 9)	(8, 12)	(10, 15)

12.

1	3	5	10	12	13
3	9	15	30	36	39
(1, 3)	(3, 9)	(5, 15)	(10, 30)	(12, 36)	(13, 39)

13. **Journal** Create a ratio that compares the number of boys to the number of girls in your class. Find five different ratios using your class.

Skills Checklist

In this section, you have:

☑ Learned About Ratios

☑ Learned About Patterns in Ratio Tables

☑ Explored Equal Ratios

☑ Solved Problems by Making Decisions

B Percent

You might find Jenny figure skating, playing a flute, practicing the piano, or drawing. The arts are an important part of her life!

About what percent of her day do you think Jenny might spend on music or art?

Estimating Percent of a Number

GET READY!

Review decimals. Round each number to the place of the underlined digit.

1. 1.4<u>2</u>   2. 0.5<u>6</u>   3. 7.6<u>4</u>9   4. 14.7<u>8</u>4

5. 3.<u>4</u>5   6. 0.0<u>2</u>1   7. 4.<u>9</u>9   8. 20.<u>6</u>4

9. 0.3<u>2</u>8   10. 1.<u>6</u>7   11. 18.<u>3</u>7   12. 0.<u>8</u>9

Skills Checklist

In this section, you will:

☐ Explore Percent Patterns

☐ Learn to Estimate the Percent of a Number

☐ Find the Percent of a Number

Exploring Percent Patterns

Problem Solving Connection

- Look for a Pattern
- Make a Table

Explore • • • • • • • • •

Percents are ratios in which a number is compared to 100. For example, 50% compares 50 to 100. You can use patterns to find percents.

Halves	Fourths	Eighths	Percents
		$\frac{1}{8}$	12.5%
	$\frac{1}{4}$		
$\frac{1}{2}$			
$\frac{2}{2}$			

Work Together

Copy and complete. Use patterns, addition, and subtraction.

Remember
To write a fraction as a percent, first find an equivalent fraction with a denominator of 100.

Halves	Fourths	Eighths	Percents
		$\frac{1}{8}$	12.5%
	$\frac{1}{4}$		
		$\frac{3}{8}$	
$\frac{1}{2}$			
		$\frac{5}{8}$	
		$\frac{6}{8}$	
		$\frac{7}{8}$	
$\frac{2}{2}$			100%

Talk About It

How can you use what you know about the percent for $\frac{1}{8}$ and the percent for $\frac{1}{2}$ to find the percent for $\frac{3}{8}$? For $\frac{5}{8}$?

Connect

This table shows percent patterns for halves, thirds, and sixths.

Halves	Thirds	Sixths	Percents
		$\frac{1}{6}$	$16\frac{2}{3}\%$
	$\frac{1}{3}$	$\frac{2}{6}$	$33\frac{1}{3}\%$
$\frac{1}{2}$		$\frac{3}{6}$	50%
	$\frac{2}{3}$	$\frac{4}{6}$	$66\frac{2}{3}\%$
		$\frac{5}{6}$	$83\frac{1}{3}\%$
$\frac{2}{2}$	$\frac{3}{3}$	$\frac{6}{6}$	100%

$$\frac{1}{6} \quad + \quad \frac{2}{6} \quad = \quad \frac{3}{6}$$
$$\downarrow \qquad\qquad \downarrow \qquad\qquad \downarrow$$
$$16\frac{2}{3}\% + 33\frac{1}{3}\% = 50\%$$

$$\frac{1}{3} \quad + \quad \frac{2}{3} \quad = \quad \frac{3}{3}$$
$$\downarrow \qquad\qquad \downarrow \qquad\qquad \downarrow$$
$$33\frac{1}{3}\% + 66\frac{2}{3}\% = 100\%$$

Practice

Patterns Copy and complete. You may use a calculator to help.

1. $\frac{1}{5} = $ ■%

$\frac{2}{5} = $ ■%

$\frac{3}{5} = $ ■%

$\frac{4}{5} = $ ■%

$\frac{5}{5} = $ ■%

2. $\frac{1}{10} = $ ■%

$\frac{2}{10} = $ ■%

$\frac{3}{10} = $ ■%

$\frac{4}{10} = $ ■%

$\frac{5}{10} = $ ■%

3. $\frac{1}{20} = $ ■%

$\frac{2}{20} = $ ■%

$\frac{3}{20} = $ ■%

$\frac{4}{20} = $ ■%

$\frac{5}{20} = $ ■%

4. $\frac{1}{50} = $ ■%

$\frac{2}{50} = $ ■%

$\frac{3}{50} = $ ■%

$\frac{4}{50} = $ ■%

$\frac{5}{50} = $ ■%

5. $\frac{■}{5} = 80\%$

$\frac{■}{10} = 80\%$

$\frac{■}{20} = 80\%$

$\frac{■}{40} = 80\%$

$\frac{■}{50} = 80\%$

Write the percent for each.

6. $\frac{1}{2}$ **7.** $\frac{3}{4}$ **8.** $\frac{3}{8}$ **9.** $\frac{5}{6}$ **10.** $\frac{2}{3}$

Using Data Use the data to answer **11–13**.

11. Which of the players' shooting percentages could be expressed as a fraction with a denominator of 4?

12. Give two equivalent fractions for Linda's shooting percentage.

13. In the next game, Carmen and Jen each doubled their shooting percentages. Which player's percentage is equivalent to $\frac{7}{10}$?

14. **Critical Thinking** Could 25% be equivalent to a fraction with a denominator of 12? Explain.

15. **Journal** Explain how knowing the percent equivalent of $\frac{2}{5}$ can help you to find the percent equivalent of $\frac{4}{5}$.

FREE THROW SHOOTING

Blue Cheers vs. Bears

Jen   35%
Carmen 40%
Linda   60%
Tovah   72%
Sarah   75%

Estimating Percent of a Number

You Will Learn

how to estimate the percent of a number

Learn • • • • • • •

When you play sports, what's important to you? Learning new skills? Winning? Or just having fun? A recent survey asked students around the country how they felt.

You can use percent benchmarks to estimate the survey results.

Math Tip

Common percent benchmarks include:

10% or $\frac{1}{10}$

25% or $\frac{1}{4}$

$33\frac{1}{3}$% or $\frac{1}{3}$

50% or $\frac{1}{2}$

$66\frac{2}{3}$% or $\frac{2}{3}$

75% or $\frac{3}{4}$

Example

If 400 students took part in the survey, about how many students said learning skills is very important?

73.4% of the students said learning skills is very important.

73.4% is close to 75%.

75% = $\frac{3}{4}$ $\frac{3}{4}$ of 400 is 300.

About 300 students said learning skills is very important.

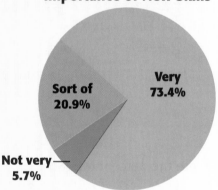

Importance of New Skills

Sort of
20.9%

Very
73.4%

Not very —
5.7%

Talk About It

Explain how you might substitute simpler numbers to help estimate 11% of 596.

Check •

Estimate.

1. 47% of 200   **2.** 72.8% of 80   **3.** 9% of 180   **4.** 65% of 180

5. 26% of 100   **6.** 47% of 240   **7.** 18% of 80   **8.** 58.7% of 40

9. Reasoning When estimating 31.5% of 38, would you estimate $33\frac{1}{3}$% of 36 or $33\frac{1}{3}$% of 40? Why?

Skills and Reasoning

Estimate.

10. 91% of 80

11. 18% of 20

12. 52% of 500

13. 26% of 199

14. $33\frac{1}{3}$% of 20

15. 30% of 110

16. 5% of 60

17. 11% of 994

18. Explain how finding 10% of 120 can help you estimate 89% of 120.

19. Explain how you would find an estimate for 82% of 60.

20. Samantha says she can use the benchmark $\frac{1}{3}$ to estimate the sale price of this soccer ball. Explain how she can do this.

Summer Sale 66% Off! $24.00

Problem Solving and Applications

Using Data Use the circle graph to answer **21** and **22**.

21. Harry surveyed students at school to find out which kind of music they liked to listen to the most. Estimate the number of students who said popular songs were their favorite.

22. **Critical Thinking** Which kinds of music listed were named by fewer than 20 students?

23. **Time** Marcus and Trevor held a contest to see who could keep a kite in the air longer. Trevor kept his in the air for an hour and a half, Marcus for 65% of that time. Estimate how many minutes Marcus' kite was in the air. Explain your answer.

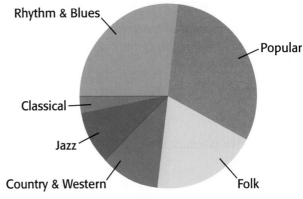

Kinds of Music Students Like to Listen To

Rhythm & Blues — Popular — Classical — Jazz — Country & Western — Folk

Survey Size: 155 Students

Mixed Review and Test Prep

Write each percent as a fraction in simplest form.

24. 60%

25. 20%

26. 23%

27. 42%

28. $16\frac{2}{3}$%

29. 80%

30. 50%

31. 49%

32. 36%

33. 25%

Find each product.

34. 0.50×190

35. 0.20×430

36. $0.83 \times 2,000$

37. 0.45×15

38. 0.36×150

39. 0.60×180

40. 0.75×58

41. 0.40×25

42. **Measurement** Change 5 ft 7 in. to inches.

Ⓐ 57 in.   Ⓑ 60 in.   Ⓒ 67 in.   Ⓓ $5\frac{7}{12}$ in.

Finding Percent of a Number

You Will Learn

how to find the percent of a number

Materials

calculator

Learn

Jenny loves ice skating, music, and drawing. She is saving for a set of colored drawing pencils that cost $40. The set is on sale for 25% off.

Example 1

How much is the 25% discount worth?

Find the percent of a number by writing the percent as a fraction or decimal and multiplying.

25% of $40 = $\frac{1}{4} \times 40$

$\frac{1}{4} \times 40 = 10$

The 25% discount is worth $10.

Example 2

Use the % key on a calculator to find percent.

What is 45% of $275.90?

Press:

4 5 % × 2 7 5 . 9 0 = | 124.155 |

Round to the nearest cent: $124.16.

Estimate to check the answer.

50% or $\frac{1}{2}$ of 280 is 140.

The answer is reasonable.

45% of $275.90 is about $124.16.

Talk About It

Math Tip

Round your answer to the nearest cent when finding percents of dollar amounts.

Explain how you would find how much to pay for colored pencils that are being sold at a 30% discount.

Check

Choose a method. Find the percent of each.

1. 50% of 75   **2.** 12% of 100   **3.** 40% of 18   **4.** 15% of $32.00

5. 30% of 60   **6.** 35% of 35   **7.** 29% of 5,000   **8.** 98% of $10,000

9. 75% of 80   **10.** 45% of 120   **11.** 60% of 30   **12.** 33% of $515.00

13. Reasoning Explain how you might use 10% of $19.95 to estimate 5% of $19.95.

Practice

Skills and Reasoning | Choose a tool

Choose a method. Find the percent of each.

14. 3% of 3.33
15. 10% of 6
16. 90% of $5.90
17. 65% of 400

18. 77% of 10
19. 54% of 750
20. 2% of $4.00
21. 17% of 40

22. 45% of $21.00
23. 5% of 200
24. 75% of 24
25. 36% of $250

26. Which number is greater: 10% of 400, 100% of 40, or 1% of 40,000? Explain.

27. Which costs less to buy a $50 computer game at 25% off or a $60 game at 30% off? Explain.

Problem Solving and Applications

28. **Money** Which set of artist's paintbrushes is less expensive? Why?

29. The art club has 60 members. 35% of the members paint; another 10% model clay. How many members don't paint or model clay?

30. **Social Studies** Before elections, polls are taken to predict which candidate will win. Suppose 1,000 people are polled and 37% say they will vote for Ms. Morgan Thomas. How many people said they would vote for Ms. Thomas?

31. **Collecting Data** Use the Data File on page 525. Conduct a class survey. Use the choices given on the double-bar graph. Have each student choose his or her favorite activity. Make a similar double-bar graph that shows the approximate percent of the class that chose each activity. How does your graph compare with the graph on page 525?

Mixed Review and Test Prep

Mental Math Estimate.

32. 99×35
33. $49.98 - $17.50
34. $368 \div 9$
35. $99 + 37 + 25 + 74$

36. 38×21
37. $376 - 263$
38. $68 + 72 + 19$
39. $429 \div 76$

40. Which of the following ratios is equal to $\frac{5}{9}$?

ⓐ $\frac{10}{27}$
ⓑ $\frac{10}{54}$
ⓒ $\frac{20}{36}$
ⓓ $\frac{50}{900}$

Review and Practice

Vocabulary Choose the correct word to complete the sentence.

1. Common percent _____ include 10%, 25%, and 50%. (ratios, benchmarks)

(Lesson 5) Patterns Copy and complete. Use patterns. You may use a calculator to help.

2. $\frac{1}{50} = \blacksquare\%$ 3. $\frac{1}{25} = \blacksquare\%$ 4. $\frac{1}{4} = \blacksquare\%$ 5. $\frac{1}{75} = \blacksquare\%$ 6. $\frac{1}{100} = \blacksquare\%$

$\frac{2}{50} = \blacksquare\%$ $\frac{2}{25} = \blacksquare\%$ $\frac{2}{4} = \blacksquare\%$ $\frac{2}{75} = \blacksquare\%$ $\frac{2}{100} = \blacksquare\%$

$\frac{3}{50} = \blacksquare\%$ $\frac{3}{25} = \blacksquare\%$ $\frac{3}{4} = \blacksquare\%$ $\frac{3}{75} = \blacksquare\%$ $\frac{3}{100} = \blacksquare\%$

$\frac{4}{50} = \blacksquare\%$ $\frac{4}{25} = \blacksquare\%$ $\frac{4}{4} = \blacksquare\%$ $\frac{4}{75} = \blacksquare\%$ $\frac{4}{100} = \blacksquare\%$

$\frac{5}{50} = \blacksquare\%$ $\frac{5}{25} = \blacksquare\%$ $\frac{6}{8} = \blacksquare\%$ $\frac{5}{75} = \blacksquare\%$ $\frac{5}{100} = \blacksquare\%$

(Lesson 6) Estimate.

7. 48% of 20   8. 9.9% of 54   9. 51% of 600   10. 23% of 100

11. $33\frac{1}{3}\%$ of 80   12. 19% of 40   13. 24% of 779   14. 78% of 50

(Lesson 7) Find the percent of each.

15. 5% of 4.6   16. 10% of 12   17. 75% of $5.00   18. 16% of 20

19. 66% of 23   20. 1% of $75.90   21. 87% of 123   22. 36% of $300

23. 97% of 100   24. 100% of 30   25. 35% of $20,000   26. 90% of 360

27. Which soccer ball is more expensive?

28. **Money** Jessica wants to buy a new dictionary. The neighborhood bookstore has a $30 dictionary on sale for 20% off. If Jessica has $25, does she have enough money to buy the dictionary? Explain.

$12.95

$15.95 25% off

29. In one class of 40 students, 20% of the students walk to school. In another class of 50 students, 18% walk to school. Which class has more students who walk?

30. **Journal** To find the cost of a $20 item marked down 25%, Mark multiplied by $\frac{1}{4}$ and Josie multiplied by $\frac{3}{4}$. Both found the right answer. Explain how this could be.

Skills Checklist

In this section you have:

☑ **Explored Percent Patterns**

☑ **Learned to Estimate the Percent of a Number**

☑ **Learned How to Find Percent of a Number**

REVIEW AND PRACTICE

Probability

Carnival games are fun! You may win a prize like a stuffed animal. Look at the information on the sign. Which sum do you think will be easier to get? Why?

CARNIVAL

LUCKY PICKS

SUM OF 3   SUM OF 5

WINS A   WINS A

6" TIGER   36" TIGER

Win Prizes

Fun For All

Skills Checklist

In this section, you will:

☐ **Explore Probability and Fairness**

☐ **Explore Predicting from Samples and Experiments**

☐ **Solve Problems By Making an Organized List**

☐ **Express Probabilities as Fractions**

☐ **Explore Expected and Experimental Results**

GET READY!

Exploring Expected and Experimental Results

Review fractions. Copy and complete.
Write >, < or =.

1. $\frac{1}{2}$ ⚪ $\frac{2}{3}$ 2. $\frac{3}{4}$ ⚪ $\frac{4}{5}$ 3. $\frac{2}{5}$ ⚪ $\frac{4}{10}$ 4. $\frac{5}{6}$ ⚪ $\frac{4}{5}$

5. $\frac{3}{5}$ ⚪ $\frac{2}{3}$ 6. $\frac{6}{7}$ ⚪ $\frac{2}{3}$ 7. $\frac{1}{3}$ ⚪ $\frac{2}{9}$ 8. $\frac{5}{8}$ ⚪ $\frac{2}{3}$

Exploring Fairness

Problem Solving Connection

Guess and Check

Materials

- spinners
- paper clips
- colored pencils or crayons

Vocabulary

probability
ratio of the number of ways an event can occur to the total number of possible outcomes

outcome
a possible result in an experiment

Explore

In each racing game, the player whose car travels the most laps wins. Are these games fair to each player?

The Two-Color Racing Game:
Player 1's car goes one lap every time the pointer lands on blue.

Player 2's car goes one lap every time the pointer lands on red.

The Five-Color Racing Game:
Player 1's car goes one lap every time the pointer lands on blue, yellow, or black.

Player 2's car goes one lap every time the pointer lands on red or green.

Work Together

1. Make 2 spinners like those shown.

2. Play the Two-Color Racing Game with a partner.

   a. Make predictions. In 50 spins, how many times will the pointer land on blue? On red?

   b. Spin 50 times. Mark your results on a tally sheet. Whose car traveled more laps?

   c. With 50 more spins, do you think the results would be similar? Explain.

   d. Is the game fair? Why or why not?

3. Play the Five-Color Racing Game with a partner.

   a. Make predictions. In 50 spins, how many times will the pointer land on green? On black?

   b. Spin 50 times. Tally your results. Whose car traveled more laps?

   c. With 50 more spins, do you think the results would be similar?

   d. Is the game fair? Why or why not?

Problem Solving Hint

In a fair game, each player has the same chance of winning.

Talk About It

How can you tell if a spinner game is fair?

Connect

Probability of an event = $\dfrac{\text{number of ways an event can occur}}{\text{total number of possible outcomes}}$

These spinners have three possible results—or **outcomes**—for each spin: red, blue, or green.

Spinner		Probability of Outcome	Fairness
Spinner 1		equally likely	fair
Spinner 2		not equal, more area for green	unfair

Practice

1. These spinners are for fantasy football games between two teams. On each spin, a touchdown is scored by either the red team or the blue team, depending on where the pointer lands. Decide whether each game is fair or unfair. Explain.

   a.   b.   c.

2. What are the possible outcomes of two spins of Spinner 1 at the top of the page?

3. Tom and Gene are tossing a pair of pennies. Tom earns one point when both coins land heads up or tails up. Gene earns one point when one coin lands heads up and one lands tails up. Do you think this is a fair game? Explain.

4. **Critical Thinking** Barbara and Sue roll two number cubes numbered 1–6. Barbara wins if the number on each cube is the same. Sue wins if each cube comes up with a different number. Who do you think will win more often? Why?

5. **Using Data** Look at the spinner on page 546 for the Five-Color Racing Game. Assign colors to 4 players so that it is a fair game.

6. Suppose you and a friend are playing a game in which you draw slips of paper from a bag. Each slip of paper has one letter written on it. There is one slip of paper for every letter in this phrase: *Who Will Win?* If you draw a *w*, you win. Your friend wins by drawing an *l*. Is this a fair game? Explain your reasoning.

 7. **Journal** Make up the rules for two games people could play with number cubes. One game should be fair, the other unfair.

Exploring Predicting from Samples

Problem Solving Connection

- Guess and Check
- Make a Table

Materials

books, magazines, old newspapers

Vocabulary

sample
a selected part of a large group

Did You Know?

Of the 26 letters in the English alphabet, Q occurs least often in English words.

Explore ●

Professional code breakers can often "crack" coded messages by tallying the frequency of the symbols or letters used in the code. In English words, certain letters are more frequently used than others.

Work Together

Make your own predictions about how often certain letters will appear.

1. Analyze a sample in a book, magazine, or newspaper.

   a. Choose the first 50 letters of a paragraph in a book, newspaper or magazine. Tally the letters. Which letter appears most frequently? Second most frequently?

   b. Predict. What will be the most common letter in a 200-letter sample? How many times will it appear? Use a ratio table to help.

2. Repeat the tally with a 200-letter sample.

   a. Compare 50-letter and 200-letter results with those of a partner. Were your results more alike in the small or the large sample?

   b. Predict the most common letter in a 400-letter sample. Use a ratio table to help you predict the number of times the letter will appear.

   c. Create a 400-letter tally by adding your own and your partner's results. How do these total results compare to the other results and your prediction?

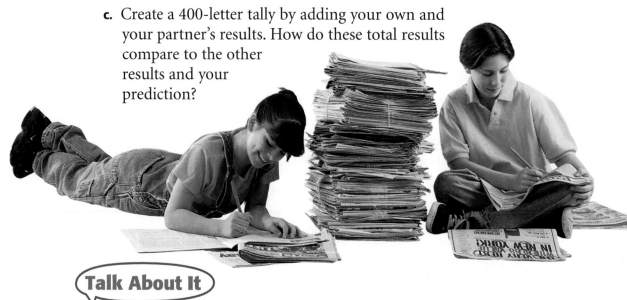

Talk About It

3. How did you use sample results and a ratio table to make a prediction?

4. Are large or small samples better for making predictions? Explain.

Connect

The 5 letters that appear most often in English words are E, T, A, O, and I. This discovery was made after testing many large **samples**. Using large samples helps you make more accurate predictions. Small samples do not supply enough data to make accurate predictions.

Sample

A sentence in a book

Letter	E	T	A	O	I
Tally		ll	l		l

Sample

Scattered words in a book

Letter	E	T	A	O	I
Tally	llll llll	llll lll	llll llll	llll llll	llll ll

Practice

This bag contains different numbers of black, white, and yellow marbles. The list below shows the results of some samples.

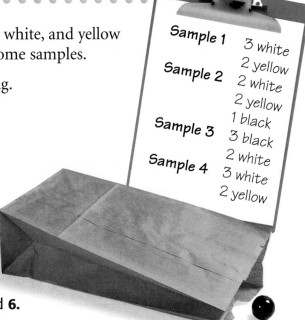

Sample 1   3 white
            2 yellow
Sample 2   2 white
            2 yellow
            1 black
Sample 3   3 black
            2 white
Sample 4   3 white
            2 yellow

1. Predict the most common color in the bag. Explain.

2. Predict the least common color.

3. If Sample 3 were the only sample, what would you predict to be the most common color?

4. Why is it better to use the total of all four samples than a single sample to make a prediction?

Use data at the top of the page to answer 5 and 6.

5. **Logic** A code often replaces one letter with another. The letters that appear most frequently in one coded note are W and P. The word that appears most frequently is PZW. What do you think PZW means?

6. **Language Arts** Look at the coded poem. Decode the poem using the following clues:

   • There are the same number of As as Ts.

   • The letters E, F, L, and R are used four times each.

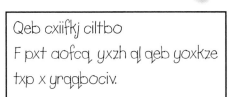

Qeb cxiifkj ciltbo
F pxt aofcq, yxzh ql qeb yoxkze
txp x yrqqbociv.

7. **Journal** Would you expect to find even one Q in a 26-letter sample? Explain your thinking.

Exploring Predicting from Experiments

All Heads   All Tails

Problem Solving Connection

- Use Objects/ Act It Out

- Make a Table

- Use Logical Reasoning

Materials

coins

Remember

A coin is equally likely to land heads or tails.

Explore

Can you make heads or tails of this? What is the likelihood of getting these results when you toss three coins?

Experiments can help you predict outcomes.

Work Together

Use three coins.

1. Predict how many "all 3 heads" or "all 3 tails" you will get in 20 tosses.

2. Make a table. Toss all 3 coins and record each result in the table. After 6 tosses, your table might look like this:

3 Heads	2 Heads/1 Tail	2 Tails/1 Head	3 Tails
I	II	III	

3. Continue until you have recorded 20 tosses. Compare your results with your prediction.

4. Combine your results with the results of the rest of the class. Which kind of toss happens most? Least?

5. Describe the chances of each outcome in a single toss of 3 coins as *very likely, somewhat likely,* or *unlikely.*

Talk About It

Do you think the class results are more accurate for making predictions than your individual results? Why or why not?

Connect

Suppose you recorded data in the table from an experiment in which two counters were tossed at the same time. One counter has a red side and a yellow side. The other has a red side and a blue side.

	Toss 1	Toss 2	Toss 3	Toss 4
Counter 1	●	●	○	○
Counter 2	●	●	●	●

Two of 4 possible outcomes have one red.

Results of 18 Tosses		
2 Red	1 Red	0 Red
|||	⦀⦀ ||	|||

One red occurred most often.

You can predict that the most likely outcome is one red.

Practice

1. You can use experiments to help you make predictions.

   a. Are you more likely to get all heads with 2 coins or 4 coins? Experiment with each 20 times. Record your results.

   b. How many tosses do you think it will take to get all heads with 10 coins?

Write the numbers 1–6 two times each on separate slips of paper. Put the slips of paper in a bag and use them to answer **2–7**.

2. Experiment with selecting 2 slips of paper and recording the sum of the numbers. Which result do you get the most? The least?

3. Which is more likely to occur: getting a sum of 4 or of 7? Explain.

4. Which do you think is more likely to occur: getting a sum of 12 or getting a sum of 9. Explain.

5. **Music** Some 20th-century composers, such as John Cage, have used chance to affect the way their music sounds. Suppose a conductor selects 2 slips of paper to decide whether clarinets, trumpets, or violins will play a melody. She uses this table to make her decision. Which instrument is most likely to play the melody?

If both numbers match	
If the sum of the numbers is six or less	
If the sum of the numbers is greater than six	

6. **Write Your Own Problem** Design an experiment that uses numbers on slips of paper. Make a table to show the possible outcomes.

7. **Journal** Describe the possible outcomes of selecting 2 slips of paper from the bag.

Problem Solving

Analyze Strategies: Make an Organized List

You Will Learn
how to solve problems by making an organized list

Learn •

You are going away for the weekend and want to take 6 of your favorite books. You have room for only 2 books in your bag. How many different combinations of 2 books can you choose?

Work Together

▶ **Understand**   What do you know?

What do you need to find out?

▶ **Plan**   How will you find the answer?

Call your books A, B, C, D, E, and F.
Make an organized list to find all the ways.

▶ **Solve**   Begin by finding all combinations for book A.

AB, AC, AD, AE, AF

Problem Solving Hint
AB and BA are the same combination, so don't list it twice!

Next, find all combinations for book B.

BC, BD, BE, BF

Complete the list.

CD, CE, CF
DE, DF
EF

What is the answer?

You can choose from 15 different combinations.

▶ **Look Back**   How can you check your answer?

How does making an organized list help in solving some problems?

Problem Solving
Understand
Plan
Solve
Look Back

Use an organized list to solve.

1. Suppose you decided which 2 books to take by writing their letters on sections of a spinner and spinning twice. When you made the spinner, however, you accidentally put only 5 sections (A to E) on it.

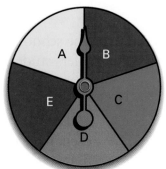

   a. Does each pair of books have an equally likely chance of occurring? Explain your answer.

   b. Which combinations of 2 books can come up on 2 spins that will not help you decide?

   c. How many combinations of books are there that include book A?

   d. How many combinations of 2 books are there for you to choose from the spinner? Make an organized list to help you decide.

Problem Solving
Practice

Problem Solving
Strategies

- Use Objects/Act It Out
- Draw a Picture
- Look for a Pattern
- Guess and Check
- Use Logical Reasoning
- Make an Organized List
- Make a Table
- Solve a Simpler Problem
- Work Backward

Choose a Tool

Use any strategy to solve.

2. You also have to pack clothes in your bag. You are packing 3 jeans, 3 sweaters, and 2 jackets.

   a. How many different outfits can you make if an outfit includes a pair of jeans, a sweater, and a jacket?

   b. If you leave one sweater home, how many different outfits are possible?

3. By leaving one sweater home, you have room for 4 books. How many combinations of 4 books are possible from the 6 books you have?

4. You have been traveling for 30 min. It is 15 mi more to the rest stop. How far have you traveled?

5. The bus ticket and the taxi fare together cost $48.45. The bus ticket is $23.45 more than the taxi fare. How much is the taxi fare?

   Ⓐ $25   Ⓑ $23.45   Ⓒ $71.90   Ⓓ $12.50   Ⓔ not here

Expressing Probabilities as Fractions

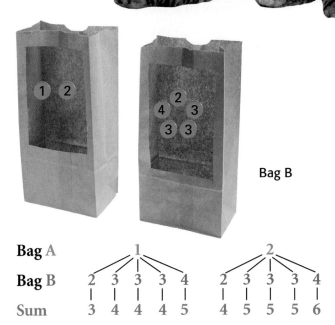

You Will Learn

to express probabilities as fractions

Math Tip
There are 10 possible outcomes.

 Learn •

The school carnival offers students the chance to win prizes. In one game, a player pulls one chip from each of two bags and finds the sum of the numbers.

Bag A

Bag B

These tree diagrams show all the possible outcomes of the game.

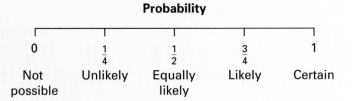

Bag A	1					2				
Bag B	2	3	3	3	4	2	3	3	3	4
Sum	3	4	4	4	5	4	5	5	5	6

Example 1

What is the probability of getting a sum of 5?

$\dfrac{4}{10}$ ←number of outcomes having a sum of 5
←total possible outcomes

The probability is 4 out of 10, or $\frac{4}{10}$, or (in simplest form) $\frac{2}{5}$.

Probability

0	$\frac{1}{4}$	$\frac{1}{2}$	$\frac{3}{4}$	1
Not possible	Unlikely	Equally likely	Likely	Certain

Some outcomes are impossible, while others are certain.

Example 2

What is the probability of getting a sum of 2?
There is no sum of 2.
$\frac{0}{10}$, or 0
So a sum of 2 is not possible.

Example 3

What is the probability of getting a sum of 3, 4, 5, or 6?
$\frac{10}{10}$, or 1
So a sum of 3, 4, 5, or 6 will certainly occur.

(**Talk About It**)

Which prize are you more likely to win? Explain your reasoning.

Check

1. Copy and complete the tree diagram to show the possible outcomes from playing the sum game with these two bags of chips.

Bag A   1   2   3

Bag B   1   2   3   3   ▢ ▢ ▢ ▢   ▢ ▢ ▢ ▢

Sum   2   3   4   4   ▢ ▢ ▢ ▢   ▢ ▢ ▢ ▢

2. **Reasoning** Use Excercise 1 to find the probability of getting either a sum of 5 **or** a sum of 6.

Bag A

Bag B

Practice

Skills and Reasoning

Each spinner is spun once. The numbers from each spinner are added. Make tree diagrams to show the possible outcomes. Give the probability of each outcome as a fraction. Simplify.

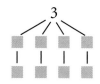

3. sum of 4   4. sum of 3   5. sum of 6   6. sum of 5   7. sum of 4 or 3

Problem Solving and Applications

8. Four of 200 students will be selected at random to attend the fair. What is the probability of any student getting selected?

9. Each guest will select a prize from a bag. Of the 25 prizes, 12 are dolls and 8 are books. What is the probability of not getting a doll or a book?

Using Data Use the Data File on page 525 to answer **10** and **11**.

10. In 1996, what was the approximate probability of a minor league baseball player substituting for a major league baseball player, if each substitution used a different minor league player?

11. What was the approximate probability of a major league player being replaced by a minor league player, if each substitution was for a different major league player?

Mixed Review and Test Prep

Find the percent of each number or amount.

12. 30% of 90   13. 82% of 200   14. 10% of 10   15. 15% of $50.00

16. **Science** Since 1 mL of water has a mass of 1 g, what is the mass of 1.4 mL of water?

Ⓐ 1.4 g   Ⓑ 14 g   Ⓒ 1.4 kg   Ⓓ 1400 kg

Exploring Expected and Experimental Results

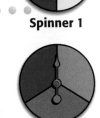

Spinner 1

Spinner 2

Problem Solving Connection

■ Guess and Check

■ Make a Table

Materials
spinners

If you spin the two spinners twelve times, how many times would you expect to get blue on the first spinner and green on the second?

How do your expected results compare with experimental ones?

Work Together

1. What is the probability of getting a blue-green (BG) combination?

   a. Copy and complete the tree diagram below. How many possible outcomes are there? How many are BG?

Remember
Large samples tend to be more accurate than smaller samples.

Spinner 1	B			Y		
Spinner 2	B	G	R			
Possible Outcomes	BB					

   b. Express the probability of a BG outcome as a fraction.

2. How many BG outcomes do you expect in a 12-spin trial? Spin each spinner 12 times. Make a table. Use tally marks. Compare results with your prediction.

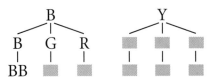

	BB	BG	BR	YB	YG	YR
Number of spins						

3. Spin each spinner 24 times and record your results. Repeat, spinning 48 times. How many times do you expect to get BG in each trial?

If you toss a coin 20 times, will the number of heads always be 10? Explain.

Connect

The probability of the pointer landing on yellow is $\frac{1}{5}$.

Suppose you held trials of 10, 50, and 100 spins.

The expected results for 50 spins would be 10 yellows.

This table shows the expected results and experimental results of your trials.

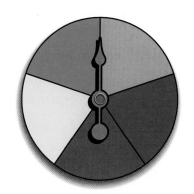

Outcome: Yellow	10 spins	50 spins	100 spins
Expected Results	2	10	20
Experimental Results	4	7	19

The 100-spin experimental results were closer to the expected results.

Practice

Use the spinner to answer **1–7.** Decide whether each result is likely or unlikely.

1. Outcome: 8
   Trial: 100 spins
   Result: get 8, 13 times

2. Outcome: 10
   Trial: 1,000 spins
   Result: get 10, 460 times

3. Outcome: red
   Trial: 10 spins
   Result: get red, 6 times

4. Outcome: blue
   Trial: 10,000 spins
   Result: get blue, 4,823 times

5. Outcome: 2
   Trial: 10 spins
   Result: get 2, 5 times

6. Outcome: red
   Trial: 1,000 spins
   Result: get red, 892 times

7. **Estimation** How many spins do you think it would take to get all 10 numbers? Do you think 10 or 20 spins is a better guess? Explain.

8. Terri and her two brothers draw straws each day to decide who will wash the dinner dishes. How many times do you expect each will have to wash the dishes in a 30-day month?

9. **Journal** Create your own probability experiment using spinners or number cubes. Make predictions for each outcome based on 20 trials. Perform the 20 trials. Then compare your results with your predictions.

SECTION C
Review and Practice

Vocabulary Match each word with its meaning.

1. outcome

    a. the ratio of the number of ways an event can occur to the total number of possible outcomes.

2. probability

    b. a possible result in a probability experiment

(Lesson 8) Use the spinner to answer **3** and **4**.
Write if each game is fair or unfair.

3. Player 1 gets 1 point if the spinner lands on a square.
Player 2 gets 1 point if the spinner lands on a circle.

4. Player 1 gets 1 point if the spinner lands on a circle or a triangle. Player 2 gets 1 point if the spinner lands on a square.

(Lesson 9) A bag contains different numbers of red, blue, black, and green marbles. Use the sample results to answer **5–7**.

Sample 1   **Sample 2**

Sample 3   **Sample 4**

5. What color do you think is the most common in the bag?

6. What color do you think is the least common in the bag?

7. If Sample 1 were the only sample, what would you predict for the most common color?

(Lessons 10, 11, and 13) Give all the outcomes for each experiment. Write whether they are equally likely or not.

8. Roll a cube numbered 1–6.

9. Spin the spinner.

10. Toss the coin.

11. Make a list of all the possible different combinations you could get from rolling 2 red cubes numbered 1–6.

(Lesson 12) The letters A, B, C, D, E, and F are in a bag. Give the probability of each outcome as a fraction.

12. of pulling out a vowel

13. of pulling out a consonant

14. of pulling out either A, B, or C

Skills Checklist

In this section you have:

☑ Explored Probability and Fairness

☑ Explored Predicting from Samples and Experiments

☑ Solved Problems by Making an Organized List

☑ Expressed Probabilities as Fractions

☑ Explored Expected and Experimental Results

YOUR CHOICE

Choose at least one. Use what you have learned in this chapter.

① Play By Your Own Rules

Create your own game based on equal probabilities and fairness for all the players. Develop a special board or spinner for your game. Be sure to write a list of rules and give each player a copy.

② Games People Play

At Home Make a list of five activities that many people enjoy. Ask ten family members or friends to rank these activities from 1 to 5, with 5 being the activity they like the most and 1 the one they like the least. Then compare the responses. What percent of the people who responded to the survey chose the same activity as their favorite? As their least favorite? Share your results with those who answered your survey.

Activity	Ranking
Playing a Sport	
Dancing	
Drawing or Painting	
Playing Chess	
Other Activity	

③ Predict the Weather

Choose a topic to access on **www.mathsurf.com/5/ch12** that will give you data on the probability of an event happening, such as weather forecasts. Express these probabilities as fractions and percents.

④ Color My World

Pick an artist whose paintings you like, or find books which show one artist's work. Make a list of the colors he or she uses most in five paintings. Then predict what colors you think the artist is likely to use in other works. Look at another painting by the same artist to see if your predictions were correct. Share your results with the class.

Henri Matisse, *Tristesse du Roi (Sadness of the King)*

REVIEW AND PRACTICE

Review/Test

Vocabulary Match each with its meaning.

1. proportion
2. ratio
3. outcome
4. probability

   a. a possible result in a probability experiment

   b. a comparison of two numbers or quantities

   c. statement that two ratios are equal

   d. the ratio of the number of ways an event can occur to the total number of possible outcomes

(Lessons 1–3) Copy and complete the ratio table. Then use it to answer **6.**

5. In a game, each player is given four chips. How many chips would be given if there were 2, 3, 4, or 5 players?

Players	2	3	4	5
Chips				

6. Look at the completed ratio table. Would a graph of these ratios form a straight line? Explain.

(Lessons 5–7) Copy and complete.

7. $\frac{8}{20} = \blacksquare\%$

8. $\frac{7}{10} = \blacksquare\%$

9. $\frac{1}{2} = \blacksquare\%$

10. $\frac{7}{25} = \blacksquare\%$

11. $\frac{2}{5} = \blacksquare\%$

Choose a method. Find the percent of each.

12. 12.5% of $30

13. 90% of $14.75

14. 21% of 15

15. $33\frac{1}{3}\%$ of 33

16. 55% of 200

17. 72% of $26.50

18. 62% of $105

19. 40% of 60

(Lessons 8, 10, 12, and 13) Use the spinner to answer **20–24.**

20. Player 1 gets 1 point if the spinner lands on a vowel. Player 2 gets 1 point if the spinner lands on a consonant. Is this game fair or unfair? Explain.

21. List all the possible outcomes of spinning the spinner. Write whether they are equally likely or not.

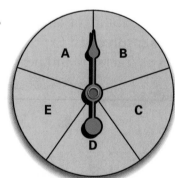

22. What is the probability of spinning the letter B? Give your answer as a fraction.

23. What is the probability of spinning a consonant? Give your answer as a fraction.

24. Make a list of all the possible different combinations you could get with 2 spins.

25. If you toss a penny 50 times, what is the expected number of heads?

Performance Assessment

A. Percent

Your city has decided to build an indoor activity center. The building will be 300 ft by 300 ft. Each of the following areas must take **at least** the following percentage of the floor space.

Basketball Courts	20%	Swings	5%
Swimming Pool	10%	Sand Area	5%
Climbing Equipment	10%	Jogging Track	10%
Offices and Restrooms	15%		

Use grid paper to make a map of the center. Label all areas. Tell how many square feet each area will have. Use 100% of the floor space.

1. **Decision Making** How will you decide how many squares to use on your grid paper? How will you decide which activities should be next to each other? Does the jogging track have any special requirements? Did you use 100% of the space?

2. **Explain Your Thinking** Explain how you determined what percentage to make each activity's area and how you used the percentages to determine the squares needed for each.

3. **Critical Thinking** Which activity required the greatest area? The least?

B. Probability

Make a set of counters like the ones shown. Put them in a bag.

Make 100 selections. Tally your results in a table like this one.

	A	B	C	Total
Red				
Blue				
Total				

1. **Recording Data** Write fractions for the parts of your selections that are red; blue; lettered A; lettered B; lettered C; and lettered B and blue.

2. **Explain Your Thinking** Explain how you determined what fractions to write.

3. **Critical Thinking** How do your fractions compare to the fractions for the part of the counters that are red; blue; lettered A; lettered B; lettered C; and lettered B and blue?

Math Magazine

Ancient African Stone Game

Kalaha, a type of Mancala, is a game that involves math. It has been played in Africa for thousands of years. Players use carved gameboards or small holes dug in the soil.

You Need: A traditional or drawn gameboard or the bottom of an egg carton with a paper cup at each end; 48 beans or pebbles

Number of Players: 2

Object: To have more beans in your *Kalaha* at the end of the game than your opponent has (Your *Kalaha* is the end cup to the right of your row of 6 cups.)

How to Play:

1. Setup: Each player chooses a side of the gameboard and places 4 beans in each of the 6 cups on his or her side. The *Kalaha* is empty until play begins and beans are moved.

2. Move: Player 1 picks up all of the beans in any cup on his or her side and places one bean in each of the next cups to the right, going counter-clockwise. This includes, if necessary, the *Kalaha* and cups on the opponent's side. Players continue the game by taking turns.

3. Special cases: If a player's last bean lands in his or her own *Kalaha,* he or she gets another turn. If a player lands in an empty cup on his or her own side, he or she can take the beans from the cup directly across and put them in his or her *Kalaha.*

4. Game ends: The game ends when the cups on one whole side of the board are empty. At that point both players count the beans in their *Kalaha.* The player with the most beans wins.

Try These!

1. Find out about some other ways Mancala is played. Remember that the game is sometimes called by different names.

2. Work with a small group to invent a new mathematical game. Play your game. Make changes in the rules, if necessary. Then trade games with another team and play.

Test Prep Strategy: Read Carefully

Watch for tricky problems.

The sign says "30% off, price reduction given at register." June sees a pair of soccer shoes with a price tag of $25.99. What is the cost for the shoes after the discount?

Ⓐ $18.19   Ⓑ $8.65   Ⓒ $7.79   Ⓓ $25.95

Write the letter of the correct answer. Choose any strategy.

1. Find the area of a rectangle 4 ft long and 6 in. wide.
   Ⓐ 24 in²   Ⓑ 24 ft²   Ⓒ 2 ft²   Ⓓ not here

2. Which figure has a volume of 60 ft³?
   Ⓐ 4 ft 3 ft 5 ft   Ⓑ 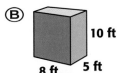 10 ft 8 ft 5 ft   Ⓒ 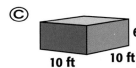 6 ft 10 ft 10 ft   Ⓓ not here

3. A class of 27 students is planning on having pizza. If each student gets $\frac{1}{3}$ of a pizza, how many pizzas need to be ordered?
   Ⓐ 162   Ⓑ 9   Ⓒ 81   Ⓓ 8

4. Miles said he ran 2,640 ft. How many miles did Miles run?
   Ⓐ 0   Ⓑ 2   Ⓒ 220   Ⓓ $\frac{1}{2}$

5. Last year Liz was $5\frac{1}{6}$ ft tall. How many inches has she grown if she is now $5\frac{1}{3}$ ft?
   Ⓐ $\frac{1}{6}$ in.   Ⓑ 2 ft   Ⓒ 2 in.   Ⓓ not here

6. A bag contains 4 blue marbles, 7 green marbles, and 3 yellow marbles. What are your chances of pulling out a blue marble?
   Ⓐ $\frac{1}{14}$ Ⓑ $\frac{1}{4}$ Ⓒ $\frac{2}{5}$ Ⓓ $\frac{2}{7}$

7. Which is not a correct statement?
   Ⓐ $\frac{5}{3} > \frac{7}{2}$ Ⓑ $\frac{7}{3} > \frac{4}{3}$ Ⓒ $\frac{5}{4} < \frac{7}{2}$ Ⓓ $\frac{2}{5} < \frac{3}{4}$

8. What is the circumference of a circle if $r = 4$ cm? Use 3.14 for π.
   Ⓐ 25.12 cm   Ⓑ 25.12 cm²   Ⓒ 12.56 cm   Ⓓ 12.56 cm²

9. Find the missing numerator. $\frac{8}{12} = \frac{\blacksquare}{3}$
   Ⓐ 32   Ⓑ 2   Ⓒ 1   Ⓓ 8

Test Prep Strategies

- Read Carefully
- Follow Directions
- Make Smart Choices
- Eliminate Choices
- Work Backward from an Answer

REVIEW AND PRACTICE

Skills Practice Bank Reviewing Skills

Set 1 For use after page 3.
Find each sum.

1. $2 + 4$
2. $5 + 3$
3. $4 + 7$
4. $9 + 6$
5. $8 + 0$

6. $7 + 5$
7. $8 + 6$
8. $5 + 9$
9. $6 + 2$
10. $7 + 3$

11. $9 + 4$
12. $6 + 3$
13. $6 + 7$
14. $5 + 4$
15. $7 + 7$

16. $7 + 8$
17. $3 + 9$
18. $8 + 3$
19. $9 + 7$
20. $7 + 9$

Set 2 For use after page 3.
Find each difference.

1. $9 - 2$
2. $5 - 2$
3. $12 - 4$
4. $10 - 5$
5. $15 - 6$

6. $13 - 8$
7. $17 - 8$
8. $10 - 4$
9. $6 - 2$
10. $11 - 4$

11. $14 - 9$
12. $6 - 3$
13. $18 - 9$
14. $5 - 4$
15. $13 - 4$

16. $10 - 8$
17. $11 - 9$
18. $17 - 9$
19. $9 - 7$
20. $16 - 8$

Set 3 For use after page 3.
Find each product.

1. 8×2
2. 3×5
3. 7×4
4. 6×3
5. 2×7

6. 9×2
7. 7×9
8. 6×5
9. 5×9
10. 8×4

11. 8×8
12. 6×6
13. 7×7
14. 5×5
15. 9×9

16. 7×8
17. 7×5
18. 6×8
19. 9×4
20. 6×7

Set 4 For use after page 3.
Find each quotient.

1. $24 \div 6$
2. $21 \div 3$
3. $16 \div 4$
4. $20 \div 5$
5. $32 \div 4$

6. $40 \div 8$
7. $72 \div 9$
8. $18 \div 6$
9. $35 \div 7$
10. $28 \div 4$

11. $45 \div 9$
12. $48 \div 6$
13. $24 \div 8$
14. $56 \div 7$
15. $42 \div 7$

16. $27 \div 3$
17. $36 \div 9$
18. $42 \div 7$
19. $64 \div 8$
20. $30 \div 6$

Set 1 For use after page 13.

Use the line graph to answer each question.

1. What was the population of Kingston in 1975?

2. During which year was the population 500?

3. In which five-year period did the greatest increase in population occur?

Population of Kingston

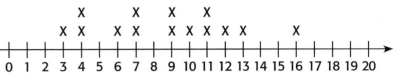

Set 2 For use after page 17.

Use the line plot to answer each question.

1. What is the
   a. range?
   b. mode?
   c. median?

2. Did Laurie score 10 or more points in half of her games?

```
                                        X
              X          X    X    X
          X   X      X   X    X  X X X X           X
    <---+---+---+---+---+---+---+---+---+---+---+---+---+---+---+---+---+---+---+---+--->
        0   1   2   3   4   5   6   7   8   9  10  11 12 13 14 15 16 17 18 19 20
```

Points Scored per Game by Laurie

Set 3 For use after page 29.

Choose a scale and make a bar graph of the data in the favorite music table.

Set 4 For use after page 31.

1. Make a line graph. Use the data in the temperature table.

2. Use the graph to estimate the temperature at 1:30 P.M.

Set 5 For use after page 33.

1. Make a stem-and-leaf plot of band member heights.

2. How many band members are between 50 and 59 inches tall?

Favorite Music of the Students at Washington School	
Music	**Votes**
Rock	75
Folk/Country	11
Jazz	25
Blues	30
Hip hop	41
Soul	39
Classical	18
Other	22

Time	Temperature (°F)
6:00 A.M.	48
9:00 A.M.	57
12:00 P.M.	70
3:00 P.M.	66
6:00 P.M.	60
9:00 P.M.	55
12:00 A.M.	51
3:00 A.M.	49

Height of Band Members (inches)
51 59 62 49 55 61 59 48 53 66 58 54 50 60 51 58 50

Set 6 For use after pages 21 and 39.

Use any strategy to solve each problem.

1. **(Page 21)** Tamara has been depositing $5 a week in her savings account. She now has $55 saved. For how many weeks has she been making a deposit?

2. **(Page 39)** Max, Kelly, Juan, and Lisette were sitting at a round table. Max did not want to sit next to Kelly. Lisette sat to the right of Kelly. How were the students arranged?

Set 1 For use after page 59.

Write each number in standard form for 1–3.

1. forty-three million
2. eight billion, eight million, two
3. ninety-nine billion
4. How many millions are in a billion?

Set 2 For use after page 71.

Write each number in decimal form for 1-3.

1. one-hundredth
2. four and fifteen-thousandths
3. nine-tenths
4. Round 1,667,129 to the nearest ten thousand.

Set 3 For use after page 77.

Copy and write $<$, $>$, or $=$ to complete.

1. 0.2 ● 0.03
2. 0.5 ● 0.51
3. 2.7 ● 2.70
4. 0.123 ● 1.123

Round each number to the place of the red digit.

5. 1.73
6. 5.83
7. 20.325
8. 0.091

Set 4 For use after page 87.

Find each sum or difference. Then estimate to check your answer.

1. 259
   + 742

2. 698
   − 169

3. 203
   + 187

4. 504
   − 396

5. 72
   9
   + 221

6. 9,000
   − 6,183

Set 5 For use after page 97.

Find each sum or difference.

1. 3.25
   + 9.68

2. 8.70
   − 7.07

3. 6.01
   + 2.4

4. 21.56 − 5.6
5. 7 + 6.1 + 5.95
6. 0.4 − 0.04

Set 6 For use after pages 79 and 101.

Solve using any strategy.

1. **(Page 79)** On the radio, four songs are played in a row. They are played in the order in which they were made. "Be Mine" was written in 1940. "Bounce" was written fifty years after "Be Mine." "Bobby" was written thirty years before "Bounce." "Betty" was written thirty years before "Bobby." Give the order in which the songs were played.

Think about which operation to use. Write the number sentence you would use, then solve the problem.

2. **(Page 101)** Magda had $40.00. She bought a hair brush for $9.95 and a dictionary for $12.45. How much money does she have left?

Set 1 For use after page 119.
Multiply.

1. 80 ×42	2. 36 ×25	3. 709 × 7	4. 91 ×16	5. 148 × 63	6. 565 × 99
7. 90 ×71	8. 33 ×27	9. 805 × 9	10. 61 ×14	11. 259 × 74	12. 675 × 88

Set 2 For use after page 127.
Find the LCM for each set of numbers.

1. 3 and 4   2. 2 and 7   3. 5 and 10   4. 4 and 10   5. 2, 6, and 9   6. 3, 6, and 7

Set 3 For use after page 139.
Find each product.

1. 3.87×4 2. 7.5×63 3. $\$9.29 \times 18$ 4. $20 \times \$6.54$

5. 4.98×5 6. 8.6×74 7. $\$7.47 \times 29$ 8. $30 \times \$7.65$

Choose the number that is closest to the actual product.

9. $\$6.05 \times 79$
   Ⓐ $48   Ⓑ $480   Ⓒ $4,800

10. 15×21.4
   Ⓐ 200   Ⓑ 400   Ⓒ 300

Set 4 For use after page 149.
Find each product. Round to the nearest hundredth or cent.

1. 3.52 × 1.4	2. $5.60 × 7.13	3. 4.1 ×0.88	4. $9.09 × 8.6	5. 0.035 × 3.6	6. $21.49 × 0.06

Set 5 For use after page 155.
Find each product. Write zeros where needed.

1. 0.09 × 3	2. 0.06 × 0.4	3. 0.002 × 7.1	4. 31 ×0.0005	5. 0.012 × 0.09	6. 0.002 ×0.003

Set 6 For use after pages 141 and 157.
Solve each problem. Choose any strategy.

1. **(Page 141)** Cereal costs $5.00 a box and $24.00 a carton. If there are 6 boxes per carton, how much do you save if you buy a carton instead of 6 individual boxes?

2. **(Page 157)** Juan's book costs $5.00 less than Birgit's book. Together the books cost $51.00. How much does each book cost?

Set 1 For use after page 179.
Divide.

1. $5\overline{)585}$
2. $2\overline{)323}$
3. $4\overline{)618}$
4. $8\overline{)987}$
5. $3\overline{)523}$

6. $6\overline{)790}$
7. $9\overline{)999}$
8. $7\overline{)880}$
9. $5\overline{)685}$
10. $4\overline{)613}$

Set 2 For use after page 185.
Divide. Check your answer.

1. $6\overline{)525}$
2. $3\overline{)734}$
3. $8\overline{)343}$
4. $5\overline{)459}$
5. $4\overline{)315}$

6. $7\overline{)970}$
7. $9\overline{)123}$
8. $4\overline{)925}$
9. $6\overline{)433}$
10. $9\overline{)765}$

Set 3 For use after page 187.
Divide. Multiply to check.

1. $3\overline{)620}$
2. $5\overline{)509}$
3. $9\overline{)5,407}$
4. $5\overline{)516}$
5. $4\overline{)1,203}$

6. $8\overline{)963}$
7. $6\overline{)1,819}$
8. $7\overline{)916}$
9. $3\overline{)1,508}$
10. $7\overline{)1,470}$

11. $6\overline{)746}$
12. $5\overline{)496}$
13. $8\overline{)3,379}$
14. $9\overline{)8,196}$
15. $4\overline{)5,603}$

Set 4 For use after page 201.
Divide.

1. $2\overline{)16.316}$
2. $5\overline{)\$32.65}$
3. $8\overline{)9.272}$
4. $3\overline{)2.40}$
5. $7\overline{)\$9.17}$

6. $3\overline{)17.652}$
7. $4\overline{)7.156}$
8. $7\overline{)\$60.34}$
9. $8\overline{)3.624}$
10. $4\overline{)\$52.32}$

Set 5 For use after page 205.
Use factor trees to find the prime factors of each number.

1. 21   2. 18   3. 24   4. 27   5. 32   6. 54   7. 22

8. 28   9. 36   10. 50   11. 15   12. 20   13. 48   14. 16

Set 6 For use after pages 181 and 211.
Use any strategy to solve.

1. (Page 181) You need 4 tickets to ride the Rambler Roller Coaster. If you have 58 tickets, how many tickets will you have left when you go on all the rides you can?

2. (Page 211) If you subtract 13 from me and then add 8, your answer will be 42. What number am I?

Skills Practice Bank Chapter 5

Set 1 For use after page 233.

Divide.

1. $31\overline{)155}$
2. $48\overline{)224}$
3. $70\overline{)516}$
4. $19\overline{)62}$

5. $93\overline{)767}$
6. $67\overline{)458}$
7. $26\overline{)234}$
8. $52\overline{)457}$

Set 2 For use after page 237.

Divide. Check your answer.

1. $29\overline{)725}$
2. $68\overline{)953}$
3. $35\overline{)1,505}$
4. $18\overline{)694}$

5. $79\overline{)4,577}$
6. $42\overline{)860}$
7. $13\overline{)386}$
8. $96\overline{)6,301}$

Set 3 For use after page 243.

Divide. Check your answer.

1. $59\overline{)612}$
2. $11\overline{)500}$
3. $34\overline{)3,655}$
4. $47\overline{)14,147}$

5. $22\overline{)5,069}$
6. $68\overline{)13,611}$
7. $74\overline{)5,215}$
8. $83\overline{)25,648}$

9. $37\overline{)9,016}$
10. $87\overline{)26,354}$
11. $52\overline{)7,163}$
12. $94\overline{)30,008}$

Set 4 For use after page 251.

Divide.

1. $18\overline{)\$82.80}$
2. $21\overline{)\$31.50}$
3. $14\overline{)\$8.68}$
4. $45\overline{)\$96.75}$

5. $70\overline{)\$231.00}$
6. $12\overline{)\$9.72}$
7. $26\overline{)\$72.02}$
8. $15\overline{)\$127.35}$

Set 5 For use after page 255.

Find each quotient. Use mental math.

1. $3.5 \div 10$
2. $568.3 \div 100$
3. $29.02 \div 10$
4. $61 \div 1,000$

5. $0.78 \div 10$
6. $\$28 \div 100$
7. $2,137.6 \div 1,000$
8. $\$35.70 \div 10$

Set 6 For use after pages 247 and 253.

Use any strategy to solve each problem.

1. **(Page 247)** Clarissa needs a fence on one side of her yard. The fence needs a post every 10 feet, including one at each end. How many posts are there if the fence is 60 feet long?

2. **(Page 253)** If 60 feet of molding costs $83.40, how much did it cost per foot?

Set 1   For use after page 273.

Trace each angle and extend its sides. Use a protractor to measure each angle.

1. 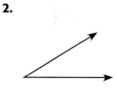 **2.**  **3.** 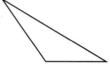 **4.**

Set 2   For use after page 275.

Classify each triangle as equilateral, isosceles, or scalene. Then classify each triangle as acute, right, or obtuse.

1.  **2.**  **3.** 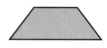 **4.**

Set 3   For use after page 277.

Write the name that best describes each figure.

1.  **2.**   **3.**   **4.**

Set 4   For use after page 285.

Match the correct polygons.

1. Which 2 polygons are similar, but not congruent?

    a.   **b.** 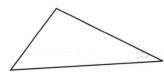 **c.**   **d.**

Set 5   For use after page 289.

Trace each figure. Draw all lines of symmetry.

1. **2.** **3.**

Set 6   For use after pages 281 and 291.

1. **(Page 281)** Six students meet at the Math Club. Each student shakes hands with all the others. How many handshakes are there?

2. **(Page 291)** Fold a piece of paper and cut a design from the folded side. Unfold the paper. Does your cut-out have symmetry?

Set 1 For use after page 307.

Find an equivalent fraction with a denominator of 12 for each.

1. $\frac{1}{2}$ 2. $\frac{1}{4}$ 3. $\frac{2}{3}$ 4. $\frac{5}{6}$ 5. $\frac{14}{24}$ 6. $\frac{15}{36}$

Set 2 For use after page 311.

Find the simplest form for each fraction.

1. $\frac{5}{10}$ 2. $\frac{3}{9}$ 3. $\frac{12}{16}$ 4. $\frac{7}{8}$ 5. $\frac{40}{48}$ 6. $\frac{6}{27}$

Set 3 For use after page 317.

Copy and write >, <, or = to complete.

1. $\frac{1}{2} \bullet \frac{2}{3}$ 2. $\frac{3}{4} \bullet \frac{3}{8}$ 3. $\frac{2}{5} \bullet \frac{3}{10}$ 4. $\frac{2}{3} \bullet \frac{3}{4}$

5. $\frac{3}{9} \bullet \frac{1}{3}$ 6. $\frac{8}{9} \bullet \frac{9}{10}$ 7. $\frac{6}{8} \bullet \frac{9}{12}$ 8. $\frac{1}{3} \bullet \frac{1}{5}$

Set 4 For use after page 327.

Write each mixed number as an improper fraction. Write each improper fraction as a mixed number.

1. $3\frac{2}{5}$ 2. $\frac{8}{3}$ 3. $1\frac{1}{8}$ 4. $\frac{15}{4}$ 5. $\frac{8}{6}$ 6. $2\frac{2}{5}$

Write in order from least to greatest.

7. $2\frac{1}{2}, \frac{9}{4}, 1\frac{11}{12}, \frac{13}{5}$ 8. $1\frac{4}{5}, \frac{14}{7}, 1\frac{1}{9}, 2\frac{1}{10}$

Set 5 For use after page 333.

Write each as a percent.

1. 25 out of 100   2. $\frac{8}{100}$ 3. 0.65   4. 0.05   5. $\frac{100}{100}$ 6. $\frac{70}{100}$

Write each as a fraction and a decimal.

7. 19%   8. 58%   9. 33%   10. 7%   11. 99%   12. 100%

Set 6 For use after pages 319 and 335.

Use any strategy to solve.

1. **(Page 319)** At Chamberlain School, 2 out of every 3 students enjoy playing basketball. If there are 96 students, how many enjoy playing basketball?

2. **(Page 335)** In a survey of 100 people for favorite flavor of ice cream, 33 people chose chocolate, 25 chose butter pecan, 10 chose strawberry, and the rest chose other flavors. What percent of the people surveyed preferred each flavor?

Set 1 For use after page 357.

Find each sum. Simplify.

1. $\dfrac{1}{2}$
   $+\dfrac{3}{7}$

2. $\dfrac{2}{5}$
   $+\dfrac{1}{6}$

3. $\dfrac{5}{6}$
   $+\dfrac{1}{3}$

4. $\dfrac{9}{10}$
   $+\dfrac{8}{15}$

5. $\dfrac{1}{6}$
   $+\dfrac{1}{8}$

6. $\dfrac{5}{9}$
   $+\dfrac{7}{12}$

Set 2 For use after page 361.

Find each difference. Simplify.

1. $\dfrac{5}{8}$
   $-\dfrac{1}{2}$

2. $\dfrac{3}{4}$
   $-\dfrac{3}{5}$

3. $\dfrac{5}{12}$
   $-\dfrac{1}{6}$

4. $\dfrac{1}{6}$
   $-\dfrac{1}{9}$

5. $\dfrac{7}{8}$
   $-\dfrac{5}{12}$

6. $\dfrac{7}{10}$
   $-\dfrac{3}{8}$

Set 3 For use after page 373.

Find each sum or difference. Simplify.

1. $3\dfrac{1}{4}$
   $-1\dfrac{1}{5}$

2. $2\dfrac{1}{2}$
   $+3\dfrac{3}{8}$

3. $1\dfrac{7}{8}$
   $-1\dfrac{2}{3}$

4. 4
   $+5\dfrac{7}{10}$

5. $8\dfrac{7}{12}$
   $-3\dfrac{3}{16}$

6. 7
   $-3\dfrac{5}{6}$

Set 4 For use after page 379.

Find each sum or difference. Simplify.

1. 6
   $-3\dfrac{1}{6}$

2. $2\dfrac{1}{2}$
   $-1\dfrac{3}{4}$

3. $4\dfrac{2}{3}$
   $2\dfrac{2}{5}$
   $+3\dfrac{1}{2}$

4. $4\dfrac{2}{5}$
   $-\dfrac{9}{10}$

5. $3\dfrac{1}{6}$
   $1\dfrac{5}{8}$
   $+2\dfrac{2}{3}$

6. $4\dfrac{3}{4}$
   $2\dfrac{1}{12}$
   $+1\dfrac{2}{3}$

Set 5 For use after page 391.

Copy and complete.

1. 9 ft = ▒ in.   2. 36 ft = ▒ yd   3. 5 mi = ▒ ft   4. 192 in. = ▒ ft

5. 3 ft 4 in. = ▒ in.   6. 9 yd 2 ft = ▒ ft   7. 100 in. = ▒ ft ▒ in.   8. 12,345 yd = ▒ mi ▒ yd

Set 6 For use after pages 365 and 393.

Use any strategy to solve. Write whether the problem has too much or too little information.

1. **(Page 365)** Brandon leaves for school at 7:35 A.M. He carpools $\dfrac{1}{3}$ of the way, takes the #25 bus for half of the trip, then walks the rest of the way. What fraction of the distance to school does Brandon walk?

Write whether you need an exact answer or an estimate.

2. **(Page 393)** Shaniqua saved $1.50 a day for two months. Did she save enough to buy inline skates that cost $92.95?

Set 1 For use after page 409.

Use rounding, benchmarks, or compatible numbers to estimate the products.

1. $\frac{2}{3} \times 32$ 2. $5\frac{1}{6} \times 10$ 3. $\frac{2}{5} \times 16$ 4. $3\frac{3}{5} \times 8$

5. $\frac{4}{7} \times 26$ 6. $1\frac{5}{6} \times 19$ 7. $3\frac{7}{15} \times 15$ 8. $9\frac{7}{8} \times 11$

Set 2 For use after page 413.

Find each product. Simplify.

1. $\frac{1}{2} \times \frac{3}{4}$ 2. $\frac{2}{5} \times \frac{3}{4}$ 3. $\frac{5}{7} \times \frac{5}{7}$ 4. $\frac{3}{8} \times \frac{1}{4}$

5. $\frac{7}{8} \times \frac{8}{11}$ 6. $\frac{1}{10} \times \frac{30}{31}$ 7. $\frac{3}{20} \times \frac{1}{6}$ 8. $\frac{1}{5} \times \frac{3}{7}$

Set 3 For use after page 421.

Find each product. Simplify.

1. $\frac{1}{2} \times 28$ 2. $\frac{3}{4} \times 12$ 3. $\frac{5}{3} \times 21$ 4. $\frac{5}{6} \times 12$

5. $\frac{3}{8} \times 32$ 6. $\frac{9}{4} \times 44$ 7. $84 \times \frac{1}{12}$ 8. $\frac{5}{8} \times 32$

Set 4 For use after page 423.

Find each product. Simplify and use estimation to check.

1. $3\frac{1}{2} \times 4$ 2. $2\frac{1}{3} \times 5$ 3. $4\frac{4}{5} \times \frac{7}{8}$ 4. $6\frac{1}{3} \times \frac{3}{4}$

5. $\frac{1}{4} \times 3\frac{2}{3}$ 6. $1\frac{1}{2} \times 2\frac{3}{4}$ 7. $4\frac{1}{6} \times 2\frac{3}{5}$ 8. $2\frac{1}{5} \times 5$

Set 5 For use after page 429.

Find each quotient.

1. $4 \div \frac{1}{3}$ 2. $5 \div \frac{1}{2}$ 3. $2 \div \frac{1}{9}$ 4. $4 \div 15$

5. $8 \div \frac{1}{6}$ 6. $3 \div \frac{1}{12}$ 7. $10 \div \frac{1}{10}$ 8. $16 \div 4$

Set 6 For use after pages 417 and 427.

Estimate. Write whether you overestimated or underestimated.

1. **(Page 417)** A teacher is reviewing papers. It takes her $\frac{2}{3}$ of an hour to review each paper. If she has 10 papers to review and starts on Saturday at 9:00 A.M. will she be finished by 4:00 P.M.?

Use logical reasoning to solve.

2. **(Page 427)** Ann, Bill, Cleo, and Don each like one of these fruits: apples, bananas, cherries, dates. No one likes fruit that begins with the first letter of his or her name. Ann and Don only like red fruits. Which fruit does each like?

Set 1 For use after page 443.

Choose the most appropriate measure.

1. length of a cassette tape

   Ⓐ 10 mm Ⓑ 10 cm Ⓒ 10 m

2. height of a door

   Ⓐ 2 cm Ⓑ 2 m Ⓒ 2 km

Copy and complete.

3. 6 m = ▇ cm

4. 8 cm = ▇ mm

5. 2 dm = ▇ mm

6. 30 cm = ▇ dm

7. 9,000 mm = ▇ m

8. 1,500 mm = ▇ cm

Set 2 For use after page 447.

Copy and complete.

1. 2.7 m = ▇ cm

2. 0.09 m = ▇ mm

3. 61 mm = ▇ cm

4. 3 cm = ▇ m

5. 838 mm = ▇ m

6. 5.5 cm = ▇ m

Set 3 For use after page 457.

Find the perimeter.

1. rectangle with length 15 ft and width 8 ft

2. square with 0.3 m sides

3. equilateral triangle with sides of 3 ft 8 in.

4. square with sides of 3 ft 8 in.

Set 4 For use after page 471.

Find the area.

1.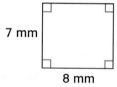

7 mm

8 mm

2.

21 yd

3.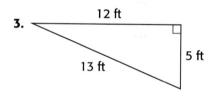

12 ft

13 ft

5 ft

4.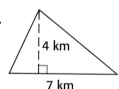

4 km

7 km

Set 5 For use after page 477.

Find the circumference. Use 3.14 for π.

5.

12 in.

2. circle with radius of 2.5 dm

3. circle with diameter of 0.1 m

Set 6 For use after pages 461 and 475.

1. **(Page 461)** A gardener wants to fence 48 ft². What are 3 sets of dimensions she could use?

2. **(Page 475)** At the dog show, each person walked 4 dogs. Below the curtain you could see 54 legs in all. How many dogs and how many people were there?

Set 1   For use after page 495.

Find the surface area of each figure.

1.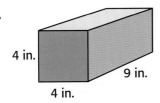

4 in.

9 in.

4 in.

2.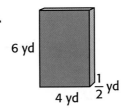

6 yd

4 yd $\frac{1}{2}$ yd

3.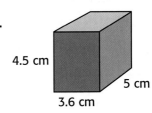

4.5 cm

5 cm

3.6 cm

4. Write a rule that relates the number of edges of each base to the number of vertices.

Set 2   For use after page 503.

Use mental math to change to kilograms or grams.

1. 2,300 g = ▨ kg

2. 0.75 kg = ▨ g

3. 5 g = ▨ kg

4. 98.1 kg = ▨ g

5. 308.4 g = ▨ kg

6. 3.45 kg = ▨ g

Set 3   For use after page 505.

Find each change in temperature. Use the thermometer on page 485.

1. 16°F to 73°F

2. 28°C to 9°C

3. 8°F to −10°F

4. 61°C to 100°C

5. 83°C to −16°C

6. -8°F to 28°F

Set 4   For use after page 509.

Copy and complete.

1. $l = 12$ in.

$w = 6$ in.

$h = 5$ in.

$v = $ ▨ in^3

2. $l = 3.2$ m

$w = 1.6$ m

$h = 2$ m

$v = $ ▨ m^3

3. $l = 6$ ft

$w = $ ▨ ft

$h = 2$ ft

$v = 48$ ft^3

4. $l = 25$ yd

$w = 12$ yd

$h = $ ▨ yd

$v = 1{,}500$ yd^3

5. $l = 16$ cm

$w = 7$ cm

$h = $ ▨ cm

$v = 392$ cm^3

Set 5   For use after page 513.

Copy and complete.

1. 10 L = ▨ mL

2. 500 mL = ▨ L

3. 2.3 L = ▨ mL

4. 19 mL = ▨ L

5. 0.5058 L = ▨ mL

6. 8 mL = ▨ L

Set 6   For use after pages 497 and 517.

1. **(Page 497)** John and Paul want to build a wooden box with an open top for their 200 LP records. If each record album is $12\frac{1}{2}$ in. by $12\frac{1}{2}$ in. and $\frac{1}{8}$ in. thick, what should the dimensions and surface area of the box be?

2. **(Page 517)** How many dots are in the figure? If there were 4 rows, what would the total be? 5 rows? Use a short cut to find the number of dots in 10 rows and 20 rows.

● ● ● ●

● ● ● ● ●

Set 1 For use after page 529.

Write each ratio in three ways. Simplify.

1. Xs to 0s

2. trapezoids to parallelograms

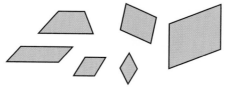

3. flour to butter

Set 2 For use after page 533.

Use grid paper. Plot the ordered pairs from the ratio table.

1.

4	8	16	20	24
3	6	12	15	18

2. What other ratio might be in the table above?

Set 3 For use after page 543.

Find the percent of each.

1. 20% of 350   2. 35% of 40   3. 8% of $12.00   4. 84% of 850
5. 17% of 5.9   6. 25% of 440   7. 6% of 42   8. 75% or $32.00

Set 4 For use after page 551.

1. Roll a cube with sides numbered 1 through 6. Which is more likely to occur, an even number or the number 3 or 5?

2. Give the outcomes for the spinner. Are they equally likely?

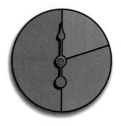

Set 5 For use after page 555.

1. In a drawer of 30 unmatched socks, 16 are black and 9 are white. What is the probability that a sock selected at random will be black? What is the probability that neither white nor black will be selected?

Set 6 For use after pages 535 and 553.

Solve using any strategy.

1. (Page 535) A map has a scale of 1 inch to 500 miles. If the United States is shown to be 6 inches long on the map, how long is that in miles? If Cleveland is 750 miles from New York, how many inches would that be on the map?

2. (Page 553) At a party, the host hands you three tape singles with one song on each side. He asks you to choose two songs. How many different combinations of two songs might you choose?

Table of Measures

Customary Units of Measure

Length
1 foot (ft)	= 12 inches (in.)
1 yard (yd)	= 36 inches (in.)
	= 3 feet (ft)
1 mile (mi)	= 5,280 feet (ft)
	= 1,760 yards (yd)

Area
1 square foot (ft^2)	= 144 square inches (in^2)
1 square yard (yd^2)	= 9 square feet (ft^2)
1 acre	= 43,560 square feet (ft^2)
	= 4,840 square yards (yd^2)
1 square mile (mi^2)	= 640 acres

Volume
1 cubic foot (ft^3)	= 1,728 cubic inches (in^3)

Capacity
1 tablespoon (tbsp)	= 3 teaspoons (tsp)
1 fluid ounce (fl oz)	= 2 tablespoons (tbsp)
1 cup (c)	= 8 fluid ounces (fl oz)
1 pint (pt)	= 2 cups (c)
1 quart (qt)	= 2 pints (pt)
1 gallon (gal)	= 4 quarts (qt)

Weight
1 pound (lb)	= 16 ounces (oz)
1 ton (T)	= 2,000 pounds (lb)

Fahrenheit Temperature
32°F	= freezing point of water
98.6°F	= normal body temperature
212°F	= boiling point of water

Metric Units of Measure

Length
1 centimeter (cm)	= 10 millimeters (mm)
1 decimeter (dm)	= 100 millimeters (mm)
	= 10 centimeters (cm)
1 meter (m)	= 1,000 millimeters (mm)
	= 100 centimeters (cm)
	= 10 decimeters (dm)
1 kilometer (km)	= 1,000 meters (m)

Area
1 square centimeter (cm^2)	= 100 square millimeters (mm^2)
1 square decimeter (dm^2)	= 100 square centimeters (cm^2)
1 square meter (m^2)	= 10,000 square centimeters (cm^2)
	= 100 square decimeters (dm^2)

Volume
1 cubic centimeter (cm^3)	= 1,000 cubic millimeters (mm^3)
1 cubic decimeter (dm^3)	= 1,000 cubic centimeters (cm^3)

Capacity
1 liter (L)	= 1,000 milliliters (mL)
	= 1 cubic decimeter (dm^3)

Mass
1 gram (g)	= 1,000 milligrams (mg)
1 kilogram (kg)	= 1,000 grams (g)
1 metric ton (t)	= 1,000 kilograms (kg)
1 cubic centimeter (cm^3)	= holds 1 milliliter (mL) of water that has a mass of 1 gram (g)

Celsius Temperature
0°C	= freezing point of water
37°C	= normal body temperature
100°C	= boiling point of water

Time
1 minute (min)	= 60 seconds (sec)
1 hour (hr)	= 60 minutes (min)
1 day (d)	= 24 hours (hr)
1 week (wk)	= 7 days (d)
1 month (mo)	= about 4 weeks (wk)
1 year (yr)	= 365 days (d)
	= 52 weeks (wk)
	= 12 months (mo)
1 decade	= 10 years (yr)
1 century	= 100 years (yr)

Formulas

Rectangle
Perimeter	$P = 2 \times (l + w)$
	$P = (2 \times l) + (2 \times w)$
Area	$A = l \times w$

Square
Perimeter	$P = 4 \times s$
Area	$A = s^2$

Triangle
Area	$A = \frac{1}{2} \times b \times h$

Prism
Volume	$V = l \times w \times h$

Circle
Circumference	$C = 2 \times \pi \times r$
	$C = \pi \times d$

Glossary

acute angle (p. 273) An angle that has a measure less than 90°.

acute triangle (p. 274) A triangle with all angles less than 90°.

addend (p. 84) A number added to find a sum.
Example: 2 + 7 = 9

Addend Addend

addition (p. 20) An operation that gives the total number when you put together two or more numbers.

algebraic expression (p. 244) An expression that contains a variable. *Example:* x + 8

angle (p. 270) Two rays with a common end point.

area (p. 450) The number of square units needed to cover a closed figure.

associative (grouping) property (p. 113) When the grouping of addends or factors is changed, the sum or product stays the same.
Examples: (5 + 2) + 3 = 5 + (2 + 3)
(3 × 2) × 1 = 3 × (2 × 1)

average (p. 192) The number found when the sum of two or more numbers is divided by the number of addends. Also called the *mean*.

bar graph (p. 10) A graph that uses bars to show data.

base (p. 56) A number used as a factor the number of times shown by an exponent. *See also* base for a plane figure (p. 464) or a solid figure (p. 489).
— Base

benchmark (p. 122) A number that is easy to work with, such as 10, 50, 100, 500, 1,000, or 1,000,000.

capacity (p. 510) The volume of a solid given in terms of liquid measurement.

center (p. 476) The point from which all points on a circle are equally distant.

centimeter (cm) (p. 440) A unit for measuring length in the metric system. *See also* Table of Measures, page 577.

1 centimeter

certain (p. 550) Definitely will happen.

chances (p. 550) The probability that a particular event will occur.

chord (p. 477) A line segment with both end points on a circle.

circle (p. 476) A plane figure in which all the points are the same distance from the center.

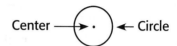
Center ——→ • ←— Circle

circle graph (p. 342) A graph in the form of a circle that is divided into sectors showing how the whole is broken into parts.

circumference (p. 476) The distance around a circle. $C = 2 \times \pi \times r$ or $C = \pi \times d$

common denominator (p. 314) A number that is a denominator of two or more fractions.

common factor (p. 308) A number that is a factor of each of two or more different numbers.

common multiple (p. 126) A number that is a multiple of two or more different numbers.

commutative (order) property (p. 113) Changing the order of addends or factors does not change the sum or product.
Examples: 8 + 5 = 5 + 8
3 × 6 = 6 × 3

compare (p. 60) To decide which of two numbers is greater.

compass (p. 342) An instrument used to make circles.

compatible numbers (p. 136) Numbers that are easy to work with mentally.
Examples: 25 + 175, 5 × 20, 360 ÷ 9

composite number (p. 204) A whole number greater than 1 that has more than two different factors.
Example: The composite number 6 has factors of 1, 2, 3, and 6.

cone (p. 486) A solid figure with one circular base.

— Base

congruent figures (p. 284) Figures that have the same size and shape.

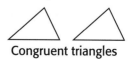
Congruent triangles

GLOSSARY

coordinates (p. 12) A pair of numbers used to locate a point on a graph. *See also* ordered pair

cube (p. 52) A solid figure whose 6 faces are all squares.

cubic centimeter (cm³) (p. 508) A cube with 1 centimeter edges. Unit for measuring volume.

cubic inch (in³) (p. 508) A cube with 1 inch edges. Unit for measuring volume.

cubic unit (p. 508) A cube with 1 unit edges. Unit for measuring volume.

cup (c) (p. 510) A unit for measuring capacity in the customary system. *See also* Table of Measures, page 577

customary units of length, weight, capacity, and temperature *See* Table of Measures, page 577

cylinder (p. 486) A solid figure with two congruent circular bases.

data (p. 10) Information used to make calculations.

decimal (p. 66) A number that uses a decimal point to show tenths, hundredths, thousands, and so on. *Example:* 4.1527

decimal point (p. 66) A symbol used to separate the ones place from the tenths place in decimals, or dollars from cents in money. *Example:* 4.57
↑ Decimal point

decimeter (dm) (p. 441) A unit for measuring length in the metric system. *See also* Table of Measures, page 577

degree (°) (p. 272) A unit of measure for angles and temperature.

degree Celsius (°C) (p. 504) A unit for measuring temperature in the metric system. *See also* Table of Measures, page 577

degree Fahrenheit (°F) (p. 504) A unit for measuring temperature in the customary system. *See also* Table of Measures, page 577

denominator (p. 302) The bottom number of a fraction that tells the number of equal parts in the whole. *Example:* $\frac{7}{8}$ ← Denominator

diameter (p. 476) A line segment that goes from one point on a circle through the center to another point on the circle.

Diameter

Center

difference (p. 20) The number that is the result of subtracting one number from another. *Example:* 6 − 4 = 2 ← Difference

digits (p. 54) The symbols used to show numbers: 0, 1, 2, 3, 4, 5, 6, 7, 8, and 9.

display (p. 130) The window on a calculator that shows the numbers as they are entered and the results of the calculations.

distributive property (p. 122) Multiplying a sum by a number is the same as multiplying each addend by the number and then adding the products.
Example: 3 × (2 + 4) = 18
(3 × 2) + (3 × 4) = 18

dividend (p. 168) The number to be divided in a division number sentence. *Example:* 63 ÷ 9 = 7
Dividend ↑

divisible (p. 202) Can be divided by another number without leaving a remainder. *Example:* 18 is divisible by 6.

division (p. 168) An operation that tells how many groups there are or how many are in each group.

divisor (p. 168) The number by which a dividend is divided. *Example:* 63 ÷ 9 = 7
Divisor ↑

edge (p. 490) A line segment at which two faces of a solid figure meet.

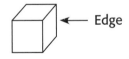

← Edge

endpoint (p. 270) A point at the end of a ray or line segment.

equally likely (p. 550) Just as likely to happen as not to happen.

equal ratios (p. 530) Ratios that give the same comparison. *Example:* $\frac{9}{27}$ and $\frac{1}{3}$ are equal ratios.

equation (p. 170) A number sentence that uses the equal sign (=) to show that two expressions have the same value. *See also* number sentence *Example:* 9 + 2 = 11

equilateral triangle (p. 274) A triangle with three equal sides.

equivalent decimals (p. 68) Decimals that name the same amount. *Example:* $0.7 = 0.70$

equivalent fractions (p. 305) Fractions that name the same part of a region, part of a set, or part of a segment. *Example:* $\frac{1}{2}$ and $\frac{2}{4}$

estimate (p. 82) To find a number that is close to an exact answer.

evaluate (p. 245) To find the number an algebraic expression names by replacing a variable with a given number. *Example:* Use $n = 3$ to evaluate $2n + 5$. Answer is $2(3) + 5 = 11$.

even number (p. 35) A whole number that has 0, 2, 4, 6, or 8 in the ones place. A whole number divisible by 2.

expanded form (p. 54) A way to write a number that shows the place value of each digit. *Example:* $9,000 + 300 + 20 + 5$

expected probability (p. 556) The probability of a certain outcome if the number of trials is extended indefinitely.

experiment (p. 550) A test or trial.

experimental probability (p. 556) Probability based on the results of an experiment.

exponent (p. 57) A number that tells how many times another number is used as a factor. *Example:* $3 \times 3 \times 3 \times 3 = 3^4 \begin{smallmatrix} \leftarrow \text{exponent} \\ \leftarrow \text{base} \end{smallmatrix}$

expression (p. 244) Numbers combined with one or more operations. *See also* algebraic expression *Example:* $4 + 5$

face (p. 489) If a solid figure has only flat surfaces, then we call each surface a face.

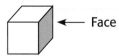
← Face

factors (p. 112) Numbers that are multiplied together to obtain a product. *Examples:* $7 \times 3 = 21$
Factor ↑ ↑ Factor

factor tree (p. 205) A diagram used to find the factors of a number.

fair game (p. 546) A game in which each player has an equal chance of winning.

flip (p. 287) To turn a plane figure over.

fluid ounce (fl oz) (p. 510) A unit for measuring capacity in the customary system. *See also* Table of Measures, page 577

foot (ft) (p. 390) A unit for measuring length in the customary system. *See also* Table of Measures, page 577

formula (p. 453) A general rule expressed by symbols. *Example:* The formula for the perimeter of a rectangle is $P = 2 \times (l + w)$.

fraction (p. 302) A way to compare equal parts with a whole. *Example:* $\frac{3}{10}$ is 3 equal parts out of 10 equal parts.

front-end estimation (p. 82) A way to estimate a sum by adding the first digit of each addend and adjusting the result based on the remaining digits.

gallon (gal) (p. 510) A unit for measuring capacity in the customary system. *See also* Table of Measures, page 577

gram (g) (p. 502) A unit for measuring mass in the metric system. *See also* Table of Measures, page 577

graph (p. 10) A picture that shows data in an organized way.

greater than (>) (p. 60) The relationship of one number being farther to the right on a number line than another number. *Examples:* $7 > 3$

"Seven is greater than three."

greatest common factor (GCF) (p. 308) The greatest number that is a factor of each of two or more numbers.

height (p. 464) The length of the perpendicular line segment from the vertex to the base of a triangle.

hexagon (p. 488) A polygon with six sides.

horizontal axis (p. 12) The left-to-right number line on a graph.

hundredth (p. 66) One out of 100 equal parts of a whole.

impossible (p. 550) Cannot happen.

improper fraction (p. 323) A fraction greater than or equal to one.

GLOSSARY

inch (in.) (p. 388) A unit for measuring length in the customary system. *See also* Table of Measures, page 577

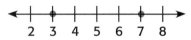
1 inch

intersecting lines (p. 270) Lines that cross at a point.

isosceles triangle (p. 274) A triangle that has at least two equal sides.

kilogram (kg) (p. 502) A unit for measuring mass in the metric system. *See also* Table of Measures, page 577

kilometer (km) (p.441) A unit for measuring length in the metric system. *See also* Table of Measures, page 577

leaf (p. 14) The part of a stem-and-leaf plot that shows the ones digit of a number.

least common denominator (LCD) (p. 352) The least common multiple of the denominators of two or more fractions.

least common multiple (LCM) (p. 127) The least number that is a multiple of two or more different numbers.

less than (<) (p. 60) The relationship of one number being farther to the left on a number line than another number. *Examples:* $3 < 7$

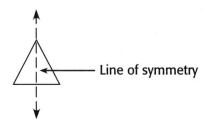
2 3 4 5 6 7 8
"Three is less than seven."

likely (p. 550) Probably will happen.

line (p. 270) A straight path that is endless in both directions.

line graph (p. 12) A graph that connects points to show how data changes over time.

line of symmetry (p. 288) A line on which a figure can be folded so that both halves are congruent.

Line of symmetry

line plot (p. 10) A graph that uses symbols above a number line to represent data.

line segment (p. 274) Part of a line that has two end points.

liter (L) (p. 512) A unit for measuring capacity in the metric system. *See also* Table of Measures, page 577

mass (p. 502) The amount of matter that something contains.

mean (p. 190) The number found when the sum of two or more numbers is divided by the number of addends. Also called the *average.*

median (p. 16) The middle number when data are arranged in order.

mental math (p. 124) Performing calculations without using pencil and paper or a calculator.

meter (m) (p. 441) A unit for measuring length in the metric system. *See also* Table of Measures, page 577

metric units of length, weight, mass, capacity, and temperature *See* Table of Measures, page 577

mile (mi) (p. 390) A unit for measuring length in the customary system. *See also* Table of Measures, page 577

milliliter (mL) (p. 512) A unit for measuring capacity in the metric system. *See also* Table of Measures, page 577

millimeter (mm) (p. 442) A unit for measuring length in the metric system. *See also* Table of Measures, page 577

mixed number (p. 323) A number that has a whole-number part and a fractional part. *Example:* $2\frac{3}{4}$

mode (p. 16) The number or numbers that occur most often in a set of data.

multiple (p. 112) The product of a given whole number and any other whole number.

multiplication (p. 20) An operation that gives the total number when you put together equal groups.

negative number (p. 504) A number that is less than zero.

net (p. 492) A pattern that can be cut out and folded into a solid.

number line (p. 10) A line that shows numbers in order using a scale.

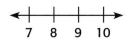
7 8 9 10

number sentence (p. 100) A way to show a relationship between numbers. *See also* equation
Examples: $2 + 5 = 7$
$6 \div 2 = 3$

numerator (p. 302) The top number of a fraction that tells the number of equal parts considered.
Example: $\frac{7}{8}$ ← Numerator

obtuse angle (p. 273) An angle with a measure greater than 90°.

obtuse triangle (p. 274) A triangle with one angle greater than 90°.

octagon (p. 488) A polygon with eight sides.

odd number (p. 35) A whole number that has 1, 3, 5, 7, or 9 in the ones place. A whole number not divisible by 2.

one property (p. 195) In multiplication, the product of a number and 1 is that number. In division, a number divided by 1 is that number.
Examples: $5 \times 1 = 5$
$3 \div 1 = 3$

operation (p. 20) Addition, subtraction, multiplication, and division.

order (p. 60) To arrange numbers from least to greatest or from greatest to least.

ordered pair (p. 12) A pair of numbers used to locate a point on a graph. *See also* coordinates

ounce (oz) (p. 500) A unit for measuring weight in the customary system. *See also* Table of Measures, page 577

outcome (p. 547) A possible result of an experiment.

parallel lines (p. 270) Lines that lie in the same plane and do not intersect.

parallelogram (p. 276) A quadrilateral with two pairs of opposite parallel sides.

pattern (p. 52) A sequence of objects, events, or ideas that repeat.

pentagon (p. 488) A polygon with five sides.

percent (%) (p. 328) Per hundred. A way to compare a number to 100. *Example:* $\frac{40}{100} = 0.40 = 40\%$

perimeter (p. 450) The distance around a closed figure.

period (p. 54) A group of 3 digits in a number. Periods are separated by a comma.

perpendicular lines (p. 270) Two lines that form right angles where they intersect.

pi (π) (p. 477) The ratio of the circumference of a circle to its diameter. The decimal for π is 3.141592…. As approximations for π, 3.14 or $3\frac{1}{7}$ are often used.

pictograph (p. 10) A graph that uses symbols to show data.

pint (p. 510) A unit for measuring capacity in the customary system. *See also* Table of Measures, page 577

place value (p. 54) The value given to the place a digit has in a number. *Example:* In 6,928, the place value of the digit 9 is hundreds.

plane figure (p. 274) A figure that lies on a flat surface.

point (p. 270) An exact position often marked by a dot.

polygon (p. 274) A closed plane figure made up of line segments.

possible (p. 550) Able to happen.

pound (lb) (p. 500) A unit for measuring weight in the customary system. *See also* Table of Measures, page 577

prediction (p. 548) An educated guess about what will happen.

prime number (p. 204) A whole number greater than 1 that has only two factors, itself and 1.

prism (p. 488) A solid figure whose bases lie in parallel planes and whose faces are parallelograms.

probability (p. 547) The ratio of the number of ways an event can occur to the total number of possible outcomes.

problem solving guide (p. 18) A process for solving a problem: Understand, Plan, Solve, Look Back.

product (p. 112) The number that is the result of multiplying two or more factors.
Example: $5 \times 6 = 30$
↑ Product

proportion (p. 530) A statement showing that two ratios are equal. *Example:* $\frac{6}{8} = \frac{3}{4}$

protractor (p. 272) An instrument used to measure the size of an angle.

pyramid (p. 488) A solid figure whose base is a polygon and whose faces are triangles with a common vertex.

quadrilateral (p. 276) A polygon with four sides.

quart (qt) (p. 510) A unit for measuring capacity in the customary system. *See also* Table of Measures, page 577

quotient (p. 168) The number other than the remainder that is the result of dividing. *Example:* 63 ÷ 7 = 9

↑Quotient

radius (p. 477) A line segment from the center of a circle to any point on the circle.

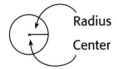

Radius

Center

range (p. 16) The difference between the greatest and least numbers in a set of data.

ratio (p. 528) A pair of numbers used to compare quantities.

ratio table (p. 530) A table that displays a set of equal ratios.

ray (p. 270) Part of a line that begins at a point and is endless in one direction.

rectangle (p. 276) A quadrilateral with four right angles and opposite sides parallel and the same length.

rectangular prism (p. 488) A solid figure whose six faces are all rectangles.

regroup (p. 84) To name a whole or decimal number in a different way. *Example:* 28 is 2 tens and 8 ones. 0.3 is 0.30 or 0.300

regular polygon (p. 450) A polygon whose sides are all equal and whose angles are all equal.

remainder (p. 168) The number less than the divisor that remains after the division is complete.

Example: 31 ÷ 7 = 4 R3

↑ Remainder

rhombus (p. 276) A quadrilateral with two pairs of parallel sides and all sides the same length.

right angle (p. 273) An angle that has a measure of 90°.

right triangle (p. 274) A triangle that has one right angle.

Roman numerals (p. 106) Numerals in a number system used by ancient Romans.
Examples: I = 1
IV = 4
V = 5
VI = 6

rounding (p. 62) Replacing a number with a number that tells about how many or how much.

sample (p. 549) A selected part of a large group.

scale (p. 12) Numbers that show the units used on a graph. Also, (p. 534) a ratio that shows the relationship between a scale drawing and the actual object.

scalene triangle (p. 274) A triangle with no sides the same length.

similar figures (p. 284) Figures that have the same shape and may or not have the same size.

Similar hexagons

simplest form (p. 310) A fraction where the greatest common factor of the numerator and denominator is 1.

skew (p. 490) Lines that are not parallel and do not intersect.

slide (p. 287) To move a plane figure in one direction.

solid figure (p. 488) A figure that has three dimensions and volume.

Cube   Cylinder

square (p. 276) A quadrilateral that has four equal sides and four right angles.

square centimeter (cm²) (p. 459) A square with 1 centimeter sides. Unit used for measuring area.

square unit (p. 468) A square with 1 unit sides; Unit used for measuring area.

standard form (p. 54) A way to write a number that shows only its digits. *Example:* 9,325

stem (p. 14) The part of a stem-and-leaf plot that shows all but the last digit of a number.

stem-and-leaf plot (p. 14) A graph for organizing data that, with 2-digit data, groups together all data with the same number of tens.

straight angle (p. 273) An angle that has a measure of 180°.

strategy (p. 4) A plan or method used to solve a problem. *Example:* Work Backward

subtraction (p. 20) An operation that tells the difference between two numbers or how many are left when some are taken away.

sum (p. 20) The number that is the result of adding two or more addends. *Example:* 7 + 9 = 16
Sum ↑

surface area (p. 494) The sum of the areas of all the faces of a solid.

symbol (p. 10) A picture in a pictograph that stands for a given number of objects.

symmetry (p. 288) A figure has symmetry if it can be folded along a line so that both parts match exactly. *See also* line of symmetry

tablespoon (tbsp) (p. 510) A unit for measuring capacity in the customary system. *See also* Table of Measures, page 577

teaspoon (tsp) (p. 510) A unit for measuring capacity in the customary system. *See also* Table of Measures, page 577

tenth (p. 66) One out of 10 equal parts of a whole.

thousandths (p. 70) One out of 1,000 equal parts of a whole.

ton (p. 500) A unit for measuring weight in the customary system. *See also* Table of Measures, page 577

trapezoid (p. 276) A quadrilateral that has exactly one pair of parallel sides.

tree diagram (p. 554) A diagram showing all possible outcomes of an event.

triangle (p. 274) A polygon with three sides.

turn (p. 287) To rotate a plane figure.

unit (p. 388) A quantity used as a standard of measure.

unit fraction (p. 406) A fraction with a numerator of 1.

unlikely (p. 550) Probably will not happen.

variable (p. 23) A letter that stands for a number or a range of numbers.

vertex (plural, vertices) (p. 270) The point that two rays of an angle have in common. Also, (p. 490) a point where two or more edges meet.

Vertex →

vertical axis (p. 12) The up-and-down number line on a graph.

volume (p. 508) The number of cubic units needed to fill a solid figure.

word form (p. 54) A way to show a number using words. *Example:* nine thousand, three hundred twenty-five

yard (yd) (p. 390) A unit for measuring length in the customary system. *See also* Table of Measures, page 577

zero property (p. 195) In addition, the sum of a number and 0 is that number. In multiplication, the product of a number and 0 is 0.
Examples: 7 + 0 = 7
        7 × 0 = 0

Credits

Photographs

Cover   Steve Ewert*

Front Matter   i Steve Ewert*   **ivC** Rick Friedman*   **viT** Rhoades Morrell Communications/Children's Garbage Museum   **viCR** Courtesy of Children's Garbage Museum   **1TR** UPI/Corbis-Bettmann   **1CR** GHP Studio*   **1C** Tony Arrowsmith*   **1CRB** Leonard Lee Rue III, The National Audubon Society Collection/Photo Researchers   **1BR** Jeff Foott/ Bruce Coleman Inc.   **1BL** Jenny Thomas*   **2T** David Leeson*   **2B** Scott Miller*

Chapter 1   6TR NASA   **9** Lloyd Litsey*   **10** ZEFA/The Stock Market   **15** Alain Chambon/ The Image Bank   **25** James Keyser*   **26** Juan Silva/The Image Bank   **29** Dennis O'Clair/ Tony Stone Images   **30** James Keyser*   **31** ©SuperStock, Inc.   **33** Mitchell Layton/Duomo   **46T** Niki Glen

Chapter 2   51 Rick Friedman/Black Star*   **53** E. R. Degginger/Bruce Coleman Inc.   **54** Rick Friedman/Black Star*   **62** Steve Payne*   **65** Ben Van Hook/Duomo   **66** Ben Van Hook/ Duomo   **71** Charles Bowman/Leo de Wys, Inc.   **81** John Greilick/The Courier News   **82** David P. Gilkey/Detroit Free Press   **86** USPS   **87** UPI/Corbis-Bettmann   **92** John Greilick/ The Courier News   **93T** ©CNRI/SPL, Science Source/Photo Researchers   **93B** ©Biology Media, Science Source/Photo Researchers   **97** Barbara Puorro Galasso/George Eastman House

Chapter 3   108BL UPI/Corbis-Bettmann   **111** Corbis-Bettmann   **114** National Baseball Library & Archive, Cooperstown, N.Y.   **115** UPI/Corbis-Bettmann   **116** Lou Mudd*   **119** American Stock Photos/Archive Photos   **120T** Donovan Reese/Tony Stone Images   **122** Corbis-Bettmann   **127L** Ramond A. Mendez/Animals Animals   **127R** Jeff Lepore, The National Audubon Society Collection/ Photo Researchers   **128** Photograph by Ansel Adams. Copyright ©1997 by the Trustees of the Ansel Adams Publishing Rights Trust. All rights reserved.   **133** Katherine Lambert*   **135** NASA/Science Source/Photo Researchers   **136** Bublitz Photography*   **138** ® & ©1997, Paramount Parks Inc. All rights reserved.   **139** Jay Brousseau/The Image Bank   **140** Katherine Lambert*   **143(inset)** ©USPS   **143(background)** Harald Sund/The Image Bank   **146** Caryn Levy*   **148** ©USPS   **149** Hans Reinhard/OKAPIA, The National Audubon Society Collection/Photo Researchers   **152** ©USPS   **154** Hagley Museum and Library

Chapter 4   165T Jeff Foott/Bruce Coleman Inc.   **165(bleed)** NASA Planetarium Armagh-N. Ireland/A NASA/JPL Photo   **167** Courtesy of Children's Garbage Museum   **168** Courtesy of Children's Garbage Museum   **171** Andy Levin, The National Audubon Society Collection/Photo Researchers   **172T** Scott Miller*   **173** Peter Gridley/FPG International Corp.   **175** C. Kucine*   **178L** Leonard Lee Rue III, The National Audubon Society Collection/Photo Researchers   **178R** Dan Suzio, The National Audubon Society Collection/Photo Researchers   **179** Tom McHugh, The National Audubon Society Collection/Photo Researchers   **183** Jeff Greenberg, The National Audubon Society Collection/Photo Researchers   **185L** Benn Mitchell/The Image Bank   **185R** Stephen Derr/The Image Bank   **186** C. Kucine*

193 Joe Traver*   **196** Jason Olson*   **199T** Peter C. Jones/Alex Gotfryd/Corbis-Bettmann   **199B** Renee Lynn, The National Audubon Society Collection/Photo Researchers   **200** Joe Traver*   **202** Brent Jones*   **203L** Stephen Dalton, The National Audubon Society Collection/Photo Researchers   **203R** Kenneth M. Highfill, The National Audubon Society Collection/Photo Researchers   **216C** Public Information Office, City of Virginia Beach, VA, Photograph by Carole Arnold

Chapter 5   218 Richard T. Nowitz/Photo Researchers   **220** NASA/Science Photo Libary, Science Source/Photo Researchers   **221** Ben Van Hook   **223** Luis Castaneda/The Image Bank   **225** NASA/Science Photo Library, Science Source/Photo Researchers   **226** Ben Van Hook   **227T** NASA/Courtesy of the Ames Research Center   **227B** Richard Elliott/Tony Stone Images   **229** Greg Kiger*   **230L** Jet Propulsion Laboratory. Copyright © California Institute of Technology, Pasadena, CA. All rights reserved.   **230R** Greg Kiger*   **233** M.H. Sharp, The National Audubon Society Collection/Photo Researchers   **234** NASA, Science Source/Photo Researchers   **237** Courtesy of the Library of Congress   **238** NASA   **239** The Planetarium, Armagh-N. Ireland/NASA   **242** NASA, Science Source/Photo Researchers   **243** Hank Morgan, Science Source/Photo Researchers   **246** First Light   **249–250** Rick Friedman*   **251** Planetarium Armagh-N. Ireland/ A NASA/JPL Photo   **252TR** Jim Mendenhall/ National Geographic Society   **252C** C. Russo/ NASM   **252B** C.Russo/NASM   **253R** Bill Carter/The Image Bank   **255** Biophoto Associates, The National Audubon Society Collection/Photo Researchers   **257** A. T. Willet/ The Image Bank   **258** NASA   **259** NASA   **263** Ken Tannenbaum/The Image Bank   **264L** UPI/Corbis-Bettmann   **264BR** NASA, Science Source/Photo Researchers

Chapter 6   267(inset 1) Shelburne Museum, Shelburne, VT, Photograph by Ken Burris   **267(inset 3)** Courtesy of W.E. Channing & Co., Santa Fe, N.M.   **267(inset 4)** America Hurrah Archive, New York, NY   **268** M.C. Escher's "Symmetry Drawing E 73" © 1997 Cordon Art - Baarn - Holland. All rights reserved.   **269–270** Jenny Thomas*   **273** Scott Camazine/Photo Researchers   **274L** Dale Wittner*   **274R** Joseph Nettis/Photo Researchers   **276** Adrienne McGrath   **278** Taro Yamacaki   **281T** Tom Prettyman/PhotoEdit   **281B** David Young-Wolf/ PhotoEdit   **283** Renee Lynn*   **284** Jerry Jacka Photography/Courtesy, Hubbell Trading Post, Ganado, AZ   **288L** Boltin Picture Library   **288M** Boltin Picture Library   **288TR** Vanessa Vick/Photo Researchers   **288TB** Boltin Picture Library   **291R** Lisa J. Goodman/The Image Bank   **295** Siqui Sanchez/The Image Bank   **296T** Richard Howard   **296B** William R. Sallaz/ Duomo

Chapter 7   302 Jenny Thomas*   **306L** Hans Reinhard/Bruce Coleman Inc.   **306R** Rick Olivier*   **308** A. Power/Bruce Coleman Inc.   **309** Carl Roessler/Bruce Coleman Inc.   **321** Joe Morreale*   **330T** Joe Morreale*   **330B** Lawrence Migdale, The National Audubon Society Collection/Photo Researchers   **332** John Hyde/Bruce Coleman Inc.   **334** Ron & Valerie Taylor/Bruce Coleman Inc.   **335** Carl Roessler/ Bruce Coleman Inc.

Chapter 8   345B G. C. Kelley, The National Audubon Society Collection/Photo Researchers   **347–348** David Leeson*   **349** Harald Sund/ The Image Bank   **357** Tim Davis, The National Audubon Society Collection/Photo Researchers   **360** Casey Cronin*   **363** Larry West/Bruce Coleman Inc.   **364** Will McIntyre/ Photo Researchers   **367** Jenny Thomas*   **372** Tony Tilford/Animals Animals   **374** Jenny Thomas*   **376TL** David Peterson*   **376B** Grant Heilman/ Grant Heilman Photography   **379** Andre Gallant/The Image Bank   **387** David Leeson*   **388** George B. Fry III   **390** David Leeson*   **392** Tony Arrowsmith*

Chapter 9   400TC Planetarium Armagh-N. Ireland/A NASA/JPL Photo   **403** Steve Payne*   **408TL** Steve Payne*   **419** Edward McCain*   **422** Edward McCain*   **423** Photofest

Chapter 10   439 Jenny Thomas*   **440TL** Ramond A. Mendez/Animals Animals   **440TC** Patti Murray/Animals Animals   **440TB** Rod Planck, The National Audubon Society Collection/Photo Researchers   **442R** Jenny Thomas*   **443** Michael Dick/ Animals Animals   **444L** David Madison/Duomo   **444R** Rick Rickman/Duomo   **445L** Tim Davis/ Photo Researchers   **445L** Tim Davis, The National Audubon Society Collection/ Photo Researchers   **446** Malcolm Yunker*   **447L** Jose Luis G. Grande, The National Audubon Society Collection/Photo Researchers   **447R** Rod Planck, The National Audubon Society Collection/Photo Researchers   **449** Katherine Lambert*   **453** Private Collection   **454T** Bruce Kluckhorn*   **454C** Joe McDonald/Animals Animals   **455** Joe McDonald/Animals Animals   **457** Catherine Lambert*   **460T** Tim Davis, The National Audubon Society Collection/Photo Researchers   **467** Lisa J. Goodman/The Image Bank   **475** ©1997, Comstock, Inc.   **477** Heather R. Davidson   **482TL** Tom & Pat Leeson, The National Audubon Society Collection/Photo Researchers   **482BL** Gerard Lacz/Animals Animals

Chapter 11   487 Carolyn Brown/The Image Bank   **488** Andrea Pistolesi/The Image Bank   **489TL** Luis Castaneda/The Image Bank   **489TC** Andrea Pistolesi/The Image Bank   **489BR** Guido A. Rossi/The Image Bank   **493** Alain Choisnet/The Image Bank   **497R** Anthony Merciega, The National Audubon Society Collection/Photo Researchers   **499** Phil Long/AP Photo   **502** Larry Justinus*   **503** *San Antonio Express-News* Collection, The Institute of Texan Cultures, San Antonio, Texas   **504L** Herbert W. Booth III/Liaison International   **504R** Hugh Grannum*   **508TR** Geoffrey Nilsen*   **515** Mella Panzella/Animals Animals   **516T** ©1997, Comstock, Inc.

Chapter 12   526 America Hurrah Archive, New York, NY   **527** George Linblade*   **530** John McGrail   **532** George Linblade*   **533** Ralph H. Wetmore II/Tony Stone Images   **534** Joseph Sohm/Tony Stone Images   **537** Steve Payne   **540** D. Young-Wolf/PhotoEdit   **542** Steve Payne*   **559** Erich Lessing/Art Resource, NY/© 1997 Succession H. Matisse, Paris/Artists Rights Society (ARS), New York

Richard Hutchings* iiiB, ivBL, viC, viiC, viiiT, viiiB, ixB, xiTR, xiiB, xivTR, xivBL, 6B, 7–8, 18, 20, 22, 32, 35, 36–37, 46C, 48–49, 73, 100, 106, 108R, 164, 165B, 170, 172B, 182, 190, 194, 208, 211, 219, 253L, 266, 267R, 296M, 298–299, 324,

Illustrations

Index

INDEX

are shown: 35, 52, 99, 145, 151, 182, 189, 218, 238, 257, 410, 538

Numbers. *See also* specific operations; Estimation; Fractions; Percent; Rounding
  comparing and ordering, 60–61, 74–75
  compatible, 136–137
  expanded form of, 54–55
  expression, 244–245
  mixed, 322–323
  odd and even, 35
  place value, 56, 57, 58, 66, 68, 70, 90
  prime, 204–205
  Roman numerals, 106
  standard form of, 54–55
  word form of, 54–55

Number theory
  even and odd numbers, 35
  prime and composite numbers, 204–205

Numerator, 302

O

Obtuse angle. *See* Angles
Obtuse triangle. *See* Triangles
Odd numbers, 35
One property of multiplication, 195
Operations. *See* Addition; Division; Multiplication; Order of operations; Subtraction
Order (commutative) property, 99, 112
Ordered pairs, 30–31, 46, 532–533
Ordering. *See* Comparing and ordering
Outcomes. *See* Probability

P

Parallel lines, 270–271, 491
Parallelogram, 276–277, 470–471
Patterns, 15, 33, 112
  in decimals, 134–135, 445
  divisibility, 170, 171, 195, 198, 309
  with equivalent fractions, 306
  length, standard, 391
  measurement, metric units, 445
  number, 3, 52–53, 57, 77, 363, 407, 409, 415, 474–475
  percent, 538–539
  in place-value chart, 66, 67

  in problem solving, 4–5, 67
  in ratio tables, 530–531
  with solids, 490, 491

Pentagon, 488
Pentomino, 286–287
Percent, 328, 525
  calculator and, 336–337
  as decimal or fraction, 321, 330–331, 336–337
  estimation with, 540–541
  of a number, 328–329, 542–543
  patterns, 538–539

Performance Assessment, 45, 105, 161, 215, 263, 295, 341, 397, 433, 481, 521, 561

Perimeter, 450–457
  and area relationships, 437, 452–453
  converting mixed units, 454–455

Period, 54
Perpendicular Lines, 270
Pictograph. *See* Graphs/graphing
Place value, 51–63, 66–71
Planning, 295
Polygon, 267, 274, 283–285, 450–451
  congruent, 284–285, 292
  similar, 284–285, 292

Powers of ten, 57
Practice. *See* specific lessons; Mixed Review and Test Prep; Skills Practice Bank; Stop and Practice

Practice Game, 88–89, 120–121, 206–207, 240–241, 380–381, 424–425

Pre-algebra. *See* Algebra readiness
Predictions, 490, 548–551
Prime number, 204–205
Prism, 488–489, 491
Probability, 524–525
  certain outcome, 554
  expected, 556–557
  experimental, 550–551, 556–557
  fairness, 546–547
  as fractions, 554–555
  impossible outcome, 554
  outcomes, 546, 547
  predictions, 548–549, 550–551

Problem, multiple-step, 140–142
Problem solving. *See also* Problem solving, analyze word problems;

Problem solving, compare strategies; Problem solving, decision making; Problem solving strategies
  and careers, 29, 185, 457
  and geography, 119
  and health, 281
  and history, 119, 237
  and literature, 199, 357
  and math history, 379
  and science, 149, 211, 233, 333
  and social studies, 87
  and technology, 39–41, 97

Problem solving, analyze word problems
  choose an operation, 20–21, 100–101
  exact or estimate, 392–393
  interpreting remainders, 180–181
  introduction to the problem solving guide, 18–19
  multiple-step problems, 140–141
  overestimating and underestimating, 416–417
  too much or too little information, 364–365

Problem Solving and Applications, 13, 17, 55, 61, 63, 71, 73, 77, 83, 86, 93, 96, 115, 123, 125, 137, 139, 148, 153, 169, 173, 179, 184, 187, 198, 203, 225, 227, 232, 236, 239, 243, 277, 285, 307, 309, 311, 325, 332, 349, 353, 361, 371, 373, 375, 378, 389, 407, 409, 413, 423, 445, 456, 501, 503, 505, 513, 515, 529, 531, 541, 543

Problem solving, compare strategies
  logical reasoning/draw a picture, 426–427
  solve a simpler problem/draw a picture, 516–517
  work backward/draw a picture, 382–383

Problem Solving Connection
  draw a picture, 30, 32, 52, 68, 74, 286, 288, 326, 452, 458, 494
  guess and check, 22, 56, 546, 548, 556
  look for a pattern, 22, 30, 32, 45, 52, 112, 126, 134, 144, 170, 204, 222, 254, 288, 304, 314,

326, 410, 428, 452, 458, 464, 470, 472, 476, 490, 532, 538
make an organized list, 56
make a table, 190, 452, 458, 464, 476, 532, 548, 550, 556
solve a simpler problem, 134, 358
use logical reasoning, 194, 204, 244
use objects/act it out, 90, 144, 176, 272, 286, 322, 326, 350, 358, 368, 404, 410, 440, 450, 464, 466, 468, 470, 476, 488, 490, 492, 494, 508, 550

Problem solving, decision making, 128–129, 252–253, 290–291, 334–335, 460–461, 496–497, 534–535

Problem Solving Hint, 16, 22, 78, 194, 251, 272, 280, 318, 364, 452, 468, 496, 534, 546, 552

Problem solving strategies
draw a picture, 4, 52, 74, 78–80, 426–427, 516–517
guess and check, 56, 156–157
logical reasoning, 5, 36–39, 426–427
look for a pattern, 4–5, 52, 474–475
make an organized list, 5, 56, 552–553
make a table, 5, 318–319
solve a simpler problem, 278–281, 516–517
use objects/act it out, 246–247
work backward, 208–211, 382–383

Properties of operations. *See* Number properties

Proportion, 530
ratio and, 524

Proportional thinking. Proportional thinking is found throughout the book. A few instances are shown. 82, 110, 201, 211, 309, 318, 446, 474, 528–535

Protractor, 272, 399

Pyramids, 484, 486, 488, 489, 490, 493

Q

Quadrilaterals, 276–277
Quotient, 168, 172–173, 215, 222

R

Radius, 476–477
Range, 16–17
Ratio, 528–529
equal, 530, 532–533
and proportion, 524, 530–531
tables, 524, 530–531, 532–533
Ray, 270
Reasoning, 10, 12, 14, 16, 36–38, 41, 54, 58, 60, 62, 66, 70, 72, 76, 85, 89, 92, 95, 114, 117, 121, 122, 125, 131, 136, 138, 147, 152, 155, 169, 172, 183, 186, 197, 201, 207, 224, 226, 231, 235, 239, 241, 243, 251, 275, 277, 284, 303, 306, 308, 310, 324, 328, 331, 348, 355, 360, 370, 373, 377, 381, 388, 390, 406, 446, 455, 501, 502, 505, 513, 514, 528, 531, 540, 542. *See also* Number sense; Skills and Reasoning; Stop and Practice
Rectangle, 276–277, 292
area, 458–459
perimeter, 452–453
Remainder, 168–167, 174, 176–177, 178–179, 182, 185, 186–187
Remember, 26, 30, 60, 66, 68, 74, 84, 99, 112, 114, 134, 154, 190, 196, 222, 230, 234, 254, 274, 276, 286, 304, 308, 314, 316, 322, 326, 330, 336, 360, 368, 412, 442, 454, 458, 464, 466, 470, 488, 490, 493, 494, 512, 514, 538, 550, 556
Review/Test, 44, 104, 160, 214, 262, 294, 340, 396, 432, 480, 520, 560
Rhombus, 276–277
Right angle, 273, 274–275 *See* Angles
Right triangle, 274–275, 282. *See* Triangles
Roman numerals, 106
Rotation (turn), 286–287, 288–289
Rounding
decimals, 65, 76–77
fractions, 407
whole numbers, 62–64, 82

S

Scale, 12, 26–27
in diagrams, 496–497, 534–535
on maps, 110, 120–121, 351
Scale, drawing, 534–535
Scalene triangle. *See* Triangles

Science, 31, 39, 55, 57, 93, 102, 118, 127, 153, 171, 179, 181, 198, 199, 203, 236, 239, 255, 273, 300, 309, 311, 317, 332, 359, 369, 373, 391, 443, 447, 503, 505, 511, 515, 533, 555
Sequence. *See* Patterns
Similar polygons, 284–285, 292
Simplest form fraction. *See* Fractions
Simulation. *See* Probability
Skew lines, 490–491
Skills Practice Bank, 564–576
Skills and Reasoning
addition, 356, 375, 456
addition and subtraction, 86, 93, 349, 371, 373
algebra readiness, 96, 169, 325, 413
angles, 271
critical thinking, 169
decimals, 67, 71, 73, 137, 139, 148, 153, 155, 201, 332
division, 169, 173, 179, 184, 187, 198, 201, 225, 227, 232, 236, 239, 243, 251
estimation, 83, 115, 118, 137, 153, 172, 179, 187, 225, 226, 236, 251, 303, 329, 378, 501, 541
factors, 203
fractions, 303, 307, 309, 311, 317, 325, 332, 349, 353, 356, 361, 371, 413
line plot, 17
lines, 270–271
measurement, 11, 389, 391, 443, 445, 447, 456, 501, 511, 513, 515
mental math, 137, 251, 356, 407
mixed numbers, 373, 375
multiplication, 115, 118, 123, 125, 137, 139, 148, 153, 155, 407, 409, 413, 421, 423, 456
number line, 63, 73
patterns, 15, 391, 407
percent, 329, 332, 543
perimeters, 456
place-value blocks, 66–67, 68, 90
polygons, classifying, 285
probability, 555
quadrilaterals, classifying, 277
ratio, 529, 531
rounding, 77, 409

INDEX